# LAW AND PHILOSOPHY

# LAW AND PHILOSOPHY

## READINGS IN LEGAL PHILOSOPHY

Edited by

### Edward Allen Kent

BROOKLYN COLLEGE,
CITY UNIVERSITY OF NEW YORK

Prentice-Hall, Inc., Englewood Cliffs, New Jersey

Printed in the United States of America

ISBN: 0-13-526459-6

Library of Congress Catalog Card Number: 70-121302

10 9 8 7 6 5

PRENTICE-HALL INTERNATIONAL, INC., *London*
PRENTICE-HALL OF AUSTRALIA, PTY. LTD., *Sydney*
PRENTICE-HALL OF CANADA, LTD., *Toronto*
PRENTICE-HALL OF INDIA PRIVATE LIMITED, *New Delhi*
PRENTICE-HALL OF JAPAN, INC., *Tokyo*

# Preface

It was not business of the law in the time of Jefferson to come into my house and see how I kept house. But when my house, when my so-called private property, became a great mine, and men went along dark corridors amidst every kind of danger in order to dig out of the bowels of the earth things necessary for the industries of the whole nation, and when it came about that no individual owned these mines, that they were owned by great stock companies, then all the old analogies absolutely collapsed and it became the right of government to go down into these mines to see whether human beings were properly treated in them or not. . . . These, again, are merely illustrations of conditions. We are in a new world, struggling under old laws. As we go inspecting our lives today, surveying this new scene of centralized and complex society, we shall find many more things out of joint.

Woodrow Wilson, The New Freedom

Contrary to the structural appearance of the traditional political philosophy course, the impulse to generate new social strategies and goals did not expire some time in the late 19th century with the ideological standoff between Marx and his critics. Yet, as Margaret Macdonald so acutely pointed out in her well-known critique delivered to the Aristotelian Society at the beginning of World War II, the 'language of political theory' had by that time come to have very little relation to the concrete issues upon which governments and citizens were being called to render momentous and far-ranging decision. The reasons for the decline in the classic mode of Anglo-American political analysis were manifold: certainly not the least had been the institution of new divisions of labor both among academic disciplines and the very instrumentalities of government itself. Positivism had called for the relegation of normative concerns to the several social sciences; to statesmen and judges—particularly the British Parliament and the American Supreme Court—had fallen most of the burden of formulating and evaluating new legal and political structures appropriate to the complexities of modern technological-industrial states where one still finds 'many more things out of joint'.

This volume and the newly rediscovered discipline of philosophy of law are dedicated to the proposition that philosophers do have an active role to play in shaping public policy and, more narrowly, that both law and philosophy stand to gain from dialogue. On the side of philosophy, normative value theory (and by implication conceptual elucidation) is incomplete until it has stood the hard test of legal decision and the multiplicity of paradigm and counter-example of which the law is such a rich store. Contemporary legal practice, for its part, stands desperately in need of the conceptual clarification and general policy elucidation and justification of which philosophy is traditionally a master. Bridges which have been built between the two disciplines only in recent decades (and which are still in the building) promise to lead the way to an expanded field, of political *and* *legal* philosophy, which has caught the imagination of a new generation of philosophers on both sides of the Atlantic.

This collection has been designed with two immediate aims in mind: to make readily available significant field materials which in surprising instances are virtually inaccessible; and to provide a text suitable with some supplements for graduate and undergraduate courses in legal philosophy and related fields. Some compromise between these two aims has been necessary: footnotes have been stripped from several of the older law journal articles that would undoubtedly have been useful for the specialist; a few widely reprinted classics from political theory have been included for reasons of topical balance. Some colleagues will object to an Anglo-American bias which has meant the exclusion of some Continental materials valuable in their own right but less directly influential in the formation of native ('provincial'?) theory; an attempt has been made to make partial restitution in more widely ranging topical bibliographies. A balance between normative and conceptual issues and the limitations of a single readable volume have imposed further restrictions; the traditional coda of legal philosophy texts, 'international law', has been omitted, as have selections from available contemporary classics (e.g. H. L. A. Hart's *The Concept of Law*) which should be read in their entirety. Chapter introductions place the selections in context, suggest wider ramifications of the topics under consideration, and undoubtedly reflect some biases of the editor. In most (but not all) instances selection headings follow the original titles of book, chapter, article or section; sources and editing excisions are footnoted on the first page of each selection.

Special thanks are owed those who have assisted in many ways in the preparation of the volume, including the City University of New York for a generous grant of research funds.

E. A. K.

*New York City*

# Contents

# LAW AND PHILOSOPHY

CHAPTER I

# GENERAL LEGAL THEORY

The life of the law has not been logic; it has been experience. The felt necessities of the time, the prevalent moral and political theories, intuitions of public policy, avowed or unconscious, even the prejudices which judges share with their fellow-men, have had a good deal more to do than the syllogism in determining the rules by which men should be governed.

Holmes, *The Common Law*, 1881

In law as elsewhere, we can know and yet not understand. Shadows often obscure our knowledge which not only vary in intensity but are cast by different obstacles to light. These cannot all be removed by the same methods and till the precise character of our perplexity is determined we cannot tell what tools we shall need.

Hart, "Definition and Theory in Jurisprudence," 1953

It may be fairly said of at least the years spanned by the two citations above, that an ancient, honorable and fruitful dialogue between law and philosophy, jurists and philosophers, had been (with a few notable exceptions) all but suspended in Anglo-American circles. Perhaps the felt necessities of the time—public attention upon the dramatic emergence of new executive powers and their conflict with traditional legislative prerogative—left little energy for philosophic encounter with purely legal problems. The period witnessed, if anything, a dispiriting decline in the two great legal traditions stemming out

1

of the late scholastic debates. With its faith in reason and a stable cosmic order already shaken by centuries of nominalist critique, the Catholic natural law tradition, following a conservative triumph at the first Vatican Council (1869-70), was severely compromised by factional divisions along national and 'special interest' lines, its long-standing consensus shattered over a host of substantial issues (e.g. the status of private property, the justice of rebellion against tyranny, the so-called 'just' war). The abortive possibilities of the command or imperative theory of law—Hobbes' absolute sovereign, enlarged by a continuing separation of law and morals, made respectable by the utilitarians—were to be unmasked finally in the garb of National Socialism. Marx's critique of law as bourgeois ideology—the mere rationalization of ruling class interests—weighed heavily on both traditions. The Nuremberg trial of Nazi war criminals found legal positivism virtually discredited, and natural law, a pale and shadowy corpse, resuscitated to handle the ugly business at hand.

Whatever the full reasons for their temporary divergence, the past two decades have once again found law and philosophy engaged in active dialogue—a dialogue which admittedly has required extensive preliminary negotiation even to set the terms of conversation. By World War II American jurisprudence had laid the theoretical basis for a radical redrafting of the legal assumptions of the previous century, with practical consequences that are just beginning to be realized. Specifically traditional dependence upon precedent (*stare decisis*) had been countermanded by new ground rules for the operation of judicial discretion; the balance of protected interests had begun to shift from adamant defense of private property to new respect and appreciation for the rights of person; new court channels had been opened through which changing economic and social conditions could make their impact directly felt; in short, basic alterations in the wider political structure itself had gradually taken place (e.g. One man, one vote).

For its part, philosophy has undergone several revolutions since the time when 'law and metaphysics' could constitute a central chapter in a text on jurisprudence. An early attempt on the part of Morris R. Cohen and his followers in this country to draft a scientific axiom system as the basis of law has seemingly given way to the more congenial (to legal practitioners) pattern of ordinary language analysis. Under the stimulus of seminal British philosophers, especially J. L. Austin and H. L. A. Hart, law has now been added to ethics and political philosophy as a requisite factor in philosophic value analysis. With the assimilation of new linguistic tools, traditional topics (natural law, natural rights, punishment, justice, property, legal reasoning, negligence, legal rights) are currently being subjected to extensive review and reconstruction; are being reframed ('excuse and justification' for 'free will and determinism'); and even rephrased (the 'concept' for the 'nature' of law, 'defeasible' for 'defined' legal concept, 'ascribed' for 'discovered' legal right).

For the student of philosophy, entrance into this 'new' field presents multiple difficulties: the traditionally arcane labyrinths of the legal guild demand extensive investigation of legal language and practice; there is also the challenge of taking a philosophic stance towards unrefined materials already overlaid by successive theoretical encrustations and diverse historic and national traditions. Fortunately, during the nineteen sixties, two strands of expanding legal awareness have begun to run together in the common sphere of Anglo-American jurisprudence. One, initiated by Justice Holmes, spiritual father of both major American schools of jurisprudence in this century (American legal realism and sociological jurisprudence), has brought effective recognition of diverse extra-legal (and inescapable) influences upon a living legal tradition: the social, political, moral or even personal factors that condition the balance of social interests. Judicial decision has been increasingly recognized as an independent instrument for effecting (or retarding) social change. The other strand, deriving from British analytical jurisprudence, made contemporary by H. L. A. Hart more than any other single figure, has exposed a morass of conceptual shadows and ambiguities lingering in habitual legal usage and calling for programmatic clarification in the interest of a mature and humane legal system.

This confluence has not been without turbulence or mutual misunderstanding, as the on-going debate between Hart of Oxford and Fuller of Harvard is all too vivid a witness. Professor Hart still defends a somewhat narrow British view of the rule of law capped by parliamentary supremacy, an 'ultimate rule of recognition,' which virtually limits the judicial function to mere clarification of accepted rules and lines of authority. American energies have been caught up in a multiplicity of concrete issues in disparate areas of law not readily assimilable to general principle or broad conceptual analysis: individual American jurists have tended to develop concepts eclectically and according to their individual lights (e.g. Fuller speaks of a 'morality of duty' and a 'morality of aspiration'; Pound's term, 'public interest', initially utilized as a working concept in a tripartite classification of individual, social and public claims, is later virtually abandoned to endure only as a vague and occasional substitute for 'public policy').

Any legal anthology can do but partial justice to the wide range of positions in the field, can offer only a limited perspective on the depth and detail of any single position. The general theories of the great jurists and jurisprudes characteristically bear the stamp of the man which can only be fully appreciated by perusing legal briefs and decisions, collected papers, critical reviews, testimonials and correspondence as well as formal theoretical statements. Holmes' "The Path of the Law" was written early and touches on only some of the themes developed throughout his distinguished career: his sense that good law is the slave of neither precedent nor formal logic; that the 'bad man' should be judged according to his acts and not his character or intentions; that political and economic factors should be taken into full account in 'predicting' future rights and duties, themselves only established when a court has spoken; his suspicion of, yet recognition of the need for, general theory in law is set against the background of his special awareness of the case by case development of legal precedent *(The Common Law,* first published in 1881, is still the great classic in that field).

John Courtney Murray, S.J. was until his recent death America's leading Catholic natural law theorist. His own distinctive attempt to make that doctrine contemporary should be set against the background of selections from Aquinas in later chapters, the French formulation of Jean Dabin, the orthodox Thomistic line of Heinrich Rommen, the critical analyses of A. P. D'Entrèves who takes to task what he calls 'technological' (e.g. Fuller) and 'metaphysical' (e.g. Aquinas) versions of the doctrine. As Father Murray argues, natural law is scarcely dead, and in particular his own notion of 'consensus', developed in detail elsewhere as the foundation of law in the collective wisdom of good and rational men, can be discovered under other rubrics in much contemporary ethical theory. In a recent updating of his own theory of justice *(Justice,* Random House Studies in Philosophy, 1967), Chaim Perelman has backed away from the scepticism of his earlier study (reprinted in Chapter VIII below) to base law in natural reason.

John Austin's 'command' or 'imperative' theory should really be read against the background of Hobbes' *Leviathan,* its archetype, and from the foreground of Hart's *The Concept of Law,* which is in some respects its 'new revised version'. Hart, too, argues the sharp separation of law and morals, and attempts in his own work to substitute an 'ultimate rule of recognition' for Austin's sovereign and a new definition of legal obligation for 'habitual obedience to orders backed by threats'.

The outlines of Hans Kelsen's own general theory are given in the selection from *General Theory of Law and State* reprinted in Chapter VI. As the only general theorist widely read and respected in both Western and Soviet circles, he is perhaps uniquely qualified to comment on Marx's widely scattered and all-too-brief asides on law. *Soviet Legal Philosophy* (Harvard University Press, 1951. Translated by Hugh Babb and with an introduction by John Hazard) and a series of detailed studies of contemporary Soviet legal practice by John Hazard (see bibliography) offer intriguing evidence of growing Soviet respect for law as an institution, as the influence of Marx's early critique wanes.

Pound's social interest theory has appeared in many published versions including his most recent massive, five-volume elaboration, *Jurisprudence* (St. Paul, 1959). The title 'sociological jurisprudence' which has been adopted by Pound and his followers is somewhat misleading, but was probably intended to distinguish the American version from German social interest theory. Pound himself actually had reservations about the contribution to law of sociology as an academic discipline, and intended the term to encompass the widest range of social-political-economic factors. Deservedly recognized as the 'Dean of American Jurisprudence', Pound nevertheless compounded confusion in many an area of critical analysis by rough and ready application of crude conceptual categories.

Karl Llewellyn's summary analysis of American legal realism (composed with the assistance of Jerome Frank who withheld his name from the venture at the last moment) was actually prepared in rebuttal of a sweeping caricature of the school by Pound. The 'realism' of this title has nothing to do with philosophical realism; it is rather a label intended by its adherents to stress their hope of penetrating the 'realities' of legal practice by close scrutiny of specific subdivisions of the law. Neither was realism's divorce between 'is' and 'ought' more than a limiting methodological caution, since a dominant concern of the school has been to bring new moral values to bear upon inequitable legal practices (see selections by Harry Jones and Lon Fuller in later chapters).

'Analytical' as applied to jurisprudence is also a term with wide and varied reference. British jurists of all persuasions have generally focused a good deal of attention upon analysis of conceptual issues. The American Wesley Newcomb Hohfeld, who died quite early in this century, is, however, claimed as one of their own by both analysts and American realists on the basis of his only partially completed study of fundamental legal conceptions. As the Singer-on-Hart selection in this chapter indicates, American analytical philosophers are working out of a somewhat more pragmatic or normative *Geist* than their English counterparts. Apart from trans-Atlantic ideological tensions that will be taken up in later introductions, schisms within contemporary philosophic schools are also reflected in legal studies. Are basic legal terms indefinable? logical primitives? 'family' concepts? Can adequate legal models be constructed? If so, are they *sui generis* (Hart)? Should they be borrowed from other contexts— the logic of science (Morris Cohen), normative economics (John Rawls), or even psychoanalysis (Jerome Frank)? Should analysis merely clarify established usage or prescribe new normative foundations?

For the time being these and many more specifics seem largely open questions despite substantial recent contributions to the field. A new generation of legal philosophers working from many platforms (the new politics, the new economics, planning theory, the law school, ethics, and even theology) seems united only in a common rejection of the niceties and simplistic emotional appeals of traditional ideologies of all persuasions. It can be argumentatively claimed, however, that one can no longer do ethics, political philosophy or even philosophy of mind without a thorough grounding in the issues raised by contemporary philosophy of law—an almost infinite supply of paradigms and counter-examples which in turn demand a new synthesis of data emerging from the widest sweep of contemporary human endeavor.

# 1

# Oliver Wendell Holmes, Jr.

Justice Holmes (1841–1935), native New Englander, professor of law at Harvard University, appointed Associate Justice of the Supreme Court in 1902, was as theorist and judge the author of modern American jurisprudence.

# THE PATH OF THE LAW*

When we study law we are not studying a mystery but a well-known profession. We are studying what we shall want in order to appear before judges, or to advise people in such a way as to keep them out of court. The reason why it is a profession, why people will pay lawyers to argue for them or to advise them, is that in societies like ours the command of the public force is intrusted to the judges in certain cases, and the whole power of the state will be put forth, if necessary, to carry out their judgments and decrees. People want to know under what circumstances and how far they will run the risk of coming against what is so much stronger than themselves, and hence it becomes a business to find out when this danger is to be feared. The object of our study, then, is prediction, the prediction of the incidence of the public force through the instrumentality of the courts.

The means of the study are a body of reports, of treatises, and of statutes, in this country and in England, extending back for six hundred years, and now increasing annually by hundreds. In these sibylline leaves are gathered the scattered prophecies of the past upon the cases in which the axe will fall. These are what properly have been called the oracles of the law. Far the most important and pretty nearly the whole meaning of every new effort of legal thought is to make these prophecies more precise, and to generalize them into a thoroughly connected system. The process is one, from a lawyer's statement of a case, eliminating as it does all the dramatic elements with which his client's story has clothed it, and retaining only the facts of legal import, up to the final analyses and abstract universals of theoretic jurisprudence. The reason why a lawyer does not mention that his client wore a white hat when he made a contract, while Mrs. Quickly would be sure to dwell upon it along with the parcel gilt goblet and the sea-coal fire, is that he foresees that the public force will act in the same way whatever his client had upon his head. It is to make the prophecies easier to be remembered and to be understood that the teachings

*An address delivered by Mr. Justice Holmes, of the Supreme Judicial Court of Massachusetts, at the dedication of the new hall of the Boston University School of Law, on January 8, 1897. Copyrighted by O. W. Holmes. 1897. *Harvard Law Review*, X(1897), 457.

of the decisions of the past are put into general propositions and gathered into text-books, or that statutes are passed in a general form. The primary rights and duties with which jurisprudence busies itself again are nothing but prophecies. One of the many evil effects of the confusion between legal and moral ideas, about which I shall have something to say in a moment, is that theory is apt to get the cart before the horse, and to consider the right or the duty as something existing apart from and independent of the consequences of its breach, to which certain sanctions are added afterward. But, as I shall try to show, a legal duty so called is nothing but a prediction that if a man does or omits certain things he will be made to suffer in this or that way by judgment of the court; and so of a legal right.

The number of our predictions when generalized and reduced to a system is not unmanageably large. They present themselves as a finite body of dogma which may be mastered within a reasonable time. It is a great mistake to be frightened by the ever-increasing number of reports. The reports of a given jurisdiction in the course of a generation take up pretty much the whole body of the law, and restate it from the present point of view. We could reconstruct the corpus from them if all that went before were burned. The use of the earlier reports is mainly historical, a use about which I shall have something to say before I have finished.

I wish, if I can, to lay down some first principles for the study of this body of dogma or systematized prediction which we call the law, for men who want to use it as the instrument of their business to enable them to prophesy in their turn, and, as bearing upon the study, I wish to point out an ideal which as yet our law has not attained.

The first thing for a business-like understanding of the matter is to under-stand its limits, and therefore I think it desirable at once to point out and dispel a confusion between morality and law, which sometimes rises to the height of conscious theory, and more often and indeed constantly is making trouble in detail without reaching the point of consciousness. You can see very plainly that a bad man has as much reason as a good one for wishing to avoid an encounter with the public force, and therefore you can see the practical importance of the distinction between morality and law. A man who cares nothing for an ethical rule which is believed and practised by his neighbors is likely nevertheless to care a good deal to avoid being made to pay money, and will want to keep out of jail if he can.

I take it for granted that no hearer of mine will misinterpret what I have to say as the language of cynicism. The law is the witness and external deposit of our moral life. Its history is the history of the moral development of the race. The practice of it, in spite of popular jests, tends to make good citizens and good men. When I emphasize the difference between law and morals I do so with reference to a single end, that of learning and understanding the law. For that purpose you must definitely master its specific marks, and it is for that I say you for the moment to imagine yourselves indifferent to other and greater things.

I do not say that there is not a wider point of view from which the distinction between law and morals becomes of secondary or no importance, as all mathematical distinctions vanish in presence of the infinite. But I do say that that distinction is of the first importance for the object which we are here to consider—a right study and mastery of the law as a business with well understood limits, a body of dogma enclosed within definite lines. I have just shown the practical reason for saying so. If you want to know the law and nothing else, you must look at it as a bad man, who cares only for the material consequences which such knowledge enables him to predict, not as a good one, who finds his reasons for conduct, whether inside the law or outside of it, in the vaguer sanctions of conscience. The theoretical importance of the distinction is no less, if you would reason on your subject aright. The law is full of phraseology drawn from morals, and by the mere force of language continually invites us to pass from one domain to the other without perceiving it, as we are sure to do unless we have the boundary constantly before our minds. The law talks about rights, and duties, and malice, and intent, and negligence, and so forth, and nothing is easier, or, I may say, more common in legal reasoning, than to take these words in their moral sense, at some stage of the argument, and so to drop into fallacy. For instance, when we speak of the rights of man in a moral sense, we mean to mark the limits of interference with individual freedom which we think are prescribed by conscience, or by our ideal, however reached. Yet it is certain that many laws have been enforced in the past, and it is likely that some are enforced now, which are condemned by the most enlightened opinion of the time, or which at all events pass the limit of interference as many consciences would draw it. Manifestly, therefore, nothing but confusion of thought can result from assuming that the rights of man in a moral sense are equally rights in the sense of the Constitution and the law. No doubt simple and extreme cases can be put of imaginable laws which the statute-making power would not dare to enact, even in the absence of written constitutional prohibitions, because the community would rise in rebellion and fight; and this gives some plausibility to the proposition that the law, if not a part of morality, is limited by it. But this limit of power is not coextensive with any system of morals. For the most part it falls far within the lines of any such system, and in some cases may extend beyond them, for reasons drawn from the habits of a particular people at a particular time. I once heard the late Professor Agassiz say that a German population would rise if you added two cents to the price of a glass of beer. A statute in such a case would be empty words, not because it was wrong, but because it could not be enforced. No one will deny that wrong statutes can be and are enforced, and we should not all agree as to which were the wrong ones.

The confusion with which I am dealing besets confessedly legal conceptions. Take the fundamental question, What constitutes the law? You will find some text writers telling you that it is something different from what is decided by the courts of Massachusetts or England, that it is a system of reason, that it is a deduction from principles of ethics or admitted axioms or what not, which may or may not coincide with the decisions. But if we take the view of our friend the bad man we shall find that he does not care two straws for the axioms or deductions, but that he does want to know what the Massachusetts or English courts are likely to do in fact. I am much of his mind. The prophecies of what the courts will do in fact, and nothing more pretentious, are what I mean by the law.

Take again a notion which as popularly understood is the widest conception which the law contains—the notion of legal duty, to which already I have referred. We fill the word with all the content which we draw from morals. But what does it mean to a bad man? Mainly, and in the first place, a prophecy that if he does certain things he will be subjected to disagreeable consequences by way of imprisonment or compulsory payment of money. But from his point of view, what is the difference between being fined and being taxed a certain sum for doing a certain thing? That his point of view is the test of legal principles is shown by the many discussions which have arisen in the courts on the very question whether a given statutory liability is a penalty or a tax. On the answer to this question depends the decision whether conduct is legally wrong or right, and also whether a man is under compulsion or free. Leaving the criminal law on one side, what is the difference between the liability under the mill acts or statutes authorizing a taking by eminent domain and the liability for what we call a wrongful conversion of property where restoration is out of the question. In both cases the party taking another man's property has to pay its fair value as assessed by a jury, and no more. What significance is there in calling one taking right and another wrong from the point of view of the law? It does not matter, so far as the given consequence, the compulsory payment, is concerned, whether the act to which it is attached is described in terms of praise or in terms of blame, or whether the law purports to prohibit it or to allow it. If it matters at all, still speaking from the bad man's point of view, it must be because in one case and not in the other some further disadvantages, or at least some further consequences, are attached to the act by the law. The only other disadvantages thus attached to it which I ever have been able to think of are to be found in two somewhat insignificant legal doctrines, both of which might be abolished without disturbance. One is, that a contract to do a prohibited act is unlawful, and the other, that, if one of two or more joint wrongdoers has to pay all the damages, he cannot recover contribution from his fellows. And that I believe is all. You see how the vague circumference of the notion of duty shrinks and at the same time grows more precise when we wash it with cynical acid and expel everything except the object of our study, the operations of the law.

Nowhere is the confusion between legal and moral ideas more manifest than in the law of contract. Among other things, here again the so called primary rights and duties are invested with a mystic significance beyond what can be assigned and explained. The duty to keep a contract at common law means a prediction that you must pay damages if you do not keep it—and nothing else. If you commit a tort, you are liable to pay a compensatory sum. If you commit a contract, you are liable to pay a compensatory sum unless the promised event comes to pass, and that is all the difference. But such a mode of looking at the matter stinks in the nostrils of those who think it advantageous to get as much ethics into the law as they can. It was good enough for Lord Coke, however, and here, as in many other cases, I am content to abide with him. In *Bromage v. Genning*,[1] a prohibition was sought in the King's Bench against a suit in the marches of Wales for the specific performance of a covenant to grant a lease, and Coke said that it would subvert the intention of the covenantor, since he intends it to be at his election either to lose the damages or to make the lease. Sergeant Harris for the plaintiff confessed that he moved the matter against his conscience, and a prohibition was granted. This goes further than we should go now, but it shows what I venture to say has been the common law point of view from the beginning, although Mr. Harriman, in his very able little book upon Contracts, has been misled, as I humbly think, to a different conclusion.

I have spoken only of the common law, because there are some cases in which a logical justification can be found for speaking of civil liabilities as imposing duties in an intelligible sense. These are the relatively few in which equity will grant an injunction, and will enforce it by putting the defendant in prison or otherwise punishing him unless he complies with the order of the court. But I hardly think it advisable to shape general theory from the exception, and I think it would be better to cease troubling ourselves about primary rights and sanctions altogether, than to describe our prophecies concerning the liabilities commonly imposed by the law in those inappropriate terms.

I mentioned, as other examples of the use by the law of words drawn from morals, malice, intent, and negligence. It is enough to take malice as it is used in the law of civil liability for wrongs—what we lawyers call the law of torts— to show that it means something different in law from what it means in morals, and also to show how the difference has been obscured by giving to principles which have little or nothing to do with each other the same name. Three hundred years ago a parson preached a sermon and told a story out of Fox's *Book of Martyrs* of a man who had assisted at the torture of one of the saints, and afterward died, suffering compensatory inward torment. It happened that Fox was wrong. The man was alive and chanced to hear the sermon, and thereupon he sued the parson. Chief Justice Wray instructed the jury that the defendant was not liable, because the story was told innocently, without malice. He took malice in the moral sense, as importing a malevolent motive. But nowadays no one doubts that a man may be liable, without any malevolent motive at all, for false statements manifestly calculated to inflict temporal damage. In stating the case in pleading, we still should call the defendant's conduct malicious; but, in my opinion at least, the word means nothing about motives, or even about the defendant's attitude toward the future, but only signifies that the tendency of his conduct under the known circumstances was very plainly to cause the plaintiff temporal harm.[2]

[1] Roll. Rep. 368.
[2] See Hanson *v.* Globe Newspaper Co., 159 Mass. 293, 302.

In the law of contract the use of moral phraseology has led to equal confusion, as I have shown in part already, but only in part. Morals deal with the actual internal state of the individual's mind, what he actually intends. From the time of the Romans down to now, this mode of dealing has affected the language of the law as to contract, and the language used has reacted upon the thought. We talk about a contract as a meeting of the minds of the parties, and thence it is inferred in various cases that there is no contract because their minds have not met; that is, because they have intended different things or because one party has not known of the assent of the other. Yet nothing is more certain than that parties may be bound by a contract to things which neither of them intended, and when one does not know of the other's assent. Suppose a contract is executed in due form and in writing to deliver a lecture, mentioning no time. One of the parties thinks that the promise will be construed to mean at once, within a week. The other thinks that it means when he is ready. The court says that it means within a reasonable time. The parties are bound by the contract as it is interpreted by the court, yet neither of them meant what the court declares that they have said. In my opinion no one will understand the true theory of contract or be able even to discuss some fundamental questions intelligently until he has understood that all contracts are formal, that the making of a contract depends not on the agreement of two minds in one intention, but on the agreement of two sets of external signs— not on the parties' having *meant* the same thing but on their having *said* the same thing. Furthermore, as the signs may be addressed to one sense or another —to sight or to hearing—on the nature of the sign will depend the moment when the contract is made. If the sign is tangible, for instance, a letter, the contract is made when the letter of acceptance is delivered. If it is necessary that the minds of the parties meet, there will be no contract until the acceptance can be read—none, for example, if the acceptance be snatched from the hand of the offerer by a third person.

This is not the time to work out a theory in detail, or to answer many obvious doubts and questions which are suggested by these general views. I know of none which are not easy to answer, but what I am trying to do now is only by a series of hints to throw some light on the narrow path of legal doctrine, and upon two pitfalls which, as it seems to me, lie perilously near to it. Of the first of these I have said enough. I hope that my illustrations have shown the danger, both to speculation and to practice, of confounding morality with law, and the trap which legal language lays for us on that side of our way. For my own part, I often doubt whether it would not be a gain if every word of moral significance could be banished from the law altogether, and other words adopted which should convey legal ideas uncolored by anything outside the law. We should lose the fossil records of a good deal of history and the majesty got from ethical associations, but by ridding ourselves of an unnecessary confusion we should gain very much in the clearness of our thought.

So much for the limits of the law. The next thing which I wish to consider is what are the forces which determine its content and its growth. You may assume, with Hobbes and Bentham and Austin, that all law emanates from the sovereign, even when the first human beings to enunciate it are the judges, or you may think that law is the voice of the Zeitgeist, or what you like. It is all one to my present purpose. Even if every decision required the sanction of an emperor with despotic power and a whimsical turn of mind, we should be interested none the less, still with a view to prediction, in discovering some order, some rational explanation, and some principle of growth for the rules which he laid down. In every system there are such explanations and principles to be found. It is with regard to them that a second fallacy comes in, which I think it important to expose.

The fallacy to which I refer is the notion that the only force at work in the development of the law is logic. In the broadest sense, indeed, that notion would be true. The postulate on which we think about the universe is that there is a fixed quantitative relation between every phenomenon and its antecedents and consequents. If there is such a thing as a phenomenon without these fixed quantitative relations, it is a miracle. It is outside the law of cause and effect, and as such transcends our power of thought, or at least is something to or from which we cannot reason. The condition of our thinking about the universe is that it is capable of being thought about rationally, or, in other words, that every part of it is effect and cause in the same sense in which those parts are with which we are most familiar. So in the broadest sense it is true that the law is a logical development, like everything else. The danger of which I speak is not the admission that the principles governing other phenomena also govern the law, but the notion that a given system, ours, for instance, can be worked out like mathematics from some general axioms of conduct. This is the natural error of the schools, but it is not confined to them. I once heard a very eminent judge say that he never let a decision go until he was absolutely sure that it was right. So judicial dissent often is blamed, as if it meant simply that one side or the other were not doing their sums right, and, if they would take more trouble, agreement inevitably would come.

This mode of thinking is entirely natural. The training of lawyers is a training in logic. The processes of analogy, discrimination, and deduction are those in which they are most at home. The language of judicial decision is mainly the language of logic. And the logical method and form flatter that longing for certainty and for repose which is in every human mind. But certainty generally is illusion, and repose is not the destiny of man. Behind the logical form lies a judgment as to the relative worth and importance of competing legislative grounds, often an inarticulate and unconscious judgment, it is true, and yet the very root and nerve of the whole proceeding. You can give any conclusion a logical form. You always can imply a condition in a contract. But why do you imply it? It is because of some belief as to the practice of the community or of a class, or because of some opinion as to policy, or, in short, because of some attitude of yours upon a matter not capable of exact quantitative measurement, and therefore not capable of founding exact logical conclusions. Such matters really are battle grounds where the means do not exist for determinations that shall be good for all time, and where the decision can do no more than embody the preference of a given body in a given time and place. We do not realize how large a part of our law is open to reconsideration upon a slight change in the habit of the public mind. No concrete proposition is self evident, no matter how ready we may be to accept it, not even Mr. Herbert Spencer's "Every man has a right to do what he wills, provided he interferes not with a like right on the part of his neighbors."

Why is a false and injurious statement privileged, if it is made honestly in giving information about a servant? It is because it has been thought more important that information should be given freely, than that a man should be protected from what under other circumstances would be an actionable wrong. Why is a man at liberty to set up a business which he knows will ruin his neighbor? It is because the public good is supposed to be best subserved by free competition. Obviously such judgments of relative importance may vary in different times and places. Why does a judge instruct a jury that an employer is not liable to an employee for an injury received in the course of his employment unless he is negligent, and why do the jury generally find for the plaintiff if the case is allowed to go to them? It is because the traditional policy of our law is to confine liability to cases where a prudent man might have foreseen the injury, or at least the danger, while the inclination of a very large part of the community is to make certain classes of persons insure the safety of those with whom they deal. Since the last words were written, I have seen the requirement of such insurance put forth as part of the programme of one of the best known labor organizations. There is a concealed, half conscious battle on the question of legislative policy, and if anyone thinks that it can be settled deductively, or once for all, I only can say that I think he is theoretically wrong, and that I am certain that his conclusion will not be accepted in practice *semper ubique et ab omnibus*.

Indeed, I think that even now our theory upon this matter is open to reconsideration, although I am not prepared to say how I should decide if a reconsideration were proposed. Our law of torts comes from the old days of isolated, ungeneralized wrongs, assaults, slanders, and the like, where the damages might be taken to lie where they fell by legal judgment, But the torts with which our courts are kept busy to-day are mainly the incidents of certain well known businesses. They are injuries to person or property by railroads, factories, and the like. The liability for them is estimated, and sooner or later goes into the price paid by the public. The public really pays the damages, and the question of liability, if pressed far enough, is really the question how far it is desirable that the public should insure the safety of those whose work it uses. It might be said that in such cases the chance of a jury finding for the defendant is merely a chance, once in a while rather arbitrarily interrupting the regular course of recovery, most likely in the case of an unusually conscientious plaintiff, and therefore better done away with. On the other hand, the economic value even of a life to the community can be estimated, and no recovery, it may be said, ought to go beyond that amount. It is conceivable that some day in certain cases we may find ourselves imitating, on a higher plane, the tariff for life and limb which we see in the *Leges Barbarorum*.

I think that the judges themselves have failed adequately to recognize their duty of weighing considerations of social advantage. The duty is inevitable, and the result of the often proclaimed judicial aversion to deal with such considerations is simply to leave the very ground and foundation of judgments inarticulate, and often unconscious, as I have said. When socialism first began to be talked about, the comfortable classes of the community were a good deal frightened. I suspect that this fear has influenced judicial action both here and in England, yet it is certain that it is not a conscious factor in the decisions to which I refer. I think that something similar has led people who no longer hope to control the legislatures to look to the courts as expounders of the Constitutions, and that in some courts new principles have been discovered outside the bodies of those instruments, which may be generalized into acceptance of the economic doctrines which prevailed about fifty years ago, and a wholesale prohibition of what a tribunal of lawyers does not think about right. I cannot but believe that if the training of lawyers led them habitually to consider more definitely and explicitly the social advantage on which the rule they lay down must be justified, they sometimes would hesitate where now they are confident, and see that really they were taking sides upon debatable and often burning questions.

So much for the fallacy of logical form. Now let us consider the present condition of the law as a subject for study, and the ideal toward which it tends. We still are far from the point of view which I desire to see reached. No one has reached it or can reach it as yet. We are only at the beginning of a philosophical reaction, and of a reconsideration of the worth of doctrines which for the most part still are taken for granted without any deliberate, conscious, and systematic questioning of their grounds. The development of our law has gone on for nearly a thousand years, like the development of a plant, each generation taking the inevitable next step, mind, like matter, simply obeying a law of spontaneous growth. It is perfectly natural and right that it should have been so. Imitation is a necessity of human nature, as has been illustrated by a remarkable French writer, M. Tarde, in an admirable book, *Les Lois de l'Imitation*. Most of the things we do, we do for no better reason than that our fathers have done them or that our neighbors do them, and the same is true of a larger part than we suspect of what we think. The reason is a good one, because our short life gives us no time for a better, but it is not the best. It does not follow, because we all are compelled to take on faith at second hand most of the rules on which we base our action and our thought, that each of us may not try to set some corner of his world in the order of reason, or that all of us collectively should not aspire to carry reason as far as it will go throughout the whole domain. In regard to the law, it is true, no doubt, that an evolutionist will hesitate to affirm universal validity for his social ideals, or for the principles which he thinks should be embodied in legislation. He is content if he can prove them best for here and now. He may be ready to admit that he knows nothing about an absolute best in the cosmos, and even that he knows next to nothing about a permanent best for men. Still it is true that a body of law is more rational and more civilized when every rule it contains is referred articulately and definitely to an end which it subserves, and when the grounds for desiring that end are stated or are ready to be stated in words.

At present, in very many cases, if we want to know why a rule of law has taken its particular shape, and more or less if we want to know why it exists at all, we go to tradition. We follow it into the Year Books, and perhaps beyond them to the customs of the Salian Franks, and somewhere in the past, in the German forests, in the needs of Norman kings, in the assumptions of a dominant class, in the absence of generalized ideas, we find out the practical motive for what now best is justified by the mere fact of its acceptance and that men are accustomed to it. The rational study of law is still to a large extent the study of history. History must be a part of the study, because without it we cannot know the precise scope of laws which it is our business to know. It is a part of the rational study, because it is the first step toward an enlightened scepticism, that is, towards a deliberate reconsideration of the worth of those rules. When you get the dragon out of his cave on to the plain and in the daylight, you can count his teeth and claws, and see just what is his strength. But to get him out is only the first step. The next is either to kill him, or to tame him and make him a useful animal. For the rational study of the law the black-letter man may be the man of the present, but the man of the future is the man of statistics and the master of economics. It is revolting to have no better reason for a rule of law than that so it was laid down in the time of Henry IV. It is still more revolting if the grounds upon which it was laid down have vanished long since, and the rule simply persists from blind imitation of the past. I am thinking of the technical rule as to trespass *ab initio,* as it is called, which I attempted to explain in a recent Massachusetts case.[3]

Let me take an illustration, which can be stated in a few words, to show how the social end which is aimed at by a rule of law is obscured and only partially attained in consequence of the fact that the rule owes its form to a gradual historical development, instead of being reshaped as a whole, with conscious articulate reference to the end in view. We think it desirable to prevent one man's property being misappropriated by another, and so we make larceny a crime. The evil is the same whether the misappropriation is made by a man into whose hands the owner has put the property, or by one who wrongfully takes it away. But primitive law in its weakness did not get much beyond an effort to prevent violence, and very naturally made a wrongful taking, a trespass, part of its definition of the crime. In modern times the judges enlarged the definition a little by holding that, if the wrong-doer gets possession by a trick or device, the crime is committed. This really was giving up the requirement of a trespass, and it would have been more logical, as well as truer to the present object of the law, to abandon the requirement altogether. That, however, would have seemed too bold, and was left to statute. Statutes were passed making

[3] Commonwealth *v.* Rubin, 165 Mass. 453.

embezzlement a crime. But the force of tradition caused the crime of embezzlement to be regarded as so far distinct from larceny that to this day, in some jurisdictions at least, a slip corner is kept open for thieves to contend, if indicted for larceny, that they should have been indicted for embezzlement, and if indicted for embezzlement, that they should have been indicted for larceny, and to escape on that ground.

Far more fundamental questions still await a better answer than that we do as our fathers have done. What have we better than a blind guess to show that the criminal law in its present form does more good than harm? I do not stop to refer to the effect which it has had in degrading prisoners and in plunging them further into crime, or to the question whether fine and imprisonment do not fall more heavily on a criminal's wife and children than on himself. I have in mind more far-reaching questions. Does punishment deter? Do we deal with criminals on proper principles? A modern school of Continental criminalists plumes itself on the formula, first suggested, it is said, by Gall, that we must consider the criminal rather than the crime. The formula does not carry us very far, but the inquiries which have been started look toward an answer of my questions based on science for the first time. If the typical criminal is a degenerate, bound to swindle or to murder by as deep seated an organic necessity as that which makes the rattlesnake bite, it is idle to talk of deterring him by the classical method of imprisonment. He must be got rid of; he cannot be improved, or frightened out of his structural reaction. If, on the other hand, crime, like normal human conduct, is mainly a matter of imitation, punishment fairly may be expected to help to keep it out of fashion. The study of criminals has been thought by some well known men of science to sustain the former hypothesis. The statistics of the relative increase of crime in crowded places like large cities, where example has the greatest chance to work, and in less populated parts, where the contagion spreads more slowly, have been used with great force in favor of the latter view. But there is weighty authority for the belief that, however this may be, "not the nature of the crime, but the dangerousness of the criminal, constitutes the only reasonable legal criterion to guide the inevitable social reaction against the criminal."[4]

The impediments to rational generalization, which I illustrated from the law of larceny, are shown in the other branches of the law, as well as in that of crime. Take the law of tort or civil liability for damages apart from contract and the like. Is there any general theory of such liability, or are the cases in which it exists simply to be enumerated, and to be explained each on its special ground, as is easy to believe from the fact that the right of action for certain well known classes of wrongs like trespass or slander has its special history for each class? I think that there is a general theory to be discovered, although resting in tendency rather than established and accepted. I think that the law regards the infliction of temporal damage by a responsible person as actionable, if under the circumstances known to him the danger of his act is

[4] Havelock Ellis, *The Criminal*, 41, citing Garofalo. See also Ferri, *Sociologie Criminelle, passim.* Compare Tarde, *La Philosophie Pénale.*

manifest according to common experience, or according to his own experience if it is more than common, except in cases where upon special grounds of policy the law refuses to protect the plaintiff or grants a privilege to the defendant.[5] I think that commonly malice, intent, and negligence mean only that the danger was manifest to a greater or less degree, under the circumstances known to the actor, although in some cases of privilege malice may mean an actual malevolent motive, and such a motive may take away a permission knowingly to inflict harm, which otherwise would be granted on this or that ground of dominant public good. But when I stated my view to a very eminent English judge the other day, he said: "You are discussing what the law ought to be; as the law is, you must show a right. A man is not liable for negligence unless he is subject to a duty." If our difference was more than a difference in words, or with regard to the proportion between the exceptions and the rule, then, in his opinion, liability for an act cannot be referred to the manifest tendency of the act to cause temporal damage in general as a sufficient explanation, but must be referred to the special nature of the damage, or must be derived from some special circumstances outside of the tendency of the act, for which no generalized explanation exists. I think that such a view is wrong, but it is familiar, and I dare say generally is accepted in England.

Everywhere the basis of principle is tradition, to such an extent that we even are in danger of making the role of history more important than it is. The other day Professor Ames wrote a learned article to show, among other things, that the common law did not recognize the defence of fraud in actions upon specialties, and the moral might seem to be that the personal character of that defence is due to its equitable origin. But if, as I have said, all contracts are formal, the difference is not merely historical, but theoretic, between defects of form which prevent a contract from being made, and mistaken motives which manifestly could not be considered in any system that we should call rational except against one who was privy to those motives. It is not confined to specialties, but is of universal application. I ought to add that I do not suppose that Mr. Ames would disagree with what I suggest.

However, if we consider the law of contract, we find it full of history. The distinctions between debt, covenant, and assumpsit are merely historical. The classification of certain obligations to pay money, imposed by the law irrespective of any bargain as quasi contracts, is merely historical. The doctrine of consideration is merely historical. The effect given to a seal is to be explained by history alone. Consideration is a mere form. Is it a useful form? If so, why should it not be required in all contracts? A seal is a mere form, and is vanishing in the scroll and in enactments that a consideration must be given, seal or no seal. Why should any merely historical distinction be allowed to affect the rights and obligations of business men?

[5] An example of the law's refusing to protect the plaintiff is when he is interrupted by a stranger in the use of a valuable way, which he has travelled adversely for a week less than the period of prescription. A week later he will have gained a right, but now he is only a trespasser. Example of privilege I have given already. One of the best is competition in business.

   Since I wrote this discourse I have come on a very good example of the way in which tradition not only overrides rational policy, but overrides it after first having been misunderstood and having been given a new and broader scope than it had when it had a meaning. It is the settled law of England that a material alteration of a written contract by a party avoids it as against him. The doctrine is contrary to the general tendency of the law. We do not tell a jury that if a man ever has lied in one particular he is to be presumed to lie in all. Even if a man tried to defraud, it seems no sufficient reason for preventing him from proving the truth. Objections of like nature in general go to the weight, not to the admissibility, of evidence. Moreover, this rule is irrespective of fraud, and is not confined to evidence. It is not merely that you cannot use the writing, but that the contract is at an end. What does this mean? The existence of a written contract depends on the fact that the offerer and offeree have interchanged their written expressions, not on the continued existence of those expressions. But in the case of a bond, the primitive notion was different. The contract was inseparable from the parchment. If a stranger destroyed it, or tore off the seal, or altered it, the obligee could not recover however free from fault, because the defendant's contract, that is, the actual tangible bond which he had sealed, could not be produced in the form in which it bound him. About a hundred years ago Lord Kenyon undertook to use his reason on this tradition, as he sometimes did to the detriment of the law, and, not understanding it, said he could see no reason why what was true of a bond should not be true of other contracts. His decision happened to be right, as it concerned a promissory note, where again the common law regarded the contract as inseparable from the paper on which it was written, but the reasoning was general, and soon was extended to other written contracts, and various absurd and unreal grounds of policy were invented to account for the enlarged rule.

   I trust that no one will understand me to to be speaking with disrespect of the law, because I criticise it so freely. I venerate the law, and especially our system of law, as one of the vastest products of the human mind. No one knows better than I do the countless number of great intellects that have spent themselves in making some addition or improvement, the greatest of which is trifling when compared with the mighty whole. It has the final title to respect that it exists, that it is not a Hegelian dream, but a part of the lives of men. But one may criticise even what one reveres. Law is the business to which my life is devoted, and I should show less than devotion if I did not do what in me lies to improve it, and, when I perceive what seems to me the ideal of its future, if I hesitated to point it out and to press toward it with all my heart.

   Perhaps I have said enough to show the part which the study of history necessarily plays in the intelligent study of the law as it is to-day. In the teaching of this school and at Cambridge it is in no danger of being undervalued. Mr. Bigelow here and Mr. Ames and Mr. Thayer there have made important contributions which will not be forgotten, and in England the recent history of early English law by Sir Frederick Pollock and Mr. Maitland has lent the

out that the plaintiff had granted a license to a person whom he reasonably supposed to be the defendant's agent, although not so in fact, and therefore had assumed that the use of the way was permissive, in which case no right would be gained. Has the defendant gained a right or not? If his gaining it stands on the fault and neglect of the landowner in the ordinary sense, as seems commonly to be supposed, there has been no such neglect, and the right of way has not been acquired. But if I were the defendant's counsel, I should suggest that the foundation of the acquisition of rights by lapse of time is to be looked for in the position of the person who gains them, not in that of the loser. Sir Henry Maine has made it fashionable to connect the archaic notion of property with prescription. But the connection is further back than the first recorded history. It is in the nature of man's mind. A thing which you have enjoyed and used as your own for a long time, whether property or an opinion, takes root in your being and cannot be torn away without your resenting the act and trying to defend yourself, however you came by it. The law can ask no better justification than the deepest instincts of man. It is only by way of reply to the suggestion that you are disappointing the former owner, that you refer to his neglect having allowed the gradual dissociation between himself and what he claims, and the gradual association of it with another. If he knows that another is doing acts which on their face show that he is on the way toward establishing such an association, I should argue that in justice to that other he was bound at his peril to find out whether the other was acting under his permission, to see that he was warned, and if necessary, stopped.

I have been speaking about the study of the law, and I have said next to nothing of what commonly is talked about in that connection—text-books and the case system, and all the machinery with which a student comes most immediately in contact. Nor shall I say anything about them. Theory is my subject, not practical details. The modes of teaching have been improved since my time, no doubt, but ability and industry will master the raw material with any mode. Theory is the most important part of the dogma of the law, as the architect is the most important man who takes part in the building of a house. The most important improvements of the last twenty-five years are improvements in theory. It is not to be feared as unpractical, for, to the competent, it simply means going to the bottom of the subject. For the incompetent, it sometimes is true, as has been said, that an interest in general ideas means an absence of particular knowledge. I remember in army days reading of a youth who, being examined for the lowest grade and being asked a question about squadron drill, answered that he never had considered the evolutions of less than ten thousand men. But the weak and foolish must be left to their folly. The danger is that the able and practical minded should look with indifference or distrust upon ideas the connection of which with their business is remote. I heard a story, the other day, of a man who had a valet to whom he paid high wages, subject to deduction for faults. One of his deductions was, "For lack of imagination, five dollars." The lack is not confined to valets. The object of ambition, power, generally presents itself nowadays in the form of money alone. Money is the most immediate form, and is a proper object of desire. "The fortune," said Rachel, "is the measure of the intelligence." That is a good text to waken people out of a fool's paradise. But, as Hegel says,[6] " It is in the end not the appetite, but the opinion, which has to be satisfied." To an imagination of any scope the most far-reaching form of power is not money, it is the command of ideas. If you want great examples, read Mr. Leslie Stephen's *History of English Thought in the Eighteenth Century*, and see how a hundred years after his death the abstract speculations of Descartes had become a practical force controlling the conduct of men. Read the works of the great German jurists, and see how much more the world is governed to-day by Kant than by Bonaparte. We cannot all be Descartes or Kant, but we all want happiness. And happiness, I am sure from having known many successful men, cannot be won simply by being counsel for great corporations and having an income of fifty thousand dollars. An intellect great enough to win the prize needs other food besides success. The remoter and more general aspects of the law are those which give it universal interest. It is through them that you not only become a great master in your calling, but connect your subject with the universe and catch an echo of the infinite, a glimpse of its unfathomable process, a hint of the universal law.

[6] Phil. des Rechts, § 190.

## 2

# John Courtney Murray, S.J.

Father Murray (1904–1967), noted liberal Catholic theologian and natural law theorist, taught until his death at Woodstock College, a distinguished Jesuit seminary in Maryland.

# WE HOLD THESE TRUTHS*

The news reported in the last chapter—that the tradition of natural law is dead—calls for some verification, before it is accepted as true. For one thing, it may be a case of mistaken identity; perhaps it was for some contrefaçon of the doctrine that the funeral rites were held. This is possible. So many misunderstandings have conspired to obscure the true identity of the doctrine that it is often mistaken for what it is not. Some of the misunderstandings are naive; others are of the learned sort. Some are the product of ignorance; others result from polemic bias.

The doctrine is accused of abstractionism, as if it disregarded experience and undertook to pull all its moral precepts like so many magician's rabbits out of the metaphysical hat of an abstract human "essence". The doctrine is also interpreted as an intuitionism, as if it maintained that all natural-law precepts were somehow "self-evident." It is also derided as a legalism, as if it proclaimed a detailed code of particularized do's and don'ts, nicely drawn up with the aid of deductive logic alone, absolutely normative in all possible circumstances, ready for automatic application, whatever the factual situation may be. The theory is also rejected for its presumed immobilism, as if its concept of an immutable human nature and an unchanging structure of human ends required it to deny the historicity of human existence and forbade it to recognize the virtualities of human freedom. It should already be clear from the earlier chapter on the origins of the public consensus that these conceptions are caricatures of the doctrine of natural law.

There is also the biologist interpretation, which imputes to natural-law theory a confusion of the "primordial," in a biological sense, with the "natural." This is a particularly gross and gratuitous misinterpretation, since nothing is clearer in natural-law theory than its identification of the "natural" with the "rational," or perhaps better, the "human." Its whole effort is to incorporate

*John Courtney Murray, S.J., from *We Hold These Truths* (New York: © Sheed and Ward, 1960), pp. 295–301, 327–336, reprinted by permission of the publishers.

the biological values in man, notably his sexual tendencies, into the fuller human order of reason, and to deny them the status of the primordial. The primordial in man—that which is first in order—is his rational soul, the form of humanity, which informs all that is biological in him. Natural-law argument against sexual aberrations (including artificial contraception) indicts them precisely because in them man succumbs to his own biological inclinations in violation of the primordial inclinations of reason and real love.

There is also the objectivist-rationalist interpretation, which is the premise from which natural-law theory is criticized for its supposed neglect of the values of the human person and for its alleged deafness to the resonances of intersubjectivity. In point of fact, the theory never forgets that the "nature" with which it deals has no existence except in the person, who is a unique realization of the nature, situated in an order of other unique realizations, whose uniqueness, nevertheless, does not make them atomistic monads, since it is in each instance a form of participation and communication in the one common nature.

Finally, there is the charge that natural-law doctrine is not Christian. If it be meant that the doctrine in structure and style is alien to the general Protestant moral system, in so far as there is such a thing, the charge is true enough. The last chapter will have made this clear. It would not, of course, be difficult to show that the doctrine is, in germinal fashion, scriptural. However, I shall be content here to make only four comments.

First, natural-law theory does not pretend to do more than it can, which is to give a philosophical account of the moral experience of humanity and to lay down a charter of essential humanism. It does not show the individual the way to sainthood, but only to manhood. It does not promise to transform society into the City of God on earth, but only to prescribe, for the purposes of law and social custom, that minimum of morality which must be observed by the members of a society, if the social environment is to be human and habitable. At that, for a man to be reasonably human, and for a society to be essentially civil—these are no mean achievements. The ideal of the reasonable man, who does his duty to God, to others, and to himself, is not an ignoble one. In fact, it puts such a challenge to the inertness and perversity which are part of the human stuff, that Christian doctrine from the day of St. Augustine has taught the necessity of divine grace for this integral fulfillment of the natural law.

Second, beyond the fulfillment of the ideal of the reasonable man there lies the perennial question of youth, whatever its age. It is asked in the Gospel: "What do I still lack?" (Matthew 19:21). And there remains the Gospel's austere answer, put in the form of an invitation, but not cast in the categories of ethics, which are good and evil and the obligation to choose between them. The invitation opens the perspectives of a higher choice, to "be a follower of mine." For the making of this choice there is no other motive, no other inner impulse, than the free desire to respond to the prior choice of Him whom one chooses because one has been first chosen.

Third, the mistake would be to imagine that the invitation, "Come, follow me," is a summons somehow to forsake the universe of human nature, somehow to vault above it, somehow to leave law and obligation behind, somehow to enter the half-world of an individualist subjectivist "freedom" which pretends to know no other norm save "love." In other words, the Gospel invitation, in so far as it is a summons to the moral life, is not a call to construct a "situation ethics" that knows no general principles of moral living but only particular instances of moral judgment, each one valid only for the instance: and that recognizes no order of moral law that is binding on freedom, but only a freedom that is free and moral singly in so far as it is sheer spontaneity.

Fourth, the law of nature, which prescribes humanity, still exists at the interior of the Gospel invitation, which summons to perfection. What the follower of Christ chooses to perfect is, and can only be, a humanity. And the lines of human perfection are already laid down in the structure of man's nature. Where else could they be found? The Christian call is to transcend nature, notably to transcend what is noblest in nature, the faculty of reason. But it is not a call to escape from nature, or to dismantle nature's own structure, and least of all to deny that man is intelligent, that nature is intelligible, and that nature's intelligibilities are laws for the mind that grasps them. In so far as they touch the moral life, the energies of grace, which are the action of the Holy Spirit, quicken to new and fuller life the dynamisms of nature, which are resident in reason. Were it otherwise, grace would not be supernatural but only miraculous.

I list these misunderstandings of natural law only to make the point that those who dislike the doctrine, for one reason or another, seem forever to be at work, as it were, burying the wrong corpse. For my part, I would not at all mind standing with them, tearless, at the grave of any of the shallow and distorted theories that they mistake for the doctrine of natural law. The same point will come clearer from a bit of history. At about the turn of the century it was rather generally believed in professional circles that the Scholastic idea of natural law, as an operative concept in the fields of ethics, political theory, and law and jurisprudence, was dead. In other words, it was generally assumed that the great nineteenth-century attack on natural law had been successful.

In this respect, of course, the nineteenth century exhibited those extensive powers of learned misunderstanding which it possessed to an astonishing degree. In its extraordinary ignorance of philosophical and legal history, it supposed that the "law of nature" of the Age of the Enlightenment was the *ius naturale* of an earlier and in many ways more enlightened age. It supposed therefore that in doing away with the former, it had likewise done away with the latter. This was by no means the case. The theory of the "law of nature" that was the creature of the Enlightenment was as fragile, time-conditioned, and transitory a phenomenon as the Enlightenment itself. But the ancient idea of the natural law is as inherently perennial as the *philosophia perennis* of which it is an integral part. Its reappearance after its widely attended funeral is one of the interesting intellectual phenomena of our generation.

Admittedly, the phenomenon is not yet as plain as the old hill of Houth; but it is discernible. In 1902, when Sir John Salmond published his well-known book, *Jurisprudence,* he wrote: "The idea of a law of nature or moral law *(lex naturalis, lex naturae)* . . . has played a notable part in the history of human thought in the realm of ethics, theology, politics and jurisprudence. It was long the accepted tradition of those sciences, but it has now fallen on evil days, and it can no longer be accepted as in harmony with modern thought on those matters." However, when Parker edited the ninth edition in 1927 he was impelled to add the cautious footnote: "Sir John Salmond's view that the doctrine in all its forms is now discredited cannot be considered correct." Today, thirty years later, when modern thought has caught up a bit more with the past, one might perhaps transcend the timidity of this footnote. As a matter of fact, it would seem that the anceint tradition of natural law is beginning to climb out of the footnotes of the learned books into the very text of our time, as the conviction dawns that there are resources in the idea that might possibly make the next page of the text sound less like a tale told by an idiot.

Here then might be an approach to the whole subject of natural law. It would be an historical approach, on the theme indicated by Heinrich Rommen in the title of his book, *Die ewige Wiederkehr des Naturrechts.* The idea would be to describe, first, the origins and political significance of the Western tradition of natural law; secondly, the supplanting of this tradition by a newly conceived "law of nature" that had its greatest intellectual popularity in the Age of the Enlightenment and its highest political success in the Era of Revolution; thirdly, the reaction against this law of nature, that resulted in the victory of juridical positivism (the triumph of the idea that "law is will" over the ancient idea that "law is reason"), behind whose success lay all the forces that came to power in the nineteenth century—scientific empiricism, sociologism, psychologism, historical and philosophical materialism; fourthly, today's reaction against the positivist theory, as the ideas of justice and of human rights have had a rebirth in the face of the problems raised by totalitarian government and by the multiple aspects of the social conflict and the international conflict. It is this reaction, which is in fact a progress, that has effected the latest *Wiederkehr* of the idea of natural law.

Another approach to the problem of natural law is possible—a more directly philosophical approach. The idea of natural law goes back to the remotest origins, not only of political thought, but of ethical thought—to the day when man first began to reflect on the problem, whether there be something that intrinsically distinguishes right from wrong, whether what is right ought to be, and (on the political plane) whether laws ought to be just, and whether what is just ought to be law. These problems raise the basic ethical question, whether there is a connection between "being" and "oughtness," whether the moral order is a reflex and prolongation of a metaphysical order. In consequence, they bring man to the heart of philosophy itself. In fact, every system of natural law, whether it be Aristotle's or St. Thomas's or Locke's or Pufendorf's, has its premises; it supposes an epistemology, and therefore a metaphysic (or the absence of one). On the other hand, every system of natural law has its conclusions; it issues in a political philosophy—a concept of the nature of the state, its end, scope, and functions. Consequently, to inquire what natural law is, means to inquire, on the one hand, what the human mind is and what it can know, and on the other hand, what human society is and to what ends it should work. But, as is obvious, all this is to inquire what man himself is— what this human "nature" is of which one predicates a law "natural" . . .

## THE PREMISES OF NATURAL LAW

The whole metaphysic involved in the idea of natural law may seem alarmingly complicated; in a sense it is. Natural law supposes a realist epistemology, that asserts the real to be the measure of knowledge, and also asserts the possibility of intelligence reaching the real, *i.e.,* the nature of things—in the case, the nature of man as a unitary and constant concept beneath all individual differences. Secondly, it supposes a metaphysic of nature, especially the idea that nature is a teleological concept, that the "form" of a thing is its "final cause," the goal of its becoming; in the case, that there is a natural inclination in man to become what in nature and destination he is—to achieve the fullness of his own being. Thirdly, it supposes a natural theology, asserting that there is a God, Who is eternal Reason, *Nous,* at the summit of the order of being, Who is the author of all nature, and Who wills that the order of nature be fulfilled in all its purposes, as these are inherent in the natures found in the order. Finally, it supposes a morality, especially the principle that for man, a rational being, the order of nature is not an order of necessity, to be fulfilled blindly, but an order of reason and therefore of freedom. The order of being that confronts his intelligence is an order of "oughtness" for his will; the moral order is a prolongation of the metaphysical order into the dimensions of human freedom.

This sounds frightfully abstract: but it is simply the elaboration by the reflective intelligence of a set of data that are at bottom empirical. Consider, for instance, the contents of the consciousness of a man who is protesting against injustice, let us say, in a case where his own interests are not touched and where the injustice is wrought by technically correct legislation. The contents of his consciously protesting mind would be something like these. He is asserting that there is an idea of justice; that this idea is transcendent to the actually expressed will of the legislator; that it is rooted somehow in the nature of things; that he really *knows* this idea; that it is not made by his judgment but is the measure of his judgment; that this idea is of the kind that ought to be realized in law and action; that its violation is injury, which his mind rejects as unreason; that this unreason is an offense not only against his own intelligence but against God, Who commands justice and forbids injustice.

Actually, this man, who may be no philosopher, is thinking in the categories of natural law and in the sequence of ideas that the natural-law mentality (which is the human mentality) follows. He has an objective idea of the "just" in contrast to the "legal." His theoretical reason perceives the idea as true; his practical reason accepts the truth as good, therefore as law; his will acknowledges the law as normative of action. Moreover, this man will doubtless seek to ally others in his protest, in the conviction that they will think the same as he does. In other words, this man, whether he be protesting against the Taft-Hartley Act or the Nazi genocidal laws, is making in his own way all the metaphysical affirmations that undergird the concept of natural law. In this matter philosophical reflection does not augment the data of common sense. It merely analyzes, penetrates, and organizes them in their full abstractness; this does not, however, remove them from vital contact with their primitive source in experience.

## LAW IMMANENT AND TRANSCENDENT

From the metaphysical premises of natural law follow its two characteristics. It is a law immanent in the nature of man, but transcendent in its reference. It is rational, not rationalist. It is the work of reason, but not of an absolutely autonomous reason. It is immanent in nature in the sense that it consists in the dictates of human reason that are uttered as reason confronts the fundamental moral problems of human existence. These are the problems of what I, simply because I am a man and apart from all other considerations, ought to do or avoid in the basic situations in which I, again simply because I am a man, find myself. My situation is that of a creature before God; that of a "self" possessed of freedom to realize its "self"; that of a man living among other men, possessing what is mine as the other possesses what is his. In the face of these situations, certain imperatives "emerge" (if you like) from human nature. They are the product of its inclinations, as these are recognized by reason to be conformed to my rational nature. And they are formed by reason into dictates that present themselves as demanding obedience. Appearing, as they do, as dictates, these judgments of reason are law. Appearing, as they do, in consequence of an inclination that reason recognizes as authentically human, they are "natural" law.

However, these dictates are not simply emergent in the rationalist sense. Reason does not create its own laws, any more than man creates himself. Man has the laws of his nature given to him, as nature itself is given. By nature he is the image of God, eternal Reason; and so his reason reflects a higher reason; therein consists its rightness and its power to oblige. Above the natural law immanent in man stands the eternal law immanent in God transcendent; and the two laws are in intimate correspondence, as the image is to the exemplar. The eternal law is the Uncreated Reason of God; it appoints an order of nature— an order of beings, each of which carries in its very nature also its end and purposes; and it commands that this order of nature be preserved by the steady pursuit of their ends on the part of all the natures within the order. Every created nature has this eternal law, this transcendent order of reason, imprinted on it by the very fact that it is a nature, a purposeful dynamism striving for the fullness of its own being. In the irrational creation, the immanence of the eternal law is unconscious; the law itself is a law of necessity. But in the rational creature the immanent law is knowable and known; it is a moral law that authoritatively solicits the consent of freedom. St. Thomas, then, defines the natural law as the "rational creature's participation in the eternal law." The participation consists in man's possession of reason, the godlike faculty, whereby man knows himself—his own nature and end—and directs himself freely, in something of divine fashion but under God, to the plenitude of self-realization of his rational and social being.

Evidently, the immanent aspect of natural law relieves it of all taint of tyrannical heteronomy. It is not forcibly imposed as an alien pattern; it is discovered by reason itself as reason explores nature and its order. Moreover, it is well to note that in the discovery there is a necessary and large part reserved to experience, as St. Thomas insists: "What pertains to moral science is known mostly through experience" *(Eth.,* I, 3*)*. The natural law, Rommen points out, "is not in the least some sort of rationalistically deduced, norm-abounding code of immediately evident or logically derived rules that fits every concrete historical situation." Like the whole of the *philosophia perennis,* the doctrine of natural law is orientated toward constant contact with reality and the data of experience. The point was illustrated above, in the chapter on public consensus.

The "man" that it knows is not the Lockean individual, leaping full grown into abstract existence in a "state of nature," but the real man who grows in history, amid changing conditions of social life, acquiring wisdom by the discipline of life itself, in many respects only gradually exploring the potentialities and demands and dignities of his own nature. He knows indeed that there is an order of reason fixed and unalterable in its outlines, that is not at the mercy of his caprice or passion. But he knows, too, that the order of reason is not constructed in geometric fashion, apart from consultation of experience, and the study of "the customs of human life and . . . all juridical and civil matters, such as are the laws and precepts of political life," as St. Thomas puts it. The natural-law philosopher does not indeed speak of a "natural law with a changing content," as do the Neo-Kantians, to whom natural law is a purely formal category, empty of material content until it be filled by positive law and its process of legalizing the realities of a given sociological situation. However, the natural-law philosopher does speak of a "natural law with changing and progressive applications," as the evolution of human life brings to light new necessities in human nature that are struggling for expression and form. Natural law is a force conservative of all acquired human values; it is also a dynamic of progress toward fuller human realization, personal and social. Because it is law, it touches human life with a firm grasp, to give it form; but because it is a living law, it lays upon life no "dead hand," to petrify it into formalism.

In virtue of its immanent aspect, therefore, the natural law constantly admits the possibility of "new orders," as human institutions dissolve to be replaced by others. But in virtue of its transcendent aspect, it always demands that the new orders conform to the order of reason, which is structured by absolute and unalterable first principles.

## NATURAL LAW AND POLITICS

In the order of what is called *ius naturae* (natural law in the narrower sense, as regulative of social relationships), there are only two self-evident principles: the maxim, *"Suum cuique,"* and the wider principle, "Justice is to be done and injustice avoided." Reason particularizes them, with greater or less evidence, by determining what is "one's own" and what is "just" with the aid of the supreme norm of reference, the rational and social nature of man. The immediate particularizations are the precepts in the "Second Table" of the Decalogue. And the totality of such particularizations go to make up what is called the juridical order, the order of right and justice. This is the order (along with the orders of legal and distributive justice) whose guardianship and sanction is committed to the state. It is also the order that furnishes a moral basis for the positive legislation of the state, a critical norm of the justice of such legislation, and an ideal of justice for the legislator.

This carries us on to the function of natural law in political philosophy—its solution to the eternally crucial problem of the legitimacy of power, its value as a norm for, and its dictates in regard of, the structures and processes of society. The subject is much too immense. Let me say, first, that the initial claim of natural-law doctrine is to make political life part of the moral universe, instead of leaving it to wander as it too long has, like St. Augustine's sinner, *in regione dissimilitudinis.* There are doubtless a considerable number of people not of the Catholic Church who would incline to agree with Pius XII's round statement in *Summi Pontificatus* that the "prime and most profound root of all the evils with which the City is today beset" is a "heedlessness and forgetfulness of natural law." Secretary of State Marshall said practically the same thing, but in contemporary idiom, when he remarked that all our political troubles go back to a neglect or violation of human rights.

For the rest, I shall simply state the major contents of the political ideal as it emerges from natural law.

One set of principles is that which the Carlyles and others have pointed out as having ruled (amid whatever violations) the political life of the Middle Ages. First, there is the supremacy of law, and of law as reason, not will. With this is connected the idea of the ethical nature and function of the state *(regnum* or *imperium* in medieval terminology), and the educative character of its laws as directive of man to "the virtuous life" and not simply protective of particular interests. Secondly, there is the principle that the source of political authority is in the community. Political society as such is natural and necessary to man, but its form is the product of reason and free choice; no ruler has a right to govern that is inalienable and independent of human agency. Thirdly, there is the principle that the authority of the ruler is limited; its scope is only political, and the whole of human life is not absorbed in the polis. The power of the ruler is limited, as it were, from above by the law of justice, from below by systems of private right, and from the sides by the public right of the Church, Fourthly, there is the principle of the contractual nature of the relations between ruler and ruled. The latter are not simply material organized for rule by the *rex legibus solutus*, but human agents who agree to be ruled constitutionally, in accordance with law.

A second set of principles is of later development, as ideas and in their institutional form, although their roots are in the natural-law theories of the Middle Ages.

The first is the principle of subsidiarity. It asserts the organic character of the state—the right to existence and autonomous functioning of various sub-political groups, which unite in the organic unity of the state without losing their own identity or suffering infringement of their own ends or having their functions assumed by the state. These groups include the family, the local community, the professions, the occupational groups, the minority cultural or linguistic groups within the nation, etc. Here on the basis of natural law is the denial of the false French revolutionary antithesis, individual versus state, as the principle of political organization. Here too is the denial of all forms of state totalitarian monism, as well as of Liberalistic atomism that would remove all forms of social or economic life from any measure of political control. This principle is likewise the assertion of the fact that the freedom of the individul is secured at the interior of institutions intermediate between himself and the state (*e.g.*, trade unions) or beyond the state (the church).

The second principle is that of popular sharing in the formation of the collective will, as expressed in legislation or in executive policy. It is a natural-law principle inasmuch as it asserts the dignity of the human person as an active co-participant in the political decisions that concern him, and in the pursuit of the end of the state, the common good. It is also related to all the natural-law principles cited in the first group above. For instance, the idea that law is reason is fortified in legislative assemblies that discuss the reasons for laws. So, too, the other principles are fortified, as is evident.

## CONCLUSION

Here then in briefest compass are some of the resources resident in natural law, that would make it the dynamic of a new "age of order." It does not indeed furnish a detailed blueprint of the order; that is not its function. Nor does it pretend to settle the enormously complicated technical problems, especially in the economic order, that confront us today. It can claim to be only a "skeleton law," to which flesh and blood must be added by that heart of the political process, the rational activity of man, aided by experience and by high professional competence. But today it is perhaps the skeleton that we mostly need, since it is precisely the structural foundations of the political, social, and economic orders that are being most anxiously questioned. In this situation the doctrine of natural law can claim to offer all that is good and valid in competing systems, at the same time that it avoids all that is weak and false in them.

Its concern for the rights of the individual human person is no less than that shown in the school of individualist Liberalism with its "law of nature" theory of rights, at the same time that its sense of the organic character of the community, as the flowering in ascending forms of sociality of the social nature of man, is far greater and more realistic. It can match Marxism in its concern for man as worker and for the just organization of economic society, at the same time that it forbids the absorption of man in matter and its determinisms. Finally, it does not bow to the new rationalism in regard of a sense of history and progress, the emerging potentialities of human nature, the value of experience in settling the forms of social life, the relative primacy in certain respects of the empirical fact over the preconceived theory; at the same time it does not succumb to the doctrinaire relativism, or to the narrowing of the object of human intelligence, that cripple at their root the high aspirations of evolutionary scientific humanism. In a word, the doctrine of natural law offers a more profound metaphysic, a more integral humanism, a fuller rationality, a more complete philosophy of man in his nature and history.

I might say, too, that it furnishes the basis for a firmer faith and a more tranquil, because more reasoned, hope in the future. If there is a law immanent in man—a dynamic, constructive force for rationality in human affairs, that works itself out, because it is a natural law, in spite of contravention by passion and evil and all the corruptions of power—one may with sober reason believe in, and hope for, a future of rational progress. And this belief and hope is strengthened when one considers that this dynamic order of reason in man, that clamors for expression with all the imperiousness of law, has its origin and sanction in an eternal order of reason whose fulfillment is the object of God's majestic will.

## 3

# John Austin

John Austin (1790–1859), strongly influenced by the utilitarians, professor of jurisprudence at London University and a member of the British Criminal Law Commission of 1833, played a central role in the reformation of English legal practice as well as in the formulation of the command theory of law.

# THE PROVINCE OF JURISPRUDENCE DETERMINED*

The matter of jurisprudence is positive law: law, simply and strictly so called: or law set by political superiors to political inferiors. But positive law (or law, simply and strictly so called) is often confounded with objects to which it is related by *resemblance,* and with objects to which it is related in the way of *analogy:* with objects which are *also* signified, *properly* and *improperly,* by the large and vague expression *law.* To obviate the difficulties springing from that confusion, I begin my projected Course with determining the province of jurisprudence, or with distinguishing the matter of jurisprudence from those various related objects: trying to define the subject of which I intend to treat, before I endeavour to analyse its numerous and complicated parts.

A law, in the most general and comprehensive acceptation in which the term, in its literal meaning, is employed, may be said to be a rule laid down for the guidance of an intelligent being by an intelligent being having power over him. Under this definition are concluded, and without impropriety, several species. It is necessary to define accurately the line of demarcation which separates these species from one another, as much mistiness and intricacy has been infused into the science of jurisprudence by their being confounded or not clearly distinguished. In the comprehensive sense above indicated, or in the largest meaning which it has, without extension by metaphor or analogy, the term *law* embraces the following objects: Laws set by God to his human creatures, and laws set by men to men.

The whole or a portion of the laws set by God to men is frequently styled the law of nature, or natural law: being, in truth, the only natural law of which it is possible to speak without a metaphor, or without a blending of objects which ought to be distinguished broadly. But, rejecting the appellation Law of Nature as ambiguous and misleading, I name those laws or rules, as considered collectively or in a mass, the *Divine law,* or the *law of God.*

*Lecture I from *The Province of Jurisprudence Determined,* first published in 1932.

Laws set by men to men are of two leading or principal classes: classes which are often blended, although they differ extremely; and which, for that reason, should be severed precisely, and opposed distinctly and conspicuously.

Of the laws or rules set by men to men, some are established by _political superiors_, sovereign and subject: by persons exercising supreme and subordinate _government_, in independent nations, or independent political societies. The aggregate of the rules thus established, or some aggregate forming a portion of that aggregate, is the appropriate matter of _jurisprudence_, general or particular. To the aggregate of the rules thus established, or to some aggregate forming a portion of that aggregate, the term _law_, as used simply and strictly, is exclusively applied. But, as contradistinguished to _natural_ law, or to the law of _nature_ (meaning, by those expressions, the law of God), the aggregate of the rules, established by political superiors, is frequently styled _positive_ law, or law existing _by position._ As contradistinguished to the rules which I style _positive morality_, and on which I shall touch immediately, the aggregate of the rules, established by political superiors, may also be marked commodiously with the name of _positive law._ For the sake, then, of getting a name brief and distinctive at once, and agreeably to frequent usage, I style that aggregate of rules, or any portion of that aggregate, _positive law:_ though rules, which are _not_ established by political superiors, are also _positive,_ or exist _by position,_ if they be rules or laws, in the proper signification of the term.

Though _some_ of the laws or rules, which are set by men to men, are established by political superiors, _others_ are _not_ established by political superiors, or are _not_ established by political superiors, in that capacity or character.

Closely analogous to human laws of this second class, are a set of objects frequently but _improperly_ termed _laws,_ being rules set and enforced by _mere opinion,_ that is, by the opinions or sentiments held or felt by an indeterminate body of men in regard to human conduct. Instances of such a use of the term _law_ are the expressions—'The law of honour'; 'The law set by fashion'; and rules of this species constitute much of what is usually termed 'International law.' _(same distinction as in ~~Golding~~ Hart, The Concept of Law, p 9)_

The aggregate of human laws properly so called belonging to the second of the classes above mentioned, with the aggregate of objects _improperly_ but by _close analogy_ termed laws, I place together in a common class, and denote them by the term _positive morality._ The name _morality_ severs them from _positive law,_ while the epithet _positive_ disjoins them from the _law of God._ And to the end of obviating confusion, it is necessary or expedient that they _should_ be disjoined from the latter by that distinguishing epithet. For the name _morality_ (or _morals_), when standing unqualified or alone, denotes indifferently either of the following objects: namely, positive morality _as it is,_ or without regard to its merits; and positive morality _as it would be,_ if it conformed to the law of God, and were, therefore, deserving of _approbation._

Besides the various sorts of rules which are included in the literal acceptation of the term law, and those which are by a close and striking analogy, though improperly, termed laws, there are numerous applications of the term

law, which rest upon a slender analogy and are merely metaphorical or figurative. Such is the case when we talk of *laws* observed by the lower animals; of
*laws* regulating the growth or decay of vegetables; of *laws* determining the
movements of inanimate bodies or masses. For where *intelligence* is not, or where
it is too bounded to take the name of *reason,* and, therefore, is too bounded to
conceive the purpose of a law, there is not the *will* which law can work on, or
which duty can incite or restrain. Yet through these misapplications of a *name,*
flagrant as the metaphor is, has the field of jurisprudence and morals been
deluged with muddy speculation.

Having suggested the *purpose* of my attempt to determine the province of
jurisprudence: to distinguish positive law, the appropriate matter of jurisprudence, from the various objects to which it is related by resemblance, and to
which it is related, nearly or remotely, by a strong or slender analogy: I shall
now state the essentials of *a law* or *rule* (taken with the largest signification
which can be given to the term *properly*).

Every *law* or *rule* (taken with the largest signification which can be given
to the term *properly*) is a *command.* Or, rather, laws or rules, properly so called,
are a *species* of commands. *laws are species of commands (cf., Hart, (3-17)*

Now, since the term *command* comprises the term *law,* the first is the simpler
as well as the larger of the two. But, simple as it is, it admits of explanation.
And, since it is the *key* to the sciences of jurisprudence and morals, its meaning
should be analysed with precision.

Accordingly, I shall endeavour, in the first instance, to analyse the meaning
of '*command*': an analysis which I fear, will task the patience of my hearers, but
which they will bear with cheerfulness, or, at least, with resignation, if they
consider the difficulty of performing it. The elements of a science are precisely
the parts of it which are explained least easily. Terms that are the largest, and,
therefore, the simplest of a series, are without equivalent expressions into which
we can resolve them *concisely.* And when we endeavour to *define* them, or to
translate them into terms which we suppose are better understood, we are
forced upon awkward and tedious circumlocutions.

*command include threat?*

If you express or intimate a wish that I shall do or forbear from some act,
and if you will visit me with an evil in case I comply not with your wish, the
*expression* or *intimation* of your wish is a *command.* A command is distinguished
from other significations of desire, not by the style in which the desire is signified,
but by the power and the purpose of the party commanding to inflict an evil
or pain in case the desire be disregarded. If you cannot or will not harm me in
case I comply not with your wish, the expression of your wish is not a command,
although you utter your wish in imperative phrase. If you are able and willing
to harm me in case I comply not with your wish, the expression of your wish
amounts to a command, although you are prompted by a spirit of courtesy to
utter it in the shape of request. '*Preces* erant, sed *quibus contradici non posset.*'
Such is the language of Tacitus, when speaking of a petition by the soldiery to a
son and lieutenant of Vespasian.

A command, then, is a signification of desire. But a command is distinguished from other significations of desire by this peculiarity: that the party to whom it is directed is liable to evil from the other, in case he comply not with the desire.

*obliged*    Being liable to evil from you if I comply not with a wish which you signify, I am *bound* or *obliged* by your command, or I lie under a *duty* to obey it. If, in spite of that evil in prospect, I comply not with the wish which you signify, I am said to disobey your command, or to violate the duty which it imposes.

*command and duty*    Command and duty are, therefore, correlative terms: the meaning denoted by each being implied or supposed by the other. Or (changing the expression) wherever a duty lies, a command has been signified; and whenever a command is signified, a duty is imposed.

Concisely expressed, the meaning of the correlative expressions is this. He who will inflict an evil in case his desire be disregarded, utters a command by expressing or intimating his desire: He who is liable to the evil in case he disregard the desire, is bound or obliged by the command.

*sanction*    The evil which will probably be incurred in case a command be disobeyed or (to use an equivalent expression) in case a duty be broken, is frequently called a *sanction*, or an *enforcement of obedience*. Or (varying the phrase) the command or the duty is said to be *sanctioned* or *enforced* by the chance of incurring the evil.

Considered as thus abstracted from the command and the duty which it enforces, the evil to be incurred by disobedience is frequently styled a *punishment*. But, as punishments, strictly so called, are only a *class* of sanctions, the term is too narrow to express the meaning adequately.

I observe that Dr. Paley, in his analysis of the term *obligation*, lays much stress upon the *violence* of the motive to compliance. In so far as I can gather a meaning from his loose and inconsistent statement, his meaning appears to be this: that unless the motive to compliance be *violent* or *intense*, the expression or intimation of a wish is not a *command*, nor does the party to whom it is directed lie under a *duty* to regard it.

If he means, by a *violent* motive, a motive operating with certainty, his proposition is manifestly false. The greater the evil to be incurred in case the wish be disregarded, and the greater the chance of incurring it on the same event, the greater, no doubt, is the *chance* that the wish will *not* be disregarded. But no conceivable motive will *certainly* determine to compliance, or no conceivable motive will render obedience inevitable. If Paley's proposition be true, in the sense which I have now ascribe to it, commands and duties are simply impossible. Or, reducing his proposition to absurdity by a consequence as manifestly false, commands and duties are possible, but are never disobeyed or broken.

If he means by a *violent* motive, an evil which inspires fear, his meaning is simply this: that the party bound by a command is bound by the prospect of an evil. For that which is not feared is not apprehended as an evil: or (changing the shape of the expression) is not an evil in prospect.

The truth is, that the magnitude of the eventual evil, and the magnitude of the chance of incurring it, are foreign to the matter in question. The greater the eventual evil, and the greater the chance of incurring it, the greater is the efficacy of the command, and the greater is the strength of the obligation: Or (substituting expressions exactly equivalent), the greater is the *chance* that the command will be obeyed, and that the duty will not be broken. But where there is the smallest chance of incurring the smallest evil, the expression of a wish amounts to a command, and, therefore, imposes a duty. The sanction, if you will, is feeble or insufficient; but still there *is* a sanction, and therefore, a duty and a command.

By some celebrated writers (by Locke, Bentham, and, I think, Paley), the term *sanction, or enforcement of obedience,* is applied to conditional good as well as to conditional evil; to reward as well as to punishment. But, with all my habitual veneration for the names of Locke and Bentham, I think that this extension of the term is pregnant with confusion and perplexity.

Rewards are, indisputably, *motives* to comply with the wishes of others. But to talk of commands and duties as *sanctioned* or *enforced* by rewards, or to talk of rewards as *obliging* or *constraining* to obedience, is surely a wide departure from the established meaning of the terms.

If *you* expressed a desire that *I* should render a service, and if you proffered a reward as the motive or inducement to render it, *you* would scarcely be said to *command* the service, nor should *I*, in ordinary language, be *obliged* to render it. In ordinary language, *you* would *promise* me a reward, on condition of my rendering the service, whilst *I* might be *incited* or *persuaded* to render it by the hope of obtaining the reward. *The sanction is not getting the reward.*

Again: If a law hold out a *reward* as an inducement to do some act, an eventual *right* is conferred, and not an *obligation* imposed, upon those who shall act accordingly: The *imperative* part of the law being addressed or directed to the party whom it requires to *render* the reward.

In short, I am determined or inclined to comply with the wish of another, by the fear of disadvantage or evil. I am also determined or inclined to comply with the wish of another, by the hope of advantage or good. But it is only by the chance of incurring *evil,* that I am *bound* or *obliged* to compliance. It is only by conditional *evil,* that duties are *sanctioned* or *enforced.* It is the power and the purpose of inflicting eventual *evil,* and *not* the power and the purpose of imparting eventual *good,* which gives to the expression of a wish the name of a *command.*

If we put *reward* into the import of the term *sanction,* we must engage in a toilsome struggle with the current of ordinary speech; and shall often slide unconsciously, notwithstanding our efforts to the contrary, into the narrower and customary meaning.

It appears, then, from what has been premised, that the ideas or notions comprehended by the term *command* are the following. 1. A wish or desire conceived by a rational being, that another rational being shall do or forbear. 2. An evil to proceed from the former, and to be incurred by the latter, in case the latter comply not with the wish. 3. An expression or intimation of the wish by words or other signs.

It also appears from what has been premised, that *command, duty,* and *sanction* are inseparably connected terms: that each embraces the same ideas as the others, though each denotes those ideas in a peculiar order or series.

'A wish conceived by one, and expressed or intimated to another, with an evil to be inflicted and incurred in case the wish be disregarded,' are signified directly and indirectly by each of the three expressions. Each is the name of the same complex notion.

But when I am talking *directly* of the expression or intimation of the wish, I employ the term <u>*command*</u>: The expression or intimation of the wish being presented *prominently* to my hearer; whilst the evil to be incurred ,with the chance of incurring it, are kept (if I may so express myself) in the background of my picture.

When I am talking *directly* of the chance of incurring the evil, or (changing the expression) of the liability or obnoxiousness to the evil, I employ the term *duty,* or the term <u>*obligation*</u>: The liability or obnoxiousness to the evil being put foremost, and the rest of the complex notion being signified implicitly.

When I am talking *immediately* of the evil itself, I employ the term <u>*sanction,*</u> or a term of the like import: The evil to be incurred being signified directly; whilst the obnoxiousness to that evil, with the expression or intimation of the wish, are indicated indirectly or obliquely.

To those who are familiar with the language of logicians (language unrivalled for brevity, distinctness, and precision), I can express my meaning accurately in a breath: Each of the three terms *signifies* the same notion; but each *denotes* a different part of that notion, and *connotes* the residue.

Commands are of two species. Some are *laws* or *rules.* The others have not acquired an appropriate name, nor does language afford an expression which will mark them briefly and precisely. I must, therefore, note them as well as I can by the ambiguous and inexpressive name of '*occasional* or *particular* commands.'

The term *laws* or *rules* being not unfrequently applied to occasional or particular commands, it is hardly possible to describe a line of separation which shall consist in every respect with established forms of speech. But the distinction between laws and particular commands may, I think, be stated in the following manner.

By every command, the party to whom it is directed is obliged to do or to forbear.

Now where it obliges *generally* to acts or forbearances of a *class,* a command is a law or rule. But where it obliges to a *specific* act or forbearance, or to acts or forbearances which it determines *specifically* or *individually,* a command is occasional or particular. In other words, a class or description of acts is determined by a law or rule, and acts of that class or description are enjoined or forbidden generally. But where a command is occasional or particular, the act or acts, which the command enjoins or forbids, are assigned or determined by their specific or individual natures as well as by the class or description to which they belong.

The statement which I have given in abstract expressions I will now endeavour to illustrate by apt examples.

If you command your servant to go on a given errand, or *not* to leave your house on a given evening, or to rise at such an hour on such a morning, or to rise at that hour during the next week or month, the command is occasional or particular. For the act or acts enjoined or forbidden are specially determined or assigned.

But if you command him *simply* to rise at that hour, or to rise at that hour *always,* or to rise at that hour *till further orders,* it may be said, with propriety, that you lay down a *rule* for the guidance of your servant's conduct. For no specific act is assigned by the command, but the command obliges him generally to acts of a determined class.

If a regiment be ordered to attack or defend a post, or to quell a riot, or to march from their present quarters, the command is occasional or particular. But an order to exercise daily till further orders shall be given would be called a *general* order, and *might* be called a *rule.*

If Parliament prohibited simply the exportation of corn, either for a given period or indefinitely, it would establish a law or rule: a *kind* or *sort* of acts being determined by the command, and acts of that kind or sort being *generally* forbidden. But an order issued by Parliament to meet an impending scarcity, and stopping the exportation of corn *then shipped and in port,* would not be a law or rule, though issued by the sovereign legislature. The order regarding exclusively a specified quantity of corn, the negative acts or forbearances, enjoined by the command, would be determined specifically or individually by the determinate nature of their subject.

As issued by a sovereign legislature, and as wearing the form of a law, the order which I have now imagined would probably be *called* a law. And hence the difficulty of drawing a distinct boundary between laws and occasional commands.

Again: An act which is not an offence, according to the existing law, moves the sovereign to displeasure: and, though the authors of the act are legally innocent or unoffending, the sovereign commands that they shall be punished. As enjoining a specific punishment in that specific case, and as not enjoining generally acts or forbearances of a class, the order uttered by the sovereign is not a law or rule.

Whether such an order would be *called* a law, seems to depend upon circumstances which are purely immaterial: immaterial, that is, with reference to the present purpose, though material with reference to others. If made by a sovereign assembly deliberately, and with the forms of legislation, it would probably be called a law. If uttered by an absolute monarch, without deliberation or ceremony, it would scarcely be confounded with acts of legislation, and would be styled an arbitrary command. Yet, on either of these suppositions, its nature would be the same. It would not be a law or rule, but an occasional or particular command of the sovereign One or Number.

To conclude with an example which best illustrates the distinction, and which shows the importance of the distinction most conspicuously, *judicial commands* are commonly occasional or particular, although the commands which they are calculated to enforce are commonly laws or rules.

For instance, the lawgiver commands that thieves shall be hanged. A specific theft and a specified thief being given, the judge commands that the thief shall be hanged, agreeably to the command of the lawgiver.

Now the lawgiver determines a class or description of acts; prohibits acts of the class generally and indefinitely; and commands, with the like generality, that punishment shall follow transgression. The command of the lawgiver is, therefore, a law or rule. But the command of the judge is occasional or particular. For he orders a specific punishment, as the consequence of a specific offence.

According to the line of separation which I have now attempted to describe, a law and a particular command are distinguished thus:—Acts or forbearances of a *class* are enjoined *generally* by the former. Acts *determined specifically,* are enjoined or forbidden by the latter.

A different line of separation has been drawn by Blackstone and others. According to Blackstone and others, a law and a particular command are distinguished in the following manner:—A law obliges *generally* the members of the given community, or a law obliges *generally* persons of a given class. A particular command obliges a *single* person, or persons whom it determines *individually*.

That laws and particular commands are not to be distinguished thus, will appear on a moment's reflection.

For, *first,* commands which oblige generally the members of the given community, or commands which oblige generally persons of given classes, are not always laws or rules.

Thus, in the case already supposed; that in which the sovereign commands that all corn actually shipped for exportation be stopped and detained; the command is obligatory upon the whole community, but as it obliges them only to a set of acts individually assigned, it is not a law. Again, suppose the sovereign to issue an order, enforced by penalties, for a general mourning, on occasion of a public calamity. Now, though it is addressed to the community at large, the order is scarcely a rule, in the usual acceptation of the term. For, though it obliges generally the members of the entire community, it obliges to acts which it assigns specifically, instead of obliging generally to acts or forbearances of a class. If the sovereign commanded that *black* should be the dress of his subjects, his command would amount to a law. But if he commanded them to wear it on a specified occasion, his command would be merely particular.

And, *secondly,* a command which obliges exclusively persons individually determined, may amount, notwithstanding, to a law or a rule.

For example, A father may set a *rule* to his child or children: a guardian, to his ward: a master, to his slave or servant. And certain of God's *laws* were as binding on the first man, as they are binding at this hour on the millions who have sprung from his loins.

Most, indeed, of the laws which are established by political superiors, or most of the laws which are simply and strictly so called, oblige generally the members of the political community, or oblige generally persons of a class. To frame a system of duties for every individual of the community, were simply impossible: and if it were possible, it were utterly useless. Most of the laws established by political superiors are, therefore, *general* in a twofold manner: as enjoining or forbidding generally acts of kinds or sorts; and as binding the whole community, or, at least, whole classes of its members.

But if we suppose that Parliament creates and grants an office, and that Parliament binds the grantee to services of a given description, we suppose a law established by political superiors, and yet exclusively binding a specified or determinate person.

Laws established by political superiors, and exclusively binding specified or determinate persons, are styled, in the language of the Roman jurists, *privilegia*. Though that, indeed, is a name which will hardly denote them distinctly: for, like most of the leading terms in actual systems of law, it is not the name of a definite class of objects, but of a heap of heterogeneous objects.[1]

It appears, from what has been premised, that a law, properly so called, may be defined in the following manner.

A law is a command which obliges a person or persons.

But, as contradistinguished or opposed to an occasional or particular command, a law is a command which obliges a person or persons, and obliges *generally* to acts or forbearances of a *class*.

In language more popular but less distinct and precise, a law is a command which obliges a person or persons to a *course* of conduct.

Laws and other commands are said to proceed from *superiors*, and to bind or oblige *inferiors*. I will, therefore, analyse the meaning of those correlative expressions; and will try to strip them of a certain mystery, by which that simple meaning appears to be obscured.

*Superiority* is often synonymous with *precedence* or *excellence*. We talk of superiors in rank; of superiors in wealth; of superiors in virtue: comparing certain persons with certain other persons; and meaning that the former precede or excel the latter in rank, in wealth, or in virtue.

But, taken with the meaning wherein I here understand it, the term *superiority* signifies *might*: the power of affecting others with evil or pain, and of forcing them, through fear of that evil, to fashion their conduct to one's wishes.

For example, God is emphatically the *superior* of Man. For his power of affecting us with pain, and of forcing us to comply with his will, is unbounded and resistless.

---

[1] Where a *privilegium* merely imposes a duty, it exclusively obliges a determinate person or persons. But where a *privilegium* confers a right, and the right conferred *avails against the world at large*, the law is *privilegium* as viewed from a certain aspect, but is also *a general law* as viewed from another aspect. In respect of the right conferred, the law exclusively regards a determinate person, and, therefore, is *privilegium*. In respect of the duty imposed, and corresponding to the right conferred, the law regards generally the members of the entire community.
This I shall explain particularly at a subsequent point of my Course, when I consider the peculiar nature of so-called *privilegia*, or so-called *private laws*.

*superior is he who obliges*

To a limited extent, the sovereign One or Number is the superior of the subject or citizen: the master, of the slave or servant: the father, of the child.

In short, whoever can *oblige* another to comply with his wishes, is the *superior* of that other, so far as the ability reaches: The party who is obnoxious to the impending evil, being, to that same extent, the *inferior*.

*two relativity of obligation*

The might or superiority of God, is simple or absolute. But in all or most cases of human superiority, the relation of superior and inferior, and the relation of inferior and superior, are reciprocal. Or (changing the expression) the party who is the superior as viewed from one aspect, is the inferior as viewed from another.

For example, To an indefinite, though limited extent, the monarch is the superior of the governed: his power being commonly sufficient to enforce compliance with his will. But the governed, collectively or in mass, are also the superior of the monarch: who is checked in the abuse of his might by his fear of exciting their anger: and of rousing to active resistance the might which slumbers in the multitude.

A member of a sovereign assembly is the superior of the judge: the judge being bound by the law which proceeds from that sovereign body. But, in his character of citizen or subject, he is the inferior of the judge: the judge being the minister of the law, and armed with the power of enforcing it.

*superiority*

It appears, then, that the term *superiority* (like the terms *duty* and *sanction*) is implied by the term *command*. For superiority is the power of enforcing compliance with a wish: and the expression or intimation of a wish, with the power and the purpose of enforcing it, are the constituent elements of a command.

'That *laws* emanate from *superiors*' is, therefore, an identical proposition. For the meaning which it affects to impart is contained in its subject.

If I mark the peculiar source of a given law, or if I mark the peculiar source of laws of a given class, it is possible that I am saying something which may instruct the hearer. But to affirm of laws universally 'that they flow from *superiors*,' or to affirm of laws universally 'that *inferiors* are bound to obey them,' is the merest tautology and trifling.

Like most of the leading terms in the sciences of jurisprudence and morals, the term *laws* is extremely ambiguous. Taken with the largest signification which can be given to the term properly, *laws* are a species of *commands*. But the term is improperly applied to various objects which have nothing of the imperative character: to objects which are *not* commands; and which, therefore, are *not* laws, properly so called.

Accordingly, the proposition 'that laws are commands' must be taken with limitations. Or, rather, we must distinguish the various meanings of the term *laws;* and must restrict the proposition to that class of objects which is embraced by the largest signification that can be given to the term properly.

I have already indicated, and shall hereafter more fully describe, the objects improperly termed laws, which are *not* within the province of jurisprudence (being either rules enforced by opinion and closely analogous to laws properly so called, or being laws so called by a metaphorical application of the term merely). There are other objects improperly termed laws (not being commands) which yet may properly be included within the province of jurisprudence. These I shall endeavour to particularise:— **DECLATORY**

1. Acts on the part of legislatures to *explain* positive law, can scarcely be called laws, in the proper signification of the term. Working no change in the actual duties of the governed, but simply declaring what those duties *are*, they properly are acts of *interpretation* by legislative authority. Or, to borrow an expression from the writers on the Roman Law, they are acts of *authentic* interpretation.

But, this notwithstanding, they are frequently styled laws; *declaratory* laws, or declaratory statutes. They must, therefore, be noted as forming an exception to the proposition 'that laws are a species of commands.'

It often, indeed, happens (as I shall show in the proper place), that laws declaratory in name are imperative in effect: Legislative, like judicial interpretation, being frequently deceptive; and establishing new law, under guise of expounding the old. **REPEALS**

2. Laws to repeal laws, and to release from existing duties, must also be excepted from the proposition 'that laws are a species of commands.' In so far as they release from duties imposed by existing laws, they are not commands, but revocations of commands. They authorize or permit the parties, to whom the repeal extends, to do or to forbear from acts which they were commanded to forbear from or to do. And, considered with regard to *this*, their immediate or direct purpose, they are often named *permissive laws,* or, more briefly and more properly, *permissions.*

Remotely and indirectly, indeed, permissive laws are often or always imperative. For the parties released from duties are restored to liberties or rights: and duties answering those rights are, therefore, created or revived.

But this is a matter which I shall examine with exactness, when I analyse the expressions 'legal right,' 'permission by the sovereign or state,' and 'civil or political liberty.' **IMPERFECT**

3. Imperfect laws, or laws of imperfect obligation, must also be excepted from the proposition 'that laws are a species of commands.'

An imperfect law (with the sense wherein the term is used by the Roman jurists) is a law which wants a sanction, and which, therefore, is not binding. A law declaring that certain acts are crimes, but annexing no punishment to the commission of acts of the class, is the simplest and most obvious example.

Though the author of an imperfect law signifies a desire, he manifests no purpose of enforcing compliance with the desire. But where there is not a purpose of enforcing compliance with the desire, the expression of a desire is not a command. Consequently, an imperfect law is not so properly a law, as counsel, or exhortation, addressed by a superior to inferiors.

Examples of imperfect laws are cited by the Roman jurists. But with us in England, laws professedly imperative are always (I believe) perfect or obligatory. Where the English legislature affects to command, the English tribunals not unreasonably presume that the legislature exacts obedience.

And, if no specific sanction be annexed to a given law, a sanction is supplied by the courts of justice, agreeably to a general maxim which obtains in cases of the kind.

The imperfect laws, of which I am now speaking, are laws which are imperfect, in the sense of *the Roman jurists*: that is to say, laws which speak the desires of political superiors, but which their authors (by oversight or design) have not provided with sanctions. Many of the writers on *morals,* and on the so called *law of nature,* have annexed a different meaning to the term *imperfect.* Speaking of imperfect obligations, they commonly mean duties which are *not legal*: duties imposed by commands of God, or duties imposed by positive morality, as contradistinguished to duties imposed by positive law. An imperfect obligation, in the sense of the Roman jurists, is exactly equivalent to no obligation at all. For the term *imperfect* denotes simply, that the law wants the sanction appropriate to laws of the kind. An imperfect obligation, in the other meaning of the expression, is a religious or a moral obligation. The term *imperfect* does not denote that the law imposing the duty wants the appropriate sanction. It denotes that the law imposing the duty is *not* a law established by a political superior: that it wants that *perfect,* or that surer or more cogent sanction, which is imparted by the sovereign or state.

I believe that I have now reviewed all the classes of objects, to which the term *laws* is improperly applied. The laws (improperly so called) which I have here lastly enumerated, are (I think) the only laws which are not commands, and which yet may be properly included within the province of jurisprudence. But though these, with the so called laws set by opinion and the objects metaphorically termed laws, are the only laws which *really* are not commands, there are certain laws (properly so called) which may *seem* not imperative. Accordingly, I will subjoin a few remarks upon laws of this dubious character.

1. There are laws, it may be said, which *merely* create *rights*: And, seeing that every command imposes a *duty,* laws of this nature are not imperative.

But, as I have intimated already, and shall show completely hereafter, there are no laws *merely* creating *rights.* There are laws, it is true, which *merely* create *duties*: duties not correlating with correlating rights, and which, therefore may be styled *absolute.* But every law, really conferring a right, imposes expressly or tacitly a *relative* duty, or a duty correlating with the right. If it specify the remedy to be given, in case the right shall be infringed, it imposes the relative duty expressly. If the remedy to be given be not specified, it refers tacitly to pre-existing law, and clothes the right which it purports to create with a remedy provided by that law. Every law, really conferring a right, is, therefore, imperative: as imperative, as if its only purpose were the creation of a duty, or as if the relative duty, which it inevitably imposes, were merely absolute.

The meanings of the term *right,* are various and perplexed; taken with its proper meaning, it comprises ideas which are numerous and complicated; and the searching and extensive analysis, which the term, therefore, requires, would occupy more room than could be given to it in the present lecture. It is not, however, necessary, that the analysis should be performed here. I purpose, in my earlier lectures, to determine the province of jurisprudence; or to distinguish the laws established by political superiors, from the various laws, proper and improper, with which they are frequently confounded. And this I may accomplish exactly enough, without a nice inquiry into the import of the term *right*.

*custom*

2. According to an opinion which I must notice *incidentally* here, though the subject to which it relates will be treated *directly* hereafter, *customary laws* must be excepted from the proposition 'that laws are a species of commands.'

By many of the admirers of customary laws (and, especially, of their German admirers), they are thought to oblige legally (independently of the sovereign or state), *because* the citizens or subjects have observed or kept them. Agreeably to this opinion, they are not the *creatures* of the sovereign or state, although the sovereign or state may abolish them at pleasure. Agreeably to this opinion, they are positive law (or law, strictly so called), inasmuch as they are enforced by the courts of justice: But, that notwithstanding, they exist *as positive law* by the spontaneous adoption of the governed, and not by position or establishment on the part of political superiors. Consequently, customary laws, considered as positive law, are not commands. And, consequently, customary laws, considered as positive law, are not laws or rules properly so called.

An opinion less mysterious, but somewhat allied to this, is not uncommonly held by the adverse party: by the party which is strongly opposed to customary law; and to all law made judicially, or in the way of judicial legislation. According to the latter opinion, all judge-made law, or all judge-made law established by *subject* judges, is purely the creature of the judges by whom it is established immediately. To impute it to the sovereign legislature, or to suppose that it speaks the will of the sovereign legislature, is one of the foolish or knavish *fictions* with which lawyers, in every age and nation, have perplexed and darkened the simplest and clearest truths.

I think it will appear, on a moment's reflection, that each of these opinions is groundless: that customary law is *imperative*, in the proper signification of the term; and that all judge-made law is the creature of the sovereign or state.

At its origin, a custom is a rule of conduct which the governed observe spontaneously, or not in pursuance of a law set by a political superior. The custom is transmuted into positive law, when it is adopted as such by the courts of justice, and when the judicial decisions fashioned upon it are enforced by the power of the state. But before it is adopted by the courts, and clothed with the legal sanction, it is merely a rule of positive morality: a rule generally observed by the citizens or subjects; but deriving the only force, which it can be said to possess, from the general disapprobation falling on those who transgress it. *why is not this an evil?*

Now when judges transmute a custom into a legal rule (or make a legal rule not suggested by a custom), the legal rule which they establish is established by the sovereign legislature. A subordinate or subject judge is merely a minister. The portion of the sovereign power which lies at his disposition is merely delegated. The rules which he makes derive their legal force from authority given by the state: an authority which the state may confer expressly, but which it commonly imparts in the way of acquiescence. For, since the state may reverse the rules which he makes, and yet permits him to enforce them by the power of the political community, its sovereign will 'that his rules shall obtain as law' is clearly evinced by its conduct, though not by its express declaration.

The admirers of customary law love to trick out their idol with mysterious and imposing attributes. But to those who can see the difference between positive law and morality, there is nothing of mystery about it. Considered as rules of positive morality, customary laws arise from the consent of the governed, and not from the position or establishment of political superiors. But, considered as moral rules turned into positive laws, customary laws are established by the state: established by the state directly, when the customs are promulged in its statutes; established by the state circuitously, when the customs are adopted by its tribunals.

The opinion of the party which abhors judge-made laws, springs from their inadequate conception of the nature of commands.

Like other significations of desire, a command is express or tacit. If the desire be signified by *words* (written or spoken), the command is express. If the desire be signified by conduct (or by any signs of desire which are *not* words), the command is tacit.

Now when customs are turned into legal rules by decisions of subject judges, the legal rules which emerge from the customs are *tacit* commands of the sovereign legislature. The state, which is able to abolish, permits its ministers to enforce them: and it, therefore, signifies its pleasure, by that its voluntary acquiescence, 'that they shall serve as a law to the governed.'

My present purpose is merely this: to prove that the positive law styled *customary* (and all positive law made judicially) is established by the state directly or circuitously, and, therefore, is *imperative*. I am far from disputing, that law made judicially (or in the way of improper legislation) and law made by statute (or in the properly legislative manner) are distinguished by weighty differences. I shall inquire, in future lectures, what those differences are; and why subject judges, who are properly ministers of the law, have commonly shared with the sovereign in the business of making it.

I assume, then, that the only laws which are not imperative, and which belong to the subject-matter of jurisprudence, are the following:—1. Declaratory laws, or laws explaining the import of existing positive law. 2. Laws abrogating or repealing existing positive law. 3. Imperfect laws, or laws of imperfect obligation (with the sense wherein the expression is used by the Roman jurists).

But the space occupied in the science by these improper laws is comparatively narrow and insignificant. Accordingly, although I shall take them into account so often as I refer to them directly, I shall throw them out of account on other occasions. Or (changing the expression) I shall limit the term *law* to laws which are imperative, unless I extend it expressly to laws which are not.

# 4

# Hans Kelsen

Hans Kelsen (1881–    ), formerly head of the School of Law at Vienna
University, and now Emeritas Professor of Political Science at the University of California, has been uniquely influential in the formulation of
both Western and Soviet legal theory.

# THE MARX—ENGELS THEORY OF LAW*

### PRIMACY OF ECONOMICS OVER POLITICS IN THE MARXIAN THEORY OF THE BOURGEOIS (CAPITALIST) STATE

The Marxian theory of law is inseparably connected with the theory of
state.[1] It is based on the assumption that the economic production and the
social relationships constituted by it (the *Produktionsverhaeltnisse*) determine the
coming into existence as well as the disappearance of state and law. Neither
phenomenon is an essential element of human society; they exist only under
definite economic conditions, namely when the means of production are at the
exclusive disposition of a minority of individuals who use or misuse this privilege
for the purpose of exploiting the overwhelming majority. This implies the
division of society into two groups of antagonistic economic interests, two
'classes', the class of the exploiting owners of the means of production and the
class of the exploited workers.

This is especially the situation of a society where the economic system of
capitalism prevails and society is split into the two classes of the bourgeois
(capitalists) and the proletariat. The state together with its law is the coercive
machinery for the maintenance of exploitation of one class by the other, an
instrument of the class of exploiters which, through the state and its law,
becomes the politically dominant class. The state is the power established for
the purpose of keeping the conflict between the dominant and the dominated
class 'within the bounds of "order"'.[2] This 'order' is the law, which—
according to this view—although something different from the state, is in
essential connection with the state. The state is 'normally the state of the most
powerful economically ruling class, which by its means becomes also the

---

*Hans Kelsen, *The Communist Theory of Law* (New York: Praeger, 1955), pp. 1–12, 33–38,
reprinted by joint permission of Praeger of New York and Stevens & Sons of London. Footnotes
have been renumbered from 37.
[1] Cf. my *Sozialismus und Staat*, 2. Aufl., Leipzig, 1923, and my *The Political Theory of Bolshevism*,
University of California Press, Berkeley and Los Angeles, 1948.
[2] Friedrich Engels, *Der Ursprung der Familie, des Privateigentums und des Staates*. Internationale
Bibliothek, Stuttgart, 1920, p. 177 *et seq.*

politically ruling class, and thus acquires new means of holding down and exploiting the oppressed class'.[3] That means that the political power of the bourgeoisie is the effect of its economic power, that the bourgeoisie becomes the politically ruling class because it is the economically ruling class. This primacy of economics over politics is quite consistent with Marx' economic interpretation of history in general and of present society in particular. A society split into classes, says Engels, 'needs the state, that means an organisation of the exploiting class for maintaining the external conditions of its production, especially for holding down by force the exploited class'.[4] The dominance of one class over the other, which is the essence of the state, is identical with the exploitation of one class by the other, the dominant class being essentially the exploiting class.

### REALITY AND IDEOLOGY

The interdependence which according to this economic or materialistic interpretation of society exists between the economic conditions on the one hand, and state and law on the other, is of decisive importance for the theory of state and in particular for the theory of law. It is usually assumed that Marx describes this interdependence in the well-known metaphor of a political and legal 'superstructure' set up above the relationships of production constituting the economic structure of society. 'Ideologies' form the superstructure, whereas the basis, the substructure, represents social reality. In his work *Zur Kritik der politischen Oekonomie* (Contribution to the Critique of Political Economy) he says:
'In the social production which men carry on they enter into definite relations that are indispensable and independent of their will; these relations of production correspond to a definite stage of development of their material powers of production. The sum total of these relations of production constitutes the economic structure of society—the real foundation, on which rise legal and political superstructures and to which correspond definite forms of social consciousness'.[5]
The 'superstructures' are 'forms of social consciousness', which he later characterises as 'ideological forms in which men become conscious' of social reality. It is usually assumed that Marx understands by 'legal and political superstructures' law and state. Engels, *e.g.*, interprets the Marxian formula in the statement that 'the economic structure of society forms the real basis, by which the total superstructure of legal and political institutions as well as religious, philosophical and other ideas *(Vorstellungsweisen)* of each historical period in the last analysis may be explained'.[6] If this interpretation is correct

[3] Engels, *Der Ursprung der Familie etc.*, p. 180.
[4] Engels, *Herrn Eugen Dührings Umwälzung der Wissenschaft (Anti-Dühring)*, Stuttgart, 1919, p. 302.
[5] Karl Marx, *Zur Kritik der politischen Oekonomie*, herausgeg v. Karl Kautsky, Stuttgart, 1919, p. lv.
[6] Friedrich Engels, *Die Entwicklung des Sozialismus von der Utopie zur Wissenschaft*, 6 Aufl., Berlin, 1911, p. 33.

and, hence, law has the nature of an ideology, the meaning of this term is of the utmost importance for a Marxian theory of law.

In his fragmentary work *Einleitung zu einer Kritik der politischen Oekonomie* (Introduction to the Critique of Political Economy) Marx says that in the study of social science it must be borne in mind that society is given 'as in reality so in our mind'.[7] Social ideology as a form of social consciousness is society as it is given in the human mind, in contradistinction to society as it is given in reality. In *Das Kommunistische Manifest* (Communist Manifesto) Marx and Engels refer to 'the charges against communism made from a religious, a philosophical and, generally, from an ideological standpoint', thus meaning by ideology in the first place religion and philosophy. Then, they maintain that 'man's ideas, views, and conceptions, in one word, man's consciousness changes with every change in the conditions of his material existence, in his social relations and his social life'. Hence 'ideology' means the content of man's consciousness, the ideas man forms in his mind of reality, especially of social reality.

But mostly Marx uses the term 'ideology' not in this wider sense as identical with 'idea', but in a narrower and decidedly deprecatory sense. By ideology he means a false consciousness, an incorrect—in contradistinction to a scientifically correct—idea of social reality. He says, in considering social transformations:

'the distinction should always be made between the material transformation . . . which can be described with the precision of natural science, and the legal, political, religious, aesthetic or philosophic—in short ideological forms in which men become conscious' of these transformations. 'Just as our opinion of an individual is not based on what he fancies himself, so we cannot judge such a period of transformation by its own consciousness'.[8]

The 'ideological' consciousness is false because it is determined by the social situation of the man whose mind reflects the social reality, especially by the interests of the social group, or class, to which the man belongs. Marx has the rather naïve epistemological view according to which man's consciousness reflects—like a mirror—the real objects. In his main work, *Das Kapital*, Marx says, in opposition to Hegel's view that reality is a reflex of idea:

'With me, on the contrary, the idea (*das Ideelle*) is nothing but the material transformed and translated in the mind of man (*das im Menschenkopf umgesetzte und uebersetzte Materielle*)'.[9]

And Engels writes in his pamphlet *Ludwig Feuerbach und der Ausgang der klassischen Philosophie*[10]: 'We conceive of ideas . . . as pictures of real things': and in his *Die Entwicklung des Sozialismus von der Utopie zur Wissenschaft*[11]:

---

[7] Marx, *Zur Kritik der politischen Oekonomie*, p. xliii.
[8] *Loc. cit.*, p. lv–lvi.
[9] Marx, *Das Kapital* (Volksausgabe, herausgeg. von Kautsky, 8. Aufl. 1928), I, p. xlvii.
[10] Friedrich Engels, *Ludwig Feuerbach und der Ausgang der klassischen Philosophie*, **Marxistische Bibliothek**, Bd. 3, p. 51.
[11] Engels, *Die Entwicklung des Sozialismuss von der Utopie etc.*, p. 31.

'thoughts are only more or less abstract images of the real things and events'. An ideology is a form of consciousness that reflects social reality in a distorted way, it counterfeits something that, in reality, does not exist, it veils reality or something in it instead of unveiling it, it is a deception and even self-deception and, above all, it is an illusive consciousness. Hence there is always an antagonism or conflict between the reality and the ideological consciousness man has of this reality; and, since Marx speaks of conflicts or antagonisms as of 'contradictions', there is always a contradiction between reality and ideology.

The epistemological doctrine which is at the basis of Marx' theory of ideology is formulated in these famous statements:

'The mode of production in material life determines the general character of the social, political and spiritual process of life. It is not the consciousness (Bewusstsein) of men that determines their existence (Sein) but, on the contrary, their social existence (gesellschaftliches Sein) determines their consciousness'.[12]

Although the second sentence is supposed to express the same idea as the first, the two are not quite the same. In the first sentence only the 'mode of production' is the determining factor, in the second, it is the entire 'social existence'. In the first sentence not only the 'spiritual' but also the 'social' and 'political' process of life is the determined factor; in the second, it is only the 'consciousness' which is identical with the spiritual process of life. By the 'social' and 'political' process of life law and state as social institutions may be understood; and this 'social' and 'political' process of life—as distinguished from the 'spiritual' process of life in the first sentence—may very well be conceived of as part of the 'social existence' of men referred to in the second sentence. Hence there is a strange ambiguity as to the meaning of the relationship between reality and ideology, which makes the foundation of Marx' theory of cognition highly problematical. This ambiguity plays a particular part in the theory of state and law when the question arises whether these social phenomena belong to the substructure, i.e., the real basis, or to the ideological superstructure.

If Marx' sociological theory of knowledge is taken in its second version (the social existence of men determining their consciousness) the question arises whether a consciousness other than an ideological, i.e., false, illusive consciousness is possible at all. Since man's consciousness is 'ideological' in this sense because it is determined by man's social existence, the answer must be in the negative. Hence there can be no true, i.e., objective theory of reality in general and of social reality in particular. It is evident that Marx cannot maintain his fundamental position, for the very statement that the social existence determines the consciousness of men must claim to be a true and that means an objective theory of the human consciousness, not determined by the social existence of the one who makes this statement. There can be no doubt that Marx presents his own social theory as a non-ideological, correct description of social reality, as a 'science'.

---

[12] *Zur Kritik der politischen Oekonomie*, p. lv.

In an above-quoted statement Marx makes a clear distinction between a description of reality performed 'with the precision of natural science', that is to say a 'scientific' consciousness, and 'ideological forms' in which man becomes conscious of social reality, that is to say, an ideological consciousness. As we shall see later, Marx explains the deficiency of an ideological consciousness by the deficiency of the social reality producing such an ideological consciousness. In the communist society of the future, which represents a perfect social reality, there will be no 'ideological' consciousness; but there will be a consciousness, there will certainly be science; and if science, as a content of consciousness, is to be conceived of as ideology, not in the derogatory sense of the term but as something different from its object, *i.e.*, from reality reflected in the consciousness, the term 'ideology' may be used not only in the sense of a false, illusive, but also in the sense of a scientifically correct, consciousness.

Marx was evidently aware of the fact that his doctrine of ideology endangers his own social theory. It is probably for the purpose of defending his theory against the objection to be a mere 'ideology' in the derogatory sense of the term that in *Das Kommunistische Manifest,* he asserts that at a certain stage of the class struggle 'the bourgeoisie itself supplies the proletariat with weapons for fighting the bourgeoisie', that 'a portion of the bourgeoisie goes over to the proletariat and, in particular, a portion of the bourgeois ideologists, who have raised themselves to the level of comprehending theoretically the historical movement as a whole'. Thus, these 'bourgeois ideologists' cease to produce ideologies and develop a true science of the historical movement. But how is such a metamorphosis possible, how can they escape the fundamental law that their social existence, that is their belonging to the bourgeois class, determines their social consciousness? This is—seen from the point of view of Marx' social theory—a miracle.

## STATE AND LAW AS REALITY

The typical and most characteristic ideology is religion. 'Religion', says Marx, 'is the general theory of this world'; and of religion he says that it is a 'perverted consciousness of the world',[13] the 'opium of the people', an 'illusion'.[14] It is significant that Marx, when he denounces religion as an illusive ideology, defines it as a 'theory'. In a letter to Ruge he speaks of 'religion and science' as of the 'theoretical existence of man'[15] in contradistinction to his practical existence, that is, the 'reality' of his true existence. In this sense only a theory, a function of cognition a form of consciousness, not the object of theory or cognition, not reality—correctly or incorrectly—reflected in man's consciousness, could be characterised as ideological. Marx frequently speaks of ideology

---

[13] Karl Marx, 'Zur Kritik der Hegelschen Rechtsphilosophie'. *Karl Marx–Friedrich Engels. Historisch-kritische Gesamtausgabe,* erste Abteilung, Bd. I-1, Frankfurt, 1927, p. 607.
[14] *Loc. cit.,* Bd. I-1, p. 608.
[15] *Loc. cit.,* Bd. I-1, pp. 573–574.

as a mere 'expression' *(Ausdruck)* of reality and denounces as an ideological fallacy to take what is a mere 'expression' of the reality for reality,[16] whereby he evidently presupposes that the expression is false, illusive. Hence, only a certain —namely a false—theory of the state or a certain —namely illusive—philosophy of law, not the state or the law, could be conceived of as an ideology. In accordance with his thesis that the social existence of man, that is, his social reality, determines man's social consciousness, Marx says that the state 'produces religion as a perverted consciousness'[17] and opposes 'the state together with the social reality connected with it' to the 'legal consciousness, the most distinguished, most universal, to the rank of science elevated expression of which is the speculative philosophy of law'.[18] Here the state is presented as social reality upon which an illusive legal philosophy as an ideological superstructure is set up.

In his *Zur Kritik der politischen Oekonomie* he identifies the relationships of production, that is, the social reality in opposition to the social ideology, with legal relations. 'At a certain stage of their development the material forces of production in society come in conflict with the existing relations of production— or what is but a legal expression for the same thing—with the property relations within which they had been at work before'[19] Property relations, that is, legal relations, are relations of production, that is, economic relations. 'Property' or 'legal' relations is only another name for relations of production, economic relations.[20] Marx, it is true, characterises here the law, just as he characterises ideology, as an 'expression' of the relations of production, *i.e.*, an expresison of the social reality. But the law is not—as an ideology by its very nature must be—a false, illusive expression, an expression which is in contradiction to the object that it expresses. The expression of economic reality which is the law, is in harmony with reality, corresponds to reality.

Marx rejects the view that sovereigns make law for the economic conditions. 'Legislation, political as well as civil, could do no more than give expression to the will of the economic relations'.[21] That economic relations have a 'will' is a rather problematical metaphor. But the meaning of it is: that the law corresponds to the economic conditions which it 'expresses', that the law is a correct and hence not an ideological, expression of economic reality. 'Law is only the official recognition of fact'.[22] Marx says of the forms of division of labour: 'Originally born of the conditions of material production, it was not till much later that they were established as laws'.[23] The law prescribing division of labour

---

[16] *Loc. cit.*, Bd. V, p. 453.
[17] *Loc. cit.*, Bd. I–1, p. 607.
[18] *Loc. cit.*, Bd. I–1, pp. 613–614.
[19] Marx, *Zur Kritik der politischen Oekonomie*, p. lv.
[20] On the basis of this identification of legal relationships with economic relationships, some Marxian writers define the law as an aggregate of economic relationships in opposition to the bourgeois definition of the law as a system of norms.
[21] Karl Marx *Misere de la Philosophie*. Gesamtausgabe, erste Abteilung, VI, p. 160.
[22] *Loc. cit.*, p. 163.
[23] *Loc. cit.*, p. 198.

is in perfect harmony with division of labour in economic reality. That the law is an 'expression' of economic conditions means that it is the product of economic reality, that it is its effect. But—according to Marx—the law is not only the effect of economic reality; the law has itself effects on this reality. In *Das Kapital* we read:

'By maturing the material conditions and the combination on a social scale of the process of production, it (the law) matures the contradictions and antagonisms of the capitalist form of production, and thereby provides, along with the elements for the formation of a new society, the force for exploding the old one'.[24]

In his *Einleitung zu einer Kritik der politischen Oekonomie*[25] Marx writes:

'Laws may perpetuate an instrument of production, *e.g.*, land, in certain families. These laws assume an economic importance if large landed property is in harmony with the system of production prevailing in society, as is the case *e.g.*, in England'.

In stressing the 'harmony' of the law with the relationships of production, Marx goes as far as to characterise the positive law as 'natural' law. He says of the English Factory Acts, they are 'just as much the necessary product of modern industry as cotton yarns, self-actors, and electric telegraph'.[26] 'They develop gradually out of the circumstances as natural laws of the modern mode of production'.[27] Marx expressly refers to 'the effect of legislation on the maintenance of a system of distribution and its resultant influence on production If the law is not 'in harmony' with the conditions of production, it ceases to be effective, as *e.g.*, in France, where in spite of the 'legislative attempts to perpetuate the minute subdivision of land' achieved by the revolution, 'land ownership is concentrating again'. In so far as the law—or the fact Marx has in mind when he refers to 'law'—is an effect of economic reality and has itself effects on this reality, that is to say, if the law is within the chain of cause and effect, it is within reality, and hence belongs to the substructure of the ideological superstructure.

STATE AND LAW AS IDEOLOGY

However, on the other hand Marx refers to the real state and the existing law, and not to a theory of the state or a philosophy of law, as to ideologies. In *Das Kommunistische Manifest* the charges against communism made from an ideological standpoint are formulated as follows: 'Undoubtedly—it will be said—religious, moral, philosophical and juridical ideas have been modified in the course of historical development. But religion, morality, philosophy, political science, and law constantly survived this change'. Here morality and law are placed as ideologies on the same plane with philosophy and science. In

[24] Marx, *Das Kapital*, I p. 443.
[25] Marx, *Zur Kritik der politischen Oekonomie*, p. xxxii *et seq.*
[26] *Das Kapital*, I, p. 422.
[27] *Loc. cit.*, p. 231.

*Die deutsche Ideologie*,[28] which is an important source for an understanding of Marx' doctrine of ideology, Marx refers to 'morality, religion, metaphysics, and other ideologies'. Morality is an effective normative order regulating human behaviour; and if morality is an ideology on the same level as religion and metaphysics, then law, too, may be conceived of in this way. Marx says of the 'laws' as well as of 'morality' that they are the *'ideele* expression of the conditions of the existence' of the dominant class (conditioned by the development of production) and by the *'ideele'* expression he means an ideological expression in opposition to the economic reality thus expressed.

It is characteristic of 'ideologists', says Marx, that 'they take their ideology for the creative force and the purpose of all social relationships, although they are only their expression and symptom'.[29] 'The law', says Marx, 'is only symptom, expression of other relationships, on which the power of the state is based'. The real bases are the relationships of production.[30] It is especially the legal institution of property which is the 'legal expression' of 'certain economic conditions, which are dependent on the development of the forces of production'[31] for 'the relationships of production among the individuals must also express themselves as political and legal relationships'.[32] In his critique of Stirner, Marx reproaches this philosopher of having taken 'the ideological-speculative expression of reality, separated from its empirical basis, for the very reality'; and as one of these ideological expressions of reality, mistaken as reality by Stirner, Marx points to the law.[33]

According to this view, the law—and not an illusive legal philosophy—is an ideological superstructure set up above the social reality, the relationships of production. Hence one is quite justified to interpret the 'legal and political superstructures' referred to in *Zur Kritik der politischen Oekonomie* to mean the law and the state—as pointed out, Engels himself and consequently almost all interpreters of Marx do so[34]—although Marx, a few lines later, identifies the

28 *Gesamtausgabe*, Bd. V, p. 16; cf. also pp. 21, 49.
29 *Lo cit.*, p. 398.
30 *Loc. cit.*, p. 307; cf. also p. 321.
31 *Loc. cit.*, p. 335.
32 *Loc. cit.*, p. 342.
33 *Loc. cit.*, pp. 261, 294.
34 Cf. e.g. Hans Barth, *Wahrheit und Ideologie, Zurich*, 1945, who defines Marx's concept of 'ideology'—in conformity with Marx—as a specific, namely false or illusive, form of cognition *(Erkenntnis)* and, nevertheless, speaks—in conformity with Marx—of state and law as of ideologies, although he—again in conformity with Marx—deals with them also as with social realities. Cf. also M. M. Bober, *Karl Marx' Interpretation of History*, 2nd ed., Cambridge, 1948. Bober (p. 115 *et seq.*) assumes that the Marxian 'superstructure' is composed of 'institutions and ideas'. He does not stress the difference between the two elements since he is not particularly concerned with the problem of the 'ideological consciousness'. He misinterprets Marx' theory in this respect. He assumes that according to Marx 'illusionism' is to be explained by the fact that 'the generality of men are mentally sluggish'; that 'with the multitude, observation is a superficial performance, and appearances are allowed to pass undistorted into an inactive mental medium'; that 'the ordinary person confuses cause and effect, and mistakes symptoms for causes; . . . fails to perceive that his beliefs are merely the product of class tradition. . . In brief the "ordinary mind" exemplifies precisely what dialectical materialism repudiates. The "ordinary

law with the relationships of production, and, in other connections, characterises the state as a specific social reality producing ideology, and not as an
ideology produced by a specific social reality.

If the law is part of the ideological superstructure as something different
from and opposed to its substructure, the social reality constituted by economic
relationships, then the law cannot be the effect of these relationships and,
especially, cannot itself have effect on them. When Marx—in the above-
quoted statements—admits an interaction between law and economics, he
deals with law as with a social reality. If the law is a social reality in the same
sense as economic production, then the scheme of super- and sub-structure is not
applicable to the relationship between the two social phenomena. But it is just
of the ideological superstructure that Engels maintains that it 'influences' the
substructure. In a letter to J. Bloch[35] he writes:

> 'The economic situation is the basis, but the various elements of the
> superstructure—political forms of the class struggle and its consequences,
> constitutions established by the victorious class after a successful battle,
> etc.—forms of law and then even the reflexes of all these actual struggles
> in the brains of the combatants: political, legal, philosophical theories,
> religious ideas and their further development into systems of dogma—
> also exercise their influence upon the course of the historical struggles'.

That means that the ideological superstructure, especially the law as element
of this superstructure, has effects on the substructure. Hence 'ideology' is
'reality' in the same sense as the economic relationships which Marx identifies
with reality; and he must identify reality with economic relationships in order
to oppose these relationships as 'reality' to that which he wants to disparage
as 'ideology': above all, to religion. Since the identification of social reality
with economic relationships is the essence of his economic interpretation of
society, this interpretation breaks down as soon as 'ideologies' are recognised as
'realities'. A very characteristic application of this interpretation is Marx'
statement:

> 'Society is not based upon law; this is a juridical fiction. On the
> contrary, the law must rest on society. It must be the expression of its
> common interests and needs arising from the actual methods of material
> production against the caprice of the single individual'.[36]

The bourgeois doctrine, rejected by Marx, that society is based on law, means,
if not intentionally misinterpreted, that the law —or more exactly formulated,
certain acts by which law is created or applied—influences social life, without

mind" lives in a world of illusionism' (p. 121). But, according to Marx, it is not the 'ordinary
mind', the 'multitude', but the philosophers and scientists of the bourgeois class, and among
them the most outstanding thinkers who produce the illusions.
Karl Mannheim, *Ideology and Utopia*, 1952, uses the term 'ideology' only for a certain type of
thinking and characterises the relationship between substructure and superstructure as the
relationship between differentiated social groupings and 'the corresponding differentiations in
concepts, categories, and thought-models' (p. 248).
[35] Marx-Engels, *Correspondence* 1846–1895. A Selection. New York, 1935, 0p. 475.
[36] *Karl Marx vor den Koelner Geschworenen*, Berlin, 1895, p. 15.

excluding that social life influences the formation of the law. Hence the rejected doctrine is not a juridical fiction. It is the description of social reality within which economic and legal elements are in a relationship of interaction or interdependence, a fact which Marx and Engels in the above-quoted statements admit. . .

THE FUTURE OF THE LAW

As to the future of the law, there are only very few statements in the writings of Marx and Engels. They were probably of the opinion that what they said about the state applied also to the law, which they considered to be a coercive order issued by the state. It is obviously the law that Engels has in mind when he, in the above-quoted statement, refers to an 'order' within the bounds of which the class conflict is kept by the state as an organisation of the ruling class. Neither Marx nor Engels had a clear idea of the relationships between state and law. That state and law are essentially connected with one another, they probably considered as self-evident; but they were more interested in the state aspect of society than in its law aspect. It may be assumed that according to the Marx-Engels doctrine of the state, the law as a coercive order and specific instrument of the state exists only in a society divided into two classes, a dominant exploiting and a dominated exploited class. In one of his most frequently quoted statements, Marx says that in the phase of transition from the proletarian revolution to the establishment of perfect communism, that is to say, during the period of the dictatorship of the proletariat, there will be still a law, but that this law, in spite of its progress as compared with the bourgeois law, will still be 'infected with a bourgeois barrier *(mit einer buergerlichen Schranke behaftet)*'.[37] By this not very fortunate metaphor he expresses the idea that the law of the socialist state will still have a certain bourgeois character, because there will still be a ruling class and a ruled class and hence a class antagonism; and that only 'in the highest phase of communist society', that is, that phase where the socialisation of the means of production is completely achieved and all class antagonisms radically abolished, 'can the narrow horizon of bourgeois law be completely overcome, and only then will society inscribe on its banner: from each according to his capacities and to each according to his needs'. This may be interpreted to mean that in this phase of the development of communism there will be no law, because the law is by its very nature bourgeois law, and that means class law. It must, however, be admitted that the statement is ambiguous and that it may also be interpreted to mean that even in the perfect communist society there will be law, but not bourgeois law, meaning a coercive order guaranteeing the exploitation of one class by another, presented by an ideological doctrine to be the realisation of justice. Communist society will

---

[37] This statement is made in a letter Marx wrote on May 5, 1875, to Bracke, concerning the draft of the Gotha Programme of the German Social-Democratic Party. The letter is published: *Neue Zeit,* IX–1, 1890–1891, p. 561 *et seq.*

have law, but no 'legal superstructure' because no ideological superstructure at all (provided that by legal superstructure not the real law but an illusive, apologetic doctrine of the law) is to be understood. There will be no reason to pretend that communist law is just, because communist law will really be just legal reality will not be self-contradictory, its external form will be in complete harmony with its internal essence, its ideal destination, the idea of justice. Hence law may be conceived of as a normative order, and such a concept of the law will have no ideological character in the derogatory sense of the term. Since even the perfectly just reality of communist society will have a consciousness—there will be science, although no religion—the reflection of the real law in the consciousness of communist society, that is to say, the description of the law as a normative order, as a *Sollen,* will not be in conflict with its immanent idea, for the law will really be identical with justice, and justice means *Sollen,* norm.

The concept of 'norm' or *Sollen* is not in itself an ideological fraud. It assumes this character only if applied to something which, from the point of view of the interpreter, does not deserve to be interpreted as norm. From the point of view of the Marxian critique, bourgeois law only pretends to be a norm —and is therefore an illusive ideology because it is not just—and only justice is a true norm, only a just law a true *Sollen,* a genuine 'norm'. That there will be justice, and hence a true norm, in communist society cannot be denied. The norm of communist justice becomes evident in the principle inscribed on the banner of communist society: 'From each according to his capacities, to each according to his needs', which is nothing else but the principle of communist justice, the principle of true equality, in opposition to capitalist injustice, only pretending to be justice. Bourgeois law, according to Marx, pretends to be an equal law for all, but in truth it is the contrary, a law of inequality; and this applies also to the law in the transition stage. The workers will get for an equal quantity of labour an equal quantity of products. But in view of the fact that the individual workers are not equal—the one is stronger and more intelligent than the other, works more and consequently gets more than the other—'this equal law is unequal for unequal work'. It is, therefore, as far as its content is concerned, a law of inequality as all law'. This is evidently the meaning of his figure of speech 'the bourgeois barrier' of the law in the transition stage.

Marx does not say that the law during the transition period of the dictatorship of the proletariat will be bourgeois law. He says only that the law of the socialist state will be infected with an evil of bourgeois society: inequality. He seems not to exclude the possibility of a law that is not infected with this evil, a law of true equality. But he adds to the words 'a law of inequality' the words 'as all law', Here, as mentioned before, the words 'all law' may, in conformity with the preceding words, mean bourgeois law as well as the law of the socialist state; the law of the communist society guaranteeing true equality is not included, because supposed to be justice. In this connection Marx says:

'These defects (the inequality of the law) are inevitable in the first phase of communist society, when, after long travail, it first emerges from capitalist society. The law can never be on a higher level than the economic structure of society and the evolution of civilisation conditioned by this structure'.

This could be interpreted to mean: in the second phase of communist society the economic structure of which will represent the highest possible degree of civilisation, the law, too, will reach the highest possible level. However, the words 'as all law' may also mean what they say: all law whatsoever, so that there is no law even where the principle of true equality prevails.

It is important to note that the same ambiguity which characterises the view presented by Marx in his *Gotha Programme* concerning the future of the law in communist society is implied in the statements he makes in the same essay concerning the future of the state. Criticising the Programmes' postulate of a 'free state' he says:

'It is not at all the purpose of the workers . . . to make the state "free". In the German Reich the "state" is almost as "free" as in Russia. Freedom consists in transforming the state, which is not an organ superior to society, into an organ subordinated to society . . .'[38]

Marx does not say that freedom consists in eliminating the state from society, but that it consists in organising the state in a way that it will become an instrument of society. As pointed out, he formulates the question of the future of the state as follows: 'What are the changes which the state will undergo in the communist society?' He does not ask: Under what conditions will the state disappear? And he objects to the Gotha Programming that it does not deal with the revolutionary dictatorship of the proletariat, nor 'with the future state of the communist society'.[39] This statement may be interpreted to mean that there will be in the future communist society a state, although not a state which dominates society but a state dominated by society, a state which is an instrument of this society:[40] just as there will be—according to the above presented interpretation of Marx' statements about the future of the law—a just law in this society.

This interpretation of Marx' statements concerning the future, of the law may be summarised as follows: There will be in communist society no law of inequality, hence no ideological, *i.e.*, illusive, legal theory, and no law pretending to be just; consequently there will be no law as an 'ideology' in the derogatory sense of the term, but a real law of true equality, a law which will be the realisation of justice. If this law is conceived of as norm or normative order, it is an ideology in a non-derogatory sense—in the same sense as science will be an ideology of communist society. This view is confirmed by some statements he made in his *Einleitung zu einer Kritik der politischen Oekonomie.*

---

[38] *Loc. cit.*, p. 572.

[39] *Loc. cit.*, p. 573.

[40] The German text corresponding to the words 'with the future state of the communist society' runs as follows: *'mit dem zukuenftigen Staatswesen der kommunistischen Gesellschaft'*. The term *Staatswesen* means by and large the same as *Staat*, that is, state. But it is significant that Marx does not use the more precise term *Staat*.

There he says that 'there can be no society where there is no property in some form', although it would be a mistake to assume that it must be private or individual property. Since property presupposes a legal order, the statement that there is no society without some form of property implies the view that where there is society there is law, expressed in the famous formula of Roman jurisprudence *ubi societas ibi jus*. He also says 'that every form of production creates its own legal relations . . .', from which follows that also in a communist society there must be law. As a matter of fact, he asserts in this connection:

> 'All production is appropriation of nature by the individual and through a definite form of society. In that sense it is tautology to say that property (appropriation) is a condition of production. But it becomes ridiculous when from that one jumps at once to a definite form of property, *e.g.*, private property (which implies, besides, as a prerequisite the existence of an opposite form, *viz.*, absence of property). History points rather to common property (*e.g.*, among the Hindoes, Slavs, ancient Celts, etc.) as the primitive form, which still plays an important part at a much later period as communal property'.[41]

If the nationalisation of the means of production achieved during the transition period of the dictatorship of the proletariat is to be maintained within the society of perfect communism, if here the means of production must remain at the exclusive disposition of the organs of the community and private property in these goods excluded, in order to maintain true equality, that is to say, if collective property of the community in the means of production has to be an institution of the future society, then there must be a law guaranteeing this status. However, it must be admitted that the other interpretation, according to which in the perfectly communist society of the future there will be no state and consequently no law, and that means that the social order will have no coercive, even no normative character, is not only not excluded but in conformity with the anarchistic tendency prevailing in the writings of Marx and especially of Engels.

### THE UTOPIA OF A STATELESS AND LAWLESS SOCIETY OF PERFECT COMMUNISM

The prediction of the coming into existence of such a social order is based on two assumptions: first that the socialisation of the means of production will increase production to such an extent that all economic needs can be completely satisfied, or, as Marx formulates it, that 'the production forces and all the springs of social wealth will pour forth a full flow'; and, secondly, that disturbances of the social order are caused only by economic circumstances, and that is a social order guarantees the complete satisfaction of the economic needs of all members of the community, no coercive measures as reaction against violations of this order are necessary. Neither the one nor the other assumption has a basis in our social experience. As far as the effect of socialisation is concerned, it certainly implies a tendency toward increasing production, but also an

[41] Marx, *Zur Kritik der politischen Oekonomie*, p. xix.; cf. also *supra*, p. 7.

opposite tendency; and the results of socialisation, in so far as they could be observed until now, do not confirm the optimistic prediction of Marx. The extraordinary increase of production in the future communist society is all the more unlikely as according to Marx the division of labour, one of the most effective means of a qualitative as well as quantitative raising of production, will be abolished. As far as the second assumption is concerned, criminal psychology shows that economic circumstances are not only causes of disturbances of a social order, that sex and ambition play at least as great a part and may play an even greater part when the economic causes are eliminated. The prediction of a stateless and lawless society of perfect justice is a utopian prophecy like the Messianic Kingdom of God, the paradise of the future.

# 5

# Karl N. Llewellyn

Karl Llewellyn (1893–1962), major spokesman for American legal
realism, professor of law at Columbia University and the University of
Chicago, argued the 'realistic' correlation of uniform legal codes with
social and economic practice.

# SOME REALISM ABOUT REALISM*

### REAL REALISTS[1]

What, then, *are* the characteristics of these new fermenters? One thing
is clear. There is no school of realists. There is no likelihood that there will
be such a school. There is no group with an official or accepted, or even with an
emerging creed. There is no abnegation of independent striking out. We hope
that there may never be. New recruits acquire tools and stimulus, not masters,
nor over-mastering ideas. Old recruits diverge in interests from each other.
They are related, says Frank, only in their negations, and in their skepticisms,
and in their curiosity.

There is, however, a *movement* in thought and work about law. The movement, the method of attack, is wider than the number of its adherents. It
includes some or much work of many men who would scorn ascription to its
banner. Individual men, then. Men more or less interstimulated—but no more
than all of them have been stimulated by the orthodox tradition, or by that
ferment at the opening of the century in which Dean Pound took a leading
part. Individual men, working and thinking over law and its place in society.
Their differences in point of view, in interest, in emphasis, in field of work, are
huge. They differ among themselves well-nigh as much as any of them differs
from, say, Langdell. Their number grows. Their work finds acceptance.

What one does find as he observes them is twofold. First (and to be

---

* Karl N. Llewellyn, from "Some Realism About Realism," *Harvard Law Review*, XLIV
(1931), pp. 1233–1256. Copyright *Harvard Law Review*, 1931. Footnotes constituting approximately one-third of the article have been omitted. An extensive bibliography of the literature
of legal realism prepared by Llewellyn and Felix Cohen is reprinted at the conclusion of the
article.
[1] Names for them vary. I call them realists (so do Frank, Radin, and often, Yntema; Bingham
also recognizes the term. And I find it used in the˙same sense in the work of Cook, Douglas,
Frankfurter)—stressing the interest in the actuality of what happens, and the distrust of formula.
Cook prefers to speak of scientific approach to law, Oliphant of objective method—stressing
much the same features. Clark speaks of fact-research, Corbin of what courts do. "Functional
approach" stresses the interest in, and valuation by, effects. Dickinson speaks of the skeptical
movement.

expected) certain points of departure are common to them all. Second (and this, when one can find neither school nor striking likenesses among individuals, is startling) a cross-relevance, a complementing, an interlocking of their varied results "as if they were guided by an invisible hand." A third thing may be mentioned in passing: a fighting faith in their methods of attack on legal problems; but in these last years the battle with the facts has proved so much more exciting than any battle with traditionalism that the fighting faith had come (until the spring offensive of 1931 against the realists) to manifest itself chiefly in enthusiastic labor to get on.

But as with a description of an economic order, tone and color of description must vary with the point of view of the reporter. No other one of the men would set the picture up as I shall. Such a report must thus be individual. Each man, of necessity, orients the whole to his own main interest of the moment—as I shall orient the whole to mine: the workings of case-law in appellate courts. Maps of the United States prepared respectively by a political geographer and a student of climate would show some resemblance; each would show a coherent picture; but neither's map would give much satisfaction to the other. So here. I speak for myself of that movement which in its sum is realism; I do not speak of "the realists"; still less do I speak *for* the participants or any of them. And I shall endeavor to keep in mind as I go that the justification for grouping these men together lies not in that they are *alike* in belief or work, but in that from certain common points of departure they have branched into lines of work which seem to be building themselves into a whole, a whole planned by none, foreseen by none, and (it may well be) not yet adequately grasped by any.

The common points of departure are several.

(1) The conception of law in flux, of moving law, and of judicial creation of law.

(2) The conception of law as a means to social ends and not as an end in itself; so that any part needs constantly to be examined for its purpose, and for its effect, and to be judged in the light of both and of their relation to each other.

(3) The conception of society in flux, and in flux typically faster than the law, so that the probability is always given that any portion of law needs reëxamination to determine how far it fits the society it purports to serve.

(4) The *temporary* divorce of Is and Ought for purposes of study. By this I mean that whereas value judgments must always be appealed to in order to set objectives for inquiry, yet during the inquiry itself into what Is, the observation, the description, and the establishment of relations between the things described are to remain *as largely as possible* uncontaminated by the desires of the observer or by what he wishes might be or thinks ought (ethically) to be. More particularly, this involves during the study of what courts are doing the effort to disregard the question what they ought to do. Such divorce of Is and Ought is, of course, not conceived as permanent. To men who begin with a suspicion that change is needed, a permanent divorce would be impossible. The argument is simply that no judgment of what Ought to be done in the future with respect to any part of law can be intelligently made without knowing objectively, as

far as possible, what that part of law is now doing. And realists believe that experience shows the intrusion of Ought-spectacles *during the investigation of the facts* to make it very difficult to see what is being done. On the Ought side this means an insistence on informed evaluations instead of armchair speculations. Its full implications on the side of Is-investigation can be appreciated only when one follows the contributions to objective description in business law and practice made by realists whose social philosophy rejects many of the accepted foundations of the existing economic order. (*E.g.,* Handler *re* trademarks and advertising; Klaus *re* marketing and banking; Llewellyn *re* sales; Moore *re* banking; Patterson *re* risk-bearing.)

(5) Distrust of traditional legal rules and concepts insofar as they purport to *describe* what either courts or people are actually doing. Hence the constant emphasis on rules as "generalized predictions of what courts will do." This is much more widespread as yet than its counterpart: the careful severance of rules *for* doing (precepts) from rules *of* doing (practices).

(6) Hand in hand with this distrust of traditional rules (on the descriptive side) goes a distrust of the theory that traditional prescriptive rule-formulations are *the* heavily operative factor in producing court decisions. This involves the tentative adoption [better: exploration] of the theory of rationalization for [what light it can give in] the study of opinions. It will be noted that "distrust" in this and the preceding point is not at all equivalent to "negation in any given instance."

(7) The belief in the worthwhileness of grouping cases and legal situations into narrower categories than has been the practice in the past. This is connected with the distrust of verbally simple rules—which so often cover dissimilar and non-simple fact situations (dissimilarity being tested partly by the way cases come out, and partly by the observer's judgment as to how they ought to come out; but a realist tries to indicate explicitly which criterion he is applying in any particular instance).

(8) An insistence on evaluation of any part of law in terms of its effects, and an insistence on the worthwhileness of trying to find these effects.

(9) Insistence on *sustained and programmatic attack* on the problems of law along any of these lines. *None of the ideas set forth in this list is new.* Each can be matched from somewhere; each can be matched from recent orthodox work in law. New twists and combinations do appear here and there. What is as novel as it is vital is for a goodly number of men to pick up ideas which have been expressed and dropped, used for an hour and dropped, played with from time to time and dropped—to pick up such ideas and set about *consistently, persistently, insistently to carry them through.* Grant that the idea or point of view is familiar—the results of steady, sustained, systematic work with it are not familiar. Not hit-or-miss stuff, not the insight which flashes and is forgotten, but sustained effort to force an old insight into its full bearing, to exploit it to the point where it laps over upon an apparently inconsistent insight, to explore their bearing on each other by the test of fact. This urge, in law, is quite new enough over the last decades to excuse a touch of frenzy among the locust-eaters.

The first, second, third and fifth of the above items, while common to the workers of the newer movement, are not peculiar to them. But the other items (4, 6, 7, 8, and 9) are to me the characteristic marks of the movement. Men or work fitting those specifications are to me "realistic" whatever label they may wear. Such, and none other, are the perfect fauna of this new land. Not all the work cited below fits my peculiar definition in all points. All such work fits most of the points.

Bound, as all "innovators" are, by prior thinking, these innovating "realists" brought their batteries to bear in first instance on the work of appellate courts. Still wholly within the tradition of our law, they strove to improve on that tradition.

(a) An early and fruitful line of attack borrowed from psychology the concept of *rationalization* already mentioned. To recanvass the opinions, viewing them no longer as mirroring the process of deciding cases, but rather as trained lawyers' arguments made by the judges (after the decision has been reached), intended to make the decision seem plausible, legally decent, legally right, to make it seem, indeed, legally inevitable—this was to open up new vision. It was assumed that the deductive logic of opinions need by no means be either a *description* of the process of decision, or an *explanation* of how the decision had been reached. Indeed over-enthusiasm has at times assumed that the logic of the opinion *could* be neither; and similar over-enthusiasm, perceiving case after case in which the opinion is clearly almost valueless as an indication of how that case came to decision, has worked at times almost as if the opinion were equally valueless in predicting what a later court will do.

But the line of inquiry via rationalization has come close to demonstrating that in any case doubtful enough to make litigation respectable the available authoritative premises—*i.e.*, premises legitimate and impeccable under the traditional legal techniques—are at least two, and that the two are mutually contradictory as applied to the case in hand. Which opens the question of what made the court select the one available premise rather than the other. And which raises the greatest of doubts as to *how far* any supposed certainty in decision which may derive merely [or even chiefly] from the presence of accepted rules really goes.

(b) A second line of attack has been to discriminate among rules with reference to their relative significance. Too much is written and thought about "law" and "rules," lump-wise. Which part of law? Which rule? Iron rules of policy, and rules "in the absence of agreement"; rules which keep a case from the jury, and rules as to the etiquette of instructions necessary to make a verdict stick—if one can get it; rules "of pure decision" for hospital cases, and rules which counsellors rely on in their counselling; rules which affect many (and which many, and how?) and rules which affect few. Such discriminations affect the traditional law curriculum, the traditional organization of law books and, above all, the orientation of study: to drive into *the most important* fields of ignorance.

(c) A further line of attack on the apparent conflict and uncertainty among the decisions in appellate courts has been to seek more understandable statement of them by grouping the facts in new—and typically but not always narrower—categories. The search is for correlations of fact-situation and outcome which (aided by common sense) may reveal *when* courts seize on one rather than another of the available competing premises. One may even stumble on the trail of *why* they do. Perhaps, *e.g.*, third party beneficiary difficulties simply fail to get applied to promises to make provision for dependents; perhaps the pre-existing duty rule goes by the board when the agreement is one for a marriage-settlement. Perhaps, indeed, contracts in what we may broadly call family relations do not work out in general as they do in business. If so, the rules—viewed as statements of the course of judicial behaviour—as *predictions* of what will happen—need to be restated. Sometimes it is a question of carving out hitherto unnoticed exceptions. But sometimes the results force the worker to reclassify an area altogether. Typically, as stated, the classes of situations which result are narrower, much narrower than the traditional classes. The process is in essence the orthodox technique of making distinctions, and reformulating—but undertaken systematically; exploited consciously, instead of being reserved until facts which refuse to be twisted by "interpretation" force action. The departure from orthodox procedure lies chiefly in distrust of, instead of search for, the widest sweep of generalization words permit. Not that such sweeping generalizations are not desired—*if they can be made so as to state what judges do* [or ought to do].

All of these three earliest lines of attack converge to a single conclusion: *there is less possibility of accurate prediction of what courts will do than the traditional rules would lead us to suppose* (and what possibility there is must be found in good measure outside these same traditional rules). The particular kind of certainty that men have thus far thought to find in law is in good measure an illusion. Realistic workers have sometimes insisted on this truth so hard that they have been thought pleased with it. (The danger lies close, for one thinking indiscriminately of Is and Ought, to suspect announcements of fact to reflect preferences, ethically normative judgments, on the part of those who do the announcing.)

But announcements of fact are not appraisals of worth. The contrary holds. The immediate results of the preliminary work thus far described has been a further, varied series of endeavors; *the focussing of conscious attack on discovering the factors thus far unpredictable, in good part with a view to their control.* Not wholly with a view to such elimination; part of the conscious attack is directed to finding where and when and how far *un*certainty has value. Much of what has been taken for insistence on the exclusive significance of the particular (with supposed implicit denial of the existence of valid or apposite generalizations) represents in fact a clearing of the ground for such attack. Close study of particular unpredictables may lessen unpredictability. It may increase the value of what remains. It certainly makes clearer what the present situation is. "Link by link is chainmail made."

(i) There is the question of the personality of the judge. (Little has as yet been attempted in study of the jury; Frank, *Law and the Modern Mind*, makes a beginning.) Within this field, again, attempts diverge. Some have attempted study of the particular judge—a line that will certainly lead to inquiry into his social conditioning. Some have attempted to bring various psychological hypotheses to bear. All that has become clear is that our government is not a government of laws, but one of law through men.

(ii) There has been some attempt to work out the varieties of interaction between the traditional concepts (the judge's "legal" equipment for thinking, seeing, judging) and the fact-pressures of the cases. This is a question not—as above—of getting at results on particular facts, but of studying the effect, *e.g.*, of a series of cases in which the facts either press successively in the one direction, or alternate in their pressures and counteract each other. Closely related in substance, but wholly diverse in both method and aim, is study of the machinery by which fact-pressures can under our procedure be brought to bear upon the court.

(iii) First efforts have been made to capitalize the wealth of our reported cases to make large-scale quantitative studies of facts and outcome; the hope has been that these might develop lines of prediction more sure, or at least capable of adding further certainty to the predictions based as hitherto on intensive study of smaller bodies of cases. This represents a more ambitious development of the procedure described above, under (c); I know of no published results. [Here the recent University of Chicago studies need attention.]

(iv) Repeated effort has been made to work with the cases of single states, to see how far additional predictability might thus be gained.

(v) Study has been attempted of "substantive rules" in the particular light of the available remedial procedure; the hope being to discover in the court's unmentioned knowledge of the immediate consequences of this rule or that, in the case at hand, a motivation for decision which cuts deeper than any shown by the opinion. Related, but distinct, is the reassertion of the fundamental quality of remedy, and the general approach to restating "what the law is" (on the side of prediction) in terms not of rights, but of what can be done: Not only "no remedy, no right," but "precisely as much right as remedy."

(vi) The set-up of men's ways and practices and ideas on the subject matter of the controversy has been studied, in the hope that this might yield a further or even final basis for prediction. The work here ranges from more or less indefinite reference to custom (the historical school), or mores (Corbin), through rough or more careful canvasses of business practice and ideology *(e.g.,* Berle, Sturges, Isaacs, Handler, Bogert, Durfee and Duffy, Breckenridge, Turner, Douglas, Shanks, Oliphant and indeed Holmes) to painstaking and detailed studies in which practice is much more considered than is any prevailing set of ideas about what the practices are (Klaus) or—even—to studies in which the concept of "practice" is itself broken up into behavior-sequences presented with careful note of the degree of their frequency and recurrence, and in which all reference to actor's own ideas is deprecated or excluded (Moore and Sussman). While grouped here together, under one formula, these workers show differences in degree and manner of interest in the background-ways which range from one pole to the other. Corbin's main interest is the appellate case; most of the second group mentioned rely on semi-special information and readily available material from economics, sociology, etc., with occasional careful studies of their own, and carry a strong interest into drafting or counselling work; Klaus insists on full canvass of all relevant literature, buttressed by and viewed in the light of intensive personal investigation; Moore's canvass and study is so original and thorough in technique as to offer as vital and important a contribution to ethnology and sociology as to banking practice. This is not one "school"; here alone are the germs of many "schools."

(vii) Another line of attack, hardly begun, is that on the effect of the lawyer on the outcome of cases, as an element in prediction. The lawyer *in litigation* has been the subject thus far only of desultory comment. Groping approach has been made to the counsellor as field general, in the business field: in drafting, and in counselling (and so in the building of practices and professional understandings which influence court action later), and in the strategy of presenting cases in favorable series, settling the unfavorable cases, etc.

All of the above has focussed on how to tell what appellate courts will do, however far afield any new scent may have led the individual hunter. But the interest in *effects* on laymen of what the courts will do leads rapidly from this still respectably traditional sphere of legal discussion into a series of further inquiries whose legal decorum is more dubious. They soon extend far beyond what has in recent years been conceived (in regard to the developed state) as law at all. I can not stop to consider these inquiries in detail. Space presses. Each of the following phases could be, and should be, elaborated at least into such a rough sketch as the foregoing. Through each would continue to run interest in what actually eventuates; interest in accurate description of what eventuates; interest in attempting, where prediction becomes uncertain, some conscious attack on hidden factors whose study might lessen the uncertainty; and interest in effects—on laymen. Finally, insistence that Ought-judgment should be bottomed on knowledge. And that action should be bottomed on all the knowledge that can be got in time to act.

I. *There is first the question of what lower courts and especially trial courts are doing, and what relation their doing has to the sayings and doings of upper courts and legislatures.*

Here the question has been to begin to find out, to find some way, some ways, of getting the hitherto unavailable facts, to find some significant way or ways of classifying what business is done, how long it takes, how various parts of the procedural mechinery work. (*E.g.,* Warner, Sunderland, Millar, Clark, Yntema, Marshall, Oliphant, Douglas, Arnold, Morgan, Frankfurter, Greene, and Swazie.) Another attack begins by inquiry not into records, but into the processes of trial and their effects on the outcome of cases. (Frank, Green.) This, on the civil side, where we have (save for memoirs) been wholly in the dark. On the criminal side, beginnings lie further back. (Pound, Frankfurter, Moley and the Crime Surveys; where lawyers have drawn on the criminologists.)

All that is really clear to date is that until we know more here our "rules" give us no remote suggestion of *what law means* to persons in the lower income brackets, and give us misleading suggestions as to the whole body of cases unappealed. Meantime, the techniques of the social sciences are being drawn upon and modified to make the work possible.

II. *There is the question of administrative bodies*—not merely on the side of administrative law (itself a novel concept recently enough)—but including all the action which state officials take "under the law" so far as it proves to affect people. And with this we begin departing from the orthodox. To be sure, the practicing lawyer today knows his commission as he knows his court. But the trail thus broken leads into the wilds of government, and politics, and queer events in both.

III. *There is the question of legislative regulation*—in terms of what it *means in action, and to whom,* not merely in terms of what it says. And with that, the question of what goes into producing legislative change—or blocking it— especially so far as the profession participates therein; legislative history on the official record; but as well the background of fact and interest and need. And, no less vital, there is the fact-inquiry into areas of life where maladjustment capable of legal remedy exists.

IV. Finally, and cutting now completely beyond the tradition-bounded area of law, there is the matter not of describing or predicting the action of officials—be they appellate courts, trial courts, legislators, administrators— but of describing and predicting *the effects of their action on the laymen of the community.* "Law" without effect approaches zero in its meaning. To be ignorant of its effect is to be ignorant of its meaning. To know its effect without study of the persons whom it affects is impossible. Here the antecedents of court action touch its results. To know law, then, to know *anything* of what is necessary to judge or evaluate law, we must proceed into these areas which have traditionally been conceived (save by the historical school) as not-law. Not only what courts do instead of what courts say, but also what difference it makes to anybody that they do it. And no sooner does one begin such a study than it becomes clear that there can be no broad talk of "law" nor of "the community"; but that it is a question of reaching the particular part of the community relevant to some particular part of law. There are persons sought to be affected, and persons not sought to be affected. Of the former, some are not in fact materially affected (the gangster-feud); of the latter, some are (depositors in a failing bank which the bank laws have *not* controlled). There is the range of questions as to those legal "helpful devices" (corporation, contract, lease) designed to make it easier for men to get where they want and what they want. There is all the information social scientists have gathered to be explored, in its bearings on the law. There is all the information they have not been interested in gathering, likewise to be explored—but, first, to be gathered.

Here are the matters one or another of the new fermenters is ploughing into. Even the sketchy citations here are enough to make clear that their lines of work organize curiously into a whole.

But again rises the query: are the matters *new?* What realist knows so little of law or the ways of human thought as to make such a claim? Which of the inquiries has not been made, or started, or adumbrated, in the past? Which of the techniques does not rest on our prior culture? New, I repeat, is one thing only: the *systematic* effort to carry one problem through, to carry a succession of problems through, to *consistently*, not occasionally, choose the best available technique, to *consistently* keep description on the descriptive level, to *consistently* distinguish the fact basis which will feed evaluation from the evaluation which it will later feed, to *consistently* seek *all* the relevant data one can find to *add* to the haphazard single-life experience, to *add* to general common sense [—so as, in possible due course, to produce that *un*common sense we know as horse-sense].

Is it not obvious that—if this be realism—realism is a mass of trends in legal work and thinking? (1) They have their common core, present to some extent wherever realistic work is done: recognition of law as means; recognition of change in society that may call for change in law; interest in what happens; interest in effects; recognition of the need for effort toward keeping perception of the facts uncolored by one's views on Ought; a distrust of the received set of rules and concepts as adequate indications of what is happening in the courts; a drive toward narrowing the categories of description. (2) They have grown out of the study of the action of appellate courts, and that study still remains their potent stimulus. Uncertainty in the action of such courts is one main problem: to find the why of it; to find means to reduce it, where it needs reduction; to find where it needs reduction, where expansion. (3) But into the work of lower courts, of administrative bodies, of legislatures, of the life which lies before and behind "law," the ferment of investigation spreads.

Some one or other of these realistic trends takes up the whole time of many; a hundred more participate in them to various degrees who yet would scorn the appellation "realist." The trends are centered in no man, in no coherent group. There is no leader. Spokesmen are self-appointed. They speak not for the whole but for the work each is himself concerned with—at times with little or no thought of the whole, at times with the exaggeration of controversy or innovation. Yet who should know better than lawyers the exaggeration of controversy; who should have more skill than they to limit argument and dictum to the particular issue, to read it in the light thereof. One will find, reading thus, little said by realistic spokesmen that does not warrant careful pondering. Indeed, on *careful* pondering, one will find little of exaggeration in their writing. Meantime, the proof of the pudding: are there results?

There are. They are results, primarily, on the side of the descriptive sociology of law discussed thus far. They are big with meaning for attack on the field of Ought—either on what courts ought to do with existing rules, or on what changes in rules are called for.

Already we have a series, lengthening impressively, of *more accurate* reformulations of what appellate courts are doing and may be expected to do. We are making headway in *seeing* (not just "knowing" without inquiry) what effects their doing has on some of the persons interested. We are accumulating some *knowledge (i.e.,* more than guesses) on phases of our life as to which our law seems out of joint.

We have, moreover, a first attack upon the realm of the unpredictable in the actions of [appellate] courts. That attack suggests strongly that one large element in the now incalculable consists in the traditional pretense or belief (sometimes the one, sometimes the other) that there is no such area of uncertainty, or that it is much smaller than it is. To *recognize* that there are limits to the certainty sought by words and deduction, to seek to define those limits, is to open the door to that other and far more useful judicial procedure: *conscious* seeking, *within the limits laid down by precedent and statute,* for the wise decision. Decisions thus reached, *within those limits,* may fairly be hoped to be more certainly predictable than decisions are now—for today no man can tell when the court will, and when it will not, thus seek the wise decision, but hide the seeking under words. And not only more certain, but what is no whit less important: more just and wise (or more frequently just and wise).

Indeed, the most fascinating result of the realistic effort appears as one returns from trial court or the ways of laymen to the tradition-hallowed problem of appellate case-law. Criticized by those who refuse to disentangle Is and Ought because of their supposed deliberate neglect of the normative aspect of law, the realists prove the value, for the normative, of temporarily putting the normative aside. They return from their excursion into the purest description they can manage with a demonstration that the field of free play for Ought in appellate courts is vastly wider than traditional Ought-bound thinking ever had made clear. This, *within* the confines of precedent as we have it, *within* the limits and on the basis of our present order. Let me summarize the points of the brief:

(a) If deduction does not solve cases, but only shows the effect of a given premise; and if there is available a competing but equally authoritative premise that leads to a different conclusion—then there is a choice in the case; a choice to be justified; a choice which *can* be justified only as a question of policy—for the authoritative tradition speaks with a forked tongue.

(b) If (i) the possible inductions from one case or a series of cases—even if those cases really had each a single fixed meaning—are nonetheless not single, but many; and if (ii) the standard authoritative techniques of dealing with precedent range for limiting the case to its narrowest issue on facts and procedure, and even searching the record for a hidden distinguishing fact, all the way to giving it the widest meaning the rule expressed will allow, or even thrusting under it a principle which was not announced in the opinion at all— then the available leeway in *interpretation of precedent* is (relatively to what the older tradition has *consciously* conceived) nothing less than huge. And only policy considerations and the facing of policy considerations can justify "interpreting" (making, shaping, drawing conclusions from) the relevant body of precedent in one way or in another. And—the essence of all—*stare decisis* has in the past been, now is, and must continue to be, a norm of change, and a means of change, as well as a norm of staying put, and a means of staying put.

*The growth of the past has been achieved by "standing on" the decided cases;* rarely by overturning them. Let this be recognized, and precedent is clearly seen to be a way of change as well as a way of refusing to change. Let that, in turn, be recognized, and that peculiar one of the ways of working with precedent which consists in blinding the eyes to policy loses the fictitious sanctity with which it is now enveloped *some of the time:* to wit, whenever judges for any reason do not wish to look at policy.

(c) If the classification of raw facts is largely an arbitrary [better: *creative*] process, raw facts having in most doubtful cases the possibility of ready classification along various lines, then "certainty," even under pure deductive thinking, has not the meaning that people who have wanted certainty in law are looking for. The quest of this unreal certainty, this certainty unattained in result, is the major reason for one self-denying ordinance of judges: their refusal to look beyond words to things. Let them once see that the "certainty" thus achieved is *un*certainty for the non-law-tutored layman in his living and dealing, and the way is open to reach for *layman's* certainty-through-law, by seeking for the fair or wise outcome, so far as precedent and statute make such outcome *possible.* To see the problem thus is also to open the way to conscious discrimination, *e.g.,* between current commercial dealings on the one hand and real estate conveyancing or corporate indenture drafting on the other. In the latter the *lawyer's* peculiar reliance on formulae may be assumed as of course; whereas in the former cause needs to be shown for making such an assumption.

Thus, as various of the self-designated realistic spokesmen have been shouting: the temporary divorce of Is and Ought brings to the reunion a sharper eye, a fuller equipment, a sounder judgment—even a wider opportunity as to that case-law which tradition has painted as peculiarly ridden by the past. That on the fact side, as to the particular questions studied, the temporary divorce yields no less gratifying results is demonstrated by the literature.

When the matter of *program in the normative aspect* is raised, the answer is: *there is none.* A likeness of method in approaching Ought-questions is apparent. If there be, beyond that, general lines of fairly wide agreement, they are hardly specific enough to mean anything on any given issue. Partly, this derives from differences in temperament and outlook. Partly, it derives from the total lack of organization or desire to schoolify among the men concerned. But partly, it is due to the range of work involved. Business lawyers have some pet Oughts, each in the material he has become familiar with; torts lawyers have the like in torts; public lawyers in public law. And so it goes. Partly also, the lack of programmatic agreement derives from the time and effort consumed in getting at facts, either the facts strictly legal or the "foreign" facts bearing on the law. Specialized interest must alone spell absence of group-program. Yet some general points of view may be hazarded.

(1) There is fairly general agreement on the importance of personnel, and of court organization, as essential to making laws have meaning. This both as to triers of fact and as to triers of law. There is some tendency, too, to urge specialization of tribunals.

(2) There is very general agreement on the need for courts to face squarely the policy questions in their cases, and use the full freedom precedent affords in working toward conclusions that seem indicated. There is fairly general agreement that effects of rules, so far as known, should be taken account of in making or remaking the rules. There is fairly general agreement that we need improved machinery for making the facts about such effects—or about needs and conditions to be affected by a decision—available to courts.

(3) There is a strong tendency to think it wiser [for purposes of initial inquiry] to narrow rather than to widen the categories in which concepts and rules *either about judging or for judging* are made.

(4) There is a strong tendency to approach most legal problems as problems in allocation of risks, and so far as possible, as problems of their reduction, and so to insist on the effects of rules on parties who not only are not in court, but are not fairly represented by the parties who are in court. To approach not only tort but business matters, in a word, as matters of *general* policy.

And so I close as I began. What is there novel here? In the ideas, nothing. In the sustained attempt to make one or another of them fruitful, much. In the narrowness of fact-category together with the wide range of fact-inquiry, much. In the techniques availed of, much—for lawyers. But let this be noted— for the summary above runs so largely to the purely descriptive side: When writers of realistic inclination are writing in general, they are bound to stress the need of more accurate description, of Is and not of Ought. There lies the *common* ground of their thinking; there lies the area of new and puzzling development. There lies the point of discrimination which they must drive home. To get perspective on their stand about ethically normative matters one must pick up the work of each man in his special field of work. There one will find no lack of interest or effort toward improvement in the law. As to whether change is called for, on any *given* point of law, and if so, how much change, and in what direction, there is no agreement. Why should there be? A *group* philosophy or program, a *group* credo of social welfare, these realists have not. They are not a group.

## BIBLIOGRAPHY:

### THE LITERATURE CANVASSED FOR THE TEST

Bingham, W.: *What is the Law?*, 11 MICH. L. REV. 1 (1912); *Science and the Law,* 25 GREEN BAG 162 (1913); *Legal Philosophy and the Law,* 9 ILL. L. REV. 98 (1914); *The Nature and Importance of Legal Possession,* 13 MICH. L. REV. 535 (1915).

Clark, C. E.: *Relations, Legal and Others,* 5 ILL. L. J. 26 (1922); *The Code Cause of Action,* 33 YALE L. J. 817 (1924); *Fact Research in Law Administration,* 2 CONN. BAR. J. 211 (1928); *New Types of Legal Research* (June 30, 1929) BUFFALO DAILY L. J.; *Some of the Facts of Law Administration in Connecticut,* 3 CONN. BAR. J. 161 (1929); *Methods of Legal Reform,* 36 W. VA. L. Q. 106 (1929); *Legal Education and Research at Yale,* YALE ALUM. WEEKLY (March 7, 1930); *Present Status of Judicial Statistics,* 14 J. AM. JUD. SOC. 84 (Oct. 1930).

Cook, W. W.: *The Alienability of Choses in Action*, 29 HARV. L. REV. 816 (1916); *The Alienability of Choses in Action: A Reply to Professor Williston*, 30 *id.* 449 (1917); *Privileges of Labor Unions in the Struggle for Life* (1918) 27 YALE L. J. 779 (1918); *Hohfeld's Contributions to the Science of Law*, 28 *id.* 721 (1919); *The Utility of Jurisprudence in the Solution of Legal Problems* in 5 LECTURES ON LEGAL TOPICS, ASSOCIATION OF THE BAR OF THE CITY OF NEW YORK (1923–24) 335; *The Logical and Legal Bases of the Conflict of Laws*, 33 YALE L. J. 457 (1924); *Scientific Method and the Law*, 15 JOHNS HOP. ALUM. MAG. 213 (1927); *The Jurisdiction of Sovereign States and the Conflict of Laws*, 31 COLUM. L. REV. 368 (1931); Book Review, 31 *id.* 725 (1931).

Corbin, Arthur Linton: *The Law and the Judges*, 3 YALE REV. 234 (New Ser. 1914); *Legal Analysis and Terminology*, 29 YALE L. J. 163 (1919); *Jural Relations and Their Classification*, 30 YALE L. J. 226 (1921); *Democracy and Education for the Bar*, 19 PROC. AM. L. S. ASS'N 143 (1921); Book Review, 38 YALE L. J. 270 (1928); *Third Parties as Beneficiaries of Contractors' Surety Bonds*, 38 *id.* i (1928); *The Restatement of the Common Law by the American Law Institute*, 15 IOWA L. REV. 19 (1929); *Contracts for the Benefit of Third Persons*, 46 L. Q. REV. 12 (1930).

Douglas, W. O.: *Vicarious Liability and Administration of Risk*, 38 YALE L. J. 584, 720 (1929); (with C. M. Shanks) *Insulation from Liability Through Subsidiary Corporations*, 39 YALE L. J. 193 (1929); (with Wm. Clark and D. S. Thomas) *The Business Failures Project—A Problem in Methodology*, 39 YALE L. J. 1013 (1930).

Francis, J.: *Domicil of a Corporation*, 38 YALE L. J. 335 (1929).

Frank, J.: LAW AND THE MODERN MIND (1930); Book Review, 40 YALE L. J. 1120 (1931).

Green, L.: Book Review, 38 YALE L. J. 402 (1929); JUDGE AND JURY (1930).

Hutcheson, Jr., J. C.: *The Judgment Intuitive:—The Function of the "Hunch" in Judicial Decision*, 14 CORN. L. Q. 274 (1929).

Klaus, S.: *Sale, Agency and Price Maintenance*, 28 COLUM. L. REV. 312, 441 (1928); Book Review, 28 *id.* 991 (1928); *Identification of the Holder and Tender of Receipt on the Counter Presentation of Checks*, 13 MINN. L. REV. 281 (1929); *Introduction to* EX PARTE MILLIGAN (1929); *Introduction to* PEOPLE V. MOLINEUX (1929); Book Review, 30 COLUM. L. REV. 1220 (1930).

Llewellyn, K. N.: *Free Speech in Time of Peace*, 29 YALE L. J. 337 (1920); *Implied Warranties of Wholesomeness Again*, 29 *id.* 782 (1920); *C. I. F. Contracts in American Law*, 32 *id.* 711 (1923); *The Effect of Legal Institutions on Economics*, 15 AM. ECON. REV. 665 (1925); Book Review, 40 HARV. L. REV. 142 (1926); *Law Observance and Law Enforcement*, PROCEEDINGS NATIONAL CONFERENCE SOCIAL WORK 127 (1928); *A Realistic Jurisprudence —The Next Step*, 30 COLUM. L. REV. 431 (1930); *The Conditions for and the Aims and Methods of Legal Research*, Am. L. S. REV. (1930); CASES AND MATERIALS ON THE LAW OF SALES (1930); THE BRAMBLE BUSH (1930); *Law and the Modern Mind: A Symposium: Legal Illusion*, 31 COLUM. L. REV. 82 (1931); *What Price Contract?—An Essay in Perspective*, 40 YALE L. J. 704 (1931); *Legal Tradition and Social Science Method* (Brookings) ESSAYS ON RESEARCH IN THE SOCIAL SCIENCES, 89 (1931).

Lorenzen, E. G.: *The Renvoi Doctrine in the Conflict of Laws—Meaning of "Law of a Country,"* 27 YALE L. J. 509 (1918); *Causa and Consideration in the Law of Contracts*, 28 *id.* 621 (1919); *The Theory of Qualifications and the Conflict of Laws*, 20 COLUM. L. REV. 247 (1920); *The Statute of Frauds and the Conflict of Laws*, 32 YALE L. J. 311 (1923); *Territoriality, Public Policy and the Conflict of Laws*, 33 *id.* 736 (1924).

Moore, U.: *Rational Basis of Legal Institutions*, 23 COLUM. L. REV. 609 (1923); (with Hope) *An Institutional Approach to the Law of Commercial Banking*, 38 YALE L. J.

703 (1929); (with Sussman) *Legal and Institutional Methods Applied to the Debiting of Direct Discounts,* 40 *id.* 381, 555, 752, 928 (1931).

Oliphant, H.: *Mutuality of Obligation in Bilateral Contracts at Law,* 25 COLUM. L. REV. 705 (1925); 28 *id.* 997 (1928); *Trade Associations and the Law,* 26 *id.* 381 (1926); *A Return to Stare Decisis,* 14 A.B.A.J. 71, 159 (1928); (with Hewitt) *Introduction to* RUEFF, FROM THE PHYSICAL TO THE SOCIAL SCIENCES (1929).

Patterson, E. W.: *The Apportionment of Business Risks Through Legal Devices,* 24 COLUM. L. REV. 335 (1924); *Equitable Relief for Unilateral Mistake,* 28 *id.* 859 (1928); *The Transfer of Insured Property in German and in American Law,* 29 *id.* 691 (1929); *Can Law be Scientific?,* 25 ILL. L. REV. 121 (1930); (with McIntyre) *Unsecured Creditors' Insurance,* 31 COLUM. L. REV. 212 (1931); *Hedging and Wagering on Produce Exchanges,* 40 YALE L. J. 843 (1931).

Powell, T. R.: *The Study of Moral Judgments by the Case Method,* 10 J. PHIL. PSYCH. 484 (1913); *Law as a University Study,* 19 COLUM. U. Q. 106 (1917); *Law as a Cultural Study,* 4 AM. L. S. REV. 330 (1917); *The Nature of a Patent Right,* 17 COLUM. L. REV. 663 (1917); *The Logic and Rhetoric of Constitutional Law,* 15 J. PHIL. PSYCH. 645 (1918); *The Changing Law of Foreign Corporations,* 33 POL. SCI. Q. 549 (1918); *How Philosophers May be Useful to Society,* 31 INT. J. ETHICS 289 (1921); *The Business Situs of Credits,* 28 W. VA. L. Q. 89 (1922); *An Imaginary Judicial Opinion,* 44 HARV. L. REV. 889 (1931).

Radin, M.: *The Disseisin of Chattels: The Title of a Thief,* 11 CALIF. L. REV. 259 (1923); *The Theory of Judicial Decision: Or How Judges Think,* 11 A.B.A.J. 357 (1925); *Scientific Method and the Law,* 19 CALIF. L. REV. 164 (1931); *Legal Realism,* 31 COLUM. L. REV. 824 (1931).

Sturges, W. A.: *Unincorporated Associations as Parties to Actions,* 33 YALE L. J. 383 (1924); *Commercial Arbitration or Court Application of Common Law Rules of Marketing,* 34 *id.* 480 (1925); Book Review, 35 *id.* 776 (1926); Book Review, 40 HARV. L. REV. 510 (1927); (with S. O. Clark) *Legal Theory and Real Property Mortgages,* 37 YALE L. J. 691 (1928).

Tulin, L. A.: *The Role of Penalties in Criminal Law,* 37 YALE L. J. 1048 (1928).

Yntema, H. E.: *The Hornbook Method and the Conflict of Laws,* 37 YALE L. J. 468 (1928); Book Review, 39 *id.* 140 (1929); *The Purview of Research in the Administration of Justice,* 16 IOWA L. REV. 337 (1931); *Mr. Justice Holmes' View of Legal Science,* 40 YALE L. J. 696 (1931); *The Rational Basis of Legal Science,* 31 COLUM. L. REV. 925 (1931).

# 6

# Roscoe Pound

Roscoe Pound (1870–1964), considered by many the 'dean' of American jurisprudence, as well as of the Harvard Law School, gave the first, and a distinctive, expression to American sociological jurisprudence based in part upon 19th century German social interest theory founded by Rudolph von Jhering.

# A SURVEY OF SOCIAL INTERESTS*

There has been a notable shift throughout the world from thinking of the task of the legal order as one of adjusting the exercise of free wills to one of satisfying wants, of which free exercise of the will is but one. Accordingly, we must start today from a theory of interests, that is, of the claims or demands or desires which human beings, either individually or in groups or associations or relations, seek to satisfy, of which, therefore, the adjustment of relations and ordering of conduct through the force of politically organized society must take account. I have discussed the general theory of interests, the classification of interests, and the details of individual interests in other places. It is enough to say here that the classification into individual interests, public interests, and social interests was suggested by Jhering. As I should put it, individual interests are claims or demands or desires involved immediately in the individual life and asserted in title of that life. Public interests are claims or demands or desires involved in life in a politically organized society and asserted in title of that organization. They are commonly treated as the claims of a politically organized society thought of as a legal entity. Social interests are claims or demands or desires involved in social life in civilized society and asserted in title of that life. It is not uncommon to treat them as the claims of the whole social group as such.

But this does not mean that every claim or demand or desire which human beings assert must be put once for all for every purpose into one of these three categories. For some purposes and in some connections it is convenient to look at a given claim or demand or desire from one standpoint. For other purposes or in other connections it is convenient to look at the same claim or demand or the same type of claims or demands from one of the other standpoints. When it comes to weighing or valuing claims or demands with respect to other claims

* Roscoe Pound, "A Survey of Social Interests," *Harvard Law Review*, LVII (1943), pp. 1–39. Copyright 1943 by The Harvard Law Review Association. This article in Dean Pound's words "is a complete revision and rewriting of a paper entitled *A Theory of Social Interests* published in May 1921." Footnotes and bibliographies which constituted approximately one-third of the original article have been omitted.

or demands, we must be careful to compare them on the same plane. If we put one as an individual interest and the other as a social interest we may decide the question in advance in our very way of putting it. For example, in the "truck act" cases one may think of the claim of the employer to make contracts freely as an individual interest of substance. In that event, we must weigh it with the claim of the employee not to be coerced by economic pressure into making contracts to take his pay in orders on a company store, thought of as an individual interest of personality. If we think of either in terms of a policy we must think of the other in the same terms. If we think of the employee's claim in terms of a policy of assuring a minimum or a standard human life, we must think of the employer's claim in terms of a policy of upholding and enforcing contracts. If the one is thought of as a right and the other as a policy, or if the one is thought of as an individual interest and the other as a social interest, our way of stating the question may leave nothing to decide.

In general, but not always, it is expedient to put claims or demands in their most generalized form, i.e., as social interests, in order to compare them. But where the problems are relatively simple, it is sometimes possible to take account of all the factors sufficiently by comparing individual interests put directly as such. It must be borne in mind that often we have here different ways of looking at the same claims or same type of claims as they are asserted in different titles. Thus, individual interests of personality may be asserted in title of or subsumed under the social interest in the general security, or the social interest in the individual life, or sometimes from different standpoints or in different aspects, both of them. Again, individual interests in the domestic relations may be subsumed under the social interest in the security of social institutions of which domestic institutions are the oldest and by no means the least important. Again, the public interest in the integrity of the state personality may be thought of as the social interest in the security of social institutions of which political institutions are one form. When we have recognized and legally delimited and secured an interest, it is important to identify the generalized individual interest behind and giving significance and definition to the legal right. When we are considering what claims or demands to recognize and within what limits, and when we are seeking to adjust conflicting and overlapping claims and demands in some new aspect or new situation, it is important to subsume the individual interests under social interests and to weigh them as such.

Some years ago one of the justices of our highest Court, dissenting from the judgment of that Court in the *Arizona Employers' Liability Cases,* told us that there was a "menace in the . . . judgment to all rights, subjecting them unreservedly to conceptions of public policy." Undoubtedly if certain legal rights were definitely established by the Constitution there would be a menace to the general security if the Court which must ultimately interpret and apply the provisions of that instrument were to suffer a state legislature to infringe those legal rights on mere considerations of political expediency. But it was only the ambiguity of the term "right," a word of many meanings, and want of clear understanding of what our law has been seeking to achieve through the obscure conception of "public policy" that made it possible to think of the decision in question in such a way. The "rights" of which Mr. Justice McKenna spoke were not legal rights in the same sense as my legal right to the integrity of my physical person or my legal right of ownership in my watch. They were individual wants, individual claims, individual interests, which it was felt ought to be secured through legal rights or through some other legal machinery. In other words, there was a policy of securing them. The Fourteenth Amendment did not set up these or any other individual interests as absolute legal rights. It imposed a standard upon the legislator. It said to him that if he trenched upon these individual interests he must not do so arbitrarily. His action must have some basis in reason. It is submitted that that basis must be the one upon which the common law has always sought to proceed, the one implied in the very term "due process of law," namely, a weighing or balancing of the various interests which overlap or come in conflict and a rational reconciling or adjustment. Thus the public policy of which Mr. Justice McKenna spoke is seen to be something at least on no lower plane than the so-called rights. As the latter term refers to individual interests which we feel ought to be secured by law, the former refers to social interests which we feel the law ought to or which in fact the law does secure in delimiting individual interests and establishing legal rights. There is a policy in the one case as much as in the other. The body of the common law is made up of adjustments or compromises of conflicting individual interests in which we turn to some social interests, frequently under the name of public policy, to determine the limits of a reasonable adjustment.

In the common law we have been wont to speak of social interests under the name of "public policy." Thus when a great judge was called on to weigh certain claims with reference to the social interest in the security of political institutions, he said that a "great and overshadowing public policy" forbade applying to the case one of the most fundamental principles of the law. Again, when it seemed to a majority of the Supreme Court of the United States that the validity of an acquisition from the Federal Government ought to be put at rest as against a claim of fraud, although limitation did not run against the Government, the Court spoke of the "policy" behind the statute of limitations and invoked the doctrine of election of remedies as expressing the same policy. So, too, when a great teacher of law wished to say that another fundamental legal doctrine was sometimes limited in its application because of the social interest in the general security, he stated that "except in certain cases based on public policy" the law of today makes liability dependent upon fault. But this limitation of the application of principles, or setting off of exceptions, on grounds of public policy, was felt to be something abnormal. The classical expression of this feeling is in the opinions of the judges in *Egerton v. Lord Brownlow*. Although the case was decided ultimately on the ground of public policy, the remarks of the judges have colored all subsequent judicial thinking on the subject. From the seventeenth century to the end of the nineteenth, juristic theory sought to state all interests in terms of individual natural rights. Moreover, the nineteenth century, under the influence of Hegel, wrote legal history as the unfolding in human experience of an idea of liberty, as an outcome of the clash of individual free wills, leading to the discovery of the invisible bounds within which each might realize a maximum of self-assertion. Thus for a time social interests were pushed into the background. It was said that public policy was "a very unruly horse, and when once you get astride it you never know where it will carry you." It was conceived that a court should be slow and cautious in taking public policy into account, and that if rules of law were to be limited in their application, or if exercise of individual powers of action was to be held down upon such grounds, the matter ought to be left to the legislature.

Questions of public policy came up in three forms: (1) in connection with the validity of contracts or similar transactions; (2) in connection with the validity of conditions in conveyances and testamentary gifts; (3) in connection with the validity of testamentary dispositions. Thus different social interests were weighed against a policy in favor of free contract ("right" of free contract) and a policy in favor of free disposition of property which was taken to be involved in the security of acquisitions and to be a corollary of individual interests of substance (rights of property). Accordingly, distrust of public policy grew out of a feeling that security of acquisitions and security of transactions were paramount policies. ". . . if there is one thing," said Sir George Jessel, "which more than another public policy requires it is that men of full age and competent understanding shall have the utmost liberty of contracting, and that their contracts . . . shall be enforced by Courts of justice."

In truth, the nineteenth-century attitude toward public policy was itself only the expression of a public policy. It resulted from a weighing of the social interest in the general security against other social interests which men had sought to secure through an overwide magisterial discretion in the stage of equity and natural law.

Thus the conception of public policy was never clearly worked out, nor were the several policies recognized by the common law defined as were the individual interests to which the juristic thought of the last century gave substantially its whole attention. The books are full of schemes of natural rights. There are no adequate schemes of public policies. Often the weighing of social interests is disguised by reasoning about "causation," or by the drawing of what seem on their face arbitrary distinctions. But three general types of policies are clearly recognized as such in the law books of the last century. First and most numerous are policies with reference to the security of social institutions. As to political institutions, there is a recognized policy against acts promotive of crime or violation of law—in other words, a policy of upholding legal institutions— and a policy against acts prejudicially affecting the public service performed by public officers. As to domestic institutions, there is the well-known policy against acts affecting the security of the domestic relations, or in restraint of marriage. As to economic institutions, there are the policy against acts destructive of competition, the policy against acts affecting commercial freedom, and the policy against permanent or general restrictions on the free use and transfer of property. Secondly, there are policies with reference to maintaining the general morals. Thus there is a recognized policy against acts promotive of dishonesty. Also there is a recognized policy against acts offending the general morals. Thirdly, there are policies with reference to the individual social life: a policy against things tending to oppression, and a policy against general or extensive restrictions upon individual freedom of action. Some of the policies with respect to economic institutions suggest this same interest in the individual life.

In one way or another most of the social interests of which the law must take account today are at least suggested in the list of those recognized as policies in the common law. Yet one social interest which has governed the ideas of lawyers at all times and has played a controlling part in the thought of the immediate past is relatively little stressed as a policy. The social interest in the general security seems to have been thought of as something apart, as something involved in the very idea of law and entering into every legal relation as a necessary element. This appears clearly in nineteenth-century theories as to the end of law and in nineteenth-century juristic method.

Juries of the last century thought of law as involving restraints on liberty which might only be justified so far as it was necessary in order to maintain liberty. Hence, they conceived that the legal order was to be held down to the minimum which was required to protect the individual against aggression and to secure the harmonious co-existence of the free will of each and the free will of all. But this is only a way of stating a paramount social interest in the general security in terms of individual liberty. Again, men strove zealously in the last century to insure complete security through absolute certainty and uniformity in judicial administration. When the eighteenth-century idea that these things might be attained through a complete and perfect code broke down, they sought to achieve them through a method of mechanical logical deduction from fixed legal conceptions. As this also broke down at many points, lawyers sought the same ends through universal definitions of absolute rights. But behind the quest of certainty and uniformity is their real end—the social interest in the general security. Attempts to administer justice with an eye solely to that one social interest have broken down because of the pressure of other social interests which it has proved impossible to ignore. Exclusive attention to security led jurists to seek abstract, universal, eternal adjustments or harmonizings of conflicting or overlapping interests which were too abstract to prove workable. We have learned slowly that it is the problem—namely, to satisfy human claims and demands and desires—that is constant, not the exact machinery of satisfying them. To go back to the illustration of the "truck acts," in rural, pioneer, agricultural America there was no call to limit the contracts a laborer might make as to taking his pay in goods. To have imposed a limitation would have interfered with individual freedom of industry and contract without any corresponding gain in securing some other interest. On the other hand, in industrial America of the end of the nineteenth century, a regime of unlimited free contract between employer and employee in certain enterprises led not to conservation but to destruction of values. It led to sacrifice of the social interest in the human life of the individual worker. Hence we began to put limits to liberty of contract between employer and employee and to require wages to be paid in money. It was inevitable that the statutes imposing these limits should be bitterly opposed by a generation which could only think of contracts of employment in terms of individual rights and security of transactions.

Not only did our thinking in the last century deceive itself in supposing that it was proceeding solely on the basis of individual liberty and individual rights deduced therefrom, it deceived itself quite as much in its interpretation of legal development. The conception that pressure of individual interests brought about state and law and fashioned legal institutions has no historical warrant. On the contrary, from the first, the controlling factor is the need of the social group to be secure against those forms of action and courses of conduct which threaten its existence. This paramount social interest is the first interest of any sort to be given legal recognition. It is not too much to say that law in the lawyer's sense of that term arose and primitive law existed simply to maintain one narrow phase of this interest, namely, the social interest in peace and order.

It must be borne in mind that juristic thinking became fixed to no small extent in the mold of the strict law. That mold was largely shaped by the circumstance that in its beginnings law was no more than a means toward the peaceable ordering of society, a regulative agency by which men were restrained and the general security was maintained. Law retains this character of a regulative agency and means toward peaceable ordering, although other functions and other ends become manifest as it develops. Thus the interests which were paramount while law was formative left their mark upon it and fixed the lines of legal thought. In the beginning, in order to establish a peaceable ordering of society, the legal order had to undertake two tasks. It had to regulate self-redress and ultimately to supersede it. It had also to prevent aggression. The simple program of primitive law deals only with assault, homicide, and larceny, which are causes of private war, and with impiety, which it was believed might cause interposition of the gods in the form of natural calamities. In the last century it was easy to say that the former (*i.e.*, giving a remedy for aggression) is private law, the securing of individual interests, while the latter (*i.e.*, putting down impiety) is criminal law—the securing of social interests as such. It is true that putting down private war grew into private law, and in the eighteenth and nineteenth centuries we came to think of it in terms of individual interests only. When self-redress and private war had been put down for centuries, men saw only that the legal order prevented aggression, that it prevented or repaired infringements of individual interests. In primitive society, however, the chief significance of aggression on individuals was that it was certain to lead to private war. Where only the interests of the individual were involved we have another story. As such primitive law ignores him. It was only the free man, head of a household and able to disturb the peace of society, who had standing in the old Roman law to call upon the law for redress. In a society in which groups of kindred are the significant element, a wrong involves much more than the mere injury to John Doe or Richard Roe. In the stage of the strict law men have discovered how to secure the social interest in peace and order by means of legal remedies given to injured individuals.

In a later stage of legal development, the individual human being, the moral unit, becomes the legal unit, and the law seeks to transmute his moral duties into legal duties. In the maturity of law, legal rights are put behind the dnties and remedies and orderings and appear to be the ultimate ends for which the legal order exists. It was natural, in that period of legal development, to write legal history from an abstract individualist standpoint and to interpret it as a working out of restrictions upon individual aggression in order to secure individual freedom of action. On the contrary, individual freedom of action as an end is something which came into juristic thinking in modern times, as we began to be conscious of a social interest in the individual human life. Individual legal rights were worked out in the endeavor to maintain the social interest in the general security.

Thus the formal remedies of the strict law, the abstract individualist legal philosophy of the nineteenth century, the individualist interpretation of legal history by the historical jurists, in short, the whole training of the lawyer, led him to think of the legal order exclusively in terms of the general security and of the general security exclusively in terms of individual rights. When the social interest in the general security is to be weighed in the scale, the courts have had little difficulty. But when other social interests are involved, it has been usual to employ a vague conception of "policy," of which courts and lawyers are rightly mistrustful, since the policies are largely ill-defined and in their application have been felt to leave too much scope for the personal equation of the particular tribunal. Hence pressure of new social interests has given the courts pause and sometimes has led them to cast doubt upon the method of dealing with individual interests which consciously or unconsciously the law has always employed. Today, jurists are having to consider all manner of problems arising from consciousness of new social interests, or at least from new phases of old ones. In contrast to nineteenth-century attempts to state the end of the legal order in terms of security of acquisitions and security of transactions, attempts have been made to state it in terms of the social interest in the individual life, or to value that interest along with the interest in the general security on which the last century insisted almost exclusively. Nor is this change confined to legal thought. Concrete individualization rather than abstract treatment is insisted upon today in every department of human activity. In law this means increased regard for the circumstances of the actual case and results in a continually increasing resort to administrative tribunals or to administrative methods. When we try to generalize the process for legal and judicial purposes, it appears as a conscious recognition of the social interest in the individual life. In criminal law we speak of a "socialized" punitive justice.

An important phase of the social interest in the individual life calls for security to free and spontaneous self-assertion and is connected easily with the juristic thought of the immediate past. But there are many conditions in the life of today in which other phases of this interest must come into account and may call for restrictions upon abstract self-assertion. Thus American legislation restricted the power of Indian allottees to dispose of the tracts allotted to them. British legislation limited the *jus disponendi* of Irish tenants, suddenly turned into proprietors and without experience of economic freedom. Courts of equity avoided sailors' contracts, contracts with heirs and sales of reversions and expectancies, and agreements with debtors clogging their equity of redeeming mortgaged property where there was an economic pressure and only an abstract, theoretical freedom of contract. Back of these doctrines of equity was a dim recognition of a social interest of which we have come to be fully conscious. Today our statute books are full of such restrictions. We do not ask: What will promote the maximum abstract freedom of contract as an item of the general abstract freedom taken to be the end of law? We ask instead: Is it wise social engineering, under the actual social and economic conditions of the time and place, to limit free self-assertion, or what in appearance is free self-assertion, for a time in certain situations? Does it secure a maximum of our scheme of interests as a whole, with the least sacrifice, to leave persons in certain relations free to contract as they choose or as their necessities may seem to dictate, or should we rather limit what is not under actual conditions a free choice? Such a mode of thinking does not fit easily into the method of hard and fast conceptions on which the last generation relied to maintain the general security. A generation ago modern social legislation presented itself to the judicial mind as involving, on the one hand, a natural right of free contract, guaranteed by the Constitution as a part of liberty, and, on the other hand, a hard and fast conception of the police power of the state, defined in terms of public health, safety, and morals. Thus courts were not unlikely to reach an *impasse* and there were sure to be judicial dissents. The net result was to break down the method of conceptions, when used as a method of applying a standard, and to take account of an increasing number of social interests as such. In reality, the courts were using an ideal of the end of law as a measure of reasonableness or of "public purpose," since the "police power" was the power of the government to achieve its ends in ways not forbidden by the fundamental law established in the Constitution.

Perhaps enough has been said to show the practical importance of recognizing social interests as such, instead of thinking of policies, and of a more complete statement of them and a more adequate classification. Yet a satisfactory starting point for such a classification requires some consideration. A generation ago, as a matter of course, we should have relied upon logical deduction. We should have deduced the several social interests as presuppositions of generalized social existence. But schemes of necessary presuppositions of law or of legal institutions seem to me to be at bottom schemes of observed elements in actual legal systems, systematically arranged, reduced to their lowest terms, and deduced, as one might say, to order. I doubt the ability of the jurist to work out deductively the necessary jural presuppositions of society in the abstract.

At one time it seemed that a more attractive starting point might be found in social psychology. One need only turn to the list of so-called instincts in any of the older social psychologies in order to see an obvious relation between interests, as the jurist now uses that term, or what we had been wont to call natural rights or public policies, on the one hand, and these "instincts" or whatever they are now called, on the other hand. Thus in McDougall's *Social Psychology* we used to find an instinct of repugnance and "predisposition to aesthetic discrimination." In jurisprudence we must consider a social interest in aesthetic surroundings which the law is beginning grudgingly to recognize. In McDougall we used to find an instinct of self-abasement, and in jurisprudence we must consider the so-called right of privacy. Again, to take so-called instincts with which the law has always had much to do, there is evident relation between the "instinct of pugnacity" and the law as to self-defense; between the "instinct of self-assertion" and the anxiety of the law that the will of the individual shall not be trodden upon; between the "instinct of acquisition" and individual interests of substance and the social interest in the security of acquisitions; between the "instinct of gregariousness" and loyalty and veracity as tendencies or habits connected therewith, and the social interest in the security of transactions. But in the last two decades, after a bitter controversy among sociologists and social psychologists, and redefinitions and substitute categories, most of what was accepted a generation ago in this connection has been pretty much given up. Certainly we can no longer build on McDougall's scheme and such definitions and classifications as are suggested today are remote from what we need in jurisprudence.

If we may not rely upon logical deduction nor upon a theory and classification of what were formerly called instincts, there remains a less pretentious method which may none the less be upon surer ground. If legal phenomena are social phenomena, observation and study of them as such may well bear fruit for social science in general as well as for jurisprudence. Why should not the lawyer make a survey of legal systems in order to ascertain just what claims or demands or desires have pressed or are now pressing for recognition and satisfaction and how far they have been or are now recognized and secured? This is precisely what has been done in the case of individual interests, in the schemes of natural rights, although the process has usually been covered up by a pretentious fabric of logical deduction. The same method may well be applied to social interests, and this should be done consciously and avowedly, as befits the science of today. It is true that objection has been made to this because the same social interest appears behind many legal institutions and doctrines and precepts, and legal institutions and doctrines and precepts almost always have behind them, not one social interest or a simple adjustment or compromise of two, but a complex harmonizing of many. Yet it is of the first importance to perceive this, to note what those interests are, to see how they are adjusted or harmonized or compromised, and to inquire why it is done in this way rather than in another. The first step in such an investigation is a mere survey of the legal order and an inventory of the social interests which have pressed upon lawmakers and judges and jurists for recognition.

In such a survey and inventory, first place must be given to the social interest in the general security—the claim or want or demand, asserted in title of social life in civilized society and through the social group, to be secure against those forms of action and courses of conduct which threaten its existence. Even if we accept Durkheim's view that it is what shocks the general conscience, not what threatens the general security, that is repressed, I suspect that the general conscience reflects experience or superstition as to the general safety. A common-law judge observed that there would be no safety for human life if it were to be considered as law that drunkenness could be shown to negative the intent element of crime where a drunk man kills while intoxicated though he would never do such a thing when sober. It should be noted how the exigencies of the general security outweighed the traditional theory of the criminal law.

This paramount social interest takes many forms. In its simplest form it is an interest in the general safety, long recognized in the legal order in the maxim that the safety of the people is the highest law. It was recognized in American constitutional law in the nineteenth century by putting the general safety along with the general health and general morals in the "police power" as a ground of reasonable restraint to which natural rights must give way. In another form, quite as obvious today but not so apparent in the past, before the nature and causes of disease were understood, it is an interest in the general health. In another form, recognized from the very beginnings of law, it is an interest in peace and public order. In an economically developed society it takes on two other closely related forms, namely, a social interest in the security of acquisitions and a social interest in the security of transactions. The two last came to be well understood in the nineteenth century, in which they were more or less identified with individual interests of substance and individual interests in freedom of contract. Yet a characteristic difference between the law of the eighteenth century and the law of the nineteenth century brings out their true nature. Eighteenth-century courts, taking a purely individualist view, regarded the statute of limitations as something to be held down as much as possible and to be evaded in every way. Lord Mansfield in particular, under the influence of natural-law ideas and thinking of the statute only as an individual plea which enabled the individual interest of a plaintiff to be deprived of legal security, sought out numerous astute contrivances to get around its most obvious provisions. If one said, "I am ready to account, but nothing is due you," if he made provision in his will for the payment of his "just debts," if his executors advertised, notifying those who had "just debts" owing them to present their claims, in these and like cases it was held there was an acknowledgment sufficing to take a barred debt out of the statute. Modern courts came to see that there was something more here than the individual interests of plaintiff and defendant. They came to see that the basis of the statute was a social interest in the security of acquisitions, which demands that titles shall not be insecure by being open to attack indefinitely, and a social interest in the security of transactions which demands that the transactions of the past shall not be subject to inquiry indefinitely, so as to unsettle credit and disturb business and trade. If we compare the French rule, *en tout cas de meuble possession vaut titre*, with the Roman doctrine that no one can transfer a greater title than he has, if we note the growth of the idea of negotiability in the law everywhere, and in our law both by legislation and by judicial decision, we may see something of how far recognition of the social interest in the security of transactions went in the maturity of law.

Other examples of recognition of the security of transactions may be seen in the presumption as to transactions of a corporation through its acting officers, the stress which the courts put upon *stare decisis* in cases involving commercial law, and the doctrine allowing only the sovereign to challenge *ultra vires* conveyances of corporations. As to recognition of the social interest in the security of acquisitions, note the insistence of the courts upon *stare decisis* where rules of property are involved. In such cases it is an established proposition that it is better that the law be settled than that it be settled right.

Second, we may put the social interest in the security of social institutions— the claim or want or demand involved in life in civilized society that its fundamental institutions be secure from those forms of action and courses of conduct which threaten their existence or impair their efficient functioning. Looking at them in chronological order, this interest appears in three forms.

The first is an interest in the eccurity of domestic institutions, long recognized in the form of a policy against acts affecting the security of domestic relations or in restraint of marriage. Legislation intended to promote the family as a social institution has been common. There is a policy against actions by members of the family against each other. Today, although the law is becoming much relaxed, this social interest is sttll weighed heavily against the individual claims of married persons in most divorce legislation. It still weighs heavily against individual claims in the law as to illegitimate children. At times this has been carried so far that great and numerous disabilities have attached to such children lest recognition of their individual interests should weaken a fundamental social institution. The movement to give independence to married women has had collateral effects of impairing the security of this interest, and the balance is not easy to make nor to maintain. The tendency to relax the rules which formerly obtained is brought out in *Russell v. Russell,* in which two of the five law lords dissented as to application of the policy of "preservation of the sanctity of married life," and *Fender v. St. John Mildmay,* in which again two of five law lords dissented as to the rule concerning the validity of a promise of marriage before a divorce proceeding has been finally determined. There are, however, recent cases which tend to uphold the policy formerly well established.

It is no doubt too soon to be sure of even the path which juristic thought of the immediate future will follow. But increased weight given to the social interest in the individual life in the concrete, instead of upon abstract liberty, seems to be indicated. There is emphasis upon the concrete claims of concrete human beings. . . . Family law, in which there must be a balance between the security of social institutions and the individual life, is necessarily much affected by such a change.

In another part of the law, the social interest in the security of domestic institutions still weighs heavily, in comparison, however, with the general security. A wife is not to be held as accessory after the fact for harboring a felon husband or for helping him escape. The common law does not require a wife to choose between fidelity to the relation of husband and wife and duty to the state. Also legislation as to mothers' pensions proceeds at least in large part upon this interest.

A second form is an interest in the security of religious institutions. In the beginning this is closely connected with the general security. A chief point of origin of the criminal law, of that part of the law by which social interests as such are directly and immediately secured, is in religion. Sacrifice of the impious offender who has affronted the gods, and exclusion from society of the impious offender whose presence threatens to bring upon his fellows the wrath of the gods, are, in part at least, the originals of capital punishment and of outlawry. Religious organization was long a stronger and more active agency of social control than political organization. In the Anglo-Saxon laws the appeals or exhortations addressed to the people as Christians are at least as important as the threats addressed to them as subjects. One of the great English statutes of the thirteenth century recites that Parliament had met to make laws "for the common Profit of holy Church, and of the Realm." It is only in relatively recent times that we have come to think of blasphemy as involving no more than a social interest in the general morals, of Sunday laws only in terms of a social interest in the general health, of heresy as less dangerous socially than radical views upon economics or politics, or of preaching or teaching of atheism as involved in a guaranteed liberty. Today what was formerly referred to this interest is usually referred to the social interest in the general morals. Questions as to the interest in the security of religious institutions have been debated in all lands.

In a third form the interest is one in the security of political institutions. This interest has weighed heavily in much twentieth-century legislation too familiar to require more than mention. When the public called for such legislation for the security of political institutions, absolute constitutional guarantees of free speech and natural rights of individual self-assertion, which in other times had moved courts to refuse to enjoin repeated and undoubted libels, lest liberty be infringed, were not suffered to stand in the way. If the individual interests involved had been conceived less absolutely and had been looked at in another light, as identified with a social interest in the general progress, they might have fared better.

Perhaps a fourth form of the interest in the security of social institutions should be added, namely, an interest in the security of economic institutions. Formerly, these were chiefly commercial. Today industrial institutions also must be taken into account. Judicial recognitions of a social interest in the security of commercial institutions are numerous. In a leading case in which it was determined that a bank note payable to bearer passed current the same as coin, Lord Mansfield grounded the judgment "upon the general course of business, and . . . the consequences to trade and commerce: which would be much incommoded by a contrary determination." More than one decision in the last generation on labor law seems to go upon an interest in maintaining the industrial regime in the face of persistent pressure from the claims of organized workingmen. Some of the policies to be considered presently under the social interest in general progress might be referred to this head.

Third, we may put the social interest in the general morals, the claim or want or demand involved in social life in civilized society to be secured against acts or courses of conduct offensive to the moral sentiments of the general body of individuals therein for the time being. This interest is recognized in Roman law in the protection of *boni mores*. It is recognized in our law by policies against dishonesty, corruption, gambling, and things of immoral tendency; by treating continuing menaces to the general morals as nuisances; and by the common-law doctrine that acts contrary to good morals and subversive of general morals are misdemeanors. It is recognized in equity in the maxim that he who comes into equity must come with clean hands. Similar provisions are to be found in the private law and in the criminal law in other lands. Obstinately held ideas of morality may in time come in conflict with ideas arising from changed social and economic conditions or newer religious and philosophical views. In such cases we must reach a balance between the social interest in the general morals, and the social interest in general progress, taking form in a policy of free discussion. What was said above as to free speech and writing and the social interest in security of social institutions applies here also.

Fourth, there is the social interest in conservation of social resources, that is, the claim or want or demand involved in social life in civilized society that the goods of existence shall not be wasted; that where all human claims or wants or desires may not be satisfied, in view of infinite individual desires and limited natural means of satisfying them, the latter be made to go as far as possible; and, to that end, that acts or courses of conduct which tend needlessly to destroy or impair these goods shall be restrained. In its simplest form this is an interest in the use and conservation of natural resources, and is recognized in the doctrines as to *res communes,* which may be used but not owned, by the common law as to riparian rights and constitutional and statutory provisions where irrigation is practiced, by modern game laws, by the recent doctrines as to percolating water and surface water, and by laws as to waste of natural gas and oil. There has been a progressive tendency to restrict the *ius abutendi* which the maturity of law attributed to owners. A crowded and hungry world may yet weight this interest against individual claims to free action still further by preventing destruction of commodities in order to keep up prices, or even cutting off the common-law liberty of the owner of land to sow it to salt if he so desires. At times overproduction of agricultural products has led to proposals for restriction of the owner's *ius utendi* by regulation of what crops he may raise. At other times there are projects for administrative appointment of receivers of agricultural land cultivated or managed by the owner "in such manner as to prejudice materially the production of food thereon. . . ." Restrictions with respect to housing proceed on another aspect of this same social interest.

A closely related social interest is one in protection and training of dependents and defectives. It might from one point of view be called an interest in conservation of the human assets of society. In one form it was recognized long ago in the common-law system by the jurisdiction of the chancellor, representing the king as *parens patriae*, over infants, lunatics, and idiots. This jurisdiction has had a significant development in recent times in the juvenile court, and an extension to youthful offenders beyond the period of infancy is being urged. Again, there has been an extension of the idea of protection and training of dependents, on one hand to the reformation of mature delinquents, and on another hand to protection of the mature who are yet economically more or less dependent. This has gone a long way in recent times in social security or social insurance legislation and in small loan legislation. The latter has had a historical background in the interference of equity to prevent oppression of debtors and necessitous persons. Also after the first world war there was legslaitive recognition of a social interest in rehabilitation of the maimed. Much of the legislation referred to runs counter to the insistence upon abstract individual liberty in the juristic theory of the last century. It was formerly often pronounced arbitrary and so unconstitutional by courts whose dogmatic scheme could admit no social interest other than the general security. There has been a significant widening of the field of legally recognized and secured social interests. But for the most part the claims or demands here considered are better treated in connection with the social interest in the individual life.

Fifth, there is the social interest in general progress, that is, the claim or want or demand involved in social life in civilized society, that the development of human powers and of human control over nature for the satisfaction of human wants go forward; the demand that social engineering be increasingly and continuously improved; as it were, the self-assertion of the social group toward higher and more complete development of human powers. This interest appears in three main forms, an interest in economic progress, an interest in political progress, and an interest in cultural progress. The social interest in economic progress has long been recognized in law and has been secured in many ways. In the common law it is expressed in four policies: the policy as to freedom of property from restrictions upon sale or use, the policy as to free trade and consequent policy against monopoly, the policy as to free industry, which has had to give much ground in recent legislation and judicial decision, and the policy as to encouragement of invention, which is behind patent legislation and there comes in conflict with the policy as to free trade. All of these policies have important consequences in everyday law. It may be thought that some of them should be classified rather as forms of a social interest in the security of economic institutions. As I read the cases, however, these demands have pressed upon courts and jurists from the standpoint of their relation to economic progress. If that relation fails, they are not likely to maintain themselves. Likewise the law has long recognized a social interest in political progress. In American bills of rights, and in written constitutions generally, a policy of free criticism of public men, public acts, and public officers, and a policy of free formation, free holding, and free expression of political opinion are guaranteed as identified with individual rights. Moreover, at common law, the privilege of fair comment upon public men and public affairs recognizes and secures the same interest. But the third form, the social interest in cultural progress, has not been recognized in the law so clearly. It may be said to involve four policies: a policy of free science, a policy of free letters, a policy of encouragement of arts and letters, and a policy of promotion of education and learning. The last two have been recognized to some extent in copyright laws and in American constitutional provisions for the promotion of higher learning. The first two have made their way more slowly because of conflict or supposed conflict with the security of religious and political institutions.

Closely connected with the interest in cultural progress is a social interest in aesthetic surroundings, which recently has been pressing for legal recognition. Fifty years ago, Sir Frederick Pollock could say with assurance that our law ignored aesthetic relations, and, comparing the English with the French in this respect, could quote Hood's lines:

> Nature which gave them the goût
> Only gave us the gout.

In the United States, courts and legislatures were long engaged in a sharp struggle over billboard laws and laws against hideous forms of outdoor advertising. For a time also the interest pressed in another way in connection with town planning legislation. It is significant that the courts are now ready to admit a policy in favor of the aesthetic as reasonable and constitutionally permissible.

Last, and in some ways most important of all, as we now are coming to think, there is the social interest in the individual life. One might call it the social interest in the individual moral and social life, or in the individual human life. It is the claim or want or demand involved in social life in civilized society that each individual be able to live a human life therein according to the standards of the society. It is the claim or want or demand that, if all individual wants may not be satisfied, they be satisfied at least so far as is reasonably possible and to the extent of a human minimum. Three forms of this social interest have been recognized in common law or in legislation: individual self-assertion, individual opportunity, and individual conditions of life. The first, the interest in free self-assertion, includes physical, mental, and economic activity. In Spencer's scheme of natural rights, they appear as a "right of free motion and locomotion," a "right of free exchange and free contract," deduced as a sort of free economic motion and locomotion, a "right of free industry," deduced expressly as a modern outgrowth of free motion and locomotion, as a right of free economic activity, a "right of free religious belief and opinion" and a right of free political belief and opinion, the two last being deduced also as modern developments of the same natural right of free motion and locomotion. These are deduced from a "law of equal freedom" which is taken to have been discovered by observation of social phenomena and verified by further observation. Without the aid of his "law of equal freedom" he might have found them by observation of the policies set forth in the law books. The old common-law policy in favor of freedom, the doctrine that one may justify by his natural liberty of action, except where his action takes the form of aggression and so threatens the general security, and in part the policy of free industry, are examples of recognition of a social interest in individual physical self-assertion. The policy in favor of free speech and free belief and opinion, although related also to the social interest in political progress, must be referred in part to a social interest in individual mental self-assertion. Policies favoring free trade and free industry are in part referable to a social interest in free economic self-assertion.

But the most important phase of the social interest in individual self-assertion, from the standpoint of modern law, is what might be called the social interest in freedom of the individual will—the claim or interest, or policy recognizing it, that the individual will shall not be subjected arbitrarily to the will of others. This interest is recognized in an old common-law policy which is declared in the Fifth and Fourteenth Amendments. If one will is to be subjected to the will of another through the force of politically organized society, it is not to be done arbitrarily, but is to be done upon some rational basis, which the person coerced, if reasonable, could appreciate. It is to be done upon a reasoned weighing of the interests involved and reasoned attempt to reconcile them or adjust them. This policy obviously expresses political and juristic experience of what modern psychology has discovered as to the ill effects of repression. For example, it is more and more recognized today in our penal legislation and in our treatment of offenders. It has come to be recognized particularly of late as a result of pressure upon courts and lawmakers for security in the relation of employer and employee. It is coming to be recognized also in juristic thought in another connection as sociological theories of property replace metaphysical theories. There are many signs of a growing feeling that complete exclusion of all but him whom the law pronounces owner from objects which are the natural media of human existence or means of human activity, must be measured and justified by reasoned weighing of the interests on both sides and a reasoned attempt to harmonize them or to save as much as we may with the sacrifice of as little on the part of the excluded, no less than on the part of the owner, as we may.

I have called a second form the social interest in individual opportunity. It is the claim or want or demand involved in social life in civilized society that all individuals shall have fair or reasonable (perhaps, as we are coming to think, we must say equal) opportunities—political, physical, cultural, social, and economic. In American thinking we have insisted chiefly on equal political opportunities, since in the pioneer conditions in which our institutions were formative other opportunities, so far as men demanded them, were at hand everywhere. But a claim to fair physical opportunities is recognized in public provision of parks and playgrounds and in other provisions for recreation; the claim to fair cultural opportunities is recognized by laws as to compulsory education of children (although the social interests in general progress and in dependents are also recognized here) as well as by state provisions for universities and for adult education; the claim to fair social opportunities is recognized by civil rights laws; and the claim to fair economic opportunities is recognized, for example, in the legal right to "freedom of the market," and in the so-called "right to pursue a lawful calling," which is weighed with other social interests in regulating training for and admission to professions.

In a third form, an interest in individual conditions of life, the social interest in the individual life appears as a claim that each individual shall have assured to him the conditions of at least a minimum human life under the circumstances of life in the time and place. I have said minimum, which certainly was all that was recognized until relatively recent times. Bur perhaps we should now say reasonable or even equal. A claim for equal conditions of life is pressing and we can't put the matter as to what is recognized with assurance as we could have done a generation ago. Moreover, the scope of generally asserted demands with respect to the individual life is obviously growing. The Roman law recognized a policy of this sort, and it has long been recognized in American legislation. In weighing individual interests in view of the social interest in security of acquisitions and security of transactions, we must also take account of the social interest in the human life of each individual, and so must restrict the legal enforcement of demands to what is consistent with a human existence on the part of the person subjected thereto. The Roman law imposed such a limitation in a number of cases in what is called the *beneficium competentiae*. At common law there were restrictions on what could be taken in distress for rent, and the thirteenth-century statute providing for execution by writ of *elegit* exempts the debtor's oxen and beasts of the plow and half of his land. In the United States and recently in continental Europe, this policy is given effect in homestead laws and in exemptions from execution. In the latter, the social interest in the family as a social institution is also a factor. But nineteenth-century opposition to homestead and exemption laws, and in Europe to the *beneficium competentiae,* is significant. The nineteenth century sought to treat such cases as if they involved nothing more than the individual interests of the parties to the debtor-creditor relation, or, if a social interest was considered, sought to think only of the general security, which here takes the form of security of transactions. Other recognitions of this interest may be seen in restrictions on the power of debtors or contractors to saddle themselves with oppressive burdens, as in the doctrines of equity heretofore referred to, as in usury laws, and more recently in "loan shark" legislation. A notable instance in recent judicial decision may be seen in the English doctrine as to covenants not to exercise the calling for which one has trained himself. Statutes forbidding contracts by laborers to take their pay in orders on company stores, and as to conditions and hours of labor, minimum wage laws, child labor laws, and housing laws, are recognitions of the same interest.

Again, when the law confers or exercises a power of control, we feel that the legal order should safeguard the human existence of the person controlled. Thus the old-time sea law, with its absolute power of the master over the sailor, the old-time ignominious punishments, that treated the human offender like a brute, that did not save his human dignity—all such things are disappearing as the circle of recognized interests widens and we come to take account of the social interest in the individual life and to weigh that interest with the social interest in the general security, on which the last century insisted so exclusively.

Such in outline are the social interests which are recognized or are coming to be recognized in modern law. Looked at functionally, the law is an attempt to satisfy, to reconcile, to harmonize, to adjust these overlapping and often conflicting claims and demands, either through securing them directly and immediately, or through securing certain individual interests, or through delimitations or compromises of individual interests, so as to give effect to the greatest total of interests or to the interests that weigh most in our civilization, with the least sacrifice of the scheme of interests as a whole.

# 7

## Marcus G. Singer

Marcus Singer (1926–     ), American ethical and legal theorist and
Professor of Philosophy at the University of Wisconsin, sets the stage
in his review of H. L. A. Hart's The Concept of Law for continuing
dialogue—and 'normative' dissension—between American and British
analysts.

# HART'S CONCEPT OF LAW*

Since World War II, the philosophy of law has had a curious yet heartening
revival. A subject that was one of the prominent interests of many of the great
philosophers of the past was in danger, in the last hundred years, of nearly
dwindling away, and was kept alive only by the efforts and the interest of a
handful of thinkers, most of whom were primarily lawyers and jurists. Under
the heading of Jurisprudence it has been regarded for some time as only a
branch, and a minor branch, of legal study; important articles on the subject
have been buried in the pages of countless law journals, and books on the subject
have rarely been reviewed in philosophical journals, so that to discover any of
these practically required an expert knowledge of legal research. Morris R.
Cohen argued persuasively some years ago that jurisprudence is a philosophical
discipline,[1] and proceeded to exemplify this in his own writing, but otherwise
his argument did not meet with any noticeable response.

This situation has now changed. No doubt legal philosophy will never
occupy the center of the philosophical stage, and metaphysics, epistemology,
logic, and ethics are in no danger of being displaced. But legal materials offer
copious and complex illustrations of various philosophical problems and theses,
and, moreover, the law is now more widely recognized as being of philosophical
interest in its own right. The prediction is not too hazardous that this revival
of interest will receive considerable impetus by the publication of Professor
Hart's important book.† Professor Hart brings to the subject a combination of
technical legal knowledge and philosophical acumen that is practically
unrivaled, and The Concept of Law is everything one would have expected it to

---

* Marcus G. Singer, "Hart's Concept of Law," The Journal of Philosophy, LX, 8 (1963), pp.
197–220. Reprinted by permission of the author and publisher. © Copyright 1963 by Journal
of Philosophy, Inc.
[1] Morris R. Cohen, "Jurisprudence as a Philosophical Discipline," this JOURNAL, 10, 9 (April 24,
1913): 225–232; reprinted in Reason and Law (Glencoe, Ill.: The Free Press, 1950).
† H. L. A. Hart, The Concept of Law (Oxford: The Clarendon Press, 1961), x, 263 p., $3.40
[commented on in this JOURNAL, Robert S. Summers, "H. L. A. Hart on Justice," 59, 18 (Aug.
30, 1962): 479–500]. All further references, unless otherwise specified, are page references to
this book.

be from his previous articles on the subject—clear, direct, illuminating, and suggestive. There can be no doubt that it will be studied and discussed for many years to come—and will provide the material for innumerable doctoral dissertations.

Professor Hart's main aim in the book is to elucidate the concept of law, by providing an analysis of the distinctive and complex elements that go together to make up a legal system, and by so doing to provide a reasoned and informed answer to the question: What is law?, or What is the nature of law? To this end he isolates and distinguishes "three recurrent issues" which he claims underlie the persistent question: What is law?: "How does law differ from and how is it related to orders backed by threats? How does legal obligation differ from, and how is it related to, moral obligation? What are rules and to what extent is law an affair of rules?" (13), and he promises to show that "it is possible to isolate and characterize a central set of elements which form a common part of the answer to all three" (16). But the purpose of the book "is not to provide a definition of law, in the sense of a rule by reference to which the correctness of the use of the word can be tested; it is to advance legal theory by providing an improved analysis of the distinctive structure of a municipal legal system and a better understanding of the resemblances and differences between law, coercion, and morality, as types of social phenomena" (17).

By this device Hart is enabled neatly to avoid, and rightly so, the irrelevancies of the sort of last-gasp positivism represented by Glanville Williams's provocative essay "The Controversy concerning the Word 'Law'," [2] which could be squarely met by a counter-essay on "The Controversy concerning the Word 'Definition'." The question: What is law?, though it could be more nicely worded, is both significant and important, the puzzlement it represents is not the result of the influence of word magic, and it is not to be answered—or rejected—merely by adopting a definition. Humpty Dumpty, it should be remembered, eventually had a great fall; apparently he was not master of the expression 'put together again'.

Central to the idea of law is the idea of a rule, and a large part of the book consists in the elaboration of a complex distinction between two types of rules, which are called primary and secondary:

> Rules of the first type impose duties; rules of the second type confer powers, public or private. Rules of the first type concern actions involving physical movement or changes; rules of the second type provide for operations which lead not merely to physical movement or change, but to the creation or variation of duties or obligations (79).

---

[2] Originally published in *British Year Book of International Law*, **22** (1945): 146; reprinted in a revised version and under the title given, in *Philosophy, Politics and Society*, ed. by Peter Laslett (Oxford: Basil Blackwell, 1956), pp. 134–156. For scintillating criticism, see Ernest Gellner, "Contemporary Thought and Politics," *Philosophy*, **32** (October, 1957): 353–356. On the matter of "definition," see Max Black, *Problems of Analysis* (Ithaca, N.Y.: Cornell University Press, 1954), essays I and II.

"In the combination of these two types of rule," Hart goes on to say, "there lies what Austin wrongly claimed to find in the notion of coercive orders, namely, 'the key to the science of jurisprudence'." Law is presented as "the union of primary and secondary rules," and

The main theme of this book is that so many of the distinctive operations of the law, and so many of the ideas which constitute the framework of legal thought, require for their elucidation reference to one or both of these two types of rule, that their union may be justly regarded as the 'essence' of law, though they may not always be found together wherever the word 'law' is correctly used (151).

This being the central theme of the book and its major contribution to the subject, it is the topic that calls for the most thorough examination.

The effective argument of the book begins with three chapters devoted to an examination of an Austinian type theory, a theory of law corresponding to, though not representing exactly in all respects, the theory of law set forth in John Austin's *Province of Jurisprudence Determined,* according to which law consists in orders backed by threats issued by a "sovereign" (or sovereign body) habitually obeyed by those to whom the orders are issued but not in the habit of obeying others. This theory of law, usually called the "imperative" or "command" theory, has by now been subjected to rather intensive examination, and is now pretty well exploded as an adequate account of the nature of law. If there is anyone who is still disposed to find such an analysis plausible, he may be invited to consider the discussion of it presented in this book. Hart's criticism of it (though many of the points he makes are based on criticisms first presented by others) strikes me as well-nigh conclusive, and I shall say no more about it. However, it should be pointed out that in his criticism of this view Hart introduces a number of the ideas that are central to his own theory, so that an understanding of these chapters is indispensable for an understanding of the rest of the book.

## I

We may conveniently begin with a consideration of the following passage:

The idea of a union of primary and secondary rules . . . may be regarded as a mean between juristic extremes. For legal theory has sought the key to the understanding of law sometimes in the simple idea of an order backed by threats and sometimes in the complex idea of morality. With both of these law has certainly many affinities and connexions; yet . . . there is a perennial danger of exaggerating these and of obscuring the special features which distinguish law from other means of social control. It is a virtue of the idea which we have taken as central that it permits us to see the multiple relationships between law, coercion, and morality for what they are, and to consider afresh in what, if any, sense these are necessary. . . .

Though it would accord with usage to treat the existence of this characteristic union of rules as a sufficient condition for the application of the expression 'legal system', we have not claimed that the word 'law' must be defined in its terms. It is because we make no such claim to identify or regulate in this way the use of the words like 'law' or 'legal', that this book is offered as an elucidation of the *concept* of law, rather than a definition of 'law' which might naturally be expected to provide a rule or rules for the use of these expressions (208).

With regard to the distinction, to which Hart attaches so much importance, between an elucidation of the concept of law and a definition of 'law', I must confess that it is not clear to me. It is evident that nothing of value can come from starting out with a stipulation as to how the term 'law' is to be used. But those who have searched for a definition of law have surely been aware of this; they had this course open to them and did not, for the most part, attempt to follow it. I can see nothing wrong with the conclusion that Hart has provided a definition of law—not the sort of definition one starts with, but the sort of definition one ends with; and, of course, not a definition on the traditional pattern of *genus* and *differentia* (cf. 14). But the concept of definition is wider than that. The search for a definition of law, or for an adequate account of the nature of law, is not really something mysterious, though what will bring it to a successful conclusion may be; it is the search for the distinctive, central, and important features that mark off a complex and important social phenomenon. The fact of borderline cases and the fact that there may be no set of properties common and peculiar to law cannot show that the search is misguided. And surely this is what Hart has attempted to provide, for his account of the concept of law and of law as the union of primary and secondary rules can justly be regarded as a definition (whether it is an adequate one has still to be seen) of the essence of a legal system. As he himself says, this complex "union may be justly regarded as the 'essence' of law" (151) (though it is true that he adds that these two types of rules "may not always be found together wherever the word 'law' is correctly used"). But one of the problems here is that we do not always know when the word 'law' is correctly used—even though this is not one of the most important problems. Moreover, as Hart himself has said: "Definition, as the word suggests, is primarily a matter of drawing lines or distinguishing between one kind of thing and another, which language marks off by a separate word" (13), and this is surely what Hart has attempted to do in the case of law, with his concern for distinguishing law from coercion and morality.

I have my doubts whether morality—as distinct from an ethical code adopted to regulate the conduct of the members of a professional group—is appropriately regarded as a "means of social control." One might as well speak of the weather or of illness—or of the laws of nature—as means of social control. For, as Hart points out (171–172), the morality of an action, as distinct from its legality, is not something that can be created or altered by the exercise of human will, and a "means of social control," if the expression is to be significantly used, ought to be something that is itself under human or social control.

For somewhat different reasons I am not convinced that coercion is usefully to be regarded as a means of social control. Coercion is a device that is frequently used by law, though it is not, as Hart makes clear, the only one. But to speak of coercion as a distinctive means of social control, as something distinct or separate from law, is odd, to say the least. For then the factors that make for social disorganization and disruption—a bandit brandishing a gun, a madman with a bomb—would be means of social control. To eliminate morality and coercion from the class of means of social control does not mean that law is the only member left; for there are still such factors as persuasion, the force of example, and appeals to self-interest. I think Hart could have made clear his reasons for distinguishing law from coercion and morality without supposing that they are members of a common class. His reasons, in my opinion, are mainly historical: on the one hand, law has frequently been confused with or reduced to coercive devices; on the other hand, it has frequently been identified with morality.

But these are minor matters. What calls for intensive examination is the idea that "a legal system is a complex union of primary and secondary rules" (111) and that "a distinguishing, if not the distinguishing, feature of law lies in its fusion of different types of rule" (48).

This last statement is peculiar. What is this feature supposed to distinguish law from? It surely does not distinguish law from morality, which also consists of different types of rules, as well as precepts such as principles and standards that cannot without confusion also be regarded as rules. I take this point to indicate a basic unclarity in the primary thesis of the book, and I shall go on to develop this point further.

No doubt what Hart meant by this statement is not simply that law is distinguished by the fact that it consists in the fusion of different types of rules, but by the character of the different types of rules it contains. What are these two types of rules? Hart first introduces this distinction in a passage where he says:

> What are called rules . . . may have very different relationships to the conduct with which they are concerned. . . . Some rules are mandatory in the sense that they require people to behave in certain ways . . . whether they wish to or not; other rules such as those prescribing the procedures, formalities, and conditions for the making of marriages, wills, or contracts indicate what people should do to give effect to the wishes they have (8–9).

The type of law that is most analogous to the notion of a general order backed by threats and therefore provides the strongest support for the Austinian analysis is provided by a criminal statute. There is even "some analogy . . . between such general orders and the law of torts, the primary aim of which is to provide individuals with compensation for harm suffered as the result of the conduct of others" (27). Such rules are called primary rules; they impose duties or obligations, and can be spoken of as being obeyed or disobeyed. But not all rules of law have this character.

Legal rules defining the ways in which valid contracts or wills or marriages are made do not require persons to act in certain ways whether they wish to or not. Such laws do not impose duties or obligations. Instead, they provide individuals with *facilities* for realizing their wishes, by conferring legal powers upon them to create, by certain specified procedures and subject to certain conditions, structures of rights and duties within the coercive framework of the law (27).

Such laws confer powers (and do not impose duties) "on individuals to mould their legal relations with others" and cannot be likened to general orders backed by threats. An example would be the law that a will, to be legally valid, must be signed and attested to by two witnesses.

In addition, there is a "further class of laws which also confer legal powers but, in contrast to those just discussed, the powers are of a public or official rather than a private nature" (27). Examples are to be found in those "laws which lie behind the operation of a law court," such as rules determining jurisdiction and those determining the qualifications for judicial office. Other examples are to be found in "the rules which lie behind the exercise of legislative powers," such as "a statute conferring legislative powers on a subordinate legislative authority" (30, 31). Such rules differ radically in function from rules of the primary sort, which impose duties, and "the radical difference in function between such rules . . . prevents the use here of the terminology appropriate to conduct in its relation to rules of the criminal law" (31).

So the two types of rules, the union of which is at the heart of a legal system, are, on the one hand, primary rules which impose duties, and, on the other hand, secondary rules which confer powers, private and public—powers or capacities on private individuals to perform certain acts within the law with the assurance that these acts will receive legal recognition, and powers on public bodies or officials for the making of laws and the adjudication of disputes that arise under the law.

The questions with which I now wish to deal are these: Is this distinction and classification of rules sufficient for the adequate clarification of the nature of a legal system? Is it exhaustive? And is it mutually exclusive?

1. Hart constantly speaks of what he calls "primary rules" as imposing duties or obligations, and implies that it is only such rules of law that can properly or appropriately be said to be "obeyed" or "disobeyed." But surely some rules are better thought of as assigning rights rather than as imposing duties, and the granting and protection of rights is at least as important a function of a legal system as the imposing of duties and the conferring of powers. It is true that not all rules of law are mandatory; some are permissive, and I do not see how Hart has allowed for this. Moreover, not all rights that are legally exercised are exercised by authority of an explicit rule. If we restrict ourselves for the purposes of the present discussion to the field of what may be called "action rights"—rights to do certain things or act in certain ways— it seems clear that such a right can be legally acquired in any of three distinct but related ways: (1) by a legal rule expressly permitting such conduct;

(2) by a rule enjoining others, either a private party or an official body, from interfering with such conduct; and (3) by the absence of a legal rule expressly prohibiting it. Thus we can speak of *explicit* rights and *implicit* rights. (The Ninth Amendment to the Constitution of the United States says: "The enumeration in the Constitution of certain rights shall not be construed to deny or disparage others retained by the people.")

No doubt this point could be construed as merely a matter of emphasis. It could be and has been argued that every assignment of a right to one person is automatically an imposition of a duty on another, either a private person or an official body, not to interfere with the conduct in question. But I doubt very much if it is really just a difference in emphasis. The imposition of duties would be unintelligible and pointless if it were not essential to the protection of rights. Again, a rule granting someone a right to do something is also a rule that cannot sensibly be spoken of as being obeyed or disobeyed by the person to whom the right is assigned, so that it is not clear in which of his two categories of rules Hart would place rules of this kind. Still further, I have some suspicion that Hart ignores this feature of law because he is more in the grip of the Austinian metaphor of law as orders backed by threats than would otherwise appear. And finally, unless I am altogether mistaken, the concept of a right is an essential part of the concept of a legal power, which plays such an important part in Hart's analysis.

2. This brings me to my second point, which is that Hart does not sufficiently analyze—indeed, I do not think that he analyzes at all—the concept of a legal power. It is true, as Hart emphasizes, that a legal power is not identical with a legal duty (see 27–31). But what is its relationship to a legal duty and—something Hart does not even touch upon—to a legal right? So far as I can see, the closest the book comes to an analysis of "legal power" consists in the assertion, following Hohfeld's analysis,[3] that the absence of a legal power is a legal disability and not a legal duty (242). We have also the following brief passages:

A constitution which effectively restricts the legislative powers of the supreme legislature in the system does not do so by imposing (or at any rate need not impose) duties on the legislature not to attempt to legislate in certain ways; instead it provides that any such purported legislation shall be void. It imposes not legal duties but legal disabilities. 'Limits' here implies not the presence of *duty* but the absence of legal power (68).

Legal limitations on legislative authority consist not of duties imposed on the legislator to obey some superior legislator but of disabilities contained in rules which qualify him to legislate (69).

[3] Wesley N. Hohfeld, *Fundamental Legal Conceptions as Applied in Judicial Reasoning* (New Haven: Yale University Press, 1923), ch. 1. For discussion, see Julius Stone, *The Province and Function of Law* (2nd ed.; Cambridge: Harvard University Press, 1950), ch. 5.

This gives us some help, but not enough, and I also think the analysis hinted at here is oversimplified and inaccurate. For it leaves out the notion of a right, and *sometimes* to overstep the boundaries of a legal power is a legal (and not just a moral) wrong. There need not always be a sanction attached to a legal duty, and it is characteristic of legal duties imposed on courts and legislatures, in our legal system at any rate, that there usually are not.

Hart occasionally uses the language of a "right to make law" or "a right to legislate" (53, 58, 73). I think the word 'power' would be more appropriate here than 'right'. But this slip, if slip it is, has some significance. For it indicates that there is some relation between a right and a power, since it is so easy to slip from speaking of one to speaking of the other. Does an ordinary citizen, not a member of a legislature and with no troops at his disposal, have a right to make law? Does a person who is not a judge or in any way connected with the government have a right to declare a certain law unconstitutional? The first question is trickier than the second, though I think the answer to each question is yes, even though this answer is likely to be misleading without further qualification. For in each instance we are likely to think of a right as a power. It would not be wrong for a private citizen to declare that some provision is a law; it is just that this declaration will have no legal effect; it is "legislation" with no chance of passing. Similarly, any private citizen has the right to declare a given law unconstitutional, and in fact it is the duty of the executive and the legislative branches to consider the constitutionality of any proposed piece of legislation. But such declarations can have no legal effect, for only a court is authorized to make such declarations, in the sense of having the legal power. If I declare the Internal Security Act unconstitutional, there is a sense in which I may be right; this may be the conclusion arrived at by a reasonable reading of the Constitution and the language of the Act; but the Act would still be the law of the land. The Supreme Court, on the other hand, is in a privileged position with respect to such matters (as it no doubt should be); if it declares the Act unconstitutional, it is, and is no longer the law of the land. My declaration has no legal effects; the declaration of the Supreme Court does. But the difference in our positions on this matter is not well described by saying that I have no right to make such declarations whereas the Court does have this right. It is better described by saying that the Court has the requisite power, whereas I do not.

No doubt Hart would agree with at least the substance of what I have just said, and I have said it not by way of criticism, but rather to bring out the importance and the distinctive character of the concept of a legal power. A legal power has been defined as "an ability on the part of a person to produce a change in a given legal relation by doing or not doing a certain act." [4] This may be all right, so far as it goes, but I do not think it goes far enough, for it does not bring out the connection between a legal power and a legal right. I

[4] G. W. Paton, *A Text-Book of Jurisprudence* (2nd ed.; Oxford: The Clarendon Press, 1951), p. 226.

would suggest, very tentatively (for I well remember the saying about fools rushing in), that a legal power to do something may be analyzed as consisting in a legal right to do it together with something else, which, for want of a better word, I shall call a legal ability. Thus, "*A* has the power to do *x*" will be equivalent to "*A* has the right to do *x* and *A* has the legal ability to do *x*." [5] A consequence of this is that "*A* does not have the legal power to do *x*" is then equivalent not to "*A* has the legal duty not to do *x*" but to "either *A* has no right to do *x* or *A* does not have the legal ability to do *x*." (Here a *legal* ability is contrasted, not with a moral ability, but with physical ability.) Consequently, though I have a perfect right to declare or express the opinion that a certain act of Congress is unconstitutional, this declaration will have no effects within the legal system. I cannot *make* it unconstitutional by saying that it is, whereas the Supreme Court can. It has the requisite power, I do not, and neither does the President or even the Speaker of the House of Representatives. (The fact that the Constitution contains no express grant of such power to the Court is clearly irrelevant here.)

But even though the proposition that some person or body lacks the legal power to do something does not mean that he or it has the legal duty not to do it, it does not follow that limitations on legislative or judicial power are never duties—duties not to pass or attempt to pass a certain law or exert a certain power. If a given legal body is deprived of the power to act in a certain way, then it may be legally wrong for it to do so or to attempt to do so. And it is no good to say that such an act will be void, or a "nullity" with no legal effects (66). For such an act can and will have legal effects until it is officially declared a nullity by a court with power to do so, and it may never be so declared. The history of the Fifteenth Amendment to the Constitution, which states that "The right of the citizens of the United States to vote shall not be denied or abridged by the United States or by any State on account of race, color, or previous condition of servitude," provides ample illustration of this. Moreover, the language in which legal powers are granted or restricted does not always make it clear whether action in excess of these powers or in clear violation of these restrictions is merely "null and void," or also, and more basically, a violation of a duty. Taking another example from the Constitution, consider the provision in Article I, Section 9, that "No tax or duty shall be laid on articles exported from any State." Suppose Congress were to lay such a tax. It is not at all clear that, in so acting in excess of its powers, it would not be violating a legal duty imposed on it. Again, the Fourteenth Amendment says, in part, that "No State shall . . . deny to any persons within its jurisdiction the equal protection of the laws." Is it so clear that this is merely the statement of a legal disability and not the imposition of a legal duty? I think not. The many states that have so frequently

[5] A possible counterexample to this analysis may be provided by what has been referred to as "the peculiarities of criminal procedure which give the jury a power, though not a right, to disregard the law as laid down by the court in its instructions" (John Dickinson, *Administrative Justice and the Supremacy of Law in the United States* [Cambridge: Harvard University Press, 1927; reprinted 1959 by Russell & Russell, Inc., New York], p. 153, n. 79).

and flagrantly violated the spirit of this Amendment seem to me not just to have exceeded their constitutional powers—though, and this is another curious point about "legal powers," not their effective and "de facto" legal power—but also to have acted in a way that is legally wrong. When Justice Holmes said, at the end of his famous dissent in *Abrams v. U.S.* (250 U.S. 616, 624 (1919) ): "I regret that I cannot put into more impressive words my belief that in their conviction upon this indictment the defendants were deprived of their rights under the Constitution of the United States," it is a rather lame view that would interpret this only as the expression of an opinion that the Court had exceeded its legal or constitutional powers. A judge has a *duty* to decide a case in accordance with the relevant law; if he does not, his decision is liable to reversal, but in many instances this liability to reversal is the only factor even resembling a sanction attached to this duty. Moreover, his decision may not in fact be reversed, since the parties may not pursue the matter further, and no similar case may ever be brought to trial (perhaps as a consequence of the original decision). In addition, an inferior court in a precedent system is bound by (that is, has a duty to follow) the decisions of higher courts, and in some legal systems the higher courts are regarded as absolutely bound by their own precedent decisions. This does not mean that they have not the power to disregard precedent, but rather something like a duty not to do so; yet there is no sanction attached to such a duty in the sense in which a sanction is ordinarily attached to ordinary rules of the criminal law.

From these points I draw three conclusions: (1) that the Austinian analysis, according to which every rule imposing a duty must have a specific sanction attached to it, has had a greater effect on Hart's theory than is at first apparent (though not, to be sure, in all contexts—see 193–195, 213–214); and (2) that Hart's analysis of the conditions under which "rules are conceived and spoken of as imposing obligations" (84–85) is not altogether adequate, for it does not seem capable of accounting for what is meant by such expressions as 'the duty of a judge' or 'a court is bound to follow precedent' (notwithstanding the possible answer on pp. 142–143). I also conclude (3) that the classes of rules that impose duties and of rules that confer powers are not mutually exclusive, and that the distinction between the two is neither so clear nor so rigid as Hart's language (perhaps for the sake of emphasis) would imply. And I do not regard the points on pp. 109–110 and 111–112 as a sufficient answer to this. A judge can be said to break or violate the law even where the word 'disobey' would be linguistically inappropriate. 'Disobey' applies primarily to the breach of an order, but not all laws are orders. Yet to break the law is to do what is legally wrong. One cannot "disobey" a duty either.

I would add that in these important concepts of the duties of officials of government—the duty of the executive to administer the law, the duty of the legislature to abide by constitutional limitations, and the duty of courts to abide by precedent and the holdings of courts of superior jurisdiction—we have excellent evidence that, although law may be distinct from morality in the ways that Hart maintains it is (ch. IX), it is not altogether distinct. For these important duties are both legal and moral, and it follows, therefore, that the existence of a legal system, as distinct from the existence of an effective regime of coercion, presupposes and rests upon the acceptance of a more than rudimentary system of moral ideas.

3. I come now to my third main point about this distinction and union of two types of rules, which is that there seems to me to be an ambiguity in the notion of a secondary rule. As this distinction was first introduced, it was used to distinguish rules imposing duties, which could be said to be obeyed or disobeyed, from rules conferring private and public legal powers. Later on, however, the concept of a secondary rule is spoken of, it seems to me, in a somewhat different way. When Hart introduces the concepts of rules of recognition, change, and adjudication (92–95) and says that "the foundation of a legal system consist in . . . the conception of an ultimate rule of recognition which provides a system of rules with its criteria of validity" (107; cf. 97, 145), he seems to me to be shifting the use of the concept of a secondary rule. Or, at any rate, there seems to me such a difference in character and function between ordinary rules that "confer powers" both on private individuals and on official bodies and rules providing the basis on which the validity of these less fundamental power-conferring rules can be assessed, that these differences really ought to be marked off by different labels. For the "ultimate rule of recognition" is used, as Hart seems to imply (97), not just "for the identification of primary rules of obligation" but *also for the identification of rules conferring powers*. It is on a constitutional level and not just on the level of the ordinary statute or judicial determination. Consequently, instead of saying that "a legal system is a complex union of primary and secondary rules" (111), it seems to me that it would be at least somewhat better to say that a legal system consists in a complex union of rules of law, both criminal and civil and both obligation-imposing and power-conferring, with various standards, criteria, or principles for determining what is a rule of the system, its validity, its interpretation, its force, and its scope; these criteria would then be not themselves *rules* of law, but criteria of such rules.

4. But a legal system is really even more complex than this. And this brings me to my fourth and final criticism of the thesis I have been examining, which is that there are elements in a legal system, of considerable importance, which are not only not accounted for, but obscured, by the idea that law is a union of (just) two types of rule. Professor Hart has many valid criticisms to make of theories that attempt "to reduce apparently distinct varieties of legal rule to a single form" (38) or "a single simple type" (32); as he says, this effort to reduce to a "single simple form the variety of laws ends by imposing upon them a spurious uniformity" (48). But it may be said that his own view is nearly as misleading in that it attempts to reduce the variety of laws to a simple dual form and thus ends by imposing upon them a spurious duality. It is not clear to me, for example, how rules of evidence and procedure fall into Hart's scheme, or the well-known presumption of innocence or other rules that create presumptions and thus throw the burden of proof in a trial on one party or the

other. Again, I am not clear how the rule that in a criminal trial the evidence against the defendant must be such as to establish his guilt beyond all reasonable doubt or the rule that in a civil suit a preponderance of evidence amounting to probability is sufficient can be regarded either as rules imposing duties (they certainly do not impose primary duties) or as rules conferring powers.

But these points are relatively minor. More fundamental is the point that to conceive of law as made up solely or even primarily of *rules* is to make the word 'rule' cover a multitude of propositions that a just view of the matter would properly distinguish. The distinction of legal propositions into legal rules, principles, and standards—first presented. I believe, by Roscoe Pound—is now well known and, I should think, reasonably well established.[6] So, unless he is merely using the term 'rule' as a blanket and amorphous term, I am extremely puzzled why Hart should gloss over this matter and present law as a union of two types of *rules*. This is especially puzzling because there are places where Hart does permit himself the luxury of vaguely referring to "general rules, standards, and principles" (such as p.121), and there is a section of the book (127–132) in which he actually discusses the nature and importance of the distinction between "uniform, determinate rules" and "vague, variable standards" such as "the standard of due care in cases of negligence." One thing he says here is that

. . . the life of the law consists to a very large extent in the guidance both of officials and private individuals by determinate rules which, unlike the applications of variable standards, do *not* require from them a fresh judgment from case to case (132).

But one thing this implies is that the life of the law consists, at least to some extent, not in the application of determinate rules, but in the application of variable standards; and it is curious that this distinction, given the importance Hart attaches to it, is not reflected in his elucidation of the concept of law, but is rather obscured by his too frequent use of the term 'rule'.

It is only fair to add, however, that Hart does say:

If we look into the various legal rules that confer legal powers on private individuals we find that these themselves fall into distinguishable kinds. Thus behind the power to make wills or contracts are rules relating to *capacity* or minimum personal qualification (such as being adult or sane) which those exercising the power must possess. Other rules detail the manner and form in which the power is to be exercised, and settle whether wills or contracts may be made orally or in writing, and if in writing the form of execution and attestation. Other rules delimit the variety, or maximum or minimum duration, of the structure of rights and duties which individuals may create by such

---

[6] See Roscoe Pound, *An Introduction to the Philosophy of Law* (New Haven: Yale University Press, 1922), pp. 116 ff.; Dickinson, *op. cit.*, pp. 128–156; and Paton, *op. cit.*, pp. 175–181. On p. 249 Hart refers, oddly enough, to Dickinson's discussion. For a distinctively different view of the matter, see Richard Wasserstrom, *The Judicial Decision* (Stanford: Stanford University Press, 1961), pp. 99–105.

acts-in-the-law. Examples of such rules are those of public policy in relation to contract, or the rules against accumulations in wills or settlements (28).

A full detailed taxonomy of the varieties of law comprised in a modern legal system, free from the prejudice that all *must* be reducible to a single simple type, still remains to be accomplished. In distinguishing certain laws under the very rough head of laws that confer powers from those that impose duties and are analogous to orders backed by threats, we have made only a beginning (32).

These disclaimers should, of course, be kept in mind. But it seems to me very dubious whether the various kinds of rules just delimited can be placed without distortion "under the very rough head of rules that confer powers."[7] And I take these disclaimers as an admission that the elucidation of the concept of law presented in this book, as a union of these two types of rules, and, consequently, its characterization of the nature of a legal system are not fully adequate.[8]

## II

One important distinction elaborated in the book is that between what is called the "internal" and the "external" points of view with regard to rules. One reason for the importance of this distinction is that it is basic to the view presented of the concepts of legal validity and of the existence of a legal system:

> If a social rule is to exist some at least must look upon the behaviour in question as a general standard to be followed by the group as a whole. A social rule has an 'internal' aspect, in addition to the external aspect which it shares with a social habit and which consists in the regular uniform behaviour which an observer could record (55). . . . It is possible to be concerned with . . . rules, either merely as an observer who does not himself accept them, or as a member of the group which accepts and uses them as

---

[7] A distinction corresponding in a number of respects to the one emphasized by Hart was elaborated some time ago by Sir Frederick Pollock, when he distinguished what he called "determining rules" from "rules which declare duties and affirm rights": "In order to have any real working acquaintance with a system of law we must inquire, not only what duties and rights are recognized, but how rights are acquired and lost; what rights are capable of transfer, and how; by what acts and events duties are imposed. . . . The conditions defining these things are . . . an integral part of the subject-matter of law, and the rules which declare them are among the most important. . . . The statement that in England every one under the age of twenty-one years is an infant is certainly a proposition of law; but it does not state any duty or right. Legal capacity is not a right, still less is the want of it a wrong." (*A First Book of Jurisprudence* [London: Macmillan and Co., Ltd., 1896], part I, ch. 3, p. 73.) Consider also the following statement by Paton, *op. cit.*, p. 59: "Much law . . . is enabling rather than restrictive; although one law may abridge liberty, a second may give powers which otherwise a citizen would not possess."

[8] It can also lead to some anomalies, as where it is said that "Possession of these legal powers makes of the private citizen, who, if there were no such rules, would be a mere duty-bearer, a private legislator. He is made competent to determine the course of the law within the sphere of his contracts, trusts, wills, and other structures of rights and duties which he is enabled to build" (40; cf. 94). This may be true, in a certain sense, of wills, but it is surely not true, even in a stretched and metaphorical sense, of contracts. To make a contract—that is, a mutual agreement—is surely not to make a law that the other party to the contract is bound to follow; each party to a contract binds himself, and not the other party, and this is not to legislate.

guides to conduct. We may call these respectively the 'external' and the 'internal points of veiw'. . . . . The external point of view . . . limits itself to the observable regularities of behaviour (86, 88; cf. 96, 99, 244).

This distinction, in its many forms, is put to a number of uses in the book. One of them is to bring out the distinction between a "social rule" and a "social habit." Another is to bring out the distinctive features of "obligations" and to show what is wrong with "predictive" analyses of "obligation" and, consequently, with the prediction theory of law. The distinction is of considerable interest, but I do not wish to examine it on its own account. I have mentioned it mainly to provide a context for considering what Hart says about the foundations of a legal system, which are said to "consist not in a general habit of obedience to a legally unlimited sovereign, but in an ultimate rule of recognition providing authoritative criteria for the identification of valid rules of the system" (245). What I wish to consider is the claim that "the question whether a rule of recognition exists and what its content is, i.e. what the criteria of validity in any given legal system are, is . . . an empirical, though complex, question of fact" (245).

On Hart's view, to say that a given rule of a system is valid is "to recognize it as passing all the tests provided by the rule of recognition and so as a rule of the system" (100). It is not to say that the particular rule is efficacious, that is, generally obeyed; for there is no necessary or uniform connection between the efficacy and the validity of a rule of law. However, "From the inefficacy of a particular rule . . . we must distinguish a general disregard of the rules of the system. . . . One who makes an internal statement concerning the validity of a particular rule of a system may be said to presuppose the truth of the external statement of fact that the system is generally efficacious" (100–101). Thus the statement that a given rule of a system is valid is an internal statement [of law?]; the statement that the system is generally efficacious is an external statement of fact. But the concept of legal validity is applicable only to particular rules of a given legal system and is not applicable to the ultimate rule of recognition in terms of which the validity of particular rules of the system is assessed; for "there is no rule providing criteria for the assessment of its own legal validity":

> When we move from saying that a particular enactment is valid, because it satisfies the rule that what the Queen in Parliament enacts is law, to saying that in England this last rule is used by courts, officials, and private persons as the ultimate rule of recognition, we have moved from an internal statement of law asserting the validity of a rule of the system to an external statement of fact which an observer of the system might make even if he did not accept it (104).

> We only need the word 'validity', and commonly only use it, to answer questions which arise *within* a system of rules where the status of a rule as a member of the system depends on its satisfying certain criteria provided by the rule of recognition. No such question can arise as to the validity of the very rule of recognition which provides the criteria; it can neither be valid nor invalid but is simply accepted as appropriate for use in this way (105–106).

This then leads to the concept of the existence of a rule in this way:

> Whereas a subordinate rule of the system may be valid and in that sense 'exist'
> even if it is generally disregarded, the rule of recognition exists only as a complex, but
> normally concordant, practice of the courts, officials, and private persons in identifying
> the law by reference to certain criteria. Its existence is a matter of fact (107).

I take this last point as confirming something that I claimed before, that the
"ultimate rule of recognition" must be a "rule" of an entirely different type
from the ordinary rules of law. But I find this claim puzzling in other ways.
How can a *rule* be a *practice?* I should have thought that a practice would be
defined by rules, and find it odd that a rule should be *identified* with a practice.
For this seems to me to imply that it is not a rule at all, in any accepted sense.
Can such a "rule" (practice) be broken? violated? formulated? Can it be said
to require, prohibit, or permit anything? A rule can confer a power; but can a
practice, where a practice is not itself defined or constituted by rules? There may
be some simple resolution to these perplexities, but, as should be obvious, I
have no idea what it is. And my difficulties are merely reinforced by what Hart
goes on to say about the existence of a legal system:

> There are . . . two minimum conditions necessary and sufficient for the existence of
> a legal system. On the one hand those rules of behaviour which are valid according to
> the system's ultimate criteria of validity must be generally obeyed, and, on the other
> hand, its rules of recognition specifying the criteria of legal validity and its rules of
> change and adjudication must be effectively accepted as common public standards of
> official behaviour by its officials (113).[9]

> So long as the laws which are valid by the system's tests of validity are obeyed by
> the bulk of the population this surely is all the evidence we need in order to establish
> that a given legal system exists (111).

This, I think, is the crux. Hart has claimed that the question whether a
legal system exists is a question of fact. But the question whether a law is valid
is a question of law and not a question of fact, in the sense in which such a
distinction is ordinarily made. How then can the question whether a legal system
exists be just a question of fact? Though the question of obedience may be a
factual question, the assertion that the obedience referred to is obedience to
"laws which are valid by the system's tests of validity" is an assertion of law, and
if this distinction does not hold here it does not hold anywhere, and there
would be no point to the claim that Hart is making. The question whether
a legal system exists would seem to be complex in a sense of 'complex' which
Hart has failed to consider.

Of course I am assuming that Hart is using the expression 'question of fact'

[9] On Hart's own showing these cannot be sufficient, because they are not all that is necessary.
Cf. pp. 148–149: "Though every rule may be doubtful at some points, it is . . . a necessary
condition of a legal system existing, that not every rule is open to doubt on all points."

in the sense in which it is contrasted with 'question of law', and I think this is readily supported by the context. It is surely implausible to suppose that he is here contrasting a "question of fact" with a "question of logic." Two other concepts frequently contrasted with "matter of fact," and which add to the complexity of this elusive notion, are "opinion" and "value." I doubt very much whether Hart wishes to deny that the question whether a legal system exists is ever a matter of opinion. But it is quite possible that he does wish to deny that this question is ever a question of value or morality. This is borne out by his attempts in chs. VIII and IX to distinguish law from morality (see esp. 205–207), and his claim that the question of the validity of a law is to be distinguished from its morality. This raises a whole new set of issues, which I shall not enter here. So I shall simply register my opinion that the claim that the question whether a legal system exists never involves any issues of morality or any judgments of value is more complex than even Hart's admirable treatment of the subject would suggest, and requires more argument than he has given it.

The distinction between "fact" and "law" is both obscure and elastic.[10] Nonetheless some things of relative clarity can be said about it, which will bring out why I find a difficulty in what Hart has said here. The question whether a legal system exists cannot be a question of fact, as opposed to a question of law, in the sense in which this complex and shifting distinction operates *within* the law. The *legal* distinction between fact and law is a special one. No doubt it will vary from one legal system to another and will even vary within a single legal system. Even so, *a finding of fact* in a court of law is always a legally determined one, made in accordance with the rules of the system. It cannot be overturned by any mass of evidence, no matter how conclusive, accumulated outside the purview of a court of competent jurisdiction. Thus we speak of a legal "finding" of fact—the defendant is *found* or judged guilty. There may be excellent evidence, either known at the time or discovered later, to show that he is not in fact guilty, in the ordinary sense of the term; that is to say, that he did not in fact do what he was accused of doing and "found" to have done. But this does not show that he is not "guilty" in the legal sense, that in law he did not do the act in question, any more than it has any automatic tendency to release him from prison. This could only be "found" in a new trial on the basis of the new evidence, and sometimes the evidence bearing the other way will be legally inadmissible and hence without legal effect. A court or a jury is a "fact-finding body" only in a special, complex, and perhaps Pickwickian sense. This is one of the reasons why someone can be "legally" guilty and in fact not, or "legally" innocent and in fact not. But, within the law, questions of guilt or innocence are normally regarded as pure questions of fact (apart from such

[10] For a stimulating and too little known discussion of this distinction, see James Bradley Thayer, *A Preliminary Treatise on Evidence at the Common Law* (Boston: Little, Brown, and Company, 1898), ch. 5. Cf. Dickinson, *op. cit.*, pp. 50–55, 312–319. An especially interesting discussion of the concept of a fact is "On Not Worshipping Facts," by J. R. Lucas, *The Philosophical Quarterly*, **8** (April, 1958): 144–156.

complications as are imported by questions of negligence and insanity) and are said to be "for the jury." This shows that the distinction as it operates within the law is a special one, not what it would appear to be, and that the concept of "a question of fact" has different senses in different contexts. It is unfortunate, therefore, that Hart did not pursue this matter further.

For these reasons I am unconvinced by the claim that "the question what the criteria of legal validity in any legal system are is a question of fact" (245), and must confess that I have almost no idea what Hart intends by it (but see 118).

One further point on this matter. The United States Constitution spells out in some detail, though no doubt with fringes of vagueness, the conditions under which an Act of Congress "shall become a law." The question whether these conditions have been complied with, or whether some law has been passed in pursuance of the Constitution, is a question of law, which can be officially and authoritatively answered only in a court of competent jurisdiction—though, of course, anyone is entitled to have an opinion on the matter. If, however, the courts were persistently to strike down (or approve) laws passed in clear compliance with (or violation of) the appropriate provisions of the Constitution or if they paid no regard to consistency in their reference to these provisions, the legal system defined by the Constitution would break down or be transformed into something different. Furthermore, if orders of courts were generally disregarded or if orders of the Supreme Court were generally disregarded by inferior courts, then the legal system could also be said to have broken down. The assertion that such a situation exists could be construed as an assertion of fact, and this may be what Hart has in mind. But if so, I can only think that he has confused matters by asserting that "the question what the criteria of legal validity in any legal system are is a question of fact."

## III

In legal philosophy perhaps the main rival to the imperative type of theory which Hart has previously discussed (frequently and ambiguously called "legal positivism"—see 253) and which provided the springboard for the presentation of his own view has been presented by theories that maintain that there is some sort of special and necessary connection between law and morality. Hart devotes two chapters to the discussion of this matter (VIII and IX), in which, among other things, he discusses the notion of justice and the reasons for its specially close connection with law; the features that distinguish moral rules from legal rules and, hence, the distinctive characteristics of morality; and the various ways in which law and morality may be related. There is much here that is interesting and important, but I shall confine myself, on the present occasion, to a few isolated remarks.

Hart claims that "justice is a distinct segment of morality" and that "laws and the administration of laws may have or lack excellences of different kinds" (153). This last statement may be admitted without its being admitted that these other "excellences" are *moral* excellences; not all merits or defects are moral ones, and neither are all terms of appraisal. "We might," Hart says, "express our approval of a law requiring parents to send their children to school, by saying that it was a good law and our disapproval of a law forbidding the criticism of the Government . . . by calling it a bad law. Such criticisms would not normally be couched in terms of 'justice' and 'injustice' " (154). I see no force in this context in appeals to the terms in which something would or would not "normally be couched"; even so, I see nothing strange in using the terms 'just' or 'unjust' in reference to such laws. Someone might complain that the law requiring parents to send their children to school was unjust, on the grounds that it was an unwarranted interference with his liberty. The answer that it is not unjust, accompanied by appropriate reasons, would not then be odd or unintelligible, supposing, as I do not, that it would have been so in the first place. Moreover, the claim that a law is good, or bad, is normally based on an appraisal of its actual or probable effects, and is then a judgment of value and not thereby a moral judgment. If it should be, as it is sometimes, intended as a moral judgment of the law, then it is a very complex one, in which evaluative and moral factors are mixed, and then the more specific question of the justice of the law is inextricably involved.

This issue comes to a head in Hart's remark:

That just and unjust are more specific forms of moral criticism than good and bad or right and wrong, is plain from the fact that we might intelligibly claim that a law was good because it was just, or that it was bad because it was unjust, but not that it was just because good, or unjust because bad (154).

This point may be readily admitted, so far as it pertains to good and bad, for reasons already alluded to. But there is nothing unintelligible in claiming that a law is just because it is right, or unjust because it is wrong. And, questions of "intelligibility" apart, neither type of claim is one that provides adequate or sufficient reason. Furthermore, if Hart's claim is sound, then 'just' and 'unjust' would seem to be more fundamental than the other concepts mentioned, not just more specific. I also do not agree with the claim that "Justice constitutes one segment of morality primarily concerned not with individual conduct but with the ways in which *classes* of individuals are treated" (163), which such examples as the above were intended to support, because I do not admit the justice, or even the validity, of the distinction. Moral judgments of individual conduct, in my view, necessarily involve a reference to classes of cases. (This may be regarded as a poor excuse for an argument, but this is not the place for another book on the subject.)

But all this is really by the way, and I have mentioned it only to prepare the ground for a (happily) brief consideration of what Hart has to say about Natural Law. Hart's discussion of this doctrine, under the heading of "The Minimum Content of Natural Law" (189–195), is intended to show that certain simple facts, or "truisms," that he mentions "afford a *reason* why, given survival as an aim, law and morals should include a certain content," for

. . . without such a content laws and morals could not forward the minimum purpose of survival which men have in associating with each other. In the absence of this content men, as they are, would have no reason for obeying voluntarily any rules; and without a minimum of co-operation given voluntarily by those who find that it is in their interest to submit to and maintain the rules, coercion of others who would not voluntarily conform would be impossible (189).

These simple facts, which I do not intend to amplify here, are presented under the headings of "human vulnerability," "approximate equality," "limited altruism," "limited resources," and "limited understanding and strength of will," and enable Hart to show (*a*) that it is not part of the *concept* of law that a legal system must provide for sanctions, and (*b*) that it is not just a contingent and accidental fact that most legal systems do provide for sanctions.

'Sanctions' are . . . required not as the normal motive for obedience, but as a *guarantee* that those who would not voluntarily obey shall not be sacrificed to those who would not. To obey, without this, would be to risk going to the wall. Given this standing danger, what reason demands is *voluntary* co-operation in a *coercive* system (193).

Sanctions, however, though not a logical necessity, are a necessity if a legal system

. . . is to serve the minimum purposes of beings constituted as men are. . . . Given the setting of natural facts and aims, which make sanctions both possible and necessary in a municipal system . . . this is a *natural necessity;* and some such phrase is needed also to convey the status of the minimum forms of protection for persons, property, and promises which are similarly indispensable features of municipal law (195).

Now I think all this is both sound and important. But it leaves a somewhat confused impression. Is it consistent with Hart's morally neutral account of the concept of law and with the external point of view that he adopts throughout[11] for him to say, as he does (188), that "there are certain rules of conduct which any social organization must contain if it is to be viable"? For the points that Hart makes here sound suspiciously like the claim that they are necessary (though of course not *logically* necessary) parts of the content of every genuine

---

[11] The external point of view manifested throughout the book is illustrated by a statement on p. 160: "The connexion between the justice and injustice of the compensation for injury, and the principle 'Treat like cases alike and different cases differently', lies in the fact that outside the law there is a moral conviction that those with whom the law is concerned have a right to mutual forbearance from certain kinds of harmful conduct." Surely this *conviction,* even though it be a *moral* conviction, is not sufficient to establish any such connection. If it were said, rather, that "the connexion . . . lies in the fact that those with whom the law is concerned *have a moral right* to forbearance from certain kinds of harmful conduct," then there would be such a connection. But Hart, apparently, is precluded from saying this by his external point of view, and this brings out, unmistakably, another limitation of this "point of view."

(and I am tempted to add "legitimate") legal system. If so, there is a more intimate and legitimate union of morality and law than he officially allows for.

## IV

As extended as this discussion has been, there are of course a number of important features of the book on which I have not even touched. But enough, of course, is enough—at least at any one time. Yet there are two or three of these other features that ought to be mentioned. Hart's discussion of "rule-skepticism," the doctrine, characteristic of what is known as "legal realism," which maintains that law does not really consist in rules, which are an unnecessary and misleading appendage, seems to me masterly; and his criticism of the doctrine that "the law (or the constitution) is what the courts say it is" (138–144) is both brilliant and definitive. The same applies to his discussions of various behaviorist and prediction theories of law, which maintain that the law consists simply in the prophecies of what the courts will do in fact or in the behavior of certain officials called "judges." He has also given the most convincing account available of what is wrong with the various theories of law that maintain that law consists in the rules that courts apply in deciding cases, so that statutes are not them-selves law, but only sources of law. Finally, his discussion of the question whether international law is "really law" is one of the most sensible and illumin-ating I have ever seen on the subject, though I think more elaboration is needed of the claim that the analogies between international and municipal law are "those of function and content, not of form" (231). (The reverse statement sounds to me just as plausible; consider a similar remark on p. 179.)

Not everything Hart has to say, even in connection with his central doctrine, is original with him, and this is not always brought out even by the useful bibliographical notes and comments at the back of the book.[12] But this is no great defect. As William James once said, "Any fool can be original." What counts is the value of the distinctive product that results. The book does not have the comprehensive coverage one is accustomed to find in works on this topic, such as is provided in the usual works on "jurisprudence." But this is a good thing, for the belief has prevailed too long, as Hart says, that "a book on legal theory is primarily a book from which one learns what other books contain" (viii). Moreover, the book is in the tradition of "analytical juris-prudence," and, despite its success in showing the interest and utility of this

---

[12] For example, his distinctions of two types of laws, and of two types of powers, were fore-shadowed by Salmond. Cf. Stone, *op. cit.,* p. 119: "This separation off of 'powers' was developed in the British literature by John Salmond . . . who classified 'a power' separately from a right . . . defined it . . . as an 'ability conferred upon a person by the law to determine, by his own will directed to that end, the rights, duties, liabilities or other legal relations either of himself or of other persons'. He pointed out that such a power might be either 'public' as vested in an official, or private; and that in the latter case 'a power' to determine another's relation is commonly called an *authority,* and power to determine one's own, a capacity." Cf. John W. Salmond, *Jurisprudence, or The Theory of the Law* (3rd ed.; London: Stevens and Haynes, 1910), p. 196.

approach, it needs to be supplemented by an approach from the point of view of what I prefer to call "normative jurisprudence" (which would rest on the basis of an adequate ethical theory).[13] Nevertheless, I trust enough—indeed, more than enough—has been said to demonstrate the value and importance of the book. It is one of the few books of which it can truly be said that it is indispensable reading for all students of the philosophy of law.

[13] A good beginning has been provided by Wasserstrom, in *The Judicial Decision*.

# CHAPTER II

# LEGAL RIGHTS

Even a casual perusal of the law journals reveals that fundamental legal concepts are thoroughly entangled with contextual, linguistic and historical ambiguities. The basic term, right, for instance, may carry normative as well as descriptive significance. In translation from Continental systems confusion is further compounded, since 'right' (*jus, droit, diritto, Recht*) also translates 'law' or even 'corpus of law' and requires a host of special qualifiers (sometimes omitted in actual usage) to distinguish several possible meanings.

Even within single systems right may change its intension from one context to another. For Hobbes, right in the state of nature consisted in 'the liberty each man hath to use his own power', but in civil society it 'lieth therefore only in those things which in regulating their actions, the sovereign hath pretermitted. . . .' Locke and Kant, on the other hand, defended the continuity of natural rights in political society, although Kant was obliged to introduce a series of complicated qualifications to explain successive levels of obligation operative in these very different contexts. Right, in short, has been the locus of ideological dispute between successive generations of natural and positive law theorists.

Even where value commitments are not at stake, however, no dominant standard has yet emerged to sort out a whole family of terms used indiscriminately by the legal profession. 'Liberty' and 'privilege' are sometimes considered synonyms of 'right' (and usually so defined by dictionaries). However, in other major schemes either 'liberty' *or* 'privilege' may be stipulated as antonym of 'right' — the alternative term as well as a postulated *definiendum* of 'right' being abandoned to ideological limbo.

Such a scheme was proposed early in this century by a Yale jurist, Wesley Newcomb Hohfeld, who unfortunately died before his position could be elaborated. Hohfeld apparently was attempting to remove rights analysis from the polemical field of irreconcilable party interests: Holmes was arguing at the time that rights were no more than 'prophecies of what the courts will do'; positivists were preparing the ground for denying the very existence of rights (the Scandinavian realist, Karl Olivecorona, would later claim that the legal right was only a 'fictitious power, an ideal or imaginary power'); and idealists and natural law theorists were purporting to discover rights in a pot pourri of alleged 'facts' ranging from the will of God to popular custom.

Amidst this turmoil Hohfeld sought to organize basic legal terms in a formal structure of opposites and correlatives consisting of two clusters ('rights' and 'powers') with four members each. There were several startling features of this schema that particularly bothered many of Hohfeld's contemporaries:

(i) two new or barely recognized concepts, 'no-right' and 'disability', were introduced;

(ii) the schema carried what we might view in retrospect as radical ideological implications. For instance, the older rights-duties contract model of private property was now universalized to reveal that ownership of property entailed not only duties but also 'no-rights' for each member of a given society. Put graphically in contemporary terms, the rights of property of the suburban landowner entail the 'no-rights' to the same property of every landless ghetto dweller.

(iii) Whereas legal powers had been recognized prior to Hohfeld the notion of correlative 'disabilities' or 'no-powers' was now made explicit (e.g. so-called 'right to work' laws which allow management to hire non-union labor entail special disabilities for the union organizer).

(iv) Privilege (or 'liberty') as a function of right was distinguished from 'special' privilege or a weaker sense of right subject to revocation. (The latter usage still causes some confusion in legal analysis: 'Are welfare benefits a 'right' or 'privilege'?)

After its posthumous publication in 1921 Hohfeld's schema immediately became a center of controversy and was abused by both its proponents (mainly American realists who tampered with its working structure) and critics such as Pound who accused Hohfeld of Hegelian logicism (Holmes' injunction undoubtedly ringing in his ears: 'the life of the law is not logic'). A growing body of American practitioners, however, has lately shown signs of rediscovering Hohfeld; the 1966 (12th) edition of the classic English text, *Salmond on Jurisprudence*, adopts the schema with only the substitution of the term 'liberty' for Hohfeld's 'privilege' (actually the term Hohfeld first used but later dropped to avoid emotive overtones). Even H. L. A. Hart gives Hohfeld credit for his elaboration, though he regrets Hohfeld's failure to render the 'significance' as well as the consequences of basic legal concepts.

Hart, himself, has taken several somewhat tentative flyers into the arena of rights elucidation. Readers should be aware, however, that he now eschews one much reprinted article, "The Ascription of Responsibility and Rights" (*Proc. of the Arist. Soc.* 1948–49) and is reluctant to have a second, "Definition and Theory in Jurisprudence" (originally delivered as an inaugural lecture at Oxford in 1953), reprinted before final revision. In the latter Hart tendered a tentative analysis of legal right:

"(1) A statement of the form 'X has a right' is true if the following conditions are satisfied:

(a) there is in existence a legal system;

(b) under a rule or rules of the system some other person Y is, in the events which have happened, obliged to do or abstain from some action;

(c) this obligation is made by law dependent on the choice either of X or some other person authorized to act on his behalf so that either Y is bound to do or abstain from some action only if X (or some authorized person) so chooses or alternately only until X (or such person) chooses otherwise.

(2) A statement of the form 'X has a right' is used to draw a conclusion of law in a particular case which falls under such rules."

However, this elucidation is minimal and leaves open significant questions: What is the status of an 'imperfect' or unenforceable right? What is the role of official discretion in the determination (or abuse) of rights? The definition has also been criticized for neglecting the political dimensions of legal rights (see the exchange between Hart and Jonathan Cohen, "Theory and Definition in Jurisprudence," *Proc. of the Arist. Soc. Suppl. Vol.*, 1955 [Problems in Psych. and Juris.]). With the sanction of Dean Pound, American legal practitioners still tend to muddle along in relative conceptual innocence in their usage of basic terms:

> One may feel that Occam's razor may well be applied to the hypertrophy of categories which analysis of 'a right' produced for a time, and in fact, current usage has pretty well settled down to caution in the use of conventional terms and realization that the four or five significant conceptions must be clearly understood, whatever they are called. ("Fifty Years of Jurisprudence," 1937.)

With the resumption of transatlantic debate, perhaps rapprochement between American pragmatic and British ordinary language analysis offers the most suggestive line for future right elucidation. Certainly any adequate account of legal rights must at least consider:

(1) the normal procedures for discovering legal rights in settled sources (whether Constitution, statute or case precedent) — too frequently lost sight of in the polemics of American realists;

(2) the significant normative effects of ideological and other value sources on the considerable discretionary powers of judicial and otner public and semi-public officials — minimized by Hart;

(3) the special extra-legal economic, social and political factors which condition formal rights variously in specific times and circumstances.

Possibly (but possibly not), some common conceptual pattern will emerge from continuing investigation; but it is as likely that irreconcilable, if overlapping, families of usage will be discovered amidst the wide variety of conceptual types of separate legal systems. At the time of writing, a number of theorists and at least one field seminar are intensively engaged in the analysis of legal rights and a new round of statements of position may be expected shortly. The article by Joel Feinberg which concludes this section represents an early and suggestive foray into the topic, which will shortly be followed up by a book now in preparation.

# 8
# Immanuel Kant

Immanuel Kant (1724–1804) wrote, relatively late in his lifetime, a philosophy of law which has only recently been rediscovered as a model for contemporary ethical and legal theory.

# THERE IS ONLY ONE INNATE RIGHT*

## DIVISION OF THE THEORY OF JUSTICE

### A. GENERAL DIVISION OF THE DUTIES OF JUSTICE

In this division, we can well use Ulpian's formulas provided that we give them a meaning that he himself indeed may not have had in mind but that can still be developed from them or given to them.

(1) *Be an honorable man (honeste vive).* Juridical honor consists in asserting one's own worth as a human being in relation to others, and this duty is expressed in the proposition: "Do not make yourself into a mere means for others, but be at the same time an end for them." This duty will be explained later as an obligation resulting from the right of humanity in our own person (*lex justi*).

(2) *Do no one an injustice (neminem laede)*, even if on this account you should have to stop associating with others and to avoid society altogether (*lex juridica*).

(3) (If you cannot avoid the latter [i.e., society]), enter into a society with others in which each person can get and keep what is his own (*suum cuique tribue*). If the original formula is translated literally as "give to each what is his own," it would be nonsense, inasmuch as one cannot give to someone something that he already has. In order to make sense of this formula, it must be interpreted to mean: "Enter into a condition under which what is his own is guaranteed to each person against everyone else" (*lex justitiae*).

Thus, these three classical formulas serve at the same time as principles of the division of the system of duties of justice into internal, external, and those that contain the derivation of the latter from the former through subsumption.

---

* From Immanuel Kant: *The Metaphysical Elements of Justice,* translated by John Ladd, copyright © 1965, by The Bobbs-Merrill Company, Inc., pp. 42-48, 76-77. Translator's footnotes omitted. Reprinted by permission of the publishers.

## B. GENERAL DIVISION OF JUSTICE

(1) [Justice in the sense of Law.] Law considered as a system [of laws] [*systematische Lehren*] can be divided into natural Law, which rests on nothing but a priori principles, and positive (statutory) Law, which proceeds from the Will of a legislator.

(2) [Justice in the sense in which it refers to rights.] Rights, considered as (moral) capacities [*moralische Vermögen*] to bind others, provide the lawful ground for binding others (*titulum*). The main division of rights is into innate rights and acquired rights. An innate right is one that belongs to everyone by nature, independently of any juridical act; an acquired right requires such an act.

Innate property can also be called internal property (*meum vel tuum internum*), for what is external must always be acquired.

### There Is Only One Innate Right

Freedom (independence from the constraint of another's will), insofar as it is compatible with the freedom of everyone else in accordance with a universal law, is the one sole and original right that belongs to every human being by virtue of his humanity.

[This principle of innate freedom contains within itself all the following rights:] Innate equality, that is, independence from being bound by others to do more than one can also reciprocally bind them to do; hence also the attribute of a human being's being his own master (*sui juris*) and of being an irreproachable man (*justi*), inasmuch as, prior to any juridical act, he has done no injustice to anyone; finally, also the authorization [or liberty] to do anything to others that does not by itself detract from what is theirs and that would not detract if only they themselves were not willing to submit themselves to it; an example of this would be merely sharing one's thoughts with others or telling or promising them something, no matter whether what is said is true and honest or false and dishonest (*veriloquium aut falsiloquium*), for it is entirely up to them whether they want to believe him.[1] All these authorizations are already contained in the principle of innate freedom and are really not (as species in a division under a higher concept of right) distinct from it.

The purpose of introducing this further division of the system of natural

---

[1] Indeed, the deliberate telling of a falsehood, even if it is done in a frivolous manner, is ordinarily called a lie (*mendacium*), because at the very least it can harm him who, after faithfully repeating the lie to others, thereby becomes a laughingstock on account of his gullibility. In the juridical sense, however, a falsehood is called a lie only if it is immediately prejudicial to the right of another; such as, for example, the false allegation that a contract has been concluded with someone in order to deprive him of what is his (*falsiloquium dolosum*). This distinction between closely related concepts is not ungrounded, because, when a person simply states his thoughts, the other always remains free to accept them as he pleases. Nevertheless, the well-founded rumor that such a person is one whose talk cannot be believed comes so close to calling him a liar that here the borderline that separates what belongs to *jus* [justice] from what belongs to Ethics is scarcely discernible.

Law with respect to innate rights was that, when a controversy arises over an acquired right and the question is raised as to who has the burden of proof (*onus probandi*)—either with respect to a disputed fact or, if this is settled, with respect to a disputed right—someone who denies this obligation [to prove his case] can methodically appeal to his innate right of freedom (which can now be specified according to his various relations) as though he were invoking various titles of right.

Since with regard to innate, internal property there are not [several] rights, but only one, the two parts that make up this superior division are utterly unequal and dissimilar. Hence it can be put among the prolegomena, the preliminary observations; and the division of the elements of justice [jurisprudence] will be concerned with external property only.

## DIVISION OF THE METAPHYSICS OF MORALS IN GENERAL

### I

All duties are either duties of justice (*officia juris*), that is, those for which external legislation is possible, or duties of virtue (*officia virtutis s. ethica*), for which such legislation is not possible. The latter cannot be the subject matter of external legislation because they refer to an end that is (or the adoption of which is) at the same time a duty, and no external legislation can effect the adoption of an end (because that is an internal act of the mind), although external actions might be commanded that would lead to this [end], without the subject himself making them his end.

Inasmuch as duties and rights are related to each other, why is moral (*Moral*) philosophy usually (for example, by Cicero) labeled the theory of duties and not also of rights? The reason for this is that we know our own freedom (from which all moral laws and hence all rights as well as duties are derived) only through the moral imperative, which is a proposition commanding duties; the capacity to obligate others to a duty, that is, the concept of a right, can be subsequently derived from this imperative.

### II

In the theory of duties, man can and should be represented from the point of view of the property of his capacity for freedom, which is completely supersensible, and so simply from the point of view of his humanity considered as a personality, independently of physical determinations (*homo noumenon*). In contradistinction to this, man can be regarded as a subject affected by these determinations (*homo phaenomenon*). Accordingly, [the ideas of] right and end, which are related to duty under these two aspects, will in turn give us the following division.

*Division According to the Objective Relationship of the
Law to Duty*

Perfect Duty

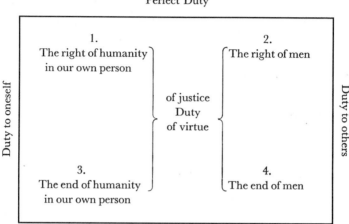

Imperfect duty

### III

Inasmuch as subjects may be related to one another in several ways with respect to the relationship of right to duty (genuinely or spuriously), a division can also be made from this point of view.

*Division According to the Subjective Relationship Between the Subject Who
Imposes the Duty and the Subject Bound by the Duty*

| 1. | 2. |
|---|---|
| The juridical relationship of man to beings who have neither rights nor duties. | The juridical relationship of man to beings who have both rights and duties. |
| *Vacat,*[2] since these are nonrational beings who do not bind us, nor could we be bound by them. | *Adest,*[3] since this is a relationship of men to men. |

| 3. | 4. |
|---|---|
| The juridical relationship of man to beings who have only duties but no rights. | The juridical relationship of man to a being who has only rights but no duties (God). |
| *Vacat,* since these would be beings without personality (serfs, slaves). | *Vacat;* that is, in pure philosophy, because it is not an object of possible experience. |

[2] [*Vacat* = "has no members."]
[3] [*Adest* = "has members."]

Thus a real relationship between right and duty can occur only under Number Two. The reason that such a relationship is not to be found under Number Four is that it would require a transcendent duty, that is, a duty for which no external subject imposing the duty can be given. Hence, the relationship is only ideal from the theoretical point of view; that is, it is a relationship to an object of thought that we make for ourselves, although the concept thereof is not completely empty, but one that is fruitful from an internal, practical point of view in relation to ourselves and to maxims of internal morality, inasmuch as our whole immanent (accomplishable) duty consists of this purely imagined relationship.

*Division of Morality as a System of Duties in General*

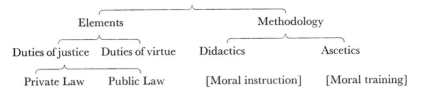

and so on, everything

that comprises, not only the matter [content], but also the architectonic form of a systematic moral philosophy [*wissenschaftliche Sittenlehre*] until the metaphysical elements will have laid completely bare the universal principles.

The supreme division of the Law of nature should be, not into natural and social Law (as it is sometimes thought to be), but into natural and civil Law. The first of these is called private Law; the second, public Law. The state of nature is not opposed and contrasted to the state of society, but to the civil society, for within a state of nature there can indeed be a society, but there can be no civil society (that guarantees property through public law). Therefore, Law in the state of nature is called private Law.

. . .

## §44 [RIGHTS IN A STATE OF NATURE]

Although experience teaches us that men live in violence and are prone to fight one another before the advent of external compulsive legislation, it is not experience that makes public lawful coercion necessary. The necessity of public lawful coercion does not rest on a fact, but on an a priori Idea of reason, for, even if we imagine men to be ever so good natured and righteous before a public lawful state of society is established, individual men, nations, and states can never be certain that they are secure against violence from one another, because each will have his own right to do what *seems just and good to him,* entirely independently of the opinion of others. Consequently, the first decision

*Kant's answer on how to tame Hobbes savage man*

that he must make, if he does not wish to renounce all concepts of justice, is to accept the principle that one must quit the state of nature, in which everyone follows his own judgment, and must unite with everyone else (with whom he comes in contact and whom he cannot avoid), subjecting himself to a public lawful external coercion; in other words, he must enter a condition of society in which what is to be recognized as belonging to him must be established lawfully and secured to him by an effective power that is not his own, but an outside power. That is, before anything else, he ought to enter a civil society.

*contra Hobbes, Austin*

Certainly, a state of nature need not be a condition of injustice [*Ungerechtigkeit*) *(injustus)* in which men treat one another solely according to the amount of power they possess; it is, however, still a state of society in which justice is absent [*Rechtlosigkeit*] (*status justitiae vacuus*) and one in which, when there is a controversy concerning rights (*jus controversum*), no competent judge can be found to render a decision having the force of law. For this reason, everyone may use violent means to compel another to enter into a juridical state of society. Although according to everyone's concept of justice and right an external thing can be acquired by occupation or by contract, such acquisition is still only provisional as long as there is no sanction of a public law for it, for the acquisition is not determined by any public legal (distributive) justice and is not guaranteed by any authority executing the Law.

*argument against Hobbes*

If it were held that no acquisition, not even provisional acquisition, is juridically valid before the establishment of a civil society, then the civil society itself would be impossible. This follows from the fact that, as regards their form, the laws concerning property in a state of nature contain the same things that are prescribed by the laws in civil society insofar as they are considered merely as pure concepts of reason; the only difference is that, in the civil society, the conditions are given under which the [right of] acquisition can be exercised (in conformity with distributive legal justice). Accordingly, if there were not even provisional property in a state of nature, there would be no duties of justice with respect to them, and, consequently, there would be no command to quit the state of nature.

# 9

# Oliver Wendell Holmes, Jr.

Justice Holmes considered over-elaboration, and especially excessive logical or metaphysical speculation in what he called the realm of "Can't Thinks", one of the worst sins that the jurist could commit.

# A LEGAL RIGHT IS NOTHING BUT . . .*

A legal right is nothing but a permission to exercise certain natural powers, and upon certain conditions to obtain protection, restitution, or compensation by the aid of the public force. Just so far as the aid of the public force is given a man, he has a legal right, and this right is the same whether his claim is founded in righteousness or iniquity. Just so far as possession is protected, it is as much a source of legal rights as ownership is when it secures the same protection.

Every right is a consequence attached by the law to one or more facts which the law defines, and wherever the law gives any one special rights not shared by the body of the people, it does so on the ground that certain special facts, not true of the rest of the world, are true of him. When a group of facts thus singled out by the law exists in the case of a given person, he is said to be entitled to the corresponding rights; meaning, thereby, that the law helps him to constrain his neighbors, or some of them, in a way in which it would not, if all the facts in question were not true of him. Hence, any word which denotes such a group of facts connotes the rights attached to it by way of legal consequences, and any word which denotes the rights attached to a group of facts connotes the group of facts in like manner.

*[handwritten margin note: rights are attached to a group of facts]*

The word "possession" denotes such a group of facts. Hence, when we say of a man that he has possession, we affirm directly that all the facts of a certain group are true of him, and we convey indirectly or by implication that the law will give him the advantage of the situation. Contract, or property, or any other substantive notion of the law, may be analyzed in the same way, and should be treated in the same order. The only difference is, that, while possession denotes the facts and connotes the consequence, property always, and contract with more uncertainty and oscillation, denote the consequence and connote the facts. When we say that a man owns a thing, we affirm directly that he has the

*Oliver Wendell Holmes, Jr., *The Common Law,* first published in 1881 while Holmes was still a teacher at Harvard Law School and editor of *The American Law Review.* The book established Holmes' reputation as a legal scholar and was followed a year later by his appointment to the highest Massachusetts court, of which he became Chief Justice prior to his appointment to the United States Supreme Court.

benefit of the consequences attached to a certain group of facts, and, by implication, that the facts are true of him. The important thing to grasp is, that each of these legal compounds, possession, property, and contract, is to be analyzed into fact and right, antecedent and consequent, in like manner as every other. It is wholly immaterial that one element is accented by one word, and the other by the other two. We are not studying etymology, but law. There are always two things to be asked: first, what are the facts which make up the group in question; and then, what are the consequences attached by the law to that group. The former generally offers the only difficulties.

legal compounds    fact    antecedent
                   right   consequent

# 10

# Wesley Newcomb Hohfeld

Wesley Newcomb Hohfeld (1879–1918) unfortunately died before he could complete a proposed program of reconstruction of fundamental legal conceptions.

# FUNDAMENTAL LEGAL CONCEPTIONS*

## FUNDAMENTAL JURAL RELATIONS CONTRASTED WITH ONE ANOTHER

One of the greatest hindrances to the clear understanding, the incisive statement, and the true solution of legal problems frequently arises from the express or tacit assumption that all legal relations may be reduced to "rights" and "duties," and that these latter categories are therefore adequate for the purpose of analyzing even the most complex legal interests, such as trusts, options, escrows, "future" interests, corporate interests, etc. Even if the difficulty related merely to inadequacy and ambiguity of terminology, its seriousness would nevertheless be worthy of definite recognition and persistent effort toward improvement; for in any closely reasoned problem, whether legal or non-legal, chameleon-hued words are a peril both to clear thought and to lucid expression. As a matter of fact, however, the above mentioned inadequacy and ambiguity of terms unfortunately reflect, all too often, corresponding paucity and confusion as regards actual legal conceptions. That this is so may appear in some measure from the discussion to follow.

The strictly fundamental legal relations are, after all, *sui generis;* and thus it is that attempts at formal definition are always unsatisfactory, if not altogether useless. Accordingly, the most promising line of procedure seems to consist in exhibiting all of the various relations in a scheme of "opposites" and "correlatives," and then proceeding to exemplify their individual scope and application in concrete cases. An effort will be made to pursue this method:

| Jural Opposites | $\begin{cases} \text{right} \\ \text{no-right} \end{cases}$ | privilege<br>duty | power<br>disability | immunity<br>liability |
|---|---|---|---|---|
| Jural Correlatives | $\begin{cases} \text{right} \\ \text{duty} \end{cases}$ | privilege<br>no-right | power<br>liability | immunity<br>disability |

*Wesley Newcomb Hohfeld, from *Fundamental Legal Conceptions as Applied to Judicial Reasoning*, first published in 1919 and reissued by Yale University Press, New Haven, 1964, pp. 35–64. Reprinted by permission of the publisher. Copyright © 1919 by Yale University Press. Footnotes omitted.

## Rights and Duties

As already intimated, the term "rights" tends to be used indiscriminately to-cover what in a given case may be a privilege, a power, or an immunity, rather than a right in the strictest sense, and this looseness of usage is occasionally recognized by the authorities. As said by Mr. Justice Strong in *People v. Dikeman*:

"The word 'right' is defined by lexicographers to denote, among other things, *property, interest, power, prerogative, immunity, privilege* (Walker's Dict. word 'Right'). In law it is most frequently applied to property in its restricted sense, but it is often used to designate *power, prerogative,* and *privilege,* . . ."

Recognition of this ambiguity is also found in the language of Mr. Justice Jackson, in *United States v. Patrick*:

"The words 'right' or 'privilege' have, of course, a variety of meanings, according to the connection or context in which they are used. Their definition, as given by standard lexicographers, include 'that which one has a *legal claim to do*,' '*legal power*,' '*authority*,' '*immunity* granted by authority,' 'the investiture with special or peculiar rights.' "

And similarly, in the language of Mr. Justice Sneed, in *Lonas v. State*:

"The state, then, is forbidden from making and enforcing any law which shall abridge the *privileges* and *immunities* of citizens of the United States. It is said that the words *rights, privileges* and *immunities,* are abusively used, as if they were synonymous. The word *rights* is generic, common, embracing whatever may be lawfully claimed."

It is interesting to observe, also, that a tendency toward discrimination may be found in a number of important constitutional and statutory provisions. Just how accurate the distinctions in the mind of the draftsman may have been it is, of course, impossible to say.

Recognizing, as we must, the very broad and indiscriminate use of the term "right," what clue do we find, in ordinary legal discourse, toward limiting the word in question to a definite and appropriate meaning? That clue lies in the correlative "duty," for it is certain that even those who use the word and the conception "right" in the broadest possible way are accustomed to thinking of "duty" as the invariable correlative. As said in *Lake Shore & M. S. R. Co. v. Kurtz*:

"A duty or a legal obligation is that which one ought or ought not to do. 'Duty' and 'right' are correlative terms. When a right is invaded, a duty is violated."

In other words, if X has a right against Y that he shall stay off the former's land, the correlative (and equivalent) is that Y is under a duty toward X to stay off the place. If, as seems desirable, we should seek a synonym for the term "right" in this limited and proper meaning, perhaps the word "claim" would prove the best. The latter has the advantage of being a monosyllable. In this connection, the language of Lord Watson in *Studd v. Cook* is instructive:

"Any words which in a settlement of moveables would be recognized by the law of Scotland as sufficient to create a right *or claim* in favor of an executor . . . must receive effect if used with reference to lands in Scotland."

## Privileges and "No-Rights"

As indicated in the above scheme of jural relations, a privilege is the opposite of a duty, and the correlative of a "no-right." In the example last put, whereas X has a *right* or *claim* that Y, the other man, should stay off the land, he himself has the *privilege* of entering on the land; or, in equivalent words, X does not have a duty to stay off. The privilege of entering is the negation of a duty to stay off. As indicated by this case, some caution is necessary at this point; for, always, when it is said that a given privilege is the mere negation of a *duty*, what is meant, of course, is a duty having a content or tenor precisely *opposite* to that of the privilege in question. Thus, if, for some special reason, X has contracted with Y to go on the former's own land, it is obvious that X has, as regards Y, both the privilege of entering and the *duty of entering*. The privilege is perfectly consistent with this sort of duty,—for the latter is of the *same* content or tenor as the privilege;—but it still holds good that, as regards Y, X's privilege of entering is the precise negation of a duty to *stay off*. Similarly, if A has not contracted with B to perform certain work for the latter, A's privilege of *not* doing so is the very negation of a duty of *doing* so. Here again the duty contrasted is of a content or tenor exactly opposite to that of the privilege.

Passing now to the question of "correlatives," it will be remembered, of course, that a duty is the invariable correlative of that legal relation which is most properly called a right or claim. That being so, if further evidence be needed as to the fundamental and important difference between a right (or claim) and a privilege, surely it is found in the fact that the correlative of the latter relation is a "no-right," there being no single term available to express the latter conception. Thus, the correlative of X's right that Y shall not enter on the land is Y's duty not to enter; but the correlative of X's privilege of entering himself is manifestly Y's "no-right" that X shall not enter.

In view of the considerations thus far emphasized, the importance of keeping the conception of a right (or claim) and the conception of a privilege quite distinct from each other seems evident; and, more than that, it is equally clear that there should be a separate term to represent the latter relation. No doubt, as already indicated, it is very common to use the term "right" indiscriminately, even when the relation designated is really that of privilege; and only too often this identity of terms has involved for the particular speaker or writer a confusion or blurring of ideas. Good instances of this may be found even in unexpected places. Thus Professor Holland, in his work on *Jurisprudence*, referring to a different and well-known sort of ambiguity inherent in the Latin *"Ius,"* the German *"Recht,"* the Italian *"Diritto,"* and the French *"Droit,"*—terms used to express "not only 'a right,' but also 'Law' in the abstract,"—very aptly observes:

"If the expression of widely different ideas by one and the same term resulted only in the necessity for . . . clumsy paraphrases, or obviously inaccurate paraphrases, no great harm would be done; but unfortunately the identity of terms seems irresistibly to suggest an identity between the ideas expressed by them."

Curiously enough, however, in the very chapter where this appears, —the chapter on "Rights,"—the notions of right, privilege and power seem to be blended, and that, too, although the learned author states that "the correlative of . . . legal right is legal duty," and that "these pairs of terms express . . . in each case the same state of facts viewed from opposite sides." While the whole chapter must be read in order to appreciate the seriousness of this lack of discrimination, a single passage must suffice by way of example:

"If . . . the power of the State will protect him in so carrying out his wishes, and will compel such acts or forbearances on the part of other people as may be necessary in order that his wishes may be so carried out, then he has a 'legal right' so to carry out his wishes."

The first part of this passage suggests privileges, the middle part rights (or claims), and the last part privileges.

Similar difficulties seem to exist in Professor Gray's able and entertaining work on *The Nature and Sources of Law*. In his chapter on "Legal Rights and Duties" the distinguished author takes the position that a right always has a duty as its correlative; and he seems to define the former relation substantially according to the more limited meaning of "claim." Legal privileges, powers, and immunities are *prima facie* ignored, and the impression conveyed that all legal relations can be comprehended under the conceptions "right" and "duty." But, with the greatest hesitation and deference, the suggestion may be ventured that a number of his examples seem to show the inadequacy of such mode of treatment. Thus, e.g., he says:

"The eating of shrimp salad is an interest of mine, and, if I can pay for it, the law will protect that interest, and it is therefore a right of mine to eat shrimp salad which I have paid for, although I know that shrimp salad always gives me the colic."

This passage seems to suggest primarily two classes of relations: *first,* the party's respective privileges, as against A, B, C, D and others in relation to eating the salad, or, correlatively, the respective "no-rights" of A, B, C, D and others that the party should not eat the salad; *second,* the party's respective rights (or claims) as against A, B, C, D and others that they should not interfere with the physical act of eating the salad, or, correlatively, the respective duties of A, B, C, D and others that they should not interfere.

These two groups of relations seem perfectly distinct; and the privileges could, in a given case, exist even though the rights mentioned did not. A, B, C, and D, being the owners of the salad, might say to X: "Eat the salad, if you can; you have our license to do so, but we don't agree not to interfere with you." In such a case the privileges exist, so that if X succeeds in eating the salad, he has violated no rights of any of the parties. But it is equally clear that if A had succeeded in holding so fast to the dish that X couldn't eat the contents, no right of X would have been violated.

Perhaps the essential character and importance of the distinction can be shown by a slight variation of the facts. Suppose that X, being already the legal owner of the salad, contracts with Y that he (X) will never eat this particular food. With A, B, C, D and others no such contract has been made. One of the relations now existing between X and Y is, as a consequence, fundamentally different from the relation between X and A. As regards Y, X has no privilege of eating the salad; but as regards either A or any of the others, X has such a privilege. It is to be observed incidentally that X's right that Y should not eat the food persists even though X's own privilege of doing so has been extinguished.

On grounds already emphasized, it would seem that the line of reasoning pursued by Lord Lindley in the great case of *Quinn v. Leathem* is deserving of comment:

"The plaintiff had the ordinary *rights* of the British subject. He was *at liberty* to earn his living in his own way, provided he did not violate some special law prohibiting him from so doing, and provided he did not infringe the rights of other people. This *liberty* involved *the liberty* to deal with other persons who were willing to deal with him. *This liberty* is *a right* recognized by law; its *correlative* is the general *duty* of every one not to prevent the free exercise of this *liberty* except so far as his own liberty of action may justify him in so doing. But a person's *liberty* or *right* to deal with others is nugatory unless they are at liberty to deal with him if they choose to do so. Any interference with their liberty to deal with him affects him."

A "liberty" considered as a legal relation (or "right" in the loose and generic sense of that term) must mean, if it have any definite content at all, precisely the same thing as *privilege;* and certainly that is the fair connotation of the term as used the first three times in the passage quoted. It is equally clear, as already indicated, that such a privilege or liberty to deal with others at will might very conceivably exist without any peculiar concomitant rights against "third parties" as regards certain kinds of interference. Whether there should be such concomitant rights (or claims) is ultimately a question of justice and policy; and it should be considered, as such, on its merits. The only correlative logically implied by the privileges or liberties in question are the "no-rights" of "third parties." It would therefore be a *non sequitur* to conclude from the mere existence of such liberties that "third parties" are under a *duty* not to interfere, etc. Yet in the middle of the above passage from Lord Lindley's opinion there is a sudden and question-begging shift in the use of terms. First, the "liberty" in question is transmuted into a "right"; and then, possibly under the seductive influence of the latter word, it is assumed that the "correlative" must be "the general duty of every one not to prevent," etc.

Another interesting and instructive example may be taken from Lord Bowen's oft-quoted opinion in *Mogul Steamship Co. v. McGregor.*

"We are presented in this case with an apparent conflict or antinomy between two rights that are equally regarded by the law—the right of the plaintiffs to be protected in the legitimate exercise of their trade, and the right of the defendants to carry on their business as seems best to them, provided they commit no wrong to others."

As the learned judge states, the conflict or antinomy is only apparent; but this fact seems to be obscured by the very indefinite and rapidly shifting meanings with which the term "right" is used in the above quoted language. Construing the passage as a whole, it seems plain enough that by "the right of the plaintiffs" in relation to the defendants a legal right or claim in the strict sense must be meant; whereas by "the right of the defendants" in relation to the plaintiffs a legal privilege must be intended. That being so, the "two rights" mentioned in the beginning of the passage, being respectively claim and privilege, could not be in conflict with each other. To the extent that the defendants have privileges the plaintiffs have no rights; and, conversely, to the extent that the plaintiffs have rights the defendants have no privileges ("no-privilege" equals duty of opposite tenor).

Thus far it has been assumed that the term "privilege" is the most appropriate and satisfactory to designate the mere negation of duty. Is there good warrant for this?

In Mackeldey's *Roman Law* it is said:

"Positive laws either contain general principles embodied in the rules of law . . . or for especial reasons they establish something that differs from those general principles. In the first case they contain a common law *(jus commune)*, in the second a special law *(jus singulare s. exorbitans)*. The latter is either favorable or unfavorable . . . according as it enlarges or restricts, in opposition to the common rule, the rights of those for whom it is established. The favorable special law *(jus singulare)* as also the right created by it . . . in the Roman law is termed benefit of the law *(beneficium juris)* or privilege *(privilegium)* . . . "

First a special law, and then by association of ideas, a special advantage conferred by such a law. With such antecedents, it is not surprising that the English word "privilege" is not infrequently used, even at the present time, in the sense of a special or peculiar legal advantage (whether right, privilege, power or immunity) belonging either to some individual or to some particular class of persons. There are, indeed, a number of judicial opinions recognizing this as one of the meanings of the term in question. That the word has a wider signification even in ordinary non-technical usage is sufficiently indicated, however, by the fact that the term "*special* privileges" is so often used to indicate a contrast to ordinary or general privileges. More than this, the dominant specific connotation of the term as used in popular speech seems to be mere *negation of duty*. This is manifest in the terse and oft-repeated expression, "That is your privilege,"—meaning, of course, "You are under no duty to do otherwise."

Such being the case, it is not surprising to find, from a wide survey of judicial precedents, that the *dominant* technical meaning of the term is, similarly, negation of *legal duty*. There are two very common examples of this, relating respectively to "privileged communications" in the law of libel and to "privileges against self-crimination" in the law of evidence. As regards the first case, it is elementary that if a certain group of operative facts are present, a privilege exists which, without such facts, would not be recognized. It is, of course, equally clear that even though all such facts be present as last supposed, the superadded fact of malice will, in cases of so-called "conditional privilege," negative the privilege that otherwise would exist. It must be evident also, that whenever the privilege does exist, it is not special in the sense of arising from a special law, or of being conferred as a special favor on a particular individual. The same privilege would exist, by virtue of general rules, for any person whatever under similar circumstances. So, also, in the law of evidence, the privilege against self-crimination signifies the mere negation of a duty to testify,—a duty which rests upon a witness in relation to all ordinary matters; and, quite obviously, such privilege arises, if at all, only by virtue of general laws.

As already intimated, while both the conception and the term "privilege" find conspicuous exemplification under the law of libel and the law of evidence, they nevertheless have a much wider significance and utility as a matter of judicial usage. To make this clear, a few miscellaneous judicial precedents will now be noticed. In *Dowman's Case,* decided in the year 1583, and reported by Coke, the court applied the term to the subject of waste:

"And as to the objection which was made, that the said privilege to be without impeachment of waste can not be without deed, etc. To that it was answered and resolved, that if it was admitted that a deed in such case should be requisite, yet without question all the estates limited would be good, although it is admitted, that the clause concerning the said privilege would be void."

In the great case of *Allen v. Flood* the opinion of Mr. Justice Hawkins furnishes a useful passage for the purpose now in view:

"Every person has a privilege . . . in the interests of public justice to put the criminal law in motion against another whom he *bona fide,* and upon reasonable and probable cause, believes to have been guilty of a crime. . . . It must not, however, be supposed that hatred and ill-will existing in the mind of a prosecutor must of necessity *destroy* the *privilege,* for it is not impossible that such hatred and ill-will may have very natural and pardonable reasons for existing. . . ."

Applying the term in relation to the subject of property, Mr. Justice Foster, of the Supreme Court of Maine, said in the case of *Pulitzer v. Livingston:*

"It is contrary to the policy of the law that there should be any outstanding titles, estates, or powers, by the existence, operation or exercise of which, at a period of time beyond lives in being and twenty-one years and a fraction thereafter, the complete and unfettered enjoyment of an estate, *with all the rights, privileges and powers incident to ownership*, should be qualified or impeded."

As a final example in the present connection, the language of Baron Alderson in *Hilton v. Eckerley* may be noticed:

"*Prima facie* it is the privilege of a trader in a free country, in all matters not contrary to law, to regulate his own mode of carrying them on according to his discretion and choice."

The closest synonym of legal "privilege" seems to be legal "liberty" or legal "freedom." This is sufficiently indicated by an unusually discriminating and instructive passage in Mr. Justice Cave's opinion in *Allen v. Flood:*

"The personal rights with which we are most familiar are: 1. Rights of reputation; 2. Rights of bodily safety and freedom; 3. Rights of property; or, in other words, rights relating to mind, body and estate, . . .
"In my subsequent remarks the word 'right' will, as far as possible, always be used in the above sense; and it is the more necessary to insist on this as during the argument at your Lordship's bar it was frequently used in a much wider and more indefinite sense. Thus it was said that a man has a perfect right to fire off a gun, when all that was meant, apparently, was that a man has a *freedom* or *liberty* to fire off a gun, so long as he does not violate or infringe any one's rights in doing so, which is a very different thing from a right, the violation or disturbance of which can be remedied or prevented by legal process."

While there are numerous other instances of the apt use of the term "liberty," both in judicial opinions and in conveyancing documents, it is by no means so common or definite a word as "privilege." The former term is far more likely to be used in the sense of physical or personal freedom (i.e., absence of physical restraint), as distinguished from a legal relation; and very frequently there is the connotation of *general* political liberty, as distinguished from a particular relation between two definite individuals. Besides all this, the term "privilege" has the advantage of giving us, as a variable, the adjective "privileged." Thus, it is frequently convenient to speak of a privileged act, a privileged transaction, a privileged conveyance, etc.

The term "license," sometimes used as if it were synonymous with "privilege," is not strictly appropriate. This is simply another of those innumerable cases in which the mental and physical facts are so frequently confused with the legal relation which they create. Accurately used, "license" is a generic term to indicate a group of *operative* facts required to create a particular privilege,—this being especially evident when the word is used in the common phrase "leave and license." This point is brought out by a passage from Mr. Justice Adams's opinion in *Clifford v. O'Neill*:

"A license is merely a *permission* to do an act which, *without such permission,* would amount to a trespass . . . nor will the continuous enjoyment of the *privilege conferred,* for any period of time cause it to ripen into a tangible interest in the land affected."

## Powers and Liabilities

As indicated in the preliminary scheme of jural relations, a legal power (as distinguished, of course, from a mental or physical power) is the opposite of legal disability, and the correlative of legal liability. But what is the intrinsic nature of a legal power as such? Is it possible to analyze the conception represented by this constantly employed and very important term of legal discourse? Too close an analysis might seem metaphysical rather than useful; so that what is here presented is intended only as an approximate explanation, sufficient for all practical purposes.

A change in a given legal relation may result (1) from some superadded fact or group of facts not under the volitional control of a human being (or human beings); or (2) from some superadded fact or group of facts which are under the volitional control of one or more human beings. As regards the second class of cases, the person (or persons) whose volitional control is paramount may be said to have the (legal) power to effect the particular change of legal relations that is involved in the problem.

This second class of cases—powers in the technical sense—must now be further considered. The nearest synonym for any ordinary case seems to be (legal) "ability,"—the latter being obviously the opposite of "inability," or "disability." The term "right," so frequently and loosely used in the present connection, is an unfortunate term for the purpose,—a not unusual result being confusion of thought as well as ambiguity of expression. The term "capacity" is equally unfortunate; for, as we have already seen, when used with discrimination, this word denotes a particular group of operative facts, and not a legal relation of any kind.

Many examples of legal powers may readily be given. Thus, X, the owner of ordinary personal property "in a tangible object" has the power to extinguish his own legal interest (rights, powers, immunities, etc.) through that totality of operative facts known as abandonment; and—simultaneously and correlatively —to create in other persons privileges and powers relating to the abandoned object,—e.g., the power to acquire title to the latter by appropriating it. *Similarly,* X has the power to transfer his interest to Y,—that is, to extinguish his own interest and concomitantly create in Y a new and corresponding interest. So also X has the power to create contractual obligations of various kinds. Agency cases are likewise instructive. By the use of some *metaphorical* expression such as the Latin, *qui facit per alium, facit per se,* the true nature of agency relations is only too frequently obscured. The creation of an agency relation involves, *inter alia,* the grant of legal powers to the so-called agent, and the creation of correlative liabilities in the principal. That is to say, one party, P, has the power to create agency powers in another party, A,—for example, the power to convey P's property, the power to impose (so-called) contractual obligations on P, the power to discharge a debt owing to P, the power to "receive" title to property so that it shall vest in P, and so forth. In passing, it may be well to observe that the term "authority," so frequently used in agency cases, is very ambiguous and slippery in its connotation. Properly employed in the present connection, the word seems to be an abstract or qualitative term corresponding to the concrete "authorization,"—the latter consisting of a particular group of operative facts taking place between the principal and the agent. All too often, however, the term in question is so used as to blend and confuse these operative facts with the powers and privileges thereby created in the agent. A careful discrimination in these particulars would, it is submitted, go far toward clearing up certain problems in the law of agency.

Essentially similar to the powers of agents are powers of appointment in relation to property interests. So, too, the powers of public officers are, intrinsically considered, comparable to those of agents,—for example, the power of a sheriff to sell property under a writ of execution. The power of a donor, in a gift *causa mortis,* to revoke the gift and divest the title of the donee is another clear example of the legal quantities now being considered; also a pledgee's statutory power of sale.

There are, on the other hand, cases where the true nature of the relations involved has not, perhaps, been so clearly recognized. Thus, in the case of a conditional sale of personalty, assuming the vendee's agreement has been fully performed except as to the payment of the last instalment and the time for the latter has arrived, what is the interest of such vendee as regards the property? Has he, as so often assumed, merely a contractual right to have title passed to him by consent of the vendor, on final payment being made; or has he, irrespective of the consent of the vendor the power to divest the title of the latter and to acquire a perfect title for himself? Though the language of the cases is not always so clear as it might be, the vendee seems to have precisely that sort of power. Fundamentally considered, the typical escrow transaction in which the performance of conditions is within the volitional control of the grantee, is somewhat similar to the conditional sale of personalty; and, when reduced to its lowest terms, the problem seems easily to be solved in terms of legal powers. Once the "escrow" is formed, the grantor still has the legal title; but the grantee has an irrevocable power to divest that title by performance of certain conditions (i.e., the addition of various operative facts), and concomitantly to vest title in himself. While such power is outstanding, the grantor is, of course, subject to a correlative liability to have his title divested. Similarly, in the case of a conveyance of land in fee simple subject to condition subsequent, after the condition has been performed, the original grantor is commonly said to have a "*right* of entry." If, however, the problem is analyzed, it will be seen that, as of primary importance, the grantor has two legal quantities, (1) the privilege of entering, and (2) the power, by means of such entry, to divest the estate of the grantee. The latter's estate endures, subject to the correlative liability of being divested, until such power is actually exercised.

Passing now to the field of contracts, suppose A mails a letter to B offering to sell the former's land, Whiteacre, to the latter for ten thousand dollars, such letter being duly received. The operative facts thus far mentioned have created a power as regards B and a correlative liability as regards A. B, by dropping a letter of acceptance in the box, has the power to impose a potential or inchoate obligation *ex contractu* on A and himself; and, assuming that the land is worth fifteen thousand dollars, that particular legal quantity—the "power *plus* liability" relation between A and B—seems to be worth about five thousand dollars to B. The liability of A will continue for a reasonable time unless, in exercise of his power to do so, A previously extinguishes it by that series of operative facts known as "revocation." These last matters are usually described by saying that A's "offer" will "continue" or "remain open" for a reasonable time, or for the definite time actually specified, unless A previously "withdraws" or "revokes" such offer. While, no doubt, in the great majority of cases no harm results from the use of such expressions, yet these forms of statement seem to represent a blending of non-legal and legal quantities which, in any problem requiring careful reasoning, should preferably be kept distinct. An offer, considered as a series of physical and mental operative facts, has spent its force and become *functus officio* as soon as such series has been completed by the "offeree's receipt." The real question is therefore as to the *legal effect*, if any, at that moment of time. If the latter consist of B's power and A's correlative liability, manifestly it is those *legal relations* that "continue" or "remain open" until modified by revocation or other operative facts. What has thus far been said concerning contracts completed by mail would seem to apply, *mutatis mutandis*, to every type of contract. Even where the parties are in the presence of each other, the offer creates a liability against the offerer, together with a correlative power in favor of the offeree. The only distinction for present purposes would be in the fact that such power and such liability would expire within a very short period of time.

Perhaps the practical justification for this method of analysis is somewhat greater in relation to the subject of options. In his able work on *Contracts*, Langdell says:

"If the offerer stipulates that his offer shall remain open for a specified time, the first question is whether such stipulation constitutes a binding contract. . . . When such a stipulation is binding, the further question arises, whether it makes the offer irrevocable. It has been a common opinion that it does, but that is clearly a mistake. . . . An offer is merely one of the elements of a contract; and it is indispensable to the making of a contract that the wills of the contracting parties do, in legal contemplation, concur at the moment of making it. An offer, therefore, which the party making it has no power to revoke, is a legal impossibility. Moreover, if the stipulation should make the offer irrevocable, it would be a contract incapable of being broken; which is also a legal impossibility. The only effect, therefore, of such a stipulation is to give the offeree a claim for damages if the stipulation be broken by revoking the offer."

The foregoing reasoning ignores the fact that an ordinary offer *ipso facto* creates a legal relation—a legal power and a legal liability,—and that it is this relation (rather than the physical and mental facts constituting the offer) that "remains open." If these points be conceded, there seems no difficulty in recognizing a unilateral option agreement supported by consideration or embodied in a sealed instrument as creating in the optionee an irrevocable power to create, at any time within the period specified, a bilateral obligation as between himself and the giver of the option. Correlatively to that power, there would, of course, be a liability against the option-giver which he himself would have no power to extinguish. The courts seem to have no difficulty in reaching precisely this result as a matter of substance; though their explanations are always in terms of "withdrawal of offer," and similar expressions savoring of physical and mental quantities.

In connection with the powers and liabilities created respectively by an ordinary offer and by an option, it is interesting to consider the liabilities of a person engaged in a "public calling"; for, as it seems, such a party's characteristic position is, one might almost say, intermediate between that of an ordinary contractual offerer and that of an option-giver. It has indeed been usual to assert that such a party is (generally speaking) under a present *duty* to all other parties; but this is believed to be erroneous. Thus, Professor Wyman, in his work on *Public Service Companies,* says:

"The duty placed upon every one exercising a public calling is primarily *a duty* to serve every man who is a member of the public. . . . It is somewhat difficult to place this exceptional duty in our legal system. . . . The truth of the matter is that the obligation resting upon one who has undertaken the performance of public duty is *sui generis.*"

It is submitted that the learned writer's difficulties arise primarily from a failure to see that the innkeeper, the common carrier and others similarly "holding out" are under present *liabilities* rather than present *duties.* Correlative to those liabilities are the respective powers of the various members of the public. Thus, for example, a traveling member of the public has the legal power, by making proper application and sufficient tender, to impose a duty on the innkeeper to receive him as a guest. For breach of the duty *thus* created an action would of course lie. It would therefore seem that the innkeeper is, to some extent, like one who had given an option to every traveling member of the public. He differs, as regards net legal effect, only because he can extinguish his present liabilities and the correlative powers of the traveling members of the public *by going out of business.* Yet, on the other hand, his liabilities are more onerous than that of an ordinary contractual offerer, for he cannot extinguish his liabilities by any simple performance akin to revocation of offer.

As regards all the "legal powers" thus far considered, possibly some caution is necessary. If, for example, we consider the ordinary property owner's power of alienation, it is necessary to distinguish carefully between the _legal_ power, the _physical_ power to do the things necessary for the "exercise" of the legal power, and, finally, the _privilege_ of doing these things—that is, if such privilege does really exist. It may or may not. Thus, if X, a landowner, has contracted with Y that the former will not alienate to Z, the acts of X necessary to exercise the power of alienating to Z are privileged as between X and every party other than Y; but, obviously, as between X and Y, the former has no privilege of doing the necessary acts; or conversely, he is under a duty to Y not to do what is necessary to exercise the power.

In view of what has already been said, very little may suffice concerning a _liability_ as such. The latter, as we have seen, is the correlative of power, and the opposite of immunity (or exemption). While no doubt the term "liability" is often loosely used as a synonym for "duty," or "obligation," it is believed, from an extensive survey of judicial precedents, that the connotation already adopted as most appropriate to the word in question is fully justified. A few cases tending to indicate this will now be noticed. In _McNeer v. McNeer,_ Mr. Justice Magruder balanced the conceptions of power and liability as follows:

> "So long as she lived, however, his interest in her land lacked those _elements of property,_ such as _power of disposition_ and _liability to sale on_ execution which had formerly given it the character of a vested estate."

In _Booth v. Commonwealth,_ the court had to construe a Virginia statute providing "that all free white male persons who are twenty-one years of age and not over sixty, shall be _liable_ to serve as jurors, except as hereinafter provided." It is plain that this enactment imposed only a _liability_ and not a _duty._ It is a liability to have a duty created. The latter would arise only when, in exercise of their powers, the parties litigant and the court officers had done what was necessary to impose a specific duty to perform the functions of a juror. The language of the court, by Moncure, J., is particularly apposite as indicating that liability is the opposite, or negative, of immunity (or exemption):

> "The word both expressed and implied is 'liable,' which has a very different meaning from 'qualified' . . . Its meaning is 'bound' or 'obliged.' . . . A person exempt from serving on juries is not liable to serve, and a person not liable to serve is exempt from serving. The terms seem to be convertible."

A further good example of judicial usage is to be found in _Emery v. Clough._ Referring to a gift _causa mortis_ and the donee's liability to have his already vested interest divested by the donor's exercise of his power of revocation, Mr. Justice Smith said:

> "The title to the gift _causa mortis_ passed by the delivery, defeasible only in the lifetime of the donor, and his death perfects the title in the donee by terminating the donor's right or _power of defeasance._ The property passes from the donor to the donee directly . . . and after his death it is _liable_ to be _divested_ only in favor of the donor's creditors. . . . His right and power ceased with his death."

Perhaps the nearest synonym of "liability" is "subjection" or "responsibility." As regards the latter word, a passage from Mr. Justice Day's opinion in *McElfresh v. Kirkendall* is interesting:

> "The words 'debt' and 'liability' are not synonymous, and they are not commonly so understood. As applied to the pecuniary relations of the parties, liability is a term of broader significance than debt. . . . Liability is responsibility."

While the term in question has the broad generic connotation already indicated, no doubt it very frequently indicates that specific form of liability (or complex of liabilities) that is correlative to a power (or complex of powers) vested in a party litigant and the various court officers. Such was held to be the meaning of a certain California statute involved in the case of *Lattin v. Gillette*. Said Mr. Justice Harrison:

> "The word 'liability' is the condition in which an individual is placed after a breach of his contract, or a violation of any obligation resting upon him. It is defined by Bouvier to be responsibility."

### Immunities and Disabilities

As already brought out, immunity is the correlative of disability ("nopower"), and the opposite, or negation, of liability. Perhaps it will also be plain, from the preliminary outline and from the discussion down to this point, that a power bears the same general contrast to an immunity that a right does to a privilege. A right is one's affirmative claim against another, and a privilege is one's freedom from the right or claim of another. Similarly, a power is one's affirmative "control" over a given legal relation as against another; whereas an immunity is one's freedom from the legal power or "control" of another as regards some legal relation.

A few examples may serve to make this clear. X, a landowner, has, as we have seen, power to alienate to Y or to any other ordinary party. On the other hand, X has also various immunities as against Y, and all other ordinary parties. For Y is under a disability (i.e., has no power) so far as shifting the legal interest either to himself or to a third party is concerned; and what is true of Y applies similarly to every one else who has not by virtue of special operative facts acquired a power to alienate X's property. If, indeed, a sheriff has been duly empowered by a writ of execution to sell X's interest, that is a very different matter: correlative to such sheriff's power would be the *liability* of X,—the very opposite of immunity (or exemption). It is elementary, too, that as against the sheriff, X might be immune or exempt in relation to certain parcels of property, and be liable as to others. Similarly, if an agent has been duly appointed by X to sell a given piece of property, then, as to the latter, X has, in relation to such agent, a liability rather than an immunity.

For over a century there has been, in this country, a great deal of important litigation involving immunities from powers of taxation. If there be any lingering misgivings as to the "practical" importance of accuracy and discrimination in legal conceptions and legal terms, perhaps some of such doubts would be dispelled by considering the numerous cases on valuable taxation exemptions coming before the United States Supreme Court. Thus, in *Phoenix Ins. Co. v. Tennessee*, Mr. Justice Peckham expressed the views of the court as follows:

"In granting to the De Soto Company 'all the rights, privileges, and immunities' of the Bluff City Company, all words are used which could be regarded as necessary to carry the exemption from taxation possessed by the Bluff City Company; while in the next following grant, that of the charter of the plaintiff in error, the word 'immunity' is omitted. Is there any meaning to be attached to that omission, and if so, what? We think some meaning is to be attached to it. The word 'immunity' expresses more clearly and definitely an intention to include therein an exemption from taxation than does either of the other words. Exemption from taxation is more accurately described as an 'immunity' than as a privilege, although it is not to be denied that the latter word may sometimes and under some circumstances include such exemptions."

In *Morgan v. Louisiana* there is an instructive discussion from the pen of Mr. Justice Field. In holding that on a foreclosure sale of the franchise and property of a railroad corporation an immunity from taxation did not pass to the purchaser, the learned judge said:

"As has been often said by this court, the whole community is interested in retaining the power of taxation undiminished. . . . The exemption of the property of the company from taxation, and the exemption of its officers and servants from jury and military duty, were both intended for the benefit of the company, and its benefit alone. In their personal character they are analogous to exemptions from execution of certain property of debtors, made by laws of several of the states."

So far as immunities are concerned, the two judicial discussions last quoted concern respectively problems of interpretation and problems of alienability. In many other cases difficult constitutional questions have arisen as the result of statutes impairing or extending various kinds of immunities. Litigants have, from time to time, had occasion to appeal both to the clause against impairment of the obligation of contracts and to the provision against depriving a person of property without due process of law. This has been especially true as regards exemptions from taxation and exemptions from execution.

If a word may now be permitted with respect to mere terms as such, the first thing to note is that the word "right" is overworked in the field of immunities as elsewhere. As indicated, however, by the judicial expressions already quoted, the best synonym is, of course, the term "exemption." It is instructive to note, also, that the word "impunity" has a very similar connotation. This is made evident by the interesting discriminations of Lord Chancellor Finch in *Skelton v. Skelton*, a case decided in 1677:

"But this I would by no means allow, that equity should enlarge the restraints of the disabilities introduced by act of parliament; and as to the granting of injunctions to stay waste, I took a distinction where tenant hath only *impunitatem*, and where he hath *jus in arboribus.* If the tenant have only a bare indemnity or *exemption* from an action (at law), if he committed waste, there it is fit he should be restrained by injunction from committing it."

In the latter part of the preceding discussion, eight conceptions of the law have been analyzed and compared in some detail, the purpose having been to exhibit not only their intrinsic meaning and scope, but also their relations to one another and the methods by which they are applied, in judicial reasoning, to the solution of concrete problems of litigation. Before concluding this branch of the discussion a general suggestion may be ventured as the great practical importance of a clear appreciation of the distinctions and discriminations set forth. If a homely metaphor be permitted, these eight conceptions,—rights and duties, privileges and no-rights, powers and liabilities, immunities and disabilities,—seem to be what may be called "the lowest common denominators of the law." Ten fractions (1-3, 2-5, etc.) may, *superficially*, seem so different from one another as to defy comparison. If, however, they are expressed in terms of their lowest common denominators (5-15, 6-15, etc.), comparison becomes easy, and fundamental similarity may be discovered. The same thing is of course true as regards the lowest generic conceptions to which any and all "legal quantities" may be reduced.

Reverting, for example, to the subject of powers, it might be difficult at first glance to discover any essential and fundamental similarity between conditional sales of personalty, escrow transactions, option agreements, agency relations, powers of appointment, etc. But if all these relations are reduced to their lowest generic terms, the conceptions of legal power and legal liability are seen to be dominantly, though not exclusively, applicable throughout the series. By such a process it becomes possible not only to discover essential similarities and illuminating analogies in the midst of what appears superficially to be infinite and hopeless variety, but also to discern common principles of justice and policy underlying the various jural problems involved. An indirect, yet very practical, consequence is that it frequently becomes feasible, by virtue of such analysis, to use as persuasive authorities judicial precedents that might otherwise seem altogether irrelevant. If this point be valid with respect to powers, it would seem to be equally so as regards all of the other basic conceptions of the law. In short, the deeper the analysis, the greater becomes one's perception of fundamental unity and harmony in the law.

# 11

## Joel Feinberg

Joel Feinberg (1929–    ) of Rockefeller University is currently engaged
in a major study of rights and now considers this article an over-
simplified but still useful introduction to contemporary rights analysis.

# DUTIES, RIGHTS AND CLAIMS*†

Among the questions that still divide philosophers who are concerned
with problems about rights are (1) whether, or to what extent, rights and duties
are logically correlative, and (2) whether it is theoretically illuminating
generally, and in particular, whether in considering question (1) it is strategically
useful to treat rights as *claims*. Although question (1) is in a familiar sense a
logical question (Do statements of duties *entail* statements of other people's
rights, and do statements of rights *entail* statements of other people's duties?),
this paper is more a descriptive or impressionistic study than a formalistic one.
Part I consists of an examination of the many kinds of normative relations
called "duty" with the aim of distinguishing those that are clearly correlated
with other people's rights from those that apparently are not. The second part
of the paper shifts the focus to rights and argues that there is at least one kind
of talk about rights-as-claims that is neither reducible to, nor in any clear logical
relation with, talk about duties. The word "claim" of course is ambiguous.
Claims *to* (I shall argue) are not always expressible as claims *against,* and
"having a claim to . . ." "making claim to . . ." are different sorts of things
from "claiming that. . . ." The paper concludes, however, that each of the
ideas capable of being expressed by the word "claim" is essential either to the
understanding or the just appreciation of rights.

## I. DUTIES AND RIGHTS

Which of the various kinds of duty are necessarily correlated with the
rights of other people? Consider first the relation between a debtor and his
creditor. Indebtedness is the clearest example of one person *owing* something
to another; and owing, in turn, is a perspicuous model for the interpretation

*Reprinted by permission of the Editor and the author from: Joel Feinberg, "Duties, Rights
and Claims," *American Philosophical Quarterly*, Vol. 3, No. 2 (1966), pp. 137ff.
†A slightly expanded revision of a paper contributed to a Symposium on Human Rights at the
meeting of the Eastern Division of the American Philosophical Association, December 27, 1964.

of that treacherous little preposition "to" as it occurs in the phrase "obligation *to* someone." Now it is unquestionably true that when one party *owes* something to another, the latter has a *right* to what he is owed. The debtor's obligation is his creditor's right seen from a different vantage point. A *duty of indebtedness*, moreover, entails a right of a very specific kind, called, in the jargon of jurisprudence, a positive *in personam right*, that is, a right against one specific person requiring him to perform a "positive act," not a mere omission.

A second class of duties, being based on promises, is also more properly called "obligations,"[1] but we can call them (other) *duties of commitment*. In discussing these, we must not be misled by the preposition "to." When a debtor owes money to a creditor, he can be said to have an obligation *to* the creditor; but the preposition here is ambiguous and obscures the distinction between two different offices the creditor occupies. On the one hand he is the one to whom the obligation is *owed*, and the one therefore who can claim it as his due. On the other hand, he is the intended beneficiary of his debtor's promised act. This dual role is also played sometimes by persons owed other kinds of duties of commitment. If Abel promises Baker to meet him at a certain time, or to shine his shoes, or favorably review his book, then Baker is both claimant and intended beneficiary of Abel's duty. There may, of course, be others who stand to gain, if only indirectly, from Abel's discharge of his obligation, but in most cases these so-called "third party beneficiaries" will profit in merely picayune and remote ways.

Sometimes, however, there is a separation of offices, and the intended direct beneficiary is not the promisee, but instead some third party designated by the promisee. This class of transactions can be further subdivided: In some cases, only the promisee is the claimant, or right-holder, while in other cases, both the promisee and the third-party beneficiary have rights to the promisor's performance. If Abel promises Baker to look after Baker's dog Fido, then Fido is the direct beneficiary of the promised services, while Baker himself, and probably only Baker, is the claimant. On the other hand, if Baker designates his wife or mother (or dog?) as beneficiary on his life insurance policy, then *both* Baker as promisee and the designated beneficiary can be said to have a right that the benefit-payment go to the beneficiary. (Even after Baker is dead, it can be said that the insurance company *owes it to him* to pay the beneficiary.)

Philosophers[2] have sometimes found it useful to direct their attention primarily to those cases where third-party beneficiaries do *not* derive rights from promises, for such cases illustrate most clearly that promisee and intended beneficiary *are* distinct moral offices. Furthermore, in cases of that kind, the distinction between the two offices is not totally obscured by ordinary language which distinguishes (sometimes) between duties *to* claimants and duties *toward*,

---

[1] For subtle discussions of the distinction between obligations and duties, see E. J. Lemmon, "Moral Dilemmas," *The Philosophical Review,* vol. 71 (1962), pp. 139–158; and Richard B. Brandt, "The Concepts of Obligation and Duty," *Mind,* vol. 73 (1964), pp. 374–393.
[2] Most notably, H. L. A. Hart, "Are There Any Natural Rights?" *The Philosophical Review,* vol. 64 (1955), pp. 179–182.

or in respect to, beneficiaries. But total preoccupation with this kind of case is as dangerous as it is unnecessary. The danger is that it might blind us to the large class of cases where third-party beneficiaries, both in law [3] and morals, do have a claim-right against the promisor; and in any case, the distinction between the offices of promisee and beneficiary can be equally well made out in the case where the third-party beneficiary and the promisee are both claimants. For in these cases, it does not *follow necessarily* from the fact that a person is an intended <u>beneficiary of a promised service</u> that he has a right to it, whereas it always follows necessarily from the fact that a person is a <u>promisee</u> that he has a right to what is promised. This difference, of course, would not be possible if beneficiary and promisee were not distinct offices. Another way of putting the point is to say that the rights of third-party beneficiaries, unlike those of promisees, are not logically correlated with the obligations of the promisor, but correlated only in virtue of moral or judicial policies and rules. In those cases where there is some temptation to say that the right of a third-party beneficiary is logically correlated with a promisor's duty, the temptation will be at least as great to say that the promisor made a *tacit promise* to the beneficiary in addition to the express promise to his promisee. I have in mind those cases where the parties to the promise allow the promise to be known to the third-party beneficiary, and the latter acts in reliance on its performance.

In all of these cases, the important relation for our present purposes is that between promisor and *claimant,* whether the latter be promisee, or beneficiary, or both. This relation is another proper and familiar case of owing, although it is already one step removed from what we might call the "paradigm case" of indebtedness. Duties of commitment, like the standard cases of owing, are obviously correlated with other people's *in personam* rights. The claimant has a right *in personam* against the promisor to either a positive performance, as in the case of feeding Fido, or else a forebearance, as when I promise to waive my right to keep you off my land, giving you thereby a claim to my non-interference, that is, a negative *in personam* right.

Similar remarks can be made about a third class of duties, the *duties of reparation.* When your loss is "my fault," that is, when it was caused by my negligence, recklessness, impulsiveness, carelessness, dishonesty, malevolence, or the like, then I have a duty to you to repair the harm or otherwise make good the loss. I "owe" reparation to you in much the same manner as I would

---

[3] For a subtle and detailed discussion of this complex topic see *Corbin on Contracts* (St. Paul, Minn., West, 1952), pp. 723–783. Corbin writes on p. 733: "The following is an attempt at a consistent statement of the generally prevailing law: A third party who is not a promisee and who gave no consideration has an enforceable right by reason of a contract made by two others (1) if he is a creditor of the promisee or of some other person and the contract calls for a performance by the promisor in satisfaction of the obligation; or (2) if the promised performance will be of pecuniary benefit to him and the contract is so expressed as to give the promisor reason to know that such benefit is contemplated by the promisee as one of the motivating causes of his making the contract. A third party may be included within both of these provisions at once, but need not be. One who is included within neither of them has no right, even though performance will incidentally benefit him."

owe you the return of something I borrowed or took from you without your permission. My duty, in these examples, is to return to you what is really your own, or where this is impossible, something of equivalent value; and your correlative right is a claim *in personam* to my positive services.

④ *need fulfillment*  A fourth class of duties also permits talk of "owing" something to someone, although we are now at least two steps away from the example of indebtedness. "Mr. Churchill feels that he owes this legacy to the world," said a 1964 advertisement for a set of recordings by Winston Churchill of public and private speeches, letters, and reminiscences. Presumably, Sir Winston did not feel that he must simply return what he had borrowed or keep some sort of promise, express or implied. I suspect rather that he felt a duty to give to the world something that it needs, but which he, at age 90, no longer had reason to keep his exclusive possession. I propose to call this, and other more worldly examples of the duty abundance owes to need, *duties of need fulfillment*. Such duties clearly give rise to positive *in personam* rights, often in many claimants.

⑤ *reciprocation*  A fifth class of duties is related to gratitude, but had better be called *duties of reciprocation*, since gratitude, a feeling, is a less appropriate subject for duty than reciprocation, which is, after all, action. There are, moreover, other confusions commonly infecting the idea of a "duty of gratitude." Many writers speak of duties of gratitude as if they were special instances, or perhaps informal analogues, of duties of indebtedness. But gratitude, I submit, feels nothing at all like indebtedness. When a person under no duty to me does me a service or helps me out of a jam, from what I imagine to be benevolent motives, my feelings of gratitude toward him bears no important resemblance to the feeling I have toward a merchant who ships me ordered goods before I pay for them. The cause of the widespread confusion of gratitude with moral indebtedness, I suspect, is a disposition, allegedly characteristic of but certainly not peculiar to the Japanese, to feel some loss of status when helped by others, and some consequent resentment of the benefactor under the respectable mask of "gratitude." We feel impelled to pay back a benefactor sometimes because we feel that his benefaction has made him "one up" and we want to get even.

The expression "duty of reciprocation" is better used for a different kind of case: My benefactor once freely offered me his services when I needed them. There was, on that occasion, nothing for me to do in return but express my deepest gratitude to him. (How alien to gratitude any sort of *payment* would have been!) But now circumstances have arisen in which he needs help, and I am in a position to help him. Surely, I *owe* him my services now, and he would be entitled to resent my failure to come through. In short, he has a right to my help now, and I have a correlative duty to proffer it to him. Like the other examples, the right in this case is *in personam* and typically positive.

I think I have now enumerated the main classes of duties that permit talk of one person owing something to another. Of course, there may be a very wide sense of "owe" in which it goes with all talk of duty, perhaps as a kind of synonym for the feeling of requirement or "must do" that goes with all duty. But still in respect to the remaining classes of duties, while one must do something, this is not because he *owes* it to someone to do it. ⑥

The sixth kind of duty is typified by the duty we all have to stay off a landowner's property. I don't think we would naturally speak of this duty as something "owed" to the landowner, although I admit the law doesn't hesitate to speak that way. In acknowledging a duty not to interfere with another's property, we show our respect for his interest in the exclusive possession and control of it. Such duties of noninterference with the person or (prototypically) the property of another, I propose to call *duties of respect*. This use of the word "respect" is not the only one, but it is, I think, a familiar one. Webster's dictionary puts it thus, ". . . to esteem; value; hence to refrain from obtruding upon or interfering with; as to respect a person's privacy."

The rights correlative with duties of respect are typically negative, that is, rights to other people's abstentions, forebearances, or noninterference, and unlike the rights discussed in our earlier examples, they are what lawyers call *in rem* rather than *in personam* rights. An <u>*in rem* right</u> holds, not against some specific namable person or persons but rather, in the legal phrase, against the world at large. In saying that "the whole world" has a duty to stay off my land, all I can mean, of course, is that any person in a position to enter my property has a duty to stay out. That implies that even General De Gaulle, if I wished to keep him out, would have to stop at my gate. My right *in rem*, in imposing on others a duty of respect, is itself no respecter of persons. ⑦

Are all *in rem* rights negative? There is no denying that negative *in rem* rights, modeled after the proprietary right and then extended to cover personal interests as well, have had an enormous influence on political thought, especially in America. They dominated lists of "natural rights," for example, in various eighteenth-century manifestos. Still there are positive *in rem* rights too, whose importance has come to be appreciated anew only in recent decades. Consider, for example, the duty of care that every citizen is said to owe to any and every person in a position to be injured by his negligence. I have this duty to some degree even to the uninvited trespasser on my land. Or consider the duty (not equally recognized in our law) that every citizen has to come to the aid of accident victims. These unfortunates have a right to be assisted that holds against every or any person in a position to help. I propose to call such positive *in rem* rights, *rights of community membership*, because it is their recognition, more than anything else, that molds a society into a cohesive community.

An eighth class of duties, which I shall call *duties of status*, is perhaps the ⑧ original from which many of the others derive. In the Middle Ages, a "duty" was something <u>due</u> a feudal lord, in virtue of his role and its status in the social system, from one of his inferiors, a vassal or a serf, <u>in virtue of *his* status</u>. A person, in being born into his relatively fixed position in the social order, was at the same time born into the duties that went with, and indeed defined, that position. One's duty was conceived as a kind of payment of one's proper share to the general economy of interests, and of course there were different shares to be extracted from different ranks and stations. Doing one's duty might be paying in crops or livestock, or performing assigned tasks at periodic intervals, or for the higher ranks contributing troops, horses, and weapons. Very likely these payments were made in a spirit similar to that in which club members pay their dues, especially in a club whose rules prescribe different types of payment for different types of members.

It was not difficult, in a rigidly hierarchical society, to know *to whom* one's duty was owed, for payments were generally from lower rank to higher, with the occupant of the higher rank always capable of exacting payment, if necessary, by force. With the decline of feudalism, however, it became increasingly difficult to find a specific claimant for every status duty. Offices and roles, of course, still survived, and carried with them their attached duties, but there was no longer a single clear line of direction in which they were owed, or single source of sanctions for their enforcement. To be sure, later when contract came to supplant status as a primary principle of social organization, one could in theory come to think of the duties of his job as derived from the "employment contract" and therefore *owed as obligations* to the boss, as promisee. This was, however, seldom a convincing myth. Employment contracts were often unfairly bargained, and by the time conditions improved in that respect, the employer was so vast and impersonal he could hardly be conceived as the claimant of a personal obligation. Hence, duties of status have come less and less to be thought of as *owed* to anyone.

The concept of a duty, however, has by no means completely forgotten its past. It still preserves its ancestral connection with offices, stations, and jobs;[4] it is still bound up, however remotely, with the idea of coercion, and it still commonly suggests the idea of a fair share of burdens, imposed on one as a levy, for the promotion of socially shared interests. In group undertakings, it is often said that "if only everybody pitches in and does his *share*, the job will be done." The share we are thereby exhorted to contribute is, of course, the very same as our duty, and it will be greater for the rich than the poor and lesser for the weak than the strong.

Does it still make sense to ask *to whom* one's duty of status is owed? Perhaps, but we can no longer always expect a simple answer mentioning some specific person, such as "one's feudal lord," or "one's employer." To whom does the left tackle on a football team owe his assigned duty to block the player opposing him? In a case like this it is odd to say that the duty is owed to anyone but "the team." And similarly we often hear of status-duties owed "to the company," or "to the university," or "to one's country." And in still other cases, for example the duty of a janitor to sweep the corridors, it might plausibly be urged

---

[4] If the phrase "moral duty," unlike "moral obligation," sounds odd in our ears, it is, I submit, because it suggests that there is an office or job of "man as such"—a most dubious metaphysical idea (*pace* Plato and Aristotle). Generally speaking, it is difficult to find plausible analogies between our moral problems as men and our moral problems as office holders. There are no analogies of this kind to compare with the close analogy between our obligations as contract signers and our moral commitments as promisors. Hence, the appropriateness of the phrase "moral obligation" and the oddness of "moral duty."

that the duty is owed to *no one at all*, although it is no less a duty for that.

Perhaps the most important feature of our talk about duties I have only mentioned up to now, and that is the alliance of the idea of duty with the idea of coercion. A duty, whatever else it be, is something *required* of one. That is to say first of all that a duty, like an obligation, is something that *obliges*. It is something we conceive of as *imposed* upon our inclinations, something we must do *whether we want to or not*. Second, a requirement is, in a perfectly good sense, a *liability*, something *we must do or else* "face the consequences" (punishment, firing, guilt feelings). When the coercive element common to duties and obligations is in clear focus, it is likely to seem so centrally important as to dim the various differences between the two conceptions, as when the lawbooks, for example, speak interchangeably of imposing duties and obligations. Moreover, both terms, "duty" and "obligation," have developed extended senses in which *only* the coercive feature is essential, as when we speak, for example, of an action, fitting perhaps as a "gesture," or symbolic expression of feeling, as a duty when it seems to have a "compelling" appropriateness. "Duty" and "obligation" both tend now to be used for any action we feel we must (for whatever reason) do.

*Duties of compelling appropriateness* are perhaps only duties in an extended sense, but still there is no harm in labeling them and including them in our catalogue.[5] The class probably includes such philosophically puzzling specimens as "duties of perfection," "duties of self-sacrifice," "duties of love," "duties of vicarious gratitude," and so on. It is clear, I think, that people who feel that they have duties of this kind do not feel them as owed to anyone.[6]

In speaking of a duty as a liability, we should take care to distinguish it from another kind of liability also imposed by roles and jobs, namely those that have come to be called *responsibilities*. A responsibility, like a duty, is both a burden and a liability; but unlike a duty it carries considerable discretion (sometimes called "authority") along with it. A goal is assigned and the means of achieving it are left to the independent judgment of the responsible party. Moreover, the liability to unwanted consequences in the case of a responsibility

---

[5] It would be going too far, however, to include "duties of compelling attractiveness," which could be duties in no proper sense, paradigmatic or extended.

[6] H. B. Acton gives several examples of persons who act "on a conception of duty that requires [them] to give benefits to others much in excess of what is [believed to be] their right." "Thus Celia in Eliot's *The Cocktail Party* must have considered she had duties to savages who certainly had no right to services from her. The man who, in Malraux's novel, gave all his supply of poison to his fellow-prisoners to enable them by suicide to escape the burning alive which was to be their fate and his, probably did not think that they had more right to the poison than he had, though he thought it his duty to give it to them. Some of these supererogatory acts may be a form of disguised egoism, the agent regarding himself as worthy of a much stricter code of behaviour than the majority of people. Others are the result of compassion or benevolence, and in that way, perhaps outside the sphere of rights and duties. But some of the more impressive acts of moral heroism appear to be performed at the behest of an exacting sense of duty without their being [I should add 'any sense of'] corresponding rights on the part of the beneficiaries." H. B. Acton, "Symposium on 'Rights'," *Proceedings of the Aristotelian Society*, Supplementary Volume 24 (1950), pp. 107–108.

tends to be "stricter" than in the case of a mere duty. That a man tried his best is more likely to be accepted as an excuse for failure to perform one's duty than for failure to fulfill one's responsibility. Indeed, the more discretion allowed in the responsibility assignment, the stricter the liability for failure is likely to be. In general, the closer the resemblance of a task assignment to the purely non-discretionary cases, where for example, the officer's command "Fire!" imposes the duty to pull the trigger, or where the annual dues notice imposes the duty to pay, the more likely we are to characterize it as a duty, and the less likely to call it a responsibility. A "duty to obey" makes sense; but there could be no such thing as a "responsibility to obey." [7]

This leads us to our final class of duties, the *duties of obedience*. The medieval lord was, in relation to his serf's duty, both beneficiary, claimant, and enforcing authority. In the complication of social roles that followed the collapse of feudalism, the separation of these three offices became common. In particular, the man who can, in some institutions, command the performance of duty from us, and back up his command with sanctions, is not always the same as the person, if there is one, to whom that duty is *owed*. It appears then to be a quite different sense of the preposition "to" in which we have duties *to* a commanding authority. And yet we commonly enough hear talk of "owing obedience" to parents, police officers, and bosses, and these authorities speak readily enough of having a claim to our obedience. Does an authority then have a *right* to be obeyed by his inferiors?

A traffic cop blows his whistle, points, and shouts "Stop!" This, of course, imposes a (legal) duty on a motorist to stop. Still it is not true that the policeman can claim the motorist's stopping as *his* due or that the motorist owes it to *him* to stop. Perhaps the policeman has an *official* right, derived from his status *qua* policeman, rather than a *personal* right, that the motorist stop. I suspect, however, that this is simply a roundabout way of saying that the policeman's office confers on him the authority to command motorists to stop, which of course is beyond question, yet does nothing to settle the further question whether authorities can be said to have a right that persons do as they command. In any case, many duties of obedience are "owed" to impersonal authority like "the law," or a painted stop sign. Here it is especially difficult to find an assignable person who can claim another's stopping as his due. Some duties of obedience, then, seem to entail no correlative rights; and if my suspicion is correct, none of them do. For if the preposition "to" in the phrase "duty (or obedience) to one's superior" means the same as it does in the

---

[7] The title of a current paperback book found in most drugstores is *The Sexual Responsibility of Woman*. The book spends several hundred pages describing the many kinds of situations in married life that call for the exercise of intelligence, judgment, and adaptability on the part of the wife. On the other hand, there could be no doubt what might be meant by a book, published say in Victorian England, with the title *The Sexual Duty of Woman*, for the sexual duty of a wife, if there could be such a thing, could only be to submit. There could be no such thing as a "responsibility to submit." This kind of point was made with great clarity and precision by J. Roland Pennock in "The Problem of Responsibility" in *Nomos III, Responsibility* (New York: Liberal Arts Press, 1960).

expression "answerable to so-and-so for his failure," and I suspect that this is so, then the authority to whom one "owes" obedience is not a *claimant* in the manner of (say) a creditor, but rather simply the one who may properly command performance of duty and apply sanctions in case of failure. The little preposition "to" then is triply ambiguous when used with "duty." One can have a duty *to* his claimant, *to* (or toward) a mere beneficiary, and be liable for failure *to* an authority; but it is only the claimant who can properly be said to have a right to one's performance.

In summary, duties of indebtedness, commitment, reparation, need-fulfillment, and reciprocation are necessarily correlated with other people's *in personam* rights. Duties of respect and community membership are necessarily correlated with other people's *in rem* rights, negative in the case of duties of respect, positive in the case of duties of community membership. Finally, duties of status, duties of obedience, and duties of compelling appropriateness are not necessarily correlated with other people's rights.

## II. RIGHTS AS CLAIMS TO . . .

Having described the various kinds of duties that *are* correlated with rights, have we thereby done all that is necessary to elucidate the concept of a right? Many writers seem to think so.[8] I am inclined, however, to agree with Richard Wasserstrom [9] that we have not until we have said something further about rights as *claims*. It will not help to attempt a formal definition of rights in terms of claims, for the idea of a right is already included in that of a claim, and we would fall into a circle. Nevertheless, certain facts about rights, more easily, if not solely, expressible in the language of claims and claiming, are necessary to a full understanding of what rights are and why they are so vitally important.

There may at first sight be grounds for holding that claims are always *against* someone, and therefore necessarily correlated with the duties of those against whom they hold; but there is a sense of "claim," closely related to "need," in which this is not always so. Imagine a hungry, sickly, fatherless infant, one of a dozen children of a desperately impoverished and illiterate mother in a squalid Mexican slum. Doesn't this child have a *claim* to be fed, to be given medical care, to be taught to read? Can't we know this before we have any idea where correlative duties lie? Won't we still believe it even if

---

[8] Howard Warrender speaks of rights as "merely the shadows cast by [other people's] duties" (*The Political Philosophy of Hobbes* [Oxford, Clarendon Press, 1957], p. 19); S. I. Benn and Richard Peters write that "Right and duty are different names for the same normative relation, according to the point of view from which it is regarded" (*Social Principles and the Democratic State* [London, Allen & Unwin, 1959], p. 89); and Richard Brandt writes that "a society with a language that had no term corresponding to 'a right' might still be said to have the *concept* of a right, if it were recognized that people have the *obligations* toward others which are the ones that correspond with rights" (*Ethical Theory* [Englewood Cliffs, N.J., Prentice-Hall, 1959], p. 441). In his sensitive discussion, Professor Brandt does allow, however, that there are important differences in emphasis and "overtone" between talk of rights and equivalent talk of duties.

[9] "Rights, Human Rights, and Racial Discrimination," *The Journal of Philosophy,* vol. 61 (1964), pp. 628–641.

we despair of finding anyone whose duty it is to provide these things? Indeed, if we do finally *assign* the duty to someone, I suspect we would do so because there *is* this prior claim, looking, so to speak, for a duty to go with it.

In our time it is commonplace to speak of *needs* as "constituting claims." William James thought that every interest is a kind of claim against the world and that the validity of an interest *qua* claim lies "in its mere existence as a matter of fact." [10] This probably goes too far. We don't think of every desire or even every need as a claim, but important needs are another matter. They "cry out," we say, for satisfaction. (Note the etymological connection of "claim" with "clamor.") And when they cry no proper name but only their own need, we speak of their claims "against the world"; but this is but a rhetorical way of saying "claim against no one at all." (Or perhaps a "claim against the world" is like an explosion in the desert—there is no one to hear it, but were anyone to get close to it what a commotion he would hear, and what an impact he would feel! So it is perhaps with my little Mexican urchin. Perhaps her claim is like a "permanent possibility of sensation," real enough, though no one comes within its range. Still note what one does hear, if he is not morally deaf, when he comes close enough: He hears a *crying need*, a claim *to* . . . that is so strong it may be felt as a claim *against*. . . .)

The right to education, like other positive *in rem* rights peculiar to twentieth-century manifestos, has caused much confusion and dissension, partly because theorists, in their eagerness to provide schematic translations for all rights in terms of other people's duties, have simply overlooked the sense of "right" uppermost in the minds of manifesto writers. Professor Brandt, for instance, says of "my having a right to an education" that it "implies roughly that each individual in my community has an obligation to do what he can [in another formulation Brandt says "to cooperate substantially"] in view of his opportunities and capacities and other obligations, to secure and maintain a system in which I and persons in my position are provided with an opportunity for education." [11] But surely there is a familiar sense of "right" that requires more than that others try, or "do what they can" (considering of course how *busy* they all are) or "cooperate substantially." My right in this sense is *to* the education (there is that preposition again in still a fourth sense) and not simply to other people's dutiful efforts. More likely my right in this case (if I have one) entails not simply a duty to try but a responsibility to succeed; but even this doesn't do the whole job of translation, for there is a MUST HAVE here not wholly translatable into any number of MUST DO's. [12]

---

[10] William James, "The Moral Philosopher and the Moral Life," *International Journal of Ethics* (1891), reprinted in *Essays in Pragmatism*, ed. A. Castell (New York, Hafner, 1948), p. 73.
[11] Brandt, *Ethical Theory, op. cit.,* p. 437.
[12] No doubt this is an extended sense of "right." I insist only that it is a proper and important one. Note that there are parallel extended senses of "claim" and "demand" both in quite general circulation. Webster's gives as its fourth sense of "demand," for example, "to call for or require as necessary or useful; to be in urgent need of, as in the phrase 'the case demands care'." It is in this sense, *at the very least*, that children require education, sickness calls for medicine, and hunger demands food.

## III. CLAIMING THAT ONE HAS A RIGHT

I wish finally to emphasize the importance of the verb "to claim," not to the analysis of a right, but to an understanding of why rights are, in Wasserstrom's phrase, such "valuable commodities." [13] To claim that one has a right (or for that matter that one has any of the other things one might claim—knowledge, ability, whatever) is to *assert* in such a manner as to demand or insist that what is asserted be *recognized*. It is my contention that for every right there is a further right to claim, in appropriate circumstances,[14] that one has that right. Why is the right to demand recognition of one's rights so important? The reason, I think, is that if one begged, pleaded, or prayed for recognition merely, at best one would receive a kind of beneficent treatment easily confused with the acknowledgment of rights, but in fact altogether foreign and deadly to it.

There are in general two quite distinct kinds of moral transaction. On the one hand there are gifts and services and favors motivated by love or pity or mercy and for which gratitude is the sole fitting response. On the other hand there are dutiful actions and omissions called for by the rights of other people. These can be demanded, claimed, insisted upon, without embarrassment or shame. When not forthcoming, the appropriate reaction is indignation; and when duly done there is no place for gratitude, an expression of which would suggest that it is not simply one's own or one's due that one was given.[15] Both kinds of transaction are important, and any world with one but not the other would—in Wasserstrom's phrase—be "morally impoverished." A world without loving favors would be cold and dangerous; a world full of kindness, but without universal rights, would be one in which self-respect would be rare

---

13 Wasserstrom, *op. cit.*, p. 629.

14 G. J. Warnock in a useful article ("Claims to Knowledge," *Proceedings of the Aristotelian Society*, Supplementary Volume 36 [1962], p. 21) says that when I claim to others that I *know* something, I am not merely asserting it, but rather I am "obtruding my putative knowledge upon their attention, demanding that it be recognized, that appropriate notice be taken of it by those concerned. . . ." This sounds like the behavior of a perfect boor! I don't wish to contend that all rights confer the additional right to be boorish, but only that one may insist, in the appropriate circumstances and with only an appropriate degree of vehemence, that one's right be recognized.

A list of "appropriate circumstances" would include occasions when one is challenged, when his rights are explicitly denied, when he must make application for them, where his possession seems insufficiently acknowledged or appreciated, etc. There may even be appropriate circumstances for one's demanding recognition of his second-level right to claim ground-level rights; but circumstances would rarely be appropriate for claiming third-level rights, and probably never for levels higher than that. So the contention in the text that for every right there is a right to claim *in appropriate circumstances* that one has that right leads to no kind of vicious regress.

15 The obverse of this point is worth noting too. Gratitude often *is* the appropriate response to a person's deliberate *failure* to press for his rights. I quote from a perceptive editorial in *The New Yorker* (June 3, 1961, p. 23): ". . . Conceivably it is in the national interest to persuade Negro leaders to set a slower pace, but the argument is one that does not permit a high moral tone. One can hardly, with justice, inform a Negro that he has a duty as a citizen to refrain from sharing in the rights of citizenship. We can imagine asking it, under special circumstances, but only as the immense favor that it would be, rather than as the obligation it certainly is not."

and difficult. Too much gratitude is a very bad thing, leading donors to be complacent and hypocritical, and doing worse harm still to the recipients. If the rugged individualist who boasts in his blindness that he owes nothing to any man is no moral paragon, neither is he who feels gratitude for everything, for that is a kind of self-abasement; and from men who respect not their own interests nor feel even their most basic needs as claims, little good, and probably considerable mischief, can be anticipated.

# CHAPTER III

# LEGAL LIABILITY

Traditionally, legal wrongs have been classified under headings so loosely defined as to become themselves a major source of controversy in the field. Crime, for example, has usually been characterized either, in circular fashion, as an 'act or omission that violates penal laws' (i.e. those that carry sanctions of imprisonment or fines paid to the state) or even more vaguely as a 'violation of the rights and interests of the community as a whole'. Since specific criminal prohibitions vary widely from jurisdiction to jurisdiction, the first alternative provides no clear cut definition of crime; with the advent of the nation state and the so-called 'political crime', the second has lent itself to severe abuses of individual rights and long-standing safeguards of the accused (e.g. the notorious 'conspiracy' charge).

A second major domain, 'civil' wrongs, has been distinguished from crime on the basis that the injuries involved are done to private parties and call only for a financial settlement of damages by those held legally responsible. A further line is drawn in this latter sphere between injuries resulting from 'breach of contract' and all others loosely grouped together under the rubric of 'legal torts'. Negligence, the major subdivision within torts (with which this chapter is primarily concerned), has drawn the special attention of legal philosophers in recent years in response both to significant changes in social policy and also to new conceptions of human action which have arisen in contemporary philosophy and psychoanalysis.

The central policy issue in contemporary negligence theory involves the proper assignment of liability for injury. In the older tradition of the common law the burden of proof in negligence cases rested with the injured party. By general rule of thumb, losses were allowed to rest with the injured party unless he could prove:

(1) the defendant's failure to do something which a reasonable and prudent man would do, or the unintentional doing of something which such a person would not do, which constitutes the proximate cause of actual injury;

(2) that he, himself, had in no way been at fault in contributing to his own injury.

A few exceptions to this fault rule were acknowledged on the basis of a limited class of special role responsibilities: those of innkeepers or public carriers for the welfare of their clients, of masters for the acts of their servants, of owners of dangerous chattels for their property, etc.

More recently a second rule of negligence, variously entitled 'absolute' or 'strict' liability, has been expanded on the base of such exceptions to the point where two potentially conflicting negligence standards operate in the field today. A theory of strict liability has never really been adequately formalized and the rule follows from two quite distinct assumptions:

(1) stronger parties should bear the burden of injuries;

(2) liabilities may justly be assigned to parties on the basis of special role responsibilities apart from proximate fault.

Strict liability has become a hotly debated issue between British and American theorists—the former defending the fault criterion, the latter experimenting with new forms of role responsibility.

Since strict liability seems to run against the normal moral intuition that one should only be held responsible when immediately at fault in some respect, it is perhaps only fair that a few words be said in defense of the new rule. It may be unfortunate that strict liability was given that title, or that the practice developed by historical accident from precedents in negligence law. Strictly speaking, what is involved here is not a revised standard of negligence at all but rather a new economic institution, namely, social insurance with all its attendant complexities. In fact, the first major exemplification of so-called strict liability in this country was the Workman's Compensation Law which established corporation responsibility—regardless of fault—for the compensation of workers injured on the job. As the Calabresi and Blum and Kalven selections exemplify, American attention is directed to the balance of broad social interests, not principles of private morality. Should fault be retained as a liability criterion, as a general deterrent to reckless driving? Should drivers, pedestrians or society at large bear the collective burden of insurance? In a recent collection of essays *(Punishment and Responsibility,* Oxford, 1967, pp. 254–55), H. L. A. Hart, however, still defends the older fault rule and cites with approbation a recent British decision absolving from damages the driver of an automobile who severely injured a pedestrian while suffering from automism (an unusual form of temporary unconsciousness). Hart offers no solace to the pedestrian, whereas Americans—whatever the special anomalies of the case in hand—would be concerned with the assignment of collective insurance responsibilities.

On another tack, questions raised by philosophy of mind are also shadowed in contemporary jurisprudence. What constitutes an 'action'? How (if at all) do we read an individual's motives and intentions—his state of mind? Since the latter half of the 19th century jurists have debated whether objective conduct or subjective states of mind should be given primary weight in determining negligence. Americans, following Holmes, have tended to favor the former position, Englishmen, generally, the latter. There are significant practical considerations further complicating the workings of either standard:

(1) Is negligence a simple state or should degrees of responsibility be established, taking into account consequences as well as conduct or mental state to distinguish negligence from recklessness or even criminal negligence carrying penal as well as civil sanctions?

(2) If a guilty state of mind ('*mens rea*') is a necessary criterion for legal sanction, is it also a sufficient one? Should or may individuals be 'punished' for their state of mind apart from an overt criminal act? At first appearance a positive answer to this question would seem a moral abomination. Nevertheless, in the relativistic world of the law cases do arise that verge on punishment for mental crime. The third-time loser may be sentenced to life imprisonment on a lesser charge on the presumption that he is an incorrigible criminal. The mere utterance of a threat against the life of an American President, or a suggestion of bombing a public carrier, may bring severe fines and jail sentences (to the shock of more than a few practical jokers). Involuntary commitment to a mental hospital, while not termed a punishment, may nevertheless constitute a graver evil, being without fixed term, than a major penal sanction. Such issues, by another unfortunate quirk of legal language, have been lumped together under the phrase, 'strict criminal liability', hinting of punishment without fault. The chapter reprinted from the 12th edition of the standard British text, *Salmond on Jurisprudence,* also notes recent philosophical developments in this field; the American contributions reflect new departures in policy speculation and should be read with an imaginative eye to wider implications in related areas, as an example of the early stages of policy in the process of formation.

# 12

# Salmond On Jurisprudence

Sir William Salmond's *Jurisprudence*, a standard British text first published in 1902, has become a collective product in the hands of successive
distinguished editors. The present selection from the 12th edition (1966)
includes both philosophic survey and extensive revision of basic liability
theory by the present editor, P. J. Fitzgerald, M.A., Barrister-at-law of
Lincoln's Inn and Professor of Law in the University of Leeds.

# LIABILITY*

## 80. THE NATURE AND KINDS OF LIABILITY

He who commits a wrong is said to be liable or responsible for it. Liability
or responsibility is the bond of necessity that exists between the wrongdoer and
the remedy of the wrong. Where the remedy is a civil one, the party wronged
has a right to demand the redress allowed by law, and the wrongdoer has a duty
to comply with this demand. In the case of a criminal remedy the wrongdoer is
under a duty to pay such penalty as the law through the agency of the courts
prescribes.[1]

The purpose of this chapter and of the two which follow it is to consider the
general theory of liability. We shall investigate the leading principles which
determine the existence, the incidence, and the measure of responsibility for
wrongdoing. The special rules which relate exclusively to particular kinds of
wrongs will be disregarded.

Liability is in the first place either civil or criminal, and in the second place
either remedial or penal. The nature of these distinctions has been already
sufficiently considered in a previous chapter on the Administration of Justice.[2]
Here it need only be recalled that in the case of penal liability the purpose of the
law, direct or ulterior, is or includes the punishment of a wrongdoer; in the case
of remedial liability, the law has no such purpose at all, its sole intent being the
enforcement of the plaintiff's right, and the idea of punishment being wholly
irrelevant. The liability of a borrower to repay the money borrowed by him
is remedial; that of the publisher of a libel to be imprisoned, or to pay damages
to the person injured by him, is penal. All criminal liability is penal; civil
liability, on the other hand, is sometimes penal and sometimes remedial.

*Sir William Salmond, *Jurisprudence*, first published in 1902, 12th edition edited by P. J.
Fitzgerald, M.A., Sweet & Maxwell, London, 1966, pp. 349–410. Reprinted by permission of
the publisher and editor.
[1] We have already seen that the term liability has another sense in which it is the correlative of
any legal power. *Supra*, § 42.
[2] *Supra*, §§ 14–16.

## 81. THE THEORY OF REMEDIAL LIABILITY

The theory of remedial liability presents little difficulty. It might seem at first sight that, whenever the law creates a duty, it should enforce the specific fulfilment of it. There are, however, several cases where, for various reasons, duties are not specifically enforced. They may be classified as follows:

1. In the first place, there are duties of imperfect obligation—duties the breach of which gives no cause of action, and creates no liability at all, either civil or criminal, penal or remedial. A debt barred by the statute of limitations is a legal debt, but the payment of it cannot be compelled by any legal proceedings.[3]

2. Secondly, there are many duties which from their nature cannot be specifically enforced after having once been broken. When a libel has already been published, or an assault has already been committed, it is too late to compel the wrongdoer to perform his duty of refraining from such acts. Wrongs of this description may be termed transitory; once committed they belong to the irrevocable past. Others, however, are continuing; for example, the non-payment of a debt, the commission of a nuisance, or the detention of another's property. In such cases the duty violated is in its nature capable of specific enforcement, notwithstanding the violation of it.

3. In the third place, even when the specific enforcement of a duty is possible, it may be, or be deemed to be, more expedient to deal with it solely through the criminal law, or through the creation and enforcement of a substitutive sanctioning duty of pecuniary compensation. It is only in special cases, for example, that the law will compel the specific performance of a contract, instead of the payment of damages for the breach of it.

## 82. THE THEORY OF PENAL LIABILITY

We now proceed to the main subject of our inquiry, namely, the general principles of penal liability. We have to consider the legal theory of punishment, in its application both to the criminal law and to those portions of the civil law in which the idea of punishment is relevant and operative. We have already, in a former chapter, dealt with the purposes of punishment, and we there saw that either its end is the protection of society or else that punishment is looked on as an end in itself. We further saw that the aim of protecting society is sought to be achieved by deterrence, prevention and reformation. Of these three methods the first, deterrence, is usually regarded as the primary function of punishment, the others being merely secondary. In our present investigation, therefore, we shall confine our attention to punishment as deterrent. The inquiry will fall into three divisions, relating (1) to the conditions, (2) to the incidence, and (3) to the measure of penal liability.[4]

---

[3] *Supra,* § 43.
[4] Division (1) is considered from this section to § 104; division (2) in § 105; and division (3) in §§ 106 and 107.

The general conditions of penal liability are indicated with sufficient accuracy in the legal maxim, *Actus non facit reum, nisi mens sit rea*—The act alone does not amount to guilt; it must be accompanied by a guilty mind. That is to say, there are two conditions to be fulfilled before penal responsibility can rightly be imposed. The one is the doing of some *act* by the person to be held liable. A man is to be accounted responsible only for what he himself does, not for what other persons do, or for events independent of human activity altogether. The other is the *mens rea* or guilty mind with which the act is done. It is not enough that a man has done some act which on account of its mischievous results the law prohibits; before the law can justly punish the act, an inquiry must be made into the mental attitude of the doer. For although the act may have been objectively wrongful, the mind and will of the doer may have been innocent.

Generally speaking, a man is penally responsible only for those wrongful acts which he does either wilfully or recklessly. Then and only then is the *actus* accompanied by the *mens rea*. But this generalisation is subject to two qualifications. First, the criminal law may include provisions penalising mere negligence, even though this may result simply from inadvertence. Secondly, the law may create offences of strict liability, where guilt may exist without intention, recklessness or even negligence.[5] Where neither *mens rea* nor inadvertent negligence is present, punishment is generally unjustifiable. Hence inevitable accident or mistake—the absence both of wrongful intention or recklessness and of culpable negligence—is in general a sufficient ground of exemption from penal responsibility. *Impunitus est,* said the Romans, *qui sine culpa et dolo malo casu quodam damnum committit.*[6]

We shall consider separately these conditions of liability, analysing, first, the conception of an act, and, secondly, that of *mens rea* in its forms of intention, recklessness and negligence.

### 83. ACTS [7]

The term act is not capable of being defined with any great precision, since in ordinary language it is used at different times to point different contrasts. Acts may be contrasted with natural occurrences, with thoughts, with omissions or with involuntary behaviour. And in any rational system of law we shall expect to find liability attaching to the act rather than to its opposite. We shall not

---

[5] Sir John Salmond regarded inadvertent negligence as a form of *mens rea*. The previous editor preferred to regard inadvertent negligence as outside the scope of *mens rea*, since it is not necessarily a state of mind. See Williams, *Criminal Law* (2nd ed.), s. 14. In so far as it is useful to distinguish crimes of strict liability as crimes requiring no *mens rea*, it is better to include negligence along with intention and recklessness under the general concept.

[6] Gaius, III, 211.

[7] See Dias, *Jurisprudence* (2nd ed.), Chap. 10; Paton, *A Textbook of Jurisprudence* (3rd ed.), Chap. 13; Fitzgerald, "Voluntary and Involuntary Acts" in *Oxford Essays in Jurisprudence* (ed. Guest), 1; Hart, "The Ascription of Responsibility and Rights" (1948–1949) 49 Proc. Arist. Soc. 171; Hart "Acts of Will and Responsibility" in *The Jubilee Lectures* (ed. Marshall), 115.

expect to find a man held liable for gales, thunderstorms and other natural phenomena beyond human control. Nor shall we expect to see him held liable for his thoughts and intentions, which are by themselves harmless, hard to prove and difficult to discipline.

Omissions, on the other hand, may attract liability.[8] An omission consists in not performing an act which is expected of you either because you normally do it or because you ought to do it, and it is the latter type of omission with which the law is concerned. But while omissions incur legal liability where there is a duty to act, such a duty will in most legal systems be the exception rather than the rule, for it would be unduly oppressive and restrictive to subject men to a multiplicity of duties to perform positive acts. It is for this reason that rights *in rem*, which are rights against everyone, are negative and correspond to duties not to do something rather than to duties to confer positive benefits on the holder of such rights.

The most important distinction for legal purposes, however, is that between voluntary and involuntary acts. Examples of the latter are (1) activities outside normal human control, *e.g.*, the beating of one's heart; (2) automatic reflexes, such as sneezes and twitches, which, though normally spontaneous, can sometimes with difficulty be controlled; and (3) acts performed by persons suffering from some abnormal condition, *e.g.*, acts done in sleep, under hypnosis or in the course of a fit of automatism. In so far as a man cannot help committing acts in these categories, it would be unjust and unreasonable that he should be penalised for them; and in common law such a man would normally be regarded as not having committed the *actus reus* of an offence. Since the majority of these involuntary acts (*e.g.*, those in categories (1) and (2)) are harmless while the rest (*e.g.*, those in category (3)) are rare, the law relating to them is relatively undeveloped. Difficulty arises, however, where a man performs some dangerous act which is involuntary but which he might have avoided committing if he had not allowed himself to fall into such a condition as to be liable to behave in this involuntary way. On the one hand there is no *actus reus* for which to hold him liable but on the other hand he ought to be held responsible for the state into which he permitted himself to fall. What is needed is a general provision to the effect that the involuntariness of the defendant's behaviour shall constitute a defence to a criminal charge unless it is the result of previous deliberate or negligent conduct on his part.[9]

Now one attempt to provide an account of what distinguishes voluntary from involuntary acts is made by the theory which regards an act as being divisible into (1) a willed muscular contraction, (2) its circumstances and (3) its

---

[8] See Hughes, "Criminal Omissions" (1957–58) 67 Yale L.J. 590.
[9] Recent developments show that the courts intend to restrict the defence of automatism and that they are inclined to assimilate it as far as possible to insanity in many cases: *R.* v. *Kemp* (1957) 1 Q.B. 399, *Bratty* v. *Att.-Gen. for Northern Ireland* (1963) A.C. 386. See also Williams, *Criminal Law* (2nd ed.), s. 157; Edwards, "Automatism and Criminal Responsibility" (1958) 21 M.L.R. 375.

consequences.[10] In its true sense a voluntary act is said to consist in a willed muscular contraction, which incurs moral or legal liability only by virtue of the circumstances in which it is committed or the consequences which it produces. An involuntary act is regarded therefore as one where the muscular contraction is not willed, its involuntariness consisting precisely in this absence of willing.

This theory, however, creates more difficulties than it solves. In the first place, it rest on dubious psychology. If we consider and examine ordinary examples of what are usually described as acts, we shall fail to find evidence of anything in the nature of a prior act of willing or of desiring either the muscular contraction or its consequences. Abnormal cases, where people find themselves unable to perform actions, may display the actor as willing, setting himself to do the action, contracting his muscles and so on, but the important thing to remember is that these are abnormal cases; we cannot necessarily infer that what occurs in the abnormal must also occur in the normal instance.

Secondly, the theory is utterly inappropiate for the problem of omissions. These negative acts can be either voluntary or involuntary. I may fail to perform an act required by law through forgetfulness or by design; for example I may just forget to make a return of income to the tax authorities, or I may refuse to do so. Alternatively, my failure to carry out my legal duty may result from some condition which prevents me: I may fail to rescue my child from danger because I have fallen asleep or because I am suffering from a fit of epileptic automatism. But in neither case is there any question of muscular contractions; and consequently we cannot contend that the difference between the two kinds of omission is that a muscular contraction was willed in the first case and unwilled in the second.

The different kinds of involuntary behaviour are indeed linked by a common feature, but this consists not in the absence of an actual exercise of will but in the lack of ability to control one's behaviour. If I just forget to file a return of income, my omission will not qualify as involuntary because I could have filed a return had I remembered. We may say then that involuntary acts are those where the actor lacks the power to control his actions, and involuntary omissions are those where the actor's lack of power to control his actions renders him unable to do the act required.

Thirdly, and quite apart from failing to explain the nature of the difference between voluntary and involuntary behaviour, the theory imposes on the meaning of the term *act* a limitation which seems no less inadmissible in law than contrary to the common usage of speech. We habitually include all material and relevant circumstances and consequences under the name of the act. The act of the murderer is the shooting or poisoning of his victim, not merely the muscular contractions by which this result is effected. To trespass on another man's land is a wrongful act, but the act includes the circumstance that the land belongs to

---

[10] This theory, derived from Thomas Brown, was held by Austin, Stephen and Holmes amongst others, and has greatly influenced criminal law theory on this point. See Austin, *Lectures on Jurisprudence*, Lecture 18; Stephen, *A General View of the Criminal Law of England*, Chap. 5; Holmes, *The Common Law*, 54, 91.

another man, no less than the bodily movements by which the trespasser enters upon it. An act has no *natural* boundaries, any more than an event or place has. Its limits must be artificially defined for the purpose in hand for the time being. It is for the law to determine, in each particular case, what circumstances and what consequences shall be counted within the compass of the act with which it is concerned. To ask what act a man has done is like asking in what place he lives.

### 84. TWO CLASSES OF WRONGFUL ACTS

Every wrong is an act which is mischievous in the eye of the law—an act to which the law attributes harmful consequences. These consequences, however, are of two kinds, being either actual or merely anticipated. In other words, an act may be mischievous in two ways—either in its actual results or in its tendencies. Hence it is that legal wrongs are of two kinds. The first consists of those in which the act is wrongful only by reason of accomplished harm which in fact ensues from it. The second consists of those in which the act is wrongful by reason of its mischievous tendencies, as recognised by the law, irrespective of the actual issue. In the first case there is no wrong or cause of action without proof of actual damage; in the second case it is sufficient to prove the act itself, even though in the event no harm has followed it.

For example, if A breaks his contract with B, it is not necessary for B to prove that he was thereby disappointed in his reasonable expectations, or otherwise suffered actual loss, for the law takes notice of the fact that breach of contract is an act of mischievous tendency, and therefore treats it as wrongful irrespective of the actual issue. The loss, if any, incurred by B is relevant to the measure of damages, but not to the existence of a cause of action. So if I walk across another man's field, or publish a libel upon him, I am responsible for the act without any proof of actual harm resulting from it. For trespass and libel belong to the class of acts which are judged wrongful in respect of their tendencies, and not merely in respect of their results. In other cases, on the contrary, actual damage is essential to the cause of action. Slander, for example, is in general not actionable without proof of some loss sustained by the plaintiff, although libel is actional *per se*. So if by negligent driving I expose others to the risk of being run over, I am not deemed guilty of any civil wrong until an accident actually happens. The dangerous tendency of the act is not in this case considered a sufficient ground of civil liability.

With respect to this distinction between wrongs which do and those which do not, require proof of actual damage, it is to be noticed that criminal wrongs commonly belong to the latter class. Criminal liability is usually sufficiently established by proof of some act which the law deems dangerous in its tendencies, even though the issue is in fact harmless. The formula of the criminal law is usually: "If you do this, you will be held liable in all events", and not: "If you do this you will be held liable if any harm ensues". An unsuccessful attempt is a ground of criminal liability, no less than a completed offence. So also dangerous and careless driving are criminal offences, though no danger ensues[11]. This, however, is not invariably so, for criminal responsibility, like civil, sometimes depends on the accident of the event. If I am negligent in the use of firearms, and kill some one in consequence, I am criminally liable for manslaughter; but if by good luck my negligence results in no accomplished mischief, I am free from all responsibility.

As to civil liability, no corresponding general principle can be laid down. In some cases proof of actual damage is required, while in other cases there is no such necessity; and the matter pertains to the detailed exposition of the law, rather than to legal theory. It is to be noted, however, that whenever this requirement exists, it imports into the administration of civil justice an element of capriciousness from which the criminal law is commonly free. In point of criminal responsibility men are judged by their acts and by the mischievous tendencies of them, but in point of civil liability they are often judged by the actual event. If I attempt to execute a wrongful purpose, I am criminally responsible whether I succeed or not; but my civil liability will often depend upon the accident of the result. Failure in a guilty endeavour amounts to innocence. Instead of saying: "Do this, and you will be held accountable for it", the civil law often says: "Do this if you wish, but remember that you do it at your peril, and if evil consequences chance to follow, you will be answerable for them."

### 85. DAMNUM SINE INJURIA

Although all wrongs are, in fact or in legal theory, mischievous acts, the converse is not true. All damage done is not wrongful. There are cases in which the law will suffer a man knowingly and wilfully to inflict harm upon another, and will not hold him accountable for it. Harm of this description—mischief that is not wrongful because it does not fulfil even the material conditions of responsibility—is called *damnum sine injuria*, the term *injuria* being here used in its true sense of an act contrary to law (*in jus*), not in its modern and currupt sense of harm.

Cases of *damnum sine injuria* fall under two heads. There are, in the first place, instances in which the harm done to the individual is nevertheless a gain to society at large. The wrongs of individuals are such only because, and only so far as, they are at the same time the wrongs of the whole community; and so far as this coincidence is imperfect, the harm done to an individual is *damnum sine injuria*. The special result of competition in trade may be ruin to many; but the general result is, or is deemed to be, a gain to society as a whole. Competitors, therefore, do each other harm but not injury. So a landowner may do many things on his own land which are detrimental to the interests of adjoining proprietors. He may so excavate his land to withdraw the support required by the buildings on the adjoining property; he may prevent the

[11] Road Traffic Act, 1960, ss. 2–3.

access of light to the windows of those buildings; he may drain away the water which supplies his neighbour's well. These things are harmful to individuals; but it is held to serve the public interest to allow a man, within wide limits, to do as he pleases with his own.[12]

The second head of *damnum sine injuria* includes all those cases in which, although real harm is done to the community, yet, owing to its triviality, or to the difficulty of proof, or to any other reason, it is considered inexpedient to attempt its prevention by the law. The mischief is of such a nature that the legal remedy would be worse than the disease.[13]

## 86. THE PLACE AND TIME OF AN ACT

Chiefly, though not exclusively, in consequence of the territorial limits of the jurisdiction of courts, it is often material to determine the place in which an act is done. In general this inquiry presents no difficulty, but there are two cases which require special consideration. The first is that in which the act is done partly in one place and partly in another. If a man standing on the English side of the Border fires at and kills a man on the Scottish side, has he committed murder in England or in Scotland? If a contract is made by correspondence between a merchant in London and another in Paris, is the contract made in England or in France. If by false representations made in Melbourne a man obtains goods in Sydney, is the offence of obtaining goods by false pretences committed in Victoria or in New South Wales? As a matter of fact and of strict logic the correct answer in all these cases is that the act is not done either in the one place or in the other. He who in England shoots a man in Scotland commits murder in Great Britain, regarded as a unity, but not in either of its parts taken in isolation. But no such answer is allowable in law; for, so long as distinct territorial areas of jurisdiction are recognised, the law must assume that it is possible to determine with respect to every act the particular area within which it is committed.

What locality, therefore, does the law attribute to acts which thus fall partly within one territorial division and partly within another? There are three possible answers. It may be said that the act is committed in both places, or solely in that in which it has its commencement, or solely in that in which it is completed. The law is free to choose such one of these three alternatives as it thinks fit in the particular case. The last of them seems to be that which is adopted for most purposes. It has been held that murder is committed in the place in which the death occurs,[14] and not also in the place in which the act

[12] For the relevance of evil motive, see *infra*, § 93.
[13] In the sphere of criminal law only certain acts are made crimes, all other harmful kinds of conduct belonging to the class of *damnum sine injuria*. It is disputed whether a similar principle holds true of tort, or whether there is a general theory of tortious liability for harmful acts. See Winfield, *Textbook of the Law of Tort* (7th ed.), 13; Goodhart, "The Foundation of Tortious Liability" (1938) 2 M.L.R. 1; Williams, "The Foundation of Tortious Liability" (1939) 7 C.L.J. 111.
[14] *Reg.* v. *Coombes* (1786) 1 Lea.Cr.C. 388.

causing the death is done, but the law on these points is not free from doubt.[15] A contract is made in the place where it is completed, that is to say, where the offer is accepted[16] or the last necessary signature to the document is affixed.[17] The offence of obtaining goods by false pretences is committed in the place in which the goods are obtained[18] and not in the place where the false pretence is made.[19]

A second case in which the determination of the locality of an act gives rise to difficulty is that of negative acts. In what place does a man omit to pay a debt or to perform a contract? The true answer is apparently that a negative act takes place where the corresponding positive act *ought* to have taken place. An omission to pay a debt occurs in the place where the debt is payable.[20] If I make in England a contract to be performed in France, my failure to perform it takes place in France and not in England. The presence of a negative act is the absence of the corresponding positive act, and the positive act is absent from the place in which it ought to have been present.

## The Time of an Act

The position of an act in time is determined by the same considerations as its position in space. An act which begins today and is completed tomorrow is in truth done neither today nor tomorrow, but in that space of time which includes both. But if necessary the law may date it from its commencement, or from its completion, or may regard it as continuing through both periods. For most purposes the date of an act is the date of its completion, just as its place is the place of its completion.[21]

[15] *Reg.* v. *Armstrong* (1875) 13 Cox C.C. 184; *Reg.* v. *Keyn* (1876) 2 Ex.D. 63. Berge, "Criminal Jurisdiction and the Territorial Principle" (1932) 30 Mich.L.Rev. 238, argues that every state in which part of the act or its consequence occurs has or should have concurrent jurisdiction. See also Hanbury in (1951) 37 Trans. Grotius Society 171.
[16] *Cowan* v. *O'Connor* (1888) 20 Q.B.D. 640.
[17] *Muller & Co's Margarine Ltd.* v. *Inland Revenue Commissioners* (1900) 1 Q.B. 310; (1901) A.C. 217.
[18] *Reg.* v. *Ellis* (1899) 1 Q.B. 230; *R.* v. *Harden* (1963) 1 Q.B. 8.
[19] The question is fully discussed in the case of *Reg.* v. *Keyn* (1876) 2 Ex. D. 63, in which the captain of a German steamer was tried in England for manslaughter by negligently sinking an English ship in the Channel and drowning one of the passengers. One of the minor questions in the case was that of the place in which the offence was committed. Was it on board the English ship or on board the German steamer, or on board neither of them? Four of the Judges of the Court for Crown Cases Reserved, namely, Denman J., Bramwell B., Coleridge C. J. and Cockburn C.J., agreed that if the offence had been wilful homicide it would have been committed on the English ship. Denman J. and Coleridge C. J. applied the same rule to negligent homicide. Cockburn C. J. doubted as to negligent homicide. Bramwell B. said (p. 150): "If the act was wilful, it is done where the will intends it should take effect: aliter when it is negligent". For a further discussion of the matter, see Stephen's *History of Criminal Law*, II. 9–12, and Oppenhoff's annotated edition of the *German Criminal Code* (13th ed. 1896) 28. The German doctrine is that an act is committed in the place where it is begun. See also Terry, *Principles of Anglo-American Law*, 598–606, and *Edmundson* v. *Render* (1905) 2 Ch. 320.
[20] *Northey Stone Co.* v. *Gidney* (1894) 1 Q.B. 99.
[21] If the law dates the commission of a wrong from the completion of it, it follows that there are cases in which a man may commit a wrong after his death. If A excavates his own land so as to cause, after an interval, the subsidence of the adjoining land of B, there is no wrong done until the subsidence happens: *Backhouse* v. *Bonomi* (1861) 9 H.L.C. 503; *Darley Mail Colliery Co.* v. *Mitchell* (1886) 11 App.Cas. 127. What shall be said, then, if A is dead in the meantime? The

A negative act is done at the time at which the corresponding positive act ought to have been done. The date of the nonpayment of a debt is the day on which it becomes payable.

## 87. CAUSATION [22]

A system of law, as we have seen, may hold a man liable either for performing acts which are dangerous in tendency or for causing actual damage or injury. In the latter type of case liability is imposed on him for the damage in fact resulting from his act; he will not normally be held accountable for damage in no way caused by his own behaviour. Causation then is a concept which plays an important part in legal discourse.

It is, however, a difficult concept, and the common law cases on causation do not make the discussion of the problem any easier. For though courts readily agree that such questions must be decided on common-sense principles rather than on the basis of abstruse philosophical theory, the language which they use in actually deciding them is often of a highly metaphorical and figurative character, owing little to common sense or common speech. So intractable at times has the problem of causation seemed, that there is a temptation to suggest that lawyers should discard inquiries into causation and concentrate rather on the question of responsibility. Instead of investigating whether the defendant's act was the cause of the plaintiff's injuries, they should inquire whether the defendant ought to be held responsible; and this type of question can be answered, it is said, according to policy and without regard to the conceptual difficulties inherent in the notion of cause.[23]

Tempting as this suggestion is, it offers hopes which are in fact illusory. It is hard to see how questions of responsibility can be decided without first deciding questions of causation. If A carelessly drops a lighted match on the floor of B's house and the house is burned to the ground, we should not hold A liable if it transpired that C had simultaneously been setting fire to another part of the house or that the house had at that very moment been struck by lightning. If A is to be held responsible for the damage to B's house, he must first be shown to have caused it. Indeed the idea of compensation is that of making amends for damage which one has *caused* to another, not that of being an insurer of all the damage which may befall that other from any cause. Similar principles obtain in the criminal law. If X shoots at Y and Y falls dead, we should not, despite X's wrongful intention, convict him of the murder or manslaughter of Y if we found that the death had been caused by a shot fired from

wrong, it seems, is not done by his successors in title: *Hall* v. *Duke of Norfolk* (1900) 2 Ch. 493; *Greenwell* v. *Low Beechburn Colliery* (1897) 2 Q.B. 165. The law, therefore, must hold either that there is no wrong at all, or that it is committed by a man who is dead at the date of its commission.

[22] The leading monograph on the subject is Hart and Honoré, *Causation in the Law;* see also by the same authors articles of the same title in (1956) 72 L.Q.R. 58, 260, 398, and further discussion by Williams in "Causation in the Law" (1961) C.L.J. 62.

[23] See expressions of this view quoted by Hart and Honoré (1956) 72 L.Q.R. 58. See also Hart and Honoré, *Causation in the Law*, 3–7, 83–102, 230–276.

some other gun or by a sudden heart attack occurring before the shot was fired.

But while in criminal and civil cases responsibility often depends on causation, no rule of logic dictates this principle. In logic other solutions are equally possible. In civil law a man could be held liable to another whenever he is careless and regardless of whether he has caused damage to him or not. In criminal law a man could be held equally guilty whether he has succeeded or not in his intentions. But this is not the position adopted by the common law.

Now the legal concept of causation is often said to be based on the common sense notion of cause. On this point three observations may be made. First, while this notion   plays a considerable part in common speech, common speech itself provides no neat analysis of the concept. We can look to common sense for the usage of the term *cause* but not for an explanatory description of this usage; the latter is to be found by philosophical reflection on such usage. Consequently in so far as the legal concept is built on the foundation of the ordinary notion, it is built on a notion which has not been explicitly defined or analysed by common sense. Secondly, the legal concept, though based on the ordinary notion, will diverge from it on account of the need for lawyers to provide answers to questions for which common sense has no solution. If A wrongfully loads B's luggage on the wrong train and the train is derailed and the luggage damaged, has A caused this damage? This is not the sort of question which arises in ordinary day-to-day conversation, nor is it one which could be readily answered according to the ordinary notion of causation. It is, however, just the sort of problem that courts and lawyers have to grapple with.

Thirdly, a distinction must be drawn between explanatory and attributive inquiries, both of which are involved in causal investigations. If a house has been burnt down, the main point of an inquiry may be to discover how this happened; if a man is found dead, the *post mortem* inquiry serves to investigate what he died of. This sort of explanatory inquiry is complete when all the facts leading up to the incident have been discovered. The inquiry about the house in the example above would be complete once we knew the house was full of inflammable gas, that a stone was thrown through the window, and that its impact on the floor inside caused a spark which ignited the gas. The *post mortem* would be complete if it was established that the man had been stabbed, that he had been taken to hospital and injected with an antibiotic to which he was allergic and that the injection had set up a fatal reaction. But attributive inquiries begin where explanations leave off. Once we know what happened to the house, we are now in a position to ask whether the conflagration was caused by the throwing of the stone. Once we know how the man died, we can inquire whether the stabbing caused the death. And here the scientist, the pathologist and the detective can no longer assist, for at this stage we no longer need more facts; we need to assess the situation in the light of the facts we have.

Now law courts often have to engage in both kinds of investigation. First, evidence may have to be heard to establish how the accident happened. Then in the light of its findings of fact, a court may have to decide whether the defendant's act or omission should be regarded as the cause of the plaintiff's damage or the victim's injury; and it is this second sort of question which constitutes the legal question about causation and which involves the problem of defining what counts as a cause for legal purposes. Typically the lawyer is concerned to decide whether, in a case where damage results to B from a conjunction of A's act and some other circumstance, as in the examples given, A can be said to have caused the damage. Here the legal problem is to discover the criteria for asserting that the additional circumstance prevents the act from being the cause of the damage; and this is another facet of the general problem of finding out the criteria for regarding one event as the cause of another, because where some combining circumstance prevents an act from qualifying as the cause of some resulting damage, such a circumstance will usually itself be regarded as the cause.

Ordinarily, where some event results from a combination of factors and we wish to identify one of these factors as the cause, we fasten on two different types of occurrence which we tend to regard as causes. We look upon (a) abnormal factors and (b) human acts (and perhaps those of animals) as causes. If a house burns down, the fire obviously results from a combination of factors, one of which is the presence of oxygen. This, however, would not be regarded as the cause of the fire unless its presence was abnormal in the circumstances. A fire in a laboratory might be said to be caused by the presence of oxygen, if this was a part of the laboratory from which oxygen was generally excluded and into which oxygen was introduced by accident. But what will be considered to be the cause of the burning of the house is, not the presence of oxygen, but either some unusual event or circumstance (*e.g.*, an electrical short-circuit) or else some human act (*e.g.*, the setting fire to the house by some person).

Why it is that abnormal events and human acts are regarded as causes *par excellence* is more a question for philosophy than for jurisprudence, but where either of such factors is to be found, it is clear that a special point has been reached by any investigation. For once either of these has been detected, we have a factor which we can seek to eliminate from future situations, thereby avoiding such incidents later on, and part of the point of identifying such factors as causes is to single them out as final stopping-places of the inquiry.

In law, where we have the typical problem of deciding whether event A is the cause of event B or whether "the chain of causation has been snapped" by some *novus actus interveniens*, X, we may expect to find that the event X is regarded as severing the causal connection wherever X is either some abnormal circumstance or some deliberate human act. If A stabs B and B is taken to hospital, where, despite the fact that he is shown to be allergic to terramycin, he is nevertheless injected with a large dose of it, then his treatment and not the stab wound would qualify in common law as the cause of B's death; for the treatment was quite abnormal in the circumstances.[24] Or if on his way to hospital B had

[24] As in the case of *R. v. Jordan* (1956) 40 Cr.App.R. 152. *Cf. R. v. Smith* (1959) 2 Q.B. 35, where subsequent treatment combined with the previous injury to cause the victim's death but where such treatment was not wholly abnormal and therefore did not operate to break the causal connection between the wound given by the accused and the victim's death.

been strangled by C, here again A's attack would be prevented from being the cause; for the cause of the death would now be C's deliberate act.

Many of the reported cases appear to work on these principles without explicitly acknowledging them. Where an abnormal circumstance or event is not held to sever the causal connection, it will usually be found that the circumstance, though abnormal, was known to the defendant, who sought to take advantage of it. As the law puts it, intended consequences are never too remote. A difficult case to fit into any theory is that of *Re Polemis*,[25] where the defendants were held liable for damage resulting from a combination of factors. The defendants' servant carelessly dropped a plank into the ship's hold, the plank struck a spark, and the spark ignited petrol vapour whose presence in the hold was unsuspected. The defendants were held liable for the loss by fire of the ship. Hart and Honoré suggested that while an abnormal circumstance or event normally "snaps the chain of causation", an abnormal circumstance will only do so if its occurrence is subsequent to the defendant's act and not if it is simultaneous with it. Here the abnormal circumstance, the presence of the vapour, already existed before the defendants' servant dropped the plank. But *Re Polemis* has since been disapproved by the Privy Council in the case of the *Wagon Mound*,[26] which, it seems, will be taken as depriving the former case of any binding authority in English law.[27] It seems then that any abnormal circumstance contributing to the result may sever the causal connection, regardless of the time of its occurrence. To this there is one exception, enshrined in the common law rule that you must take the plaintiff as you find him. If you wrongfully injure someone and it turns out that he has some condition of which you are unaware and which renders the injury more serious, you will nevertheless be held responsible for all the damage suffered. If you wilfully or negligently bump into a man who, unknown to you, has an egg-shell skull and who thereby suffers grave injury, you are liable for all the injury suffered. Where the abnormal circumstance consists in a condition of the plaintiff himself, it will not sever the causal link, for in this respect the law takes the view that if you injure people by negligence or by design, then you act at your peril.[28]

Cases in which the alleged *novus actus interveniens* consists of some human act are often cases in which the defendant contends that the plaintiff himself caused the damage which he suffered. The decisions on these and other cases on this problem suggest that though the courts regard a human act by the plaintiff or some third party as preventing the defendant's act from being the cause, they will not so regard an act (whether by the plaintiff or a third party) as severing the causal link if this act was in some way not wholly free. If, as in the rescue cases, the act was done out of a legal or a moral duty; if the act was forced on the plaintiff by the danger in which the defendant placed him; or if

[25] [1921] 3 K.B. 560.
[26] [1961] A.C. 388.
[27] See *Doughty* v. *Turner Manufacturing Co. Ltd.* [1964] 1 Q.B. 518: *Smith* v. *Leech Brain & Co. Ltd.* [1962] 2 Q.B. 405.
[28] Salmond, *Torts* (14th ed.), 719–720.

the act was an automatic and natural reaction—in such cases it will not suffice to prevent the defendant's act from counting as the cause of the damage.

## 88. MENS REA

We have seen that the conditions of penal liability are sufficiently indicated by the maxim, *Actus non facit reum, nisi mens sit rea.* A man is responsible, not for his acts in themselves, but for his acts coupled with the *mens rea* or guilty mind with which he does them. Before imposing punishment, the law must be satisfied of two things: first, that an act has been done which by reason of its harmful tendencies or results is fit to be repressed by way of penal discipline; and secondly, that the mental attitude of the doer towards his deed was such as to render punishment effective as a deterrent for the future, and therefore just. The form which *mens rea* assumes will depend on the provisions of the particular legal system. Criminal liability may require the wrongful act to be done intentionally or with some further wrongful purpose in mind, or it may suffice that it was done recklessly; and in each case the mental attitude of the doer is such as to make punishment effective. If he intentionally chose the wrong, penal discipline will furnish him with a sufficient motive to choose the right instead for the future. If, on the other hand, he committed the forbidden act without wrongful intent, but yet realising the possibility of the harmful result, punishment will be an effective inducement to better conduct in the future.

Yet there are other cases in which, for sufficient or insufficient reasons, the law is content with a lower form of *mens rea*. This is the case, as was already noticed, with crimes of negligence.[29] A person may be held responsible for some crimes if he did not do his best as a reasonable man to avoid the consequence in question. Sometimes, however, the law goes even beyond this; holding a man responsible for his acts, independently altogether of any wrongful state of mind or culpable negligence. Wrongs which are thus independent of fault may be distinguished as wrongs of *strict liability*.

It follows that in respect of the requirments of fault, wrongs are of three kinds:—

(1) Intentional or Reckless Wrongs, in which the *mens rea* amounts to intention, purpose, design, or at least foresight. In such wrongs defences like mistake operate to negative the existence of *mens rea*.

(2) Wrongs of Negligence, in which the *mens rea* assumes the less serious form of mere carelessness, as opposed to wrongful intent or foresight. With these wrongs defences such as mistake will only negative *mens rea* if the mistake itself is not negligent.

---

[29] Sir John Salmond regarded inadvertent negligence as a form of *mens rea*, although inadvertent negligence does not require any particular state of mind; and this is surely reasonable, since negligent offences differ sharply from offences not requiring *mens rea*, *i.e.*, offences of strict liability, which make no allowance for the fact that the accused may have had no fair chance of conforming to the law's requirements; offences of negligence penalise those who ought to have and could have conformed and were therefore at fault.

(3) Wrongs of Strict Liability, in which the *mens rea* is not required, neither wrongful intent nor culpable negligence being recognised as a necessary condition of responsibility; and here defences like mistake are of no avail.

We shall deal with these three classes of wrongs, and these three forms of liability, in the order mentioned.

## 89. INTENTION [30]

An intention is the purpose or design with which an act is done. This may consist of an intention to perform some further act, an intention to bring about certain consequences or perhaps merely an intention to do the act itself. My intention in buying a gun may be to kill someone with it; my intention in shooting at him may be to cause his death; but if the latter act is described not as shooting at him but as killing him, then my intention can be said to be to do this very thing, to kill him.

An unintentional act is one lacking such purpose or design. To do something unintentionally is to do it without meaning to do it. Through inadvertence I may disregard a traffic signal; through forgetfulness I may omit to pay a debt. An act such as killing, which consists of a cause and an effect, may be unintentional when the actor brings about consequences which he does not intend. I may shoot X dead by accident, being unaware that the wind will alter the direction of my shot. I may kill him by mistake, wrongly imagining him to be someone else. In the former case I fail to foresee the consequences, in the latter I am ignorant of some of the circumstances.

Whether an act is to be termed intentional or unintentional must depend partly on the description of the act itself. If in the latter case above my act is described as shooting at X, then it qualifies as intentional. If it is described as killing X, it must qualify as unintentional, for I did not intend to kill X. In a sense such acts are partly intentional and partly unintentional, and many acts fall into this category. If I trespass on A's land believing it to be my own, I intend to enter upon land which in fact belongs to A but I do not intend to enter-upon-land-belonging-to-A. If a woman marries again during the lifetime of her husband believing him to be dead, she does not commit bigamy, for though she intends to marry again while her husband is in fact alive, she does not intend to marry-again-during-her-husband's-lifetime. Where an act is in part intentional and in part unintentional, liability, if it exists at all, must either be absolute or be based on recklessness or negligence.

Where the intention consists of an intention to produce certain consequences, this is sometimes explained as a combination of foresight and desire.[31] But while intended consequences must be foreseen—for one cannot aim at a

---

[30] See Passmore and Heath, "Intentions" (1955) 29 Arist.Soc.Supp. 131; Anscombe, "Intention" (1956–57) 57 Proc.Arist.Soc. 321. Legal writers have often defined intention as consisting of foresight of consequences together with a desire of such consequences: *e.g.*, Holmes, *The Common Law*, 53; Salmond, *Jurisprudence* (7th ed.), § 133.
[31] *Supra*, note *(d)*.

consequence which is unforeseen—the converse is not true. Consequences can be foreseen without being intended. A doctor may administer certain treatment, knowing that it will be painful but that it will cure the patient. To show that in such a case the doctor cannot be said (without further evidence) to intend to cause the patient pain, we may construct another example where the pain would be intended. Suppose for instance that the doctor pricks the patient's skin to test his perception of pain: here there is a deliberate intention to cause pain as a means to some further end.

Where a consequence is expected, it is usually intended but this need not be the case. An operating surgeon may know very well that his patient will probably die of the operation; yet he does not intend the fatal consequence which he expects. He intends the recovery which he hopes for but does not expect.

Consequences which are intended are normally also expected, but this is not always so. One can be said to intend a consequence which is foreseen as possible but highly improbable. If I fire a rifle in the direction of a man a mile away, I may know perfectly well that the chance of hitting him is not one in a thousand; I may fully expect to miss him; nevertheless I intend to hit him if this is what I am trying to do.

Finally intention is not identical with desire. I may desire something with all my heart, but unless I do something by way of aiming at it I cannot be said to intend it. Conversely I can be said to intend something without desiring it. A thing may be intended, not for its own sake but merely as the means to an end. Here the end is intended and desired, while the means, though intended may perhaps not be desired; indeed it may be utterly indifferent to me or even undesired. If I kill a man in order to rob him, it may be that I do not desire his death but would much prefer to be able to achieve my objective in some other way. The doctor who inflicts pain to test for pain perception will not normally have an actual desire to inflict pain but will on the contrary regret the necessity of it.

We have seen that consequences which are foreseen as certain or highly probable need not be, but usually are, intended. A system of law, however, could provide that a man be held liable for such consequences, even though he did not intend them. In the first place, such a rule would obviate the need for difficult inquiries into the mental element. But secondly, and more important, the rule could be justified on the ground that a man should not do acts which he foresees will involve consequential harm to others, whether or not he intends to cause this harm. Such behaviour is clearly reckless or blameworthy, unless the risk can be justified by reason of the social interest of the act itself. An operation which is known to be likely to prove fatal will be justifiable if it is carried out to remedy some highly dangerous condition; it would hardly be justified if performed simply to remove a birthmark or scar. With regard to murder English law adopts the rule that a person is responsible for consequences foreseen as the certain or highly probable outcome of his act, regardless of whether he intended them. Thus, if I do an act which I know is very likely to kill Smith and he dies as a result, I cannot be heard to say that I did not intend his death. Indeed the law has gone further and provided that one may be liable for consequences foreseeable by the reasonable man as certain or highly probable, whether or not the actor himself foresaw them.[32] Thus if I intentionally do some unlawful act on a man which I do not realise, but which a reasonable man would realise, is highly likely to cause death or serious injury to him, this is enough to render me guilty of murder if he dies. In this respect foreseen, and even foreseeable consequences, are put on the same footing as consequences which are intended.

This, however, does not apply to cases involving mere knowledge of statistical probability where there is no certainty in the concrete instance. A manufacturer establishes a factory in which he employs many workmen who are daily exposed to the risk of dangerous machinery or processes. He knows for a certainty that from time to time fatal accidents will, notwithstanding all precautions, occur to the workmen so employed. A military commander orders his troops into action, well knowing that many of them will lose their lives. Such consequences are certainly not intended and would hardly qualify as the result of recklessness. For it is not necessarily reckless to incur a risk if an adequate social advantage is to be gained from the enterprise.

Both in this special connection and generally then it is to be observed that the law may, and sometimes does, impute liability, outside the strict definition of intention, for what is called constructive intention. Consequences which are in fact the outcome of negligence merely are sometimes in law dealt with as intentional. Thus he who intentionally does grievous bodily harm to another, though with no desire to kill him, or certain expectation of his death, is guilty of murder if death ensues. It does not seem possible to lay down any general principle as to the cases in which such a constructive intention beyond the scope of his actual intention is thus imputed by law to a wrongdoer. This is a matter pertaining to the details of the legal system. It is sometimes said, indeed, that a person is presumed in law to intend the natural or necessary results of his actions.[33] This, however, is much too wide a statement, for, if true, it would eliminate from the law the distinction between intentional and negligent wrongdoing, merging all negligence in constructive wrongful intent. A statement much nearer the truth is that the law frequently—though by no means invariably—treats as intentional all consequences due to that form of negligence which is distinguished as recklessness—all consequences, that is to say, which the actor foresees as the probable results of his wrongful act.[34] We have seen that on

[32] *D.P.P.* v. *Smith* [1961] A.C. 290.

[33] *R.* v. *Harvey* (1823) 2 B. & C. 264: "A party must be considered in point of law to intend that which is the necessary or natural consequence of that which he does." *Cf. Freeman* v. *Pope* (1870) 5 Ch.App. 540; *Ex parte Mercer* (1886) 17 Q.B.D. 298. See the discussion in Williams, *op. cit.* (2nd ed.), § 35.

[34] Thus, in criminal law, crimes of "malice" can be committed either intentionally or recklessly *(infra,* § 91); but some crimes, such as attempt, conspiracy, rape and treason, generally require intention and cannot be committed by recklessness merely (Williams, *op. cit.,* § 22). In the law of tort, recklessness is equated with intention in deceit (*Derry* v. *Peek* (1889) 14 App. Cas. 337).

occasions the law may even dispense with the need for actual foresight on the part of the actor, and provide that the latter shall be deemed to foresee such consequences as a reasonable man in the actor's position would have foreseen.[35] The foresight of the reasonable man is of course an obviously useful evidential test whereby to infer what the actor himself foresaw, but the rule just mentioned has transformed it into a presumption of law which cannot, it seems, be rebutted. The result is the existence in law of a type of constructive recklessness.

It may also be observed that in English law, especially criminal law, the intention that is material is usually the generic and not the specific intent. Thus if A shoots at B intending to kill him, but the shot actually kills C, this is held to be murder of C. So also if A throws a stone at one window and breaks another, it is held to be malicious damage to the window actually broken.[36] This doctrine, which is known as the doctrine of transferred malice, applies only where the harm intended and the harm done are of the same kind. If A throws a stone at a human being and unintentionally breaks a window, he cannot be convicted of malicious damage to the window.[37]

## 90. MOTIVES[38]

A wrongful act is seldom intended and desired for its own sake. The wrongdoer has in view some ulterior object which he desires to obtain by means of it. The evil which he does to another, he does and desires only for the sake of some resulting good which he will obtain for himself. The desire for this good is the motive of his act.

Motives, though closely related and similar to intentions, differ from intentions in certain respects. First, an intention relates to the immediate objectives of an act, while a motive relates to the object or series of objects for the sake of which the act is done. The immediate intent of the thief is to appropriate another person's money, while his ulterior objective may be to buy food with it or to pay a debt. Secondly, a man's motive for an act consists in a desire for something which will confer a real or imagined benefit of some kind on the actor himself, whereas his intention need not relate to some personal interest of this kind. The point of asking what a man intends is to discover what he is trying to achieve. The point of asking for his motive is to find out

[35] *D.P.P.* v. *Smith* [1961] A.C. 290. See Williams, *op. cit.*, s. 35. It seems, however, that the courts may minimise the effect of this case and require proof of actual foresight on the part of the actor himself and regard the "reasonable man" test as evidential only: *Hardy* v. *Motor Insurers' Bureau* [1964] 2 Q.B. 745. See also Buxton, "The Retreat from Smith" (1966) Cr.L.R. 195.
[36] *Cf. R.* v. *Latimer* (1886) 17 Q.B.D. 359 (maliciously striking at B and wounding C held to be a malicious wounding of C).
[37] *R.* v. *Pembliton* (1874) 2 C.C.R. 119. *Cf.* Williams, *op. cit.*, Chap. 4. For a discussion of the concept of "kind", see Williams, "Language and the Law" (1945) 61 L.Q.R. 189 *et seq.*, especially at 193–194. For a further discussion of intention and recklessness in criminal law, see J. W. C. Turner, "*Mens Rea* and Motorists" (1933) 5 C.L.J. 61; same, "The Mental Element in Crimes at Common Law", in *The Modern Approach to Criminal Law*, 195.
[38] See J. F. Lever, "Means, Motives, and Interests in the Law of Tort" in *Oxford Essays in Jurisprudence* (ed. Guest), 50.

what personal advantage he is seeking to gain; and a motiveless act is one aimed at no such personal advantage.

In explaining a man's motives we may sometimes describe them in either specific or general terms. The thief in the example above may be said to steal to buy food, or to steal out of necessity. So acts may be said to be done for revenge, out of curiosity and so on, all of which are common mental states relating to a future state of affairs desired by the actor as in some way benefiting him. Intentions cannot be described in such general terms.

The objective of one wrongful act may be the commission of another. I may make a die with intent to coin bad money; I may coin bad money with intent to utter it; I may utter it with intent to defraud. Each of these acts is or may be a distinct criminal offence, and the intention of any one of them is immediate with respect to that act itself, but ulterior with respect to all that go before it in the series.

A person's ulterior intent may be complex instead of simple; he may act from two or more concurrent motives instead of from one only. He may institute a prosecution, partly from a desire to see justice done, but partly also from ill-will towards the defendant. He may pay one of his creditors preferentially on the eve of bankruptcy, partly from a desire to benefit him at the expense of the others, and partly from a desire to gain some financial advantage for himself. Now the law, as we shall see later, sometimes makes liability for an act depend on the motive with which it is done. The Bankruptcy Act, for example, regards as fraudulent any payment made by a debtor immediately before his bankruptcy with intent to prefer one of his creditors to the others. In all such cases the presence of mixed or concurrent motives raises a difficulty of interpretation. The phrase "with intent to", or its equivalents, may mean any one of at least four different things:—(1) That the intent referred to must be the sole or exclusive intent; (2) that it is sufficient if it is one of several concurrent intents; (3) that it must be the chief or dominant intent, any others being subordinate or incidental; (4) that it must be a determining intent, that is to say, an intent in the absence of which the act would not have been done, the remaining purposes being insufficient motives by themselves. It is a question of construction which of those meanings is the true one in the particular case.[39]

## 91. MALICE

Closely connected with the law and the theory of intentional wrongdoing is the legal use of the word malice. In a narrow and popular sense this term means ill-will, spite, or malevolence; but its legal signification is much wider. Malice means in law wrongful intention or recklessness.[40] Any act done

[39] For a discussion of this matter, see *Ex p. Hill* (1883) 23 Ch.D. 695 at 704, *per* Bowen L.J.; also *Ex p. Taylor* (1886) 18 Q.B.D. 295; *Crofter Hand Woven Harris Tweed Co.* v. *Veitch* [1942] A.C. 435 at 445, *per* Viscount Simon L.C., and at 473, *per* Lord Wright.
[40] See J. Ll. J. Edwards, *Mens Rea in Statutory Offences* (1955), Chap. 1; Williams, *Criminal Law: The General Part* (2nd ed.), § 30.

with one of these mental elements is, in the language of the law, malicious, and this legal usage has etymology in its favour. The Latin *malitia* [41] means badness, physical or moral—wickedness in disposition or in conduct—not specifically or exclusively ill-will or malevolence; hence the malice of English law, including all forms of evil purpose, design, intent or motive.

We have seen, however, that we must distinguish between the immediate intention with which an act is done and its ulterior purpose or motive. The term malice is applied in law to both these, and the result is a somewhat puzzling ambiguity which requires careful notice. When we say that an act is done maliciously, we mean one of two distinct things. We mean either that it is done intentionally (or alternatively recklessly) or that it is done with some wrongful motive. In the phrases malicious homicide and malicious injury to property, malicious is merely a collective term for intention and recklessness. I burn down a house maliciously if I burn it on purpose, or realising the possibility that what I do will set it on fire. There is here no reference to any ulterior purpose or motive. But, on the other hand, malicious prosecution does not mean any intentional prosecution; it means, more narrowly, a prosecution inspired by some motive of which the law disapproves. A prosecution is malicious, for example, if its ulterior intent is the extortion of money from the accused. So, also, with the malice which is needed to make a man liable for defamation on a privileged occasion; I do not utter defamatory statements maliciously simply because I utter them intentionally.[42]

Although the word *malitia* is not unknown to the Roman lawyers, the usual and technical name for wrongful intent is *dolus*, or more specifically *dolus malus*. *Dolus* and *culpa* are the two forms of *mens rea*. In a narrower sense, however, *dolus* includes merely that particular variety of wrongful intent which we term fraud—that is to say, the intent to deceive.[43] From this limited sense it was extended to cover all forms of wilful wrongdoing. The English term fraud has never received an equally wide extension. It resembles *dolus*, however, in having a double use. In its narrower sense it means deceit, as we have just said, and is commonly opposed to force. In a wider sense it includes all forms of dishonesty, that is to say, all wrongful conduct inspired by a desire to derive profit from the injury of others. In this sense fraud is commonly opposed to malice in its popular sense. I act fraudulently when the motive of my wrongdoing is to derive some material gain for myself, whether by way of deception, force, or otherwise. But I act maliciously when my motive is the pleasure of doing harm to another rather than the acquisition of any material advantage for myself. To steal property is fraudulent; to damage or destroy it is malicious.

---

[41] See for example D. 4. 3. 1 pr.
[42] It is to malice in one only of these two uses that the well-known definition given in *Bromage* v. *Prosser* (1825) 4 Barn. & C. 247, is applicable: "Malice in common acceptation means ill-will against a person; but in its legal sense it means a wrongful act done intentionally, without just cause or excuse". See, to the same effect, *Mogul Steamship Co.* v. *McGregor, Gow & Co.* (1889) 23 Q.B.D. at p. 612, *per* Bowen L.J.; and *Allen* v. *Flood* [1898] A.C. at p. 94, *per* Lord Watson.
[43] D. 4. 3. 1. 2.

## 92. RELEVANCE AND IRRELEVANCE OF MOTIVES

We have already seen in what way and to what extent a man's immediate intent is material in a question of liability. As a general rule no act is a sufficient basis of responsibility unless it is done either wilfully or negligently. Intention and negligence are the two alternative conditions of penal liability.

We have now to consider the relevance or materiality, not of the immediate, but of the ulterior intent. To what extent does the law take into account the motives of a wrongdoer? To what extent will it inquire, not merely what the defendant has done, but why he has done it? To what extent is malice, in the sense of improper motive, an element in legal wrongdoing?

In answer to this question we may say generally (subject, however, to very important qualifications) that in law a man's motives are irrelevant. As a general rule no act otherwise lawful becomes unlawful because done with a bad motive; and conversely no act otherwise unlawful is excused or justified because of the motives of the doer, however good. The law will judge a man by what he does, not by the reasons for which he does it.

"It is certainly," says Lord Herschell,[44] "a general rule of our law that an act prima facie lawful is not unlawful and actionable on account of the motives which dictated it." So it has been said[45]: "No use of property which would be legal if due to a proper motive can become illegal because it is prompted by a motive which is improper or even malicious." "Much more harm than good," says Lord Macnaghten,[46] "would be done by encouraging or permitting inquiries into motives when the immediate act alleged to have caused the loss for which redress is sought is in itself innocent or neutral in character and one which anybody may do or leave undone without fear of legal consequences. Such an inquisition would I think be intolerable."

An illustration of this irrelevance of motives is the right of a landowner to do harm to adjoining proprietors in certain defined ways by acts done on his own land. He may intercept the access of light to his neighbour's windows, or withdraw by means of excavation the support which his land affords to his neighbour's house, or drain away the water which would otherwise supply his neighbour's well. His right to do all these things depends in no way on the motive with which he does them. The law cares nothing whether his acts are inspired by an honest desire to improve his own property, or by a malevolent impulse to damage that of others. He may do as he pleases with his own.[47]

---

[44] *Allen* v. *Flood* [1898] A.C. at p. 123.
[45] *Corporation of Bradford* v. *Pickles* [1895] A.C. 587, at p. 598.
[46] *Allen* v. *Flood* [1898] A.C. 92, at p. 152.
[47] The Roman law as to the rights of adjoining proprietors was different. Harm done *animo nocendi*, that is to say, with a malicious motive, was frequently actionable. D. 39. 3. 1. 12. The German Civil Code, sect. 226, provides quite generally that the exercise of a right is unlawful when its only motive is to harm another person, and a similar rule has been recognised in France to some extent. See Gutteridge, "Abuse of Rights" (1933) 5 C.L.J. 22. The English rule has been subjected to a great deal of adverse academic criticism: see Gutteridge, *op. cit.;*

## 93. EXCEPTIONS TO THE IRRELEVANCE OF MOTIVES

Criminal attempts constitute the first of the exceptions to the rule that a person's ulterior intent or motive is irrelevant in law. Every attempt is an act done with intent to commit the offence so attempted. The existence of this ulterior intent or motive is the essence of an attempt, and can render unlawful an otherwise lawful act. So, if a man standing beside a haystack strikes a match, this act, which will be quite lawful and innocent if done with the purpose of lighting his pipe, will be unlawful and criminal if done with the purpose of setting fire to the haystack; for then it will constitute the crime of attempted arson. A second exception comprises all those cases in which a particular intent forms part of the definition of a criminal offence. Burglary, for example, consists in breaking and entering a dwelling-house by night with intent to commit a felony therein. So forgery consists in making a false document with intent to defraud. In all such instances the ulterior intent is the source, in whole or part, of the mischievous tendency of the act, and is therefore material in law.

In civil as opposed to criminal liability the ulterior objective is very seldom relevant. In almost all cases the law looks to the act alone, and makes no inquiries into the motives from which it proceeds. There are, however, certain exceptions even in the civil law. There are cases where it is thought expedient in the public interest to allow certain specified kinds of harm to be done to individuals, so long as they are done for some good and sufficient reason; but the ground of this privilege falls away so soon as it is abused for bad ends. In such cases, therefore, malice is an essential element in the cause of action. Examples of wrongs of this class are defamation (in cases of privilege) and malicious prosecution. In these instances the plaintiff must prove malice, because in all of them the defendant's act is one which falls under the head of *damnum sine injuria* so long, but so long only, as it is done with good intent.

It should also be observed that though motives are seldom relevant to determine the legality or otherwise of an act, yet, once it is shown that an illegal act has been committed, the motives of the defendant may become highly relevant. In a criminal case, where the penalty for the offence is not fixed by law, the defendant's motives may be an important factor for the court to take into account in deciding on sentence. In a civil case the defendant's motives may be taken into account where the court decides to award aggravated damages.

### 94. JUS NECESSITATIS

We shall conclude our examination of the theory of wilful wrongdoing by considering a special case in which motive operates as a ground of excuse.

Allen, "Legal Morality and the *Jus Abutendi*", *Legal Duties* 95 *et seq.*, reprinted from (1924) 40 L.Q.R. 164; Williams, "The Foundation of Tortious Liability" (1939) 7 C.L.J. 111, at 125 *et seq.*, and literature there cited; Pound, *The Spirit of the Common Law* 209; Sullivan in (1955) 8 *Current Legal Problems*, 61.

This is the case of the *jus necessitatis*. So far as the abstract theory of responsibility is concerned, an act which is necessary is not wrongful, even though done with full and deliberate intention. It is a familiar proverb that necessity knows no law: *Necessitas non habet legem*.

Necessity, however, does not mean inevitability. An act which can in no possible manner be avoided and as to which the actor has no choice cannot properly be regarded as an act in the full sense at all. An act which is necessary, on the other hand, is one where the actor could have chosen otherwise but where he had highly compelling reasons for the choice he made. A situation of so-called necessity is, in analysis, one in which there is a competition of values— on the one hand, the value of obedience to the general principles of law, and, on the other hand, some value regarded as possessing a higher claim in the particular circumstances. Here, the law itself permits a departure from its own general rules. For example, it would be lawful in an emergency to damage the property of another in order to save life.

Another factor operating to admit the defence of necessity is that it commonly involves the presence of some motive of such exceeding strength as to overcome any fear that can be inspired by the threat of legal penalties. The *jus necessitatis* is the right of a man to do that from which he cannot be dissuaded by any terror of legal punishment. Where threats are necessarily ineffective, they should not be made, and their fulfilment is the infliction of needless and uncompensated evil.[48]

The common illustration of this right of necessity where punishment would be ineffective is the case of two drowning men clinging to a plank that will not support more than one of them. It may be the moral duty of him who has no one dependent on him to sacrifice himself for the other who is a husband or a father; it may be the moral duty of the old to give way to the young. But it is idle for the law to lay down any other rule save this, that it is the right of the stronger to use his strength for his own preservation. Another familiar case of necessity is that in which shipwrecked sailors are driven to choose between death by starvation on the one side and murder and cannibalism on the other. A third case is that of crime committed under the pressure of illegal threats of death or grievous bodily harm. "If", says Hobbes,[49] "a man by the terror of present death be compelled to do a fact against the law, he is totally excused; because no law can oblige a man to abandon his own preservation."

It is to be noticed that the test of necessity in these cases is not the power-lessness of any possible, but that of any reasonable punishment. It is enough if the lawless motives to an act will necessarily countervail the fear of any penalty which it is just and expedient that the law should threaten. If burning alive were a fit and proper punishment for petty theft, the fear of it would

---

[48] Though the threats are ineffective, their fulfilment is not necessarily so. The punishment of those acting out of necessity might be an additional deterrent to those not acting out of necessity: if the law does not excuse the former, the latter can entertain no hope of excuse or acquittal.
[49] *Leviathan*, Chap. 27: *Eng. Works*. III. 288.

probably prevent a starving wretch from stealing a crust of bread; and the *jus necessitatis* would have no place. But we cannot place the rights of property at so high a level. There are cases, therefore, in which the motives to crime cannot be controlled by any reasonable punishment. In such cases morality demands that no punishment be administered, since it seems morally unjust to punish a man for doing something which he or any ordinary man could not resist doing—*i.e.,* could not morally resist doing, even given the countervailing motive of the maximum punishment reasonable for the offence.

It may be submitted that where necessity involves a choice of some value higher than the value of obedience to the letter of the law, it is always a legal defence. Where, however, the issue is merely one of the futility of punishment, evidential difficulties prevent any but the most limited scope being permitted to the *jus necessitatis.* In how few cases can we say with any approach to certainty that the possibility of self-control is really absent, that there is no true choice between good and evil, and that the deed is one for which the doer is rightly irresponsible. In this conflict between the requirements of theory and the difficulties of practice the law has resorted to compromise. While in some few instances necessity is admitted as a ground of excuse, as for example in treason,[50] it is in most cases regarded as relevant to the measure rather than to the existence of liability. It is acknowledged as a reason for the reduction of the penalty, even to a nominal amount, but not for its total remission. Homicide in the blind fury of irresistible passion is not innocent, but neither is it murder; it is reduced to the lower level of manslaughter. Shipwrecked sailors who kill and eat their comrades to save their own lives are in law guilty of murder itself; but the clemency of the Crown will commute the sentence to a short term of imprisonment.[51]

## 95. NEGLIGENCE[52]

We have considered the first of the three classes into which injuries are divisible, namely those which are intentional or wilful, and we have now to deal with the second, namely wrongs of negligence.[53]

Negligence is culpable carelessnesses. "It is", says Willes J.,[54] "the absence of such care as it was the duty of the defendant to use." What then is meant by carelessness? It is clear, in the first place, that it excludes wrongful intention. These are two contrasted and mutually inconsistent mental attitudes of a

---

[50] *R.* v. *M'Growther* (1746) Foster 13; 18 St.Tr. 391.
[51] *R.* v. *Dudley* (1884) 14 Q.B.D. 273. The law as to compulsion and necessity is discussed by Williams in (1953) 6 *Current Legal Problems,* 216 and in *Criminal Law: The General Part* (2nd ed.), Chaps. 17, 18.
[52] On care and the lack of it, see A. R. White, *Attention,* Chap. 5.
[53] In Roman law negligence is signified by the terms *culpa* and *negligentia,* as contrasted with *dolus* or wrongful intention. Care, or the absence of *negligentia,* is *diligentia.* The use of the word diligence in this sense is obsolete in modern English, though it is still retained as an archaism of legal diction. In ordinary usage, diligence is opposed to idleness, not to carelessness.
[54] *Grill* v. *General Iron Screw Colliery Co.* (1866) L.R. 1 C.P. at p. 612.

person towards his acts and their consequences. No result which is due to carelessness can have been also intended. Nothing which was intended can have been due to carelessness.[55]

It is to be observed, in the second place, that carelessness or negligence does not necessarily consist in thoughtlessness or inadvertence. This is doubtless the commonest form of it, but it is not the only form. If I do harm, not because I intended it, but because I was thoughtless and did not advert to the dangerous nature of my act, or foolishly believed that there was no danger, I am certainly guilty of negligence. But there is another form of negligence, in which there is no thoughtlessness or inadvertence whatever. If I drive furiously down a crowded street, I may be fully conscious of the serious risk to which I expose other persons. I may not intend to injure any of them, but I knowingly and intentionally expose them to the danger. Yet if a fatal accident happens, I am liable, at the most, not for wilful, but for negligent homicide. When I consciously expose another to the risk of wrongful harm, but without any wish to harm him, and harm actually ensues, it is inflicted not wilfully, since it was not desired, nor inadvertently, since it was foreseen as possible or even probable, but nevertheless negligently.[56]

Negligence then is failure to use sufficient care, and this failure may result from a variety of factors. A negligent motorist for example may be careless in several different ways. Through inadvertence he may fail to notice what is happening and what the probable consequence of his conduct will be. Through miscalculation he may misjudge his speed, that of other road-users, the width of the road and other conditions. He may drive carelessly by reason of poor vision, innate clumsiness or lack of motoring skill. Or he may err in none of these ways; he may simply appreciate the risks involved and decide to take them, and insofar as we deem it wrong to take the risk we shall hold him negligent in so doing. This latter type of negligence differs from the others in that the defendant deliberately takes a risk which he fully appreciates; and the greater our feeling that the risk should not have been incurred, the grosser in our estimation is the negligence, until we arrive at the point where a flagrantly unjustifiable risk has been incurred and this we stigmatize as recklessness. The practical importance of this is that, as already seen, recklessness is frequently for legal purposes classed with intention.

---

[55] *Kettlewell* v. *Watson* (1882) 21 Ch.D. 685, at p. 706: "Fraud imports design and purpose; negligence imports that you are acting carelessly and without that design."
[56] It is held by some that negligence consists essentially in inadvertence. See Austin, Lecture XX; Birkmeyer, *Strafrecht,* § 17; Clark, *Analysis of Criminal Liability,* Chap. 9. The issue seems to be purely one of terminology. There are in reality three forms of fault: namely, (1) that in which the consequences are foreseen and wrongfully intended; (2) that in which they are not intended but are foreseen and should have been avoided; and (3) that in which they are neither foreseen nor intended, but ought to have been foreseen and avoided. The suggestion now being considered is that the term negligence should be confined to case (3) alone. The objection to the suggestion is that it runs counter to ordinary usage and that it would, if accepted, rob us of a useful generic term for cases (2) and (3), which are sometimes, though by no means always, classed together in law.

## 96. THE DUTY OF CARE

Carelessness is not culpable, or a ground of legal liability, save in those cases in which the law has imposed a duty of carefulness. In all other cases complete indifference as to the interests of others is allowable. No general principle can be laid down, however, with regard to the existence of this duty, for this is a matter pertaining to the details of the concrete legal system, and not to abstract theory. Carelessness is lawful or unlawful, as the law sees fit to provide. In the criminal law liability for negligence is quite exceptional. Speaking generally, crimes are wilful wrongs, the alternative form of *mens rea* being deemed an insufficient ground for the rigour of criminal justice. This, however, is not invariably the case, negligent homicide, for example, being a criminal offence. In the civil law, on the other hand, no such distinction is commonly drawn between the two forms of *mens rea*. In general we may say that whenever an act would be a civil wrong if done intentionally, it is also a civil wrong if done negligently. When there is a legal duty not to do a thing on purpose, there is commonly a legal duty to take care not to do it accidentally. To this rule, however, there are certain exceptions—instances in which wrongful intent, or at least recklessness, is the necessary basis even of civil liability. In these cases a person is civilly responsible for doing harm wilfully, but is not bound to take any care not to do it. He must not, for example, deceive another by any wilful or reckless falsehood, but unless there are special circumstances giving rise to a duty of care, he is not answerable for false statements which he honestly believes to be true, however negligent he may be in making them.[57]

## 97. THE STANDARD OF CARE

Carelessness may exist in any degree, and in this respect it differs from the other form of *mens rea*. Intention either exists or it does not; there can be no question of the degree in which it is present. The degree of carelessness varies directly with the risk to which other persons are exposed by the act in question. He is careless, who, without intending evil, nevertheless exposes others to the danger of it, and the greater the danger the greater the carelessness. The risk depends, in its turn, on two things: first, the magnitude of the threatened evil, and second, the probability of it. The greater the evil is, and the nearer it is, the greater is the carelessness of him who creates the danger.

Inasmuch, therefore, as carelessness varies in degree, it is necessary to know what degree of it is requisite to constitute culpable negligence. What measure of care does the law demand? What amount of anxious consideration for the interests of others is a legal duty, and within what limits is indifference lawful?

We have first to notice a possible standard of care which the law might have adopted but has not. It does not demand the highest degree of care of which

[57] The law on this topic was fully reviewed by the House of Lords in *Hedley Byrne & Co. Ltd.* v. *Heller & Partners Ltd.* [1964] A.C. 465.

human nature is capable. I am not liable for harm ignorantly done by me, merely because by some conceivable exercise of prudential foresight I might have anticipated the event and so avoided it. Nor am I liable because, knowing the possibility of harm, I fail to take every possible precaution against it. The law demands not that which is possible, but that which is reasonable in view of the magnitude of the risk. Were men to act on any other principle than this, excess of caution would paralyse the business of the world. The law, therefore, allows every man to expose his feelings to a certain measure of risk, and to do so even with full knowledge. If an explosion occurs in my powder mill, I am not necessarily liable to those injured inside the mill,[58] even though I established and carried on the industry with full knowledge of its dangerous character. This is a degree of indifference to the safety of other men's lives and property which the law deems permissible because not excessive. Inasmuch as the carrying of firearms and the driving of automobiles are known to be the occasions of frequent harm, extreme care and the most scrupulous anxiety as to the interest of others would prompt a man to abstain from those dangerous forms of activity. Yet it is expedient in the public interest that those activities should go on, and therefore that men should be exposed to the incidental risks of them. Consequently the law does not insist on any standard of care which would include them within the limits of culpable negligence. It is for the law to draw the line as best it can, so that while prohibiting unreasonable carelessness, it does not at the same time demand unreasonable care.

On the other hand it is not sufficient that I have acted in good faith to the best of my judgment and belief, and have used as much care as I myself believed to be required of me in the circumstances of the case. The question in every case is not whether I honestly thought my conduct sufficiently careful, but whether in fact it attained the standard of due care established by law.

What standard then does the law actually adopt? It demands the amount of care which is reasonable in the circumstances of the particular case.[59] This obligation to use reasonable care is very commonly expressed by reference to the conduct of a "reasonable man" or of an "ordinarily prudent man", meaning thereby a reasonably prudent man. "Negligence", it has been said,[60] "is the omitting to do something that a reasonable man would do, or the doing something which a reasonable man would not do." "We ought", it has been said,[61] "to adhere to the rule which requires in all cases a regard to caution such as a man of ordinary prudence would observe. . . . The care taken by a prudent man has always been the rule laid down." The reference to the "ordinary man" does not mean that it is in all cases a defence to show that the defendant behaved as the average man would have behaved, for there are instances where the court has considered that even the usual standard of

---

[58] *Read* v. *Lyons* [1947] A.C. 156.
[59] *Ford* v. *L. & S.W. Ry.* (1862) 2 F. & F. 730.
[60] *Blyth* v. *Birmingham Water Works Co.* (1856) 25 L.J.Ex. at 213.
[61] *Vaughan* v. *Menlove* (1837) 3 Bing.N.C. 475.

conduct falls short of the "reasonable" minimum.[62] "Reasonable" in short, seems to refer not to the average standard, but to the standard that the jury or judge think ought to have been observed in the particular case.

In determining the standard to be required, there are two chief matters for consideration. The first is the magnitude of the risk to which other persons are exposed, while the second is the importance of the object to be attained by the dangerous form of activity. The reasonableness of any conduct will depend upon the proportion between these two elements. To expose others to danger for a disproportionate object is unreasonable, whereas an equal risk for a better cause may lawfully be run without negligence. By driving trains at the rate of fifty miles an hour, railway companies have caused many fatal accidents which could quite easily have been avoided by reducing the speed to ten miles, but this additional safety would be attained at too great a cost of public convenience, and therefore in neglecting this precaution the companies do not fall below the standard of reasonable care and are not guilty of negligence.[63]

In conclusion, a word may be said upon the maxim *Imperitia culpae adnumeratur*.[64] It is a settled principle of law that want of skill or of professional competence amounts to negligence. He who will exercise any trade or profession must bring to the exercise of it such a measure of skill and knowledge as will suffice for reasonable efficiency, and he who has less than this practises at his own risk. At first sight this maxim may seem to require a degree of care far in excess of what is reasonably to be expected of the ordinary person, but further consideration will show that this is not so. The ignorant physician who kills his patient, or the unskilled blacksmith who lames the horse shod by him, is legally responsible, not because he is ignorant or unskilful—for skill and knowledge may be beyond his reach—but because, being unskilful or ignorant, he ventures to undertake a business which calls for qualities which he does not possess. No man is bound in law to be a good surgeon or a capable attorney, but all men are bound not to act as surgeons or attorneys until and unless they are good and capable as such.

### 98. DEGREES IN NEGLIGENCE

Where a system of law recognises only one standard of care, it does not follow that it must recognise only one degree of negligence. For since negligence consists in falling below the standard of care recognised by law, the further the defendant falls below this, the greater his negligence.

We have already seen that in assessing whether a man is guilty of negligence regard must be had to the seriousness of the danger to which his actions expose others, to the degree of probability that the danger would occur and to the importance of the object of the defendant's own activity. Clearly the greater the danger and the greater its likelihood, the greater the defendant's carelessness

---

[62] Salmond, *Torts* (14th ed.), 296–297.
[63] *Ford* v. *L. & S.W. Ry.* (1862) 2 F. & F. 730.
[64] Just. *Inst.* 4. 3. 7.

in not taking precautions against it; and conversely the more important and socially valuable his own objective, the smaller his carelessness. There are degrees of negligence then and these could be taken into account by law for both criminal and civil purposes. In crimes of negligence the law could provide that the greater the negligence the greater the punishment. We have seen that English law does not recognise many offences of negligence, but an acceptance of the different gradations of carelessness can be found in the law relating to road traffic. Here a distinction is drawn between ordinary negligence, criminal negligence and gross negligence. Ordinary negligence is such failure to use care as would render a person civilly but not criminally liable; criminal negligence is a greater failure and a greater falling below the standard of care, and renders a man guilty of a driving offence—and even within this category the law distinguishes between the less negligent offence of careless driving and the more negligent offence of dangerous driving; gross negligence is a yet greater fall below the standard and is such a wholly unreasonable failure to take care as to make the defendant guilty not only of a driving offence but also, in the event of his conduct resulting in another person's death, of manslaughter.

Equally for civil purposes the law could take account of different degrees of negligence. It could provide that the greater the defendant's negligence, the greater the compensation he must make to the plaintiff. This, however, is not the position adopted by English law, which for civil purposes recognises only one standard of care and therefore only one degree of negligence. Whenever a person is under a duty to take any care at all, he is bound to take that amount of it which is deemed reasonable under the circumstances; and the absence of this care is culpable negligence. Although this is probably a correct statement of English law, attempts have been made to establish two or even three distinct standards of care and degrees of negligence. Some authorities, for example, distinguish between gross negligence *(culpa lata)* and slight negligence *(culpa levis)*, holding that a person is sometimes liable for the former only, and at other times even for the latter. In some cases we find even a threefold distinction maintained, negligence being either gross, ordinary, or slight.[65] These distinctions are based partly upon Roman law, and partly upon a misunderstanding of it, and notwithstanding some judicial dicta to the contrary we may say with some confidence that no such doctrine is known to the law of England.[66]

---

[65] See, for example, Smith's *Leading Cases* (13th ed.), I. 190 (Notes to *Coggs* v. *Bernard*).
[66] See *Hinton* v. *Dibbin* (1842) 2 Q.B. at p. 661, *per* Denman C.J.: "It may well be doubted whether between gross negligence and negligence merely any intelligible distinction exists". *Wilson* v. *Brett* (1843) 11 M. & W. at p. 113, *per* Rolfe B.: "I said I could see no difference between negligence and gross negligence, that it was the same thing with the addition of a vituperative epithet". *Grill* v. *General Iron Screw Colliery Co.* (1866) L.R. 1 C.P. at p. 612, *per* Willes J.: "No information has been given us as to the meaning to be attached to gross negligence in this case, and I quite agree with the *dictum* of Lord Cranworth in *Wilson* v. *Brett* that gross negligence is ordinary negligence with a vituperative epithet, a view held by the Exchequer Chamber in *Beal* v. *South Devon Ry.*" *Doorman* v. *Jenkins* (1834) 2 Ad. & El. at p. 265, *per* Denman C.J.: "I thought and I still think it impossible for a judge to take upon himself to say whether negligence is gross or not". Salmond, *Torts* (14th ed.), 298–299; Pollock, *Torts* (15th ed.), 339; Street, *Foundations of Legal Liability*, I. 98. See, however, for a full discussion of the matter, and an expression of the contrary opinion, *Beven on Negligence*, I. Chap. II.

The distinctions so drawn are hopelessly indeterminate and impracticable. On what principle are we to draw the line between gross negligence and slight? Even were it possible to establish two or more standards, there seems no reason of justice or expediency for doing so. The single standard of English law is sufficient for all cases. Why should any man be required to show more care than is reasonable under the circumstances, or excused if he shows less?

In connection with this alleged distinction between gross and slight negligence it is necessary to consider the celebrated doctrine of Roman law to the effect that the former *(culpa lata)* is equivalent to wrongful intention *(dolus)*— a principle which receives occasional expression and recognition in English law also. *Magna culpa dolus est*,[67] said the Romans. In its literal interpretation, indeed, this is untrue, for we have already seen that the two forms of *mens rea* are wholly inconsistent with each other, and that no degree of carelessness can amount to design or purpose. Yet the proposition, though inaccurately expressed, has a true signification. Although *real* negligence, however gross, cannot amount to intention, *alleged* negligence may. Alleged negligence which, if real, would be exceedingly gross, is probably not negligence at all, but wrongful purpose. Its grossness raises a presumption against its reality. For we have seen that carelessness is measured by the magnitude and imminence of the threatened mischief. Now the greater and more imminent the mischief, the more probable is it that it is intended. Genuine carelessness is very unusual and unlikely in extreme cases. Men are often enough indifferent as to remote or unimportant dangers to which they expose others, but serious risks are commonly avoided by care unless the mischief is desired and intended. The probability of a result tends to prove intention and therefore to disprove negligence. If a new-born child is left to die from want of medical attention or nursing, it *may* be that its death is due to negligence only, but it is more probable that it is due to wrongful purpose and malice aforethought. He who strikes another on the head with an iron bar *may* have meant only to wound or stun, and not to kill him, but the probabilities are the other way.[68]

In certain cases, as has already been indicated in dealing with the nature of intention, the presumption of fact that a person intends the probable consequences of his actions has hardened into a presumption of law and become irrebuttable. In those cases that which is negligence in fact is deemed wrongful intent in law. It is constructive, though not actual intent. The law of homicide supplies us with an illustration. Murder is wilful homicide, and manslaughter

---

[67] D. 50. 16. 226. See also D. 17. 1. 29. pr., D. 47. 4. 1. 2., D. 11. 6. 1. 1.: *Lata culpa plane dolo comparabitur.*

[68] In *Le Lievre* v. *Gould* [1893] 1 Q.B. at p. 500, it is said by Bowen L.J.: "If the case had been tried with a jury, the judge would have pointed out to them that gross negligence might amount to evidence of fraud, if it were so gross as to be incompatible with the idea of honesty, but that even gross negligence, in the absence of dishonesty, did not of itself amount to fraud". Literally read, this implies that, though gross negligence cannot *be* fraud, it may be *evidence* of it, but this of course is impossible. If two things are inconsistent with each other, one of them cannot be evidence of the other. The true meaning is that alleged or admitted negligence may be so gross as to be a ground for the inference that it is in reality fraud and not negligence at all: see also *Kettlewell* v. *Watson* (1882) 21 Ch.D. at p. 706, *per* Fry J.

is negligent homicide, but the boundary line as drawn by the law is not fully coincident with that which exists in fact. Thus, an intent to cause grievous bodily harm is imputed as an intent to kill, if death ensues. The justification of such conclusive presumptions of intent is twofold. In the first place, as already indicated, very gross negligence is probably in truth not negligence at all, but wrongful purpose; and in the second place, even if it is truly negligence, yet by reason of its grossness it is as bad as intent, in point of moral deserts, and therefore may justly be treated and punished as if it were intent. The law, accordingly, will sometimes say to a defendant: "Perhaps, as you allege, you were merely negligent and had no actual wrongful purpose; nevertheless you will be dealt with just as if you had, and it will be conclusively presumed against you that your act was wilful. For your deserts are no better than if you had in truth intended the mischief which you have so recklessly caused. Moreover it is exceedingly probable, notwithstanding your disclaimer, that you did indeed intend it; therefore no endeavour will be made on your behalf to discover whether you did or not."

### 99. THE SUBJECTIVE AND OBJECTIVE THEORIES OF NEGLIGENCE

There are two rival theories of the meaning of the term negligence. According to the one, negligence is a state of mind; according to the other, it is not a state of mind but merely a type of conduct. These opposing views may conveniently be distinguished as the subjective and objective theories of negligence. The one view was adopted by Sir John Salmond, the other by Sir Frederick Pollock. We shall consider in turn the arguments for each view, and then attempt an evaluation of them.

#### (1) *The Subjective Theory of Negligence*

Sir John Salmond's view was that a careless person is a person who does not *care*. Although negligence is not synonymous with thoughtlessness or inadvertence, it is nevertheless, on this view, essentially an attitude of *indifference*. Now indifference is exceedingly apt to produce thoughtlessness or inadvertence; but it is not the same thing, and may exist without it. If I am indifferent as to the results of my conduct, I shall very probably fail to acquire adequate foresight and consciousness of them; but I may, on the contrary, make a very accurate estimate of them, and yet remain equally indifferent with respect to them.

Negligence, therefore, on this view, essentially consists in the *mental attitude of undue indifference with respect to one's conduct and its consequences*.[69]

#### (2) *The Objective Theory of Negligence*

The other theory is that negligence is not a subjective, but an objective fact. It is not a particular state of mind or form of the *mens rea* at all, but a

---

[69] Sir John Salmond quoted Merkel's *Lehrbuch des deutschen Strafrechts*, sects. 32 and 33.

particular kind of conduct. It is a breach of the duty of taking care, and to take care means to take precautions against the harmful results of one's actions, and to refrain from unreasonably dangerous kinds of conduct.[70] To drive at night without lights is negligence, because to carry lights is a precaution taken by all reasonable and prudent men for the avoidance of accidents. To take care, therefore, is no more a mental attitude or state of mind than to take cold is. This view obtains powerful support from the law of tort, where it is clearly settled that negligence means a failure to achieve the objective standard of the reasonable man.[71] If the defendant has failed to achieve this standard it is no defence for him to show that he was anxious to avoid doing harm and took the utmost care of which *he* was capable. The same seems to hold good in criminal law.

The truth contained in the subjective theory is that in certain situations any conclusions as to whether a man had been negligent will depend partly on conclusions as to his state of mind. In criminal law a sharp distinction is drawn between intentionally causing harm and negligently causing harm, and in deciding whether the accused is guilty of either we must have regard to his knowledge, aims, motives and so on. Cases of apparent negligence may, upon examination of the party's state of mind, turn out to be cases of wrongful intention. A trap door may be left unbolted, in order that one's enemy may fall through it and so die. Poison may be left unlabelled, with intent that some one may drink it by mistake. A ship's captain may wilfully cast away his ship by the neglect of the ordinary rules of good seamanship. A father who neglects to provide medicine for his sick child may be guilty of wilful murder, rather than of mere negligence. In none of these cases, nor indeed in any others, can we distinguish between intentional and negligent wrongdoing, save by looking into the mind of the offender and observing his subjective attitude towards his act and its consequences. Externally and objectively, the two classes of offences are indistinguishable.

The subjective theory then has the merit of making clear the distinction between intention and negligence. The wilful wrongdoer desires the harmful consequences, and therefore does the act in order that they may ensue. The negligent wrongdoer does not desire the harmful consequences, but in many cases is careless (if not wholly, yet unduly) whether they ensue or not, and therefore does the act notwithstanding the risk that they may ensue. The wilful wrongdoer is liable because he desires to do the harm; the negligent wrongdoer may be liable because he does not sufficiently desire to avoid it. He who will excuse himself on the ground that he meant no evil is still open to the reply: Perhaps you did not, but at all events you might have avoided it if you had sufficiently desired so to do; and you are held liable not because you

---

[70] Pollock, *Torts* (15th ed.), 336: "Negligence is the contrary of diligence, and no one describes diligence as a state of mind." It may be answered that this simply plays upon two meanings of the word "diligence". Diligence to-day means activity, which is not a state of mind; but originally and in contrast to negligence it meant care, which has at least a mental element.
[71] *Supra,* § 97.

desired the mischief, but because you were careless and indifferent whether it ensued or not.

But to identify negligence with any one state of mind is a confusion and an oversimplification. We have seen that negligence consists in failure to comply with a standard of care and that such failure can result from a variety of factors, including ignorance, inadvertence and even clumsiness. Now while it is true that these may often result from indifference, there is no reason to suppose that they must in all cases arise from this source. To imagine otherwise is to salvage the subjective theory that negligence consists in the mental attitude of indifference at the expense of adopting a hypothesis which has no particular plausibility and no special merit other than that of supporting the subjective theory itself. In fact if wrongful intention is not in issue, and the question is simply whether the defendant caused the harm without any fault on his part or by his unintentional fault, the question is to be settled by ascertaining whether his conduct conformed to the standard of the reasonable man. In this case the state of his mind is not quite irrelevant. For the standard of care represents the degree of care which should be used in the circumstances, and his knowledge or lack of knowledge may be relevant in assessing what the circumstances were. The question may then be whether a reasonable man, knowing only what the defendant knew, would have acted as did the defendant.

But his state of mind is not conclusive. In certain circumstances it may be held in law that a reasonable man would know things that the defendant did not know, and the defendant will be blamed for not knowing and held liable because he ought to know. In such cases the law relating to negligence requires the defendant at his peril to come up to an objective standard and declines "to take his personal equation into account".[72]

### 100. THE THEORY OF STRICT LIABILITY

We now proceed to consider the third class of wrongs, namely, those of strict liability.[73] These are the acts for which a man is responsible irrespective of the existence of either wrongful intent or negligence. They are the exceptions to the general requirement of fault. It may be thought, indeed, that in the civil as opposed to the criminal law, strict liability should be the rule rather than the exception. It may be said: "It is clear that in the criminal law liability should in all ordinary cases be based upon the existence of *mens rea*. No man

---

[72] Holmes, *The Common Law*, 108. On negligence and recklessness see the controversy between White (1961) 24 M.L.R. 592; Fitzgerald (1962) 25 M.L.R. 49; Williams, *ibid;* White *ibid.* 437. For a discussion and criticism of the view that the idea of degrees of negligence is nonsensical see Hart, "Negligence, Mens Rea and Criminal Responsibility," *Oxford Essays in Jurisprudence* (ed. Guest), 29.

[73] The expression formerly used was "absolute" liability, but since exceptions are always recognised to so-called absolute liability, Sir Percy Winfield suggested that a better term was "strict" liability ("The Myth of Absolute Liability" (1926) 42 L.Q.R. 37), and this suggestion has since been judicially adopted *(Northwestern Utilities* v. *London Guarantee, etc., Co.* [1936] A.C. 108, 118, 119, 126).

should be punished criminally unless he knew that he was doing wrong, or unless, at least, a reasonable person in his shoes could have avoided the harmful result by taking reasonable care. Inevitable mistake or accident should be a good defence. But why should the same principle apply to civil liability? If I do another man harm, why should I not be made to pay for it? What does it matter to him whether I did it wilfully, or negligently, or by inevitable accident? In either case I have actually done the harm, and therefore should be bound to *undo* it by paying compensation. For the essential aim of civil proceedings is redress for harm suffered by the plaintiff, not punishment for wrong done by the defendant; therefore the rule of *mens rea* should be deemed inapplicable."

It is clear, however, that this is not the law of England, and it seems equally clear that there is no sufficient reason why it should be. For unless damages are at the same time a deserved penalty inflicted upon the defendant, they are not to be justified as being a deserved recompense awarded to the plaintiff. In the first place they in no way undo the wrong or restore the former state of things. The wrong is done and cannot be undone. If by accident I burn down another man's house, the only result of endorcing compensation is that the loss has been transferred from him to me; but it remains as great as ever for all that. The mischief done has been in no degree abated. Secondly, the idea of compensation is related to that of fault, for it consists in the restoring of a balance by the person who has disturbed it; but if the defendant from whom compensation is sought is not at fault, he can hardly be taken to have disturbed the balance which needs to be redressed. If I am not in fault, there is no more reason why I should insure other persons against the harmful issues of my own activity, than why I should insure them against lightning or earthquakes. Unless some definite gain is to be derived by transferring loss from one head to another, sound reason, as well as the law, requires that the loss should lie where it falls.[74]

### 101. THE EXTENT OF STRICT LIABILITY

Although the requirement of fault is general throughout the civil and criminal law, there are numerous exceptions to it. The considerations on which these are based are various, but the most important is the difficulty of procuring adequate proof of intention or negligence. In the majority of instances, indeed, justice requires that this difficulty be honestly faced; but in certain special cases it is circumvented by a provision that proof of intention or negligence is unnecessary and that liability is strict. In this way we shall certainly punish some who are innocent, but in the case of civil liability this is not a very serious matter—since men know that in such cases they act at their peril, and are content to take the risk—while in respect of criminal liability such a provision

---

[74] The question is discussed in Holmes's *Common Law*, 81–96, and in Pollock's *Law of Torts* (15th ed.), 96 *et seq*.

applies only in the case of less serious offences.[75] Whenever, therefore, the strict doctrine of *mens rea* would too seriously interfere with the administration of justice by reason of the evidential difficulties involved in it, the law tends to establish a form of strict liability. Nevertheless, strict liability in criminal law remains open to serious objection. A man should, we feel, be given a reasonable chance to conform his conduct to the requirements of law. It is true that some mistakes and some accidents are culpable and would not have occurred but for the defendant's negligence. Others, however, could not have been avoided however much care had been taken, and to penalise a man for unavoidable mistakes or accidents is to fail to afford him a reasonable opportunity of complying with the law. The difficulty of procuring adequate proof of intention or negligence could be met quite simply by allowing the defendant to shoulder the burden of proving his innocence. In this event it would be for him to show that he acted neither intentionally nor through negligence and that any accident or mistake on his part was not culpable. This unfortunately is not the present position in English law, which recognises many offences of strict liability.

In proceeding to consider the chief instances of strict liability we find that the matter falls into three divisions, namely—(1) Mistake of Law, (2) Mistake of Fact, and (3) Accident.

### 102. MISTAKE OF LAW

It is a principle recognised not only by our own but by other legal systems that ignorance of the law is no excuse for breaking it. *Ignorantia juris neminem excusat*. The rule is also expressed in the form of a legal presumption that every one knows the law. The presumption is irrebuttable: no diligence of inquiry will avail against it, and no inevitable ignorance or error will serve for justification. Whenever a man is thus held accountable for breaking a law which he did not know, and which he could not by due care have acquired a knowledge of, we have a type of strict liability.

The reasons rendered for this somewhat rigorous principle are three in number. In the first place, the law is in legal theory definite and knowable; it is the duty of every man to know that part of it which concerns him; therefore innocent and inevitable ignorance of the law is impossible. Men are conclusively presumed to know the law, and are dealt with as if they did know it, because in general they can and ought to know it.

In the second place, even if invincible ignorance of the law is in fact possible, as indeed it is, the evidential difficulties in the way of the judicial recognition of such ignorance are insuperable, and for the sake of any benefit derivable therefrom it is not advisable to weaken the administration of justice

---

[75] As to *mens rea* in criminal responsibility, see *R. v. Tolson* (1873) 23 Q.B.D. 168; *R. v. Prince* (1875) L.R. 2 C.C. 154; *Chisholm* v. *Doulton* (1889) 22 Q.B.D. 736; Kenny, *Outlines of Criminal Law* (ed. Turner 1962), 23 *et seq.*; R. M. Jackson, "Absolute Prohibition in Statutory Offences" in *The Modern Approach to Criminal Law*, 262, reprinted from (1936) 6 C.L.J. 83. The arguments for and against strict liability in criminal law are carefully reviewed in Howard, *Strict Responsibility*.

by making liability dependent on well-nigh inscrutable conditions touching knowledge or means of knowledge of the law. Who can say of any man whether he knew the law, or whether during the course of his past life he had an opportunity of acquiring a knowledge of it by the exercise of due diligence?

Thirdly and lastly, the law is in most instances derived from and in harmony with the rules of natural justice. It is a public declaration by the state of its intention to maintain by force those principles of right and wrong which have already a secure place in the moral consciousness of men. The common law is in great part nothing more than common honesty and common sense. Therefore although a man may be ignorant that he is breaking the law, he knows very well in most cases that he is breaking the rule of right. If not to his knowledge lawless, he is at least dishonest and unjust. He has little ground of complaint, therefore, if the law refuses to recognise his ignorance as an excuse, and deals with him according to his moral deserts. He who goes about to harm others when he believes that he can do so within the limits of the law, may justly be required by the law to know those limits at his peril. This is not a form of activity that need be encouraged by any scrupulous insistence on the formal conditions of legal responsibility.

It must be admitted, however, that while each of these considerations is valid and weighty, they do not constitute an altogether sufficient basis for so stringent and severe a rule.[76] None of them goes the full length of the rule. That the law is knowable throughout by all whom it concerns is an ideal rather than a fact in any system as indefinite and mutable as our own. That it is impossible to distinguish invincible from negligent ignorance of the law is by no means wholly true. It may be doubted whether this inquiry is materially more difficult than many which courts of justice undertake without hesitation; and here again the difficulty of proving the defendant's knowledge of the law could be surmounted by providing that the defendant should bear the burden of establishing non-negligent ignorance.[77] That he who breaks the law of the land disregards at the same time the principles of justice and honesty is in many instances far from the truth. In a complex legal system a man requires other guidance than that of common sense and a good conscience. The fact seems to be that the rule in question, while in general sound, does not in its full extent and uncompromising rigidity admit of any sufficient justification. Indeed, it may be said that certain exceptions to it are in course of being developed, particularly in respect of the defence of "claim of right" in criminal law.[78]

### 103. MISTAKE OF FACT

In respect of the influence of ignorance or error upon legal liability, we

---

[76] The rule is not limited to civil and criminal liability, but extends to other departments of the law. It prevents, for example, the recovery of money paid under a mistake of law, though that which is paid under a mistake of fact may be reclaimed.

[77] See Andenaes "*Ignorantia Legis* in Scandinavian Criminal Law" in *Essays in Criminal Science* (ed. Mueller), 217.

[78] For an extended discussion, see Williams, *Criminal Law: The General Part* (2nd ed.), Chap. 8.

have inherited from Roman law a familiar distinction between law and fact. By reason of his ignorance of the law no man will be excused, but it is commonly said that inevitable ignorance of fact is a good defence.[79] This, however, is far from an accurate statement of English law. It is much more nearly correct to say that mistake of fact is an excuse only within the sphere of the criminal law, while in the civil law responsibility is commonly strict in this respect. So far as civil liability is concerned, it is a general principle of our law that he who intentionally or semi-intentionally (see § 89) interferes with the person, property, reputation, or other rightful interests of another does so at his peril, and will not be heard to allege that he believed in good faith and on reasonable grounds in the existence of some circumstance which justified his act. If I trespass upon another man's land, it is no defence to me that I believed it on good grounds to be my own. If in absolute innocence and under an inevitable mistake of fact I meddle with another's goods, I am liable for all loss incurred by the true owner.[80] If, intending to arrest A, I arrest B by mistake instead, I am liable to him, notwithstanding the greatest care taken by me to ascertain his identity. If I falsely but innocently make a defamatory statement about another, I am liable to him, however careful I may have been to ascertain the truth. There are, indeed, exceptions to this rule of strict civil liability for mistake of fact, but they are not of such number or importance as to cast any doubt on the validity of the general principle.[81]

In the criminal law, on the other hand, the matter is otherwise, and it is here that the contrast between mistake of law and mistake of fact finds its true application. Absolute criminal responsibility for a mistake of fact is quite exceptional. An instance of it is the liability of him who abducts a girl under the legal age of consent. Inevitable mistake as to her age is no defence; he must take the risk.[82]

A word may be said as to the historical origin of this failure of English law to recognise inevitable mistake as a ground of exemption from civil liability. Ancient modes of procedure and proof were not adapted for inquiries into mental conditions. By the practical difficulties of proof early law was driven to attach exclusive importance to overt acts. The subjective elements of wrong-doing were largely beyond proof or knowledge, and were therefore disregarded as far as possible. It was a rule of our law that intent and knowledge were not matters that could be proved or put in issue. "It is common learning", said one of the judges of King Edward IV, "that the intent of a man will not be tried, for the devil himself knoweth not the intent of a man".[83] The sole question

---

[79] *Regula est juris quidem ignorantiam cuique nocere, facti vero ignorantiam non nocere.* D. 22. 6. 9. pr.

[80] *Hollins* v. *Fowler* (1874) L.R. 7 H.L. 757; *Consolidated Co.* v. *Curtis* [1892] 1 Q.B. 495.

[81] It may be noted that, as regards the tort of negligence, an entirely innocent error as to facts may make an act which would otherwise be negligent non-negligent. Thus an act which would be negligent if it were known that a third party was present and would be imperilled may not be negligent if the defendant was innocently *(i.e.,* without breach of duty to come to know) ignorant of this fact.

[82] *R.* v. *Prince* (1875) L.R. 2 C.C. 154.

[83] Y.B. 17 Edw. IV. 2.

which the courts would entertain was whether the defendant did the act complained of. Whether he did it ignorantly or with guilty knowledge was entirely immaterial. This rule, however, was restricted to civil liability. It was early recognised that criminal responsibility was too serious a thing to be imposed upon an innocent man simply for the sake of avoiding a difficult inquiry into his knowledge and intention. In the case of civil liability, on the other hand, the rule was general. The success with which it has maintained itself in modern law is due in part to its undeniable utility in obviating inconvenient or even impracticable inquiries, and in part to the influence of the conception of redress in minimising the importance of fault as a condition of penal liability.

## 104. ACCIDENT

Unlike mistake, inevitable accident is commonly recognised by our law as a ground of exemption from liability. It is needful, therefore, to distinguish accurately between these two things, for they are near of kin. Every act which is not done intentionally is done either accidentally or by mistake. It is done accidentally when the consequences are unintended. It is done by mistake, when the consequences are intended but the actor is ignorant of some material circumstance.[84] If I drive over a man in the dark because I do not know that he is in the road, I injure him accidentally; but if I procure his arrest, because I mistake him for some one who is liable to arrest, I injure him, not accidentally, but by mistake. In the former case I did not intend the harm at all, while in the latter case I fully intended it, but falsely believed in the existence of a circumstance which would have served to justify it. So if by insufficient care I allow my cattle to escape into my neighbour's field, their presence there is due to accident; but if I put them there because I wrongly believe that the field is mine, their presence is due to mistake. In neither case did I intend to wrong my neighbour, but in the one case my intention failed as to the consequence, and in the other as to the circumstance.

Accident, like mistake, is either culpable or inevitable. It is culpable when due to negligence, but inevitable when the avoidance of it would have required a degree of care exceeding the standard demanded by the law. Culpable accident is no defence, save in those exceptional cases in which wrongful intent is the exclusive and necessary ground of liability. Inevitable accident is commonly a good defence, both in the civil and in the criminal law.

To this rule, however, there are, at least, in the civil law, important exceptions. These are cases in which the law insists that a man shall act at his peril, and shall take his chance of accidents happening. If he desires to keep wild beasts,[85] or to construct a reservoir of water,[86] or to accumulate upon his land any substance which will do damage to his neighbours if it escapes,[87]

---

[84] The distinction between accident and mistake is neatly explained in Austin, "A Plea for Excuse" (1956–57) 57 Proc.Arist.Soc. 1.
[85] *Filburn* v. *Aquarium Co.* (1890) 25 Q.B.D. 258.
[86] *Rylands* v. *Fletcher* (1868) L.R. 3 H.L. 330.
[87] *Pickard* v. *Smith* (1861) 10 C.B. (N.S.) 470.

he will do all these things *suo periculo* (though none of them are *per se* wrongful), and will answer for all ensuing damage, notwithstanding consummate care. So also every man is strictly responsible for the trespasses of his cattle.[88] If my horse or my ox escapes from my land to that of another man, I am answerable for it without any proof of negligence.[89]

## 105. VICARIOUS RESPONSIBILITY

Hitherto we have dealt exclusively with the conditions of liability, and it is needful now to consider its incidence. Normally and naturally the person who is liable for a wrong is he who does it. Yet both ancient and modern law admit instances of vicarious liability in which one man is made answerable for the acts of another. In more primitive systems, however, the impulse to extend vicariously the incidence of liability receives free scope in a manner altogether alien to modern notions of justice. It is in barbarous times considered a very natural thing to make every man answerable for those who are kin to him. In the Mosaic legislation it is deemed necessary to lay down the express rule that "Fathers shall not be put to death for the children, neither shall the children be put to death for the fathers; every man shall be put to death for his own sin".[90] Plato in his *Laws* does not deem it needless to emphasise the same principle.[91] Furthermore, so long as punishment is conceived rather as expiative, retributive, and vindictive, than as deterrent and reformative, it might seem reasonable for the incidence of liability to be determined by *consent,* and for a guilty man to provide a substitute to bear his penalty and to provide the needful satisfaction to the law. Guilt must be wiped out by punishment but there is no reason why the victim should be one person rather than another.

Morally, however, such proceedings would be indefensible. Most people would agree that punishment, since it consists of the infliction of pain, must be justified, for to inflict pain without justification is immoral and itself an evil. Now it is justifiable to punish an offender, provided that the punishment is not out of all proportion to the offence, because the evil inflicted is a means to a

---

[88] *Ellis* v. *Loftus Iron Co.* (1874) L.R. 10 C.P. 10.
[89] The history of the principle of strict liability has been the subject of some controversy. It is universally agreed that in primitive law a man was, in general, strictly liable for his own acts, though there were cases where the law came quite early to make some inquiry into the question of fault. The dispute has turned on the question of liability for the acts of one's slaves or servants, animals, and inanimate objects. According to one view, early law started with strict liability for these acts also, and the course of legal development was in the direction of a relaxation of the early rules. According to the other view the opposite was the case: early law had in general no conception of vicarious liability for servants or of liability for chattels, and the course of legal development was in the direction of establishing and strengthening such liability. The first view was propounded in the United States by Dean Wigmore, and in England adopted by Sir John Salmond and Sir William Holdsworth, and received the somewhat hesitating adherence of Pollock and Maitland. The second view was held in the United States by Mr. Justice Holmes, and supported by Glanville Williams.
[90] *Deut.* xxiv. 16.
[91] *Laws* 856. On the vicarious responsibility of the kindred in early law, see Lea, *Superstition and Force* (4th ed.), 13–20, and Tarde, *La Philosophie Pénale,* 136–140.

greater good, *i.e.*, the protection of society; because the wrongdoer has forfeited, of his own volition, the right not to have evil inflicted on him, since he might have abstained from his wrongdoing; and because the punishment may serve to turn him away from his wrongdoing. But where punishment is inflicted on some person other than the actual offender, the law is treating the victim as a mere means to an end. In such a case the victim's own conduct is not in question, nor is there any suggestion of reforming the victim himself; he is being penalised merely for the greater good of others. And this is to regard him as less than a person; it is to use him as a thing. In so far as the law is in harmony with morality it will avoid vicarious liability in criminal law, and in English criminal law vicarious liability, though existing, is exceptional.[92]

Modern civil law recognises vicarious liability in two chief classes of cases. In the first place, masters are responsible for the acts of their servants done in the course of their employment. In the second place, representatives of dead men are liable for deeds done in the flesh by those whom they represent. We shall briefly consider each of these two forms.

It has been sometimes said that the responsibility of a master for his servant has its historical source in the responsibility of an owner for his slave. This, however, is certainly not the case. The English doctrine of employer's liability is of comparatively recent growth. It has its origin in the legal presumption, gradually become conclusive, that all acts done by a servant in and about his master's business are done by his master's express or implied authority, and are therefore in truth the acts of the master for which he may be justly held responsible.[93] No employer will be allowed to say that he did not authorise the act complained of, or even that it was done against his express injunctions, for he is liable none the less. This conclusive presumption of authority has now, after the manner of such presumptions, disappeared from the law, after having permanently modified it by establishing the principle of employer's liability. Historically, as we have said, this is a fictitious extension of the principle, *Qui facit per alium facit per se*. Formally, it has been reduced to the laconic maxim, *Respondeat superior*.

The rational basis of this form of vicarious liability is in the first place evidential. There are such immense difficulties in the way of proving actual authority, that it is necessary to establish a conclusive presumption of it. A word, a gesture, or a tone may be a sufficient indication from a master to his servant that some lapse from the legal standard of care or honesty will be deemed acceptable service. Yet who could prove such a measure of complicity? Who could establish liability in such a case, were evidence of authority required, or evidence of the want of it admitted?[94]

---

[92] See Williams, *Criminal Law* (2nd ed.), Chap. 7.
[93] Salmond, *Essays in Jurisprudence and Legal History*, 161–163; Wigmore, "Responsibility for Tortious Acts", *Select Essays in Anglo-American Legal History*, III. 520–537; Street, *Foundations of Legal Liability*, II., Chaps. 41–43; Holdsworth, *H.E.L.*, VIII. 472 *et seq.*
[94] Here again a possible solution would be to require the master to undertake the burden of disproving complicity.

A further reason for the vicarious responsibility of employers is that employers usually are, while their servants usually are not, financially capable of the burden of civil liability. It is felt, probably with justice, that a man who is able to make compensation for the hurtful results of his activities should not be enabled to escape from the duty of doing so by delegating the exercise of these activities to servants or agents from whom no redress can be obtained. Such delegation confers upon impecunious persons means and opportunities of mischief which would otherwise be confined to those who are financially competent. It disturbs the correspondence which would otherwise exist between the capacity of doing harm and the capacity of paying for it. It is requisite for the efficacy of civil justice that this delegation of powers and functions should be permitted only on the condition that he who delegates them shall remain answerable for the acts of his servants, as he would be for his own.[95]

A second form of vicarious responsibility is that of living representatives for the acts of dead men. There is no doubt that criminal responsibility must die with the wrongdoer himself, but with respect to penal redress the question is not free from difficulty. For in this form of liability there is a conflict between the requirements of the two competing principles of punishment and compensation. The former demands the termination of liability with the life of the wrongdoer, while the latter demands its survival. In this dispute the older common law approved the first of those alternatives. The received maxim was: *Actio personalis moritur cum persona*.[96] A man cannot be punished in his grave; therefore it was held that all actions for penal redress, being in their true nature instruments of punishment, must be brought against the living offender and must die with him. Modern opinion rejects this conclusion, and by various statutory provisions the old rule has been almost entirely abrogated. It is considered that although liability to afford redress ought to depend in point of *origin* upon the requirements of punishment, it should depend in point of *continuance* upon those of compensation. For when this form of liability has once come into existence, it is a valuable right of the person wronged; and it is expedient that such rights should be held upon a secure tenure, and should not be subject to extinction by a mere irrelevant accident such as the death of the offender. There is no sufficient reason for drawing any distinction in point of survival between the right of a creditor to recover his debt and the right of a man who has been injured by assault or defamation to recover compensation for the loss so suffered by him.

As a further argument in the same sense, it is to be observed that it is not strictly true that a man cannot be punished after his death. Punishment is effective not at the time it is inflicted, but at the time it is threatened. A threat of evil to be inflicted upon a man's descendants at the expense of his estate will

---

[95] This reason is not given full effect to by the law, for vicarious liability in English law does not generally extend to the acts of independent contractors. For a further discussion of the justifications, real or supposed, of vicarious liability, see Baty, *Vicarious Liability*.
[96] On the history of this maxim see Holdsworth, *H.E.L.*, III. 576–584.

undoubtedly exercise a certain deterrent influence upon him; and the apparent injustice of so punishing his descendants for the offences of their predecessor is in most cases no more than apparent. The right of succession is merely the right to acquire the dead man's estate, subject to all charges which, on any grounds, and apart altogether from the interests of the successors themselves, may justly be imposed upon it.[97]

### 106. THE MEASURE OF CRIMINAL LIABILITY

We have now considered the conditions and the incidence of penal liability. It remains to deal with the measure of it, and here we must distinguish between criminal and civil wrongs, for the principles involved are fundamentally different in the two cases.

In considering the measure of criminal liability it will be convenient to bestow exclusive attention upon the deterrent purpose of the criminal law, remembering, however, that the conclusions so obtained are subject to possible modification by reference to those other purposes of punishment which we thus provisionally disregard.

Were men perfectly rational, so as to act invariably in accordance with an enlightened estimate of consequences, the question of the measure of punishment would present no difficulty. A draconian simplicity and severity would be perfectly effective. It would be possible to act on the Stoic paradox that all offences involve equal guilt, and to visit with the utmost rigour of the law every deviation, however slight, from the appointed way. In other words, if the deterrent effect of severity were certain and complete, the most efficient law would be that which by the most extreme and undiscriminating severity effectually extinguished crime. Were human nature so constituted that a threat of burning all offenders alive would with certainty prevent all breaches of the law, then this would be an effective penalty for all offences from high treason to petty larceny. So greatly, however, are men moved by the impulse of the moment, rather than by a rational estimate of future good and evil, and so ready are they to face any future evil which falls short of the inevitable, that the utmost rigour is sufficient only for the diminution of crime, not for the extinction of it. It is needful, therefore, in judging the merits of the law, to subtract from the sum of good which results from the partial prevention of offences, the sum of evil which results from the partial failure of prevention and the consequent necessity of fulfilling those threats of evil by which the law had hoped to effect its purpose. The perfect law is that in which the difference

---

[97] There is a second application of the maxim, *Actio personalis moritur cum persona*, which seems equally destitute of justification. According to the common law an action for penal redress died not merely with the wrongdoer but also with the person wronged. This rule also has been abrogated by statute in large part. There can be little doubt that in all ordinary cases, if it is right to punish a person at all, his liability should not cease simply by reason of the death of him against whom his offence was committed. The right of the person injured to receive redress should descend to his representatives like any other proprietary interest.

between the good and the evil is at a maximum in favour of the good, and the rules as to the measure of criminal liability are the rules for the attainment of this maximum. It is obvious that it is not attainable by an indefinite increase of severity. To substitute hanging for imprisonment as the punishment for petty theft would doubtless diminish the frequency of this offence,[98] but it is certain that the evil so prevented would be far outweighed by that which the law would be called on to inflict in the cases in which its threats proved unavailing.

In every crime there are three elements to be taken into account in determining the appropriate measure of punishment. These are (1) the motives to the commission of the offence, (2) the magnitude of the offence, and (3) the character of the offender.

### 1. *The Motive of the Offence*

Other things being equal, the greater the temptation to commit a crime the greater should be the punishment. This is an obvious deduction from the first principles of criminal liability. The object of punishment is to counteract by the establishment of contrary and artificial motives the natural motives which lead to crime. The stronger these natural motives the stronger must be the counteractives which the law supplies. If the profit to be derived from an act is great, or the passions which lead men to it are violent, a corresponding strength or violence is an essential condition of the efficacy of repressive discipline. We shall see later, however, that this principle is subject to a very important limitation, and that there are many cases in which extreme temptation is a ground of extenuation rather than of increased severity of punishment.

### 2. *The Magnitude of the Offence*

Other things being equal, the greater the offence, that is to say the greater the sum of its evil consequences or tendencies, the greater should be its punishment. At first sight, indeed, it would seem that this consideration is irrelevant. Punishment, it may be thought, should be measured solely by the profit derived by the offender, not by the evils caused to other persons; if two crimes are equal in point of motive, they should be equal in point of punishment, notwithstanding the fact that one of them may be many times more mischievous than the other. This, however, is not so, and the reason is twofold.

*(a)* The greater the mischief of any offence the greater is the punishment which it is profitable to inflict with the hope of preventing it. For the greater this mischief the less is the proportion which the evil of punishment bears to the good of prevention, and therefore the greater is the punishment which

---

[98] In fact such a substitution might only diminish the frequency of conviction and punishment for juries and courts might well be loth to bring in findings of guilt. See Page, *Crime and the Community*, 54.

can be inflicted before the balance of good over evil attains its maximum. Assuming the motives of larceny and of homicide to be equal, it may be profitable to inflict capital punishment for the latter offence, although it is certainly unprofitable to inflict it for the former. The increased measure of prevention that would be obtained by such severity would, in view of the comparatively trivial nature of the offence, be obtained at too great a cost.

*(b)* A second and subordinate reason for making punishment vary with the magnitude of the offence is that, in those cases in which different offences offer themselves as alternatives to the offender, an inducement is thereby given for the preference of the least serious. If the punishment of burglary is the same as that of murder, the burglar has obvious motives for not stopping at the lesser crime. If an attempt is punished as severely as a completed offence, why should any man repent of his half-executed purposes?

### 3. *The Character of the Offender*

The worse the character or disposition of the offender the more severe should be his punishment. Badness of disposition is constituted either by the strength of the impulses to crime, or by the weakness of the impulses towards law-abiding conduct. One man may be worse than another because of the greater strength and prevalence within him of such anti-social passions as anger, covetousness, or malice; or his badness may lie in a deficiency of those social impulses and instincts which are the springs of right conduct in normally constituted men. In respect of all the graver forms of law-breaking, for one man who abstains from them for fear of the law there are thousands who abstain by reason of quite other influences. Their sympathetic instincts, their natural affections, their religious beliefs, their love of the approbation of others, their pride and self-respect, render superfluous the threatenings of the law. In the degree in which these impulses are dominant and operative, the disposition of a man is good; in the degree in which they are wanting or inefficient, it is bad.

In both its kinds badness of disposition is a ground for severity of punishment. If a man's emotional constitution is such that normal temptation acts upon him with abnormal force, it is for the law to supply in double measure the counteractive of penal discipline. If he is so made that the natural influences towards well-doing fall below the level of average humanity, the law must supplement them by artificial influences of a strength that is needless in ordinary cases.

Any fact, therefore, which indicates depravity of disposition is a circumstance of aggravation, and calls for a penalty in excess of that which would otherwise be appropriate to the offence. One of the most important of these facts is the repetition of crime by one who has been already punished. The law rightly imposes upon habitual offenders penalties which bear no relation either to the magnitude or to the profit of the offence. A punishment adapted for normal men is not appropriate for those who, by their repeated defiance of it, prove their possession of abnormal natures.[99] A second case in which the same principle is applicable is that in which the mischief of an offence is altogether disproportionate to any profit to be derived from it by the offender. To kill a man from mere wantonness, or merely in order to facilitate the picking of his pocket, is a proof of extraordinary depravity beyond anything that is imputable to him who commits homicide only through the stress of passionate indignation or under the influence of great temptation. A third case is that of offences from which normal humanity is adequately dissuaded by such influences as those of natural affection. To kill one's father is in point of magnitude no worse a crime than any other homicide, but it has at all times been viewed with greater abhorrence, and by some laws punished with greater severity, by reason of the depth of depravity which it indicates in the offender. Lastly it is on the same principle that wilful offences are punished with greater rigour than those which are due merely to negligence.

An additional and subordinate reason for making the measure of liability depend upon the character of the offender is that badness of disposition is commonly accompanied by deficiency of sensibility. Punishment must increase as sensibility diminishes. The more depraved the offender the less he feels the shame of punishment; therefore the more he must be made to feel the pain of it. A certain degree of even physical insensibility is said to characterise those who commit crimes of violence; and the indifference with which death itself is faced by those who in the callousness of their hearts have not scrupled to inflict it upon others is a matter of amazement to normally constituted men.

We are now in a position to deal with a question which we have already touched upon but deferred for fuller consideration, namely the apparent paradox involved in the rule that punishment must increase with the temptation to the offence. As a general rule this proposition is true; but it is subject to a very important qualification. For in certain cases the temptation to which a man succumbs may be of such a nature as to rebut that presumption of bad disposition which would in ordinary circumstances arise from the commission of the offence. He may, for example, be driven to the act not by the strength of any bad or self-regarding motives, but by that of his social or sympathetic impulses. In such a case the greatness of the temptation, considered in itself, demands severity of punishment, but when considered as a disproof of the degraded disposition which usually accompanies wrongdoing it demands leniency; and the latter of these two conflicting considerations may be of sufficient importance to outweigh the other. If a man remains honest until he is driven in despair to steal food for his starving children, it is perfectly consistent with the deterrent theory of punishment to deal with him less severely than with him who steals from no other motive than cupidity. He who commits homicide from motives of petty gain, or to attain some trivial purpose, deserves to be treated with the utmost severity, as a man thoroughly callous and

---

[99] The preventive function of punishment is an additional reason for sentencing habitual offenders to such punishments as long terms of imprisonment.

depraved. But he who kills another in retaliation for some intolerable insult or injury need not be dealt with according to the measure of his temptations, but should rather be excused on account of them.

### 107. THE MEASURE OF CIVIL LIABILITY

We have seen that penal redress involves both the compensation of the person injured and the punishment, in a sense, of the wrongdoer. Yet in measuring civil liability the law attaches more importance to the principle of compensation than to that of fault. For it is measured exclusively by the magnitude of the offence, that is to say, by the amount of loss inflicted by it. Apart from some exceptions[100] it takes no account of the character of the offender, and so visits him who does harm through some trivial want of care with as severe a penalty as if his act had been prompted by deliberate malice. Similarly it takes no account of the motives of the offence; he who has everything and he who has nothing to gain are equally punished, if the damage done by them is equal. Finally, it takes no account of probable or intended consequences, but solely of those which actually ensue; wherefore the measure of a wrong-doer's liability is not the evil which he meant to do, but that which he has succeeded in doing. If one man is made to pay higher damages than another, it is not because he is more guilty, but because he has had the misfortune to be more successful in his wrongful purposes, or less successful in the avoidance of unintended issues.

Yet it is not to be suggested that this form of civil liability is unjustifiable. Penal redress possesses advantages more than sufficient to counterbalance any such objections to it. More especially it possesses this, that while other forms of punishment, such as imprisonment, are uncompensated evil, penal redress is the gain of him who is wronged as well as the loss of the wrongdoer. Further, this form of remedy gives to the persons injured a direct interest in the efficient administration of justice—an interest which is almost absent in the case of the criminal law. It is true, however, that the law of penal redress, taken by itself, falls so far short of the requirements of a rational scheme of punishment that it would by itself be totally insufficient. In all modern and developed bodies of law its operation is supplemented, and its deficiencies made good, by a co-ordinate system of criminal liability. These two together, combined in due proportions, constitute a very efficient instrument for the maintenance of justice.

---

100 In certain cases higher damages may be awarded, where the defendant's motives, malice or conduct have increased the plaintiff's suffering. In others higher damages may be awarded to punish the defendant for his behaviour. For the difference between aggravated and exemplary damages *Cf. Rookes* v. *Barnard* [1964] A.C. 1129.

# 13

## Guido Calabresi

Guido Calabresi (1932–    ), Professor of Law at Yale University, initiates in this article a major policy dispute over guidelines for auto liability law with Professors Walter Blum and Harry Kalven, both of the University of Chicago.

# FAULT, ACCIDENTS AND THE WONDERFUL WORLD OF BLUM AND KALVEN*†

This year Professors Walter Blum and Harry Kalven of the University of Chicago Law School published in book form the Shulman lectures they had previously given at Yale.[1] These lectures expounded the thesis that fault might, after all, be a sound basis for liability in automobile accident cases. And, perhaps more important, they contended that none of the myriad plans which had recently been proposed, and which in one way or the other sought their basis in some form of "risk spreading," could be supported. The breadth of the attack as well as the eminence of its authors would by themselves require a careful examination of this thesis. The fact that their position is essentially contrary to most current academic thought and, nonetheless, on the whole wrong makes such examination essential.[2]

What then in essence is it that Blum and Kalven are saying? The main outline of their analysis can be stated simply. First they say that there is no evidence that any automobile compensation plan can, out of its own economies,

*Guido Calabresi, "Fault, Accidents and the Wonderful World of Blum and Kalven." Reprinted by permission of The Yale Law Journal Company and Fred B. Rothman & Company from *The Yale Law Journal*, Vol. 75 (1965), pp. 216–238.

†Many of the ideas in this article were expressed by me at the Association of American Law Schools Torts Roundtable held in December of 1964. The other participants were Professors Addison Mueller of U.C.L.A., moderator, Robert Keeton of Harvard, and Walter Blum and Harry Kalven of Chicago. Professor Luke Cooperrider of Michigan was the chairman of the panel. I should especially like to thank the Walter E. Meyer Research Institute of Law, whose generous support is making possible my continued research in this area, and Jon Hirschoff, a student at the Yale Law School, whose help has been particularly significant.

[1] BLUM & KALVEN, PUBLIC LAW PERSPECTIVES ON A PRIVATE LAW PROBLEM (1965) [hereinafter cited as BLUM & KALVEN]; originally published in 31 U. CHI. L. REV. 641 (1964) as a revised version of the Shulman lectures.

[2] I have not attempted in this short piece to examine all the arguments which Blum and Kalven make. The scope of their work would make that impossible. I have attempted to concentrate on what, to me, is the key weakness in their approach. As a result, many of their elegant contributions and some rather surprising lapses are left unmentioned. Since writing this article I have received page proofs of a book review of BLUM & KALVEN by Professor A. M. Linden due to appear at 53 CALIF. L. REV. 1098 (1965). Professor Linden's piece more than fills many of these gaps.

pay the added costs of non-fault compensation. If there were, and if these economies could not be achieved in another way, Blum and Kalven, like good classical economists, would accept the notion that such a plan was worthwhile. The gainers would be able to compensate the losers, and in some traditional economic sense a more efficient arrangement would be available.[3] There are in fact difficulties both with the way Blum and Kalven reach their conclusion that no plan can pay for itself,[4] and with the view that if it could that would end the matter.[5] But for the moment I am willing to accept their premises.

Second they say: since no plan can pay for itself, we must next ask whether there is any theoretical justification for placing the total cost of accidents on a different group of people from those who currently pay. This question, in effect, assumes a totality of accident costs, and asks whether there is any reason for dividing them up in any way different from the present way. They describe the present way as one in which sometimes victims and sometimes involved non-victims bear all the loss, the decision turning on the rough and ready, but allegedly workable concept of fault. They, at times, depict this way as a vertical division of losses rather than a horizontal one, which would spread the loss among victims and involved non-victims leaving no one as a 100% loser and no one as a 100% winner. Although their categorization is only approximately accurate, given the existence of insurance and their occasional flirting with compulsory insurance of drivers, it is, at least temporarily, acceptable.

---

[3] BLUM & KALVEN 44–54; especially at 51.
[4] One key to their conclusion is that adoption of any non-fault plan would result in increased claims consciousness, and that even if the economies of a plan could pay for current claims regardless of fault, they could not pay for the higher level of claims thus brought about. *Id.* at 46–54. There is, however, an interesting irony in their handling of this problem. At times their whole approach seems to be based on the "justice" of the current system. They say that it is better that worthy (non-fault) victims be *fully* compensated than that less worthy (faulty) victims (or victims injured by non-faulty drivers?) receive some recoveries at the cost of reducing the recoveries of "worthy" victims. *Id.* at 34. Yet when they discuss claims consciousness, they admit that there are many "worthy" victims—fault-free people injured by faulty drivers—who currently *do not* sue and *do not* recover. And it is the fact that these people (who in Blum and Kalven's terms *ought* to recover today) would probably recover under a plan (because of increased claims consciousness) which convinces them that a plan cannot pay for itself out of its own economies. In fact, if this were the only reason that a plan could not pay for itself, then Blum and Kalven would have given a good reason for a plan. For surely if a plan only costs more—and therefore reduces recoveries of "worthy" victims—because it gives recoveries to *equally* worthy victims currently left in the cold, and in addition manages to give something to other "less worthy" types, it would certainly meet Blum and Kalven's requirements. Actually there are other reasons to think that such plans could not pay for themselves just out of economies, and Blum and Kalven's conclusion that the money would have to come from somewhere is probably correct. Needless to say, I find the whole concept of "worthy" victims hard to swallow and would continue to do so even if "fault" meant as much as Blum and Kalven think it means.
[5] Economic literature is full of discussion of when a change is clearly an improvement. And while the start of such discussions is usually the statement that the winners can compensate the losers, that is just the start. Then arguments begin to rage over how to handle situations where compensation of losers, though possible, would not in fact take place, and how such situations relate to income distribution. While such arguments can reach a remarkable degree of mathematical elegance, see, *e.g.*, Mishan, *Welfare Criteria for External Effects*, 51 AM. ECON. REV. 594 (1961) and works there cited, we lawyers can, in this context at least, accept Blum and Kalven's formulation.

Third, and most important, they answer no to the question they have posed; there is no better group of "payers," they say, at least under any plans so far presented. The reasons for this answer are really the core of their analysis. There are, they suggest, two significant grounds usually given for dividing accident costs on non-fault bases. The first is that we wish to compensate victims in such a way that no one is crushed by the loss. The second is that in some sense "economic theory" requires that one of the parties bear the costs it has caused. What they do not say is that the two bases of liability which follow from these grounds share a key element with fault: all three are derived from a common general goal—the reduction of total costs of automobile accidents to society.[6] Fault, in theory, tries to reduce total costs by deterring specific conduct which is felt to be dangerous. "Letting the party which causes the cost bear it" attempts to decrease accident costs either by reducing the cost-causing activity by making it more expensive, or by inducing the introduction of safety devices to the extent that they cost less than paying for the damages which they prevent. "Spreading the loss broadly" attempts to reduce costs in a secondary sense. It does not, like the first two bases of liability, seek to reduce the number or gravity of accidents, but by spreading the burden of accidents it attempts to reduce the bad effects that accidents have—their secondary costs.[7]

At first glance then, the other bases of liability would seem to merit at least as much adherence as fault.[8] But Blum and Kalven decide otherwise. The reasons why they reject each are quite different. They discard risk spreading (compensation of the victim) as a goal of accident law because the same result can be accomplished better through social insurance paid out of general taxes. This solution is better than any accident-law solution because it is more efficient (cheaper), because it makes both the degree of burden (taxes can be adjusted) and the degree of compensation (payments can too) exactly what we want them to be and because we can choose the payor and payee in accordance with their means (with the *goal* of compensation-spreading in mind), whereas accident law at best hits classes of good risk bearers but might include a fair number of bad ones, as well. Of course, if risk spreading is the goal, any serious injury or disease is worthy of the same treatment, and the problem seems to become, as Blum and Kalven view it, one of "poverty" or "distribution of wealth" and not at all one of accidents.[9]

---

6 See Calabresi, *The Decision for Accidents: An Approach to Nonfault Allocation of Costs*, 78 HARV. L. REV. 713, 713–16 (1965). On the relation of fault to this general goal *cf.* HOLMES, THE COMMON LAW 76–77 (Howe ed. 1963).
7 Blum and Kalven, among others (*e.g.*, Calabresi, *supra* note 6 at 714, 734), fail at times to keep in mind that it is minimization of total accident *costs*, *not* minimization of accidents, which is the goal. See, *e.g.*, BLUM & KALVEN 61. Usually minimization of accidents is just used as a short-hand way of saying minimization of accident costs. Occasionally, however, that short-hand may lead to conclusions which would be harder to justify if the goal of minimizing *costs* and not just accidents were kept in the forefront. See, *e.g.*, BLUM & KALVEN 63.
8 Each is, in a sense, a sub-goal of the general goal of minimization of accident costs.
9 See, *e.g.*, BLUM & KALVEN 37–38, 41–43, 83.

Blum and Kalven reject allocating the accident cost to the party which "causes" it because, they contend, any accident cost is in fact caused in an economic sense by all those involved in the accident. Since there is no meaningful way of deciding to what extent a car-pedestrian accident is in fact a cost of driving or walking, we cannot hope correctly to burden one activity with its proper share of the cost in order to reduce it or to induce it to introduce safety measures to a proper degree. Therefore, they conclude, economic theory does not give us a workable standard for allocating losses.

Since the goals of risk spreading and letting the party who causes the cost bear it are either meaningless, or can best be accomplished outside of accident law, we are left, Blum and Kalven suggest, with fault, which, in a rough and ready way, divides losses according to a sense of justice (which, they assert, we have) and, to a degree, reduces total accident costs through specific deterrence. They never really ask—as they do with compensation—whether the goals of fault can better be accomplished outside of accident law. And they treat on the whole unsatisfactorily the questions whether there is any meaning to the sense of justice which fault supposedly vindicates, and whether fault in fact accomplishes any specific deterrence.

So much for the thesis. What does it in fact show? The first thing to note is that, rather unintentionally, the one "plan" which comes out best as a result of Blum and Kalven's dissections is *not* the current fault system—which is left alive, if cadaverous, more for want of a better way than from its own merit— since its "merit" is left largely unexplained. Rather it is social insurance, which emerges as a cheap and effective way of meeting a problem which Blum and Kalven admit exists, that of compensation, or spreading of losses.

And this result is not surprising. For if we deny a meaning to what I have elsewhere termed resource allocation, or general deterrence, as a reason for accident law,[10] if we feel that accident law has no part to play in influencing whether manufacturers, for instance, should use a more expensive but safer material rather than a cheaper more dangerous one, or whether teen-agers should drive as much as 45-year-olds, then there is mighty little reason for accident law at all. It would then be true that the only goals of the law in this area would be a) deterring specific acts of wrongdoing (acts we wish to forbid *even to those willing to pay for the costs which result)*,[11] b) satisfying our "sense of justice" and c) compensating victims. The first two would hardly require the existing massive apparatus of torts and fault. They would best be handled outside of torts law by some more modern semi-criminal device involving,

---

[10] Calabresi, *Some Thoughts on Risk Distribution and the Law of Torts*, 70 YALE L.J. 499, 502 (1961) [hereinafter cited as Calabresi, *Risk Distribution*]; Calabresi, *supra* note 6, at 718, 725 n.18, 742.
[11] We do not permit the individual to exercise independent judgment on the value of drunken driving by offering to pay for all the damage he causes while intoxicated. But even under our present fault system, such specific deterrence is attempted largely through the criminal law. See generally Calabresi, *supra* note 6, at 716–21.

perhaps, non-insurable fines.[12] The last goal would, as Blum and Kalven suggest, best be handled through social insurance rather than through our cumbersome system of torts laws. Since Blum and Kalven reject the general deterrence thesis and make only weak arguments for the necessity of retaining our current fault system, it is only natural that the one conclusion most will draw from their discussion is that we are well on our way to generalized social insurance, despite Blum and Kalven's seeming personal distaste for the loss of freedom that system may entail!

What then are the problems with their analysis? As I see it there are two major problems, and they are related. The first, and more specific one, is that their rejection of "allocation of resources," "general deterrence" or "economic theory" (all really words for the same thing as a guide of *any* usefulness at all is premature. This is far from saying that "general deterrence" presents the answer to the problem. It is only to say that despite Blum and Kalven's attack, general deterrence is, as I hope to show, an element which must be given consideration together with compensation and the "specific deterrence" supposedly induced by fault liability in arriving at a sensible solution. The second problem is that Blum and Kalven reject most proposed "plans" because they do not do as good a job of meeting a *specific* goal as an extreme or ideal solution; but these plans are never examined as ways of accomplishing a complex mixture of goals. Each plan is rejected because it does not do *perfectly* some *one* thing we desire, although it may do the combination of things we want pretty well. The current fault system is, of course, not subjected to a similar test. For example, plans

[12] I assume that, to the extent that we want to deter specific acts directly, a non-insurable fine will be more of a deterrent than a potentially large but fully insured torts judgment. I assume also that at least within the context of *actual* accidents it would not be as expensive to levy such fines as to go through civil torts trials. We might incur added expense if we extended semi-criminal fines to situations where no accident had occurred, for then the cost of discovering the situation would be added. But fault-torts makes no attempt to deal with such questions today. The proper comparison is between specific deterrence accomplished by fault-torts today and the specific deterrence which would be accomplished by having substantial non-insurable fines levied on wrongdoers in accident situations. If we then wanted to expand this deterrence, at added cost, to non-accident situations, that would be another matter.

I am, of course, weaseling to some extent when I talk of a "more modern semi-criminal device." To discuss the form of such a sanction, the procedure for applying it, and its relation to current criminal law would require, at least, a full article. But enough writers have discussed the concept that it is not unfair to suggest that some form of that device may provide a better answer to specific deterrence than is given by fault and insurance in torts today. See, *e.g.*, BLUM & KALVEN 63–64.

The question remains, however, whether such a device would satisfy our sense of justice as fully as fault liability. This I find hard to answer, for I do not fully understand the term "sense of justice." To many people it seems to mean something in the nature of revenge, beyond deterrence and compensation. It is hard for me to swallow this in straight criminal situations, and, of course, even harder in torts situations. But even assuming some meaning for it, would we not get more "adequate" or "just" revenge if the wrongdoer were assessed according to his wrong and not according to chance and size of his insurance policy? On the receiving end, too, one could have a different scale of compensation if one wished, depending on the innocence of the recipient. But why should compensation depend on the *relative* innocence of the victim and the particular injurer, and on the injurer's particular insurance coverage? Surely our sense of justice has advanced somewhat beyond the rather medieval "duel" stage.

designed to increase loss spreading or compensation are ruled out because
"social insurance" can do it better (given social insurance, all are equally
good risk bearers). But social insurance could equally be rejected for failing
to effectuate some of the deterrence goals we wish of accident law. And the
key question, whether fault or any given non-fault system best accomplishes
the *mixture* of goals we in fact want, is never really asked!

I have said that these two problems with the book are related, and before
I discuss them in detail, it may be well to explain generally what the relationship is. In the first place, the more goals we want accident law to accomplish,
the more likely the kind of unilateral comparison Blum and Kalven engage in
will be misleading. If general deterrence is added to specific deterrence, compensation and undigested "justice" as an aim of tort law, an analysis which
rejects one plan because it does not compensate as well as social insurance, and
rejects another plan because it does not give us a good undigested "justice" as
fault might, becomes even less satisfactory. The more valid aims we have, the
more we must look to see which system or combination of systems does the
best job of reconciling them all.

The second aspect of this relationship follows from the fact that the validity
of "general deterrence" as a goal of tort law may depend in part on the existence
of a variety of other valid goals. Blum and Kalven say that economic theory
can not tell us whether it is better for cars or pedestrians to bear the cost of
car-pedestrian accidents. Even if that statement were completely true (which
it is not),[13] if economic theory suggested no more than that the cost should be
borne by cars *or* by pedestrians, then, although fault might be as good a ground
for dividing the cost between them as any (from a general deterrence point
of view), social insurance, which removes the cost from *both* pedestrians and
cars, would not! Thus, if compensation motives led us to remove (externalize
is the economists' term) part or all of the cost from both pedestrians and
drivers and cover it by social insurance, we would substantially violate the goal
of general deterrence. In short, we might find that fault failed because it gave
inadequate compensation, while social insurance failed because it removed
the cost from the combined cost causers (pedestrians and drivers) and, therefore,
gave no general deterrence. Instead, a combined plan which picked the best
loss spreader *between* pedestrians and drivers, although not giving as good
compensation as social insurance, or any better general deterrence than
fault,[14] might still give the best combination of both.

I do not mean this to be the answer, not yet at least. For I have left out
of the mixture those goals which fault supposedly accomplishes best—specific
deterrence and gratifying our sense of justice—and if I were to support a system

---

[13] See Calabresi, *supra* note 6, at 725–42, especially 726–27 and 734–36.
[14] I have argued elsewhere that various combined non-fault plans would, in fact, give better
general deterrence than fault, because they would tend to deter activities prone to serious
accidents rather than just activities prone to fault-caused serious accidents. Calabresi, *supra*
note 6, at 719–20. I still hold to that, *cf.* note 37 *infra,* and am only taking the "weaker" position
here, *arguendo,* for the sake of remaining close to Blum and Kalven's argument.

on such analysis, I would be guilty of the same fault of which I accuse Blum and Kalven. The only conclusions to be derived from the above analysis at this stage are: 1) it is incorrect to reject systems which seek to accomplish a variety of goals because a single-minded system can meet one goal more fully; and, conversely, 2) a goal which by itself may not be so capable of definition as to determine a *single* perfect solution may nevertheless be clear enough and important enough to rule out *some* solutions, and therefore to militate for mixed rather than single-minded systems.

These conclusions would be enough for a book review and perhaps I should stop here. But to do so would leave substantially unanswered the *specific* criticisms which Blum and Kalven make of "general deterence" or, in their words, of "economic theory," as a guide to allocation of losses. There is no need to go to great length in reiterating what the "general deterrence" thesis is.[15] Essentially it is the notion that in our society what is produced is by and large the result of market choices by individuals. These choices are influenced by the relative prices of competing goods. To the extent that these prices reflect the costs of producing the product involved, people get as near to what they want as is possible in a fallible world; but to the extent that these prices understate the actual cost to society of producing a product, more of that product gets made and bought (relative to other goods) than we in fact want, and unnecessary costs are undertaken. And finally, accident costs are as much costs to society and as worthy of being considered in deciding what goods we want as, say, the cost of the metal it takes to make a product. Specifically, the thesis holds that although, for instance, we may not want the *safest* possible product, we do want the manufacturer to choose a means of production which may be somewhat more expensive in terms of materials used if this expense is made up by savings in accident costs. Similarly, although we do not wish to abandon cars altogether (they give us more pleasure than they cost us—despite accident costs), we may, if we are made to pay for car-caused accidents, drive less, or less at night, or less when we are of accident-prone ages, or with more safety devices, than if we are not made to pay for accident costs when we decide to use a car. I call this thesis general deterrence, because it seeks to diminish accident costs not by directly attacking specific occasions of danger, but (like workmen's compensation) by making more expensive those activities which are accident prone and thereby making more attractive their safer substitutes.

Blum and Kalven divide general deterrence into two areas: situations arising from injuries where the choice of loss bearers is between related parties—

---

[15] See generally Calabresi, *Risk Distribution* at 500–17; Calabresi, *supra* note 6, especially at 719–20.

This thesis has, as I have pointed out elsewhere, many limitations. These involve, among others, the existence of monopoly power and the problem of income distribution. See Calabresi, *Risk Distribution* 503, & n.17, 507–14. These limitations would be enough to preclude making general deterrence our sole goal. But as I tried to show in the above article, they do not render it invalid as one of our aims.

for example, buyers and sellers—and situations arising from injuries where the choice of loss bearers is between independent parties. The first is exemplified by a workmen's compensation accident, a *Vincent v. Lake Erie* situation,[16] or a simple products liability—with privity—case; the second by a car-pedestrian accident. Blum and Kalven conclude that, on the whole, it makes no difference (in terms of economics) who bears the loss in the first case, and that economics can give no guide as to who ought to bear the loss in the second. Needless to say, while I agree fully with their division of the problem into what I have elsewhere called "bargaining" and "non-bargaining" situations, I do not agree with their conclusions as to the relevance of economics to each.

The first and easier case is the bargaining situation. Blum and Kalven contend that it makes no difference which of the two bargaining parties bears the loss. And, in theory, they are correct. How the theory works has been clearly stated by Blum and Kalven in their book and perhaps less clearly by me in an earlier article,[17] so there is little point in restating it fully. The short of it is that the price ultimately established between the parties to the bargain will—under perfect competition—necessarily reflect who bears the risk of loss and, therefore, the same share of the loss will be borne by each regardless of who the original loss bearer is. Moreover, the party who is made to bear the loss initially will try to minimize his loss (if minimization is possible) by installing safety devices or by dealing only with parties who do, whichever is cheaper. Consequently, the cheapest way of minimizing the loss will result, whoever the initial risk bearer is. The use of safety devices is, of course, only one example of how such losses may be minimized.

That this theory is an insufficient answer is patent. If nothing else, the effect workmen's compensation had on industrial accidents (a classic "bargaining situation") made this clear once and for all. Part of the reason for this insufficiency is, as I have attempted to say elsewhere, that the theory presupposes two things: a) the equal ability of the parties to the bargain to estimate and value the risk of accidents properly and to act on their evaluations, and b) the equal ability of the parties to insure—or self-insure—at an equal cost. In addition, the theory excludes a third thing: c) that the initial placing of all or part of the loss on one of the two bargaining parties rather than on the other may result, for political, compensation or other reasons, in the removal of this portion of the loss from *both* bargaining parties, with the result that the pressure toward minimizing the loss would be lost. In practice, the two assumptions made by the theory are often invalid, and the excluded situation is very real. And whenever *one* of these contingencies occurs, "economic theory" or "general deterrence," taken not as an exercise in economic "model" making, but as a practical tool, suggests very definite preferences as to loss bearers in bargaining situations.

[16] Vincent v. Lake Erie Transp. Co., 109 Minn. 456, 124 N.W. 221 (1910). Defendant kept its vessel tied to plaintiff's dock during an "unforeseeably" violent storm, and was held liable for damage to the dock.
[17] BLUM & KALVEN 58–59 (the watch case). Calabresi, *supra* note 6.

Economic theory suggests, first of all, that the party who can better evaluate the risk of accidents is the better loss bearer, because his evaluation will bring about a more accurate determination of the point up to which changes to avoid accident costs (such as safety measures or reduction in an activity) are cheaper than the accident costs which would result without these changes. It suggests, secondly, that the party who can insure or self-insure more cheaply is the better loss bearer, because the other party would be influenced, in making the decision as to the changes suggested above, by an unnecessary administrative cost, the extra cost of providing *him* with insurance. Finally, it suggests that the better loss bearer is the party whose initial bearing of the liability does not result, for compensation or other reasons, in removal of the loss from both parties. For such removal would destroy the incentive to adopt the changes previously mentioned.[18] These three preferences, of course, will not necessarily be consistent in any given case. But they each represent criteria based on general deterrence which must be taken into account in a deciding who is the better loss bearer in a bargaining situation.

Blum and Kalven, although starting from the position that generally it makes no difference in a bargaining situation who the initial loss bearer is, do admit one, and only one, reason why this theory does not work perfectly. This reason, somewhat different from any of the three that I have suggested, has some validity, but is inadequately analyzed by them. The reason given by Blum and Kalven for doubting this theory is this: "Placing liability on the [manufacturer rather than the victim in a product liability, industrial accident, or other bargaining case] is tantamount to compelling [potential victims] to buy insurance against the loss through paying a higher price."[19] Moreover, they suggest, this insurance necessarily fails to take into account the different accident proneness of different potential victims and therefore makes the safe user pay as much as the unsafe one. At first glance this argument seems compelling. But it turns out that the first point, "compulsory insurance," is, strictly speaking, false, and the second, while it does suggest a valid criterion for determining the better loss bearer in a bargaining situation, names it as the sole one, when it is only a criterion of the same type and general significance as the three I have suggested.

---

[18] This result would occur whenever one of the parties (on whom all or part of the loss is placed) received assistance (such as a government subsidy) in paying for the portion of the loss initially placed on him. To the extent that a party received such assistance, he would not consider minimization of the loss worthwhile, since *he* would be paying for the minimization (*i.e.*, he would pay for the safety devices, or would pay more by dealing only with parties who used safety devices), while only the *assisting party (e.g.*, the government) would benefit by the reduction in loss. The assisting party might, of course, try to bring pressure on the assisted party to minimize the loss—query, however, how expensive and how effective such pressure would be. *Cf.* Calabresi, *supra* note 6, at 727–28.

The result under discussion assumes, it must be remembered, only assistance which is triggered by the placement of loss upon the party, not subsidies generally. A party receiving, for example, a yearly subsidy, which is not affected by his accident costs, would react exactly like a non-subsidized party.

[19] BLUM & KALVEN 59. See also note 23 *infra*.

It is of course true that if we make manufacturers of a product compulsorily liable with no right to "opt out" (exculpate themselves) for a price discount, the user will, in effect, be forced to insure against accidents. Part of the cost of all accidents will be included in the price he pays, and he will be covered if he is the one hurt. That is what insurance is. But it is equally true that if manufactures are not liable and have no right to "opt in" to liability for a higher price (indemnify the user), then *manufacturers* will, in effect, be forced to insure against accidents, and users will be the insurers.[20] A manufacturer (according to the theory Blum and Kalven accept) will have to charge less for the product than if he were liable, since users will be aware of the risk they take in buying the product. This reduction in price represents the "cost" of the "compulsory" insurance to the manufacturer.

This case, where manufacturers cannot assume liability, strikes us as unlikely, and in practice perhaps it is. For we do not usually think of manufacturing situations where we would not allow the seller to agree to indemnify the buyer. The typical manufacturing situation, however, is just one selected example of the bargaining problem. Consider, instead, a large number of small farmers selling wheat, which occasionally explodes, to the gigantic "Incorporated Millers Company"—or more realistically, small parts manufacturers selling to a large industrial user.[21] In these cases the notion of forbidding the seller from "opting into" liability (from agreeing to a "form" indemnification contract), with the resulting "compulsory insurance" of the seller, seems quite plausible. The cases of the farmers and the small parts manufacturers are, in fact, exactly the same as Blum and Kalven's reversed. The only difference is that in my examples we may want to make insurance of the seller compulsory, while in Blum and Kalven's example we seem to want to make insurance of the buyer compulsory. In either case it is our decision to exclude contractual arrangements designed to shift the initial loss from one bargainer to the other which makes the insurance compulsory, *not* the fact that the loss is originally placed by law on one or the other.[22]

The fact of the matter is simply this—whenever we determine, as a matter of law, which of two bargaining parties will bear the initial undivided

---

[20] The users could, of course, farm out the risk; that is, they could insure with parties outside the bargain, in short, insurance companies. Similarly, if the manufacturer were originally held liable, he too could farm out the risk. These facts in no way affect the analysis in the text, for the insured is, in either case, compelled to be *insured;* they just mean that the original insurer is not compelled to be a final *insurer.* It is still true, however, that the cost of avoiding being a compulsory insurer, *i.e.,* the cost of farming out the risk as against self-insuring or taking a lump loss, is, and ought to be, an important factor in deciding who the better risk bearer is.

[21] *Cf.,* United States v. New York Great A & P Co., 173 F.2d 79 (7th Cir. 1949), also a monopsonistic situation in an area where we usually think and speak in terms of monopolistic power.

[22] Opting in may be different from opting out. Opting in sounds as if the assumer of liability has a greater awareness of what he is doing. (But imagine my "Incorporated Millers Company" using a form contract requiring opting into liability.) In any case, this difference is but another illustration that knowledge or awareness of risk may affect the choice of whom we wish to hold initially liable and whether we wish to allow such a party to exculpate himself. *(Cf.,* the criteria I suggest as relevant, text accompanying note 27 *infra.)*

cost of an accident, and forbid the shifting of that liability to the other in exchange for a fee, we are *compelling* the party who is not held liable to insure against the loss with the party who is liable.[23] This is not to say that we are indifferent as to which party we wish to compel to insure, or that we are indifferent as to whether we wish to *compel* insurance at all or to make it optional by allowing exculpatory or indemnificatory clauses. The point is only that the argument which Blum and Kalven make from compulsory insurance is false, for *whether compulsory insurance results from a liability scheme depends not, as they say, on which party is held liable, but on whether once we decide to hold one party liable in the first instance* (for any of the reasons I have previously suggested) *we let that party exculpate itself*—that is shift the risk of undivided loss to the other—*for a price.* Nor does the fact that we are more likely to let one party exculpate itself than the other change my point at all. For this fact just suggests that reasons *not* discussed by Blum and Kalven for assigning liability in a bargaining situation (such as unequal awareness of risks or unequal bargaining power) are sufficiently strong to impel compulsory insurance of the non-liable party.

This argument leaves unanswered, however, Blum and Kalven's point that the compulsory insurance which comes about in a bargaining situation is a particularly noxious one since it charges all those who are insured the same premium. All users of Brand X (which occasionally explodes) pay the same additional amount for the product once it is decided that Brand X will compensate the injured buyer, even though people over 45 are more likely to suffer serious injury than nimble 33 year-olds. But why would all parties pay the same amount for this insurance? In the wonderful world of Blum and Kalven, where all parties know and evaluate all risks equally well, and insurance costs stand in the same proportion to risk for all parties—in the world of their theory without my limitations on it, in other words—there would be no such equality.[24] The manufacturer of Brand X would charge different users different

[23] Strictly speaking, "held liable" is not used in the normal sense. I am using the term to identify the party who under the law bears the initial undivided loss, whether that party is the party who is originally injured or the party who through a legal judgment must compensate the injured party and thereby becomes the financially injured party. I use the term this way to emphasize the fact that whether the originally injured party or some other party is made to bear the undivided loss, in the first instance, is the result of a legal judgment, a "holding liable," and not of metaphysics. Failure to recognize this fact leads easily to the error Blum and Kalven make—that compulsory insurance in this area is a one-way street.

[24] If Blum and Kalven are troubled that in some cases compulsory insurance results in the same premium to each insured, they should (in the wonderful world of their theory) be dismayed at the very existence of insurance! For differentiation in premiums is only movement along a spectrum which begins at total social insurance (no differentiation among risks) and ends at the absence of insurance (total differentiation among risks, or total predictability). At one end there is perfect loss spreading; at the other there is perfect general deterrence, since each individual undertakes each act fully aware of its costs and perfectly willing to pay those costs. In the latter case, there may still be "intertemporal insurance" through saving but never "interpersonal insurance."

In a world where predictability is limited, however, each individual must either undertake actions at the risk of their costing more than he had anticipated, or be willing, to some extent, to pool his risks with those of others. He may sometimes even be *compelled* to pool his risks; see text preceding note 23 *supra*. This pooling may take place through farming the risk out to an "insurance company," or through dealings between a group of parties "not held liable" and

prices depending on their accident proneness. He would, in effect, charge them different insurance premiums according to their risk categories. The fact that the manufacturer does not distinguish among his purchasers in this way is simply a sign that the distinction is not worth the cost, a not unusual fact in insurance. Indeed, if Brand X were used in making toilet paper (hardly any explosive potential) and airplane bodies (very high explosive potential), and if the maker of Brand X were the party held liable, we can be sure that the prices charged to the two types of buyers would be very different and would reflect the different accident proneness of the uses.

The reverse is similarly true. If users of goods are uncompensated for injuries—that is if manufacturers are "forced" to insure with their buyers— and if different manufacturers have different accident records, they may or may not be able to command different prices for their goods. This ability will depend on how significantly different their accident records are and on the feasibility of having a price structure with differing prices. If the manufacturers can command different prices, then the case is like Brand X toilet paper and airplanes reversed. If they cannot, then it is like the "horror" Blum and Kalven pose, for here the safe manufacturer (in Blum and Kalven it was the safe user) is forced to pay the same "compulsory insurance premium" as the accident-prone one.

Having said all this, I must admit that Blum and Kalven have a point—if a small one. It is certainly true, in *fact,* though not in Blum and Kalven's theory, that in most bargaining situations one of the parties is better able to differentiate than the other. It may be more difficult or expensive for manufacturers who are held liable to charge different prices to users in accordance with the latters' accident proneness, than it is for users who are held liable [25] to command different prices from manufacturers according to the manufac-

parties "held liable." (See note 23 *supra.*) (The latter situation is illustrated by Blum and Kalven's watch case. See note 17 *supra.)* If an individual wishes to pool his risks, he can never insist on total differentiation in premiums (that would mean the absence of risk pooling), or on the particular differentiation which suits him; he must accept that differentiation in premiums which is set by the insurance company or by the party "held liable." Of course, under relatively pure competition the insurance company or the party held liable would have to differentiate so long as greater differentiation was worth more to the insureds or non-liable parties than it cost the insurer or liable party. In all cases, moreover, the amount of differentiation in premiums, or movement along the spectrum I have described, must be related to the costs of such movement faced by the insurance company or party held liable. Why Blum and Kalven should be so concerned about lack of differentiation when a "party held liable" is concerned, and not when an "insurance company" is involved, is not clear to me.

We may make a collective judgment that we want more general deterrence, or, instead, more loss spreading, than is provided at the equilibrium point reached on the spectrum through private dealings. If so, we can take action resulting in more or less differentiation, as the case may be. Consider, for example, subsidized special risk categories to enable employment of physically handicapped, and hence accident-prone, workers. But we *cannot* have both more loss spreading and more general deterrence; hence the constant tension between them. Of course, the point on the spectrum desired by society might well be the same as arrived at through the process of private decision making described above. Indeed, the more we accept the basic postulates of "free market" economy, the more this is likely to be so. I am indebted to Mr. Jon Hirschoff for the thoughts awkwardly expressed by me in this footnote.

[25] See note 23 *supra.*

turers' accident proneness.[26] If this difference exists in fact, then a small argument (based on general deterrence) exists for user rather than manufacturer liability. But it exists despite the theory which says that it makes no difference who is held liable, as the argument is of exactly the same nature and weight as the three arguments I suggested previously for deciding who in a bargaining situation ought to bear the loss. Indeed the criterion Blum and Kalven suggest may be no more than a restatement in a slightly different context of one of the criteria I suggested: "which party can more efficiently insure against the loss." But whatever the context, this is not the sole criterion. For surely it is equally important to know whether the various manufacturers are better aware of the accident risks involved in their products than are the users, as it is to know whether they can distinguish the accident proneness of users more easily than the users can distinguish the accident proneness of the manufacturers.

In other words, in theory it makes no difference, for *general deterrence*, which of two parties to a bargain bears the accident costs which may result. In practice it might also make no difference (usually when the bargainers are of approximately equal size, number, expertise and wealth). But it may make a great deal of difference. Among the factors which operate to determine who is the better loss bearer from a general deterrence point of view are: 1) which of the parties can better evaluate the risk involved; 2) which of the parties can better evaluate the accident proneness of potential parties on the other side; 3) which of the parties can better let this knowledge, when significant, be reflected in the prices it can command; 4) which of the parties can more cheaply insure against the liability; and 5) placing liability on which of the two parties is less likely to cause the loss to be removed from both, for compensation or other reasons.[27]

So viewed, the "bargaining" situation, far from being the throw away which Blum and Kalven make it out to be, becomes a situation where general deterrence gives definite guidelines. And Blum and Kalven's ultimate conclusions on the bargaining case show the error of not keeping these general deterrence guidelines in mind. For they conclude that when you deal with a bargaining case, in theory it does not matter who bears the loss, and in practice it matters

---

[26] This is not unlikely in what we think of as the normal situation with respect to manufacturers and users, because of the numbers involved (it may be easier for many users to inform themselves about the products of a few manufacturers than it is for the manufacturers to inform themselves about the habits of each user), and perhaps because it may be easier to determine characteristics of products than to determine habits of individuals. But manufacturing cases are only one instance of the "bargaining" situation. And, especially in non-manufacturing cases, the person we think of as the user may be in the opposite position. See, for example, Vincent v. Lake Erie Transp. Co., *supra* note 16, where the dock owners could probably estimate with relative ease the damage which a given boat would inflict to a dock during a violent storm, while boat owners might find it difficult to say which dock would most likely be hit by a violent storm.

The passage of time may affect our estimate. Whereas it was once easier for the employer (held liable for injuries to employees) to adjust the wages of the employee according to his safety record than it was for the employee (made to bear the cost of his injuries) to command higher wages from more accident-prone employers, today in industries where labor unions are strong the reverse might even be true. *Cf.* Calabresi, *supra* note 6, at 728 n.22.

[27] See also note 22 *supra*.

only in the sense of finding who is the more readily available and cheaper insurer. Furthermore, they say, there is no reason to believe that the manufacturer is a better loss bearer than the consumer, because social insurance can make the consumer a better insurer than the manufacturer. The trouble is that social insurance removes the cost from *both* the bargaining parties and, according to the theory Blum and Kalven accept, it is important to the diminution (general deterrence) of accident costs to keep these costs on *one or the other*. The relevant question, then, may not be who can insure more cheaply in an absolute sense, but what allocation of liability results in finding the cheaper insurer while keeping the cost on the bargaining parties. The answer is *not* social insurance, but may be manufacturers' liability. I say may be, because general deterrence guidelines cannot by themselves determine where we want to place liability. We cannot, however, ignore these guidelines in comparing how well different systems or plans (including fault) meet our combined complex of goals.

The more difficult case Blum and Kalven pose is that of non-bargaining parties, such as the car-pedestrian accident. Here Blum and Kalven are prepared to say that it may make a good deal of difference, from a general deterrence point of view, which of the two parties bears the loss; but they claim economic theory is of no help at all in deciding this question. They first, properly I fear, reject the ingenious attempt of Professor Coase to resolve this case into the bargaining case.[28] They then assert that since we do not know the extent to which the costs of car-pedestrian accidents are due to cars and the extent to which they are due to pedestrians, economics can give us no way of dividing the costs of these accidents that is more precise than fault.

But once again, I think, Blum and Kalven have moved too quickly. For again our general deterrence motives do tell us that, in theory, even if we could not tell what part of the cost to put on cars and what part to put on pedestrians, it would be better to put the cost on one or the other, or partially on both, than to externalize it from both and make it a general cost of living (as social insurance would do). Indeed economic theory would go further and say that the more we can sub-categorize (the more we can put the cost not just on "cars" but on old cars or old cars driven by people under 21, etc.), the more adequate general deterrence we get.[29] Of course, since it costs money to

---

[28] Professor Coase suggested the possibility of independent parties involved in accidents or other joint-cost causing activities entering into bargaining relationships and concluded that where the cost of establishing such relationships was not too great the independent situation would, in theory, resolve itself exactly as the bargaining one did. Blum and Kalven, however, and indeed Coase himself, feel that the practical limitations on such "artificial" bargains are significant enough to exclude their being the answer. BLUM & KALVEN 61–62. See generally Coase, *The Problem of Social Cost*, 3 J. LAW & ECON. 1 (1960). I agree—and feel that there may be some theoretical limitations as well. See Calabresi, *supra* note 6, at 724–31 and accompanying footnotes. This is too bad, because were Coase's theory frequently workable, the guidelines for liability derived in the bargaining case would apply here as well. As it is, more work is needed, though it still helps to know that egregious mistakes made in assigning liability in non-bargaining situations may, at least in part, be mitigated through Coasian "deals" between independent parties.

[29] See generally Calabresi, *supra* note 6, at 733–34.

sub-categorize, we shall finally reach the point at which the added general deterrence achieved is not worth the cost of the added sub-categorization.[30]

If, moreover, we knew that we wanted the cost to be distributed among the smallest sub-categories of pedestrians or drivers which can efficiently be drawn, then we would tend to rule out those loss allocation systems which, for either compensation or political reasons or for just practical reasons of how the insurance industry works, tend to put the cost on broad categories rather than small categories, or ultimately remove it from both parties to the accident and put it on the broadest category of all, "the taxpayers." A few examples may help. Suppose that we have no theoretical guidelines indicating whether pedestrians or drivers ought to bear the costs of car-pedestrian accidents. Suppose also that we know that drivers can insure cheaply against such accidents at prices which relate to their driving record and relevant characteristics (age, type of car, etc.), but that pedestrians can insure cheaply against such accidents only by taking out broad "all accidents of living" policies. Placing the cost on drivers would in this situation tend to cause a proper general deterrence effect (it would influence the amount and type of driving in relation to pedestrian accidents caused), while placing it on pedestrians would not result in general deterrence. Though the theory would not tell us in the abstract which party ought to bear the loss, the theory would, in practice, tell us that drivers should.

We would reach the same result if placing the cost on pedestrians would not affect the amount or type of walking chosen because walking is (let us assume) an activity which is virtually fixed and has no safer substitutes. The pedestrian would, therefore, have no alternative choices if some forms of walking were made more expensive than others.[31] If driving, instead, were more flexible, or had more substitutes, drivers would once again be better loss bearers. Furthermore, even if walking were not "fixed" but we wanted it to be fixed and unaffected (for various political or philosophical reasons) then we could best minimize car-pedestrian accidents by placing the loss on drivers.

Finally, and most important of all, if placing the loss on pedestrians results in such an unpalatable situation, from a compensation point of view, that the loss is removed from the pedestrians, and is shifted to a general social insurance fund, then we know that from a general deterrence point of view

---

[30] Among the costs of sub-categorization are those of fact-finding and record keeping. Whenever the parties involved are benefited (or suffer loss) by virtue of their category, the cost of determining the facts on which to base categorization is likely to be substantial, because one cannot rely on statements of facts by the parties. Compare the problem under workmen's compensation of whether an injury is work-related.

The point at which added general deterrence is not worth the cost of sub-categorization may even be at social insurance in some areas. See CONARD et al., AUTOMOBILE ACCIDENT COSTS AND PAYMENTS, 52 (1964), and Conard, *The Economic Treatment of Automobile Injuries,* 63 MICH. L. REV. 279, 289–91 (1964).

[31] The assumption now is different from that in the previous paragraph. I am assuming here that pedestrians can insure against car-pedestrian accidents at prices geared to their individual characteristics as pedestrians. The new assumption is, however, that this will have almost no effect on "walking."

the pedestrian is a poor loss bearer. If, in addition, putting the loss on drivers has no similar effect, then general deterrence tells us quite clearly that the driver is the better loss bearer.[32]

This last example is particularly germane in view of the conclusions which Blum and Kalven reach with regard to the problem of compensation (risk spreading) in the context of automobile accidents. They pose the question: "Are motorists as a class superior risk bearers to the tax paying public?" "The very existence of social security indicates that the answer is obviously no."[33] But if it is only a form of social insurance which can make auto victims as good risk bearers as motorists (from a compensation point of view), then, in practice, from the point of view of general deterrence or economic theory, motorists are much better loss bearers than pedestrians, since putting the loss on pedestrians means putting the loss *outside* the motorist-pedestrian pair.

---

[32] It may not be readily apparent why, if economics cannot tell us how to divide pedestrian-car accident costs between pedestrians and cars, it is better, from a general deterrence point of view, that cars bear all the cost than that cars bear part and the rest be removed from both. The reason we have difficulty in determining a proper division of costs between the two is that we cannot say how much the presence of cars, as against a substitute, adds to the cost of walking; and how much walking, as against a substitute, adds to the cost of cars. All we know is that together they have certain costs. See *Calabresi, supra* note 6, 725, 737–39. It is probable that the best way (the cheapest from the point of view of society) of reducing these costs would be to affect both cars and walking somewhat (both as to the amount of each which is done and as to the way in which it is done—the latter means driving new cars rather than old, driving older people, etc.). But we do not know, at least on the Blum and Kalven assumptions, how much we should try to affect cars and how much walking. Since we do know, however, that together they cost society a certain amount, we can say that, from an allocation of resources or general deterrence point of view, we are always better off if we reduce or alter the combined activities, either jointly or severally, up to the point where people would rather pay for the accident costs than suffer the reduction or alteration. Up to that point, the change "costs" people less than the accidents avoided, and so is worth doing. It is worth doing, moreover, even if the change is *all* at the expense of one activity and a cheaper (less painful) change could be accomplished *in theory* by affecting both. For this last premise does not deny that the original change "cost" people less than it saved them; all it shows is that a theoretically *better* change was possible. But this theoretically better change is, under the original assumptions, not available in practice. For the situation we are examining is one where whatever part of the accident cost is not put on cars is removed from both cars and pedestrians and borne in a way which affects neither. The result is that instead of getting the theoretically better combined effect on both activities by dividing the costs, we end up getting no diminution in one and some in the other in a situation where *ex hypothesis* a greater diminution would save more than it would cost.

For a discussion of how placing costs on activities bring about the optimal result from a general deterrence point of view, and how this general deterrence optimum may nonetheless differ from what we want, see Calabresi, *supra* note 6, 716–21.

Ironically, if it were true, as Blum and Kalven argue, that we do not know at all how to divide car-pedestrian costs between walking and driving, it would follow that even if putting part of the cost on cars and part on pedestrians did not result in externalization we could not show that the change brought about was better than that resulting from putting all the costs on driving. What Blum and Kalven must mean, therefore, is that while we cannot know precisely how to divide accident costs between cars and pedestrians so as to accomplish the best general deterrence, we can take a rough guess, and that rough guess is the fault division. See BLUM & KALVEN 63. Apart from the problem that that rough guess may well result in a removal of part of the cost from both and, therefore, a clear error, there is very little reason for believing that "fault," with all the moral luggage it carries, is at all equipped for making even an adequate, let alone the best, rough guess. See note 37 *infra*.

[33] BLUM & KALVEN, at 56. See also *id.* at 83.

Once again, Blum and Kalven's error is to talk general deterrence just long enough to show that it gives no complete answer, but to forget, when the discussion turns to compensation, the indications general deterrence is able to give. For if the choice is among three types of systems, the first of which gives general deterrence and *some* compensation (as in a motorist liability plan), the second of which gives optimal compensation but no general deterrence (as in social insurance) and the third of which gives general deterrence but inadequate compensation (as in a pedestrian liability, or a fault-based plan), we may well and properly choose the first. In other words, we may prefer a mixed-goals system to single-minded systems.

The above conclusion follows even on the most negative of assumptions about what we can learn from economic theory concerning the division of costs of accidents between their joint causers, and gives rise to some interesting possibilities in the way of mixed systems which it may be worthwhile to mention. A complete analysis, however, is far beyond the scope of the present discussion. Let us continue to assume for the moment that economics does not tell us how best to divide accident costs between cars and pedestrians, but does, as I have suggested, tell us that it is better that either bear all of the cost than that one bear part and the remainder be removed from both.[34] If we feel that it is better from the point of view of "justice" to try to divide the cost between cars and pedestrians, then the way to do it might not be through the "vertical" fault system Blum and Kalven suggest which, because of its bad compensation effects, might result in removal of part of the cost from both. The way to divide the cost might be through those very "horizontal" plans Blum and Kalven reject.

Take for example the suggestion made by Jaffe, and in a slightly different way by Keeton and O'Connell, that as liability moves further away from fault, pain and suffering damages become anachronistic.[35] If leaving pain and suffering on auto victims while putting other damages on drivers brought about a result which was acceptable from a compensation point of view, and if leaving pain and suffering on victims did not bring about an externalization or nullification of their "costs" for any of the other reasons I have suggested, then such a plan would be acceptable from a general deterrence point of view and, *ex hypothesis,* adequate from the standpoint of compensation.[36] If in addition such a division of costs between "drivers" and "victims" had the effect of minimizing the expense of administering the system, it might turn out to be quite a good plan for meeting our goals of accident law.

---

[34] See note 32 *supra.*

[35] Jaffe, *Damages for Personal Injury: The Impact of Insurance,* 18 LAW & CONTEMP. PROB. 219, 235 (1953); Keeton & O'Connell, *Basic Protection—A Proposal for Improving Automobile Claims Systems,* 78 HARV. L. REV. 329, 356–57, 371, 381–82 (1964). The authors do not provide compensation for pain and suffering under their proposed plan. They do suggest self-insurance, and they allow supplementary recoveries (including pain and suffering damages) based on the fault principle in cases of "serious injury."

[36] This assumes that the prospect of bearing the monetary cost of pain and suffering would affect the habits of potential victims. This assumption implies both that potential victims who wished

But, as I have said, this is not the place to examine systems. And such a division of costs might be inadequate because it failed to meet other goals such as specific deterrence, or our sense of justice. It might also be inadequate if economics gives a more specific answer as to how to divide costs between cars and pedestrians than we have here admitted for the sake of staying close to Blum and Kalven's argument.[37] If economics does provide a more specific answer, agnostic splitting between cars and pedestrians might not be the best we could do, although general deterrence being only one of our aims, failure to meet all the requirements of general deterrence would certainly not rule out such a plan. Still, the best that can be said for Blum and Kalven's attempt to show these "horizontal" plans to be unsatisfactory is that they fail to prove their case.

to insure against pain and suffering would obtain, such insurance for pain and suffering specifically resulting from automobile accidents and not as part of an all-encompassing pain and suffering insurance policy, and that the prospect of no compensation for pain and suffering would affect their habits. If potential victims could not insure separately for pain and suffering resulting from specific activities, then placing pain and suffering costs on them would result in externalization.

If we assume, instead, that the habits of potential victims would be the same whether or not they were made to bear some monetary cost of pain and suffering, because it is the prospect of bearing the pain and suffering *itself*, not the lack of compensation for it, which influences potential victims, then externalization of pain and suffering would, in a sense, be impossible. Potential victims, it would seem, would always be affected by the prospect.

While externalization would be impossible, this is no guarantee that the effect that the prospect of pain and suffering would have on the habits of potential victims would be optimal. Such optimal effect would require that potential victims correctly evaluate the risk of pain and suffering coming about, which is most unlikely. Indeed, I would guess that, *ex ante*, potential victims evaluate the risk of pain and suffering coming about at a lower value than that at which they, when serving on juries, are willing to compensate others, after accidents, for similar pain and suffering. If I am right, an argument may exist for putting at least the difference between these *ex post* and *ex ante* valuations on non-victims (drivers). *Cf.* note 32 *supra*. How strong the argument is would depend not only on the validity of the basic assumption that it is the prospect of the pain and suffering itself, and not its cost, which influences the habits of potential victims, but also on the extent of the discrepancy between individuals' *ex ante* valuations and *ex post* "jury type" valuations, and on the cost of making such *ex post* valuations. See Calabresi, note 6 *supra*, 721–24.

[37] In the last paragraph of note 32, *supra*, I have suggested that Blum and Kalven, despite themselves, do feel that some rough guess as to the proper division of costs between cars and pedestrians is possible from a general deterrence point of view. And I have suggested that they feel that division is fault. *Cf.*, BLUM & KALVEN at 63. This is not the place to analyze how much more can be said on the question of how to divide costs in such situations. In 78 HARV. L. REV. 713, 734–42, I make some suggestions in that regard. Whether the answer lies in the "involvement" test there suggested, or in a more sophisticated division based on involvement but in proportion to other, non-accident, costs attributable to the parties involved, or in some totally different division, requires much more than a footnote.

Among possible totally different divisions is one that might be termed "ease of avoidance" or non-fault fault. Such a division would involve a rough and ready guess as to the degree to which each of the various parties involved could have avoided the accident costs most cheaply, and would contemplate a *division* of costs between the parties which would reflect this. This guess is, despite its sound, very different from "fault." Some of the more obvious differences are: (1) This guess can, if efficiency justifies it, be made by classes or activities ("driving" as against "walking") and is *not* restricted, as fault is, to a more expensive individual case-by-case basis. (2) Even if the division were made on a case-by-case basis, some party would always be found who could have avoided the cost more easily. Or, if both could have avoided the cost as

I have, however, been hard on Blum and Kalven long enough. And it is time to try to point out how truly significant and impressive their small book is—despite its wrong conclusions. In the first place, their work should make it impossible for scholars or courts blithely to say "risk spreading" and assume that they have solved the very complex question of who ought to bear what share of the cost of accidents, or, indeed, that they have said very much at all. In the second place, this book will require those shcolars who tend to hide behind economics to make clear just how far their economics carries them. In the third place, by highlighting social insurance as a feasible alternative against which all accident plans must be judged, Blum and Kalven force us to consider what goals of accident law social insurance, cheap and effective as it is, *fails* to accomplish. In so doing, they necessarily cause us to consider which mixed plan, or mixture of plans, does in fact best accomplish our goals.

They, themselves, fail to make this investigation,[38] despite their protests to the contrary, and therefore end up supporting a system which they do not show to be at all superior to any other discussed. But this failure does not detract from their accomplishment. Hereafter any plan proposed will have to be examined in a much more thorough way than we have admitted in the past. The fact is that to varying extends we all want our laws dealing with automobile accidents (and all accidents really): a) to give compensation sufficient to minimize secondary losses and to make the loss burden politically tolerable; b) to provide specific deterrence sufficient to prevent "useless acts" reasonably well;[39] c) to provide a certain amount of internalization of costs, so that costs of accidents do not just become a "cost of living" and are made, instead, to affect both the degree to which we engage in activities which tend

easily, there would be a 50–50 split (*i.e.,* the situation of a total burden on the "innocent" victim because the party who injured him did not meet the criteria of being at "fault", though that party, or the activity he engaged in, could have avoided the cost more easily than the victim, would not exist). (3) There would, *ex hypothesis,* be a "comparative" ease-of-avoidance test (by individuals or activities involved) and not an all-or-nothing ease-of-avoidance test. (In effect this would be like moving to comparative negligence, and then dropping the *negligence* aspect.) (4) The "moral luggage" of fault would be irrelevant.

The advantage of this form of division is that it would concentrate on the question of minimizing *social costs* caused by *all* accidents and would not concentrate, as fault today does, on minimizing *fault-caused* accident costs. *Cf.* Coase *op. cit. supra,* note 28, at 27–28; BLUM & KALVEN 63–64 text and notes. But compare Calabresi, note 6 *supra,* 732, 739, with *id.* at 741. Whether such a division is acceptable, even from a general deterrence point of view, depends on whether it causes externalization of part of the cost. This in turn depends on whether such a division is acceptable from a risk spreading point of view. See notes 29–33 *supra* and accompanying text. Whether this guess is best done by "categories" (driving as against walking, driving as against motorcycles) or on a case-by-case basis is a question of, on the one hand, how much better general deterrence we get by individualization and, on the other hand, how expensive this individualization is. In other words, is individualization worth its cost?

[38] Except for one brief and rather superficial but interesting attempt at 83–85, where the authors mention various proposals combining the approaches of social security and fault.

[39] BLUM & KALVEN, at 63–64, are quick to point out that criminal penalties and licensing controls might hold down accident waste more efficiently than liability rules which attempt to make activities related to motoring bear their appropriate shares of accident costs. Whatever the validity of their argument, it is amusing that it should come from such devoted advocates of the free market system.

to result in accidents and the way in which we perform those activities; d) to satisfy certain "justice" and "revenge" requirements (some of which are undifferentiated and some of which are for me just plain unintelligible); and e) to do each of the above in a sufficiently efficient and and inexpensive way that we do not spend more in achieving the goal than it is worth.[40] It is also true that even if Blum and Kalven have shown that most compensation schemes heretofore suggested do not accomplish each of these goals perfectly, they have failed to show that the current fault scheme accomplishes any of them optimally. And they certainly fail to show that fault meets the combination of these goals better than any of the schemes they criticize. Nevertheless, as a result of their book we can begin to compare how well different plans or combinations of plans give us what we want. And perhaps within what we currently think of as the area of accident law, or perhaps, in whole or in part outside that area, we can find a somewhat more satisfactory solution than that which we have so far been given.

[40] *Cf.*, 2 HARPER & JAMES, TORTS 742–43 (1956).

# 14
# Walter J. Blum and Harry Kalven, Jr.

Walter Blum (1918–    ) and Harry Kalven (1914–    ), Professors of Law at the University of Chicago and collaborators on several major books spanning the spheres of public and private law, defend and expand the policy position outlined in their major study, *"Public Law Perspectives on a Private Law Problem – Auto Compensation Plans."*

# AUTO ACCIDENTS AND GENERAL DETERRENCE*

*"If Yale is against us, who will be for us?"*†
C. O. Gregory

The notable renaissance of writing about auto compensation plans in the past few years calls for a strong reason for adding still another essay to the stream.[1] In his article last year in the *Yale Law Journal*,[2] Professor Calabresi has prodded us, we believe, with two such reasons. First, he has been so effectively witty in reviewing our own position as put forth in *Public Law Perspectives on a Private Law Problem*[3] that under the stern conventions of academic gamesmanship we are impelled to reply. But more important, in focusing on the auto accident problem he has crystallized the economic analysis of liability which he has been developing in his writings over the past several years.[4] The analysis

---

*Walter J. Blum and Harry Kalven, Jr., "The Empty Cabinet of Dr. Calabresi: Auto Accidents and General Deterrence," *University of Chicago Law Review,* Vol. 34, No. 2 (1967), pp. 239–273. Reprinted by permission of the authors and through the courtesy of the University of Chicago Law School.

†Personal letter, dated 6/6/66, to Harry Kalven, Jr. The letter is no longer on file.

[1] The principal writings during the past three years, in addition to those of Calabresi, collected *infra* note 4, include KEETON & O'CONNELL, BASIC PROTECTION FOR THE TRAFFIC VICTIM (1965), which contains an extensive bibliography at pages 543–66; CONARD, MORGAN, PRATT, VOLTZ, & BOMBAUGH, AUTOMOBILE ACCIDENT COSTS AND PAYMENTS—STUDIES IN THE ECONOMICS OF INJURY REPARATIONS (1964); Conard, *The Economic Treatment of Automobile Injuries,* 63 MICH. L. REV. 279 (1964); James, *An Evaluation of the Fault Concept,* 32 TENN. L. REV. 394 (1965).

For two especially relevant pieces by economists, see Demsetz, *The Exchange and Enforcement of Property Rights,* 7 J. L. & ECON. 11 (1964); Rottenberg, *Liability in Law and Economics,* 55 AM. ECON. REV. 107 (1965).

There has also been an exceptionally important and lively book review "literature" on the various books involved.

[2] Calabresi, *Fault, Accidents, and the Wonderful World of Blum and Kalven,* 75 YALE L.J. 216 (1965).

[3] BLUM & KALVEN, PUBLIC LAW PERSPECTIVES ON A PRIVATE LAW PROBLEM—AUTO COMPENSATION PLANS (1965); Blum & Kalven, *Public Law Perspectives on a Private Law Problem—Auto Compensation Plans,* 31 U. CHI. L. REV. 641 (1964).

[4] Calabresi, *Some Thoughts on Risk Distribution and the Law of Torts,* 70 YALE L.J. 499 (1961); Calabresi, *The Decision for Accidents: An Approach to Nonfault Allocation of Costs,* 78 HARV. L. REV. 713 (1965); Calabresi, *Fault, Accidents, and the Wonderful World of Blum and Kalven,* 75 YALE L.J. 216 (1965) [hereinafter cited as Calabresi].

deserves careful attention because it may have a reach far transcending the auto problem and because, although couched in the idiom of superior risk bearing, it strikes us as saying something quite new for the legal discussion.

I

It is a tribute to Calabresi's rhetorical skill that he manages both to kid us for being in the wonderful world of classical economics and to criticize us for favoring an extension of social security to cover auto accident victims. Seeing how he got there will serve to throw light on the soundness of his analysis generally.

Our earlier essay was occasioned by our feeling that, although auto compensation plans were popular among academic commentators, the arguments offered on behalf of them lacked rigor. Indeed, it had never been clear why anyone would oppose what was made out to be such a totally desirable reform. The argument for a plan was that it would eliminate the costs and delays of litigation under the fault system, and that it would provide prompt, adequate compensation for all victims. What we had hoped to do was point up that the issue was not that simple: there was an inescapable countervailing factor. The increased number of victims covered with compensation under a plan would necessarily entail additional costs. Therefore the pivotal question about a plan, to us, was how these additional costs would be met. We were not persuaded that they could be met by the increased efficiency of administering a plan as compared to the common law system; we were not persuaded that they should be met by a lowering of damage awards across the board; and we concluded that it would be impractical to compel the victims to insure themselves by buying first party insurance. We therefore confronted the alternative that the additional costs should be absorbed by the motorists. Here again, even after a detour into economic analysis, we were unable to locate a satisfying rationale for charging the motorists.

In the end we felt that the fault liability system was not indefensible and that it should be retained until a better touchstone had been found to guide in allocating the neeessary additional costs of a plan.

We saw the problem as a hard choice between less than satisfactory alternatives. We could stay with our present system; or we could move to a plan at the price of arbitrarily allocating the costs to motorists via higher insurance premiums, or to victims via lower awards, or to some combination of both.[5] We submitted, however, that if the value of having all victims compensated was paramount, that goal could best be achieved by extending social security. This view seemed especially cogent for those concerned about human misfortunes,

---

[5] In our earlier piece we emphasized that there is no simple way of contrasting the present fault liability system with motorist compensation plans because of the variety of possible plans and because of the variety of common law rules. Only in a rough sense is the difference captured by the opposition between fault liability and strict liability. BLUM & KALVEN, *op. cit. supra* note 3, at 4.

since there is nothing distinctive about the misfortune of being hit by an auto-mobile.

The Calabresi critique moves on different levels. The broadest line of attack is that we display a basically unsound approach to issues of law and public policy, and that this flaw—more than any specific weakness in our analysis of the auto accident problem—brings us out with the wrong answer. There are, he would emphasize, a multiplicity of goals to be served by the law in this area. No single alternative will in an imperfect world achieve them all satisfactorily. Sound policy judgement therefore seeks the legal measure that will achieve the best mix among the goals.[6]

When applied to the auto accident problem, his multi-goal analysis runs like this. There are three main legal measures: the common law fault system, a compensation plan paid for by motorists, and social security financed out of general tax revenues. Further, there are several goals for the law here: justice (which he professes not to understand and largely dismisses); compensation of the injured; wide distribution of costs so as to avoid the impact of jarring losses; and holding to a minimum the net waste of resources for society—that is, bringing accident-associated costs to an optimal level. Calabresi never quite shows us his scorecard; but there is a strong intimation that had we tested the fault system against the mixture of goals, as he argues we should have done, it would have finished a poor third.[7] It is not superior in the achievement of any of the goals, and it is admittedly inferior in providing compensation.[8] The motorist compensation plan is also not superior when measured separately against each goal; but since in each of these ratings it is never the poorest, always being at least second best, it emerges as the overall soundest solution.

If all that Calabresi means is that one should weigh the various competing considerations in reaching a policy conclusion, no one would ever disagree. But he seems to be saying something more precise, to have developed his own Occam's razor for assessing issues of public policy: achieving two goals is always better than achieving one. Whether or not he meant to be so flat footed about it, there are pitfalls in being schematic about the goals of law. It is not easy to locate what the goals of a law are. Nor is it easy to know when we can prop-erly split one goal into two. And it cannot be assumed that all goals are of coordinate importance. Often the achieving of one important goal will out-weigh the achieving of two lesser goals. For all these reasons any apparent quantification is likely to be illusory.

In our specific case of the auto compensation plan, multiple goal scoring

---

[6] "The second problem is that Blum and Kalven reject most proposed 'plans' because they do not do as good a job of meeting a *specific* goal as an extreme or ideal solution; but these plans are never examined as ways of accomplishing a complex mixture of goals. Each plan is rejected because it does not do *perfectly* some *one* thing we desire, although it may do the combination of things we want pretty well." Calabresi 221.

[7] "And the key question, whether fault or any given non-fault system best accomplishes the *mixture* we in fact want, is never really asked!" *Ibid.*

[8] It is inferior in the sense that by the very nature of the fault criterion, not all victims will be able to shift their losses.

turns out to be especially awkward. It is symptomatic of the difficulties that Calabresi is reluctant to keep justice in as a goal and constantly professes to find the concept unintelligible.[9] If one looks only to the benefit side or aspirations of almost any welfare scheme, surely the scheme will appear attractive. In large part what tension there is in debate over such policies will arise over the justice issue—the question of how the costs of the measure are to be met. We submit that the avoidance of injustice or arbitrariness in allocating costs is also a goal; moreover, it is a goal likely to conflict with the other goals put forward. And the slipperiness of multiple goal quantification is nowhere better seen than when one attempts to score a proposal by whether it was gloriously just, tolerably just, tolerably unjust, or just plain lousy. If a proposal fails to satisfy a sense of justice in the allocation of its costs, it will, we suggest, be decisively impeached regardless of how fully it may achieve its other goals.

Initially, we had urged that the only critical question to be answered with respect to auto compensation plans was how they were to be paid for. When the dust has finally settled on the multiple goal analysis, the critical question remains unchanged. This perhaps explains why Calabresi does not rest his case with the multiple goal rhetoric but acknowledges a responsibility for justifying the allocation of the additional costs to motorists.

II

Before turning to what Calabresi argues is the economic justification for assessing the costs against motorists, we must pause briefly for another unusual rhetorical ploy in his article.[10] The question before the house in our earlier essay was whether a compensation plan was sufficiently superior to the common law system to justify a shift. Calabresi's answer is a firm yes—because a compensation plan is superior to social security!

His conclusion rests on a general economic insight with which we agree. A possible weakness of social security is that it takes the costs of auto accidents off the participants and places them on taxpayers indifferently. The result is that whatever pressures toward safety there might have been on the participants because of their sensitivity to bearing some part of the costs of accidents are eliminated. To use Calabresi's idiom, social security "externalizes" from the activities that produce accidents the costs of those accidents—bringing in its wake a loss of "general deterrence."

What is arresting here is not the content of his economic analysis, but rather his feeling that the point about externalization of costs under social

---

[9] "The fact is that to varying extents we all want our laws dealing with automobile accidents . . . to satisfy certain 'justice' and 'revenge' requirements (some of which are undifferentiated and some of which are for me just plain unintelligible). . . ." Calabresi 238. Compare, however, the somewhat different reaction of Holmes: "The undertakings to redistribute losses simply on the ground that they resulted from the defendant's act would not only be open to these objections, but, as it is hoped the preceding discussion has shown, to the still graver one of offending the sense of justice." HOLMES, THE COMMON LAW 96 (1881).
[10] See especially Calabresi 219–22.

security virtually disposes of the basic issue about auto plans. Surely, members of the bar and bench· who are bracing themselves for debate, see the choice as between the common law system and the various forms of compensation schemes, including social security. Yet Calabresi is quite serious in asserting that this misframes the issue. He is persuaded that the compensation shortcomings of the common law system are too great to be tolerated much longer by society. The wave of the future therefore will bring a compensation scheme in some form, and at this time the only policy issue for sensible men to debate is what that form should be.

What disturbs us is that Calabresi achieves the appearance of having won the case against the common law system by making a point of economic analysis. But in fact what he has done at most is to win a case against social security by his economic point and then to claim a win by default against the common law system on the basis of a political hunch.

Nor is this quite all. There is at least an implication that by scoring on economic grounds against the social security system he has also scored on economic grounds against the common law system. Although he is careful and in full command of the analysis, his emphasis obscures the point that externalization of costs—the economic shortcoming of social security—does not carry over to the common law system. It too avoids externalizing costs. The comparison *in economic terms* of a motorist compensation plan and the common law system is a far more subtle and difficult matter than is the comparison of a motorist plan and social security.

As a means of providing compensation, a social security approach has the great merit of admitting of a candid rationale for who should bear the cost of the benefits and a coherent rationale for who the beneficiaries should be. It can, that is, provide an open weighing of costs against benefits and a clear test of the depth of the public consensus on welfare measures. One can therefore only wonder how heavily Calabresi would under other circumstances weigh the loss of general deterrence involved in social security. If we already had auto accidents under social security, would Calabresi then be disposed to argue that they should be taken out and handled separately under a compensation plan financed by motorists? And further, would he say the same about victims of motorboat or bicycle accidents?[11] In these instances, too, social security would externalize the costs of the accidents and would eliminate whatever inducement the bearing of these costs might have on the participants to reduce the loss from accidents. Surely there are limits to the attractiveness of atomizing social security in the quest for general deterrence.

---

[11] It is tempting to add victims of lightning, lung cancer and bathtub tumbles. However, there is a difficulty in devising a compensation plan which is an alternative to social security. Compare Calabresi, *supra* note 4, 78 HARV. L. REV. at 715. See text accompanying notes 71–73 *infra*.

III

Near the end of his article,[12] Calabresi does address himself directly to what we have urged is the central issue about compensation plans: What is the rationale for charging the new costs against motorists? The justification is to be found, he suggests, in utilizing the criterion of general deterrence. By way of preface to the argument, we pause for a look at the general deterrence thesis in the large.

There is for the law world a certain freshness about the Calabresi analysis. Although focusing on deterrence, he is not working over old notions about the use of sanctions to discourage antisocial behaviour;[13] he would distinguish sharply between specific deterrence, which has been the traditional hope of the law, and general deterrence, which is for him the new hope for the law borrowed from economics. Moreover, while building his liability theory on economic analysis, he relies very little on the idea of a wide distribution of losses which has been so fashionable in other economics—oriented legal commentary.[14] His concern is rather with the allocation of costs, including accident losses.

The law has not been a complete stranger to the concern with allocation of costs. For the most part in a market society with private property, the allocation of costs is noncontroversial and appears to be automatic. The cost of steel in buildings constructed of steel, for example, is reflected without controversy [15] and without the intervention of law other than to protect the market institution. When the allocation of costs has appeared controversial,

---

[12] Calabresi 231–37.

[13] See, *e.g.*, GREGORY & KALVEN, CASES ON TORTS 690–702 (1959); Morris, *Punitive Damages in Tort Cares,* 44 HARV. L. REV. 1173 (1931).

[14] It would be a worthwhile task to write the intellectual history of economic ideas in tort liability theory, beginning perhaps with Holmes' remark that "The state might conceivably make itself a mutual insurance company against accidents and distribute the burden of its citizens' mishaps among all its members." HOLMES, THE COMMON LAW 96 (1881). In rough profile, the ferment begins with the debate over workmens' compensation legislation at the turn of the century, when it is argued that the costs of industry should be placed on industry. A decade or so later Laski, Smith and Douglas, seek to rationalize vicarious liability rules by analogy to workmen's compensation. The point changes somewhat, the emphasis being placed on the wide distribution of losses through use of the market mechanism and liability insurance, and the phrase "enterprise liability" is exploited. After the passage of another decade or two, tort scholars, in particular James, Morris, Ehrenzweig, and Green, attempt to adapt the agency analysis to tort liability rules. Again the emphasis changes slightly, and the concern is with the customary patterns of carrying insurance and relative accessibility to insurance. The quest is for the "superior risk bearer." Finally, in the current decade the stimulus to use of economics is found mainly in the auto compensation discussion.

In his earliest essay, *supra* note 4, 70 YALE L.J. at 499 (1961), Calabresi differentiates the various economic ideas behind the phrase "risk distribution." His focus is not primarily on achieving wide distribution of losses. What is distinctive about his approach, although there are faint echoes of it in the writings of Douglas, is his attention to the possibility of changing behavior so as to reduce the net loss to society from accidents.

[15] Perhaps this isn't such a good example after all. See Youngstown Sheet & Tube Co. v. Sawyer, 343 U.S. 579 (1952), discussed in Kurland, *Guidelines and the Constitution: Some Random Observations on Presidential Power to Control Prices and Wages,* in SHULTZ & ALIBER, GUIDELINES, INFORMAL CONTROLS AND THE MARKET PLACE 209 (1966).

there usually have been direct intrusions into this process by way of governmental subsidies or special taxes not designed to raise revenues. In the subsidy
situation, part of the cost would have been shifted from the users of steel buildings
to the tax-paying public; in the tax situation, costs would have been added to
the users of steel buildings. In both cases the objectives are clear: in the one it is
to encourage the use of steel in buildings; in the other it is to discourage it. All
this is, of course, very familiar. But the point to be stressed is that for the economist cost is instrumental, and the allocation of it always reflects some government
policy. There is nothing more "natural" in having the users of steel buildings
bear the cost of steel than there is in having the tax-paying public bear that cost.
The choice simply defines the nature of the society and its institutions.

The destruction of persons or property in the course of some activity is
also a cost. The allocating of these costs has been a basic concern of law and
liability theory, and the traditional legal formulas for allocating the costs of
accidents have been embodied in the rules of torts and agency.[16] When the
lawyer turns to the economist and asks that he evaluate these rules in cost
allocation terms, the discussion is likely to be at cross purposes. The lawyer
hopes to be told about "proper" or "improper" allocation of costs; the
economist can only repeat that these costs, like all costs, are instrumental, and
therefore he will ask the lawyer what purposes he wishes to achieve in allocating
them.

Calabresi is very clear about all this.[17] He sets out a purpose he wishes to
achieve in allocating the costs of auto accidents to motorists. His goal is to
optimize the costs of auto accidents to society, and he proposes to do so by
utilizing what he thinks are the possibilities for general deterrence which can be
exploited by placing liability costs on motorists. Although in theory we today
might have either too much or too little general deterrence pressure, Calabresi
proceeds on the assumption that we have too little because no part of losses in
non-fault accidents is now charged against motorists. Thus he assumes that
moving toward optimization of costs calls for reducing the number of auto
accidents.[18]

An extended illustration of how liability law can be made to serve the
objective of general deterrence is needed at this point. Whatever the economist's
phrasing, what is being discussed is human behavior and ways of changing it.
To put the problem in a formal way, for liability law the choice is between
placing liability for a loss on Group A or leaving the loss on Group B upon whom
it initially falls. In general deterrence terms, there is only one argument for
imposing liability on Group A: we should do so if the behavior of Group A
and of Group B will be different than when we leave the loss where it falls,
and if this difference in behavior will reduce the net loss to society.

16 HOLMES, THE COMMON LAW 77–79 (1881).
17 See, e.g., Calabresi, supra note 4, 78 HARV. L. REV. at 725.
18 "[N]on-fault plans would, in fact, give better deterrence than fault, because they would tend
to deter activities prone to serious accidents rather than just activities prone to fault-caused
serious accidents." Calabresi 222 n.14. See also the discussion infra, Part V, on optimizing
auto accidents.

The tracing of such behavioral consequences can be quite complex. To use again an illustration from our earlier essay, we will assume that Group A are manufacturers of a watch with a radium dial that will cause distinctive skin damage to some users. The policy issue is who is to bear the cost of the skin damage—the manufacturers or the users, who as a class can be looked upon as Group B. The situation thus posed looks promising for various strategies of reducing the net losses from skin damage. Without working through these exhaustively, attention should be called to the possibilities that a substitute product not having radium on the dial might be developed, that a shield might be designed to protect against skin irritation, or that users might change their habits of wearing the watch continuously so as to reduce the hazards of exposure. Several things should be noted. None of the behavior listed has yet occurred, but is merely a future possibility. Each will represent a net gain in productivity to society so long as the cost of it does not exceed the reduction in losses it can effect. Further, independent of liability law there are strong motivations present to come up with safer products. Economic self-interest suggests that there must already be a race among manufacturers to develop a safer watch, especially when we look to the competition from substitute products. It would thus be a pretty fair prediction that sooner or later one of these possible lines of improvement will materialize, whatever the law does or does not do about the liability problem.

What Calabresi must show here is that the process will go faster [19]—that the motivations toward safety will be deepened—if the law intervenes by placing liability on the manufacturers. And indeed he sketches what could be a plausible case in this situation.[20] By making the manufacturer liable for all such losses, the law forces him to become aware of his recurring experience with the loss. Being an enterpriser he presumably can also calculate the costs of any given "remedy." The result is that he should be in a position to make a calculus of safety versus cost. Moreover, at least in the short run, it will be to his economic advantage to innovate safety measures that, by reducing his liability losses, will reduce the net costs of his operations, and thereby increase his net profit.

Assuming that the strategy of holding the manufacturers liable will induce them to seek out desirable safety measures, are there offsets in the motivation of users to minimize injuries? While they can now shift the loss of skin damage back to the manufacturer, it would seem that on balance the positive impact on manufacturers will be greater than the negative impact on users. The users are not centralized; they are unlikely to have technical expertise; they are less likely to perceive the incidence of damage; and for the individual user, the cost of seeking alternatives must outweigh the advantage to him. Whether the losses are left on users or are shifted off of them is not likely to make a perceptible difference in their behavior.

---

[19] Once again the assumption is that we have too many accidents and too little investment in safety. Conceivably, the economic calculus might call for *slowing down* the investment in safety.
[20] Calabresi 224–31.

From the view pointof general deterrence there is another advantage in placing liability on the manufacturer, an advantage which is paradoxical from the perspective of the common law.[21] If liability is placed on the manufacturer by law, the accepted economic analysis is that through the operation of market forces this additional cost on the producer ultimately will be passed on to the users in the form of increased prices.[22] Whichever way the law jumps here, the users of radium dial watches as a class will end up bearing the cost of losses from skin damage; yet there is a gain in having the loss placed on the manufacturer and shifted back to the users.[23] The point is that the individual user is more likely to perceive the increase in his purchase price than to perceive his share of the risk of skin damage. In this sense he is more accurately confronted with the costs of using radium dail watches and gets to cast a more intelligent consumer vote. As a result, any "over consumption" of radiumdial watches due to unawareness of the true costs of using them is eliminated.

We have dwelt at some length on this example to give a "feel" for the subtleties of the behaviorial analysis on which general deterrence theory rests. In the radium watch situation we think it is likely that a case can be made out for placing liability on the manufacturer.[24] Perhaps a vague perception of such a general deterrence calculus is at the source of the contemporary revolution in products liability laws.[25] This is not to say that a case for general enterprise liability to consumers has been established regardless of context. Consider, for example, the commercial airline. Motivation of the airline enterpriser to seek out safety may already be so close to optimum that change in liability law could not be justified by the argument that it would make a difference in behavior.

There is one final characteristic of the radium watch dial type of case that needs to be underscored. It is seen that the choice here is not ultimately between placing the loss on the consumer or relieving him of it; it is rather between placing the loss on him by one method or by another—either by leaving the loss on him initially or by shifting it to the manufacturer via liability rules in the expectation that it will be shifted back to the consumer via market forces in the form of increased prices.[26] In this special context even a slight advantage in

[21] We noted the paradox in our earlier essay, BLUM & KALVEN, *op. cit. supra* note 3, at 60.

[22] Due to time lags, monopolies, and lack of perfect knowledge, the passing on of costs through increased prices will often be less than perfect. See Calabresi, *supra* note 4, 70 YALE L.J. at 499.

[23] We confess error here. In our earlier essay we overstated the degree to which consumers would have knowledge to properly assess the risks of radiation injury. We failed to take our assumption of "perfect" knowledge to its logical terminus. Calabresi has now done so at our expense, giving point to his "Wonderful World" title. Calabresi 228.

[24] The facts in the radium watch dial example have been kept overly simple by assuming that the radium on the dial is the only cause of the particular skin disease. In the real world, complications about causation may make it difficult to isolate the contribution of the product from the contribution of the other possible causes of the particular harm, thus making it arbitrary to shift such losses to the manufacturer. Consider the current problem of lung cancer and cigarette manufacturers.

[25] See Kalven, *Torts: The Quest for Appropriate Standards*, 53, CALIF. L. REV. 189 205–06 (1965); RESTATEMENT (SECOND), TORTS § 402A (1965) (suggesting a possible limit in the revolution in tort liability for injurious products).

[26] Because the parties are in a position to bargain with each other, there is another possibility. The manufacturer could give the consumer a choice of buying the product at a lower price

general deterrence may be persuasive. The strains on general deterrence analysis, however, may be considerably greater when the choice is whether or not to place the costs on a group that would not otherwise bear them.

IV

We must acknowledge that Calabresi has not as yet attempted to make a complete analysis of the possibilities for general deterrence in the auto accident situation. He has only argued that the possibilities are promising enough to call for careful consideration of them in any policy decisions about the auto problem. We propose here to attempt to think through in some detail where the pursuit of general deterrence in the auto case might lead. In thus going beyond the analysis Calabresi has so far offered on general deterrence, we run the risk of committing some errors in its name.

Since we presumably are talking about a change in the existing law, that law provides the baseline against which any gains in general deterrence have to be measured. The law now places the cost of negligently caused accidents on motorists and does so on the theory that motorists are having accidents a reasonable man would not have had. A proposal to place all costs on motorists on general deterrence grounds must therefore seek its justification in the likelihood that such an allocation of costs will reduce the accidents that even a reasonable man would otherwise have had, and will do so without excessive offsetting costs.[27] To state the matter this way suggests that to establish the general deterrence thesis in respect to auto accidents will be something of an uphill fight.

There are other reasons why the auto field may prove an unfertile one for a general deterrence approach, both of which become apparent when we compare the auto case to the radium dial watch case. That there may have been a valid reason for placing all accident costs on the watch manufacturer does not establish a comparable reason for placing all accident costs on motorists. In very large part the cost savings that were expected to be achieved in the watch situation depended upon two circumstances. First, the manufacturer as an enterpriser is presumably in a position to make a economic calculus both about the probability of accidents from the watches and about the cost of alternative means of reducing them. He can therefore be expected to invest in safety up to the appropriate degree. Second, since as a result of market forces the consumer will in the end inevitably bear the cost of accidents from the watches, it is desirable to place him in a position where he will confront and recognize these costs as directly as possible, and will regulate his purchases

without recourse against the manufacturer for harm or of buying at a higher price which reflects the manufacturer's strict liability for harm. Arguably, this arrangement has the advantages of the other possibilities without their disadvantages. It maximizes consumer choice and nevertheless confronts the consumer with "proper" prices. *But see* Calabresi 225–30.

[27] "It is sometimes said that the study of negligence is the study of the mistakes a reasonable man might make." GREGORY & KALVEN, CASES ON TORTS 89 (1959).

accordingly. Neither of these points holds for the auto case. The driving of autos is not basically a business; and, as we shall see, it is far more difficult for the individual driver to make an economic calculus of accident losses and accident risks. Moreover, the decisive fact about auto accidents is that market forces do not inexorably place the costs of these accidents on any group. If the law elects to leave them on victims, they will be left on victims. If the law elects to place them on motorists, they will remain on motorists.[28] There is therefore no point in talking about confronting any group with the costs of auto accidents on a theory that such a confrontation makes explicit to them what they must bear in any event.

Since the costs will not fall on motorists through the operation of market forces but will do so only if the law decides to place them on motorists, it may be useful to conceive of the issue as if it were one of taxation. The questions is: Should motorists be taxed to pay for all the losses suffered by auto accident victims? We would agree with Calabresi that a case for such a tax might be made if it can be shown that once the levy is imposed the behavior of motorists and potential victims will be so altered that there will be a significant improvement in achieving an optimum number of auto accidents for society as a whole.

As far as we can see, there are just three routes through which general deterrence can be expected to operate on auto accidents. It can lead to the discovery of safety devices or techniques. It can induce an improvement in driving habits. It can cause a discriminating reduction in the level of driving and a substitution of safer activities in place of driving. As Calabresi has summarized the prospects: "we may, if we are made to pay for car-caused accidents, drive less, or less at night, or less when we are of accident-prone ages, or with more safety devices than if we are not made to pay for accident costs when we decide to use a car."[29] And he adds: "I call this thesis general deterrence, because it seeks to diminish accident costs not by directly attacking specific occasions of danger, but (like workmen's compensation) by making more expensive those activities which are accident prone and thereby making more attractive their safer substitutes."[30]

It may be true, as James and now Calabresi have argued,[31] that the advent of workmen's compensation did provide a stimulus for discovery of safety measures for coping with the industrial accident. But even if this reading of a complex history is correct, it does not help us much in tracing through why taxing motorists will lead to the discovery of safety measures for coping with the auto accident. The theory must be that motorist-consumer awareness of accident costs will create an increased demand by them for safer cars, thus putting the pressure on manufacturers to increase their level of innovation concerning safety features in autos. This sequence of behavior seems quite

---

[28] Theoretically there is one conceivable qualification: the parties in a limited number of instances might strike private bargains and shift the loss. See note 53 *infra*.
[29] Calabresi 223.
[30] *Ibid.*
[31] James, *Accident Liability Reconsidered: The Impact of Liability Insurance*, 57 YALE, L.J. 549 (1948).

unpromising in view of the long history of consumer unwillingness to pay for safety in the purchase of autos.[32] In any event, if one is serious about taking this route, it might make more sense to place the costs on manufacturers of autos directly.[33]

As an aid to analysis we proceed to test our reactions to an auto compensation plan which imposes strict liability on the manufacturer for all accidents involving its cars. Let us assume that this "plan" would be appropriately qualified to take account of various outrageous accidents, such as those caused by drunken driving of old, secondhand, beat-up cars. The auto case might then be seen as in line with the radium watch case or workmen's compensation—that is, there would be economic pressure put on the manufacturer, and these costs would be passed on to motorist-consumers via the market. Some intractable difficulties remain, nevertheless. It appears likely that a majority of accidents are traceable to the driver and not to the car.[34]

[32]However, consumer interest in safety appears to have increased during the past year. See NADER, UNSAFE AT ANY SPEED (1965); O'CONNELL & MYERS, SAFETY LAST (1966).

[33] Our purpose in positing a plan which puts accident costs on auto manufacturers is only to test the strongest case for the Calabresi analysis. We recognize that there may be a new disadvantage introduced in limiting the freedom of choice of car purchasers. See not 26 *supra*.

[34] Fifteen years ago James and Dickinson reported that only $3\frac{1}{2}$ per cent of the cars involved in accidents had mechanical defects, and only in $\frac{1}{4}$ of 1 per cent of the accidents were they thought to be a contributing factor. James & Dickinson, *Accident Proneness and Accident Law*, 63 HARV. L. REV. 769, 770 (1950).

Our colleague, Hans Zeisel, has advised us as follows regarding the contribution of mechanical defects to auto accidents:

"Just how many accidents are caused by mechanical defects of the automobile—that is, how many accidents would not happen if the defect had not existed—is an unknown figure. Only one research design could reveal it, and that design has never been used. It calls for taking a random sample of accidents, and then ascertaining for each accident all the facts, including a sufficiently thorough examination of the car or cars involved. This research design is feasible; the experts for it are available; but it is costly because it would often involve stripping a car beyond the needs of immediate repair.

"The paradigm of such a research design was developed many years ago in a study sponsored by the United States Department of Commerce:

ANALYSIS OF IMMEDIATE CAUSES OF 30 ACCIDENTS

| Driver Violations | | % |
|---|---|---|
| Excessive Speed | 20 | |
| Improper Turns | 10 | |
| Improper passing and others | 5 | |
| | — | |
| Total | | 35 |
| Driver Errors | | 41 |
| Car defects | | 5 |
| Road properties | | 11 |
| Miscellaneous | | 8 |
| | | — |
| Total | | 100% |

"This is a slightly modified and simplified version of a table reproduced in H.R. Doc. No. 462, 75th Cong., 3d Sess. 11 (1938). Unfortunately, this study was not based on a represen-

Certainly this kind of major change in liability policy ought not be predicated on the futuristic possibility of a driver-proof car. Even when we acknowledge, as we must, that changes in construction and design will have a greater impact on the gravity of accidents than on their incidence,[35] it seems that the possibility of reducing auto accidents in major part falls beyond the reach of this strategy.

Further, it is well to recognize what we are talking about. The objective is to encourage inventiveness, research, discovery. And what are sought are not safer devices simply, but safer devices which are roughly the economic equivalent of those now in use. It is true that placing economic pressure on the manufacturer works in the right direction. But if we are willing to tax on behalf of this objective, we confront the difficulty that there are altenative ways of stimulating such research that might well be more effective dollar for dollar. We might, for example, utilize government subsidies of research laboratories and perhaps a scheme of honorific government prizes. But whatever might be the best technique, once the quest is avowedly for stimulating inventiveness it is no longer clear why motorists alone are the proper group to call upon to pay for the stimulus.

In the end, the strategy seems to come down to this: motorists, who on hypothesis are driving cars that could have been built safer, are to be made to pay for the losses from accidents caused by those cars in the hope of inducing someone else to be more inventive or persistent about designing safer cars.

One final point of perspective might be added. Once a safety discovery has been made and has become economically feasible, the compulsion of an accident compensation plan is not required to bring it into use. The existing law is capable of quite quickly absorbing the change as a matter of the common law calculus of negligence; and if that is thought too slow a process, society can always turn to specific safety legislation.

tative sample, nor was the mechanical examination of the cars sufficiently thorough.

"In recent years several approximations to the suggested research design have been achieved. The Swedish government, through one of its agencies, undertook such a study, but only for single car accidents—accidents that involve no collision with another car. While the report on this study has not been made available, upon informal inquiry the figure for mechanical causation, including tire failures, was tentatively placed around 25 per cent. In evaluating this finding one must keep in mind that mechanical failures are probably higher in single car accidents than in collisions, and that conditions in Sweden might differ from those in the United States.

"Another study based on a random sample of accidents was done in upstate New York, but it was limited to determining the part alcohol played. Autopsies were performed on some one hundred consecutive death casualties in auto accidents; some fifty per cent. were found to be inebriated beyond the legally allowed alcohol limit.

"Another such partial assessment study concerning the contribution of faulty tires in a random sample of auto accidents is now under way at the Traffic Institute of Northwestern University under the direction of J. Stannard Baker, who was also responsible for the United States Department of Commerce study reported above."

One could get to a logical problem in deciding when an accident is caused by the driver or is caused by a defect in the car. A good driver, knowing he has bad brakes, might be able to adjust his driving pattern so as to take account of the defect. Presumably the reported statistics are based on much cruder notions of defects and causation.

[35] See Katz, *Liability of Automobile Manufacturers for Unsafe Design of Passenger Cars*, 69 HARV. L. REV. 863 (1956); Noel, *Manufacturer's Negligence of Design or Directions for Use of a Product*, 71 YALE L.J. 816 (1962).

The second route for general deterrence in the auto case is one that sounds more familiar to the legal ear. It is that we might by law change the conduct of motorists. No one doubts that an enormous reduction in auto accidents would be effected if we could devise some way of altering the habits of motorists. The theory although Calabresi does not seem to rely on it, must be that by imposing the "liability tax" on those involved in auto accidents without regard to fault, we can make them more sensitive to the connections between their driving behavior and the accidents, and thus induce a change in their habits. Since the law already imposes on them the obligation to drive with reasonable care, the hope here is to induce what might well be called super-care. In brief, the thesis is that economic pressures may be able to mould conduct better than law using criminal fines, licence suspensions, and tort liability keyed to negligence. The target at this point in the analysis is not the more effective screening of potential drivers, but rather the interstitial improvement in the behavior of those who are already driving.[36]

At the threshold this approach runs into a major obstacle. It is surely commonplace knowledge that any driver is always risking not simply the safety of others, but equally his own personal safety. Inasmuch as the situation thus already seems to present a very high inducement to safety, it is hard to see what additional incentive to super-care will be added by economic pressure.

If we go on to assume that there may be some people who would react to the change in costs, there are some less obvious difficulties to consider. There is the circumstance that any motorist compensation plan will operate through use of auto insurance. The economic pressure or tax we seek to impose consequently will appear in the form of premiums. In turn this means that the premiums will have to be differentiated so as to show the individual motorist that if he engages in super-care, he will be rewarded by a smaller premium. Just how one does this is not clear. Presumably, since we are not going to introduce the fault system all over again in order to graduate insurance premiums, the allocation will be on the basis of some test such as involvement in accidents. If the motorist understands that this is the way premiums are graded, he may learn the wrong lesson or be discouraged when he realizes that, no matter how careful he is, he will not get his "reward" if he is the victim of another's carelessness.

But beyond this, there is a further sense in which the motorist's fate is linked to the behaviour of others. The nature of insurance requires that we deal with classes of persons representing different degrees of risk. Any one motorist is therefore stuck with a kind of guilt by association. The extent to which he gets his premium adjusted downward for his super-care always turns in part on the incidence of accident involvement by strangers.

---

[36] For clarity of analysis we distinguish here between the objective of improving the behavior of those who drive and the objective of dissuading riskier drivers from taking the wheel. The general deterrence theory aspires to achieve both objectives simultaneously. The second objective is discussed later.

These difficulties are no surprise. They reflect those characteristics of insurance which critics of the current common law system have pointed to in arguing that, because of the dilution of impact due to insurance, even the fault system does not deter.[37] Further, if some way of making auto insurance a more discriminating mechanism among insured motorists could be devised, there is nothing that would keep us from using it under the existing system of negligence law without waiting upon a compensation plan.

But even if we assume for the sake of argument that adjustment of insurance premiums can have an impact on motorist conduct, the quest for super-care is still left with one last difficulty. The aim of general deterrence strategy, it may bear repeating, is an overall net reduction of costs. Super-care may generate offsetting costs.

From the point of view of society, the simple facts are that people can drive too carefully, and excessive care may produce problems of its own. Since the impact on driving habits very likely will be most evident with respect to speed, let us look briefly at the consequences of a widespread but not universal reduction in speed below what is now under the negligence calculus thought to be a reasonable maximum. There is a distinct possibility that this change may work to increase the number of accidents. It is becoming a commonplace that the slow driver on a throughway is as much of a hazard as his excessively speedy brother, largely because his pattern does not mesh easily with that of most drivers, thus resulting in periodic foul-ups of the traffic flow. Moreover, if super-care causes a significant number of drivers to change habits, there will on the average be a general slowing up of traffic. This can be counted on to set off a chain of cost consequences, such as loss of time of those being transported or the building of additional roads or the altering of existing ones.

Society of course can always change the speed limits when it is persuaded that slower traffic is more desirable. The puzzle is why we would ever use indirect stimuli to induce people to drive slower than the legal limit. The quest for super-care may, it is true, work better on other aspects of motorist conduct than speed, but we think the analysis has been carried far enough to suggest that there are troublesome problems of offsetting costs to be taken into account. We may in our argument be doing no more than repeating a concern the common law has always had against overinhibiting an activity.[38] The point is more widely understood in a different context: the overanxious parent is not the model.

We come to the third route through which general deterrence may be expected to operate: the discriminating reduction in the level of motoring. It is probably accurate to say that this represents Calabresi's best hope for general deterrence in the automobile field. In contrast to stimulating safety discovery or to inducing super-care in driving, there is little doubt but that imposing higher charges on motoring will affect behaviour significantly. This is simply

---

[37] KEETON & O'CONNELL, op. cit. supra note 1, at 252.
[38] See Seavey, Principles of Torts, 56 HARV. L. REV. 72, 73 (1943).

to say that we have another illustration of the great axiom of economics that price will affect demand.[39]

Calabresi, as we might anticipate, has a more interesting idea in mind than lessening auto accidents by a blunt reduction in the overall level of motoring. He would seek to reduce the level of driving in a discriminating way by forcing the motorist to attend to the distinctive costs of driving under various definable conditions. If, for example, teen-age driving shows a distinctively higher than average rate of involvement in auto accidents, these costs can be placed on such driving by means of differential insurance premiums. We can then expect that "by making more expensive those activities which are accident prone" [40] we would discourage them. Presumably under this scheme there would be fewer teenagers driving, and consequently costs in the society would be reduced.

This is indeed an attractive prospect. It links legal control to the free market mechanism and thereby achieves its social goals with a minimum of direct restraints on individual freedom and with a minimum of reliance on the political process and majority vote. It accommodates with little friction a wide variety of judgments as to whether the activity remains worthwhile at higher prices. As a matter of affecting behavior it will, we repeat, work.

Insofar as we can follow Calabresi at this point, his thinking runs this way. Under a motorist compensation plan it will be possible for insurance purposes to group motorists into specific categories and to base rates on involvement in accidents regardless of fault. Thus premiums for teenagers will be based on the number of accidents in which teenagers are involved, wholly apart from the number in which they are at fault. This process of dealing with specific subcategories of driving could be extended so long as using smaller breakdowns proved to be feasible.[41]

To turn these points into an argument against the common law system and in favor of liability without fault, an important further step is required. It must be shown that this scheme of accident accounting can be exploited to a greater extend under a strict liability system than under a fault system. It is this prospect that we find unpersuasive. Today the differentials in insurance rates are in large measure based on the incidence of involvement and not of ultimate

---

[39] Once again we have an example of inconsistent rationales for a particular rule of law. Consider the rule of liability for ultrahazardous activities. Calabresi's analysis might justify liability without fault as a means of holding down the number of accidents from a given line of activity. RESTATEMENT (SECOND), TORTS § 520 (1965), would single out the ultrahazardous activity cases because they involve a risk "which cannot be eliminated by the utmost care." Compare Keeton, *Conditional Fault in the Law of Torts*, 72 HARV. L. REV. 401 (1959).

[40] Calabresi 223.

[41] It might not be easy to combine, in a single strategy of grading insurance premiums, the goal of inducing super-care and the goal of selectively reducing motoring activity. The first goal would seem to call for setting premiums on the basis of accident involvement of the individual motorist; the second, by accident involvement of some class of which he is a member. For example, in dealing with a teenage driver, "super-care" premiums would reward him for staying out of accidents by lowering his costs, while activity repressing premiums would discourage him from driving by increasing his costs because he is a teenager.

liability due to fault. Further, there is nothing in the nature of things to prevent the insurance institution under a negligence liability law from more fully utilizing such an accounting in setting its rates. The main subcategories in use today—age, urban/rural, sex—are not wedded to fault; and whatever subcategories might be developed under a motorist compensation plan could just as readily be developed today. Hence, all that would be accomplished along these lines by shifting from fault to strict liability would be to increase the total charge placed on motoring but not to place it any more discriminatingly among motorists.

On our view, the argument stumbles over this initial hurdle; nevertheless, it may be useful to push the analysis a little deeper. Thus far we have been concerned with discriminating among motoring activities solely in terms of seeking to repress those which carry the greater risk of accident—that is, we have been exploring the possibility of maximizing the amount of accident loss reduction for every dollar of "tax" imposed on the motorist.[42] One might, however, misunderstand Calabresi to be saying something further, to be suggesting that there may be another dimension to the discrimination he advocates. Is it possible to locate as targets for repression those categories of motoring which are of lesser value to society? It will be remembered that the objective is not simply to reduce accidents, but rather to reduce the net costs of accidents. If qualitative discrimination could be made to work, it would have the benign consequence of holding down the level of accident-producing activity at what would seem to be the lowest offsetting cost. But this happy prospect quickly evaporates upon analysis. There is no likelihood that the driving categories which have the highest accident potential are those which have the lowest social value, as is sufficiently shown by the case of the urban fire engine or police car. In any event, there is no palatable way of ranking driving activity in terms of its social utility. Is driving on weekends less socially useful than driving to work? Undoubtedly some people would be willing to rank the activity for all of us, but we obviously run afoul here of the basic issue of sumptuary legislation.[43]

We are left then, as we compare behavior under the existing system with behavior under the proposed system, with the prospect of an across-the-board reduction in the level of motoring, and a consequent reduction in the overall number of auto accidents. Under these circumstances, whether or not the change-over is desirable turns on weighing the offsetting costs that flow from reducing the general level of the activity. Many are obvious though difficult to trace in any detail. There will be a loss of either work time or leisure time

---

[42] We ignore here another variable which in principle ought to be considered. Not all subcategories of driving will have the same elasticity of demand. Teenage driving may be riskier, but not as responsive to price changes as other categories of driving. Would general deterrence strategy call for pushing relatively harder on riskier but inelastic categories or on less risky but more elastic ones?

[43] For another instance of a latent preference for sumptuary legislation, see the discussion in BLUM & KALVEN, THE UNEASY CASE FOR PROGRESSIVE TAXATION 68 (1st ed. 1953).

insofar as people shift to slower forms of transportation; there may be an increase in hazard in the more intensive use of some forms of substitute transportation such as car pools or helicopters; there may be increased investment in mass transportation and underuse of investment already committed to auxiliary motoring facilities like garages and parking lots; there may even be a change in driving habits as traffic flows lessen. In brief, this one change will set off a chain reaction of other changes, not all obviously advancing the goal of economizing on resources; and all of these consequences must be taken into account in appraising whether the changeover in liability rules will yield in the end a net reduction in costs to the society.[44]

One of the possible consequences is interesting enough to stop for. In the radium watch example, it will be recalled, we were concerned not only with the conduct of the manufacturer, but also with the conduct of the victim-consumer. Similarly, in the auto case we should look not exclusively at the behavior of motorists, but at the behavior of potential victims (for convenience, pedestrians) as well. Is there any likelihood that changing the behavior of the one will produce any offsetting change in the behavior of the other? More specifically, as we shift all costs off victims in order to encourage super-care in motorists or to reduce the level of motoring, will we be lifting existing restraints on pedestrians, causing them to become more careless or to engage more freely in risky alternatives such as riding motor bikes? We would readily agree that there is a lack of perfect symmetry here. The motorist and the pedestrian are not literally on a see-saw; any legal change on the one that affects his conduct in the desired direction does not necessarily produce an equal change in the wrong direction in the conduct of the other. Nevertheless, in the grand toting up of all pluses and minuses which the general deterrence analysis calls for, we would expect to find some additional costs due to liberating pedestrians to be more careless.[45]

---

[44] The common law has its own formulation. Under the well-known Hand calculus for risk, the law does not shift a loss where the burden or cost to the actor of avoiding the risk of loss is thought, "objectively," to outweigh the cost of the loss. See United States v. Carroll Towing Co., 159 F.2d 169 (2d Cir. 1947). Thus the negligence system might be said to impose liability only where doing so will not result in a net loss. At first glance, it might seem that the common law here has already made the very calculation which interests Calabresi, and that any further imposition of liability beyond the negligence line will result in a net loss to society. But see Calabresi, *supra* note 4, 78 HARV. L. REV. at 719. The common law formulation looks at a single case at a time and views the economic problem only from the point of view of the particular actor. The economic pluses and minuses for the whole society need not be the sum of the pluses and minuses in all the individual cases. For example, society may legislate a certain speed limit reflecting a judgment that it would be wasteful to insist that every one drive slower. But as Calabresi would argue, it may nevertheless be advisable to impose pressures of general deterrence in order to induce slower driving by some people.

[45] It is convenient to note here that coverage of the single car accident under an auto compensation plan—which so greatly troubled the proponents of the Columbia Plan of 1932—is not anomalous under the Calabresi analysis. In the aggregate accounting for society as a whole, it is as important to reduce such accidents as it is to reduce those involving other cars.

There may be an additional complication, however. The aim of the law under the Calabresi analysis is to effect the behavior of drivers, including those who are destined to be the drivers involved in single car accidents. Under currently proposed motorist compensation plans, such

Much of our argument has dwelt on the conjectural aspects of tracing costs, and on the point that Calabresi has not sufficiently persuaded us that a change in liability rules would yield a net reduction in the cost of auto accidents to society. It remains to acknowledge that Calabresi has a major rejoinder to the argument in this posture. And in facing it, we revisit a point we have already partially looked at.[46] He argues that the real choice is between a motorist compensation plan of some sort and a social security system, since on political grounds the existing fault system, failing as it does to compensate all accident victims, cannot survive. Then, on grounds of general deterrence, he finds a decisive case for the motorist plan as against social security, regardless of our degree of ignorance about the economic consequences of placing all costs on motorists. As Calabresi puts it: "[A] though it is unclear whether an accident cost is attributable to driving or walking, in terms of general accident deterrence it is better to allocate it to one or the other or both than to pay it out of general taxes. . . . [W]here accident costs are not readily divisible between the activities involved, it is clear that placing the costs on them is better than externalizing the costs." [47] Since the existing tort system allocates accident costs between driving and walking and does not cover them out of general taxes, this cannot be offered as an economic argument against the present system. Calabresi is staying within the confines of his political prediction that the real choice will be between a motorist compensation plan and social security. We have already noted his rhetorical gambit of offering a political guess under the cover of an economic argument. We look here for a moment at whether the economic argument in its own right is all that good.

In essence, the argument is the comforting one that we cannot go wrong by not externalizing accident costs, however arbitrary and unconvincing our allocation of them between driver and pedestrian may be. There is no reason to doubt that in terms of sheer numbers, there will be fewer accidents if we do not externalize costs, but instead keep the cost pressures on motorists and pedestrians. The chance of going wrong therefore turns on the offsetting costs.[48] Putting all costs on motorists runs the hazard of repressing driving so much that the net costs of accidents to society will increase.[49] There is nothing in the nature of the case that makes it impossible to go wrong.

---

drivers would, as victims, be assured compensation. The pressures generated by such a law would thus seem to work in opposite directions.

The overlap between those who drive and those who are victims of auto accidents is, as has been widely observed, very great. This fact has caused some to be skeptical whether it can be worthwhile to worry about who should pay for auto accident damage—the driver as driver or the driver as victim. See BLUM & KALVEN, *op. cit. supra* note 3, at 43-44. Under the Calabresi approach there may thus be a general problem of offsetting stimuli along the lines of that suggested by the case of the driver who is involved in a single car accident.

[46] See text accompanying notes 10-11 *supra*.

[47] Calabresi, *supra* note 4, 78 HARV. L. REV. at 734.

[48] The chance of going wrong also depends on the absence of any possibility that the parties involved in accidents can shift the loss through private bargaining. See note 53 *infra*.

[49] Motorists in effect would be called on to subsidize all others who contribute to auto accidents.

V

One trouble with the Calabresi approach is that in a curious way he has been provincial about it all. He has opened legal analysis to broad new horizons, but he has refused, perhaps wisely, to speculate about radically new approaches implicit in his own argument. He has, if we may risk the phrase, been too tied down to the private law problem without maintaining the appropriate public law perspective.

Calabresi's approach, as we have stressed, has two basic features: he would use net reduction of the costs of auto accidents to society as the criterion by which to judge various measures; and he would utilize, under what he calls general deterrence, the pricing system as a mechanism for controlling behavior.

It might help at this point to rename the game. The objective is to optimize the number of auto accidents by using controls which preserve the the maximum amount of individual choice. However jarring it may be to the legal ear to talk of optimizing accidents, this formulation will have a familiar and congenial ring for the economist.

The idea of course is that there is some balance point between the losses from accidents and the offsetting costs of inhibiting the activity. If we fall on one side, we have more accidents than is desirable in the sense that the costs of reducing them are overshadowed by the benefits in cutting losses. On the other side, the analysis makes intelligible the apparently shocking remark that we may have too few auto accidents. What is meant is that the costs of repressing the activity outweigh the benefits.

Calabresi argues that a motorist compensation plan as contrasted to other viable alternatives [50] will move us further in the direction of optimizing accidents. He has, however, been willing to play the game only with limited stakes. The dollar magnitudes he wishes to use under a motorist compensation plan to control driver behavior are determined by the number of dollars that will be needed to compensate victims under the plan. As we shall see, there is no likely relationship between the amount of repressant on motorists required to optimize accidents and the amount of compensation needed to pay victims. We may still have too many auto accidents, and thus still be short of the goal. Or, as we have already indicated, the opposite may well turn out to be the case, leaving us with too few accidents.

This line of thought invites readdressing ourselves to the goal of bringing about the optimum number of auto accidents. If we liberate ourselves for the moment from conventional uses of law in the accident area, how might we conceivably arrange matters so as to come closer to that goal? The answer admittedly takes on a science-fiction flavor.

If we were to assume a kind of omniscience giving us full knowledge

---

[50] Once again it should be emphasized that under Calabresi's analysis there is only one viable alternative—social insurance paid out of general revenues. And again it should be emphasized that in his view the defect of the common law is not that it fails to move towards optimizing accidents but that it is not politically viable.

relevant to auto accident costs—data we clearly do not now have—we could build a mathematical model for stating the optimization problem in precise quantitative terms. Once we reached this stage, there would be no difficulty in solving the mathematical problem thus posed. To set up the model, our omniscience would have had to provide the answers to the following questions: (1) What factors have a bearing on auto accident costs? (2) How should these factors be priced or translated into dollar terms? (3) What is the price curve for each of the factors—that is, how does its contribution to accident costs vary with increases and decreases in its magnitude? (4) How do these curves interact on each other? When the computer finally ground to a halt, it would tell us what pattern of factors would given us the optimum allocation of resources for the auto accident problem. The law would thereby be told exactly where it should be going. The legal problem would then be how best to apply pressures so as to bring about this mix.

In order to leave the widest area for individual choice and to achieve our goal in the most efficient, frictionless way, we would want to use the price mechanism as the control wherever possible. This would call for intruding into the market with taxes or subsidies as conditions required: for example, if optimization called for a certain number of autos on the road, we could, by adjusting the price of motoring up or down, get to the desired number, while leaving to each individual the choice of driving or not. In making these moves no consideration would be given to the compensation of victims. Compensation payments would be made under the social security system, and there would be no need to draw any balance between the "prices" the motorists would pay for driving and the size of the fund required for compensation. The final result would be a perfection of general deterrence—a Utopian use of the strategy.[51]

It is worth noting that this fantasy serves among other things to illuminate the meaning of the key phrase, "costs of driving." In our Utopia it is more than possible that the costs of driving will be greater than under any motorist compensation plan. They will, however, be costs of driving in just as valid a sense as they are asserted to be costs of driving under a motorist compensation plan. Since in the auto accident situation costs are instrumental and since there is no way of relying on the market to fix them, they can only be assigned by some authority, for this reason it can never be helpful to talk of placing the costs of driving on driving.

There is no mystery over why Calabresi has not elected to push general deterrence toward Utopia. He tells us explicitly:

> [M]ost important, the world is infinitely more complex than the example. The choice is not between fewer pedestrians or fewer cars. It is among fewer old cars, new cars, cars driven by teenagers and aged ladies, fewer old pedestrians and crippled pedestrians,

---

[51] Calabresi at this point might well be tempted to invoke the old Hungarian bon mot: "If you have a Hungarian for a friend, you don't need an enemy." He might also come to recognize just how wonderful our world really is.

and all of these in relation to fewer buses and trains and better streets, better street lighting, and so on forever.

In other words, we cannot begin by determining the combination of activities that, given what we consider to be real costs of accidents, brings about the degree of reduction of accidents that we want in the cheapest possible way. . . .

This difficulty, though, is not grounds for abandoning an otherwise valuable approach if partial answers may be discovered and if the partial resolution is better than none at all.[52]

At this point we fundamentally part company. Calabresi urges that despite our deep ignorance in these matters, it is proper in order to implement general deterrence to impose the costs of all auto accidents on drivers, thus in effect adding the costs of non-fault accidents as a tax on driving. The acid test, we suggest, would be a proposal to go further in the same direction by doubling this tax on motorists. We can only surmise that he would be unwilling to take this step. Whether or not he would call it "unfair" to add the surtax, it is our deep hunch he would argue that it was imprudent to do so and that society would risk moving away from optimization of accident costs. Our position is in sharp contrast. We see the reasons for having doubts about the surtax as equally cogent reasons for having doubts about the tax required by a motorist compensation plan.

But perhaps we should not dismiss quite so quickly the possibilities of Utopia.[53] Putting the problem of auto accidents in terms of the optimization of resources has the special virtue of stating a legal problem in a form which is familiar and congenial to the economist. In this form he can at long last understand what our liability problems are about. It may not be too much to hope that gradually he will find some strands of the problem amenable to his measurements. As one economist has recently observed in discussing the auto accident problem: "To ask an economist how costs should be borne is to ask him what kind of property and social system we ought to have. Give us another 3,000 centuries."[54]

---

[52] Calabresi, *supra* note 4, 78 Harv. L. Rev. at 732-33.

[53] In the eyes of the bar another Utopian approach to the auto accident problem coming from economics would be an effort to adopt the general analysis offered by Ronald Coase. The Coase approach would seek to minimize the difference between cases like our radium watch dial example, and auto accident cases where there is no market nexus between the parties. He has succeeded in demonstrating that some cases, always thought of as outside the market, can be treated as market situations if the parties are in a position to strike private bargains as to paying for the cost of injuries resulting from an activity—as in the instance of the example he utilizes involving cattle raisers and crop farmers. See Coase, *The Problem of Social Costs,* 3 J. L. & Econ. 1 (1960). As far as we can see, the relationship between the parties involved in auto accidents is too remote from any conceivable bargaining arrangement to make this analysis usable. Calabresi seems to agree. See Calabresi 231-32. See also Blum & Kalven, *op. cit. supra* note 3, at 61-62; Demsetz, *supra* note 1.

[54] Alchian, *Review of Public Law Perspectives on a Private Law Problem,* 34 Geo. Wash. L. Rev. 820, 823 (1966).

VI

It is time to bring justice back into the discussion. We noted at the outset that Calabresi, finding the idea largely unintelligible, had virtually ruled it out as a goal for the legal system. And in so doing he was echoing the views of fellow economists who would distinguish sharply between justice and economic efficiency as guides to social policy. We stumble here upon what we suspect is a fundamental issue which goes well beyond auto compensation. There are various ways in which the basic query may be put: Is there any meaning "left over" for justice once efficiency goals have been attended to? Can efficiency ever conflict with justice?

Whatever the full range of such questions, they are vividly framed by the controversy over general deterrence and the auto accident. If society is coercively to impose a burden on citizens, we submit that there must be some justification for imposing it on one group rather than another. In this context we mean by justice the avoidance of what will be perceived as an arbitrary imposition of a burden.

The difficulty with general deterrence as a justification for shifting non-fault auto accident losses to motorists is that it is too fragile to carry the weight that would be put on in. Where the burdens are clear, certain, and not trivial, something more than conjecture about possible patterns of behavior is needed as a countervalue. To put the disagreement in a nutshell: when we know as little as we appear to know now about the prophecies of general deterrence, it is unjust to tax motorists on behalf of it.[55]

A more critical difficulty turns on the relative magnitude of the gains and the burdens involved. Let us assume that we know enough to devise a general deterrence strategy and to put it into operation, and that when it is implemented there will be at the end of the year be an increase in the gross national product of $1000 as a result of a reduction in the net costs of auto accidents by that amount. Let us assume further that to achieve this social good it is necessary to levy an additional tax of $100 on each motorist. We pick an example as extreme as this in order to raise a key question: Is there not some point at which even an unqualified gain in the efficient allocation of resources, achievable only through this particular route, is not of sufficient importance to justify the burdens which it calls for placing on particular individuals?

Although we recognize that the most rigorous and austere economic analysis might insist that the answer is no, we are quite confident that most people, and especially those in the traditions of law, would say that the answer must be yes. We therefore have a final difficulty with the Calabresi thesis. Even if we are to resolve all doubts in favor of the ability of a general deterrence strategy to bring about a net reduction in the costs of auto accidents, we may still confront a disturbing imbalance between the social gain achieved and the individual burdens imposed. Where the social gain seems small and the individual burdens in the aggregate seem relatively large, we find ourselves

---

[55] Put another way, it is unjust not also to tax others who contribute to the accidents.

thinking of the dangers of reversing Churchill's famous epigram: "Never have so many owed so much to so few." If we were to put our reaction into somewhat less personal terms, it would be that there very likely are hidden values that cannot be translated into economic costs, such as the value of having individuals understand why they are being subjected to a special tax and the value of not departing too lightly from traditional and accepted ways of doing things.[56]

## VII

In concentrating on Calabresi and the theory of general deterrence, our discussion of the auto compensation problem admittedly has been badly skewed.[57] We have singled out his writings not only in retaliation, but also because we have found his analysis to be most intellectually stimulating and the most promising for general tort theory. The fact of the matter is, however, that the auto accident problem is being widely discussed and that general deterrence has not been salient in the recent literature.[58] A review of recent developments is not now in order. But there is one feature in current thinking about auto plans that clamors for a further word. Turning to it will serve to move this essay toward a close.

The dominant view today among proponents of compensation plans is that the plans should be what might be called "two level." Originally, as in the Columbia Plan of the early thirties, the idea was to replace the tort system for auto accidents in toto with a compensation scheme. The new view is to provide an underlying plan that will compensate *all* victims but only up to some ceiling level of awards; and to leave the existing fault system alive while abolishing the collateral benefits rule, under which welfare payments could not be deducted from damages in tort suits.[59] The result is two levels of compensation: automatic but limited compensation to all victims, plus

---

[56] In the science-fiction world discussed in part V, it would be "possible" to avoid the difficulty noted here by collecting the special tax simply as a way of controlling the behavior of those individuals in the class of motorists, and then refunding that same aggregate amount to the class on a per capita basis out of general revenues. The class would not be worse off financially, thus erasing our difficulty as to the imbalance between burden and gain. Some motorists would be better off and some worse off; for example, the special tax on teenage motorists might exceed their share of the per capita "repayment" out of general revenues.

[57] Other reasons being advanced for adopting a motorist compensation plan are at very different levels. These include: (1) reducing the amount of fraud associated with proving fault; (2) reducing the size of legal and other fees in pressing a claim; (3) reducing the congestion of courts in various metropolitan areas; (4) providing prompt compensation for needy victims; (5) simplifying the handling of insurance and thereby reducing the cost of insurance; (6) reforming the present structure of damage awards. Proponents of plans have weighed these factors differently.

[58] Perhaps a sufficient indication of this is the attention paid by Keeton and O'Connell to Green, to Ehrenzweig, to Morris and Paul, to Conrad—and to Blum and Kalven, as contrasted to their single footnote reference to Calabresi. KEETON AND O'CONNELL, *op. cit. supra* note 1, at 259.

[59] The collateral benefits rule states that where an accident loss is compensated by insurance proceeds, employment fringe benefits, or outright gifts by a third party, the law will treat such payments as coming from collateral sources and therefore as not relevant to the computation of damages.

unlimited compensation to victims who can establish a fault basis for recovery.[60]

A first reaction might well be that such arrangements are politically ingenious but wholly unprincipled. The absence of clear principle is suggested by twin circumstances: the proponents have argued the need for a compensation plan on the weaknesses of the common law fault criterion and have viewed some aspects of common law damages as excessive; they nevertheless end up by keeping the fault system alive and giving common law damages.[61] The cleverness of the arrangement is that it makes possible a plan under which no victim as a victim can be worse off than he was at common law and under which some function is still left for the tort system. Thus any sense of grievance over the proposed change is abated for those parties most likely to complain —the victims and the lawyers.[62]

On fuller examination, however, it appears there need be no inconsistency in the two level arrangement; and further, whatever the practical motivation for such plans, the two level concept may be the route to a sound solution to the whole problem. The key lies in the separation of two functions of tort damages that have always been tied together in the past—the welfare function of providing relief for the injured and the corrective justice function of righting a private wrong. So long as the functions are lumped together, the welfare function is likely to be seen as dominant given present concerns. By separating the functions, the two level plans may test sharply whether the corrective justice function is worth preserving.

In our earlier essay we found it instructive to think about the tort field being overlaid by the adoption of a broad social security system that covered a large variety of human ills and misfortunes. And we maintained that, insofar as we are concerned with compensation of victims, there is no alternative superior to extension of social security. It alone can provide a coherent and equal treatment of deserving beneficiaries, and it alone is capable of furnishing a rationale for distributing burdens and for determining benefits. What the

---

[60] The clearest instance of this two level approach is the Saskatchewan Plan. See GREGORY & KALVEN, CASES ON TORTS 757-60 (1959). Another instance, although a more complicated version, is that in KEETON & O'CONNELL, op. cit. supra note 1, at 273.

[61] These inconsistencies are frequently raised in bar association discussions in criticism of the Keeton-O'Connell Plan. See, e.g., Green, Basic Protection and Court Congestion, 52 A.B.A.J. 926 (1966).

[62] A distinctive aspect of the Keeton-O'Connell Plan is that it deliberately leaves some victims worse off and thus does not follow the strategy of the Saskatchewan Plan. The principal loss of rights are the elimination of the first $5000 of damages for pain and suffering; the elimination of the collateral benefits rule for most claims; the elimination in many cases of wages losses in excess of $750 a month; the elimination of the first $100 of any loss (which is borne by the victim). See Marryott, The Tort System and Automobile Claims: Evaluating the Keeton-O'Connell Proposal, 52 A.B.A.J. 639 (1966). Marryott concludes that as a result of these provisions "in a state like New York 80 per cent or so of the basic protection claimants will have their benefits substantially reduced, [and] the net effect is that a large majority of the persons injured in automobile accidents will be looking to non-basic protection benefits (self-provided, government-provided, employer-provided) as the principal sources of reparation of automobile accident injuries." Id., at 642. Compare BLUM & KALVEN, op. cit. supra note 3, at 32-40.

two level plans ultimately put in issue is whether even under such extensive welfare guarantees there is a function left over for the tort system.[63]

The answer is not without its difficulties. There are two wings to the problem: the case for corrective justice with respect to accident injuries that fall below the ceiling for social security payments, and the case for it in the more serious accidents. The two level plans that are now being offered preserve the tort function in the more serious accidents but eliminate it in the less serious.

This handling of the less serious accident cases is probably inescapable, but it is worth working through the analysis. There are three possibilities that merit consideration: the victim can recover only from the welfare fund, but the fund can recover over from the tortfeasor; the victim can recover both from the fund and from the tortfeasor; once the victim has recovered from the fund, neither he nor the fund can recover from the tortfeasor. In this matrix the problem has been thoroughly analyzed elsewhere by others, and there is no need to restate it here.[64] One point, however, is of special interest to us. In large part corrective justice is concerned not with deterring the wrongdoer, but with satisfying the victim's feeling of indignation.[65] If the victim recovers only from the fund, he will not gain the satisfaction of seeing his wrong righted, Nor will it be much different if, after paying the victim, the fund later recovers from the tortfeasor. We come then to the question of whether it is worth allowing the victim to have a double recovery merely to satisfy his sense of indignation—with the tort recovery becoming in effect a form of punitive damages.

Several reasons converge on the conclusion that double recovery would be unwarranted. To leave the victim with his tort action in addition to his social security payments would be to continue to burden the adjudication system with all the costs today associated with litigation and settlement. Inasmuch as motorists would continue to run the risk of tort liability for negligence, the demand for liability insurance would be little changed, and hence there would be the cost of keeping the insurance arrangements alive. Moreover, because of the presence of insurance the corrective justice lesson would be lost in many cases on the tortfeasor; often he might never even learn how the case came out.[66] Nor in allowing a double recovery can we ignore the

---

[63] As a matter of history, the English reached this issue when they adopted the Beveridge national welfare plan which provided for broad social insurance. The proposal precipitated wide debate on whether to abolish the tort remedy altogether or to abolish the collateral benefits rule with respect to the welfare plan payments. The English "solved" the problem by doing neither. See Friedman, *Social Insurance and the Principles of Tort Liability*, 63 HARV. L. REV. 241 (1949).

[64] See James, *Social Insurance and Tort Liability: The Problem of Alternative Remedies*, 27 N.Y.U.L. REV. 537 (1952).

[65] Compare ARISTOTLE, NICOMACHEAN ETHICS V (iv) (Loeb transl. 1926); HART, THE CONCEPT OF LAW 160 (1961).

[66] CONARD, MORGAN, PRATT, VOLTZ, & BOMBAUGH, *op. cit. supra* note 1, at 296-99, Included in their elaborate survey of some 86,000 accident losses were questionnaires to a sample of 183 insured defendants. In 33% of the cases the defendant did not know whether the claim against him had been paid or not; if, however, the case went to trial, only 5% of the defendants remained unaware of the outcome of the claim.

traditional view that punitive damages in any form are not appropriate for negligent conduct. Finally, there is the telling point that the double recovery is likely to spoil the corrective justice adjustment from the viewpoint of the victim as well. Since he has been made whole by the social security payments, he is apt to perceive the tort recovery more as a windfall than as the correction of a loss wrongfully caused.

But do the arguments change when we shift attention to the more serious injuries—those in which the social security payments are not thought to make the victim whole? Only one point is really different. To withdraw the tort remedy in this context would be to leave the victim with some uncompensated loss wrongfully caused him by another. Conversely, to give him a remedy would be perceived as correcting a wrong and not as a windfall. The tort remedy can thus serve to satisfy his sense of moral indignation.

Undoubtedly people will weigh these arguments differently. Many are likely to hold to the view that the vagaries of the fault criterion, the costs of litigation and of insurance arrangements, the obscuring of corrective justice adjustments because of liability insurance, and the oddity of pain and suffering as damages all combine to make the game not worth the candle.[67] There is assuredly much to be said for striking the balance this way, but we would conclude otherwise.

To us there remains great force in the notion that no one should be worse off because of the wrongdoing of another so long as the wrongdoer, or his insurer, is in a position to make redress.[68] The law ought not to break sharply with the moral traditions of the society, as it would do were it no longer to recognize fault and personal responsibility. And we would urge that not all reflection of moral values should be left to the criminal law. The tort system can share some of the burden of satisfying indignation.

The two level arrangement, whereby welfare underwriting for all accidents is supplied by social security and the tort system is left "on top" of that underwriting, has one paramount advantage. It permits the society to make independent judgments on matters that cannot be cleanly handled together—the setting of welfare payment levels and the setting of corrective justice damage levels.[69] On the one side, welfare payments should be set by some general standard deemed appropriate for victims of all misfortunes. They clearly should not be set differently for victims of auto accidents and other victims.

---

[67] The opponents of plans have frequently asserted that a two level arrangement, by its victim protection underwriting, will serve to finance tort suits, and that this will have a very undesirable effect on claims consciousness and on court congestion. On the other side, it has been suggested that once the urgency of compensation is satisfied by victim protection, pressure will be taken off the tort system to expand the concept of fault. The assumption is that if the tort system had to serve only a corrective justice function, the fault criteria could be kept narrow and pure. See EHRENZWEIG, "FULL AID" INSURANCE FOR THE TRAFFIC VICTIM (1954).

[68] We would take this position even if insurance premiums remain as undifferentiated as they are now. But any increase in differentiation probably would increase the perception that corrective justice is being done.

[69] See BLUM & KALVEN, op. cit. supra note 3, at 36-39. Compare Calabresi's discussion of what is "appropriately" a cost of an accident. Calabresi, op. cit. supra note 4, 78 HARV. L. REV. at 721-24.

And they should, as a matter of policy, be set without contagion from common law damages and the settlement practices of insurance companies. On the other side, it should be observed that there is a basic compatibility between pain and suffering as a recognition of the dignitary aspects of accident injuries and a liability system keyed to fault. From a welfare point of view awards for pain and suffering may well be regarded as a quixotic luxury; from a corrective justice point of view such damages may be at the heart of the matter.[70]

VIII

By a curious route we are led back to Calabresi and general deterrence. We earlier showed that Calabresi is much too sanguine that a motorist plan will move in the direction of optimizing auto accident costs, but we have not examined fully [71] his position that social security is from a general deterrence viewpoint the worst of all possible worlds. We turn to it now.

Once again Calabresi seems to have narrowed his sights too much. It is by no means true that the welfare objective must be satisfied in a form which externalizes accident costs. In our society it is becoming less and less utopian to think of adopting a social welfare system under which payments would not be for specific items, but rather would be calculated to provide everyone with a minimum level of annual income, out of which individuals would be free to insure themselves against catastrophic losses.[72]

As a final twist of the analysis of the auto problem, let us posit for a moment a "two level" plan under which the social welfare underwriting would be in this form and all accident losses due to fault would remain actionable under tort law. Such a regime might well rank highest even under Calabresi's point system. It would provide for all needy victims; it would maximize the range of individual choice; it would satisfy the demands for corrective justice; and most important, it would not externalize any auto accident costs.[73] It would, moreover, have the added feature of eliminating all questions about overlaps between payments under the tort system and under the social welfare system. Victims of fault losses would continue to recover their losses in full from the tortfeasors or their insurers. Welfare payments would be made to adjust for inadequacies of income and not for particular accident losses. Neither these losses nor the compensating payments would be counted in determining the right to welfare payments pursuant to the minimum income schedules.

---

[70] This view suggests a solution to the dilemma which Jaffe argued the tort system faced as it sought both to "honor" pain and suffering and to compensate ever more widely. See Jaffe, *Damages for Personal Injury: The Impact of Insurance,* 18 LAW & CONTEMP. PROB. 219 (1953).
[71] Earlier we suggested that placing all additional costs on motorists might be worse than externalizing them. See note 49 *supra* and accompanying text.
[72] See FRIEDMAN, CAPITALISM AND FREEDOM (1962).
[73] It does not externalize non-fault accident costs because they are left on the victim. If the victim is entitled to receive welfare payments, it is because he is poor and not because he was injured in an automobile.

But would this regime be "fair" to the victim of a non-fault accident who was unable to recover anything for his loss? To us the answer is clearly yes. We find that his case for recovery is no more (and no less) appealing than those of the victims of other misfortunes, including being born badly handicapped or having a heart attack or being struck by lightning. The answer becomes even more persuasive when we ask ourselves whether we would allow the victim of a non-fault accident to shift his loss if everyone had ample economic means. Once we are freed of concerns about poverty, is there any case for compensating victims of misfourtune apart from working corrective justice in redressing humanly caused wrongs?

*          *          *

In these reflections we have explored a continuum encompassing four solutions to the auto accident problem: the common law fault liability system; a two level plan consisting of a tort action for fault on top of non-fault compensation to all victims, financed by motorists; a two level plan, this time with the non-fault underwriting provided by social insurance that cover a wide range of misfortunes and is paid for out of general revenues; and finally, a two level plan in which there is no underwriting for specific misfortunes but a general underwriting of income up to some level. Two points should be emphasized. Under all four alternatives for solving the auto problem, the fault system remains alive, albeit only for some purposes. And while the most obvious difference is between the common law system and the two level arrangements, we would urge that the differences among the two level arrangements are also critical.[74] Against this backdrop, it may be useful to once more summarize the basic position we have been advancing in these essays.

The tort system should be kept alive for auto accidents not as a compromise to make change politically palatable, but because it has a distinctive function to perform in the handling of indignation. Insofar as society is being moved by the needs of uncompensated victims of auto accident, the law should group the beneficiaries of its intervention rationally and should not single out the auto victims for preferential treatment; better still, it should address itself directly to the problem of poverty. The award levels should be set in terms of the function being performed by payment: welfare awards should be keyed to general welfare criteria, and damages for being wronged should permit recognition of indignation. Finally, the method of financing awards should also be selected in terms of the functions being performed by the payments.

---

[74] Two "political" points have been raised against the position that if welfare is the goal, social security and not a motorist compensation plan is the appropriate route. On the one hand, it is argued that a motorist plan is a halfway house on the road to social security; on the other hand, it is argued that since adequate expansion of social security will never be forthcoming, half a loaf is better than none. It should be clear from the text that we are hopeful that it is possible to separate one's policy judgments from one's political predictions. Indeed, a chief objection to the Calabresi analysis is that he has failed to do so.

General welfare payments should be financed from general taxes,[75] and corrective justice payments should be assessed against those guilty of flawed conduct.

There has been a good deal of development of the topic in the two years since we first attempted to think through the auto compensation problem. Important new research has been published; thoughtful legislative proposals have been made; Calabresi has advanced the analysis of general deterrence; and there has been much debate in the law school world and in bar forums. As a result, we have had occasion to reexamine, to restudy, and repeatedly to adjust our position to new insights. There is, however, a sentence about motorists plans that seems to us as pertinent now as it did two years ago. The sentence will come as a surprise to no one, and we end with it. "If the expanded coverage in operation will cost more than the present system, what justification is there for placing such additional costs on those who own or operate vehicles?"[76]

---

[75] There may even be a few problems of distributive justice in this area. See, BLUM & KALVEN, THE UNEASY CASE FOR PROGRESSIVE TAXATION (1st Phoenix ed. 1963). Afficianados of this issue might be interested in the reports of the American Institute of Legal Jurimetrics, published in 43 TAXES 636 (1965) and 44 TAXES 737 (1966).

[76] BLUM & KALVEN, op. cit. supra note 3, at 54.

# CHAPTER IV

# LEGAL RESPONSIBILITY

Both moral obligation and causal agency are contributing factors in the elucidation of legal responsibility; but neither singly nor together do they supply necessary or sufficient conditions for assigning legal liability in the face of complex and sometimes idiosyncratic legal conventions. Two cases, one hypothetical, the other a landmark in American jurisprudence, illustrate some of the special anomalies apparent in this sphere:

(1) Let us suppose that X, an able-bodied adult male, calmly watches a child drown who could have been rescued with slight risk and effort on his part. Scarcely any moral system would find such inaction less than reprehensible. Yet the law would not hold such an individual legally responsible unless he could be assigned some special role responsibility, say that of parent or acting lifeguard. The law has been reluctant to impose legal duties in such cases not only because of difficulties of proof but also in accordance with a long-standing legal policy that individuals are not to be held accountable for the general welfare of others, except in stipulated circumstances. In fact, would-be good Samaritans – even doctors acting without specific authorization – may be subject to damage suits if their actions in any way contribute to injury.

(2) In 1916, while serving with the New York Court of Appeals, Benjamin Cardozo (later to inherit Holmes' mantle as the leading shcolar on the United States Supreme Court) overturned a significant line of precedent when he awarded damages to an injured party in the famous case, *MacPherson v. Buick Motor Co.* The case is a masterful illustration of the logic of development in law – the gradual displacement of an established principle through successive exemptions leading to the formation of a new standard in a decisive judgment. The circum-

stances of the case were these: faulty wooden spokes in a wheel of MacPherson's new Buick had given way, causing a serious accident. The wheel had not been manufactured by Buick but by a subcontractor. Prior to the decision, according of the common law principle of "privity", injured parties had generally only been allowed to sue the immediate contractual party from whom faulty goods had been purchased, and then only if the fault in question could be directly attributed to this same party. MacPherson would have had no claim because he had purchased the automobile in question from a retailer and not Buick directly, and because the subcontractor and not Buick was causally responsible for the fault. Nevertheless, Cardozo awarded damages to MacPherson on the basis that final manufacturers should now be held responsible for reasonable inspection of their product.

Taken together, these cases illustrate some (by no means all) of the difficulties involved in assigning legal responsibility. Reasons of general social policy may override both private moral principle and proximate causality in the assignment of liability. Wasn't Buick something of a scapegoat in the establishment of this new precedent? Why should't our mythical X be held as legally responsibible for his actions as a negligent landlord or a reckless driver?.

In a postscript to his collection of essays, *Punishment and Responsibility* (Oxford University Press, 1967), H. L. A. Hart sketches several disparate, if frequently overlapping, subdivisions in the legal responsibility family:

(1) "role-responsibility", a traditional but expanding class of special obligations imposed by law on individuals by virtue of their social roles – parental, official, professional, etc.;

(2) "causal-responsibility", largely self-explanatory but only operative in line with legal conventions;

(3) "liability-responsibility", frequently coincident with (1) or (2) but occasionally assigned for other policy reasons;

(4) "capacity-responsibility", usually a ground for exemption from, or mitigation of, responsibility (special legal rules affecting minors, the legally insane or those of diminished capacity), but sometimes a basis for assigning positive role-responsibilities.

As Hart acknowledges, his criteria are not necessarily exhaustive; nor does he answer fundamental questions of policy. In what cases should new forms of legal liability be assigned; in which should traditional legal patterns be retained. Modern societies seem to be entering a period of rapid expansion of special role-responsibilities in measure with the increasing social and economic complexities of industrial-technological systems. The liberties of the iniquitous X have been somewhat eroded by recent statutes and decisions: 'good Samaritans' have been increasingly absolved from the threat of damages; owners of so-called "attractive nuisances" (e.g. unlocked automobiles or unprotected bodies of water) have been held liable for injuries sustained even by acknowledged trespassers, especially when the latter are juveniles.

Nowhere are the limitations and inner conflicts of contemporary philosophies of mind or psychoanalysis more apparent then when theory is set adrift on the rough seas of the 'hard case' or even standard legal practice. Should juries search for and attribute responsibility to unconscious motives? Are motives an expression of conscious intent or a manifestation of deep-seated character traits (Ryle's "law-like proposition")? Imagine an hypothetical Mrs. X who has shot an admittedly despised husband but who claims that she mistook him for a burglar. Did she shoot her husband intentionally? Did she make an honest mistake? Did she shoot him out of unconscious desires or dispositional hostility? The adversary system has been understandably wary of *primie facie* answers to such questions'. *Pace* Ryle or Freud, Mrs. X may, indeed, have hated her husband but nevertheless have made an honest mistake.

Despite considerable dissatisfaction with traditional accounts of human behavior, the very vagueness, say, of Aristotle's definition of voluntary action ("that of which the moving principle is in the agent himself, he being aware of the particular circumstances of the action", *Nic. Ethics*, III, 1) may be considered a virtue in the eyes of the practitioner – it offers latitude for flexible interpreta-tion of the case in hand. M'Naghten's Rule for determining legal insanity ("...such a defect of reason, from disease of the mind, as not to know the nature and quality of the act he was doing, or, if he did know it, that he did not know he was doing what was wrong") still holds sway over proposed psychoanalytic alternatives because that field can offer no consensus on the question of respon-sibility (see Joseph Margolis, *Psychotherapy and Morality*, New York, Random House, 1966).

J. L. Austin's "A Plea for Excuses" suggests the range of subtleties and complexities that confronts any attempt at an adequate analysis of human responsibility in a legal context. No area in the field is more subject to contro-versy and the clash of theoretical and empirical disciplines, and definitive work is yet to be done on a number of fundamental topics. In addition to the Hart essays mentioned above, Herbert Morris' *Freedom and Responsibility* (Stanford, 1963) and Philip Davis' *Moral Duty and Legal Responsibility* (Appleton-Century-Crofts, 1966) offer extensive correlative readings focused respectively on theore-tical and case materials.

# 15

# Aristotle

Aristotle (384-322 B.C.), author of a theory of human responsibility which has endured the vicissitudes of successive waves of ideological critique, still speaks with an authoritative voice on this problematic topic.

# RESPONSIBILITY*

Acts just and unjust being as we have described them, a man acts unjustly or justly whenever he does such acts voluntarily; when involuntarily, he acts neither unjustly nor justly except in an incidental way; for he does things which happen to be just or unjust. Whether an act is or is not one of injustice (or of justice) is determined by its voluntariness or involuntariness; for when it is voluntary it is blamed, and at the same time is then an act of injustice; so that there will be things that are unjust but not yet acts of injustice, if voluntariness be not present as well. By the voluntary I mean, as has been said before, any of the things in a man's own power which he does with knowledge, i.e. not in ignorance either of the person acted on or of the instrument used or of the end that will be attained (e.g. whom he is striking, with what, and to what end), each such act being done not incidentally nor under compulsion (e.g. if A takes B's hand and therewith strikes C, B does not act voluntarily; for the act was not in his own power). The person struck may be the striker's father, and the striker may know that is is a man or one of the persons present, but not know that is is his father; a similar distinction may be made in the case of the end, and with regard to the whole action. Therefore that which is done in ignorance, or though not done in ignorance is not in the agent's power, or is done under compulsion, is involuntary (for many natural processes, even, we knowingly both perform and experience, none of which is either voluntary or involuntary; e.g. growing old or dying). But in the case of unjust and just acts alike the injustice or justice may be only incidental; for a man might return a deposit unwillingly and from fear, and then he must not be said either to do what is just or to act justly, except in an incidental way. Similarly the man who under compulsion and unwillingly fails to return the deposit must be said to act unjustly, and to do what is unjust, only incidentally. Of voluntary acts we do some by choice, others not by choice; by choice those which we do after deliberation, not by choice those which we do without previous deliberation. Thus

---

*Aristotle, *Nicomachean Ethics*, V. 8, reprinted by permission of the publisher from *The Oxford Translation of Aristotle*, Clarendon Press, Oxford, edited by W. D. Ross. The editors' footnotes have been omitted.

there are three kinds of injury in transactions between man and man; those done in ignorance are *mistakes* when the person acted on, the act, the instrument, or the end that will be attained is other than the agent supposed; the agent thought either that he was not hitting any one of that he was not hitting with this missile or not hitting this person or to this end, but a result followed other than that which he thought likely (e.g. he threw not with intent to wound but only to prick), or the person hit or the missile was other than he supposed. Now when (1) the injury takes place contrary to reasonable expectation, it is a *misadventure*. When (2) it is not contrary to reasonable expectation, but does not imply vice, it is a *mistake* (for a man makes a mistake when the fault originates in him, but is the victim of accident when the origin lies outside him). When (3) he acts with knowledge but not after deliberation, it is an *act of injustice*—e.g. the acts due to anger or to other passions necessary or natural to man; for when men do such harmful and mistaken acts they act unjustly, and the acts are acts of injustice, but this does not imply that the doers are unjust or wicked; for the injury is not due to vice. But when (4) a man acts from choice, he is an *unjust man* and a vicious man.

Hence acts proceeding from anger are rightly judged not to be done of malice aforethought; for it is not the man who acts in anger but he who enraged him that starts the mischief. Again, the matter in dispute is not whether the thing happened or not, but its justice; for it is apparent injustice that occasions rage. For they do not dispute about the occurrence of the act—as in commercial transactions where one of the two parties *must* be vicious—unless they do so owing to forgetfulness; but, agreeing about the fact, they dispute on which side justice lies (whereas a man who has deliberately injured another cannot help knowing that he has done so), so that the one thinks he is being treated unjustly and the other disagrees.

But if a man harms another by choice, he acts unjustly; and *these* are the acts of injustice which imply that the doer is an unjust man, provided that the act violates proportion or equality. Similarly, a man *is just* when he acts justly by choice; but he *acts justly* if he merely acts voluntarily.

Of involuntary acts some are excusable, others not. For the mistakes which men make not only in ignorance but also from ignorance are excusable, while those which men do not from ignorance but (though they do them *in* ignorance) owing to a passion which is neither natural nor such as man is liable to, are not excusable.

# 16

# M'Naghten's Rule

M'Naghten's Rule (1843), an enduring criterion for establishing legal insanity, often criticised for its stress on the state of knowledge of the accused, was formulated by the House of Lords in response to questions posed by the judges in the famous case of M'Naghten who was tried for the murder of the secretary to Sir Robert Peel.

# LEGAL INSANITY

(Q.I.) "What is the law respecting alleged crimes committed by persons afflicted with insane delusion in respect of one or more particular subjects or persons: as for instance, where, at the time of the commission of the alleged crime, the accused knew he was acting contrary to law, but did the act complained of with a view, under the influence of insane delusion, of redressing or revenging some supposed grievance or injury, or of producing some supposed public benefit?"

(A.I.) "Assuming that your lordships' inquiries are confined to those persons who labor under such partial delusions only, and are not in other respects insane, we are of opinion that notwithstanding the accused did the act complained of with a view, under the influence of insane delusion, of redressing or avenging some supposed grievance or injury, or of producing some public benefit, he is nevertheless punishable, according to the nature of the crime committed, if he knew at the time of committing such crime that he was acting contrary to law, by which expression we understand your lordships to mean the law of the land."

(Q.II.) "What are the proper questions to be submitted to the jury where a person alleged to be afflicted with insane delusion respecting one or more particular subjects or persons is charged with the commission of a crime (murder, for example), and insanity is set up as a defence?"

(Q.III.) "In what terms ought the question to be left to the jury as to the prisoner's state of mind at the time when the act was committed?"

(A.II and A.III.) "As these two questions appear to us to be more conveniently answered together, we submit our opinion to be that the jury ought to be told in all cases that every man is presumed to be sane, and to possess a sufficient degree of reason to be responsible for his crimes, until the contrary be proved to their satisfaction; and that to establish a defence on the ground of insanity it might be clearly proved that, at the time of committing the act, the accused was labouring under such a defect of reason, from disease of the mind, as not to know the nature and quality of the act he was doing, or, if he did know it, that he did not know he was doing what was wrong. The mode of putting the latter part of the question to the jury on these occasions has generally been whether the accused at the time of doing the act knew the difference between right and wrong: which mode, through rarely, if ever, leading to any mistake with the jury, is not, as we conceive, so accurate when put generally and in the abstract as when put with reference to the party's knowledge of right and wrong, in respect to the very act with which he is charged. If the question were to be put as to the knowledge of the accused solely and exclusively with reference to the law of the land, it might tend to confound the jury, by inducing them to believe that an actual knowledge of the law of the land was essential in order to lead to conviction: whereas, the law is administered upon the principle that everyone must be taken conclusively to know it, without proof that he does know it. If the accused was conscious that the act was one that he ought not to do, and if that act was at the same time contrary to the law of the land, he is punishable; and the usual course, therefore, has been to leave the question to the jury, whether the accused had a sufficient degree of reason to know that he was doing an act that was wrong; and this course we think is correct, accompanied with such observations and explanations as the circumstances of each particular case may require."

(Q.IV.) "If a person under an insane delusion as to existing facts commits an offence in consequence thereof, is he thereby excused?"

(A.IV.) "The answer must, of course, depend on the nature of the delusion; but making the same assumption as we did before, namely, that he labors under such partial delusion only, and is not in other respects insane, we think he must be considered in the same situation as to responsibility as if the facts with respect to which the delusion exists were real. For example, if under the influence of his delusion he supposes another man to be in the act of attempting to take away his life, and he kills that man, as he supposes in self-defence, he would be exempt from punishment. If his delusion was that the deceased had inflicted a serious injury to his character and fortune, and he killed him in revenge for such supposed injury, he would be liable to punishment."

# 17

# John Langshaw Austin

J. L. Austin (1911–1953), White's Professor of Moral Philosophy at Oxford University and one of the most penetrating minds of the school of ordinary language analysis, reshaped the problem of human responsibility in this now classic article.

# A PLEA FOR EXCUSES*

The subject of this paper, *Excuses,* is one not to be treated, but only to be introduced, within such limits. It is, or might be, the name of a whole branch, even a ramiculated branch, of philosophy, or at least of one fashion of philosophy. I shall try, therefore, first to state *what* the subject is, *why* it is worth studying, and *how* it may be studied, all this at a regrettably lofty level: and then I shall illustrate, in more congenial but desultory detail, some of the methods to be used, together with their limitations, and some of the unexpected results to be expected and lessons to be learned. Much, of course, of the amusement, and of the instruction, comes in drawing the coverts of the microglot, in hounding down the minutiae, and to this I can do no more here than incite you. But I owe it to the subject to say, that it has long afforded me what philosophy is so often thought, and made, barren of—the fun of discovery, the pleasures of cooperation, and the satisfaction of reaching agreement.

What, then, is the subject? I am here using the word "excuses" *for a title,* but it would be unwise to freeze too fast to this one noun and its partner verb: indeed for some time I used to use "extenuation" instead. Still, on the whole "excuses" is probably the most central and embracing term in the field, although this includes others of importance—"plea," "defense," "justification," and so on. When, then, do we "excuse" conduct, our own or somebody else's? When are "excuses" proffered?

In general, the situation is one where someone is *accused* of having done something, or (if that will keep it any cleaner) where someone is *said* to have done something which is bad, wrong, inept, unwelcome, or in some other of the numerous possible ways untoward. Thereupon he, or someone on his behalf, will try to defend his conduct or to get him out of it.

One way of going about this is to admit flatly that he, X, did do that very thing, A, but to argue that it was a good thing, or the right or sensible thing, or a permissible thing to do, either in general or at least in the special circum-

*J. L. Austin, *Aristotelian Society Proceedings,* LVII (1956-57), pp. 1-30, reprinted by permission of The Clarendon Press, Oxford. Footnotes renumbered.

stances of the occasion. To take this line is to *justify* the action, to give reasons for doing it: not to say, to brazen it out, to glory in it, or the like.

A different way of going about it is to admit that it wasn't a good thing to have done, but to argue that it is not quite fair or correct to say *baldly* "X did A." We may say it isn't fair just to say X did it; perhaps he was under somebody's influence, or was nudged. Or, it isn't fair to say baldly he *did* A; it may have been partly accidental, or an unintentional slip. Or, it isn't fair to say he did simply A—he was really doing something quite different and A was only incidental, or he was looking at the whole thing quite differently. Naturally these arguments can be combined or overlap or run into each other.

In the one defense, briefly, we accept responsibility but deny that it was bad: in the other, we admit that it was bad but don't accept full, or even any, responsibility.

By and large, justifications can be kept distinct from excuses, and I shall not be so anxious to talk about them because they have enjoyed more than their fair share of philosophical attention. But the two certainly can be confused, and can *seem* to go very near to each other, even if they do not perhaps actually do so. You dropped the tea tray: Certainly, but an emotional storm was about to break out: or, Yes, but there was a wasp. In each case the defense, very soundly, insists on a fuller description of the event in its context; but the first is a justification, the second an excuse. Again, if the objection is to the use of such a dyslogistic verb as "murdered," this may be on the ground that the killing was done in battle (justification) or on the ground that it was only accidental if reckless (excuse). It is arguable that we do not use the terms "justification" and "excuse" as carefully as we might; a miscellany of even less-clear terms, such as "extenuation," "palliation," "mitigation," hovers uneasily between partial justification and partial excuse; and when we plead, say, provocation, there is genuine uncertainty or ambiguity as to what we mean—is *he* partly responsible, because he roused a violent impulse or passion in me, so that it wasn't truly or merely me acting "of my own accord" (excuse)? Or is it rather that, he having done me such injury, I was entitled to retaliate (justification)? Such doubts merely make it the more urgent to clear up the usage of these various terms. But that the defenses I have for convenience labeled "justification" and "excuse" are in principle distinct can scarcely be doubted.

This then is the sort of situation we have to consider under "excuses." I will only further point out how very wide a field it covers. We have, of course, to bring in the opposite numbers of excuses—the expressions that *aggravate,* such as "deliberately," "on purpose," and so on, if only for the reason that an excuse often takes the form of a rebuttal of one of these. But we have also to bring in a large number of expressions which at first blush look not so much like excuses as like accusations—"clumsiness," "tactlessness," "thoughtlessness," and the like. Because it has always to be remembered that few excuses get us out of it *completely:* the average excuse, in a poor situation, gets us only out of the fire into the frying-pan—but still, of course, any frying-pan in a fire.

If I have broken your dish or your romance, may be the best defense I can find will be clumsiness.

Why, if this is what "excuses" are, should we trouble to investigate them? It might be thought reason enough that their production has always bulked so large among human activities. But to moral philosophy in particular a study of them will contribute in special ways, both positively towards the development of a cautious, latter-day version of conduct, and negatively towards the correction of older and hastier theories.

In ethics we study, I suppose, the good and the bad, the right and the wrong, and this must be for the most part in some connection with conduct or the doing of actions. Yet before we consider what actions are good or bad, right or wrong, it is proper to consider first what is meant by, and what not, and what is included under, and what not, the expression "doing an action" or "doing something." These are expressions still to little examined on their own accounts and merits, just as the general notion of "saying something" is still too lightly passed over in logic. There is indeed a vague and comforting idea in the background that, after all, in the last analysis, doing an action must come down to the making of physical movements with parts of the body; but this is about as true as that saying something must, in the last analysis, come down to making movements of the tongue.

The beginning of sense, not to say wisdom, is to realize that "doing an action," as used in philosophy,[1] is a highly abstract expression—it is a stand-in used in the place of any (or almost any?) verb with a personal subject, in the same sort of way that "thing" is a stand-in for any (or when we remember, almost any) noun substantive, and "quality" a stand-in for the adjective. Nobody, to be sure, relies on such dummies quite implicitly quite indefinitely. Yet notoriously it is possible to arrive at, or to derive the idea for, an over-simplified metaphysics from the obsession with "things" and their "qualities." In a similar way, less commonly recognized even in these semi-sophisticated times, we fall for the myth of the verb. We treat the expression "doing an action" no longer as a stand-in for a verb with a personal subject, as which it has no doubt some uses, and might have more if the range of verbs were not left unspecified, but as a self-explanatory, ground-level description, one which brings adequately into the open the essential features of everything that comes, by simple inspection, under it. We scarcely notice even the most patent exceptions or difficulties (is to think something, or to say something, or to try to do something, to do an action?), any more than we fret, in the *ivresse des grandes profondeurs*, as to whether flames are things or events. So we come easily to think of our behavior over any time, and of a life as a whole, as consisting in doing now action A, next action B, then action C, and so on, just as elsewhere we come to think of the world as consisting of this, that, and the other substance or material thing, each with its properties. All "actions" are, as actions

[1] This use has little to do with the more down-to-earth occurrences of "action" in ordinary speech.

(meaning what?), equal, composing a quarrel with striking a match, winning a war with sneezing: worse still, we assimilate them one and all to the supposedly most obvious and easy cases, such as posting letters or moving fingers, just as we assimilate all "things" to horses or beds.

If we are to continue to use this expression in sober philosophy, we need to ask such questions as: Is to sneeze to do an action? Or is to breathe, or to see, or to checkmate, or each one of countless others? In short, for what range of verbs, as used on what occasions, is "doing an action" a stand-in? What have they in common, and what do those excluded severally lack? Again we need to ask how we decide what is the correct name for "the" action that somebody did—and what, indeed, are the rules for the use of "the" action, "an" action, "one" action, a "part" or "phase" of an action and the like. Further, we need to realize that even the "simplest" named actions are not so simple—certainly are not the mere makings of physical movements, and to ask what more, then, comes in (intentions? conventions?) and what does not (motives?), and what is the detail of the complicated internal machinery we use in "acting"—the receipt of intelligence, the appreciation of the situation, the invocation of principles, the planning, the control of execution and the rest.

In two main ways the study of excuses can throw light on these fundamental matters. First, to examine excuses is to examine cases where there has been some abnormality or failure: and as so often, the abnormal will throw light on the normal, will help us to penetrate the blinding veil of ease and obviousness that hides the mechanisms of the natural successful act. It rapidly becomes plain that the breakdowns signalized by the various excuses are of radically different kinds, affecting different parts or stages of the machinery, which the excuses consequently pick out and sort out for us. Further, it emerges that not *every* slip-up occurs in connection with *every*thing that could be called an "action," that not every excuse is apt with every verb—far indeed from it: and this provides us with one means of introducing some classification into the vast miscellany of "actions." If we classify them according to the particular selection of breakdowns to which each is liable, this should assign them their places in some family group or groups of actions, or in some model of the machinery of acting.

In this sort of way, the philosophical study of conduct can get off to a positive fresh start. But by the way, and more negatively, a number of traditional cruces or mistakes in this field can be resolved or removed. First among these comes the problem of Freedom. While it has been the tradition to present this as the "positive" term requiring elucidation, there is little doubt that to say we acted "freely" in the philosopher's use, which is only faintly related to the everyday use) is to say only that we acted *not* unfreely, in one or another of the many heterogeneous ways of so acting (under duress, or what not). Like "real," "free" is only used to rule out the suggestion of some or all of its recognized antitheses. As "truth" is not a name for a characteristic of assertions, so "freedom" is not a name for a characteristic of actions, but the name of a dimension in which actions are assessed. In examining all the ways in which each action may not be "free," i.e., the cases in which it will not do to say simply "X did A," we may hope to dispose of the problem of Freedom. Aristotle has often been chidden for talking about excuses or pleas and overlooking "the real problem": in my own case, it was when I began to see the injustice of this charge that I first became interested in excuses.

There is much to be said for the view that, philosophical tradition apart, Responsibility would be a better candidate for the role here assigned to Freedom. If ordinary language is to be our guide, it is to evade responsibility, or full responsibility, that we most often make excuses, and I have used the word myself in this way above. But in fact "responsibility" too seems not really apt in all cases: I do not exactly evade responsibility when I plead clumsiness or tactlessness, nor, often, when I plead that I only did it unwillingly or reluctantly, and still less if I plead that I had in the circumstances no choice: here I was constrained and have an excuse (or justification), yet may accept responsibility. It may be, then, that at least two key terms, Freedom and Responsibility, are needed: the relation between them is not clear, and it may be hoped that the investigation of excuses will contribute towards its clarification.[2]

So much, then, for ways in which the study of excuses may throw light on ethics. But there are also reasons why it is an attractive subject methodologically, at least if we are to proceed from "ordinary language," that is, by examining *what we should say when,* and so why and what we should mean by it. Perhaps this method, at least as *one* philosophical method, scarcely requires justification at present—too evidently, there is gold in them thar hills: more opportune would be a warning about the care and thoroughness needed if it is not to fall into disrepute. I will, however, justify it very briefly.

First, words are our tools, and, as a minimum, we should use clean tools: we should know what we mean and what we do not, and we must forearm ourselves against the traps that language sets us. Secondly, words are not (except in their own little corner) facts or things: we need therefore to prize them off the world, to hold them apart from and against it, so that we can realize their inadequacies and arbitrariness, and can relook at the world without blinkers. Thirdly, and more hopefully, our common stock of words embodies all the distinctions men have found worth drawing, and the connections they have found worth making, in the lifetimes of many generations: these surely are likely to be more numerous, more sound, since they have stood up to the long test of the survival of the fittest, and more subtle, at least in all ordinary and reasonably practical matters, than any that you or I are likely to think up in our armchairs of an afternoon—the most favored alternative method.

---

[2] Another well-flogged horse in these same stakes is Blame. At least two things seem confused together under this term. Sometimes when I blame X for doing A, say for breaking the vase, it is a question simply or mainly of my disapproval of A, breaking the vase, which unquestionably X did: but sometimes it is, rather, a question simply or mainly of how far I think X responsible for A, which unquestionably was bad. Hence if somebody says he blames me for something, I may answer by giving a *justification,* so that he will cease to disapprove of what I did, or else by giving an *excuse,* so that he will cease to hold me, at least entirely and in every way, responsible for doing it.

In view of the prevalence of the slogan "ordinary language," and of such names as "linguistic" or "analytic" philosophy or "the analysis of language," one thing needs specially emphasizing to counter misunderstandings. When we examine what we should say when, what words we should use in what situations, we are looking again not *merely* at words (or "meanings," whatever they may be) but also at the realities we use the words to talk about: we are using a sharpened awareness of words to sharpen our perception of, though not as the final arbiter of, the phenomena. For this reason I think it might be better to use, for this way of doing philosophy, some less misleading name than those given above—for instance, "linguistic phenomenology," only that is rather a mouthful.

Using, then, such a method, it is plainly preferable to investigate a field where ordinary language, is rich and subtle, as it is in the pressingly practical matter of Excuses, but certainly is not in the matter, say, of Time. At the same time we should prefer a field which is not too much trodden into bogs or tracks by traditional philosophy, for in that case even "ordinary" language will often have become infected with the jargon of extinct theories, and our own prejudices too, as the upholders or imbibers of theoretical views, will be too readily, and often insensibly, engaged. Here too, Excuses form an admirable topic; we can discuss at least clumsiness, or absence of mind, or inconsiderateness, even spontaneousness, without remembering what Kant thought, and so progress by degrees even to discussing deliberation without for once remembering Aristotle or self-control without Plato. Granted that our subject is, as already claimed for it, neighboring, analogous, or germane in some way to some notorious center of philosophical trouble, then, with these two further requirements satisfied, we should be certain of what we are after: a good site for *field work* in philosophy. Here at last we should be able to unfreeze, to loosen up and get going on agreeing about discoveries, however small, and on agreeing about how to reach agreement.[3] How much it is to be wished that similar field work will soon be undertaken in, say, aesthetics; if only we could forget for a while about the beautiful and get down instead to the dainty and the dumpy.

There are, I know, or are supposed to be, snags in "linguistic" philosophy, which those not very familiar with it find, sometimes not without glee or relief, daunting. But with snags, as with nettles, the thing to do is to grasp them—and to climb above them. I will mention two in particular, over which the study of excuses may help to encourage us. The first is the snag of Loose (or Divergent or Alternative) Usage; and the second the crux of the Last Word. Do we all say the same, and only the same, things in the same situations? Don't usages differ? And, Why should what we all ordinarily say be the only or the best or final way of putting it? Why should it even be true?

Well, people's usages do vary, and we do talk loosely, and we do say different things apparently indifferently. But first, not nearly as much as one

---

[3] All of which was seen and claimed by Socrates, when he first betook himself to the way of Words.

would think. When we come down to cases, it transpires in the very great majority that what we had thought was our wanting to say different things of and in *the same* situation was really not so—we had simply imagined the situation *slightly* differently: which is all too easy to do, because of course no situation (and we are dealing with *imagined* situations) is ever "completely" described. The more we imagine the situation in detail, with a background of story—and it is worth employing the most idiosyncratic or, sometimes, boring means to stimulate and to discipline our wretched imaginations—the less we find we disagree about what we should say. Nevertheless, *sometimes* we do ultimately disagree: sometimes we must allow a usage to be, though appalling, yet actual; sometimes we should genuinely use either or both of two different descriptions. But why should this daunt us? All that is happening is entirely explicable. If our usages disagree, then you use "X" where I use "Y", or more probably (and more intriguingly) your conceptual system is different from mine, though very likely it is at least equally consistent and serviceable: in short, we can find *why* we disagree—you choose to classify in one way, I in another. If the usage is loose, we can understand the temptation that leads to it, and the distinctions that it blurs: if there are "alternative" descriptions, then the situation can be described or can be "structured" in two ways, or perhaps it is one where, for current purposes, the two alternatives come down to the same. A disagreement as to what we should say is not to be shied off, but to be pounced upon: for the explanation of it can hardly fail to be illuminating. If we light on an electron that rotates the wrong way, that is a discovery, a portent to be followed up, not a reason for chucking physics: and by the same token, a genuinely loose or eccentric talker is a rare specimen to be prized.

As practice in learning to handle this bogey, in learning the essential *rubrics,* we could scarcely hope for a more promising exercise than the study of excuses. Here, surely, is just the sort of situation where people will say "almost anything," because they are so flurried, or so anxious to get off. "It was a mistake," "It was an accident"—how readily these can *appear* indifferent, and even be used together. Yet, a story or two, and everybody will not merely agree that they are completely different, but even discover for himself what the difference is and what each means.[4]

Then, for the Last Word. Certainly ordinary language has no claim to be the last word, if there is such a thing. It embodies, indeed, something better than the metaphysics of the Stone Age, namely, as was said, the inherited experience and acumen of many generations of men. But then, that acumen has been concentrated primarily upon the practical business of life. If a distinc-

---

[4] You have a donkey, so have I, and they graze in the same field. The day comes when I conceive a dislike for mine. I go to shoot it, draw a bead on it, fire: the brute falls in its tracks. I inspect the victim, and find to my horror that it is *your* donkey. I appear on your doorstep with the remains and say—what? "I say, old sport, I'm awfully sorry, etc., I've shot your donkey *by accident"?* Or *"by mistake"?* Then again, I go to shoot my donkey as before, draw a bead on it, fire—but as I do so, the beasts move, and to my horror yours falls. Again the scene on the doorstep—what do I say? "By mistake"? Or "by accident"?

tion works well for practical purposes in ordinary life (no mean feat, for even ordinary life is full of hard cases), then there is sure to be something in it, it will not mark nothing: yet this is likely enough to be not the best way of arranging things if our interests are more extensive or intellectual than the ordinary. And again, that experience has been derived only from the sources available to ordinary men throughout most of civilized history: it has not been fed from the resources of the microscope and its successors. And it must be added too, that superstition and error and fantasy of all kinds do become incorporated in ordinary language and even sometimes stand up to the survival test (only, when they do, why should we not detect it?). Certainly, then, ordinary language is *not* the last word: in principle it can everywhere be supplemented and improved upon and superseded. Only remember, it *is* the *first* word.[5]

For this problem too the field of Excuses is a fruitful one. Here is matter both contentious and practically important for everybody, so that ordinary language is on its toes: yet also, on its back it has long had a bigger flea to bite it, in the shape of the Law, and both again have lately attracted the attentions of yet another, and at least a healthily growing, flea, in the shape of psychology. In the law a constant stream of actual cases, more novel and more tortuous than the mere imagination could contrive, are brought up *for decision*—that is, formulas for docketing them must somehow be found. Hence it is necessary first to be careful with, but also to be brutal with, to tortue, to fake, and to override, ordinary language: we cannot here evade or forget the whole affair. (In ordinary life we dimiss the puzzles that crop up about time, but we cannot do that indefinitely in physics.) Psychology likewise produces novel cases, but it also produces new methods for bringing phenomena under observation and study: moroever, unlike the law, it has an unbiased interest in the totality of them and is unpressed for decision. Hence its own special and constant need to supplement, to revise and to supersede the classifications of both ordinary life and the law. We have, then, ample material for practice in learning to handle the bogey of the Last Word, however it should be handled.

Suppose, then, that we set out to investigate excuses, what are the methods and resources initially available? Our object is to imagine the varieties of situation in which we make excuses, and to examine the expressions used in making them. If we have a lively imagination, together perhaps with an ample experience of dereliction, we shall go far, only we need system: I do not know how many of you keep a list of the kinds of fool you make of yourselves. It is advisable to use systematic aids, of which there would appear to be three at least. I list them here in order of availability to the layman.

First we may use the dictionary—quite a concise one will do, but the use must be *thorough*. Two methods suggest themselves, both a little tedious, but repaying. One is to read the book through, listing all the words that seem relevant; this does not take as long as many suppose. The other is to start with a widish selection of obviously relevant terms, and to consult the dictionary

---

[5] And forget, for once and for a while, that other curious question "Is it true?" May we?

under each: it will be found that, in the explanations of the various meanings of each, a surprising number of other terms occur, which are germane though of course not often synonymous. We then look up each of *these,* bringing in more for our bag from the "definitions" given in each case; and when we have continued for a little, it will generally be found that the family circle begins to close, until ultimately it is complete and we come only upon repetitions. This method has the advantage of grouping the terms into convenient clusters—but of course a good deal will depend upon the comprehensiveness of our initial selection.

Working the dictionary, it is interesting to find that a high percentage of the terms connected with excuses prove to be *adverbs,* a type of word which has not enjoyed so large a share of the philosophical limelight as the noun, substantive or adjective, and the verb: this is natural because, as was said, the tenor of so many excuses is that I did it but only *in a way,* not just flatly like that—i.e., the verb needs modifying. Besides adverbs, however, there are other words of all kinds, including numerous abstract nouns, "misconception," "accident," "purpose," and the like, and a few verbs too, which often hold key positions for the grouping of excuses into classes at a high level ("couldn't help," "didn't mean to," "didn't realize," or again "intend," and "attempt"). In connection with the nouns another neglected class of words is prominent, namely, prepositions. Not merely does it matter considerably which preposition, often of several, is being used with a given substantive, but further the prepositions deserve study on their own account. For the question suggests itself, Why are the nouns in one group governed by "under," in another by "on," in yet another by "by" or "through" or "from" or "for" or "with," and so on? It will be disappointing if there prove to be no good reasons for such groupings.

Our second sourcebook will naturally be the law. This will provide us with an immense miscellany of untoward cases, and also with a useful list of recognized pleas, together with a good deal of acute analysis of both. No one who tries this resource will long be in doubt, I think, that the common law, and in particular the law of tort, is the richest storehouse; crime and contract contribute some special additions of their own, but tort is altogether more comprehensive and more flexible. But even here, and still more with so old and hardened a branch of the law as crime, much caution is needed with the arguments of counsel and the dicta or decisions of judges: acute though these are, it has always to be remembered that, in legal cases, (1) there is the overriding requirement that a decision be reached, and a relatively black or white decision—guilty or not guilty—for the plaintiff or for the defendant; (2) there is the general requirement that the charge or action and the pleadings be brought under one or another of the heads and procedures that have come in the course of history to be accepted by the courts (These, though fairly numerous, are still few and stereotyped in comparison with the accusations and defenses of daily life. Moreover contentions of many kinds are beneath the law, as too trivial, or outside it, as too purely moral—for example, inconsiderateness); (3) there is the general requirement that we argue from and abide by

precedents (The value of this in the law is unquestionable, but it can certainly
lead to distortions of ordinary beliefs and expressions). For such reasons as
these, obviously closely connected and stemming from the nature and function
of the law, practicing lawyers and jurists are by no means so careful as they
might be to give to our ordinary expressions their ordinary meanings and
applications. There is special pleading and evasion, stretching and strait-
jacketing, besides the invention of technical terms, or technical senses for
common terms. Nevertheless, it is a perpetual and salutary surprise to discover
how much is to be learned from the law; and it is to be added that if a distinction
drawn is a sound one, even though not yet recognized in law, a lawyer can be
relied upon to take note of it, for it may be dangerous not to—if he does not,
his opponent may.

Finally, the third sourcebook is psychology, with which I include such
studies as anthropology and animal behavior. Here I speak with even more
trepidation than about the Law. But this at least is clear, that some varieties
of behavior, some ways of acting or explanations of the doing of actions, are
here noticed and classified which have not been observed or named by ordinary
men and hallowed by ordinary language, though perhaps they often might
have been so if they had been of more practical importance. There is real
danger in contempt for the "jargon" of psychology, at least when it sets out to
supplement, and at least sometimes when it sets out to supplant, the language
of ordinary life.

With these sources, and with the aid of the imagination, it will go hard if
we cannot arrive at the meanings of large numbers of expressions and at the
understanding and classification of large numbers of "actions." Then we shall
comprehend clearly much that, before, we only made use of *ad hoc*. Definition,
I would add, explanatory definition, should stand high among our aims:
it is not enough to show how clever we are by showing how obscure everything
is. Clarity, too, I know, has been said to be not enough: but perhaps it will
be time to go into that when we are within measurable distance of achieving
clarity on some matter.

So much for the cackle. It remains to make a few remarks, not, I am afraid,
in any very coherent order, about the types of significant result to be obtained
and the more general lessons to be learned from the study of Excuses.

1. *No modification without aberration.* When it is stated that X did A, there is
a temptation to suppose that given some, indeed perhaps *any*, expression
modifying the verb we shall be entitled to insert either it or its opposite or
negation in our statement: that is, we shall be entitled to ask, typically, "Did X
do A Mly or not Mly?" (e.g., "Did X murder Y voluntarily or involuntarily?"),
and to answer one or the other. Or as a minimum it is supposed that if X did A
there must be at least *one* modifying expression that we could, justifiably and
informatively, insert with the verb. In the great majority of cases of the use of
the great majority of verbs ("murder" perhaps is not one of the majority) such
suppositions are quite unjustified. The natural economy of language dictates
that for the *standard* case covered by any normal verb—not, perhaps, a verb

of omen such as "murder," but a verb like "eat" or "kick" or "croquet"—
no modifying expression is required or even permissible. Only if we do the
action named in some *special* way or circumstances, different from those in
which such an act is naturally done (and of course both the normal and the
abnormal differ according to what verb in particular is in question), is a modifying expression called for, or even in order. I sit in my chair, in the usual way—
I am not in a daze or influenced by threats or the like: here, it will not do to say
either that I sat in it intentionally or that I did not sit in it intentionally,[6]
nor yet that I sat in it automatically or from habit or what you will. It is
bedtime, I am alone, I yawn: but I do not yawn involuntarily (or voluntarily!),
nor yet deliberately. To yawn in any such peculiar way is just not to just yawn.

2. *Limitation of application.* Expressions modifying verbs, typically adverbs,
have limited ranges of application. That is, given any adverb of excuse, such
as "unwittingly" or "spontaneously" or "impulsively," it will not be found that
it makes good sense to attach it to any and every verb of "action" in any and
every context: indeed, it will often apply only to a comparatively narrow range
of such verbs. Something in the lad's upturned face appealed to him, he threw
a brick at it—"spontaneously"? The interest then is to discover why some
actions can be excused in a particular way but not others, particularly perhaps
the latter.[7] This will largely elucidate the meaning of the excuse, and at the
same time will illuminate the characteristics typical of the group of "actions"
it picks out: very often too it will throw light on some detail of the machinery
of "action" in general (see 4), or on our standards of acceptable conduct
(see 5). It is specially important in the case of some of the terms most favored
by philosophers or jurists to realize that at least in ordinary speech (disregarding
backseepage of jargon) they are not used so universally or so dichotomistically.
For example, take "voluntarily" and "involuntarily": we may join the army
or make a gift voluntarily, we may hiccough or make a small gesture involuntarily, and the more we consider further actions which we might naturally
be said to do in either of these ways, the more circumscribed and unlike each
other do the two classes become, until we even doubt whether there is *any*
verb with which both adverbs are equally in place. Perhaps there are some
such; but at least sometimes when we may think we have found one it is an
illusion, an apparent exception that really does prove the rule. I can perhaps
"break a cup" voluntarily, *if* that is done, say, as an act of self-impoverishment:
and I can perhaps break another involuntarily, *if*, say, I make an involuntary
movement which breaks it. Here, plainly, the two acts described each as
"breaking a cup" are really very different, and the one is similar to acts typical
of the "voluntary" class, the other to acts typical of the "involuntary" class.

3. *The importance of Negations and Opposites.* "Voluntarily" and "involuntarily," then, are not opposed in the obvious sort of way that they are made

---

[6] Caveat or hedge: of course we can say "I did *not* sit in it "intentionally' " as a way simply of
repudiating the suggestion that I sat in it intentionally.
[7] For we are sometimes not so good at observing what we *can't* say as what we can, yet the first
is pretty regularly the more revealing.

to be in philosophy or jurisprudence. The "opposite," or rather "opposites," of "voluntarily" might be "under constraint" of some sort, duress or obligation or influence;[8] the opposite of "involuntarily" might be "deliberately" or "on purpose" or the like. Such divergences in opposites indicate that "voluntarily" and "involuntarily," in spite of their apparent connection, are fish from very different kettles. In general, it will pay us to take nothing for granted or as obvious about negations and opposites. It does not pay to assume that a word must have an opposite, or one opposite, whether it is a "positive" word like "wilfully" or a "negative" word like "inadvertently." Rather, we should be asking ourselves such questions as why there is no use for the adverb "advertently." For above all it will not do to assume that the "positive" word must be around to wear the trousers; commonly enough the "negative" (looking) word marks the (positive) abnormality, while the "positive" word, *if* it exists, merely serves to rule out the suggestion of that abnormality. It is natural enough, in view of what was said in (1) above, for the "positive" word not to be found at all in some cases. I do an act A₁ (say, crush a snail) *inadvertently* if, in the course of executing by means of movements of my bodily parts some other act A₂ (say, in walking down the public path), I fail to exercise such meticulous supervision over the courses of those movements as would have been needed to ensure that they did not bring about the untoward event (here, the impact on the snail).[9] By claiming that A₁ was inadvertent we place it, where we imply it belongs, on this special level, in a class of incidental happenings which must occur in the doing of any physical act. To lift the act out of this class, we need and possess the expression "not . . . inadvertently": "advertently," if used for this purpose, would suggest that, if the act was not done inadvertently, then it must have been done noticing what I was doing, which is far from necessarily the case (e.g., if I did it absent-mindedly), or at least that there is *something* in common to the ways of doing all acts not done inadvertently, which is not the case. Again, there is no use for "advertently" at the *same* level as "inadvertently": in passing the butter I do not knock over the cream-jug, though I do (inadvertently) knock over the teacup—yet I do not by-pass the cream-jug *advertently;* for at this level, below supervision in detail, *anything* that we do is, if you like, inadvertent, though we only call it so, and indeed only call it something we have done, if there is something untoward about it.

A further point of interest in studying so-called "negative" terms is the manner of their formation. Why are the words in one group formed with *un-*

---

8 But remember, when I sign a check in the normal way, I do not so do *either* "voluntarily" *or* "under constraint."

9 Or analogously: I do an act A₁ (say, divulge my age, or imply you are a liar) *inadvertently* if, in the course of executing by the use of some medium of communication some other act A₂ (say, reminiscing about my war service), I fail to exercise such meticulous supervision over the choice and arrangement of the signs as would have been needed to ensure that. . . . It is interesting to note how such adverbs lead parallel lives, one in connection with physical actions ("doing") and the other in connection with acts of communication ("saying"), or sometimes also in connection with acts of "thinking" ("inadvertently assumed").

or *in-*, those in another with *-less* ("aimless," "reckless," "heedless," etc.), and those in another with *mis-* ("mistake," "misconception," "misjudgment," etc.)? Why care*less*ly but *in*attentively? Perhaps care and attention, so often linked, are rather different. Here are remunerative exercises.

4. *The machinery of action*. Not merely do adverbial expressions pick out classes of actions, they also pick out the internal detail of the machinery of doing actions, or the departments into which the business of doing actions is organized. There is for example the stage at which we have actually to *carry out* some action upon which we embark—perhaps we have to make certain bodily movements or to make a speech. In the course of actually *doing* these things (getting weaving) we have to pay (some) attention to what we are doing and to take (some) care to guard against (likely) dangers: we may need to use judgment or tact: we must exercise sufficient control over our bodily parts: to take (some) care to guard against (likely) dangers: we may need to use and so on. Inattention, carelessness, errors of judgment, tactlessness, clumsiness, all these and others are ills (with attendant excuses) which affect one specific stage in the machinery of action, the *executive* stage, the stage where we *muff* it. But there are many other departments in the business too, each of which is to be traced and mapped through its cluster of appropriate verbs and adverbs. Obviously there are departments of intelligence and planning, of decision and resolve, and so on: but I shall mention one in particular, too often overlooked, where troubles and excuses abound. It happens to us, in military life, to be in receipt of excellent intelligence, to be also in self-conscious possession of excellent principles (the five golden rules for winning victories), and yet to hit upon a plan of action which leads to disaster. One way in which this can happen is through failure at the stage of *appreciation* of the situation, that is at the stage where we are required to cast our excellent intelligence into such a form, under such heads and with such weights attached, that our equally excellent principles can be brought to bear on it properly, in a way to yield the right answer.[10] So too in real, or rather civilian, life, in moral or practical affairs, we can know the facts and yet look at them mistakenly or perversely, or not fully realize or appreciate something, or even be under a total misconception. Many expression, of excuse indicate failure at this particularly tricky stage: even thoughtlessnesss inconsiderateness, lack of imagination, are perhaps less matters of failure in intelligence or planning than might be supposed, and more matters of failure to appreciate the situation. A course of E. M. Forster and we see things differently: yet perhaps we know no more and are no cleverer.

5. *Standards of the unacceptable*. It is characteristic of excuses to be "unacceptable": given, I suppose, almost any excuse, there will be cases of such a kind or of such gravity that "we will not accept" it. It is interesting to detect the standards and codes we thus invoke. The extent of the supervision we exercise

---

[10] We know all about how to do quadratics: we know all the needful facts about pipes, cisterns, hours and plumbers: yet we reach the answer "$3\frac{3}{4}$ men." We have failed to cast our facts correctly into mathematical form.

over the execution of any act can never be quite unlimited, and usually is expected to fall within fairly definite limits ("due care and attention") in the case of acts of some general kind, though of course we set very different limits in different cases. We may plead that we trod on the snail inadvertently: but not on a baby—you ought to look where you are putting your great feet. Of course it *was (really)*, if you like, inadvertence: but that word constitutes a plea, which is not going to be allowed, because of standards. And if you try it on, you will be subscribing to such dreadful standards that your last state will be worse than your first. Or again, we set different standards, and will accept different excuses, in the case of acts which are rule-governed, like spelling, and which we are expected absolutely to get right, from those we set and accept for less stereotyped actions: a wrong spelling may be a slip, but hardly an accident, a winged beater may be an accident, but hardly a slip.

6. *Combination, dissociation, and complication.* A belief in opposites and dichotomies encourages, among other things, a blindness to the combinations and dissociations of adverbs that are possible, even to such obvious facts as that we can act at once on impulse and intentionally, or that we can do an action intentionally yet for all that not deliberately, still less on purpose. We walk along the cliff, and I feel a sudden impulse to push you over, which I promptly do: I acted on impulse, yet I certainly intended to push you over, and may even have devised a little ruse to achieve it: yet even then I did not act deliberately, for I did not (stop to) ask myself whether to do it or not.

It is worth bearing in mind, too, the general rule that we must not expect to find simple labels for complicated cases. If a mistake results in an accident, it will not do to ask whether "it" was an accident or a mistake, or to demand some briefer description of "it". Here the natural economy of language operates: if the words already available for simple cases suffice in combination to describe a complicated case, there will be need for special reasons before a special new word is invented for the complication. Besides, however well-equipped our language, it can never be forearmed against all possible cases that may arise and call for description: fact is richer than diction.

7. *Regina* v. *Finney.* Often the complexity and difficulty of a case is considerable. I will quote the case of *Regina* v. *Finney:*[11]

Shrewsbury Assizes.   1874.                                            12 Cox 625.
   Prisoner was indicted for the manslaughter of Thomas Watkins.
   The Prisoner was an attendant at a lunatic asylum. Being in charge of a lunatic, who was bathing, he turned on hot water into the bath, and thereby scalded him to death. The facts appeared to be truly set forth in the statement of the prisoner made before the committing magistrate, as follows: "I had bathed Watkins, and had loosed the bath out. *I intended putting in a clean bath,* and asked Watkins if he would get out. At this time *my attention was drawn* to the next bath by the new attendant, who was aking me a question; and *my attention was taken from the bath* where Watkins was. I put my hand down to turn

[11] A somewhat distressing favorite in the class that Hart used to conduct with me in the years soon after the war. The italics are mine.

water on in the bath where Thomas Watkins was. *I did not intend to turn the hot water,* and *I made a mistake in the tap. I did not know what I had done until* I heard Thomas Watkins shout out; and *I did not find my mistake out till* I saw the steam from the water. You cannot get water in this bath when they are drawing water at the other bath; but at other times it shoots out like a water gun when the other baths are not in use. . . .''

(It was proved that the lunatic had such possession of his faculties as would enable him to understand what was said to him, and to get out of the bath.)

*A. Young* (for Prisoner). The death *resulted from accident.* There was no such *culpable negligence* on the part of the prisoner as will support this indictment. A *culpable mistake,* or some degree of *culpable negligence,* causing death, will not support a charge of manslaughter; unless the *negligence* be so gross as to be *reckless.* (R. v. *Noakes.*)

*Lush, J.* To render a person liable for *neglect of duty* there must be such a degree of culpability as to amount to *gross negligence* on his part. If you accept the prisoner's own statement, you find no such amount of *negligence* as would come within this definition. It is not every little *trip or mistake* that will make a man so liable. It was the duty of the attendant not to let hot water into the bath while the patient was therein. According to the prisoner's own account, *he did not believe that* he was letting the hot water in while the deceased remained there. The lunatic was, we have heard, a man capable of getting out by himself and of understanding what was said to him. He was told to get out. A new attendant who had come on this day, was at an adjoining bath and he *took off the prisoner's attention.* Now, if the prisoner, knowing that the man was in the bath, had turned on the tap, and turned on the hot instead of the cold water, I should have said there was gross negligence; for he ought to have looked to see. But from his own account he had told the deceased to get out, and *thought he had got out.* If you think that indicates gross *carelessness,* then you should find the prisoner guilty of manslaughter. But if you think it *inadvertence* not amounting to culpability–i.e., what is properly termed an *accident*–then the prisoner is not liable.

Verdict, Not guilty.

In this case there are two morals that I will point. (1) Both counsel and judge make very free use of a large number of terms of excuse, using several as though they were, and even stating them to be, indifferent or equivalent when they are not, and presenting as alternatives those that are not. (2) It is constantly difficult to be sure *what* act it is that counsel or judge is suggesting might be qualified by what expression of excuse. The learned judge's concluding direction is a paradigm of these faults.[12] Finney, by contrast, stands out as an evident master of the Queen's English. He is explicit as to each of his acts and states, mental and physical: he uses different, and the correct, adverbs in connection with each: and he makes no attempt to boil down.

[12] Not but what he probably manages to convey his meaning somehow or other. Judges seem to acquire a knack of conveying meaning, and even carrying conviction, through the use of a pithy Anglo-Saxon which sometimes has literally no meaning at all. Wishing to distinguish the case of shooting at a post in the belief that it was an enemy, as *not* an "attempt," from the case of picking an empty pocket in the belief that money was in it, which *is* an "attempt," the judge explains that in shooting at the post "the man is never on the thing at all."

8. *Small distinctions, and big too.* It should go without saying that terms of excuse are not equivalent, and that it matters which we use: we need to distinguish inadvertence not merely from (save the mark) such things as mistake and accident, but from such nearer neighbors as, say, aberration and absence of mind. By imagining cases with vividness and fullness we should be able to decide in which precise terms to describe, say, Miss Plimsoll's action in writing, so carefully, "DAIRY" on her fine new book: we should be able to distinguish between sheer, mere, pure, and simple mistake or inadvertence. Yet unfortunately, at least when in the grip of thought, we fail not merely at these stiffer hurdles. We equate even—I have seen it done—"inadvertently" with "automatically": as though to say I trod on your toe inadvertently means to say I trod on it automatically. Or we collapse succumbing to temptation into losing control of ourselves—a bad patch, this, for telescoping.[13]

All this is not so much a *lesson* from the study of excuses as the very object of it.

9. *The exact phrase and its place in the sentence.* It is not enough, either, to attend simply to the "key" word: notice must also be taken of the full and exact form of the expression used. In considering mistakes, we have to consider seriatim "by mistake," "owing to a mistake," "mistakenly," "it was a mistake to," "to make a mistake in or over or about," "to be mistaken about," and so on: in considering purpose, we have to consider "on," "with the," "for the," etc., besides "purposeful," "purposeless," and the like. These varying expressions may function quite differently—and usually do, or why should we burden ourselves with more than one of them?

Care must be taken too to observe the precise position of an adverbial expression in the sentence. This should of course indicate what verb it is being used to modify: but more than that, the position can also affect the *sense* of the expression, i.e., the way in which it modifies that verb. Compare, for example:

$a_1$ He clumsily trod on the snail.

$a_2$ Clumsily he trod on the snail.

$b_1$ He trod clumsily on the snail.

$b_2$ He trod on the snail clumsily.

Here, in $a_1$ and $a_2$ we describe his treading on the creature at all as a piece of clumsiness, incidental, we imply, to his performance of some other action: but with $b_1$ and $b_2$ to tread on it is, very likely, his aim or policy, what we criticize is his execution of the feat.[14] Many adverbs, though far from all (not,

---

[13] Plato, I suppose, and after him Aristotle, fastened this confusion upon us, as bad in its day and way as the later, grotesque, confusion of moral weakness with weakness of will. I am very partial to ice cream, and a bombe is served divided into segments corresponding one to one with the persons at High Table: I am tempted to help myself to two segments and do so, thus succumbing to temptation and even conceivably (but why necessarily?) going against my principles. But do I lose control of myself? Do I raven, do I snatch the morsels from the dish and wolf them down, impervious to the consternation of my colleagues? Not a bit of it. We often succumb to temptation with calm and even with finesse.

[14] As a matter of fact, most of these examples *can* be understood the other way, especially if we allow ourselves inflections of the voice, or commas, or contexts. $a_2$ might be a poetic inversion for $b_2$: $b_1$, perhaps with commas round the "clumsily," might be used for $a_1$: and so on. Still, the two senses are clearly enough distinguishable.

for example, "purposely") are used in these two typically different ways.

10. *The style of performance.* With some adverbs the distinction between the two senses referred to in the last paragraph is carried a stage further. "He ate his soup deliberately" may mean, like "He deliberately ate his soup," that his eating his soup was a deliberate act, one perhaps that he thought would annoy somebody, as it would more commonly if he deliberately ate *my* soup, and which he decided to do: but it will often mean that he went through the performance of eating his soup in a noteworthy manner or *style*—pause after each mouthful, careful choice of point of entry for the spoon, sucking of moustaches, and so on. That is, it will mean that he ate *with* deliberation rather than *after* deliberation. The style of the performance, slow and unhurried, is understandably called "deliberate" because each movement *has the typical look* of a deliberate act: but it is scarcely being said that the making of each motion *is* a deliberate act or that he is "literally" deliberating. This case, then, is more extreme than that of "clumsily," which does in both uses describe literally a manner of performing.

It is worth watching out for this secondary use when scrutinizing any particular adverbial expression: when it definitely does not exist, the reason is worth inquiring into. Sometimes it is very hard to be sure whether it does exist or does not: it does, one would think, with "carelessly," it does not with "inadvertently," but does it or does it not with "absent-mindedly" or "aimlessly"? In some cases a word akin to but distinct from the primary adverb is used for this special role of describing a style of performance: we use "purposefully" in this way, but never "purposely."

11. *What modifies what?* The judge in *Regina* v. *Finney* does not make clear what event is being excused in what way. "If you think that indicates gross carelessness, then. . . . But if you think it inadvertence not amounting to culpability—i.e., what is properly called an accident—then. . . ." Apparently he means that Finney may have *turned on the hot tap* inadvertently:[15] does he mean also that the tap may have been turned accidentally, or rather that *Watkins may have been scalded* and killed accidentally? And was the carelessness in turning the tap or in thinking Watkins had got out? Many disputes as to what excuse we should properly use arise because we will not trouble to state explicitly *what* is being excused.

To do so is all the more vital because it is in principle always open to us, along various lines, to describe or refer to "what I did" in so many different ways. This is altogether too large a theme to elaborate here. Apart from the more general and obvious problems of the use of "tendentious" descriptive

---

[15] What Finney says is different: he says he "made a mistake in the tap." This is the basic use of "mistake," where we simply, and not necessarily accountably, take the wrong one. Finney here attempts to account for his mistake, by saying that his attention was distracted. But suppose the order is "Right turn" and I turn left: no doubt the sergeant will insinuate that my attention was distracted, or that I cannot distinguish my right from my left—but it was not and I can; this was a simple, pure mistake. As often happens. Neither I nor the sergeant will suggest that there was any accident, or any inadvertence either. If Finney had turned the hot tap inadvertently, then it would have been knocked, say, in reaching for the cold tap: a different story.

terms, there are many special problems in the particular case of "actions."
Should we say, are we saying, that he took her money, or that he robbed her?
That he knocked a ball into a hole, or that he sank a putt? That he said "Done,"
or that he accepted an offer? How far, that is, are motives, intentions, and
conventions to be part of the description of actions? And more especially here,
what is *an* or *one* or *the* action? For we can generally split up what might be
named as one action in several distinct ways, into different *stretches* or *phases*
or *stages*. Stages have already been mentioned: we can dismantle the machinery
of the act, and describe (and excuse) separately the intelligence, the appreciation, the planning, the decision, the execution, and so forth. Phases are rather
different: we can say that he painted a picture or fought a campaign, or else
we can say that first he laid on this stroke of paint and then that, first he fought
this action and then that. Stretches are different again: a single term descriptive
of what he did may be made to cover either a smaller or a larger stretch of
events, those excluded by the narrower description being then called "consequences" or "results" or "effects" or the like of his act. So here we can describe
Finney's act *either* as turning on the hot tap, which he did by mistake, with the
result that Watkins was scalded, *or* as scalding Watkins, which he did *not* do by
mistake.

It is very evident that the problems of excuses and those of the different
descriptions of actions are throughout bound up with each other.

12. *Trailing clouds of etymology.* It is these considerations that bring us up
so forcibly against some of the most difficult words in the whole story of Excuses,
such words as "result," "effect," and "consequence," or again as "intention,"
"purpose," and "motive." I will mention two points of method which are,
experience has convinced me, indispensable aids at these levels.

One is that a word never—well, hardly ever—shakes off its etymology
and its formation. In spite of all changes in and extensions of and additions to
its meanings, and indeed rather pervading and governing these, there will
still persist the old idea. In an *accident* something befalls: by *mistake* you take
the wrong one: in *error* you stray: when you act *deliberately* you act after weighing
it up (*not* after thinking out ways and means). It is worth asking ourselves
whether we know the etymology of "result" or of "spontaneously," and worth
remembering that "unwillingly" and "involuntarily" come from very different
sources.

And the second point is connected with this. Going back into the history of
a word, very often into Latin, we come back pretty commonly to pictures or
*models* of how things happen or are done. These models may be fairly sophisticated and recent, as is perhaps the case with "motive" or "impulse," but one of
the commonest and most primitive types of model is one which is apt to baffle
us through its very naturalness and simplicity, We take *some very simple action,*
like shoving a stone, usually as done by and viewed by oneself, and use *this,*
with the features distinguishable in it, as our model in terms of which to talk
about other actions and events: and we continue to do so, scarcely realizing it,
even when these other actions are pretty remote and perhaps much more

interesting to us in their own right than the acts originally used in constructing the model ever were, and even when the model is really distorting the facts rather than helping us to observe them. In primitive cases we may get to see clearly the differences between, say, "results," "effects," and "consequences," and yet discover that these differences are no longer clear, and the terms themselves no longer of real service to us, in the more complicated cases where we had been bandying them about most freely. A model must be recognized for what it is. "Causing," I suppose, was a notion taken from a man's own experience of doing simple actions, and by primitive man every event was construed in terms of this model: every event has a cause, that is, every event is an action done by somebody—if not by a man, then by a quasi-man, a spirit. When, later, events which are *not* actions are realized to be such, we still say that they must be "caused," and the word snares us: we are struggling to ascribe to it a new, unanthropomorphic meaning, yet constantly, in searching for its analysis, we unearth and incorporate the lineaments of the ancient model. As happened even to Hume, and consequently to Kant. Examining such a word historically, we may well find that it has been extended to cases that have by now too tenuous a relation to the model case, that it is a source of confusion and superstition.

There is too another danger in words that invoke models, half-forgotten or not. It must be remembered that there is no necessity whatsoever that the various models used in creating our vocabulary, primitive or recent, should all fit together neatly as parts into one single, total model or scheme of, for instance, the doing of actions. It is possible, and indeed highly likely, that our assortment of models will include some, or many, that are overlapping, conflicting, or more generally simply *disparate*.[16]

13. In spite of the wide and acute observation of the phenomena of action embodied in ordinary speech, modern scientists have been able, it seems to me, to reveal its inadequacy at numerous points, if only because they have had access to more comprehensive data and have studied them with more catholic and dispassionate interest than the ordinary man, or even the lawyer, has had occasion to do. I will conclude with two examples.

Observation of animal behavior shows that regularly, when an animal is embarked on some recognizable pattern of behavior but meets in the course of it with an insuperable obstacle, it will betake itself to energetic, but quite unrelated, activity of some wild kind, such as standing on its head. This phenomenon is called "displacement behavior" and is well identifiable. If now, in

---

[16] This is by way of a general warning in philosophy. It seems to be too readily assumed that if we can only discover the true meanings of each of a cluster of key terms, usually historic terms, that we use in some particular field (as, for example, "right," "good," and the rest in morals), then it must without question transpire that each will fit into place in some single, interlocking, consistent, conceptual scheme. Not only is there no reason to assume this, but all historical probability is against it, especially in the case of a language derived from such various civilizations as ours is. We may cheerfully use, and with weight, terms which are not so much head-on incompatible as simply disparate, which just do not fit in or even on. Just as we cheerfully subscribe to, or have the grace to be torn between, simply disparate ideals—why *must* there be a conceivable amalgam, the Good Life for Man?

the light of this, we look back at ordinary human life, we see that displacement behavior bulks quite large in it: yet we have apparently no word, or at least no clear and simple word, for it. If, when thwarted, we stand on our heads or wiggle our toes, than we are not exactly *just* standing on our heads, don't you know, in the ordinary way, yet is there any convenient adverbial expression we can insert to do the trick? "In desperation"?

Take, again, "compulsive" behavior, however exactly psychologists define it, compulsive washing for example. There are of course hints in ordinary speech that we do things in this way—"just feel I have to," "shouldn't feel comfortable unless I did," and the like: but there is no adverbial expression satisfactorily pre-empted for it, as "compulsively" is. This is understandable enough, since compulsive behavior, like displacement behavior, is not in general going to be of great practical importance.

Here I leave and commend the subject to you.

CHAPTER V

# PUNISHMENT

> When men strive together, and hurt a woman with child, so that there is a mis-
> carriage, and yet no harm follows, the one who hurt her shall be fined, according as the
> woman's husband shall lay upon him; and he shall pay as the judges determine. If any
> harm follows, then you shall give life for life, eye for eye, tooth for tooth, hand for hand,
> foot for foot, burn for burn, wound for wound, stripe for stripe.
>
> *Exodus* 21:22-25

Punishment has long been a problem for legal theory. It is generally
agreed that punishment of some sort is a necessary prop for any legal system.
Some individuals will only be deterred from violating society's rules by the
threat of painful sanctions. However, two major schools of thought, which may
be loosely classified as 'retributivist' and 'utilitarian', have diverged on such
basic questions as when to punish and to what degree, and the purpose and
justification of punishment both in general and in the specific case.

At the heart of the retributivist theory lies the *lex talionis* or law of equal
punishment of which the above citation is the first mention in the *Old Testament*.
The notion that criminals should suffer sanctions equal to and no greater than
the measure of their crime appears in the most ancient Near Eastern legal
codes (e.g. the Code of Hammurabi, c.2100 B.C.) and contrary to popular
assertions of the 'savage nature' of this guide line it undoubtedly represented a
humanizing gain in historical context over wrathful and unlimited retaliation.
Retributivists have been frequently and severely criticised out of context for
maintaining this central tenet by those who forget that the *lex talionis* is a two-

283

edged sword. Kant, for instance, in the selection reprinted below argues that a society in the process of dissolution should execute its murderers as its last act before disbanding—but this assertion was put forth in the face of contemporary German legal practice which allowed high-born murderers to escape capital punishment with a mere financial settlement. The reintroduction of capital punishment into the Soviet legal code in the last decade was taken by some as a retrograde penal policy; yet it undeniably reflected a reaffirmation of the rule of law in a society where citizens had previously merely 'disappeared' when they won the displeasure of the official regime.

It is, perhaps, unfortunate that contemporary punishment debates are still framed in the context of older retributivist-utilitarian controversies. Few, if any, adherents ever maintained a 'pure' version of either theory and the following sketches of the two must be recognized as mere abstractions from actual formulations. Minimally retributivists (Kant is usually considered the archetype) have argued:

(1) that only those who have voluntarily and knowingly violated legal rules can be punished;

(2) that the degree of punishment should match the crime;

(3) that the return of evil for evil is morally permissible (if not mandatory) and needs no further justification.

The utilitarian quibble (Hobbes is a prototype for Bentham's classic formulation) begins with this last postulate. In Hobbes' words: "All evil which is inflicted without intention or possibility of disposing the delinquent or, by his example, other men to obey the laws is not punishment but an act of hostility." *(Leviathan* Chapter 28). In other words, utilitarians have argued that punishment can only be justified as a deterrent or reforming influence upon individuals and in society at large. This counter-assumption implicitly strikes at the equal-punishment criterion of the *lex talionis:* Bentham argued that sanctions should be only sufficiently severe to deter the specific crime in question and of a quality to produce reform in the character of the actual criminal. Retributivists have claimed in return that Bentham's criteria also undermine their first postulate and open the dikes of criminal sanctions against the innocent as well as the guilty, namely punishment of the 'potential' offender and excessive punishment of the so-called incorrigible criminal (both of whom will not be deterred by normal sanctions).

As Quinton's article expounds, both theories have been plagued by practical problems. Given the broad range both in crimes and human motivation, what standard establishes the proper degree of punishment in the particular case? Certainly the modern retributivist would not claim a literal eye for an eye or an automobile accident for an automobile accident, etc. Bentham failed abysmally in his attempt to formulate a common calculus of human pleasures and pains, although his speculations contributed to a reduction in the then excessive scale of sanctions operative in the British legal system.

Theorists of both persuasions also continue to agonize over the problem of the potential offender. Should he be declared legally insane and committed to a mental hospital? By a sleight of hand of retributivist logic such commitment would not technically be punishment (the return of evil for evil), although an 'evil inflicted for the purpose of deterence' by utilitarian standards. Should involuntarily committed mental patients be granted special safeguards in due process (e.g. periodic *legal* review of their cases) since inadequately-financed state institutions offer at best only custodial care after a few months of initial (and sometimes erratic) remedial treatment? Certainly such involuntary restraint—potentially indefinite—is a painful evil, whatever it is called in law.

Such practical questions take on special importance since some contemporary utilitarians (see especially Barbara Wootton, *Social Science and Social Pathology*, 1959) have recommended that the mental element in crime, personal responsibility and virtually the concept of punishment, itself, be disregarded in the evaluation of harmful acts, that courts should simply decide whether an offender should be incarcerated for 'penal' or 'therapeutic' treatment. Hart's essays, *Punishment and Responsibility* (Oxford, 1968), offer a review of central areas of contemporary dispute among legal theorists.

# 18

## Immanuel Kant

Kant's retributivist theory of punishment, and particularly the claim that societies are morally obliged to punish, have been considered a sharp contrast to his general ethical position.

# RETRIBUTIVIST THEORY*

## THE PENAL LAW AND THE LAW OF PARDON

### [THE RIGHT TO PUNISH]

The right to punish contained in the penal law [*das Strafrecht*] is the right that the magistrate has to inflict pain on a subject in consequence of his having committed a crime. It follows that the suzerain of the state cannot himself be punished; we can only remove ourselves from his jurisdiction. A transgression of the public law that makes him who commits it unfit to be a citizen is called either simply a crime *(crimen)* or a public crime *(crimen publicum)*. The first (a private crime) is brought before a civil court, and the second (a public crime), before a criminal court. Embezzlement, that is, misappropriation of money or wares entrusted in commerce, and fraud in buying and selling, if perpetrated before the eyes of the party who suffers, are private crimes. On the other hand, counterfeiting money or bills of exchange, theft, robbery, and similar acts are public crimes, because through them the commonwealth and not just a single individual is exposed to danger. These crimes may be divided into those of a base character *(indolis abjectae)* and those of a violent character *(indolis violentae)*.

Judicial punishment *(poena forensis)* is entirely distinct from natural punishment *(poena naturalis)*. In natural punishment, vice punishes itself, and this fact is not taken into consideration by the legislator. Judicial punishment can never be used merely as a means to promote some other good for the criminal himself or for civil society, but instead it must in all cases be imposed on him only on the ground that he has committed a crime; for a human being can never be manipulated merely as a means to the purposes of someone else and can never be confused with the objects of the Law of things [*Sachenrecht*]. His innate personality [that is, his right as a person] protects him against such treatment, even though he may indeed be condemned to lose his civil person-

* From Immanuel Kant: *The Metaphysical Elements of Justice,* translated by John Ladd, copyright © 1965, by The Bobbs-Merrill Company, Inc., pp. 99-107. Translator's footnotes omitted. Reprinted by permission of the publisher.

ality. He must first be found to be deserving of punishment before any consideration is given to the utility of this punishment for himself or for his fellow citizens. The law concerning punishment is a categorical imperative, and woe to him who rummages around in the winding paths of a theory of happiness looking for some advantage to be gained by releasing the criminal from punishment or by reducing the amount of it—in keeping with the Pharisaic motto: "It is better that one man should die than that the whole people should perish." If legal justice perishes, then it is no longer worth while for men to remain alive on this earth. If this is so, what should one think of the proposal to permit a criminal who has been condemned to death to remain alive, if, after consenting to allow dangerous experiments to be made on him, he happily survives such experiments and if doctors thereby obtain new information that benefits the community? Any court of justice would repudiate such a proposal with scorn if it were suggested by a medical college, for [legal] justice ceases to be justice if it can be bought for a price.

What kind and what degree of punishment does public legal justice adopt as its principle and standard? None other than the principle of equalty (illustrated by the pointer on the scale of justice), that is, the principle of not treating one side more favorably than the other. Accordingly, any undeserved evil that you inflict on someone else among the people is one that you do to yourself. If you vilify him, you vilify yourself; if you steal from him, you steal from yourself; if you kill him, you kill yourself. Only the Law of retribution *(jus talionis)* can determine exactly the kind and degree of punishment; it must be well understood, however, that this determination [must be made] in the chambers of a court of justice (and not in your private judgement). All other standards fluctuate back and forth and, because extraneous considerations are mixed with them, they cannot be compatible with the principle of pure and strict legal justice.

Now, it might seem that the existence of class distinctions would not allow for the [application of the] retributive principle of returning like for like. Nevertheless, even though these class distinctions may not make it possible to apply this principle to the letter, it can still always remain applicable in its effects if regard is had to the special sensibilities of the higher classes. Thus, for example, the imposition of a fine for a verbal injury has no proportionality to the original injury, for someone who has a good deal of money can easily afford to make insults whenever he wishes. On the other hand, the humiliation of the pride of such an offender comes much closer to equaling an injury done to the honor of the person offended; thus the judgment and Law might require the offender, not only to make a public apology to the offended person, but also at the same time to kiss his hand, even though he be socially inferior. Similarly, if a man of higher class has violently attacked an innocent citizen who is socially inferior to him, he may be condemned, not only to apologize, but to undergo solitary and painful confinement, because by this means, in addition to the discomfort suffered, the pride of the offender will be painfully affected, and thus his humiliation will compensate for the offence as like for like.

But what is meant by the statement: "If you steal from him, you steal from yourself"? Inasmuch as someone steals, he makes the ownership of everyone else insecure, and hence he robs himself (in accordance with the Law of retribution) of the security of any possible ownership. He has nothing and can also acquire nothing, but he still wants to live, and this is not possible unless others provide him with nourishment. But, because the state will not support him gratis, he must let the state have his labor at any kind of work it may wish to use him for (convict labor), and so he becomes a slave, either for a certain period of time or indefinitely, as the case may be.

If, however, he has committed a murder, he must die. In this case, there is no substitute that will satisfy the requirements of legal justice. There is no sameness of kind between death and remaining alive even under the most miserable conditions, and consequently there is also no equality between the crime and the retribution unless the criminal is judicially condemned and put to death. But the death of the criminal must be kept entirely free of any maltreatment that would make an abomination of the humanity residing in the person suffering it. Even if a civil society were to dissolve itself by common agreement of all its members (for example, if the people inhabiting an island decided to separate and disperse themselves around the world), the last murderer remaining in prison must first be executed, so that everyone will duly receive what his actions are worth and so that the bloodguilt thereof will not be fixed on the people because they failed to insist on carrying out the punishment; for if they fail to do so, they may be regarded as accomplices in this public violation of legal justice.

Furthermore, it is possible for punishment to be equal in accordance with the strict Law of retribution only if the judge pronounces the death sentence. This is clear because only in this way will the death sentence be pronounced on all criminals in proportion to their inner viciousness (even if the crime involved is not murder, but some other crime against the state that can be expiated only by death). To illustrate this point, let us consider a situation, like the last Scottish rebellion, in which the participants are motivated by varying purposes, just as in that rebellion some believed that they were only fulfilling their obligations to the house of Stuart (like Balmerino and others), and others, in contrast, were pursuing their own private interests. Suppose that the highest court were to pronounce as follows: Each person shall have the freedom to choose between death and penal servitude. I say that a man of honor would choose death and that the knave would choose servitude. This is implied by the nature of human character, because the first recognizes something that he prizes more highly than life itself, namely, honor, whereas the second thinks that a life covered with disgrace is still better than not being alive at all *(animam praeferre pudori)*. The first is without doubt less deserving of punishment than the other, and so, if they are both condemned to die, they will be punished exactly in proportion (to their inner viciousness); the first will be punished mildly in terms of his kind of sensibility, and the second will be punished severely in terms of his kind of sensibility. On the other hand, if both were condemned to penal servitude, the first would be punished too severely and the second too mildy for their baseness. Thus, even in sentences imposed on a number of criminals united in a plot, the best equalizer before the bar of public legal justice is death.

It may also be pointed out that no one has ever heard of anyone condemned to death on account of murder who complained that he was getting too much [punishment] and therefore was being treated unjustly; everyone would laugh in his face if he were to make such a statement. Indeed, otherwise we would have to assume that, although the treatment accorded the criminal is not unjust according to the law, the legislative authority still is not authorized to decree this kind of punishment and that, if it does so, it comes into contradiction with itself.

Anyone who is a murderer—that is, has committed a murder, commanded one, or taken part in one—must suffer death. This is what [legal] justice as the Idea of the judicial authority wills in accordance with universal laws that are grounded a priori. The number of accomplices (correi) in such a deed might, however, be so large that the state would soon approach the condition of having no more subjects if it were to rid itself of these criminals, and this would lead to its dissolution and a return to the state of nature, which is much worse, because it would be a state of affairs without any external legal justice whatsoever. Since a sovereign will want to avoid such consequences and, above all, will want to avoid adversely affecting the feelings of the people by the spectacle of such butchery, he must have it within his power in case of necessity (cassu necessitatis) to assume the role of judge and to pronounce a judgment that, instead of imposing the death penalty on the criminals, assigns some other punishment that will make the preservation of the mass of the people possible, such as for example, deportation. Such a course of action would not come under a public law, but would be an executive decree [Machtspruch], that is, an act based on the right of majesty, which as an act of reprieve, can be exercised only in individual cases.

In opposition to this view, the Marquis of Beccaria, moved by sympathetic sentimentality and an affectation of humanitarianism, has asserted that all capital punishment is illegitimate. He argues that it could not be contained in the original civil contract, inasmuch as this would imply that every one of the people has agreed to forfeit his life if he murders another (of the people); but such an agreement would be impossible, for no one can dispose of his own life.

No one suffers punishment because he has willed the punishment, but because he has willed a punishable action. If what happens to someone is also willed by him, it cannot be a punishment. Accordingly, it is impossible to will to be punished. To say, "I will to be punished if I murder someone," can mean nothing more than, "I submit myself along with everyone else to those laws which, if there are any criminals among the people, will naturally include penal laws." In my role as colegislator making the penal law, I cannot be the same person who, as subject, is punished by the law; for, as a subject who is also a criminal, I cannot have a voice in legislation.(The legislator is holy.) When, therefore, I enact a penal law against myself as a criminal it is the pure juridical legislative reason *(homo noumenon)* in me that submits myself to the penal law as a person capable of committing a crime, that is, as another person *(homo phaenomenon)* along with all the others in the civil union who submit themselves to this law. In other words, it is not the people (considered as individuals) who dictate the death penalty, but the court (public legal justice); that is, someone other than the criminal. The social contract does not include the promise to permit oneself to be punished and thus to dispose of oneself and of one's life, because, if the only ground that authorizes the punishment of an evildoer were a promise that expresses his willingness to be punished, then it would have to be left up to him to find himself liable to punishment, and the criminal would be his own judge. The chief error contained in this sophistry (πρωτον ψευδος) consists in the confusion of the criminal's own judgment (which one must necessarily attribute to his reason) that he must forfeit his life with a resolution of the Will to take his own life. The result is that the execution of the Law and the adjudication thereof are represented as united in the same person.

There remain, however, two crimes deserving of death with regard to which it still remains doubtful whether legislation is authorized to impose the death penalty. In both cases, the crimes are due to the sense of honor. One involves the honor of womanhood; the other, military honor. Both kinds of honor are genuine, and duty requires that they be sought after by every individual in each of these two classes. The first crime is infanticide at the hands of the mother *(infanticidium maternale)*; the other is the murder of a fellow soldier *(commilitonicidium)* in a duel.

Now, legislation cannot take away the disgrace of an illegitimate child, nor can it wipe away the stain of suspicion of cowardice from a junior officer who fails to react to a humiliating affront with action that would show that he has the strength to overcome the fear of death. Accordingly, it seems that, in such circumstances, the individuals concerned find themselves in a state of nature, in which killing another *(homicidium)* can never be called murder *(homicidium dolosum)*; in both cases, they are indeed deserving of punishment, but they cannot be punished with death by the supreme power. A child born into the world outside marriage is outside the law (for this is [implied by the concept of] marriage), and consequently it is also outside the protection of the law. The child has crept surreptitiously into the commonwealth (much like prohibited wares), so that its existence as well as its destruction can be ignored (because by right it ought not to have come into existence in this way); and the mother's disgrace if the illegitimate birth becomes known cannot be wiped out by any official decree.

Similarly, a military man who has been commissioned a junior officer may suffer an insult and as a result feel obliged by the opinions of his comrades in arms to seek satisfaction and to punish the person who insulted him, not by appealing to the law and taking him to court, but instead, as would be done in a state of nature, by challenging him to a duel; for even though in doing so he will be risking his life, he will thereby be able to demonstrate his military valor, on which the honor of his profession rests. If, under such circumstances, his opponent should be killed, this cannot properly be called a murder *(homicidium dolosum)*, inasmuch as it takes place in a combat openly fought with the consent of both parties, even though they may have participated in it only reluctantly.

What, then, is the actual Law of the land with regard to these two cases (which come under criminal justice)? This question presents penal justice with a dilemma; either it must declare that the concept of honor (which is no delusion in these cases) is null and void in the eyes of the law and that these acts should be punished by death or it must abstain from imposing the death penalty for these crimes, which merit it; thus it must be either too cruel or too lenient. The solution to this dilemma is as follows: the categorical imperative involved in the legal justice of punishment remains valid (that is, the unlawful killing of another person must be punished by death), but legislation itself (including also the civil constitution), as long as it remains barbaric and undeveloped, is responsible for the fact that incentives of honor among the people do not accord (subjectively) with the standards that are (objectively) appropriate to their purpose, with the result that public legal justice as administered by the state is injustice from the point of view of the people.

# 19

## Jeremy Bentham

Jeremy Bentham (1748–1832), major author of the utilitarian theory of punishment, sought a new and humane justification for penal sanctions.

## UTILITARIAN THEORY*

### CHAPTER XIII

#### CASES UNMEET FOR PUNISHMENT

§1. *General view of cases unmeet for punishment*

I. The general object which all laws have, or ought to have, in common, is to augment the total happiness of the community; and therefore, in the first place, to exclude, as far as may be, everything that tends to subtract from that happiness: in other words, to exclude mischief.

II. But all punishment is mischief: all punishment in itself is evil. Upon the principle of utility, if it ought at all to be admitted, it ought only to be admitted in as far as it promises to exclude some greater evil.[1]

III. It is plain, therefore, that in the following cases punishment ought not to be inflicted.

1. Where it is *groundless:* where there is no mischief for it to prevent; the act not being mischievous upon the whole.

2. Where it must be *inefficacious:* where it cannot act so as to prevent the mischief.

3. Where it is *unprofitable,* or too *expensive:* where the mischief it would produce would be greater than what it prevented.

---

*Jeremy Bentham, from *An Introduction to the Principles of Morals and Legislation*, first published in 1789, Chap. XIII, 1-3, Chap. XIV, 1-21. Some footnotes omitted.

[1] What follows, relative to the subject of punishment, ought regularly to be preceded by a distinct chapter on the ends of punishment. But having little to say on that particular branch of the subject, which has not been said before, it seemed better, in a work, which will at any rate be but too voluminous, to omit this title, reserving it for another, hereafter to be published, intituled *The Theory of Punishment*. To the same work I must refer the analysis of the several possible modes of punishment, a particular and minute examination of the nature of each, and of its advantages and disadvantages, and various other disquisitions, which did not seem absolutely necessary to be inserted here. A very few words, however, concerning the *ends* of punishment, can scarcely be dispensed with.

The immediate principal end of punishment is to control action. This action is either that of the offender, or of others: that of the offender it controls by its influence, either on his will, in which case it is said to operate in the way of *reformation;* or on his physical power, in which

4. Where it is *needless:* where the mischief may be prevented, or cease of itself, without it: that is, at a cheaper rate. . . .

# CHAPTER XIV

## OF THE PROPORTION BETWEEN PUNISHMENTS AND OFFENCES

I. We have seen that the general object of all laws is to prevent mischief; that is to say, when it is worth while; but that, where there are no other means of doing this than punishment, there are four cases in which it is *not* worth while.

II. When it *is* worth while, there are four subordinate designs or objects, which, in the course of his endeavours to compass, as far as may be, that one general object, a legislator, whose views are governed by the principle of utility, comes naturally to propose to himself.

III. 1. His first, most extensive, and most eligible object, is to prevent, in as far as it is possible, and worth while, all sorts of offences whatsoever: in other words, so to manage, that no offence whatsoever may be committed.

IV. 2. But if a man must needs commit an offence of some kind or other, the next object is to induce him to commit an offence *less* mischievous, *rather* than one *more* mischievous: in other words, to choose always the *least* mischievous, of two offences that will either of them suit his purpose.

V. 3. When a man has resolved upon a particular offence, the next object is to dispose him to do *no more* mischief than is *necessary* to his purpose: in other words, to do as little mischief as is consistent with the benefit he has in view.

VI. 4. The last object is, whatever the mischief be, which it is proposed to prevent, to prevent it at as *cheap* a rate as possible.

VII. Subservient to these four objects, or purposes, must be the rules or canons by which the proportion of punishments to offences is to be governed.

VIII. Rule 1. 1. The first object, it has been seen, is to prevent, in as far as it is worth while, all sorts of offences; therefore.

---

case it is said to operate by *disablement:* that of others it can influence no otherwise than by its influence over their wills; in which case it is said to operate in the way of *example*. A kind of collateral end, which it has a natural tendency to answer, is that of affording a pleasure or satisfaction to the party injured, where there is one, and, in general, to parties whose ill-will, whether on a self-regarding account, or on the account of sympathy or antipathy, has been excited by the offence. This purpose, as far as it can be answered *gratis*, is a beneficial one. But no punishment ought to be allotted merely to this purpose, because (setting aside its effects in the way of control) no such pleasure is ever produced by punishment as can be equivalent to the pain. The punishment, however, which is allotted to the other purpose, ought, as far as it can be done without expense, to be accommodated to this. Satisfaction thus administered to a party injured, in the shape of a dissocial pleasure, may be styled a vindictive satisfaction or compensation: as a compensation, administered in the shape of a self-regarding profit, or stock of pleasure, may be styled a lucrative one. Example is the most important end of all, in proportion as the *number* of the persons under temptation to offend is to *one*.

*The value of the punishment must not be less in any case than what is sufficient to outweigh that of the profit of the offence.*

If it be, the offence (unless some other considerations, independent of the punishment, should intervene and operate efficaciously in the character of tutelary motives) will be sure to be committed notwithstanding: the whole lot of punishment will be thrown away: it will be altogether *inefficacious*.

IX. The above rule has been often objected to, on account of its seeming harshness: but this can only have happened for want of its being properly understood. The strength of the temptation, *coeteris paribus*, is as the profit of the offence: the quantum of the punishment must rise with the profit of the offence: *coeteris paribus*, it must therefore rise with the strength of the temptation. This there is no disputing. True it is, that the stronger the temptation, the less conclusive is the indication which the act of delinquency affords of the depravity of the offender's disposition. So far then as the absence of any aggravation, arising from extraordinary depravity of disposition, may operate, or at the utmost, so far as the presence of a ground of extenuation, resulting from the innocence or beneficence of the offender's disposition, can operate, the strength of the temptation may operate in abatement of the demand for punishment. But it can never operate so far as to indicate the propriety of making the punishment ineffectual, which it is sure to be when brought below the level of the apparent profit of the offence.

The partial benevolence which should prevail for the reduction of it below this level, would counteract as well those purposes which such a motive would actually have in view, as those more extensive purposes which benevolence ought to have in view: it would be cruelty not only to the public, but to the very persons in whose behalf it pleads: in its effects, I mean, however opposite in its intention. Cruelty to the public, that is cruelty to the innocent, by suffering them, for want of an adequate protection, to lie exposed to the mischief of the offence: cruelty even to the offender himself, by punishing him to no purpose, and without the chance of compassing that beneficial end, by which alone the introduction of the evil of punishment is to be justified.

X. Rule 2. But whether a given offence shall be prevented in a given degree by a given quantity of punishment, is never anything better than a chance; for the purchasing of which, whatever punishment is employed, is so much expended in advance. However, for the sake of giving it the better chance of outweighing the profit of the offence.

*The greater the mischief of the offence, the greater is the expense, which it may be worth while to be at, in the way of punishment.*

XI. Rule 3. The next object is, to induce a man to choose always the least mischievous of two offences; therefore

*Where two offences come in competition, the punishment for the greater offence must be sufficient to induce a man to prefer the less.*

XII. Rule 4. When a man has resolved upon a particular offence, the next object is, to induce him to do no more mischief than what is necessary for his purpose: therefore

*The punishment should be adjusted in such manner to each particular offence, that for every part of the mischief there may be a motive to restrain the offender from giving birth to it.*

XIII. Rule 5. The last object is, whatever mischief is guarded against, to guard against it at as cheap a rate as possible: therefore

*The punishment ought in no case to be more than what is necessary to bring it into conformity with the rules here given.*

XIV. Rule 6. It is further to be observed, that owing to the different manners and degrees in which persons under different circumstances are affected by the same exciting cause, a punishment which is the same in name will not always either really produce, or even so much as appear to others to produce, in two different persons the same degree of pain: therefore

*That the quantity actually inflicted on each individual offender may correspond to the quantity intended for similar offenders in general, the several circumstances influencing sensibility ought always to be taken into account.*

XV. Of the above rules of proportion, the four first, we may perceive, serve to mark out the limits on the side of diminution; the limits *below* which a punishment ought not to be *diminished:* the fifth, the limits on the side of increase; the limits *above* which it ought not to be *increased.* The five first are calculated to serve as guides to the legislator: the sixth is calculated, in some measure, indeed, for the same purpose; but principally for guiding the judge in his endeavours to conform, on both sides, to the intentions of the legislator.

XVI. Let us look back a little. The first rule, in order to render it more conveniently applicable to practice, may need perhaps to be a little more particularly unfolded. It is to be observed, then, that for the sake of accuracy, it was necessary, instead of the word *quantity* to make use of the less perspicuous term *value.* For the word *quantity* will not properly include the circumstances either of certainty or proximity: circumstances which, in estimating the value of a lot of pain or pleasure, must always be taken into the account. Now, on the one hand, a lot of punishment is a lot of pain; on the other hand, the profit of an offence is a lot of pleasure, or what is equivalent to it. But the profit of the offence *is* commonly more *certain* than the punishment, or, what comes to the same thing, *appears* so at least to the offender. It is at any rate commonly more *immediate.* It follows, therefore, that, in order to maintain its superiority over the profit of the offence, the punishment must have its value made up in some other way, in proportion to that whereby it falls short in the two points of *certainty* and *proximity.* Now there is no other way in which it can receive any addition to its *value,* but by receiving an addition in point of *magnitude.* Wherever then the value of the punishment falls short, either in point of *certainty,* or of *proximity,* of that of the profit of the offence, it must receive a proportionable addition in point of *magnitude.*

XVII. Yet farther. To make sure of giving the value of the punishment the superiority over that of the offence, it may be necessary, in some cases, to take into the account the profit not only of the *individual* offence to which the punishment is to be annexed, but also of such *other* offences of the *same sort* as the offender is likely to have already committed without detection. This random mode of calculation, severe as it is, it will be impossible to avoid having recourse to, in certain cases: in such, to wit, in which the profit is pecuniary, the chance of detection very small, and the obnoxious act of such a nature as indicates a habit: for example, in the case of frauds against the coin. If it be *not* recurred to, the practice of committing the offence will be sure to be, upon the balance of the account, a gainful practice. That being the case, the legislator will be absolutely sure of *not* being able to suppress it, and the whole punishment that is bestowed upon it will be thrown away. In a word (to keep to the same expressions we set out with) that whole quantity of punishment will be *inefficacious.*

XVIII. Rule 7. These things being considered, the three following rules may be laid down by way of supplement and explanation to Rule 1.

*To enable the value of the punishment to outweigh that of the profit of the offence, it must be increased, in point of magnitude, in proportion as it falls short in point of certainty.*

XIX. Rule 8. *Punishment must be further increased in point of magnitude, in proportion as it falls short in point of proximity.*

XX. Rule 9. *Where the act is conclusively indicative of a habit, such an increase must be given to the punishment as may enable it to outweigh the profit not only of the individual offence, but of such other like offences as are likely to have been committed with impunity by the same offender.*

XXI. There may be a few other circumstances or considerations which may influence, in some small degree, the demand for punishment: but as the propriety of these is either not so demonstrable, or not so constant, or the application of them not so determinate, as that of the foregoing, it may be doubted whether they be worth putting on a level with the others. . . .

# 20

# A. M. Quinton

Anthony Quinton (1925–    ), a Fellow of New College, Oxford
University, attempts a logical reconciliation between the two great
theories of punishment.

# ON PUNISHMENT*

## [I] INTRODUCTORY

There is a prevailing antinomy about the philosophical justification of
punishment. The two great theories—retributive and utilitarian—seem, and
at least are understood by their defenders, to stand in open and flagrant contradiction. Both sides have arguments at their disposal to demonstrate the
atrocious consequencies of the rival theory. Retributivists, who seem to hold
that there are circumstances in which the infliction of suffering is a good thing
in itself, are charged by their opponents with vindictive barbarousness. Utilitarians, who seem to hold that punishment is always and only justified by the
good consequences it produces, are accused of vicious opportunism. Where the
former insists on suffering for suffering's sake, the latter permits the punishment
of the innocent. Yet, if the hope of justifying punishment is not to be abandoned
altogether, one of these apparently unsavory alternatives must be embraced.
For they exhaust the possibilities. Either punishment must be self-justifying, as the
retributivists claim, or it must depend for its justification on something other than
itself, the general formula of "utilitarianism" in the wide sense appropriate here.

In this paper I shall argue that the antinomy can be resolved, since retribu
tivism, properly understood, is not a moral but a logical doctrine, and that it
does not provide a moral justification of the infliction of punishment but an
elucidation of the use of the word. Utilitarianism, on the other hand, embraces
a number of possible moral attitudes toward punishment, none of which
necessarily involves the objectionable consequences commonly adduced by
retributivists, provided that the word "punishment" is understood in the way
that the essential retributivist thesis lays down. The antinomy arises from a
confusion of modalities, of logical and moral necessity and possibility, of "must"
and "can" with "ought" and "may". In brief, the two theories answer different
questions: retributivism the question "when (logically) *can* we punish?",
utilitarianism the question "when (morally) *may* we or *ought* we to punish?"
I shall also describe circumstances in which there is an answer to the question

---

*A. M. Quinton, "On Punishment," *Analysis*, XIV (1954), pp. 512-517. Reprinted by permission
of the author and publisher, Basil Blackwell & Mott Ltd.

"when (logically) *must* we punish?" Finally, I shall attempt to account for this difference in terms of a distinction between the establishment of rules whose infringement involves punishment from the application of these rules to particular cases.

The essential contention of retributivism is that punishment is only justified by guilt. There is a certain compellingness about the repudiation of utilitarianism that this involves. We feel that whatever other considerations may be taken into account, the primary and indispensable matter is to establish the guilt of the person to be punished. I shall try to show that the peculiar outrageousness of the rejection of this principle is a consequence, not of the brutality that such rejection might seem to permit, but of the fact that it involves a kind of lying. At any rate the first principle of retributivism is that it is necessary that a man be guilty if he is to be punished.

But this doctrine is normally held in conjunction with some or all of three others which are logically, if not altogether psychologically, independent of it. These are that the function of punishment is the negation or annulment of evil or wrongdoing, that punishment must fit the crime (the *lex talionis*) and that offenders have a right to punishment, as moral agents they ought to be treated as ends not means.

The doctrine of "annulment," however carefully wrapped up in obscure phraseology, is clearly utilitarian in principle. For it holds that the function of punishment is to bring about a state of affairs in which it is as if the wrongful act had never happened. This is to justify punishment by its effects, by the desirable future consequences which it brings about. It certainly goes beyond the demand that only the guilty be punished. For, unlike this demand, it seeks to prescribe exactly what the punishment should be. Holding that whenever wrong has been done it must be annulled, it makes guilt—the state of one who has done wrong—the sufficient as well as the necessary condition of punishment. While the original thesis is essentially negative, ruling out the punishment of the innocent, the annulment doctrine is positive, insisting on the punishment and determining the degree of punishment of the guilty. But the doctrine is only applicable to a restricted class of cases, the order of nature is inhospitable to attempts to put the clock back. Theft and fraud can be compensated, but not murder, wounding, alienation of affection, or the destruction of property or reputation.

Realizing that things cannot always be made what they were, retributivists have extended the notion of annulment to cover the infliction on the offender of an injury equal to that which he has caused. This is sometimes argued for by reference to Moore's theory of organic wholes, the view that sometimes two blacks make a white. That this, the *lex talionis*, revered by Kant, does not follow from the original thesis is proved by the fact that we can always refrain from punishing the innocent but that we cannot always find a punishment to fit the crime. Some indeed would argue that we can never fit punishment to wrongdoing. for how are either, especially wrongdoing, to be measured? (Though, as Ross has pointed out, we can make ordinal judgments of more or less about both punishment and wrongdoing.)

Both of these views depend on a mysterious extension of the original thesis to mean that punishment and wrongdoing must necessarily be somehow equal and opposite. But this is to go even further than to regard guilt and punishment as necessitating one another. For this maintains that only the guilty are to be punished and that the guilty are always to be punished. The equal and opposite view maintains further that they are to be punished to just the extent that they have done wrong.

Finally retributivism has been associated with the view that if we are to treat offenders as moral agents, as ends and not as means, we must recognize their right to punishment. It is an odd sort of right whose holders would strenuously resist its recognition. Strictly interpreted, this view would entail that the sole relevant consideration in determining whether and how a man should be punished is his own moral regeneration. This is utilitarian and it is also immoral, since it neglects the rights of an offender's victims to compensation and of society in general to protection. A less extreme interpretation would be that we should never treat offenders merely as means in inflicting punishment but should take into account their right to treatment as moral agents. This is reasonable enough; most people would prefer a penal system which did not ignore the reformation of offenders. But it is not the most obvious correlate of the possible view that if a man is guilty he ought to be punished. We should more naturally allot the correlative right to have him punished to his victims or society in general and not to him himself.

## [III] THE RETRIBUTIVIST THESIS

So far I have attempted to extricate the essentials of retributivism by excluding some traditional but logically irrelevant associates. A more direct approach consists in seeing what is the essential principle which retributivists hold utilitarians to deny. Their crucial charge is that utilitarians permit the punishment of the innocent. So their fundamental thesis must be that only the guilty are to be punished, that guilt is a necessary condition of punishment. This hardly lies open to the utilitarian countercharge of pointless and vindictive barbarity, which could only find a foothold in the doctrine of annulment and in the *lex talionis*. (For that matter, it is by no means obvious that the charge can be sustained even against them, except in so far as the problems of estimating the measure of guilt lead to the adoption of a purely formal and external criterion which would not distinguish between the doing of deliberate and accidental injuries.)

Essentially, then, retributivism is the view that only the guilty are to be punished. Excluding the punishment of the innocent, it permits the other three possibilities: the punishment of the guilty, the nonpunishment of the guilty, and the nonpunishment of the innocent. To add that guilt is also the sufficient condition of punishment, and thus to exclude the nonpunishment of the guilty, is another matter altogether. It is not entailed by the retributivist attack on utilitarianism and has none of the immediate compulsiveness of the doctrine that guilt is the necessary condition of punishment.

There is a very good reason for this difference in force. For the necessity of not punishing the innocent is not moral but logical. It is not, as some retributivists think, that we *may* not punish the innocent and *ought* only to punish the guilty, but that we *cannot* punish the innocent and *must* only punish the guilty. Of course, the suffering or harm in which punishment consists can be and is inflicted on innocent people, but this is not punishment, it is judicial error or terrorism or, in Bradley's characteristically repellent phrase, "social surgery." The infliction of suffering on a person is only properly described as punishment if that person is guilty. The retributivist thesis, therefore, is not a moral doctrine, but an account of the meaning of the word "punishment." Typhoid carriers and criminal lunatics are treated physically in much the same way as ordinary criminals; they are shut up in institutions. The essential difference is that no blame is implied by their imprisonment, for there is no guilt to which the blame can attach. "Punishment" resembles the word "murder"; it is infliction of suffering on the guilty and not simply infliction of suffering, just as murder is wrongful killing and not simply killing. Typhoid carriers are no more (usually) criminals than surgeons are (usually) murderers. This accounts for the flavor of moral outrage attending the notion of punishment of the innocent. In a sense a contradiction in terms, it applies to the common enough practice of inflicting the suffering involved in punishment on innocent people and of sentencing them to punishment with a lying imputation of their responsibility and guilt. Punishment *cannot* be inflicted on the innocent; the suffering associated with punishment *may* not be inflicted on them, first, as brutal and secondly, if it is represented as punishment, as involving a lie.

This can be shown by the fact that punishment is always *for* something. If a man says to another "I am going to punish you" and is asked "what for?" he cannot reply "nothing at all" or "something you have not done." At best, he is using "punish" here as a more or less elegant synonym for "cause to suffer." Either that or he does not understand the meaning of "punish." "I am going to punish you for something you have not done" is as absurd a statement as "I blame you for this event for which you were not responsible." "Punishment implies guilt" is the same sort of assertion as "ought implies can." It is not *pointless* to punish or blame the innocent, as some have argued, for it is often very useful. Rather the very conditions of punishment and blame do not obtain in these circumstances.

[IV] AN OBJECTION

But how can it be useful to do what is impossible? The innocent can be punished and scapegoats are not logical impossibilities. We do say "they punished him for something he did not do." For A to be said to have punished B it is surely enough that A thought or said he was punishing B and ensured that suffering was inflicted on B. However innocent B may be of the offense adduced by A, there is no question that, in these circumstances, he has been punished by A. So guilt cannot be more than a *moral* precondition of punishment.

The answer to this objection is that "punish" is a member of that now familiar class of verbs whose first-person-present use is significantly different from the rest. The absurdity of "I am punishing you for something you have not done" is analogous to that of "I promise to do something which is not in my power." Unless you are guilty I am no more in a position to punish you than I am in a position to promise what is not in my power. So it is improper to say "I am going to punish you" unless you are guilty, just as it is improper to say "I promise to do this" unless it is in my power to do it. But it is only *morally* improper if I do not *think* that you are guilty or that I can do the promised act. Yet, just as it is perfectly proper to say of another "he promised to do this," whether he thought he could do it or not, provided that he *said* "I promise to do this," so it is perfectly proper to say "they punished him," whether they thought him guilty or not, provided that they *said* "we are going to punish you" and inflicted suffering on him. By the first-person-present use of these verbs we prescribe punishment and *make* promises; these activities involve the satisfaction of conditions over and above what is required for *reports* or *descriptions* of what their prescribers or makers represent as punishments and promises.

Understandably "reward" and "forgive" closely resemble "punish." Guilt is a precondition of forgiveness, desert—its contrary—of reward. One cannot properly say "I am going to reward you" or "I forgive you" to a man who has done nothing. Reward and forgiveness are always *for* something. But, again, one can say "they rewarded (or forgave) him for something he had not done." There is an interesting difference here between "forgive" and "punish" or "reward." In this last kind of assertion "forgive" seems more peculiar, more inviting to inverted commas, that the other two. The three undertakings denoted by these verbs can be divided into the utterance of a more or less ritual formula and the consequences authorized by this utterance. With punishment and reward the consequences are more noticeable than the formula, so they come to be sufficient occasion for the use of the word even if the formula is inapplicable and so improperly used. But, since the consequences of forgiveness are negative, the absence of punishment, no such shift occurs. To reward involves giving a reward, to punish inflicting a punishment, but to forgive involves no palpable consequence, e.g., handing over a written certificate of pardon.

Within these limitations, then, guilt is a *logically* necessary condition of punishment and, with some exceptions, it might be held, a morally necessary condition of the infliction of suffering. Is it in either way a sufficient condition? As will be shown in the last section there are circumstances, though they do not obtain in our legal system, nor generally in extralegal penal systems (e.g., parental), in which guilt is a logically sufficient condition of at least a sentence of punishment. The parellel moral doctrine would be that if anyone is guilty of wrongdoing he ought morally to be punished. This rather futile rigorism is not embodied in our legal system with its relaxations of penalties for first offenders. Since it entails that offenders should never be forgiven it is hardly likely to commend itself in the extralegal sphere.

## [V] THE UTILITARIAN THEORY

Utilitarianism holds that punishment must always be justified by the value of its consequences. I shall refer to this as "utility" for convenience without any implication that utility must consist in pleasure. The view that punishment is justified by the value of its consequences is compatible with any ethical theory which allows meaning to be attached to moral judgments. It holds merely that the infliction of suffering is of no value or of negative value and that it must therefore be justified by further considerations. These will be such things as prevention of and deterrence from wrongdoing, compensation of victims, reformation of offenders, and satisfaction of vindictive impulses. It is indifferent for our purposes whether these are valued as intuitively good, as productive of general happiness, as conducive to the survival of the human race or are just normatively laid down as valuable or derived from such a norm.

Clearly there is no *logical* relation between punishment and its actual or expected utility. Punishment *can* be inflicted when it is neither expected, nor turns out, to be of value and, on the other hand, it can be foregone when it is either expected, or would turn out, to be of value.

But that utility is the morally necessary or sufficient condition, or both, of punishment are perfectly reputable moral attitudes. The first would hold that no one should be punished unless the punishment would have valuable consequences; the second that if valuable consequences would result punishment ought to be inflicted (without excluding the moral permissibility of utility-less punishment). Most people would no doubt accept the first, apart from the rigorists who regard guilt as a morally sufficient condition of punishment. Few would maintain the second except in conjunction with the first. The first says when you may not but not when you ought to punish, the second when you ought but not when you may not.

Neither permits or encourages the punishment of the innocent, for this is only logically possible if the word "punishment" is used in an unnatural way, for example as meaning any kind of deliberate infliction of suffering. But in that case they cease to be moral doctrine about punishment as we understand the word and become moral doctrines (respectively, platitudinous and inhuman) about something else.

So the retributivist case against the utilitarians falls to the ground as soon as what is true and essential in retributivism is extracted from the rest. This may be unwelcome to retributivists since it leaves the moral field in the possession of the utilitarians. But there is a compensation in tee fact that what is essential in retributivism can at least be definitely established.

## [VI] RULES AND CASES

So far what has been established is that guilt and the value or utility of consequences are relevant to punishment in different ways. A further understanding of this difference can be gained by making use of a distinction made by Sir David Ross in the appendix on punishment in *The Right and the Good*. This will also help to elucidate the notion of guilt which has hitherto been applied uncritically.

The distinction is between laying down a rule which attaches punishment to actions of a certain kind and the application of that rule to particular cases. It might be maintained that the utilitarian theory was an answer to the question "What kinds of action should be punished?" and the retributive theory an answer to the question "On what particular occasions should we punish?" On this view both punishment and guilt are defined by reference to these rules. Punishment is the infliction of suffering attached by these rules to certain kinds of action, guilt the condition of a person to whom such a rule applies. This accounts for the logically necessary relation holding between guilt and punishment. Only the guilty can be punished because unless a person is guilty, unless a rule applies to him, no infliction of suffering on him is properly called punishment, since punishment is infliction of suffering as laid down by such a rule. Considerations of utility, then, are alone relevant to the determination of what in general, what *kinds* of action, to punish. The outcome of this is a set of rules. Given these rules, the question of whom in particular to punish has a definite and necessary answer. Not only will guilt be the logically necessary but also the logically sufficient condition of punishment or, more exactly, of a sentence of punishment. For declaration of guilt will be a declaration that a rule applies and, if the rule applies, what the rule enjoins—a sentence of punishment— applies also.

The distinction between setting up and applying penal rules helps to explain the different parts played by utility and guilt in the justification of punishment, in particular the fact that where utility is a moral, guilt is a logical, justification. Guilt is irrelevant to the setting up of rules, for until they have been set up the notion of guilt is undefined and without application. Utility is irrelevant to the application of rules, for once the rules have been set up, punishment is determined by guilt; once they are seen to apply, the rule makes a sentence of punishment necessarily follow.

But this account is not an accurate description of the very complex penal systems actually employed by states, institutions, and parents. It is, rather, a schemea, a possible limiting case. For it ignores an almost universal feature of penal systems (and of games, for that matter, where penalties attend infractions of the rules)—discretion. For few offenses against the law is one and only one fixed and definite punishment laid down. Normally only an upper limit is set. If guilt, the applicability of the rule, is established no fixed punishment is entailed but rather, for example, one not exceeding a fine of forty shillings or fourteen days' imprisonment. This is even more evident in the administration of such institutions as clubs or libraries and yet more again in the matter of parental discipline. The establishment of guilt does not close the matter; at best it entails some punishment or other. Precisely how much is appropriate must be determined by reference to considerations of utility. The variety of things is too great for any manageably concise penal code to dispense altogether with discretionary judgment in particular cases.

But this fact only shows that guilt is not a logically *suffictent* condition of punishment; it does not affect the thesis that punishment entails guilt. A man cannot be guilty unless his action falls under a penal rule and he can only be properly said to be punished if the rule in question prescribes or permits some punishment or other. So all applications of the notion of guilt necessarily contain or include all applications of the notion of punishment.

CHAPTER VI

# LEGAL OBLIGATION AND THE RULE OF LAW

> Let every person be subject to the governing authorities. For there is no authority
> except from God, and those that exist have been instituted by God.
>
> *Letter of Paul to the Romans,* 13:1

Notwithstanding a long history of natural rights definitions of the just law, the so-called right of civil disobedients is very much a modern invention, scarcely established in the sense that civil disobedients in any major legal system can expect to escape punishment as a standard practice. The attention of legal theorists has tended to focus rather on the correlative limits of political authority and the nature and justification of legal obligation. The history of civil disobedience has been one of peculiar anomalies and possible exceptions to the general rule of law.

In the *Crito,* Plato has Socrates, the first of the great civil disobedients, voice the standard arguments in defense of the rule of law:

> But he who has experience of the manner in which we order justice and administer the state, and still remains, has entered into an implied contract that he will do as we command him. And he who disobeys us is, as we maintain, thrice wrong; first, because in disobeying his parents; secondly, because we are the authors of his education; thirdly, because he has made an agreement with us that he will duly obey our commands; and he neither obeys them nor convinces us that our commands are unjust; and we do not rudely impose them, but give him the alternative of obeying or convincing us. . . .

305

St. Thomas narrowly hedges the limits of disobedience: particular injustices should be tolerated in the interests of public order; only an illegitimate
power may be disobeyed and then only when a rule of law is not in effect.
Hobbes, generally a proponent of absolute sovereign right, allows: "[A] man
. . . commanded as a soldier to fight against the enemy, though his sovereign
have right enough to punish his refusal with death, may nevertheless in many
cases refuse, without injustice . . ." Locke, the defender of natural rights of life,
liberty, and property, nevertheless commends "absolute obedience to the
command of every superior officer, and it is justly death to disobey or dispute
the most dangerous or unreasonable of them . . ."

Recently, theorists have attempted to patch up some of the weak points
in traditional formulations. Hart, for instance, focuses on the verbal distinction
between saying 'X was obligated' which would apply to the external threat of
force of the gunmen as well as to that of the absolute sovereign, and 'X's having
an obligation' which would presumably entail his sense of obligation for internal
reasons. Rawls' 'justice as fairness' and limited defense of civil disobedience are
partially intended as correctives to the preferences for property over other civil
rights entailed by Locke's version of the social contract.

Theorists have also become divided on the criteria for validity of specific
laws as well as whole systems. For the layman this question might seem to
involve no more than a careful search through relevant statutes and case
precedents. Actually there are peculiar legal problems in this area. A legitimate
legal defense may be the fact that a law has not been enforced for some time,
though it exists on the statute books (e.g. the so-called Blue laws of several
New England states). Again, judges may enforce as law customs which have
endured but which have never been formally codified. Not infrequently statutes
—particularly when they are the product of political compromise—are
ambiguous in their intent and call for judicial interpretation. Rulings of lower
jurisdiction may conflict with higher legal authorities.

In the face of these and other contingencies St. Thomas declared a law
valid in principle ('just' in his terminology) if constituted by legitimate authority
and compatible with the common welfare and general virtue. Positivists, on
the other hand, have generally pointed to the 'efficacy' of a given law, i.e.
whether it is generally obeyed. Hart claims that an empirically discoverable
'rule of recognition' (line of deference between separate legal authorities sometimes but not always culminating in an ultimate body) combined with evidence
of general acceptance of the rule in question establishes its validity. The
Scandinavian, Alf Ross, more narrowly limits efficacy to 'official' acceptance
of the law in question. Hans Kelsen is somewhat the anomaly in this survey:
validity of a law depends not on its particular efficacy but rather upon that of
a whole system of laws authorized by a priori "basic norm" which can only be
overthrown by revolution, i.e. processes or procedures not provided for within
its own structure.

To return to the question of civil disobedience, none of the theorists cited
leaves much clear ground for limited challenge to specific laws other than through

due process. John Rawls speaks of the 'right' to engage in civil disobedience, a public, non-violent, and conscientious act contrary to law usually done with the intent to bring about a change in the policies or laws of government. However, like most other commentators, he adds a crucial fifth criterion that makes civil disobedience something less than a perfect legal right: it is done in a situation where arrest and punishment is expected and accepted without resistance.

However narrowly civil disobedience is defined, one suspects that no single set of formal criteria can treat adequately a diversity of types and degrees of injustice ranging along a broad potential spectrum. Civil disobedience, in Dean Allen's wide definition, has already taken many forms in our own country ranging from minor nuisance protest, work slow-down and strike to a Boston Tea Party, an Underground Railroad and the Suffragettes movement. As one member of a high court of appeals has pointed out in the privacy of his class-room, civil disobedients considered noteworthy and honorable in our American mythology have at times violated all the narrow criteria and appealed to conscience alone.

Current developments in theory and practice would seem to reflect a quest for more flexible and direct instruments for authorization, and repudiation of specific laws and official actions, short of the extremes of outright rebellion or passive acceptance implicit in the 'once-and-for-all-time' consent clause of older contract models. The suggestive notion of the individual as ultimate 'author' is manifest in Hobbes, though subordinated in his frame to absolute sovereign command. A reasonable distinction between general legal-political obligation and the right to protest specific injustices would seem imperative to the rule of law today, given the complex exigencies of modern social systems.

# 21

# Saint Thomas Aquinas

Saint Thomas Aquinas (1225–1274) set criteria for the 'just' law, but only slightly qualified the Church's traditional acceptance of the supremacy of secular authority.

# LEGAL AND MORAL OBLIGATION*

## SUMMA THEOLOGICA

### THE DIFFERENCE BETWEEN LEGAL AND MORAL OBLIGATION

*Law and the Practice of Virtue. (Qu. 100, Art. 9.)*

As we have shown above, a precept of law has power to compel: thus whatever is obliged by law may be said to fall directly under the precept of law. But the compulsion of law obtains through fear of penalty, as is shown in the tenth book of the *Ethics;* for those matters may be said to come strictly under the precept of law for which a legal penalty is inflicted. Hence divine law differs from human law in the imposition of its penalties. For a legal penalty is inflicted only for those matters about which the law-giver is competent to judge, since the law punishes in view of a judgment passed. Now man, the maker of human law, can pass judgment only upon external actions, because 'man seeth those things that appear,' as we are told in the first book of *Kings.* God alone, the divine Law-giver, is able to judge the inner movement of the will, as the Psalmist says, 'The searcher of hearts and reins is God.'

In view of this we must conclude that the practice of virtue is in one respect subject both to human and to divine law, while in another respect it is subject to divine but not to human law. Again there is a third sense in which it is affected neither by divine nor by human law. Now the mode of the practice of virtue consists, according to Aristotle (II *Ethics,* 4), in three things. The first of these is that a person should act knowingly. And this is subject to judgment both by divine and by human law. For whatever a man does in ignorance he does accidentally, and in consequence both human and divine law must consider the question of ignorance in judging whether certain matters are punishable or pardonable.

*Saint Thomas Aquinas, selections from the *Summa Theologica* and *Commentary on the Sentences of Peter Lombard,* reprinted by permission of the editor and publisher from *Thomas Aquinas: Selected Political Writings* (edited by A. P. d'Entreves and translated by J. G. Dawson), Basil Blackwell, Oxford, 1948, pp. 147-149, 175-185. Latin text omitted.

308

The second point is that a man should act voluntarily, deliberately choosing a particular action for its own sake. This involves a two-fold interior action of the will and of intention, and of these we have already spoken above. Divine law alone is competent to judge of these, but not human law. For human law does not punish the man who meditates murder but does not commit it, though divine law does punish him, as we are told by *St. Matthew* (V, 22): 'Whosoever is angry with his brother shall be in danger of the judgment.'

The third point is that a man should act upon a firm and unchanging principle; and such firmness proceeds strictly from habit, and obtains when a man acts from a rooted habit. In this sense the practice of virtue does not fall under the precept either of divine or of human law for no man is punished for breaking the law, either by God or by man, if he duly honours his parents, though lacking the habit of filial piety.

## OBEDIENCE. (QU. 104.)

*Obedience is a Precept of both the Divine and the Natural Law. (Art. 1, concl.)*

Just as the operations of natural agents derive from the forces of nature so do human actions derive from the human will. Now in the operations of nature it is necessary the higher things move the lower in virtue of the pre-eminence of natural powers conferred upon them by God. So also in human affairs it is necessary that superiors impose their will upon inferiors, in virtue of the authority established by God. But to impose the reason and will is the same thing as to command. So therefore, in the same way as in the natural order created by God, the lower must remain beneath the direction of the higher, in human affairs inferiors are bound to obey their superiors according to the order established by natural and divine law.

*The Limits of Obedience. (Ibid. Art. 5.)*

As we have already said, he who obeys is directed by the will of him who commands in virtue of the obligation of justice, just as things in nature are moved by that which acts upon them according to natural necessity. . . . Similarly, there can be two reasons why a subject is not obliged to obey his superior in everything. First, in virtue of the command of some higher power. The *Gloss* says with reference to the text of St. Paul (*Romans* XIII, 'Those who resist authority, bring upon themselves damnation'): 'If the Curator commands something, should you do it if it is contrary to what the Proconsul commands? And again, if the Proconsul commands one thing and the Emperor another can it be doubted that the latter is to be obeyed and the former not? Therefore, when the Emperor commands one thing and God another, one should ignore the former and obey the latter.' Another case in which the subject is not obliged to obey his superior occurs when the latter commands something in matters in which he has no authority. As Seneca says (III *De Beneficiis*, 20):

'It is a mistake to believe that slavery embraces the whole man: the best part escapes it. The body is a slave and subject to a master but the mind is free.' Therefore in those things which depend upon the interior movements of the will man is not bound by obedience to man, but only to God. Man, it is true, is bound by obedience to man with respect to the external operations of the body: but even here, in what regards the nature of the body, he is not bound to obey man, but only God, for all men are equal in nature. Such is the case with regard to sustaining the body and the procreation of children. Thus in contracting matrimony or making a vow of chastity and other similar matters, a slave is not obliged to obey his master nor children their parents. But in those matters which regard the ordering of human affairs and actions, a subject is bound to obey his superiors in virtue of their particular authority: thus the soldier obeys his general in matters of war; the slave his master with respect to the tasks allotted to him; the son his father with regard to the discipline and management of family life, and so forth.

### Obedience is a Religious Duty. *(Ibid. Art. 6.)*

The Christian faith is the principle and cause of justice, according to what St. Paul says *(Romans* III, 22*):* 'The justice of God through faith in Jesus Christ.' So the order of justice is not destroyed through faith in Jesus Christ, but is rather confirmed. Now the order of justice demands that subjects should obey their superiors: for there would otherwise be no stability in human affairs. So, therefore, the Christian faith does not dispense the faithful from the obligation of obeying temporal princes.

### Obedience and Christian Liberty. *(Ibid. ad* 1*um)*

As we have said above, slavery, by which one man is subject to another, exists in respect of the body, but not of the soul, which remains free. Now in the state of this life we are free by the grace of Christ from the defects of the soul, but not from those of the body; as we see from the words of the Apostle *(Romans* VII, 25), where he says of himself, that 'with the mind he obeys the law of God, but with the flesh the law of sin.' So, therefore, those who through grace become the sons of God are free from the spiritual slavery of sin, but not from the slavery of the body through which they are bound to earthly masters; as the *Gloss* says in the commentary upon I *Timothy* VI, 1: 'All are under the yoke of slavery,' etc.

### The Justification of Civil Disobedience. *(Ibid. ad 3um.)*

Man is bound to obey secular Rulers to the extent that the order of justice requires. For this reason if such rules have no just title to power, but have usurped it, or if they command things to be done which are unjust, their subjects are not obliged to obey them; except, perhaps, in certain special cases when it is a matter of avoiding scandal or some particular danger.

## COMMENTARY ON THE SENTENCES OF
## PETER LOMBARD

BOOK II

*The Obedience owed by Christians to the Secular Power and in particular to Tyrants.*
*(Dist. 44, Quest. 2, Art. 2.)*

1. It would seem that Christians are not bound to obey the secular powers, and particularly tyrants. For it is said, *Matthew* XVII, 25: 'Therefore the children are free.' And if in all countries the children of the reigning sovereign are free, so also should the children of that Sovereign be free, to whom all kings are subject. But Christians have become the sons of God as we read in the *Epistle to the Romans* (VIII, 16). 'For the Spirit himself giveth testimony to our spirit, that we are the sons of God.' Christians then are everywhere free, and are thus not bound to obey the secular powers.

2. Furthermore: as we have already shown, servitude began in consequence of sin. But men are cleansed from sin by baptism. Therefore they are freed from servitude. So we have the same conclusion.

3. Furthermore: a greater bond absolves from a lesser, as the new law absolved from observance of the old. But man is by baptism bound to God: and this obligation is a greater bond than that by which one man is bound to another by servitude. Therefore man is freed from servitude by baptism.

4. Furthermore: Any one is permitted, if opportunity offers, to take back what has been unjustly taken from him. But many secular princes have possessed themselves tyrannically of the lands they rule. Therefore when the opportunity of rebelling occurs, their subjects are not bound by obedience to them.

5. Furthermore: there can be no duty of obedience towards a person whom it is permissible or even praiseworthy to kill. But Cicero in the *De Officiis* (I, 26) justifies those who killed Julius Caesar, even though he was their friend and relative, because he usurped the imperial powers like a tyrant. To such, then, no obedience is owed.

But against the above arguments there is the text of the first *Epistle to St. Peter* (II, 18): 'Servants, be subject to your masters': and that of the *Epistle to the Romans* (XIII, 2): 'He that resisteth the power, resisteth the ordinance of God.' Now it is not permissible to resist the ordinance of God, neither; therefore, is it permissible to resist the secular power.

Solution. We must observe that, as has been stated already, in the observance of a certain precept, obedience is connected with the obligation to such observance. But such obligation derives from the order of authority which carries with it the power to constrain, not only from the temporal, but also from the spiritual point of view, and in conscience; as the Apostle says *(Romans* XIII): and this because the order of authority derives from God, as the Apostle says in the same passage. For this reason the duty of obedience is, for the Christian, a consequence of this derivation of authority from God, and ceases when that ceases. But, as we have already said, authority may fail to derive from God for two reasons: either because of the way in which authority has been obtained, or in consequence of the use which is made of it. There are two ways in which the first case may occur. Either because of a defect in the person, if he is unworthy; or because of some defect in the way itself by which power was acquired, if, for example, through violence, or simony or some other illegal method. The first defect is not such as to impede the acquisition of legitimate authority; and since authority derives always, from a formal point of view, from God (and it is this which produces the duty of obedience), their subjects are always obliged to obey such superiors, however unworthy they may be. But the second defect prevents the establishment of any just authority: for whoever possesses himself of power by violence does not truly become lord or master. Therefore it is permissible, when occasion offers, for a person to reject such authority; except in the case that it subsequently became legitimate, either through public consent or through the intervention of higher authority. With regard to abuse of authority, this also may come about in two ways. First, when what is ordered by an authority is opposed to the object for which that authority was constituted (if, for example, some sinful action is commanded or one which is contrary to virtue, when it is precisely for the protection and fostering of virtue that authority is instituted). In such a case, not only is there no obligation to obey the authority, but one is obliged to disobey it, as did the holy martyrs who suffered death rather than obey the impious commands of tyrants. Secondly, when those who bear authority command things which exceed the competence of such authority; as for example, when a master demands payment from a servant which the latter is not bound to make, and other similar cases. In this instance the subject is free to obey or to disobey.

So, to the first objection we may reply that authority which is instituted in the interests of those subject to it, is not contrary to their liberty; so there is no objection to those who are transformed into sons of God, by the grace of the Holy Spirit, being subject to it. Or again we can say that Christ speaks of Himself and of His disciples, who were neither of servile condition nor had they any temporal possessions for which to pay tribute to temporal lords. So it does not follow that all Christians should enjoy such liberty, but only those who follow the apostolic way of life, without possessions and free from servile condition.

With regard to the second objection we must note that baptism does not take away all the penalties which derive from the sin of our first parents, as for instance the inevitability of death, blindness, and other such evils. But it regenerates in the living hope of that life in which we shall be free from such penalties. Therefore, from the fact that a man is baptized it does not necessarily follow that he should be freed from servile condition, even though this is a consequence of sin.

To the third objection we reply that the greater bond does not absolve from the lesser, unless the two be incompatible, since error and truth cannot be found together; therefore with the coming of the truth of the Gospel the darkness of the Old Law passed away. But the bond with which one is bound in baptism is compatible with the bond of servitude, and does not in consequence absolve from it.

To the fourth objection we reply that those who attain power by violence are not truly rulers; therefore their subjects are not bound to obey them except in the cases already noted.

With regard to the fifth objection it must be noted that Cicero was speaking of a case where a person had possessed himself of power through violence, either against the will of his subjects or by compelling their consent, and where there was no possibility of appeal to a higher authority who could pass judgment on such action. In such a case, one who liberates his country by killing a tyrant is to be praised and rewarded.

*The Relation between the Temporal and the Spiritual Power. (Ibid. Dist. 44, Quest. 3, Art. 4.)*

Both the spiritual and the temporal power derive from the divine power; consequently the temporal power is subject to the spiritual only to the extent that this is so ordered by God; namely, in those matters which affect the salvation of the soul. And in these matters the spiritual power is to be obeyed before the temporal. In those matters, however, which concern the civil welfare, the temporal power should obeyed rather than the spiritual, according to what we are told in *St. Matthew* (XXII, 21) 'Render to Caesar the things that are Caesar's.' Unless, of course, the spiritual and the temporal power are identified in one person as in the Pope, whose power is supreme in matters both temporal and spiritual, through the dispensation of Him Who is both priest and king; a Priest for ever according to the order of Melchisadech, the Kings of king and Lord of lords, Whose power shall not fail and Whose dominion shall not pass away to all eternity. Amen.

# 22

# Thomas Hobbes

Thomas Hobbes (1588–1679), writing for a generation beset by civil war, contrived a version of the social contract which obligated citizen but not sovereign and granted virtually unlimited legal powers to the latter.

# THE LEVIATHAN*

# CHAPTER SIXTEEN

## OF PERSONS, AUTHORS, AND THINGS PERSONATED

*A person what*

A person is he *whose words or actions are considered either as his own or as representing the words or actions of another man or of any other thing to whom they are attributed, whether truly or by fiction.*

*Person natural and artificial.*

When they are considered as his own, then is he called a *natural person;* and when they are considered as representing the words and actions of another, then is he a *feigned* or *artificial person.*

*The word person, whence.*

The word *person* is Latin, instead whereof the Greeks have πρόσωπον which signifies the *face,* as *persona* in Latin signifies the *disguise* or *outward appearance* of a man, counterfeited on the stage, and sometimes more particularly that part of it which disguises the face, as a mask or vizard; and from the stage has been translated to any representer of speech and action, as well in tribunals as theaters. So that a *person* is the same that an *actor* is, both on the stage and in common conversation; and to *personate* is to *act* or *represent* himself or another; and he that acts another is said to bear his person or act in his name–in which sense Cicero uses it where he says, *Unus sustineo tres personas: mei, adversarii, et judicis;* I bear three persons: my own, my adversary's and the judge's– and is called in divers occasions diversely, as a *representer* or *representative, a lieutenant, a vicar,* an *attorney,* a *deputy,* a *procurator,* an *actor,* and the like.

*Actor.*

Of persons artificial, some have their words, and actions *owned* by those whom they represent. And then the person is

*Thomas Hobbes, selections from *Leviathan,* Chap, 16 (in part), Chap. 17 (in part), Chap. 18. First published, 1651.

*Author*

the *actor*, and he that owns his words and actions is the AUTHOR; in which case the actor acts by authority. For that which in speaking of goods and possessions is called an *owner*–and in Latin *dominus*, in Greek κύριος– speaking of actions is called author. And as the right of possession is called dominion *Authority* so the right of doing any action is called AUTHORITY. So that

*Authority*

by *authority* is always understood a right of doing any act; and *done by authority*, done by commission or license from him whose right it is.

*Covenants by authority bind the author.*

"*contract*" –

From hence it follows that when the actor makes a (covenant) by authority, he binds thereby the author no less than if he had made it himself, and no less subjects him to all the consequences of the same. And therefore all that has been said formerly (chap. xiv) of the nature of covenants between man and man in their natural capacity is true also when they are made by their actors, representers, or procurators that have authority from them, so far forth as is in their commission, but no further.

And therefore he that makes a covenant with the actor or representer, not knowing the authority he has, does it at his own peril. For no man is obliged by a covenant whereof he is not author, nor consequently by a covenant made against or

*But not the actor.*

beside the authority he gave. When the actor does anything against the law of nature by command of the author, if he be obliged by former covenant to obey him, not he but the author breaks the law of nature, for though the action be against the law of nature, yet it is not his; but contrarily, to refuse to do it is against the law of nature that forbids breach of covenant.

*The authority is to be shown.*

And he that makes a covenant with the author by mediation of the actor, not knowing what authority he has, but only takes his word, in case such authority be not made manifest unto him upon demand, is no longer obliged; for the covenant made with the author is not valid without his counterassurance. But if he that so covenants knew beforehand he was to expect no other assurance than the actor's word, then is the covenant valid, because the actor in this case makes himself the author. And therefore, as when the authority is evident the covenant obliges the author, not the actor, so when the authority is feigned it obliges the actor only, there being no author but himself. . . .

*A multitude of men, how one person.*

A multitude of men are made *one* person when they are by one man or one person represented, so that it be done with the consent of every one of that multitude in particular. For it is the *unity* of the representer, not the *unity* of the represented, that makes the person *one*. And it is the representer that bears the person, and but one person; and *unity* cannot otherwise be understood in multitude.

*Everyone is author.*   And because the multitude naturally is not *one* but *many*, they cannot be understood for one but many authors of everything their representative says or does in their name, every man giving their common representer authority from himself in particular and owning all the actions the representer does, in case they give him authority without stint; otherwise, when they limit him in what and how far he shall represent them, none of them owns more than they gave him commission to act.

*An actor may be many men made one by plurality of voices.*   And if the representative consist of many men, the voice of the greater number must be considered as the voice of them all. For if the lesser number pronounce, for example, in the affirmative, and the greater in the negative, there will be negatives more than enough to destroy the affirmatives; and thereby the excess of negatives, standing uncontradicted, are the only voice the representative has. . . .

### FROM CHAPTER SEVENTEEN

*The generation of a commonwealth.*   The only way to erect such a common power as may be able to defend them from the invasion of foreigners and the injuries of one another, and thereby to secure them in such sort as that by their own industry and by the fruits of the earth they may nourish themselves and live contentedly, is to confer all their power and strength upon one man, or upon one assembly of men that may reduce all their wills, by plurality of voices, unto one will; which is as much as to say, to appoint one man or assembly of men to bear their person, and everyone to own and acknowledge himself to be author of whatsoever he that so bears their person shall act or cause to be acted in those things which concern the common peace and safety, and therein to submit their wills every one to his will, and their judgments to his judgment. This is more than consent or concord; it is real unity of them all in one and the same person, made by covenant of every man with every man, in such manner as if every man should say to every man, *I authorize and give up my right of governing myself to this man, or to this assembly of men, on this condition, that you give up your right to him and authorize all his actions in like manner.* This done, the multitude so united in one person is called a COMMONWEALTH, in Latin CIVITAS. This is the generation of that great LEVIATHAN (or rather, to speak more reverently, of that *mortal god*) to which we owe, under the *immortal God,* our peace and defense. For by this

*the people give authority to the sovereign* [handwritten annotation]

authority, given him by every particular man in the commonwealth, he has the use of so much power and strength conferred
on him that, by terror thereof, he is enabled to form the wills
of them all to peace at home and mutual aid against their
enemies abroad. And in him consists the essence of the
*The definition of a*
*commonwealth.*
commonwealth, which, to define it, is *one person, of whose acts*
*a great multitude, by mutual covenants one with another, have made*
*themselves every one the author, to the end he may use the strength and*
*means of them all as he shall think expedient for their peace and*
*common defense.*

And he that carries this person is called SOVEREIGN and said
*Sovereign and*
*subject, what.*
to have *sovereign power;* and everyone besides, his SUBJECT.

The attaining to this sovereign power is by two ways. One,
by natural force, as when a man makes his children to submit
themselves and their children to his government, as being able
to destroy them if they refuse, or by war subdues his enemies to
his will, giving them their lives on that condition. The other is
when men agree among themselves to submit to some man or
assembly of men voluntarily, on confidence to be protected by
him against all others. This latter may be called a political
commonwealth, or commonwealth by *institution,* and the
former a commonwealth by *acquisition.* And first I shall speak
of a commonwealth by institution.

CHAPTER EIGHTEEN

## OF THE RIGHTS OF SOVEREIGNS BY INSTITUTION

*The act of instituting*
*a commonwealth, what.*
A *commonwealth* is said to be *instituted* when a *multitude* of men
do agree and *covenant, every one with every one,* that to whatsoever
*man* or *assembly of men* shall be given by the major part the *right*
to *present* the person of them all—that is to say, to be their
*representative*—every one, as well he that *voted for it* as he that
*voted against it,* shall *authorize* all the actions and judgments of
that man or assembly of men in the same manner as if they
were his own, to the end to live peaceably among themselves
and be protected against other men.

*The consequences to*
*such institutions, are:*
From this institution of a commonwealth are derived all
the *rights* and *faculties* of him or them on whom the sovereign
power is conferred by the consent of the people assembled.

*1. The subjects cannot*
*change the form of*
*government.*
First, because they covenant, it is to be understood they
are not obliged by former covenant to anything repugnant
hereunto. And consequently they that have already instituted
a commonwealth, being thereby bound by covenant to own the
actions and judgments of one, cannot lawfully make a new

*cannot release*
*themselves (legally?)*
*from obligation(?)*

covenant among themselves to be obedient to any other, in
anything whatsoever, without his permission. And therefore,
they that are subjects to a monarch cannot without his leave
cast off monarchy and return to the confusion of a disunited
multitude, nor transfer their person from him that bears it to
another man or other assembly of men; for they are bound,
every man to every man, to own and be reputed author of all
that he that already is their sovereign shall do and judge fit to
be done; so that any one man dissenting, all the rest should

*injustice* —→ ›
break their covenant made to that man, which is injustice;
and they have also every man given the sovereignty to him
that bears their person, and therefore if they depose him they
take from him that which is his own, and so again it is injustice.
Besides, if he that attempts to depose his sovereign be killed or
punished by him for such attempt, he is author of his own
punishment, as being by the institution author of all his
sovereign shall do; and because it is injustice for a man do do
anything for which he may be punished by his own authority,
he is also upon that title unjust. And whereas some men have
pretended for their disobedience to their sovereign a new
covenant, made not with men but with God, this also is unjust;

*covenant*
*with god*

for their is no covenant with God but by mediation of somebody that represents God's person, which none but God's
lieutenant, who has the sovereignty under God. But this
pretense of covenant with God is so evident a lie, even in the
pretenders' own consciences, that it is not only an act of an
unjust but also of a vile and unmanly disposition.

*2. Sovereign power
cannot be forfeited*

Secondly, because the right of bearing the person of them
all is given to him they make sovereign by covenant only of
one to another and not of him to any of them, there can happen
no breach of covenant on the part of the sovereign; and
consequently none of his subjects, by any pretense of forfeiture,
can be freed from his subjection. That he which is made
sovereign makes no covenant with his subjects beforehand is
manifest, because either he must make it with the whole
multitude, as one party to the covenant, or he must make a
several covenant with every man. With the whole, as one party,
it is impossible because as yet they are not one person; and if
he make so many several covenants as there be men, those
covenants after he has the sovereignty are void because what
act soever can be pretended by any one of them for breach
thereof is the act both of himself and of all the rest, because
done in the person and by the right of every one of them in
particular. Besides, if any one or more of them pretend a
breach of the covenant made by the sovereign at his institution,

and others, or one other of his subjects, or himself alone, pretend there was no such breach, there is in this case no judge to decide the controversy; it returns therefore to the sword again, and every man recovers the right of protecting himself by his own strength, contrary to the design they had in the institution. It is therefore in vain to grant sovereignty by way of precedent covenant. The opinion that any monarch receives his power by covenant—that is to say, on condition—proceeds from want of understanding this easy truth: that covenants, being but words and breath, have <u>no force to oblige</u>, contain, constrain, or protect any man but what it has from the public sword—that is, from the untied hands of that man or assembly of men that has the sovereignty, and whose actions are avouched by them all and performed by the strength of them all in him united. But when an assembly of men is made sovereign, then no man imagines any such covenant to have passed in the institution; for no man is so dull as to say, for example, the people of Rome made a covenant with the Romans to hold the sovereignty on such or such conditions, which not performed, the Romans might lawfully depose the Roman people. That men see not the reason to be alike in a monarchy and in a popular government proceeds from the ambition of some that are kinder to the government of an assembly, whereof they may hope to participate, than of monarchy, which they despair to enjoy.

3. *No man can without injustice protest against the institution of the sovereign declared by the major part.*

Thirdly, because the major part has by consenting voices declared a sovereign, he that dissented must now consent with the rest—that is, be contented to avow all the actions he shall do—or else justly be destroyed by the rest. For if he voluntarily entered into the congregation of them that were assembled, he sufficiently declared thereby his will, and therefore tacitly covenanted, to stand to what the major part should ordain; and therefore, if he refuse to stand thereto or make protestation against any of their decrees, he does contrary to his covenant, and therefore unjustly. And whether he be of the congregation or not, and whether his consent be asked or not, he must either submit to their decrees or be left in the condition of war he was in before, wherein he might without injustice be destroyed by any man whatsoever.

4. *The Sovereign's actions cannot be justly accused by the subject.*

Fourthly, because every subject is by this institution author of all the actions and judgments of the sovereign instituted, it follows that whatsoever he does, it can be no injury to any of his subjects; nor ought he to be by any of them accused of injustice. For he that does anything by authority from another does therein no injury to him by whose authority he acts; but by this institution of a commonwealth, every particular man is author of all the sovereign does; and consequently he that complains of injury from his sovereign complains of that whereof he himself is author, and therefore ought not to accuse any man but himself—no, nor himself of *faul* injury, because to do injury to one's self is impossible. It is true *109* that that they have sovereign power may commit iniquity, but not injustice or injury in the proper signification.

5. *Whatsoever the sovereign does is unpunishable by the subject.*

Fifthly, and consequently to that which was said last, no man that has sovereign power can justly be put to death or otherwise in any manner by his subjects punished. For seeing every subject is author of the actions of his sovereign, he punishes another for the actions committed by himself.

6. *The sovereign is judge of what is necessary for the peace and defense of his subjects.*

And because the end of this institution is the peace and defense of them all, and whosoever has the right to the end has right to the means, it belongs of right to whatsoever man or assembly that has the sovereignty to be judge both of the means of peace and defense and also of the hindrances and disturbances of the same, and to do whatsoever he shall think necessary to be done, both beforehand, for the preserving of peace and security by prevention of discord at home and hostility from abroad, and, when peace and security are lost, for the recovery of the same. And therefore,

*And judge of what doctrines are fit to be taught them.*

Sixthly, it is annexed to the sovereignty to be judge of what opinions and doctrines are averse and what conducing to peace, and consequently on what occasions, how far, and what men are to be trusted withal in speaking to multitudes of people, and who shall examine the doctrines of all books before they be published. For the actions of men proceed from their opinions, and in the well-governing of opinions consists the well-governing of men's actions, in order to their peace and concord. And though in matter of doctrine nothing ought to be regarded but the truth, yet this is not repugnant to regulating the same by peace. For doctrine repugnant to peace can no more be true than peace and concord can be against the law of nature. It is true that in a commonwealth, where by the negligence or unskillfulness of governors and teachers false doctrines are by time generally received, the contrary truths may be generally offensive. Yet the most sudden and rough bustling in of a new truth that can be does never break the peace but only sometimes awake the war. For those men that are so remissly governed that they dare take up arms to defend or introduce an opinion are still in war, and their condition not peace but only a cessation of arms for fear of one another, and they live, as it were, in the precincts of battle continually.

It belongs therefore to him that has the sovereign power to be judge or constitute all judges of opinions and doctrines as a thing necessary to peace, thereby to prevent discord and civil war.

*7. The right of making rules; whereby the subjects may every man know what is so his own, as no other subject can without injustice take it from him.*

Seventhly is annexed to the sovereignty the whole power of prescribing the rules whereby every man may know what goods he may enjoy and what actions he may do without being molested by any of his fellow subjects; and this is it men call *propriety*. For before constitution of sovereign power, as has already been shown, all men had right to all things, which necessarily causes war; and therefore this propriety, being necessary to peace and depending on sovereign power, is the act of that power in order to the public peace. These rules of propriety, or *meum* and *tuum*,[1] and of *good, evil, lawful,* and *unlawful* in the actions of subjects, are the civil laws—that is to say, the laws of each commonwealth in particular—though the name of civil law be now restrained to the ancient civil laws of the city of Rome, which being the head a of great part of the world, her laws at that time were in these parts the civil law.

*8. To him also belongs the right of all judicature and decision of controversy.*

Eighthly is annexed to the sovereignty the right of judicature—that is to say, of hearing and deciding all controversies which may arise concerning law, either civil or natural, or concerning fact. For without the decision of controversies, there is no protection of one subject against the injuries of another; the laws concerning *meum* and *tuum* are in vain; and to every man remains, from the natural and necessary appetite of his own conservation, the right of protecting himself by his private strength, which is the condition of war and contrary to the end for which every commonwealth is instituted.

*9. And of making war and peace as he shall think best.*

Ninthly is annexed to the sovereignty the right of making war and peace with other nations and commonwealths—that is to say, of judging when it is for the public good, and how great forces are to be assembled, armed, and paid for that end, and to levy money upon the subjects to defray the expenses thereof. For the power by which the people are to be defended consists in their armies, and the strength of an army in the union of their strength under one command, which command the sovereign instituted therefore has; because the command of the *militia*, without other institution, makes him that has it sovereign. And therefore whosoever is made general of an army, he that has the sovereign power is always generalissimo.

---

[1][Mine and thine.]

10. *And of choosing all counselors and ministers, both of peace and war.*

Tenthly is annexed to the sovereignty the choosing of all counselors, ministers, magistrates, and officers, both in peace and war. For seeing the sovereign is charged with the end, which is the common peace and defense, he is understood to have power to use such means as he shall think most fit for his discharge.

11. *And of rewarding and punishing, and that (where no former law has determined the measure of it) arbitrarily.*

Eleventhly, to the sovereign is committed the power of rewarding with riches or honor, and of punishing with corporal or pecuniary punishment or with ignominy, every subject according to the law he has formerly made; or if there be no law made, according as he shall judge most to conduce to the encouraging of men to serve the commonwealth or deterring of them from doing disservice to the same.

12. *And of honor and order.*

Lastly, considering what value men are naturally apt to set upon themselves, what respect they look for from others, and how little they value other men—from whence continually arise among them emulations, quarrels, factions, and at last war, to the destroying of one another and diminution of their strength against a common enemy—it is necessary that there be laws of honor and a public rate of the worth of such men as have deserved or are able to deserve well of the commonwealth, and that there be force in the hands of some or other to put those laws in execution. But it has already been shown that not only the whole *militia* or forces of the commonwealth, but also the judicature of all controversies is annexed to the sovereignty. To the sovereign therefore it belongs also to give titles of honor, and to appoint what order of place and dignity each man shall hold, and what signs of respect, in public or private meetings, they shall give to one another.

*These rights are indivisible.*

These are the rights which make the essence of sovereignty, and which are the marks whereby a man may discern in what man or assembly of men the sovereign power is placed and resides. For these are incommunicable and inseparable. The power to coin money, to dispose of the estate and persons of infant heirs, to have pre-emption in markets, and all other statute prerogatives may be transferred by the sovereign, and yet the power to protect his subjects be retained. But if he transfers the *militia,* he retains the judicature in vain for want of execution of the laws; or if he grant away the power of raising money, the *militia* is in vain; or if he give away the government of doctrines, men will be frighted into rebellion with the fear of spirits. And so if we consider any one of the said rights, we shall presently see that the holding of all the rest will produce no effect in the conservation of peace and justice, the end for which all commonwealths are instituted.

And this division is it whereof it is said *a kingdom divided in itself cannot stand;* for unless this division precede, division into opposite armies can never happen. If there had not first been an opinion received of the greatest part of England that these powers were divided between the King and the Lords and the House of Commons, the people had never been divided and fallen into this civil war—first between those that disagreed in politics and after between the dissenters about the liberty of religion—which has so instructed men in this point of sovereign right that there be few now in England that do not see that these rights are inseparable and will be so generally acknowledged at the next return of peace; and so continue till their miseries are forgotten, and no longer, except the vulgar be better taught than they have hitherto been.

*And can by no grant pass away without direct renouncing of the sovereign power.*

And because they are essential and inseparable rights, it follows necessarily that in whatsoever words any of them seem to be granted away, yet if the sovereign power itself be not in direct terms renounced and the name of sovereign no more given by the grantees to him that grants them, the grant is void; for when he has granted all he can, if we grant back the sovereignty all is restored as inseparably annexed thereunto.

*The power and honor of subjects vanishes in the presence of the power sovereign.*

This great authority being indivisible and inseparably annexed to the sovereignty, there is little ground for the opinion of them that say of sovereign kings, though they be *singulis majores,* of greater power than every one of their subjects, yet they be *universis minores,* or less power than them all together. For if by *all together* they mean not the collective body as one person, then *all together* and *every one* signify the same, and the speech is absurd. But if by *all together* they understand them as one person, which person the sovereign bears, then the power of all together is the same with the sovereign's power, and so again the speech is absurd; which absurdity they see well enough when the sovereignty is in an assembly of the people, but in a monarch they see it not; and yet the power of sovereignty is the same in whomsoever it be placed.

And as the power, so also the honor of the sovereign ought to be greater than that of any or all the subjects. For in the sovereignty is the fountain of honor. The dignities of lord, earl, duke, and prince are his creatures. As in the presence of the master the servants are equal, and without any honor at all, so are the subjects in the presence of the sovereign. And though they shine some more, some less, when they are out of his sight, yet in his presence they shine no more than the stars in the presence of the sun.

*Sovereign power not
so hurtful as the want
of it, and the hurt
proceeds for the
greatest part from not
submitting readily to a
less.*

But a man may here object that the condition of subjects is very miserable, as being obnoxious to the lusts and other irregular passions of him or them that have so unlimited a power in their hands. And commonly they that live under a monarch think it the fault of monarchy, and they that live under the government of democracy or other sovereign assembly attribute all the inconvenience to that form of commonwealth, whereas the power in all forms, if they be perfect enough to protect them, is the same—not considering that the state of man can never be without some incommodity or other, and that the greatest that in any form of government can possibly happen to the people in general is scarce sensible in respect of the miseries and horrible calamities that accompany a civil war or that dissolute condition of masterless men, without subjection to laws and a coercive power to tie their hands from rapine and revenge; nor considering that the greatest pressure of sovereign governors proceeds not from any delight or profit they can expect in the damage or weakening of their subjects, in whose vigor consists their own strength and glory, but in the restiveness of themselves that, unwillingly contributing to their own defense, make it necessary for their governors to draw from them what they can in time of peace that they may have means on any emergent occasion or sudden need to resist or take advantage on their enemies. For all men are by nature provided of notable multiplying glasses—that is, their passions and self-love—through which every little payment appears a great grievance, but are destitute of those prospective glasses—namely, moral and civil science—to see afar off the miseries that hang over them and cannot without such payments be avoided.

# 23

# John Locke

John Locke (1632–1704) centered the rule of law on the legislative power, limited by the natural rights of "life, liberty and estate."

# THE SECOND TREATISE OF CIVIL GOVERNMENT*

## OF THE EXTENT OF THE LEGISLATIVE POWER

134. The great end of men's entering into society being the enjoyment of their properties in peace and safety, and the great instrument and means of that being the laws established in that society: the first and fundamental positive law of all commonwealths, is the establishing of the legislative power; as the first and fundamental natural law, which is to govern even the legislative itself, is the preservation of the society, and (as far as will consist with the public good) of every person in it. This legislative is not only the supreme power of the commonwealth, but sacred and unalterable in the hands where the community have once placed it; nor can any edict of anybody else, in what form soever conceived, or by what power soever backed, have the force and obligation of a law, which has not its sanction from that legislative which the public has chosen and appointed. For without this the law could not have that, which is absolutely necessary to its being a law, the consent of the society over whom nobody can have a power to make laws; but by their own consent, and by authority received from them; and therefore all the obedience, which by the most solemn ties any one can be obliged to pay, ultimately terminates in this supreme power, and is directed by those laws which it enacts; nor can any oaths to any foreign power whatsoever, or any domestic subordinate power discharge any member of the society from his obedience to the legislative, acting pursuant to their trust; nor oblige him to any obedience contrary to the laws so enacted, or farther than they do allow; it being ridiculous to imagine one can be tied ultimately to obey any power in the society which is not the supreme.

135. Though the legislative, whether placed in one or more, whether it be always in being, or only by intervals, though it be the supreme power in every commonwealth, yet.

First, It is not nor can possibly be absolutely arbitrary over the lives and fortunes of the people. For it being but the joint power of every member of the

*John Locke, *The Second Treatise of Civil Government*, Chap. XI. First published in 1690.

society given up to that person, or assembly, which is legislator; it can be no more than those persons had in a state of nature before they entered into society, and gave it up to the community. For nobody can transfer to another more power than he has in himself; and nobody has an absolute arbitrary power over himself, or over any other to destroy his own life, or take away the life or property of another. A man, as has been proved, cannot subject himself to the arbitrary power of another; and having in the state of nature no arbitrary power over the life, liberty, or possession of another, but only so much as the law of nature gave him for the preservation of himself, and the rest of mankind; this is all he doth, or can give up to the commonwealth, and by it to the legislative power, so that the legislative can have no more than this. Their power in the utmost bounds of it, is limited to the public good of the society. It is a power that hath no other end but preservation, and therefore can never have a right to destroy, enslave, or designedly to impoverish the subjects. The obligations of the law of nature cease not in society, but only in many cases are drawn closer, and have by human laws known penalties annexed to them to enforce their observation. Thus the law of nature stands as an eternal rule to all men, legislators as well as others. The rules that they make for other men's actions must, as well as their own and other men's actions, be conformable to the law of nature, *i.e.*, to the will of God, of which that is a declaration, and the fundamental law of nature being the preservation of mankind, no human sanction can be good or valid against it.

136. Secondly, The legislative, or supreme authority, cannot assume to itself a power to rule by extemporary arbitrary decrees, but is bound to dispense justice, and decide the rights of the subject by promulgated standing laws, and known authorised judges. For the law of nature being unwritten, and so nowhere to be found but in the minds of men, they who through passion or interest shall miscite or misapply it, cannot so easily be convinced of their mistake where there is no established judge. And so it serves not, as it ought, to determine the rights, and fence the properties of those that live under it, especially where every one is judge, interpreter, and executioner of it too, and that in his own case; and he that has right on his side, having ordinarily but his own single strength hath not force enough to defend himself from injuries, or punish delinquents. To avoid these inconveniences, which disorder men's properties in the state of nature, men unite into societies that they may have the united strength of the whole society to secure and defend their properties, and may have standing rules to bound it, by which every one may know what is his. To this end it is that men give up all their natural power to the society which they enter into, and the community put the legislative power into such hands as they think fit, with this trust, that they shall be governed by declared laws, or else their peace, quiet, and property will still be at the same uncertainty as it was in the state of nature.

137. Absolute arbitrary power, or governing without settled standing laws, can neither of them consist with the ends of society and government, which men would not quit the freedom of the state of nature for, and tie

themselves up under, were it not to preserve their lives, liberites, and fortunes; and by stated rules of right and property to secure their peace and quiet. It cannot be supposed that they should intend, had they a power so to do, to give to any one, or more, an absolute arbitrary power over their persons and estates, and put a force into the magistrate's hand to execute his unlimited will arbitrarily upon them. This were to put themselves into a worse condition than the state of nature, wherein they had a liberty to defend their right against the injuries of others, and were upon equal terms of force to maintain it, whether invaded by a single man or many in combination. Whereas, by supposing they have given up themselves to the absolute arbitrary power and will of a legislator, they have disarmed themselves, and harmed him, to make prey of them when he pleases. He being in a much worse condition that is exposed to the arbitrary power of one man who has the command of 100,000, than he that is exposed to the arbitrary power of 100,000 single men; nobody being secure that his will, who hath such a command, is better than that of other men, though his force be 100,000 times stronger. And, therefore, whatever form the commonwealth is under, the ruling power ought to govern by declared and received laws, and not by extemporary dictates and undetermined resolutions. For then mankind will be in a far worse condition than in the state of nature, if they shall have armed one, or a few men, with the joint power of a multitude to force them to obey at pleasure the exorbitant and unlimited decrees of their sudden thoughts, or unrestrained, and, till that moment, unknown wills, without having any measures set down which may guide and justify their actions. For all the power the government has, being only for the good of the society, as it ought not to be arbitrary and at pleasure, so it ought to be exercised by established and promulgated laws; that both the people may know their duty and be safe and secure within the limits of the law; and the rulers too kept within their due bounds, and not be tempted by the power they have in their hands to employ it to such purposes, and by such measures as they would not have known, and own not willingly.

138. Thirdly, The supreme power cannot take from any man any part of his property without his own consent. For the preservation of property being the end of government, and that for which men enter into society, it necessarily supposes and requires that the people should have property, without which they must be supposed to lose by entering into society, which was the end for which they entered into it, too gross an absurdity for any man to own. Men, therefore, in society having property, they have such a right to the goods which by the law of the community are theirs, that nobody hath a right to take them or any part of them from them, without their own consent; without this they have no property at all. For I have truly no property in that which another can by right take from me when he pleases, against my consent. Hence it is a mistake to think that the supreme or legislative power of any commonwealth can do what it will, and dispose of the estates of the subjects arbitrarily, or take any part of them at pleasure. This is not much to be feared in governments where the legislative consists wholly, or in part, in assemblies which are variable,

whose members, upon the dissolution of the assembly, are subjects under the common laws of their country, equally with the rest. But in governments where the legislative is in one lasting assembly, always in being, or in one man, as in absolute monarchies, there is danger still, that they will think themselves to have a distinct interest from the rest of the community, and so will be apt to increase their own riches and power by taking what they think fit from the people. For a man's property is not at all secure, though there be good and equitable laws to set the bounds of it between him and his fellow subjects, if he who commands those subjects have power to take from any private man what part he pleases of his property, and use and dispose of it as he thinks good.

139. But government, into whosesoever hands it is put, being, as I have before shown, entrusted with this condition, and for this end, that men might have and secure their properties, the prince, or senate, however it may have power to make laws for the regulating of property between the subjects one amongst another, yet can never have a power to take to themselves the whole or any part of the subjects' property without their own consent. For this would be in effect to leave them no property at all. And to let us see that even absolute power, where it is necessary, is not arbitrary by being absolute, but is still limited by that reason, and confined to those ends which required it in some cases to be absolute, we need look no farther than the common practice of martial discipline. For the preservation of the army, and in it the whole commonwealth, requires an absolute obedience to the command of every superior officer, and it is justly death to disobey or dispute the most dangerous or unreasonable of them; but yet we see that neither the sergeant, that could command a soldier to march up to the mouth of a cannon, or stand in a breach, where he is almost sure to perish, can command that soldier to give him one penny of his money; nor the general, that can condemn him to death for deserting his post, or not obeying the most desperate orders, cannot yet, with all his absolute power of life and death, dispose of one farthing of that soldier's estate, or seize one jot of his goods, whom yet he can command anything, and hang for the least disobedience. Because such a blind obedience is necessary to that end for which the commander has his power, *viz.*, the preservation of the rest; but the disposing of his goods has nothing to do with it.

140. 'Tis true governments cannot be supported without great charge, and it is fit every one who enjoys a share of the protection should pay out of his estate his proportion for the maintenance of it. But still it must be with his own consent, *i.e.*, the consent of the majority giving it either by themselves or their representatives chosen by them. For if any one shall claim a power to lay and levy taxes on the people, by his own authority, and without such consent of the people, he thereby invades the fundamental law of property, and subverts the end of government. For what property have I in that which another may by right take when he pleases to himself?

141. Fourthly, The legislative cannot transfer the power of making laws to any other hands; for it being but a delegated power from the people, they who have it cannot pass it over to others. The people alone can appoint the

form of the commonwealth, which is by constituting the legislative, and appointing in whose hands that shall be. And when the people have said we will submit to rules, and be governed by laws made by such men, and in such forms, nobody else can say other men shall make laws for them; nor can the people be bound by any laws but such as are enacted by those whom they have chosen and authorised to make laws for them.

142. These are the bounds which the trust that is put in them by the society, and the law of God and nature, have set to the legislative power of every commonwealth, in all forms of government.

First, They are to govern by promulgated established laws, not to be varied in particular cases, but to have one rule for rich and poor, for the favourite at court and the countryman at plough.

Secondly, These laws also ought to be designed for no other end ultimately but the goods of the people.

Thirdly, They must not raise taxes on the property of the people without the consent of the people, given by themselves or their deputies. And this properly concerns only such governments where the legislative is always in being, or at least where the people have not reserved any part of the legislative to deputies, to be from time to time chosen by themselves.

Fourthly, The legislative neither must nor can transfer the power of making laws to anybody else, or place it anywhere but where the people have.

# 24

# Hans Kelsen

Hans Kelsen attempts to formulate a 'pure' theory of law applicable to all historical legal systems which, he argues, are based upon logically prior 'basic norms.'

# GENERAL THEORY OF LAW AND STATE*

## NOMODYNAMICS. X. THE LEGAL ORDER

### A. The Unity of a Normative Order

#### a. The Reason of Validity: the Basic Norm

The legal order is a system of norms. The question then arises: What is it that makes a system out of a multitude of norms? When does a norm belong to a certain system of norms, an order? This question is in close connection with the question as to the reason of validity of a norm.

In order to answer this question, we must first clarify the grounds on which we assign validity to a norm. When we assume the truth of a statement about reality, it is because the statement corresponds to reality, because our experience confirms it. The statement "A physical body expands when heated" is true, because we have repeatedly and without exception observed that physical bodies expand when they are heated. A norm is not a statement about reality and is therefore incapable of being "true" or "false", in the sense determined above. A norm is either valid or non-valid. Of the two statements: "You shall assist a fellowman in need," and "You shall lie whenever you find it useful," only the first, not the second, is considered to express a valid norm. What is the reason?

The reason for the validity of a norm is not, like the test of the truth of an "is" statement, its conformity to reality. As we have already stated, a norm is not valid because it is efficacious. The question why something ought to occur can never be answered by an assertion to the effect that something occurs, but only by an assertion that something ought to occur. In the language of daily life, it is true, we frequently justify a norm by referring to a fact. We say, for instance: "You shall not kill because God has forbidden it in one of the Ten Commandments"; or a mother says to her child: "You ought to go to school because your father has ordered it." However, in these statements the fact that

---

*Hans Kelsen, *General Theory of Law and State,* Translated by Anders Wedberg [© 1945] New York: Russell & Russell, 1961, pp. 110–123.

God has issued a command or the fact that the father has ordered the child to do something is only apparently the reason for the validity of the norms in question. The true reason is norms tacitly presupposed because taken for granted. The reason for the validity of the norm, You shall not kill, is the general norm, You shall obey the commands of God. The reason for the validity of the norm, You ought to go to school, is the general norm, Children ought to obey their father. If these norms are not presupposed, the references to the facts concerned are not answers to the questions why we shall not kill, why the child ought to go to school. The fact that somebody commands something is, in itself, no reason for the statement that one ought to behave in conformity with the command, no reason for considering the command as a valid norm, no reason for the validity of the norm the contents of which corresponds to the command. The reason for the validity of a norm is always a norm, not a fact. The quest for the reason of validity of a norm leads back, not to reality, but to another norm from which the first norm is derivable in a sense that will be investigated later. Let us, for the present, discuss a concrete example. We accept the statement "You shall assist a fellowman in need," as a valid norm because it follows from the statement "You shall love your neighbor." This statement we accept as a valid norm, either because it appears to us as an ultimate norm whose validity is self-evident, or–for instance–Christ has bidden that you shall love your neighbor, and we postulate as an ultimate valid norm the statement "You shall obey the commandments of Christ." The statement "You shall lie whenever you find it useful," we do not accept as a valid norm, because it is neither derivable from another valid norm nor is it in itself an ultimate, self-evidently valid norm.

A norm the validity of which cannot be derived from a superior norm we call a "basic" norm. All norms whose validity may be traced back to one and the same basic norm form a system of norms, or an order. This basic norm constitutes, as a common source, the bond between all the different norms of which an order consists. That a norm belongs to a certain system of norms, to a certain normative order, can be tested only by ascertaining that it derives its validity from the basic norm constituting the order. Whereas an "is" statement is true because it agrees with the reality of sensuous experience, an "ought" statement is a valid norm only if it belongs to such a valid system of norms, if it can be derived from a basic norm presupposed as valid. The ground of truth of an "is" statement is its conformity to the reality of our experience; the reason for the validity of a norm is a presupposition, a norm presupposed to be an ultimately valid, that is, a basic norm. The quest for the reason of validity of a norm is not – like the quest for the cause of an effect – a *regressus ad infinitum;* it is terminated by a highest norm which is the last reason of validity within the normative system, whereas a last or first cause has no place within a system of natural reality.

### b. The Static System of Norms

According to the nature of the basic norm, we may distinguish between two

*static*

different types of orders or normative systems: static and dynamic systems. Within an order of the first kind the norms are "valid" and that means, we assume that the individuals whose behavior is regulated by the norms "ought" to behave as the norms prescribe, by virtue of their contents: Their contents has an immediately evident quality that guarantees their validity, or, in other terms: the norms are valid because of their inherent appeal. This quality the norms have because they are derivable from a specific basic norm as the particular is derivable from the general. The binding force of the basic norm is itself self-evident, or at least presumed to be so. Such norms as "You must not lie," "You must not deceive," "You shall keep your promise," follow from a general norm prescribing truthfulness. From the norm "You shall love your neighbor" one may deduce such norms as "You must not hurt your neighbor," "You shall help him in need," and so on. If one asks why one has to love one's neighbor, perhaps the answer will be found in some still more general norm, let us say the postulate that one has to live "in harmony with the universe." If that is the most general norm of whose validity we are convinced, we will consider it as the ultimate norm. Its obligatory nature may appear so obvious that one does not feel any need to ask for the reason of its validity. Perhaps one may also succeed in deducing the principle of truthfulness and its consequences from this "harmony" postulate. One would then have reached a norm on which a whole system of morality could be based. However, we are not interested here in the question of what specific norm lies at the basis of such and such a system of morality. It is essential only that the various norms of any such system are implicated by the basic norm as the particular is implied by the general, and that, therefore, all the particular norms of such a system are obtainable by means of an intellectual operation, viz., by the inference from the general to the particular. Such a system is on a static nature.

### c. The Dynamic System of Norms

The derivation of a particular norm may, however, be carried out also in another way. A child, asking why it must not lie, might be given the answer that its father has forbidden it to lie. If the child should further ask why it has to obey its father, the reply would perhaps be that God has commanded that it obey its parents. Should the child put the question why one has to obey the commands of God, the only answer would be that this is a norm beyond which one cannot look for a more ultimate norm. That norm is the basic norm providing the foundation for a system of dynamic character. Its various norms cannot be obtained from the basic norm by any intellectual operation. The basic norm merely establishes a certain authority, which may well in turn vest norm-creating power in some other authorities. The norms of a dynamic system have to be created through acts of will by those individuals who have been authorized to create norms by some higher norm. This authorization is a delegation. Norm creating power is delegated from one authroity to another authority; the former is the higher, the latter the lower authority. The basic norm of a dynamic system is the fundamental rule according to which the norms of the system are to be created. A norm forms part of a dynamic system if it has been created in a way that is – in the last analysis – determined by the basic norm. A norm thus belongs to the religious system just given by way of example if it is created by God or originates in an authority having its power from God, "delegated" by God.

## B. The Law as a Dynamic System of Norms

### a. The Positivity of Law

The system of norms we call a legal order is a system of the dynamic kind. Legal norms are not valid because they themselves or the basic norm have a content the binding force of which is self-evident. They are not valid because of their inherent appeal. Legal norms may have any kind of content. There is no kind of human behavior that, because of its nature, could not be made into a legal duty corresponding to a legal right. The validity of a legal norm cannot be questioned on the ground that its contents are incompatible with some moral or political value. A norm is a valid legal norm by virtue of the fact that it has been created according to a definite rule and by virtue of the fact that it has been created according to a definite rule and by virtue thereof only. The basic norm of a legal order is the postulated ultimate rule according to which the norms of this order are established and annulled, receive and lose their validity. The statement "Any man who manufactures or sells alcoholic liquors as beverages shall be punished" is a valid legal norm if it belongs to a certain legal order. This it does if this norm has been created in a definite way ultimately determined by the basic norm of that legal order, and if it has not again been nullified in a definite way, ultimately determined by the same basic norm. The basic norm may, for instance, be such that a norm belongs to the system provided that it has been decreed by the parliament or created by custom or established by the courts, and has not been abolished by a decision of the parliament or through custom or a contrary court practice. The statement mentioned above is no valid legal norm if it does not belong to a valid legal order—it may be that no such norm has been created in the way ultimately determined by the basic norm, or it may be that, although a norm has been created in that way, it has been repealed in a way ultimately determined by the basic norm.

Law is always positive law, and its positivity lies in the fact that it is created and annulled by acts of human beings, thus being independent of morality and similar norm systems. This constitutes the difference between positive law and natural law, which, like morality, is deduced from a presumably self-evident basic norm which is considered to be the expression of the "will of nature" or of "pure reason." The basic norm of a positive legal order is nothing but the fundamental rule according to which the various norms of the order are to be created. It qualifies a certain event as the initial event in the creation of the various legal norms. It is the starting point of a norm-creating process and, thus, has an entirely dynamic character. The particular norms of the legal order cannot be logically deduced from this basic norm, as can the norm "Help your neighbor when he needs your help" from the norm "Love your neighbor." They are to be created by a special act of will, not concluded from a premise by an intellectual operation.

### b. Customary and Statutory Law

Legal norms are created in many different ways: general norms through custom or legislation, individual norms through judicial and administrative acts or legal transactions. Law is always created by an act that deliberately aims at creating law, except in the case when law has its origin in custom, that is to say, in a generally observed course of conduct, during which the acting individuals do not consciously aim at creating law; but they must regard their acts as in conformity with a binding norm and not as a matter of arbitrary choice. This is the requirement of so-called *opinio juris sive necessitatis*. The usual interpretation of this requirement is that the individuals constituting by their conduct the law-creating custom must regard their acts as determined by a legal rule; they must believe that they perform a legal duty or exercise a legal right. This doctrine is not correct. It implies that the individuals concerned must act in error: since the legal rule which is created by their conduct cannot yet determine this conduct, at least not as a legal rule. They may erroneously believe themselves to be bound by a rule of law, but this error is not necessary to constitute a law-creating custom. It is sufficient that the acting individuals consider themselves bound by any norm whatever.

We shall distinguish between statutory and customary law as the two fundamental types of law. By statutory law we shall understand law created in a way other than by custom, namely, by legislative, judicial, or administrative acts or by legal transactions, especially by contracts and (international) treaties.

### C. THE BASIC NORM OF A LEGAL ORDER

### a. The Basic Norm and the Constitution

The derivation of the norms of a legal order from the basic norm of that order is performed by showing that the particular norms have been created in accordance with the basic norm. To the question why a certain act of coercion—e.g., the fact that one individual deprives another individual of his freedom by putting him in jail—is a legal act, the answer is: because it has been prescribed by an individual norm, a judicial decision. To the question why this individual norm is valid as part of a definite legal order, the answer is: because it has been created in conformity with a criminal statute. This statute, finally, receives its validity from the constitution, since it has been established by the competent organ in the way the constitution prescribes.

The basic norm must be established by an authority or power. Kelsen fundamental premise as to how a legal order begins is very similar to Hobbes. Hobbes would say that sovereignty not only creates, but is, the basic norm.

If we ask why the constitution is valid, perhaps we come upon an older constitution. Ultimately we reach some constitution that is the first historically and that was laid down by an <u>individual usurper or by some kind of assembly</u>. The validity of this first constitution is the last presupposition, the final postulate, upon which the validity of all the norms of our legal order depends. It is postulated that one ought to behave as the individual, or the individuals, who laid down the first constitution have ordained. This is the basic norm of the legal order under consideration. The document which embodies the first constitution is a real constitution, a binding norm, only on the condition that the basic norm is presupposed to be valid. Only upon this presupposition are the declarations of those to whom the constitution confers norm-creating power binding norms. It is this presupposition that enables us to distinguish between individuals who are legal authorities and other individuals whom we do not regard as such, between acts of human beings which create legal norms and acts which have no such effect. All these legal norms belong to one and the same legal order because their validity can be traced back—directly or indirectly—to the first constitution. That the first constitution is a binding legal norm is presupposed, and the formulation of the presupposition is the basic norm of this legal order. The basic norm of a religious norm system says that one ought to behave as God and the authorities instituted by Him command. Similarly, the basic norm of a legal order prescribes that one ought to behave as the "fathers" of the constitution and the individuals—directly or indirectly—authorized (delegated) by the constitution command. Expressed in the form of a legal norm: coercive acts ought to be carried out only under the conditions and in the way determined by the "fathers" of the constitution or the organs delegated by them. This is schematically formulated, the basic norm of the legal order of a single State, the basic norm of a national legal order. It is to the national legal order that we have here limited our attention. Later, we shall consider what bearing the assumption of an international law has upon the question of the basic norm of national law.

### b. The Specific Function of the Basic Norm

That a norm of the kind just mentioned is the basic norm of the national legal order does not imply that it is impossible to go beyond that norm. Certainly one may ask why one has to respect the first constitution as a binding norm. The answer might be that the fathers of the first constitution were empowered by God. The characteristic of so-called <u>legal positivism</u> is, however, that it dispenses with any such religious justification of the legal order. The ultimate hypothesis of positivism is the norm authorizing the historically first legislator. The whole function of this basic norm is to confer law-creating power on the act of the first legislator and on all the other acts based on the first act. To interpret these acts of human beings as legal acts and their products as binding norms, and that means to interpret the empirical material which presents itself as law as such, is possible only on the condition that the basic norm is presupposed as a valid norm. The basic norm is only the necessary presupposition of any positivistic interpretation of the legal material.

The basic norm is not created in a legal procedure by a law-creating organ. It is not—as a positive legal norm is—valid because it is created in a certain way by a legal act, but it is valid because it is presupposed to be valid; and it is presupposed to be valid without this presupposition no human act could be interpreted as a legal, especially as a norm-creating, act.

By formulating the basic norm, we do not introduce into the science of law any new method. We merely make explicit what all jurists, mostly  unconsciously, assume when they consider positive law as a system of valid norms and not only as a complex of facts, and at the same time repudiate any natural law from which positive law would receive its validity. That the basic norm really exists in the juristic consciousness is the result of a simple analysis of actual juristic statements. The basic norm is the answer to the question: how—and that means under what condition—are all these juristic statements concerning legal norms, legal duties, legal rights, and so on, possible?

### c. The Principle of Legitimacy

The validity of legal norms may be limited in time, and it is important to notice that the end as well as the beginning of this validity is determined only by the order to which they belong. They remain valid as long as they have not been invalidated in the way which the legal order itself determines. This is the principle of legitimacy.

 This principle, however, holds only under certain conditions. It fails to hold in the case of a revolution, this word understood in the most general sense, so that it also covers the so-called *coup d'Etat*. A revolution, in this wide sense, occurs whenever the legal order of a community is nullified and replaced by a new order in an illegitimate way, that is in a way not prescribed by the first order itself. It is in this context irrelevant whether or not this replacement is effected through a violent uprising against those individuals who so far have been the "legitimate" organs competent to create and amend the legal order. It is equally irrelevant whether the replacement is effected through a movement emanating from the mass of the people, or through action from those in government positions. From a juristic point of view, the decisive criterion of a revolution is that the order in force is overthrown and replaced by a new order in a way which the former had not itself anticipated. Usually, the new men whom a revolution brings to power annual only the constitution and certain laws of paramount political significance, putting other norms in their place. A great part of the old legal order "remains" valid also within the frame of the new order. But the phrase "they remain valid," does not give an adequate description of the phenomenon. It is only the contents of these norms that remain the same, not the reason of their validity. They are no longer valid by virtue of having been created in the way the old constitution prescribed. That constitution is no longer in force; it is replaced by a new constitution which is not

the result of a constitutional alteration of the former. If laws which were introduced under the old constitution "continue to be valid" under the new constitution, this is possible only because validity has expressly or tacitly been vested in them by the new constitution. The phenomenon is a case of reception (similar to the reception of Roman law). The new order "receives," i.e., adopts, norms from the old order; this means that the new order gives validity to (puts into force) norms which have the same content as norms of the old order. "Reception" is an abbreviated procedure of law-creation. The laws which, in the ordinary inaccurate parlance, continue to be valid are, from a juristic viewpoint, new laws whose import coincides with that of the old laws. They are not identical with the old laws, because the reason for their validity is different. The reason for their validity is the new, not the old, constitution, and between the two continuity holds neither from the point of view of the one nor from that of the other. Thus, it is never the constitution merely but always the entire legal order that is changed by a revolution.

This shows that all norms of the old order have been deprived of their validity by revolution and not according to the principle of legitimacy. And they have been so deprived not only *de facto* but also *de jure*. No jurist would maintain that even after a successful revolution the old constitution and the laws based thereupon remain in force, on the ground that they have not been nullified in a manner anticipated by the old order itself. Every jurist will presume that the old order—to which no political reality any longer corresponds—has ceased to be valid, and that all norms, which are valid within the new order, receive their validity exclusively from the new constitution. It follows that, from this juristic point of view, the norms of the old order can no longer be recognized as valid norms.

### d. Change of the Basic Norm

It is just the phenomenon of revolution which clearly shows the significance of the basic norm. Suppose that a group of individuals attempt to seize power by force, in order to remove the legitimate government in a hitherto monarchic State, and to introduce a republican form of government. If they succeed, if the old order ceases, and the new order begins to be efficacious, because the individuals whose behavior the new order regulates actually behave, by and large, in conformity with the new order, then this order is considered as a valid order. It is now according to this new order that the actual behavior of individuals is interpreted as legal or illegal. But this means that a new basic norm is presupposed. It is no longer the norm according to which the old monarchical constitution is valid, but a norm according to which the new republican constitution is valid, a norm endowing the revolutionary government with legal authority. If the revolutionaries fail, if the order they have tried to establish remains inefficacious, then, on the other hand, their undertaking is interpreted, not as a legal, a law-creating act, as the establishment of a constitution, but as an illegal act, as the crime of treason, and this according to the old monarchic constitution and its specific basic norm.

## e. The Principle of Effectiveness

If we attempt to make explicit the presupposition on which these juristic considerations rest, we find that the norms of the old order are regarded as devoid of validity because the old constitution and, therefore, the legal norms based on this constitution, the old legal order as a whole, has lost its efficacy; because the actual behavior of men does no longer conform to this old legal order. Every single norm loses its validity when the total legal order to which it belongs loses its efficacy as a whole. The efficacy of the entire legal order is a necessary condition for the validity of every single norm of the order. A *conditio sine qua non,* but not a *conditio per quam.* The efficacy of the total legal order is a condition, not the reason for the validity of its constituent norms. These norms are valid not because the total order is efficacious, but because they are created in a constitutional way. They are valid, however, only on the condition that the total order is efficacious; they cease to be valid, not only when they are annulled in a constitutional way, but also when the total order ceases to be efficacious. It cannot be maintained that, legally, men have to behave in conformity with a certain norm, if the total legal order, of which that norm is an integral part, has lost its efficacy. The principle of legitimacy is restricted by the principle of effectiveness.

## f. Desuetudo

This must not be understood to mean that a single legal norm loses its validity, if that norm itself and only that norm is rendered ineffective. Within a legal order which as a whole is efficacious there may occur isolated norms which are valid and which yet are not efficacious, that is, are not obeyed and not applied even when the conditions which they themselves lay down for their application are fulfilled. But even in this case efficacy has some relevance to validity. If the norm remains permanently inefficacious, the norm is deprived of its validity by "desuetudo." "Desuetudo" is the negative legal effect of custom. A norm may be annulled by custom, viz., by a custom contrary to the norm, as well as it may be created by custom. Desuetudo annuals a norm by creating another norm, identical in character with a statute whose only function is to repeal a previously valid statute. The much-discussed question whether a statute may also be invalidated by desuetudo is ultimately the question whether custom as a source of law may be excluded by statute within a legal order. For reasons which will be given later, the question must be answered in the negative. It must be assumed that any legal norm, even a statutory norm, may lose validity by desuetudo.

However, even in this case it would be a mistake to identify the validity and the efficacy of the norm; they are still two different phenomena. The norm annulled by desuetudo was valid for a considerable time without being efficacious. It is only an enduring lack of efficacy that ends the validity.

The relation between validity and efficacy thus appears to be the following: A norm is a valid legal norm if (a) it has been created in a way provided for by the legal order to which it belongs, and (b) if it has not been annulled either in a way provided for by that legal order or by way of desuetudo or by the fact that the legal order as a whole has lost its efficacy.

### g. The "Ought" and the "Is"

The basic norm of a national legal order is not the arbitrary product of juristic imagination. Its content is determined by facts. The function of the basic norm is to make possible the normative interpretation of certain facts, and that means, the interpretation of facts as the creation and application of valid norms. Legal norms, as we point out, are considered to be valid only if they belong to an order which is by and large efficacious. Therefore, the content of a basic norm is determined by the facts through which an order is created and applied, to which the behavior of the individuals regulated by this order, by and large, conforms, The basic norm of any positive legal order confers legal authority only upon facts by which an order is created and applied which is on the whole effective. It is not required that the actual behavior of individuals be in absolute conformity with the order. On the contrary, a certain antagonism between the normative order and the actual human behavior to which the norms of the order must be possible. Without such a possibility, a normative order would be completely meaningless. What necessarily happens under the laws of nature does not have to be prescribed by norms: The basic norm of a social order to which the actual behavior of the individuals always and without any exception conforms would run as follows: Men ought to behave as they actually behave, or: You ought to do what you actually do. Such an order would be as meaningless as an order with which human behavior would in no way conform, but always and in every respect contradict. Therefore, a normative order loses its validity when reality no longer corresponds to it, at least to a certain degree. The validity of a legal order is thus dependent upon its agreement with reality, upon its "efficacy." The relationship which exists between the validity and efficacy of a legal order—it is, so to speak, the tension between the "ought" and the "is"—can be determined only by an upper and a lower borderline. The agreement must neither exceed a certain maximum nor fall below a certain minimum.

### h. Law and Power (Right and Might)

Seeing that the validity of a legal order is thus dependent upon its efficacy, one may be misled into identifying the two phenomena, by defining the validity of law as its efficacy, by describing the law by "is" and not by "ought" statements. Attempts of this kind have very often been made and they have always failed. For, if the validity of law is identified with any natural fact, it is impossible to comprehend the specific sense in which law is directed towards reality and thus stands over against reality. Only if law and natural reality, the system of legal norms and the actual behavior of men, the "ought" and the "is", are two different realms, may reality conform with or contradict law, can human behavior be characterized as legal or illegal.

The efficacy of law belongs to the realm of reality and is often called the power of law. If for efficacy we substitute power, then the problem of validity and efficacy is transformed into the more common problem of "right and might." And then the solution here presented is merely the precise statement of the old truth that though law cannot exist without power, still law and power, right and might, are not the same. Law is, according to the theory here presented, a specific order or organization of power.

### i. The Principle of Effectiveness as Positive Legal Norm
### (International and National Law)

The principle that a legal order must be efficacious in order to be valid is, in itself, a positive norm. It is the principle of effectiveness belonging to international law. According to this principle of international law, an actually established authority is the legitimate government, the coercive order enacted by this government is the legal order, and the community constituted by this order is a State in the sense of international law, insofar as this order is, on the whole, efficacious. From the standpoint of international law, the constitution of a State is valid only if the legal order established on the basis of this constitution is, on the whole, efficacious. It is this general principle of effectiveness, a positive norm of international law, which, applied to the concrete circumstances of an individual national legal order, provides the individual basic norm of this national legal order. Thus, the basic norms of the different national legal orders are themselves based on a general norm of the international legal order. If we conceive of international law as a legal order to which all the States (and that means all the national legal orders) are subordinated, then the basic norm of a national legal order is not a mere presupposition of juristic thinking, but a positive legal norm, a norm of international law applied to the legal order of a concrete State. Assuming the primacy of international law over national law, the problem of the basic norm shifts from the national to the international legal order. Then the only true basic norm, a norm which is not created by a legal procedure but presupposed by juristic thinking, is the basic norm of international law.

### j. Validity and Efficacy

That the validity of a legal order depends upon its efficacy does not imply, as pointed out, that the validity of a single norm depends upon its efficacy. The single legal norm remains valid as long as it is part of a valid order. The question whether an individual norm is valid is answered by recourse to the first constitution. If this is valid, then all norms which have been created in a constitutional way are valid, too. The principle of effectiveness embodied in international law refers immediately only to the first constitution of a national legal order, and therefore to this order only as a whole.

The principle of effectiveness may, however, be adopted to a certain extent also by national law, and thus within a national legal order the validity of a single norm may be made dependent upon its efficacy. Such is the case when a legal norm may lose its validity by desuetudo.

### D. The Static and the Dynamic Concept of Law

If one looks upon the legal order from the dynamic point of view, as it has been expounded here, it seems possible to define the concept of law in a way quite different from that in which we have tried to define it in this theory. It seems especially possible to ignore the element of coercion in defining the concept of law.

It is a fact that the legislator can enact commandments without considering it necessary to attach a criminal or civil sanction to their violation. If such norms are also called legal norms, it is because they were created by an authority which, according to the constitution, is competent to create law. They are law because they issue from a law-creating authority. According to this concept, law is anything that has come about in the way the constitution prescribes for the creation of law. This dynamic concept differs from the concept of law defined as a coercive norm. According to the dynamic concept, law is something created by a certain process, and everything created in this way is law. This dynamic concept, however, is only apparently a concept of law. It contains no answer to the question of what is the essence of law, what is the criterion by which law can be distinguished from other social norms. This dynamic concept furnishes an answer only to the question whether or not and why a certain norm belongs to a system of valid legal norms, forms a part of a certain legal order. And the answer is, a norm belongs to a certain legal order if it is created in accordance with a procedure prescribed by the constitution fundamental to this legal order.

It must, however, be noted that not only a norm, i.e., a command regulating human behavior, can be created in the way prescribed by the constitution for the creation of law. An important stage in the law-creating process is the procedure by which general norms are created, that is, the procedure of legislation. The constitution may organize this procedure of legislation in the following way: two corresponding resolutions of both houses of parliament, the consent of the chief of State, and publication in an official journal. This means that a specific form of law-creation is established. It is then possible to clothe in this form any subject, for instance, a recognition of the merits of a statesman. The form of a law—a declaration voted by parliament, consented to by the chief of State, published in the official journal—is chosen in order to give to a certain subject, here to the expression of the nation's gratitude, the character of a solemn act. The solemn recognition of the merits of a statesman is by no means a norm, even if it appears as the content of a legislative act, even if it has the form of a law. The law as the product of the legislative procedure, a statute in the formal sense of the term, is a document containing words, sentences; and that which is expressed by these sentences need not necessarily be a norm. As a matter of fact, many a law—in this formal sense of the term—contains not only legal norms, but also certain elements which are of no specific legal, i.e. normative, character, such as, purely theoretical views concerning certain matters, the motives of the legislator, political ideologies contained in references such as "justice" or "the will of God," etc., etc. All these are legally irrelevant contents of the statute, or, more generally, legally irrelevant products of the law-creating process. The law-creating process includes not only the process of legislation, but also the procedure of the judicial and administrative authorities. Even judgments of the courts very often contain legally irrelevant elements. If by the term "law" is meant something pertaining to a certain legal order, then law is anything which has been created according to the procedure prescribed by the constitution fundamental to this order. This does not mean, however, that everything which has been created according to this procedure is law in the sense of a legal norm. It is a legal norm only if it purports to regulate human behavior, and if it regulates human behavior by providing an act of coercion as sanction.

# 25

# John Rawls

John Rawls (1921–    ), Professor of Philosophy at Harvard University and author of several major essays in the field, offers guidelines for justified civil disobedience in a well-ordered democratic society.

# THE JUSTIFICATION OF CIVIL DISOBEDIENCE*

## I. Introduction

I should like to discuss briefly, and in an informal way, the grounds of civil disobedience in a constitutional democracy. Thus, I shall limit my remarks to the conditions under which we may, by civil disobedience, properly oppose legally established democratic authority; I am not concerned with the situation under other kinds of government nor, except incidentally, with other forms of resistance. My thought is that in a reasonably just (though of course not perfectly just) democratic regime civil disobedience, when it is justified, is normally to be understood as a political action which addresses the sense of justice of the majority in order to urge reconsideration of the measures protested and to warn that in the firm opinion of the dissenters the conditions of social cooperation are not being honored. This characterization of civil disobedience is intended to apply to dissent on fundamental questions of internal policy, a limitation which I shall follow to simplify our question.

## II. The Social Contract Doctrine:

It is obvious that the justification of civil disobedience depends upon the theory of political duty in general and so we may appropriately begin with a few comments on this question. The two chief virtues of social institutions are justice and efficiency, where by the efficiency of institutions I understand their effectiveness for certain social conditions and ends the fulfillment of which is to every one's advantage. We should comply with and do our part in just and efficient social arrangements for at least two reasons: first of all, we have a natural duty not to oppose the establishment of just and efficient institutions (when they do not yet exist) and to uphold and comply with them (when they do exist); and second, assuming that we have knowingly accepted the benefits

*Originally presented at the meetings of the American Political Science Association, September 1966. Some revisions have been made and two paragraphs have been added to the last section. Printed by permission of the author.

of these institutions and plan to continue to do so, and that we have encouraged and expect others to do their part, we also have an obligation to do our share when, as the arrangement requires, it comes our turn. Thus, we often have both a natural duty as well as an obligation to support just and efficient institutions, the obligation arising from our voluntary acts while the duty does not.

Now all this is perhaps obvious enough, but it does not take us very far. Any more particular conclusions depend upon the conception of justice which is the basis of a theory of political duty. I believe that the appropriate conception, at least for an account of political duty in a constitutional democracy, is that of the social contract theory from which so much of our political thought derives. If we are careful to interpret it in a suitably general way, I hold that this doctrine provides a satisfactory basis for political theory, indeed even for ethical theory itself, but this is beyond our present concern.[1] The interpretation I suggest is the following: that the principles to which social arrangements must conform, and in particular the principles of justice, are those which free and rational men would agree to in an original position of equal liberty; and similarly, the principles which govern men's relations to institutions and define their natural duties and obligations are the principles to which they would consent when so situated. It should be noted straightway that in this interpretation of the contract theory the principles of justice are understood as the outcome of a hypothetical agreement. They are principles which would be agreed to if the situation of the original position were to arise. There is no mention of an actual agreement nor need such an agreement even be made. Social arrangements are just or unjust according to whether they accord with the principles for assigning and securing fundamental rights and liberties which would be chosen in the original position. This position is, to be sure, the analytic analogue of the traditional notion of the state of nature, but it must not be mistaken for a historical occasion. Rather it is a hypothetical situation which embodies the basic ideas of the contract doctrine; the description of this situation enables us to work out which principles would be adopted. I must now say something about these matters.

The contract doctrine has always supposed that the persons in the original position have equal powers and rights, that is, that they are symmetrically situated with respect to any arrangements for reaching agreement, and that coalitions and the like are excluded. But it is also an essential element (which has not been sufficiently observed although it is implicit in Kant's version of the theory) that there are very strong restrictions on what the contractees are presumed to know. In particular, I interpret the theory to hold that the parties do not know their position in society, past, present, or future; nor do they know which institutions exist. Again, they do not know their own place in the distribution of natural talents and abilities, whether they are intelligent or

---

[1] By the social contract theory I have in mind the doctrine found in Locke, Rousseau, and Kant, I have attempted to give an interpretation of this view in: "Jusitce as Fairness", *Philosophical Review* (April, 1958) and "Justice and Constitutional Liberty", *Nomos* VI (1963).

strong, man or woman, and so on. Finally, they do not know their own particular interests and preferences or the system of ends which they wish to advance: they do not know their conception of the good. In all these respects the parties are confronted with a veil of ignorance which prevents any one from being able to take advantage of his good fortune or particular interests or from being disadvantaged by them. What the parties do know (or assume) is that Hume's circumstances of justice obtain: namely, that the bounty of nature is not so generous as to render cooperative schemes superfluous nor so harsh as to make them impossible. Moreover, they assume that the extent of their altruism is limited and that, in general, they do not take an interest in one another's interests. Thus, given the special features of the original position, each man tries to do the best he can for himself by insisting on principles calculated to protect and advance his system of ends whatever it turns out to be.

I believe that as a consequence of the peculiar nature of the original position there would be an agreement on the following two principles for assigning rights and duties and for regulating distributive shares as these are determined by the fundamental institutions of society: first, each person is to have an equal right to the most extensive liberty compatible with a like liberty for all; and second, social and economic inequalities (as defined by the institutional structure or fostered by it) are to be arranged so that they are both to everyone's advantage and attached to positions and offices open to all. In view of the content of these two principles and their application to the main institutions of society, and therefore to the social system as a whole, we may regard them as the two principles of justice. Basic social arrangements are just insofar as they conform to these principles; and we can, if we like, discuss questions of justice directly by reference to them. But a deeper understanding of the justification of civil disobedience requires, I think, an account of the derivation of these principles provided by the doctrine of the social contract. Part of our task is to show why this is so.

### III. The Grounds of Compliance With an Unjust Law

If we assume that in the original position men would agree both to the principle of doing their part when they have accepted and plan to continue to accept the benefits of just institutions (the principle of fairness), and also to the principle of not preventing the establishment of just institutions and of upholding and complying with them when they do exist, then the contract doctrine easily accounts for our having to conform to just institutions. But how does it account for the fact that we are normally required to comply with unjust laws as well? The injustice of a law is not a sufficient ground for not complying with it any more than the legal validity of legislation is always sufficient to require obedience to it. Sometimes one hears these extremes asserted, but I think that we need not take them seriously.

An answer to our question can be given by elaborating the social contract theory in the following way. I interpret it to hold that one is to envisage a series of agreements as follows: first, men are to agree upon the principles of justice in the original position. Then they are to move to a constitutional convention in which they choose a constitution that satisfies the principles of justice already chosen. Finally they assume the role of a legislative body and guided by the principles of justice enact laws subject to the constraints and procedures of the just constitution. The decisions reached in any stage are binding in all subsequent stages. Now whereas in the original position the contractees have no knowledge of their society or of their own position in it, in both a constitutional convention and a legislature, they do know certain general facts about their institutions, for example, the statistics regarding employment and output required for fiscal and economic policy. But no one knows particular facts about his own social class or his place in the distribution of natural assets. On each occasion the contractees have the knowledge required to make their agreement rational from the appropriate point of view, but not so much as to make them prejudiced. They are unable to tailor principles and legislation to take advantage of their social or natural position; a veil of ignorance prevents their knowing what this position is. With this series of agreements in mind, we can characterize just laws and policies as those which would be enacted were this whole process correctly carried out.

In choosing a constitution the aim is to find among the just constitutions the one which is most likely, given the general facts about the society in question, to lead to just and effective legislation. The principles of justice provide a criterion for the laws desired: the problem is to find a set of political procedures that will give this outcome. I shall assume that, at least under the normal conditions of a modern state, the best constitution is some form of democratic regime affirming equal political liberty and using some sort of majority (or other plurality) rule. Thus it follows that on the contract theory a constitutional democracy of some sort is required by the principles of justice. At the same time it is essential to observe that the constitutional process is always a case of what we may call imperfect procedural justice: that is, there is no feasible political procedure which guarantees that the enacted legislation is just even though we have (let's suppose) a standard for just legislation. In simple cases, such as games of fair division, there are procedures which always lead to the right outcome (assume that equal shares is fair and let the man who cuts the cake take the last piece). These situations are those of perfect procedural justice. In other cases it does not matter what the outcome is as long as the fair procedure is followed: fairness of the process is transferred to the result (fair gambling is an instance of this). These situations are those of pure procedural justice. The constitutional process, like a criminal trial, resembles neither of these; the result matters and we have a standard for it. The difficulty is that we cannot frame a procedure which guarantees that only just and effective legislation is enacted. Thus even under a just constitution unjust laws may be passed and unjust policies enforced. Some form of the majority principle is necessary but the majority may be mistaken, more or less willfully, in what it legislates. In agreeing to a democratic constitution (as an instance of imperfect procedural justice) one accepts at the same time the principle of majority rule. Assuming that the constitution is just and that we have accepted and plan to continue to accept its benefits, we then have both an obligation and a natural duty (and in any case the duty) to comply with what the majority enacts even though it may be unjust. In this way we become bound to follow unjust laws, not always, of course, but provided the injustice does not exceed certain limits. We recognize that we must run the risk of suffering from the defects of one another's sense of justice; and this burden we are prepared to carry as long as it is more or less evenly distributed or does not weigh too heavily. Justice binds us to a just constitution and to the unjust laws which may be enacted under it in precisely the same way that it binds us to any other social arrangement. Once we take the sequence of stages into account, there is nothing unusual in our being required to comply with unjust laws.

It should be observed that the majority principle has a secondary place as a rule of procedure which is perhaps the most efficient one under usual circumstances for working a democratic constitution. The basis for it rests essentially upon the principles of justice and therefore we may, when conditions allow, appeal to these principles against unjust legislation. The justice of the constitution does not insure the justice of laws enacted under it; and while we often have both an obligation and a duty to comply with what the majority legislates (as long as it does not exceed certain limits), there is, of course, no corresponding obligation or duty to regard what the majority enacts as itself just. The right to make law does not guarantee that the decision is rightly made; and while the citizen submits in his conduct to the judgment of democratic authority, he does not submit his judgment to it.[2] And if in his judgment the enactments of the majority exceed certain bounds of injustice, the citizen may consider civil disobedience. For we are not required to accept the majority's acts unconditionally and to acquiesce in the denial of our and others' liberties; rather we submit our conduct to democratic authority to the extent necessary to share the burden of working a constitutional regime distorted as it must inevitably be by men's lack of wisdom and the defects of their sense of justice.

## IV. The Place of Civil Disobedience in a Constitutional Democracy

We are now in a position to say a few things about civil diobedience. Is shall understand it to be a public, non violent, and conscientious act contrary to law usually done with the intent to bring about a change in the policies or laws of the government.[3] Civil disobedience is a political act in the sense that it is an act justified by moral principles which define a conception of civil society and the public good. It rests, then, on political conviction as opposed to a search for self or group interest; and in the case of a constitutional democracy, we may

---

[2] On this point see A. E. Murphy's review of Yves Simon's *The Philosophy of Democratic Government* (1951) in the *Philosophical Review* (April, 1952).

[3] Here I follow H. A. Bedau's definition of civil disobedience. See his "On Civil Disobedience," *Journal of Philosophy* (October, 1961).

assume that this conviction involves the conception of justice (say that expressed by the contract doctrine) which underlies the constitution itself. That is, in a viable democratic regime there is a common conception of justice by reference to which its citizens regulate their political affairs and interpret the constitution. Civil disobedience is a public act which the dissenter believes to be justified by this conception of justice and for this reason it may be understood as addressing the sense of justice of the majority in order to urge reconsideration of the measures protested and to warn that, in the sincere opinion of the dissenters, the conditions of social cooperation are not being honored: For the principles of justice express precisely such conditions, and their persistent and deliberate violation in regard to basic liberties over any extended period of time cuts the ties of community and invites either submission or forceful resistance. By engaging in civil disobedience a minority leads the majority to consider whether it wants to have its acts taken in this way, or whether, in view of the common sense of justice, it wishes to acknowledge the claims of the minority.

Civil disobedience is also civil in another sense. Not only is it the outcome of a sincere conviction based on principles which regulate civic life, but is it public and non-violent, that is, it is done in a situation where arrest and punishment is expected and accepted without resistance. In this way it manifests a respect for legal procedures. Civil disobedience expresses disobedience to law within the limits of fidelity to law, and this feature of it helps to establish in the eyes of the majority that it is indeed conscientious and sincere, that it really is meant to address their sense of justice.[4] Being completely open about one's acts and being willing to accept the legal consequences of one's conduct is a bond given to make good one's sincerity, for that one's deeds are conscientious is not easy to demonstrate to another or even before oneself. No doubt it is possible to imagine a legal system in which conscientious belief that the law is unjust is accepted as a defense for non-compliance, and men of great honesty who are confident in one another might make such a system work. But as things are such a scheme would be unstable; we must pay a price in order to establish that we believe our actions have a moral basis in the convictions of the community.

The nonviolent nature of civil disobedience refers to the fact that it is intended to address the sense of justice of the majority and as such it is a form of speech, an expression of conviction. To engage in violent acts likely to injure and to hurt is incompatible with civil disbedience as a mode of address. Indeed, any interference with the basic rights of others tends to obscure the civilly disobedient quality of one's act. Civil disobedience is nonviolent in the further sense that the legal penalty for one's action is accepted and resistance is not (at least for the moment) contemplated. Nonviolence in this sense is to be distinguished from nonviolence as a religious or pacifist principle. While those engaging in civil disobedience have often held some such principle, there is no necessary connection between it and civil disobedience. For on the interpreta-

---

[4] For a fuller discussion of this point to which I am indebted, see Charles Fried, "Moral Causation", *Harvard Law Review* (1964).

tion suggested, civil disobedience in a democratic society is best understood as an appeal to the principles of justice, the fundamental conditions of willing social cooperation among free men, which in the view of the community as a whole are expresssed in the constitution and guide its interpretation. Being an appeal to the moral basis of public life, civil disobedience is a political and not primarily a religious act. It addresses itself to the common principles of justice which men can require one another to follow and not to the aspirations of love which they cannot. Moreover by taking part in civilly disobedient acts one does not foreswear indefinitely the idea of forceful resistance; for if the appeal against injustice is repeatedly denied, then the majority has declared its intention to invite submission or resistance and the latter may conceivably be justified even in a democratic regime. We are not required to acquiesce in the crushing of fundamental liberties by democratic majorities which have shown themselves blind to the principles of justice upon which justification of the constitution depends.

## V. The Justification of Civil Disobedience

So far we have said nothing about the justification of civil disobedience, that is, the conditions under which civil disobedience may be engaged in consistent with the principles of justice that support a democratic regime. Our task is to see how the characterization of civil disobedience as addressed to the sense of justice of the majority (or to the citizens as a body) determines when such action is justified.

First of all, we may suppose that the normal political appeals to the majority have already been made in good faith and have been rejected, and that the standard means of redress have been tried. Thus, for example, existing political parties are indifferent to the claims of the minority and attempts to repeal the laws protested have been met with further repression since legal institutions are in the control of the majority. While civil disobedience should be recognized, I think, as a form of political action within the limits of fidelity to the rule of law, at the same time it is a rather desperate act just within these limits, and therefore it should, in general, be undertaken as a last resort when standard democratic processes have failed. In this sense it is not a normal political action. When it is justified there has been a serious breakdown; not only is there grave injustice in the law but a refusal more or less deliberate to correct it.

Second, since civil disbedience is a political act addressed to the sense of justice of the majority, it should usually be limited to substantial and clear violations of justice preferably to those which, if rectified, will establish a basis for doing away with remaining injustices. For this reason there is a presumption in favor of restricting civil disobedience to violations of the first principle of justice, the principle of equal liberty, and to barriers which contravene the second principle, the principle of open offices which protects equality of opportunity. It is not, of course, always easy to tell whether these principles are satisfied. But if we think of them as guaranteeing the fundamental equal political and civil liberties (including freedom of conscience and liberty of thought) and equality of opportunity, then it is often relatively clear whether their principles are being honored. After all, the equal liberties are defined by the visible structure of social institutions; they are to be incorporated into the recognized practice, if not the letter, of social arrangements. When minorities are denied the right to vote or to hold certain political offices, when certain religious groups are repressed and others denied equality of opportunity in the economy, this is often obvious and there is no doubt that justice is not being given. Whereas the first part of the second principle which requires that inequalities be to everyone's advantage is a much more imprecise and controversial matter. Not only is there a problem of assigning it a determinate and precise sense, but even if we do so and agree on what it should be, there is often a wide variety of reasonable opinion as to whether the principle is satisfied. The reason for this is that the principle applies primarily to fundamental economic and social policies. The choice of these depends upon theoretical and speculative beliefs as well as upon a wealth of concrete information, and all of this mixed with judgment and plain hunch, not to mention in actual cases prejudice and self-interest. Thus unless the laws of taxation are clearly designed to attack a basic equal liberty, they should not be protested by civil disobedience; the appeal to justice is not sufficiently clear and its resolution is best left to the political process. But violations of the equal liberties that define the common status of citizenship are another matter. The denial of these more or less deliberate over any extended period of time in the face of normal political protest is, in general, an appropriate object of civil disobedience. We may think of the social system as divided roughly into two parts, one which incorporates the fundamental equal liberties (including equality of opportunity) and another which embodies social and economic policies properly aimed at promoting the advantage of everyone. As a rule civil disobedience is best limited to the former where the appeal to justice is not only more definite and precise, but where, if it is effective, it tends to correct the injustices in the latter.

Third, civil disobedience should be restricted to those cases where the dissenter is willing to affirm that everyone else similarly subjected to the same degree of injustice has the right to protest in a similar way. That is, we must be prepared to authorize others to dissent in similar situations and in the same way, and to accept the consequences of their doing so. Thus, we may hold, for example, that the widespread disposition to disobey civilly clear violations of fundamental liberties more or less deliberate over an extended period of time would raise the degree of justice throughout society and would insure men's self-esteem as well as their respect for one another. Indeed, I believe this to be true, though certainly it is partly a matter of conjecture. As the contract doctrine emphasizes, since the principles of justice are principles which we would agree to in an original position of equality when we do not know our social position and the like, the refusal to grant justice is either the denial of the other as an equal (as one in regard to whom we are prepared to constrain our actions by principles which we would consent to) or the manifestation of a willingness to take advantage of natural contingencies and social fortune at his expense. In either case, injustice invites submission or resistance; but submission arouses the contempt of the oppressor and confirms him in his intention. If straightway, after a decent period of time to make reasonable political appeals in the normal way, men were in general to dissent by civil disobedience from infractions of the fundamental equal liberties, these liberties would, I believe, be more rather than less secure. Legitimate civil disobedience properly exercised is a stabilizing device in a constitutional regime tending to make it more firmly just.

Sometimes, however, there may be a complication in connection with this third condition. It is possible, although perhaps unlikely, that there are so many persons or groups with a sound case for resorting to civil disobedience (as judging by the foregoing criteria) that disorder would follow if they all did so. There might be serious injury to the just constitution. Or again, a group might be so large that some extra precaution is necessary in the extent to which its members organize and engage in civil disobedience. Theoretically the case is one in which a number of persons or groups are equally entitled to and all want to resort to civil disobedience, yet if they all do this, grave consequences for everyone may result. The question, then, is who among them may exercise their right, and it falls under the general problem of fairness. I cannot discuss the complexities of the matter here. Often a lottery or a rationing system can be set up to handle the case; but unfortunately the circumstances of civil disobedience rule out this solution. It suffices to note that a problem of fairness may arise and that those who contemplate civil disobedience should take it into account. They may have to reach an understanding as to who can exercise their right in the immediate situation and to recognize the need for special constraint.

The final condition, of a different nature, is the following. We have been considering when one has a right to engage in civil disobedience, and our conclusion is that one has this right should three conditions hold: when one is subject to injustice more or less deliberate over an extended period of time in the face of normal political protests; where the injustice is a clear violation of the liberties of equal citizenship; and provided that the general disposition to protest similarly in similar cases would have acceptable consequences. These conditions are not, I think, exhaustive but they seem to cover the more obvious points; yet even when they are satisfied and one has the right to engage in civil disobedience is still the different question of whether one should exercise this right, that is, whether by doing so one is likely to further one's ends. Having established one's right to protest one is then free to consider these tactical questions. We may be acting within our rights but still foolishly if our action only serves to provoke the harsh retaliation of the majority; and it is likely to do so if the majority lacks a sense of justice, or if the action is poorly timed or not well designed to make the appeal to the sense of justice effective. It is easy to think of instances of this sort, and in each case these practical questions have to be faced. From the standpoint of the theory of political duty we can only say that the exercise of the right should be rational and reasonably designed to advance the protestor's aims, and that weighing tactical questions presupposes that one has already established one's right, since tactical advantages in themselves do not support it.

## VI. Conclusion: Several Objections Considered

In a reasonably affluent democratic society justice becomes the first virtue of institutions. Social arrangements irrespective of their efficiency must be reformed if they are significantly unjust. No increase in efficiency in the form of greater advantages for many justifies the loss of liberty of a few. That we believe this is shown by the fact that in a democracy the fundamental liberties of citizenship are not understood as the outcome of political bargaining nor are they subject to the calculus of social interests. Rather these liberties are fixed points which serve to limit political transactions and which determine the scope of calculations of social advantage. It is this fundamental place of the equal liberties which makes their systematic violation over any extended period of time a proper object of civil disobedience. For to deny men these rights is to infringe the conditions of social cooperation among free and rational persons, a fact which is evident to the citizens of a constitutional regime since it follows from the principles of justice which underlies their institutions. The justification of civil disobedience rests on the priority of justice and the equal liberties which it guarantees.

It is natural to object to this view of civil disobedience that it relies too heavily upon the existence of a sense of justice. Some may hold that the feeling for justice is not a vital political force, and that what moves men are various other interests, the desire for wealth, power, prestige, and so on. Now this is a large question the answer to which is highly conjectural and each tends to have his own opinion. But there are two remarks which may clarify what I have said: first, I have assumed that there is in a constitutional regime a common sense of justice the principles of which are recognized to support the constitution and to guide its interpretation. In any given situation particular men may be tempted to violate these principles, but the collective force in their behalf is usually effective since they are seen as the necessary terms of cooperation among free men; and presumably the citizens of a democracy (or sufficiently many of them) want to see justice done. Where these assumptions fail, the justifying conditions for civil disobedience (the first three) are not affected, but the rationality of engaging in it certainly is. In this case, unless the costs of repressing civil dissent injure the economic self-interest (or whatsoever) of the majority, protest may simply make the position of the minority worse. No doubt as a tactical matter civil disobedience is more effective when its appeal coincides with other interests, but a constitutional regime is not viable in the long run without an attachment to the principles of justice of the sort which we have assumed.

Then, further, there may be a misapprehension about the manner in which a sense of justice manifests itself. There is a tendency to think that it is shown by professions of the relevant principles together with actions of an altruistic nature requiring a considerable degree of self-sacrifice. But these conditions are obviously too strong, for the majority's sense of justice may show itself simply in its being unable to undertake the measures required to suppress the minority and to punish as the law requires the various acts of civil disobedience. The sense of justice undermines the will to uphold unjust institutions, and so a majority despite its superior power may give way. It is unprepared to force the minority to be subject to injustice. Thus, although the majority's action is reluctant and grudging, the role of the sense of justice is nevertheless essential, for without it the majority would have been willing to enforce the law and to defend its position. Once we see the sense of justice as working in this negative way to make established injustices indefensible, then it is recognized as a central element of democratic politics.

Finally, it may be objected that this account does not settle the question of who is to say when the situation is such as to justify civil disobedience. And because it does not answer this question, it invites anarchy by encouraging every man to decide the matter for himself. Now the reply to this is that each man must indeed settle this question for himself, although he may, of course, decide wrongly. This is true on any theory of political duty and obligation, at least on any theory compatible with the principles of a democratic constitution. The citizen is responsible for what he does. If we ordinarily think that we should comply with the law, this is because our political principles normally lead to this conclusion. There is a presumption in favor of compliance in the absence of good reasons to the contrary. But because each man is responsible and must decide for himself as best he can whether the circumstances justify civil disobedience, it does not follow that he may decide as he pleases. It is not by looking to our personal interests or to political allegiances norrowly construed, that we should make up our mind. The citizen must decide on the basis of the principles of justice that underlie and guide the interpretation of the constitution and in the light of his sincere conviction as to how these principles should be applied in the circumstances. If he concludes that conditions obtain which justify civil disobedience and conducts himself accordingly, he has acted conscientiously and perhaps mistakenly, but not in any case at his convenience.

In a democratic society each man must act as he thinks the principles of political right require him to. We are to follow our understanding of these principles, and we cannot do otherwise. There can be no morally binding legal interpretation of these principles, not even by a supreme court or legislature. Nor is there any infallible procedure for determining what or who is right. In our system the Supreme Court, Congress, and the President often put forward rival interpretations of the Constitution. Although the Court has the final say in settling any particular case, it is not immune from powerful political influences that may change its reading of the law of the land. The Court presents its point of view by reason and argument; its conception of the Constitution must, if it is to endure, persuade men of its soundness. The final court of appeal is not the Court, or Congress, or the President, but the electorate as a whole. The civilly disobedient appeal in effect to this body. There is no danger of anarchy as long as there is a sufficient working agreement in men's conception of political justice and what it requires. That men can achieve such an understanding when the essential political liberties are maintained is the assumption implicit in democratic institutions. There is no way to avoid entirely the risk of divisive strife. But if legitimate civil disobedience seems to threaten civil peace, the responsibility falls not so much on those who protest as upon those whose abuse of authority and power justifies such opposition.

# 26
# Francis A. Allen

Francis A. Allen (1919–        ), Dean of the Law School and Professor of Law at the University of Michigan, records patterns of civil disobedience indigenous to the American political tradition.

# CIVIL DISOBEDIENCE AND THE LEGAL ORDER*

## PART II†

### III. OF CHALLENGE AND RESPONSE.

In 1920, when Mahatma Gandhi was asked to give testimony before a governmental commission in India, the following question was put to him in the course of his interrogation: "I ask you to look at it from the point of view of the Government. If you were Govenor yourself, what would you say to a movement that was started with the object of breaking those laws which your Committee determined?" Mr. Gandhi's answer, in part, was the following: "If I were in charge of the Government and brought face to face with a body who, entirely in search of truth, was determined to seek redress from unjust laws without inflicting violence, I would welcome it and consider that they were the best constitutionalists, and as a Governor I would take them by my side as advisers who would keep me on the right path." [1]

In this third and concluding section I propose to make use of Mahatma Gandhi's suggestion. The primary focus of attention will be neither on the problems of ethical justification of civil disobedience nor on an appraisal of its dangers to the maintenance of a legal order. Instead, I shall at the outset concede the fact of civil disobedience as one recurring aspect of modern American life and inquire into both the social processes of which it is part and the functions it performs. I shall also view the practice of civil disobedience as a criticism of American political, social, and legal institutions, and seek to discover what light it may throw on the nature and limitations of American life. Viewed as social criticism, what does the practice of civil disobedience tell us about

---

*Francis A. Allen, "Civil Disobedience and the Legal Order." Reprinted, with permission, from Volume 36 of the *University of Cincinnati Law Review*. Dean Allen's article was originally presented as the concluding portion of his 1966 Robert S. Marx Lectures at the University of Cincinnati College of Law. The footnotes have been renumbered.
†This is the second and concluding part of a two-part Article. The first part appears in 36 CIN. L. REV. 1 (1967).
[1] GANDHI, NON-VIOLENT RESISTANCE 20 (Kumarappa ed. 1961).

ourselves and about the responses required of American society for successful confrontation of the challenges of the present day? This self-imposed assignment is an ambitious one, and I have no expectation that it will be fully and successfully peformed.

In recent months a number of commentators have advanced the tempting hypothesis that the current campaigns of civil disobedience are to be understood largely as manifestations of some of the characteristic pathologies of the modern age. Thus, several of our elder statemen have seen in recent instances of conscientious law violation evidences of a general decline of morality, the erosion of American character, the loss of vitality of religious belief, and the atrophying of a sense of individual responsibility for the welfare of the community as a whole.[2] Whenever such discouraging analyses are advanced, one can be sure that a large part of the fault will be attributed to the absence of proper parental discipline in the American family. Hence, many have seen in the phenomenon of civil disobedience, particularly that practiced by our college students, the consequences of permissive child-rearing which they say has produced a generation of young persons, unusual numbers of whom are lacking in the ability to brook restraint or to tolerate frustration.[3] Accordingly, they are incapable of making terms with authority or of comprehending the validity of restraint. Other commentators have asserted that the willingness of large numbers of our citizens to engage in deliberate law violation in efforts to achieve social goals is a manifestation of an age in which the old categories are dissolving along many fronts—an age in which art is not only impatient of old forms but often makes a fetish of formlessness; an age in which efforts to contain sexual expression within the confines of the monogamous family are seen as prudery, productive of neuroses, and a denial of human rights; an age in which even grammarians have been converted (or have converted themselves) into public-opinion pollsters.

It is not my purpose to examine the validity of this indictment of modern American society. It is surely possible that at least some of these propositions contain elements of truth. But these arguments, so far as they are advanced as explanations for the present expressions of civil disobedience, are predicated on an implicit assumption that invites attention and investigation. This assumption is that the practice of civil disobedience is a distinctively modern occurrence, and that its explanations are to be found in a collection of factors that are peculiar to the modern age. Should inquiry reveal that the assumption is fallible, we may be required to reconsider our views about the nature and significance of civil disobedience in modern American society. The fact, (for it is a fact), that conscientious law violation is not unique to the mid-twentieth century, but accompanied a number of the most significant movements for social and political reform in nineteenth-century America, serves at least to raise serious questions about the adequacy of the assumptions upon which much of the contemporary analysis rests.

[2] See generally Lawrence, *The Era of Anarchy*, U.S. News & World Report, Aug. 29, 1966, p. 96; The Reporter, Feb. 23, 1967, p. 14.
[3] See, *e.g.*, Logan, *The Crisis on Our Campuses*, Reader's Digest, Feb. 1965, pp. 124, 125.

In his famous lecture entitled "Man the Reformer," delivered a century-and-a-quarter ago, Ralph Waldo Emerson asserted: "In the history of the world the doctrine of reform had never such a scope as at the present hour. . . . [There is not] a kingdom, town, statute, rite, calling, man, or woman, but is threatened by the new spirit." [4] One of the persistent strands in the fabric of American history is the impulse toward the conscious remolding of American life in order that it might conform more closely to some ideal of the good society. It is all the more remarkable, therefore, that there has been so little serious effort to discover and lay bare the dynamics of reform movements that have played such significant roles in the development of American institutions, including legal institutions. Obviously, this is not the occasion for an attempt to supply this lack. But any effort to appraise the contemporary significance of civil disobedience requires that some attention be devoted to manifestations of conscientious law violation in earlier American reform movements.

It would be a distortion of the historical record to suggest that all important reform movements in America have been accompanied by expressions of civil disobedience. Nevertheless, the instances of the advocacy and practice of conscientious law violation in the last century were sufficiently numerous and widespread to identify it as one of the persistently recurring aspects of American efforts at social and political reform. It is also significant that the movements inducing the largest resort to such tactics include some of the most important of nineteenth-century efforts of social amelioration. I shall confine myself principally to brief comments concerning conscientious law violation in two of these movements: antislavery and the struggle for the abolition of discriminations founded on sex.

It is well known that violations of law occurred on both sides of the controversies that led ultimately to the American Civil War. The arguments advanced to urge or justify the use of such means are perhaps not so familiar. The incident out of which Thoreau's essay on *Civil Disobedience* emerged was only the most publicized instance of many refusals by New England residents to give fiscal support to the Mexican War,[5] a conflict viewed as unjust and immoral because believed to be instigated by slaveholders for the purpose of advancing the cause of slaveholding. Nor was Thoreau alone in stimulating opposition. *The Biglow Papers* [6] of James Russell Lowell, for example, may be taken as a deliberate effort to obstruct military recruiting. Thus, Lowell has his farmer say:

> Whan to tackle *me* in, du ye?
> I expect you'll hev to wait;
> Wen cold led puts daylight thru ye
> You'll begin to kal' late . . .'[7]

---

[4] EMERSON, ESSAYS 46 (Harvard Classics ed. 1909).
[5] See HARDING, THE DAYS OF HENRY THOREAU 199-201 (1965).
[6] LOWELL, THE BIGLOW PAPERS (1891).
[7] *Id.* at 67.

Among the other vigorous opponents of the Mexican War was Theodore Parker, an abolitionist clergyman. Although infrequently recalled today, he was one of the towering figures of his era. Parker's language demonstrates how readily the discourse of men of his time and persuasion utilized the language and justification of the higher law:

"What shall we do . . . in regard to this present war? We can refuse to take any part in it; we can encourage others to do the same, we can aid men, if need be, who suffer because they refuse. Men will call us traitors; what then? That hurt nobody in '76. We are a rebellious nation; our whole history is treason; our blood was attained before we were born; our creeds are infidelity to the mother church; our constitution treason to our fatherland. What of that? Though all the governors in the world bid us commit treason against man, and set the example, let us never submit. Let God only be a master to control our conscience."[8]

It was perhaps the passage and enforcement of the Fugitive Slave Act of 1850 [9] that evoked the most forthright acts of resistance to the law and the most serious efforts to articulate a theory in support of the defiance. The acts of resistance, which were numerous and sometimes violent, led to riots, the confrontation of agents of law enforcement on the public streets, and the rescuing of runaway slaves from the grasp of their masters. Traffic on the Underground Railroad was accelerated. The number of escaping slaves spirited north to safety or across the border into Canada can never be known with certainty. Estimates of those reaching Canada annually during the decade of the 1850's run as high as 2,000.[10] Such an operation required the active participation of many northern residents and the tacit approval and support of many thousands more. It is said that 200 fugitives passed through the Quaker settlement of Alum Creek, Ohio, in one six-month period.[11]

The support of these various activities by the leaders of the antislavery movement was emphatic and specific. In a public address, Theodore Parker once again voiced his views of the law above law:

But the effect of a law which men cannot keep without violating conscience, is always demoralizing. There are men who know no higher law than the statute of the State. When good men cannot keep a law that is base, some bad ones will say, "Let us keep no law at all,"–then where does the blame lie? On him that enacts the outrageous law.[12]

On another occasion he said:

In cases of this kind, when justice is on one side and the court on the other, it seems

[8] COMMAGER, THEODORE PARKER 192-93 (Beacon Paperback ed. 1960).
[9] Ch. 60, 9 Stat. 462.
[10] GARA, THE LIBERTY LINE 162 (1960).
[11] Siebert, *A Quaker Section of the Underground Railroad in Northern Ohio,* 39 OHIO ARCHAEOLOGICAL & HISTORICAL Q. 479, 501 (1930).
[12] PARKER, *The State of the Nation,* in 4 COLLECTED WORKS OF THEODORE PARKER 256 (1863).

to me a conscientious man must either refuse to serve as a juror, or else return a verdict at variance with the facts and what courts declare to be his official business as juror . . . . It seems to me it is time this matter should be understood, and that it should be known that no official oath can take a man out of the jurisdiction of God's natural law of the universe.[13]

Parker, of course, was not alone. Wendell Phillips, one of the intellectuals of the abolition movement, would have elevated nullification of laws by the acts of individuals to the level of official state policy: "Massachusetts is ours, if we choose to make it so. We can nullify this Fugitive Slave Bill. We can put on the Supreme bench judges who will laugh to defiance the Congress of the United States, when they undertake to carry a fugitive slave out of Massachusetts."[14] For many of these same commentators, the step from unqualified defiance of the Fugitive Slave Act to the fervid justification of John Brown's raid on Harper's Ferry proved to be easy and short. This progression of thought is exemplified in two of Thoreau's late essays, *Slavery in Massachusetts* and *The Last Days of John Brown*.[15] To the question, "Was John Brown justified in his attempt?," William Lloyd Garrison had no hesitation in answering, "Yes, if Washington was in his . . . ."[16] In a private letter, Theodore Parker paid tribute to John Brown: "And he went on to show what was True and Right— to show that slaves had a right to revolt, and that freemen had a right to help them, 'and as a means to that end, to aid them in killing all such as oppose their natural freedom.' "[17]

It may be doubted by some, however, whether the antislavery crusade in the years before 1860 offers much of general significance for one who is interested in the dynamics of reform and the relation of law violation to efforts at social improvement. It is true that the movement to abolish human slavery in the United States was in many respects unique: in the nature of the issue of conscience posed, in the intensity and virulence of the emotions aroused, and in the magnitude of the interests—social, political, economic, and regional—that were affected. Whatever the validity of these doubts, they may be sufficient to justify a broadening of the inquiry to encompass other movements of reform presenting issues, highly significant, but perhaps less overwhelming. The feminist movements of the nineteenth and early twentieth centuries will serve this purpose.

It is interesting that the early history of the Woman's Revolution (as it was later frequently described) is closely associated with the abolition movement. For some, but by no means all, of the antislavery crusaders, the emancipation of

---

[13] PARKER, *The Function and Place of Conscience, in Relation to the Laws of Men*, in 5 *id*. at 156–57.
[14] Address by Wendell Phillips, to a Gathering at Framington, Massachusetts, July 4, 1854, in The Liberator, July 14, 1854.
[15] THOREAU, A YANKEE IN CANADA, ANTI-SLAVERY AND REFORM PAPERS 97, 278 (1891).
[16] Address by William Lloyd Garrison, to a Gathering at Tremont Temple, Boston, Massachusetts, Dec. 2, 1859, in The Liberator, Dec. 16, 1859.
[17] Quoted in COMMAGER, *op. cit. supra* note 72, at 254.

slaves and the emancipation of women presented an anlogy too clear to miss. Thus, Emily Collins, the founder of an equal suffrage society, said: " 'All through the Anti-Slavery struggle, every word of denunciation of the wrongs of the Southern slave, was, I felt, equally applicable to the wrongs of my own sex.' " [18] Frederick Douglass, the runaway slave who became one of the principal spokesmen for the abolition movement, a few months before his death in 1888 stated that he regarded his early identification with the woman suffrage movement as his most praiseworthy act. " 'When I ran away from slavery, it was for myself; when I advocated emancipation, it was for my people; but when I stood up for the rights of women, self was out of the question, and I found a little nobility in the act' " [19] From the first meeting called to devote attention exclusively to the inequality of women in American society which was held at Seneca Falls, New York, in 1848, demands for extreme forms of resistance were heard. Thus, in 1852, Elizabeth Cady Stanton posed the following question for consideration: Should not all women living in states where women have the right to hold property refuse to pay taxes, so long as she is unrepresented in the government of that State? [20]

The adoption of the fourteenth amendment in 1868 raised the hopes of those espousing the cause of woman suffrage that votes for women would be held implicit in the guarantee of the privileges and immunities of citizens of the United States. These hopes were, of course, to be dashed by the Supreme Court in the well-known case of *Minor v. Happersett*.[21] In the years prior to this case, the reformers bent their energies to establish the constitutional validity of their claim, and this history throws considerable light on the complexity of the motivations of those involved in so-called test cases. Perhaps the dominant figure in this history was one of the most remarkable American women of the last century, Susan B. Anthony. Something of her character was revealed when, ten years before the events under consideration, she assisted in the escape from a mental institution of a mother whom Miss Anthony believed to be unjustly incarcerated. Threats, exhortations, and other efforts at persuasion by her friends and associates did not move Miss Anthony from her adamant refusal to reveal the mother's hiding place.[22]

In the early 1870's, women in several states made efforts to have their names included in the polling lists and to vote. Through a combination of intelligence, wiles, and eloquence, Miss Anthony and several associates succeeded in having their names listed and in casting their ballots in a state election. Subsequently Miss Anthony was prosecuted under federal law for having

---

[18] Collins, *Reminiscences*, in 1 HISTORY OF WOMAN SUFFRAGE 89 (Anthony, Stanton & Gage ed. 1882).
[19] Quoted in FONNER, FREDERICK DOUGLASS 105 (1964) (quoting from *The Woman's Journal*, April 14, 1888).
[20] Letter From Elizabeth Cady Stanton to Gerrit Smith, in 1 HISTORY OF WOMAN SUFFRAGE 520 (Anthony, Stanton & Gage ed. 1882).
[21] 88 U.S. (21 Wall.) 162 (1894).
[22] STANTON, EIGHTY YEARS AND MORE 213–14 (1898).

illegally voted. She was convicted and fined one hundred dollars.[23] The fine was never paid. There is no reason to doubt that Susan B. Anthony sincerely believed that she possessed a legal right to cast her ballot; but it is equally clear that her purposes were not limited to that of establishing a legal position. While the prosecution was pending she stumped the countryside in an effort to rally public sentiment to the cause she represented. So effective was her advocacy that one editorial writer at the time somewhat ruefully observed that: "[S]he actually converted nearly the entire male population to the Woman Suffrage doctrine," [24] The full extent of her position is reaveled in a letter written after the trial:

> I do not complain of Judge Hunt's interpretations of the Constitution on the suffrage question. . . . What I complain of is that he did not hold as void, instead of arguing them to be valid, any words in the instrument which seemed to him to favor the disenfranchisement of woman and consequent robbery and destruction of her rights. What I complain of is that, instead of his conscientious regard for his oath, he was not prepared to ignore and scout all human law so far as it is antagonistic to natural law and natural rights . . . .[25]

After her trial she informed a correspondent:

> I owe no allegiance to the Government's penalties until I have a voice in it and shall pay none. What the Government can *exact* it may, whether of cash or imprisonment.[26]

On the whole, during the last quarter of the century the suffrage movement devoted itself to efforts at persuasion and political action. There were some instances of refusal to pay taxes; and, from time to time, resolutions were passed calling for even more extreme forms of resistance. Occasionally the efforts at persuasion took on unusual and bizarre forms. Thus, a group of suffragists, denied a place in the ceremonies at Independence Hall marking the centennial of the Declaration of Independence, succeeded in capturing the lectern at one stage of the proceedings and reading a declaration of women's rights to an astonished and, no doubt, hostile audience.[27]

After the turn of the century, there was a hardening of attitudes on the part of certain segments of the American feminist movement. The "New Woman," whose emergence was trumpeted by Ibsen and Shaw, had arrived on the scene. Many looked back on a half-century's argumentation and advocacy and concluded that too little had been achieved by these moderate means. Many were profoundly influenced by the events then occurring in England.[28] Under the direction óf Mrs. Emmeline Pankhurst and her formidable daughters, the

---

[23] FLEXNER, CENTURY OF STRUGGLE 166–67 (1959).
[24] 2 HISTORY OF WOMAN SUFFRAGE 936 (Anthony, Stanton & Gage ed. 1882) (referring to an editorial in the *Syracuse Standard*).
[25] 2 *id*, at 942.
[26] Letter From Susan B. Anthony to Dr. E. B. Foote, in 2 *id*. at 941. (Emphasis in original.)
[27] See 3 *id*. at 27–34.
[28] See MITCHELL, MONSTROUS REGIMENT 19–31 (1965).

Woman's Revolution in Britain reached excesses never approached in the United States. Frustrated by their inability to dent the apathy of public opinion and of the political leadership, the British feminists indulged in a succession of the most extreme measures to gain their ends. When the nonpayment of taxes failed to achieve perceptible results, the women resorted to the interruption of Parliamentary proceedings and invasions of the privacy of members of the government.[29] A campaign of destruction of property was launched. Paintings were slashed in public art galleries. On a single night three castle in Scotland were burned to the ground. The coronation chair in Westminster Abbey was splintered by a bomb. The slogan "No Golf, No Votes" was etched in acid on the greens of Balmoral.[31] In 1913, one enthusiast was killed when she threw herself under the hoofs of the horses at the Derby. The violence of the women was matched by the excesses of the officials. Women on occasion were left to the aggression of mobs, without police intervention. When arrested, they were frequently subjected to brutal treatment in the prisons, including the practice of forced feeding. The official response was, in short, admirably calculated to produce martyrs and revealed perhaps even less rationality than the conduct that precipitated it.[31]

The situation in the United States never deteriorated so badly as it did across the Atlantic; but with the coming of the second decade of the new century, a substantial segment of the feminist movement (although, no doubt, a small minority of all those who supported woman's suffrage) was persuaded of the need for sterner methods. The new activism was signaled in 1915, when Miss Mable Vernon, who was seated on the speaker's platform, interrupted a speech of President Woodrow Wilson by calling out in her powerful voice: "Mr. President, if you sincerely desire to foreward the interests of all the people, why do you oppose the national enfranchisement of women?"[32] After Miss Vernon stated her question a second time, she was ordered from the meeting by the police.[33] The suffrage movement was considerably hampered by the diversion of public interest produced by the entry of the United States into the European war in 1917. The strategy devised by the activists to confront this problem was to call attention to a presumed discrepancy between the administration's claim to be fighting a war to advance the democratic principle and the refusal of the administration to remove the barriers to democratic participation of women in American political life.[34] The White House was picketed, disorders occurred, and charges of police brutality were heard. By mid-1917, arrests of pickets were being made in considerable numbers.[35] The reaction of the women was expressed in a statement of Anne Martin at her trial:

[29] *Id.* at 23.
[30] *Id.* at 26.
[31] See *id.* at 29–31. See also TUCHMAN, THE PROUD TOWER 381 (1965).
[32] STEVENS, JAILED FOR FREEDOM 43 (1920).
[33] *Ibid.*
[34] *Ibid.*
[34] *Id.* at 83.
[35] See *id.* at 84–95.

As long as the government and the representatives of the government prefer to send women to jail on petty and technical charges, we will go to jail. Persecution has always advanced the cause of justice. . . . We would hinder, not help, the whole cause of freedom for women, if we weakly submitted to persecution now. Our work for the passage of the amendment must go on. It *will* go on.[36]

In the jails of the District of Columbia and in nearby Virginia the events took on a darker hue. When the arrested women complained of deplorable prison conditions and demanded improvements, they were roughly handled. As in England, hunger strikes were met by forced feeding; and, also as in England, the excesses of official response produced sympathy and support across the nation for the cause the women were advancing.[37]

The further multiplication of historical examples of the advocacy and practice of law violation by American reformers would probably serve little useful purpose, although many such additional examples could be summoned. At this point it may be more profitable to inquire whether this history reveals any significant regularities, any common patterns or tendencies, that may illuminate reflections on modern manifestations of conscientious law violation. This is treacherous ground; obviously any observations that I shall be able to advance will be highly tentative and incomplete. Nevertheless, I believe that certain patterns can be discerned.

Typical of the leaders of the great nineteenth-century reform movements was the intensity of their conviction of social sin. The theological phraseology is appropriate, for in many instances their perceptions of social evil—whether of slavery, discriminations against women, conditions in prisons and mental institutions, or any of dozens of other wrongs—reveal an almost religious quality. Making all allowances for the rhetoric of the period, one can hardly fail to detect the depth and sincerity of feeling when, for example, William Lloyd Garrison speaks of slavery:

> It is a system which has in itself no redeeming feature, but is full of blood–the blood of innocent men, women, and children; full of adultery and concupiscence; full of darkness, blasphemy and woe; full of rebellion against God and treason against the universe; full of wrath—impurity—ignorance—bruatality—and awful impiety; full of wounds and bruises and putrefying sores; full of temperal suffering and eternal damnation.[38]

Hardly less intense is the statement that appeared in Susan B. Anthony's suffragist journal: "On the idea taught by the creeds, codes, and customs of the world, that woman was made for man—his toy, drudge, subject, or even mere companion—we declare war to the death . . . ."[39]

For persons of that temperment and of that time, a conviction of evil resulted almost automatically in efforts to extirpate the evil. As Professor Oscar

[36] *Id.* at 102. (Emphasis in original.)
[37] See *id.* at 184–91.
[38] GARRISON, THOUGHTS ON AFRICAN COLONIZATION 51–53 (1832).
[39] The Revolution, Jan. 6, 1870, p. 1.

Handlin has written: "Behind all these excited endeavors was the conviction that men had the power to transform the universe in accord with their moral ideas." [40] But when the reformers moved into the arena of action, certain hard facts had to be confronted. How were the apathetic masses to be reached? How were they to be made to share the reformer's zeal, and to accede to his solutions of the social problem? The difficulties of communication and persuasion became all too apparent at the earliest stages of the abolition movement. In the first issue of the *Liberator,* William Lloyd Garrison bravely proclaimed: "I am in earnest—I will not equivocate—I will not excuse—I will not retreat a single inch—and I will be heard." [41] But being heard proved no simple matter; and when not subjected to abuse by the larger community, the abolitionist was often ignored. The same difficulties of communication bedeviled the careers of other reform movements even more seriously. A perceptive editorial writer in the *New York Post* accurately identified the central problem of the American feminist movement in its first half-century of existence, when he wrote: "In a word, it is not hostility so much as calm indifference with which the advocates of woman suffrage have to contend, and unluckily for them indifference is very largely feminine." [42] American reform movements have been characterized by the rise and speedy demise of scores of journals published, sometimes as great personal sacrifice, by editors seeking to broadcast their version of truth to an often indifferent world.

Frequently the reformers, suffused with zeal but frustrated by public apathy and the absence of favorable official response, moved to other means of communication and persuasion. As one observes the techniques of antislavery agitation in the 1840's and 1850's, he is struck by a propensity to employ dramatic and symbolic gestures in ways that suggest certain modern analogies. William Lloyd Garrison's Fourth of July address at Framingham, Massachusetts, in 1854, is perhaps the most famous instance of this sort. With all solemnity he produced a copy of the hated Fugitive Slave Law and burned it in the presence of the crowd. He repeated the ritual by burning copies of charges to juries in notorious prosecutions under the law. Then, as reported in Garrison's own periodical:

> [H]olding up the U.S. Constitution, he branded it as the source and parent of all the other atrocities,—"a covenant with death, and an agreement with hell,"—and consumed it to ashes on the spot, exclaiming, "So perish all compromises with tyranny! And let the people say, Amen!" A temendous shout of "Amen!" went up to heaven in ratification of the deed, mingled with a few hisses and wrathful exclamations from some who were evidently in a rowdyish state of mind, but who were at once cowed by the popular feeling. [43]

[40] Handlin, *Editor's Preface* to NYE, WILLIAM LLOYD GARRISON AND THE HUMANITARIAN REFORMERS at v-vi (1955).
[41] The Liberator, Jan. 1, 1831, p. 1.
[42] 3 HISTORY OF WOMAN SUFFRAGE 43 (Anthony, Stanton & Gage ed. 1882) (editorial appearing in the *New York Post*).
[43] The Liberator, July 7, 1854.

The attraction of ritualistic burnings was not confined to the antislavery advocates. While the First World War was in progress, suffragists conducted a series of symbolic burnings of the words of President Wilson. At a ceremony at Lafayette Monument in Washington, one of the leaders proclaimed: " 'The torch which I hold symbolizes the burning indignation of the women who for years have been given words without action. . . . As in ancient fights for liberty, the crusaders for freedom symbolized their protest against those responsible for injustice by consigning their hollow phrases to the flames, so we, on behalf of thousands of suffragists . . . protest.' "[44] The full significance of such ritualistic acts, some of them in violation of the law, is probably more complex than is immediately apparent. In part they reflect the frustrations experienced in other forms of communication and are intended to engage more effectively the attention of the larger community in the cause being advanced. Often they also represent efforts to gain solidarity among those already convinced and to achieve morale and sustenance for the work remaining undone.

Against this background of historical American experience with conscientious law violation and with our knowledge of its contemporary manifestations, we may be in a better position to consider more carefully the relations of civil disobedience to the American system of law and government. The problem of the conscientious violator may perhaps be profitably viewed as part of the broader problem of the political role of minority groups in a nation dedicated, in general, to the principle of majority rule. From the beginning of the Republic the strategies of dealing with minority groups have been one of our principal preoccupations. That majority rule should prevail unrestrained and unconditioned has never been the American position, as the Bill of Rights alone is sufficient to attest. But our tactics have gone much beyond promulgating and enforcing a Bill of Rights. The grand strategy has been to avoid, insofar as possible, total or serious alienation of substantial groups of citizens from the institutions and major assumptions of the society. Experience suggests that if this is to be achieved, minorities must sometimes be provided with opportunities, not only to speak, but to be heard; and that they must not be deprived of all hope of prevailing in the end. Despair of the truth prevailing within the framework of legitimate institutions is the great peril; and, with the substantial exception of the events leading to the Civil War, our political instinct has ordinarily been sound enough to avoid this result. In general, our public life has been characterized by a politics that has avoided polar positions, that welcomes compromise and seeks consensus. But the principle of majority rule has been tempered by more than the give and take of democratic politics. The law itself has created devices to frustrate the popular will as expressed by legislative bodies. Such at least is suggested by those commentators who assert that the privilege against self-incrimination may be viewed as a hedge against bad (but not necessarily invalid) law.[45] The legislative filibuster provides an

[44] STEVENS, *op. cit. supra* note 96, at 278–79.
[45] *Cf.* McNaughton, *The Privilege Against Self-Incrimination*, 51 J. CRIM. L., C. & P.S. 138, 145–46 (1960).

even more dramatic example. It is a device that ensures that a minority will not only speak, but be attended to; that holds out the hope that right, even when in the minority, will prevail; and that encourages compromise and accommodation.

My purpose is not to praise the filibuster, but to point out that the resistance to the will of the majority on grounds of conscience expressed in acts of civil disobedience may depart less drastically from the assumptions underlying much of our political practice than might at first be supposed. When analysis proceeds in purely operational terms, it may be possible to observe that civil disobedience sometimes identifies grievances and areas of sensitivity theretofore unknown to the legislative majorities, or, if known, not taken seriously by them. In short, it may disclose where the rub is, and may induce the majority to consider whether there are ways to avoid conscientious objections or, if not, whether the legislative objective is worth overriding the scruples of the minority. The problems posed for law makers and enforcement officials in several states by the Amish communities may illustrate this process.[46] The constitutional power of state legislatures to create a system of compulsory public education surely encompasses a wide discretion to stipulate the levels of education that will be made compulsory. But constitutional authority is only part of the problem. The sincere and dedicated resistance of Amish parents and children to instruction above grade-school levels has caused more than one public official to wonder whether the game is worth the candle, and to search, however unsuccessfully, for means to accommodate the eccentric convictions of these groups to the requirements of the legal order.

Nothing in the foregoing comments is to be taken as a defense or justification of civil disobedience. The fact remains that the practices to which civil disobedience has been compared and analogized have been embraced by the system and legitimated; whereas civil disobedience itself, when measured by any criteria relevant to the legal order, is illegitimate. Nevertheless, the persistence of civil disobedience in a society that has made such apparently substantial concessions to the interests and scruples of minority groups is an arresting fact. The evidence, historical and contemporary, suggests that civil disobedience is not something alien to the American system, introduced from the outside, but is rather a phenomenon indigenous to our soil, and in some sense reflective of gaps between the promise of American life and its performance.

One conclusion to be derived from historical and contemporary instances of civil disobedience is that groups possessing little political power encounter enormous difficulties both in communicating their interests and convictions to the larger community and in experiencing a sense of participation in American life. Although the element of race is an aggravating factor, this problem is not confined to racial minorities. It has become critical to city dwellers of all races when confronted by official decisions, such as those involved in programs of highway building and urban redevelopment, that profoundly

[46] See Smith, The Amish Today 288–91 (1961).

affect the individual's immediate environment and his sense of well-being. It is ironic that at the local level, where, according to traditional notions, the citizen is expected to experience the greatest sense of participation in governmental policy, he often feels most helpless to influence the measures that affect him and his family in the most direct and drastic ways. As one experienced and perceptive critic has observed: "[T]enderness should not prevent our attending the fact that one of the worst features of urban renewal and planning is the motivation and machinery available to discourage or even prevent open public discussion of its purposes and methods."[47] The problem is difficult, for one of the constant factors in these situations is the insistence of many urban neighborhoods that public works are admirable, so long as they are located in other neighborhoods. But the propensity of municipal authorities to proceed, whenever possible, without consultation with the affected populations—or worse, after conducting perfunctory and wholly meaningless hearings—has inspired angry resentment throughout the country and threatens serious alienation of urban populations from the institutions of self-government.

The recurrence of protest and civil disobedience demonstrates not only inadequacies in the legally sanctioned means available to individuals and groups to communicate their needs, aspirations, and proposals to the larger community, but a widespread conviction that the remedies provided by the legal order are inadequate to meet the problems of greatest importance to these groups. There is surely no absence of evidence to support this belief. Thus, when the Department of Justice filed its first voting cases in Dallas County in 1961, one per cent of the Negro population of voting age was registered. Two and one-half years were required to secure a court order prohibiting further discrimination. After litigation had dragged on for nearly four years, less than 400 out of 15,000 Negroes of voting age were registered, and four additional suits had been filed to protect Negro applicants from intimidation by officials and private groups.[48] It was the perception of the inadequacies of the legal remedies and the protests inspired by the resulting conditions that led to the subsequent enactment of federal voting-rights legislation.[49] But there is a wide range of problems involving the vital interests of members of impoverished and alienated groups within our society to which the law has as yet made no effective response. The adaptation of law, both substantive and remedial, to such problems—problems that are only just beginning to penetrate the consciousness of the dominant segments of the community—is one of the principal challenges confronting lawyers and law-makers in the years immediately ahead. To a very considerable degree the success of this important undertaking rests in the hands of a generation of young lawyers, some of whom are today students in the law schools.

[47] Lehman, *Thinking Small About Urban Renewal,* 1965 Wash. U.L.Q. 396, 399.
[48] Marshall, *The Protest Movement and the Law,* 51 Va. L. Rev. 785, 790–91 (1965).
[49] Voting Rights Act of 1965, 79 Stat. 437, 42 U.S.C.A. § 1973 (Supp. 1966).

In part, the task of law reform is to render the law relevant to the conditions of life in the deprived communities. The considerable irrelevancy of
the law to these problems stems from the fact that law in our society is primarily
a product of the experience and presuppositions of the middle-class. Thus, in
legal areas like those involving the family, the law frequently fails when
applied to the slum community because it is founded on assumptions about
the nature of social relationships and about human responses to legal regulations
that are at war with reality. Encompassed in the middle-class orientation is a
tendency toward paternalism, a tendency expressed when the law seeks
deliberately to confront the problems arising in the impoverished areas. The
interests of dwellers in slum tenements are sought to be protected through
public inspection and regulation, which, in general, have served the interests
of those investing in such properties more effectively than they have served
the interests of those living in them. As has recently been suggested, an approach
to these problems that creates legal remedies against the violating landlord that
may be initiated directly by the tenants might well ameliorate the conditions
of life of the slum dweller and, at the same time, demonstrate to him the
existence of remedies within the legal order.[50]

Law reform, insofar as pertinent to the issues under consideration, involves
more than the modification of legal norms and procedures. It also encompasses
the extension of legal services to members of deprived communities in order
that they may be advised of their legal rights and obligations and that they
may have access to the representation necessary to invoke appropriate legal
remedies.[51] These needs, of course, have frequently been asserted; and the
proposition as advanced contains little that is startling. There is, however, one
consideration that has not always been noted when the case for the extension
of legal services has been made. The point is that such programs involve more
than philanthropy, and constitute an essential part of the strategy of public
order. Inhabitants of any community, however affluent or impoverished,
become involved in disputes and in conflicts of interests with other persons.
Such controversies contain the potential for violence and disorder. A major
function of a system of law is to reduce this potential by providing agencies,
armed with the authority of the state, whose mission it is to resolve disputes
and to protect rights from invasion through the use of procedures that minimize
social waste and human misery. If, however, by reason of ignorance and
poverty, persons are denied access to the courts, they will devise methods of
self-help that are a threat to good order and which are productive of attitudes
and values that threaten the interests, not only of those residing in the deprived
areas, but of the entire community.

The observations just made should not be understood as constituting an
assertion that all of the problems involving modern protest movements, includ-

---

[50] Sax & Heistand, *Slumlordism as a Tort*, 65 MICH. L. REV. 869 (1967).
[51] See Pye, *The Role of Legal Services in the Antipoverty Program*, 31 LAW & CONTEMP. PROB. 211,
215 (1966).

ing the problems of civil disobedience, can be resolved by an exercise in law reform. Many critical issues posed by these movements are only incidentally legal in character; and efforts focused wholly on modifications of the legal order or on vigorous application of penal sanctions will surely prove inadequate to the challenge. Nevertheless, the legal order is inextricably involved in the problems arising from the modern protest movement and has its important contributions to make to their ultimate solution. One of the most important of these is that of rendering the law relevant to the issues of these times and accessible to those with grievances to advance.

Unfortunately, the responses of the legal order have not in all cases been constructive or intelligent. It does little good to urge upon alienated and disaffected groups the virtues of pursuing social objectives through the use of legally approved means so long as such groups, with reason, feel debarred from access to those means and from full participation in the life of a democratic society. On occasion, both in the North and in the South, official power has been employed to maintain the old patterns of exclusion. Virtually every discretionary power granted to the administration of justice has been employed to harass and suppress the activities of protest groups, regardless of their legal propriety.[52] Powers of arrest,[53] the granting and withholding of bail,[54] the revocation of licences, and even the exercise of the jurisdiction of juvenile courts, have been diverted from their proper and important purposes and converted into instrumentalities of suppression.[55]

The dangers of such distortion of legal processes are unmistakable and profound. The deterrent capacities of the criminal law rest perhaps most importantly on the moral authority of the law. But when the processes of the law are perceived as instrumentalities of oppression, the stigma of law violation evaporates; and the sense of obligation to the law is destroyed at the source. Thus, modern experience with civil disobedience has again demonstrated that the justice of a legal order is not simply a desirable embellishment. It is, on the contrary, an indispensable prerequisite to the performance of its important functions.[56]

A canvass of some of the challenges confronting American society and the legal order, such as I have attempted to make, ought not to obscure the fact that recent history also records achievement and strength. Fairness requires it to be observed that in some sense the range and intensity of criticisms of twentieth-century America are, paradoxically enough, a product of the remarkable successes of American society. Attacks on the inequalities of races and classes bite because the ideal of equality possesses vitality and is thus a dynamic

---

[52] See, *e.g.*, Life, March 19, 1965, p. 30.
[53] See KING, WHY WE CAN'T WAIT 72 (1964).
[54] See *id.* at 70.
[55] See generally KING, STRIDE TOWARD FREEDOM (1964).
[56] Compare FULLER, THE LAW IN QUEST OF ITSELF 90–91 (1940): The stability of a given legal system, its capacity to produce peace and order, will depend not simply on the lawyer's faithful adherence to its enacted rules, but also on the layman's willingness to accept those rules as being essentially right. A law which is "good" for the purpose of establishing order will have to be, or at least seem, "good" in other respects as well.

force. Our very affluence gives point to modern protests that gains in material prosperity have not narrowed the gaps in the levels of well-being separating the disadvantaged from the community as a whole. Political movements to eliminate poverty are possible only when a substantial number of people believe that poverty can be eliminated through political and social action. In short, the modern protest movement gains much of its nourishment from the conviction that iniquities and privations suffered by our lower classes are today unnecessary. Our social failures are no longer seen as innocent because avoidable, and hence, there has grown up a kind of collective *mens rea* that manifests itself in forms ranging from a vague unease, more or less consciously repressed, to a flaming conviction of social sin. The irony is that this sense of guilt is likely to grow stronger as we succeed in our efforts to mitigate the ills of our society.

This frame of mind creates its own perils for the legal order. No system of law succeeds in providing full and complete justice, and one form of subversion of the free society is to demand levels of performance that no human institution can attain. The essayist Montaigne observed: "Now laws remain in credit not because they are just, but because they are laws. That is the mystic foundation of their authority; they have no other. . . . There is nothing so grossly and widely and ordinarily faulty as the laws. Whoever obeys them because they are just, does not obey them for just the reason he should."[57] This sentiment, however overstated, expresses more than a weary cynicism. All legal systems depend on there being sufficient credit in the concept of law, or sufficient respect for the law's sanctions, to induce general compliance with bad and foolish laws—at least until the mistakes and oversights of the past can be altered through established constitutional procedures. It is difficult to see how, without a rather high level of tolerance of this kind, a system of law can function at all: which is to say, the attainment of the goals of justice, rationality, and good order through law requires a considerable tolerance of this kind.

But this is an idea from which we are able to take little comfort or repose. We live in an age in which the tolerable margins of institutional failure are narrowing; and, consequently, the maintenance of the rule of law cannot prudently be hazarded simply on the existence of a popular sense of obligation to law because it is the law. Nothing in our history, and certainly nothing that has occurred in recent years, would justify any such exclusive reliance. The challenge to the legal order that emerges from our recent experiences with civil disobedience is extreme and even unreasonable. It is that the law should proceed promptly and effectively to the task of realizing its promises of justice and rationality in the conditions of the mid-twentieth-century world. In framing the response of the legal order to this test of dedication and creativity, the contributions of the younger lawyers must inevitably be of first importance.

[57] MONTAIGNE, THE COMPLETE ESSAYS OF MONTAIGNE 821 (Frame transl. 1958).

# 27

# Douglas E. Sturm

Douglas Sturm (1929–      ), Professor of Religion at Bucknell University
and critic of Lon Fuller's philosophy of law, surveys recent international
developments in the theory of rule of law in a paper prepared at the
Institute for Advanced Legal Studies, University of London.

# RULE OF LAW AND POLITICS IN A
# REVOLUTIONARY AGE*

This is an essay on constitutionalism as the Rule of Law in a revolutionary
world. That the world is in a revolutionary state, none can doubt. Revolution
is stirring in almost every nook and cranny of the world. Even established, well-
developed, seemingly secure societies are troubled. They confront challenges
both internal and external to their pattern of existence. In some areas and at some
times, the turmoil is so confusing and the changes so rapid, it is virtually
impossible to maintain an adequate flow of information about them.

But revolutions are not always dramatic or rapid or signalled by use of arms.
It may be that the most effective and ultimately far reaching revolutions are not
at all obvious to the naked eye while they are in process. Modernization and
social and political development involve shifts in career patterns, in attitudes
and orientations, in loyalties and commitments that may not be at first blush
perceptible even to persons undergoing the change. Yet these changes may, in
the course of time, radically transform the values and the institutions of a society.

Indeed, a genuine and profound revolution, by its very nature, runs deep.
It penetrates into the soul of man even as it alters the patterns of his behavior
and the structure of his common life. It affects the forms of his understanding,
the shape of his vocabulary, the categories of his thought as much as it is
evidenced in his conduct and his associations.

Upon first reflection, law and revolution are strange partners, if they can
be understood as partners at all. Surely their immediate connotations are
antithetical. Law is a symbol of order, peace, stability, the maintenance of the
status quo. The law-abiding citizen is one whose actions are predictable and
non-disruptive. The certainty and strength of law are understood to constitute
a bulwark against any social and political forces that might threaten to alter or

*Douglas E. Sturm, "Rule of Law and Politics in a Revolutionary Age," *Soundings*, Vol. LI,4
(1968). Reprinted by permission of the author and publisher. This essay was written while the
author held a post-doctoral Fellowship for cross-disciplinary studies from the Society for Religion
in Higher Education. He is indebted to Professor William B. Gwyn for assistance in various
stages of its preparation.

undo a traditional pattern of life. In fact, it can and has been argued that while political regimes may come and go, the laws, as they affect the everyday life of the ordinary citizen remain virtually unmodified and continue to be as effectively and extensively obeyed after a political revolution as before. Thus Robert MacIver writes, "Even the most violent revolutions leave the bulk of the code intact when they overthrow the agency which hitherto guarded it. The most permanent, as it is also the most conservative character of the state is its body of law."[1] One may be modestly displeased or even profoundly offended by the character of the laws, but if they are, by and large, honored, they provide, it is said, a foundation of security and continuity, an assured structure of expectation.

So characterized—or caricatured, if you will—law is the antithesis of revolution, for revolution means change, transformation, alteration, conversion. More precisely, the term revolution is customarily reserved to designate not minor changes, but changes of a major, far reaching, profoundly shattering, radical character. Of course it is no simple matter in some instances to judge whether an upheaval is major or minor, but difficulties of classification do not detract from the applicability of the concept or from the *prima facie* contrast between law and revolution.

In the modern world, this contrast, if it holds, is of particular significance, if one accepts the force of Carl J. Friedrich's observation that "Generally speaking, the modern world is distinguished by a reasonably favorable attitude toward revolution."[2] Indeed, could it be that the emergence of this favorable attitude towards revolution, which Friedrich views as an expression of the readiness of modern man to engage in innovation, experimentation, invention, is itself the result of a revolutionary or radical change? This question is not intended to be merely a clever play on the word revolution. It is intended rather to suggest that in thought and in action there is perhaps an appreciably greater propensity nowadays to radicalize the notions of change, process, mobility, creativity, and the like and to tolerate or even encourage inventiveness in social policy and innovation in political action.

On the level of forms of thought, for instance, Eugene Fontinell has asserted that "For the contemporary man it is reality and not simply an aspect or dimension of reality which is in process. . . . process and relation rather than structure and substance are the controlling categories."[3] What causal connection, if any, there might be between the processive mode of thought to which Fontinell refers and the radical political, social, and economic revolutions that are currently twisting the world of human relations into new shapes is open to question.

But whatever the case, if it is true that innovation, process, transformation, change constitute the leitmotif of modern man's thought and action, then the

---

[1] *The Modern State* (London: Oxford University Press, 1926), p. 99.
[2] *Man and His Government* (New York: McGraw-Hill, 1963), p. 375.
[3] "Reflections on Faith and Metaphysics," *Cross Currents,* vol. XVI, no. 1, Winter 1966, p. 20.

question of the relevance of law is thrust to the fore. This is a question that in a way C. H. McIlwain formulated over twenty years ago. "Perhaps never in its long history has the principle of constitutionalism been so questioned as it is questioned today, never has the attack upon it been so determined or so threatening as it is just now. The world is trembling in the balance between the orderly procedure of law and the processes of force which seem so much more quick and effective."[4] In an age of revolution and radical change, what is the place and relevance of law?

In the medieval world, there was an uneasy balance between *gubernaculum* and *jurisdictio,* between governmental prerogative and the operation of law. In principle, the sphere of law was the preserve of the people. The scope of governmental activity was circumscribed and contained by *jurisdictio,* protecting the interests and liberties of the people. Government under law meant limited government.

Despite the extensive transformations in thought, action, and association that constitute the watershed between the medieval and the modern worlds, the principle of the Rule of Law continued to be invoked, but the consequences in the nineteenth century were not altogether the most fortunate. Law continued to function to delimit the scope of governmental activity, but the results seemed to lend evident support to the contention of Marx and Engels that law is an expression of the interests of the ruling class, that law is a tool of exploitation and oppression, that within a capitalist society law protects property but prosecutes persons. The contention is an exaggeration but sufficiently true to raise serious question about the compatibility of constitutionalism or Rule of Law and the realization of social justice in the modern world. Another form of the same question is indicated in the above citation from McIlwain. That is, where rules of law are (presumably) fixed, rigid, and certain, and where legal procedures are slow, cautious, and laden with protective principles, governmental policies in the interests of social reform and social justice must be flexible, open, often imprecise, and provision made for the exercise of discretionary and forceful power by governmental officials.

But the contrast that I have drawn in general terms between revolution and law, between governmental action for the sake of social change and social justice and the principles of legality is too stark. It is a falsification of historical realities, for law has been in fact a two-edged sword. It has been an agent of exploitation but it has also been a basic instrument of social reform.[5] Furthermore, the contrast glosses over what is possible in theory. On the latter point the notion of the Rule of Law may be intelligibly formulated as containing revolutionary potentialities, as incorporating the principles of social justice, and as consistent with the possibility of effective governmental action. If this is so, it may be possible, at least in theory, to solve what McIlwain judged to be "probably our most serious practical problem," namely, the reconciliation of

---

4 *Constitutionalism: Ancient and Modern* (Ithaca, N.Y.: Great Seal Books, 1958), p. 1.
5 See the excellent studies in legal history by James Willard Hurst.

*jurisdictio* and government. Admittedly, theoretical solutions, especially of a highly general character, are not in themselves practical solutions. But if they point a direction, if they provide a basis for understanding, they are a first step toward practical solutions.

In this light, I intend to develop the outlines of a dynamic concept of the Rule of Law, to suggest its compatibility with the "politics of growth" (Karl W. Deutsch), and throughout the analysis to indicate that law and politics, *so conceived and understood,* constitute in themselves a certain form of revolutionary change, a certain structure of the process of becoming.

I.

It must be admitted at the outset that the concept of the Rule of Law perpetuates a verbal ambiguity that has long plagued discussions of law in the English-speaking world. Where in other languages there is a verbal distinction between, for instance, *Recht* and *Gesetz, droit* and *loi, pravo* and *zakon,* the word law has been used in both indicated capacities. Thus, on the one hand, law is used to refer to the positive law of a nation, but, on the other hand, Rule of Law is taken as the cognate of *Rechtsstaat* and *du principe de Primauté du Droit.* There is a long and well-known tradition of legal thought that has attempted to make the distinction clear—often by reserving the term law for the former usage, but at least by insisting upon a precise demarcation between legal standards and moral standards.

Yet the notion of Rule of Law persists, and I suggest it persists because of another tradition, a tradition that conceives the jurist as a professional. A profession involves both specialized training and responsibility for the affairs of other men. But beyond technique and service, there is a third element in a profession, namely dedication to some ideal, which ideal constitutes the central organizing and critical principle of the profession. This is analogous to the normative element inherent in role definition,[6] except that the ideal in a profession is more deliberate and open. Law was one of the "three great professions" of the medieval world, each of which was bound to an ideal that functioned as its normative core or *telos.* In divinity it was the beatific vision, the good of the human soul; in medicine it was health, the good of the human body; in law it was justice, the good of human social conduct. A lawyer, or more broadly, a jurist is, within this framework, not merely a technician, one whose professional obligation ceases when he has applied existing laws or given advice and counsel as to the legal implications of a proposed action. He has as well a moral obligation, and this not merely as a human being or as a member of a given society, but as a jurist. To be sure, he must use and apply the laws as they are but not indiscriminately, lest he neglect his role as critic. Given the juristic role as critic the question of the constitutive elements of the notion of the Rule of Law, which from this perspective is synonymous with the question of the meaning of justice,

---

[6] See Dorothy Emmet, *Rules, Roles and Relations* (London: MacMillan, 1966).

is of central importance. It is important both in order to have a relatively precise standard by which to assess existing political and legal systems and in order to indicate the perimeters or basic character of a society informed by the Rule of Law.

In the development of the constitutive elements of a dynamic concept of the Rule of Law, I have relied heavily upon the publications of the International Commission of Jurists both because the work of the ICJ expresses the felt responsibility of a significant body of jurists, acting in their professional capacity, to the ideal of justice and because the deliberations of the ICJ about the meaning of Rule of Law are particularly apt relative to the problem of this essay.[7]

There are two major dimensions to Rule of Law, (1) the valuational and (2) the operational, the more definitive of which is the valuational.[8]

(1) The central end or value of Rule of Law is that of a free society, which Norman S. Marsh, one-time secretary general of the ICJ, has defined variously as "a society that acknowledges the supreme value of the human person and conceives all its social institutions, and in particular the State, as the servants, not the masters, of the individual" (1959)[9]; "one in which the free spirit of every member can find the fullest expression" (1961)[10]; "a convenient way of summarizing the aim of those who see in the worth and dignity of the individual the ultimate aim and purpose of all human organization" (1963).[11]

These definitions are intended to indicate that Rule of Law is humanistic and universalistic. It does not preclude distinctions among men, but it stresses first and foremost their commonality, whose fundamental character is indicated by the terms free spirit and personality. On that basis it stresses that there are certain rights, liberties, or freedoms[12] of human beings arising from their sheer humanity, all aimed at and therefore, where necessary or arguably desirable, qualified by the ultimate value of human personality.

These rights, which constitute the further extension of the valuational dimension of Rule of Law, have been roughly classified into two related sets,

---

[7] According to its Statute, Article 4, the International Commission of Jurists, since its founding in 1952, has been "dedicated to the support and advancement of those principles of justice which constitute the basis of the Rule of Law.

[8] As M. J. C. Vile wrote recently, constitutionalism (which in this essay is understood as Rule of Law) consists in the advocacy of certain kinds of *institutional arrangements* on the grounds that certain *ends or values* will be achieved in this way. (*Constitutionalism and the Separation of Powers* [Oxford: Clarendon Press, 1967] p. 8). Whether Rule of Law is the key concept, or but one of a cluster of key concepts, of constitutionalism, is, of course, a debatable point. See Charles E. Wyzanski, Jr., "Constitutionalism: Limitation and Affirmation," in Arthur E. Sutherland, ed., *Government Under Law* (Cambridge: Harvard University Press, 1956).

[9] *Le Principe de la Légalité dans une Société Libre,* prepared by Norman S. Marsh (Geneva: ICJ, 1959), p. 202.

[10] "The Rule of Law as a Supra-National Concept," in A. G. Guest, ed., *Oxford Essays in Jurisprudence* (London: Oxford University Press, 1961), p. 240.

[11] "The Rule of Law: New Delhi—Lagos—Rio de Janeiro," *Journal of the ICJ,* vol. IV, no. 2, Summer 1963, p. 265.

[12] See Carl J. Friedrich's discussion of the relative differences suggested by the three terms "rights," "liberties," and "freedoms" in *Man and his Government, op. cit.* at note 2, p. 357, and in *Transcendant Justice* (Durham, N.C.: Duke University Press, 1964), chapter 5.

(a) the negative or the political and spiritual set, and (b) the positive or the social and economic set.

(a) The first set is labelled negative because, at least *ab initio*, it was conceived as protecting the individual from the interference of the state. It expresses the medieval distinction between government and law, establishing at law a sphere of private activity beyond the legitimate reach of king or governor.

This set includes the rights usually associated with the Western liberal laissez faire state of the nineteenth century, but expanded and changed in relative emphasis with the emergence of the so-called modern state. Thus while it includes the right to freedom of religion and to own property, it also embraces the right to freedom of opinion and expression through all media of communication, the right to freedom of assembly and association including political parties and trade unions, the right of free movement, and the right to participate in the selection of representatives in government. Moreover, it includes certain rights in the area of criminal law, such as the right of the accused to know the charges brought against him, the right to have counsel and to have opportunity to prepare a defense, the right against self-incrimination, the right to a fair and public trial, the right of appeal and the right against cruel and degrading treatment before and subsequent to conviction.

Norman S. Marsh has noted that whatever rights are included in this set, they cannot be considered as "absolute," that is, as binding without exception in all circumstances. But if exception is to be made, it can be justified in the final analysis only by the fundamental value of the Rule of Law of which these rights are expressions. That is, in Marsh's terms, there should be no restrictions on these rights or freedoms *"except in so far as such restrictions are necessary to ensure as a whole the status and dignity of the individual."*[13] The fundamental value of the free society and therefore of human personality is thus both the originating principle and the limiting principle of these political and spiritual rights.

It might be possible on that basis to consider some of these rights as more crucial than others, as "preferred freedoms," as the operational key or index to the set. On this question there is some variance of judgment. Jean Graven points to the relative degree and character of the rights of the accused as the crucial indicator of whether a legal system conforms to Rule of Law.[14] Ivor Jennings, however, contends that the test of a free society is not the character of its criminal law, but whether "political power rests in the last analysis on free elections, carried out in a State where criticism of the Government is not only permissible, but a positive merit, and where parties based on competing policies or interests are not only allowed but encouraged."[15] Norman S. Marsh

---

[13] *Op. cit.* at note 11, p. 262. Italics in the original. See also *op. cit.* at note 10, p. 245, and *op. cit.* at note 9, p. 229.

[14] Quoted in *Report of the International Congress of Jurists: Athens, Greece: June* 13-20, 1955 (The Hague: ICJ, March 1956), p. 67.

[15] Sir W. Ivor Jennings, *The Law and the Constitution* (London: University of London Press, Ltd., Fifth Edition, 1959), p. 60.

agrees that the right of persons to choose their own government is first among individual liberties; but he adds that "in the second place come freedom of speech, freedom of assembly and freedom of association" of which freedom of speech is most important under modern conditions.[16] Finally Sean MacBride observes that "The surest sign of deterioration of the situation in any country is interference with the freedom of the press."[17]

But in any case it should be obvious that to describe this as a set of *negative* rights, liberties, or freedoms is a half truth. They are negative in the sense that they constitute limitations on the proper powers of government, although, even in fulfilling this function, their efficacy may well depend on governmental action. But, what I should like to stress is that they are also *positive* in the sense that they constitute the *normative foundation of the participation of the common man in the processes of government.* Through speech, press, assembly, association, elections, parties, the members of a society may press demands, indicate support, level criticisms, offer suggestions, register complaints. Through these means the people may actively participate in the processes that make up the total operation of a policital system. Thus these rights do not merely circumscribe a sphere of privacy in which officialdom is not to meddle. Beyond that they sanction a style of government that is open to the impress of the articulated desires and needs of a people and that must respond in some tolerably satisfactory way to those desires and needs in order to persist. Even the rights in the area of criminal law can be understood as providing for the participation of the accused in a process of decision-making that vitally affects his future. The Rule of Law is not simply a wall; more profoundly it is a channel of communication and participation by which and through which all persons may (where Rule of Law is fully effective) engage in processes of social and political action.

(b) The ICJ tended to stress this first and more traditional set of rights during its early years of development, when its predominate concern was the fate or portion of the Rule of Law in Communist countries.[18] But the experiences and requirements of societies in Asia and Africa provoked a broadening of the concept of Rule of Law to incorporate a set of social, economic, and cultural rights. The acknowledgment of this second set as an integral aspect of the principle of Law and the responsibility of the jurists constituted a significant turning point in the history of the ICJ's deliberations about the meaning of the Rule of Law.

The relationship between the two sets is articulated in the argument that "without a minimum standard of education and economic security, political and civil freedoms may be more formal than real."[19] That is, in the presence

---

[16] *Op. cit.* at note 10, p. 244.
[17] "Report of the Secretary-General to the ICJ Meeting," *For the Rule of Law: Bulletin of the ICJ*, No. 28, December, 1966, p. 9.
[18] See *Right vs. Injustice* (The Hague: ICJ, n.d.), a report of the International Congress of Jurists held under the aegis of the Investigating Committee of Free Jurists in West Berlin in 1952. The ICJ was formed as a result of this Congress. See also op. cit. at note 14.
[19] Quoted in "The Spirit of the New Delhi Congress," *Newsletter of the ICJ*, No. 6, March–April 1959, p. 13.

of illiteracy, ignorance, malnutrition, economic privilege, especially where maintained or aggravated by social and economic forces that could be changed, constitutional liberties against tyrannical government and provisions for participation in the political system are a sham and a pretense. So, it is properly argued, all men and women have a right to those economic, social, educational, and cultural means that are needed in order to actualize their spiritual and political liberties and to give expression to the aspirations as persons. The second set of rights is thus conceived as a condition for the first set and as bearing on the full actualizing of the fundamental value of the Rule of Law, the free society.

This set includes the right to employment, vocational guidance and training, opportunities for rest and leisure, a reasonable standard of living, favorable conditions of work, the enjoyment of high standards of physical and mental health, family assistance, social security, education, participation in cultural life, and the enjoyment of the benefits of scientific and technological progress.

These rights are called positive in the sense that their realization in the modern world is largely contingent upon the active manipulation of the social and economic order by government including in some circumstances the nationalization of property. Indeed, the reshaping of human relations and associations that is required in many societies is so extensive and radical in character that it is in import revolutionary. And yet it is called for by the Rule of Law, which, as Dr. Justino Jimenez de Arechaga points out, includes (1) *peace and order,* and is protective of (2) *individual freedom, but not to the detriment of* (3) *social justice.*[20] The balance among these three values is often uneasy and precarious, but orderliness is not inherently paramount. Deep-seated, structural changes in the social order, if toward the actualization of social justice, are warranted by the Rule of Law and are therefore among the responsibilities of the jurist.

This is affirmed by the statement of the International Congress of Jurists at Rio de Janeiro (1962) that the lawyer "cannot remain a stranger to important developments in economic and social affairs if he is to fulfil his vocation as a lawyer: he should take an active part in the process of change. He will do this by inspiring and promoting economic development and social justice."[21] The jurist is thus by dint of his professional responsibilities plunged into a maelstrom of issues that extend far beyond the strictly legal and he must work without benefit of precise, well-defined, universally valid directives. But in every instance he must continue to maintain that the fundamental political decision of the modern world is "not between social and economic progress and the retention of the traditional civil liberties of freedom of speech, association and the like but between either of these two alternatives and a free society which pursues both

---

[20] See "Some Thoughts on the Rule of Law," in *op. cit.* at note 11, pp. 275–281.
[21] "International Congress of Jurists on 'Executive Action and the Rule of Law', Rio de Janeiro (Petropolis), Brazil, December 11–15, 1962," *Newsletter of the ICJ,* No. 14, April 1963, p. 4.

ends."[22] Rule of Law thus embraces both the value of individual and associational freedom and the value of social justice.[23]

(2) The operational dimension of the Rule of Law is properly understood as the shaping of social processes in the form of these values of a free society. It includes both (a) an institutional and (b) a psychological-cultural aspect.

(a) The former aspect is emphasized in the definition of Rule of Law as adherence to those institutions, procedures, and methods not always identical, but functionally similar, which experiences and traditions in different counties of the world have shown to be important and useful to protect individuals and groups from unjust government and to enable them to actualize their powers as human persons in both public and private affairs.[24]

There is a cluster of institutions traditionally associated with the first set of rights (i.e. the so-called negative or political and spiritual rights) : a judiciary and bar independent of executive direction and public pressure, separation of governmental powers and functions, a system of checks and balances within government, a written constitution including a bill of rights, judicial review of legislative and executive action, parliamentary democracy and representative government. More recently, it has been argued especially by political theorists that the party system and a pluralistic society belong to the same cluster. And there are even more detailed methods and procedures allied to these rights, including, for instance, procedures in criminal cases, principles governing the relation among the branches of government, and, recently formulated at a Conference of Nordic Jurists under the aegis of the ICJ, a set of rules to protect the right to privacy.[25]

With respect to the second set of rights (i.e. the positive or social and economic rights), while it is generally agreed that precise criteria for the distribution or redistribution of economic and cultural goods cannot be universalized and that no single blueprint for economic and social development would be everywhere effective, there have been attempts to design methods and procedures of assuring that the principles of the free society are not violated in the process of distribution and development. Thus, for example, the Ceylon Colloquium (1966) proposed proper means to undertake the nationalization of property and strongly urged the institutionalization of an ombudsman for the Asian and Pacific region.[26] And the Rio Congress (1962) undertook to define appropriate

[22] "The Background to the Congress of New Delhi," *Journal of the ICJ,* vol. II, no. 1, Spring/Summer 1959, p. 54.
[23] Intriguingly this formulation has been accompanied by a development of the ICJ away from an earlier more rigidly anti-Communist stance to a point where the secretary-general could report that *both* Communist countries and "enlightened democracies" vary in their degree of conformity to the Rule of Law, and he suggests a "closer dialogue" between jurists in the two sets of nations. See *op. cit.* at note 17, pp. 4–10.
[24] This is a paraphrase of a formula presented by Norman S. Marsh in "Editorial: Domestic Jurisdiction and International Concern," *Journal of the ICJ,* vol. I, no. 1, Autumn/Winter 1957, p. 6.
[25] See "Nordic Conference on the Right to Privacy," *Bulletin of the ICJ,* No. 31, September 1967, pp. 1–11.
[26] "The Ceylon Colloquium on the Rule of Law," *Bulletin of the ICJ,* No. 26, June 1966, pp. 1–15.

procedures to be reasonably sure that the massive discretionary and rule-making powers that are delegated to the executive-administrative branch of government in order to realize the economic and social rights of men are so utilized and are neither misdirected nor misused.[27]

Although some jurists tend to insist, with fervor, that particularly the traditional institutions indicated above are absolutely indispensable to Rule of Law, Norman S. Marsh has more modestly (and more accurately) stated "in this pragmatic field . . . dogmatism is out of place."[28] Some institutions and procedures, of course, may be more crucial than others, and, clearly, if all of the institutions and procedures indicated are effectively absent from a given society it is doubtful if the Rule of Law can be said to exist there. But in assessing the matter, the jurist should be aware of the possible *functional equivalence* of different institutions in different systems.

The function that is crucial derives from the valuational aspect of the Rule of Law and, for the purposes of this essay, I would depict it as that of *providing for all man and women within a given society access to effective channels of communication in matters of public decision and an ability to use them*. The fulfillment of this function, which is meant to integrate the two sets of rights into one formulation, requires both negative and positive structures. *Negative structures* are those whose purpose is to restrain and to check any action or operation that would limit the full carrying out of the function. *Positive structures* are those designed actively to direct and to manipulate social, economic, political, and cultural conditions to assure its effective performance.

(b) However, it has properly been recognized that institutions and procedures are by themselves insufficient to give full effect to the Rule of Law. Vivian Bose, honorary president of the ICJ, wrote of Rule of Law as "a way of life rather than a hide-bound set of Rule and Laws and Regulations."[29] That is, Rule of Law is *fully* operational only when it infuses the ethos of a society, only when it is integral to the psychical and cultural make-up of the persons involved in a given social system. In the field of political analysis, a significant amount of attention has been devoted recently to the cognitive, emotional and valuational orientations of members of a political system to its various components, these orientations being conceived as the cultural aspect of politics.[30] This aspect is, quite properly, understood as a crucial factor in the development, maintenance, transformation, and decay of political systems. Just so, it is a crucial factor in the actualization of Rule of Law.

In a sense, this assertion is redundant or at least uninteresting, for it merely states that a given juristic moral standard is efficacious or operational only

[27] See the report on the International Congress of Jurists at Rio in *op. cit.* at note 21, pp. 1–19.
[28] "A Summary of the Working Paper on the Rule of Law" in *op. cit.* at note 22, p. 24. See also *op. cit.* at note 9, pp. 206–207.
[29] Quoted in "The Rule of Law and the Rule of Life," *op. cit.* at note 19, p. 8.
[30] See, for instance, Gabriel A. Almond and Sidney Verba, *The Civic Culture* (Boston; Little, Brown & Co., 1965) and Lucien W. Pye and Sidney Verba, editors, *Political Culture and Political Development* (Princeton: Princeton University Press, 1965).

when it in fact is embedded within the morality of a people. Nonetheless the assertion does point to the insufficiency of merely designing legal and political institutions and urging their adoption. It indicates, to exploit a phrase from H. L. A. Hart, the "internal aspect of law," or of Rule of Law. It articulates an oft neglected part of the full responsibility of the juristic profession, namely, attending to the mentality or disposition of both officials and public within a social system.

This is to say that the understandings, the sensibilities, the values of *officials* —of policeman, civil servant, judge, minister of state—constitute a major factor in the actual operation of a social system, especially where powers of rule-making and of rule-interpretation and application have been delegated and where there is wide scope for discretionary action. Exactly how to "train" officials in the ways of the Rule of Law is a sticky and difficult question. Yet it is a question of concern to jurists if, indeed, the Rule of Law is a constitutive element of their profession. And, as acknowledged by the ICJ, the formation of *public* opinion in the shape of the principles of Rule of Law is also a part of the jurists' burden.[31]

This statement about the psychological-cultural aspect of the operational dimension of Rule of Law might easily provoke a vision of a group of law-abiding officials and citizens—orderly, uniform, quiet, peaceful, all thinking, feeling, and acting exactly alike, thereby giving credence to Judith N. Shklar's charge that jurists in general are imbued with an "ideology of agreement."[32] But the accuracy of that vision is severely limited. The *only* agreement that is sought after is agreement on the principles and procedures of the Rule of Law. The *only* uniformity that is necessarily aimed at is a uniformity of acceptance of the values and institutions that are essential to or arguably desirable for the working of a genuinely free society.

Rule of Law entails orderliness to be sure, *but a type of order that is itself productive of constant innovation, change, experimentation, and diversity in policy and action.* This is what Charles E. Wyzanski, Jr., meant when he wrote that "paradoxically the merit of a constitutional regime rests upon its promotion of constant peaceful revolution."[33] And this, I take it, is what Dr. Justino Jimenez de Arechaga meant by his statement (given its context):

"We are faced with a dilemma: either we carry out a revolution *through* law, or we will have a revolution *against* law. . . . The law must meet the dominant aspirations of the community, apart entirely from the fact that in so doing it should, so far as possible respect the fundamental values on which civilized living depends. In the present circumstances, it is far less important to find suitable means of enforcing the existing body of law than to promote speedy and thorough-going changes in its actual content."[34]

---

[31] See "Public Opinion and the Rule of Law," conclusions adopted at a conference of jurists held in Dakar, 1967, reported in *Bulletin of the ICJ*, No. 29, March 1967, pp. 11–17.
[32] *Legalism* (Cambridge: Harvard University Press, 1964), *passim.*
[33] *Op. cit.* at note 8, p. 484.
[34] *Op. cit.* at note 20, p. 281.

The fact is that this dynamic concept of Rule of Law is revolutionary in two senses. First, given the existing pattern of most if not all contemporary societies, even those that presume to adhere to Rule of Law, it implies the desirability and propriety of radical institutional and cultural change. It stands in harsh criticism of the lot of human social, political, economic, and legal systems. In this sense, the Rule of Law does not condone or warrant *all* revolutionary movements; rather it formulates, albeit in general terms, the proper direction for revolutionary effort.

Secondly, since the nuclear center of the Rule of Law is the creative freedom of the human spirit, its actualization would provide social and cultural milieux within which radical, revolutionary change would be possible, the only principle of limitation being that of the Rule of Law itself. That is, in fact, the meaning of the free society, and on the basis of that meaning, it should be clear that it is not altogether accurate to refer to currently existing Western democracies, liberal and open as they may be, as free societies.

## II.

Given the particular twist of this interpretation of Rule of Law, law and politics should be understood as integrally related. Of course, the sad fact is that jurists and political analysts are notorious in keeping each other at arm's length. Jurists have long tended to eschew certain questions as "political" and therefore as outside their competence and their responsibility. On the other hand, many contemporary political scientists and policy-makers tend either to use or exploit law only when politically expedient, or to interpret law in allegedly non-legal categories, categories of a strictly conceived political or behavioral character, or even to ignore law altogether. In effect, this division between the juridical and the political perpetuatas the medieval distinction between government and law; it manifests a kind of mutual jealousy holding lawyer and politician apart.

It is without doubt desirable for some purposes to maintain the division, but I would contend, first, that *on the question of the fundamental form and operation of a good society, legal and political theory should be reconcilable and reconciled, for on that question the interest of law and politics is the same,* and, second, that there is a striking congruity between the dynamic concept of Rule of Law outlined above and the notion of a "politics of growth" particularly as developed in the writings of Karl W. Deutsch, who has pioneered in the application of the model of cybernetics, or communications and control systems, to the understanding of politics and for whom the model is laden with both empirical and normative implications.

In conjunction with Talcott Parson's theory, Deutsch defines the essence of politics as "the dependable coordination of human efforts and expectations for the attainment of the goals of the society."[35] The fulfillment of this function

[35] *The Nerves of Government* (New York: The Free Press, 1966), p. 124.

depends largely on the ability of the political system to receive and to use *information,* and that ability, in turn, is contingent upon the system's *learning capacity* and *learning performance.*

That is, in order to pursue its goals and to maintain control over its own destiny, a political system must "continue to receive a full flow of three kinds of information: first, information about the world outside; second, information from the past, with a wide range of recall and recombination; and third, information about itself and its own parts."[36] The sustained interruption of any of these sources through oppression, or secrecy, or whatever leads to a loss of self-control and a diminishment of the range of goals a system is able effectively to pursue.

The learning capacity of a system is its openness to new information, its ability to absorb new messages, its readiness to engage in a radical rearrangement of itself in the light of new information, its general plasticity. There is, Deutsch notes, a high correaltion between learning capacity and the ability of a system to survive, to grow, to continue to seek after creative purposes and goals.

But learning performance, that is the actual learning processes of a system are not, it should be noted, *ipso facto,* creative and good. They are creative only if they lead to an increase in the range of both information intake and the possibilities of internal rearrangement and constructive action. They are merely viable if they neither add to nor subtract from the system's capacity and performance. And they are pathological if they lead to a shrinking of the capacity to learn and of the control of the system over its own behavior.[37]

On this basis, Deutsch writes about the relative "health" or "pathology" of communications and control systems in general and of political systems in particular, according to whether they are able to maintain themselves and their autonomy within the context of their environment. A pathological system, at its outer extremity, is self-destructive. The crucial aspects of a system from this perspective are its operating rules, its channels of transmission, its feedback mechanisms, its ability to recall and to use data from its memory, its decision-making processes, and the character of its overriding purposes and goals. It is perhaps tautological, but not important, to observe that the overriding purpose of a healthy system is the preservation of the very process of purpose-seeking itself.

In the light of this total position, the failure of political systems to maintain their autonomy and to attain their goals is often the consequence of "their propensity to prefer self-referent symbols to new information from the outside world."[38] That is, one of the major causes of the degeneration or downfall of a political system is "self-closure" which involves the overvaluation of certain data or memories within the system, a rigidification of its rules and procedures, a diminuation or cessation of the flow of ideas, insights, and information from

---

[36] *Ibid.,* p. 129.
[37] *Ibid.,* p. 169.
[38] *Ibid.,* p. 215.

the social system of which it is a part and from the rest of the world as well, a loss in the depth of its memory, in its capacity for recall from its traditions, in its ability to rearrange and reconstruct its character.

The converse of the "self-closure" of a political system is the "politics of growth" which Deutsch contrasts with a "politics of power." Power is construed as "the ability of an individual or an organization to impose extrapolations or projections of their inner structure upon their environment."[39] It means the ability to impose one's interests and goals upon a resistant world. And this, it is often averred, is what the political game is all about, and what makes it so different from law. From that perspective, the political realist is one who, in the pursuit of the interests of his nation, party, or group attends, not to legal principles, but to the realities of the power situation, and acts accordingly.

Deutsch distinguishes growth or strength from power. Growth means, among other things, "an application of learning capacity toward an increase in openness, that is, an increase in the range, diversity, and effectiveness of an organization's channels of intake of information from the outside world. . . . an increase in an organization's ability to make effective responses to its environment and to change this environment in accordance with its needs . . . an increase in the range and diversity of goals the organization is able to follow, including the power to change goals and to add new ones."[40]

Assuming the strong probability of a continuously changing environment, the chances of the survival of a political system depends more upon its strength and growth than upon its sheer power. This is not to ignore the political relevance of power as the ability to get one's way, but it is to cast it within a more embracing context that in fact radically alters the meaning of realism. Political realism, within this context, is oriented toward the preservation of the system and therefore calls for openness to streams of information from the world at large, resiliency in its own operation, and the enhancement of subsystem autonomy.

The point is that politics is a crucial locus of decision-making within a society. As such it may either retard or accelerate social learning and innovation. It may either accentuate rigidities within the social system or may generate, quicken, and provide direction for processes of change in keeping with a changing world. But for the sake of survival it should adopt the latter course. Thus, paradoxically, if it is true that the modern world is in the grip of revolutionary change, then survival depends upon growth. Or, in other terms, preservation requires innovation, innovation not only in the environment of the political system, but in the internal structure and operation of the system as well.

Significantly, Deutsch argues that among the political techniques devised in the Western tradition for accelerating innovation, perhaps the three most important are majority rule, protection of minorities, and the institutionalization of dissent.[41] Intriguingly these techniques are indicative of the rights of the Rule

---

[39] *Ibid.,* p. 111.
[40] *Ibid.,* pp. 139–140. *Cf.* 247–248.
[41] *Ibid.,* pp. 254–256.

of Law—the rights of expression, assembly, association, participation in the selection of governments, and, as conditions for the actualization of that set, the rights to a reasonable standard of living, to education, to a high standard of mental and physical health.

In fact, in general, it could well be argued that the requirements of the politics of growth are virtually the same as the constitutive elements of the dynamic concept of Rule of Law. In brief, the rights, liberties, and freedoms of Rule of Law, if effective, would maximize the possibility of a full flow of information throughout the social and political system. The institutional structures of Rule of Law would provide organized locations for assembling, sorting out, arranging, and reacting to the flow of information. And culturally, Rule of Law is productive of persons whose characters are imbued with respect for the rights of all men —which is to say persons, both officials and citizens, dedicated to actualizing and preserving a self-steering, purpose-seeking political system inclusive of all mankind.

This means that, just as in the concept of Rule of Law uniformity and diversity, constancy and creativity are conjoined, so also in the politics of growth the presumed paradox between preservation and innovation is removed. What ought to be preserved within this understanding of law and politics is the basic pattern of relationships and action within which, by which, and through which learning, innovation, growth are possible; what ought to be maintained is the structure of creative action, the form of the process of purpose-seeking itself.

Moreover, this means that the notion of a politics of growth constructed on the model of communications and control systems is, in its normative aspects, revolutionary in the same two senses in which the dynamic concept of Rule of Law is revolutionary. First, in its import, it implies the desirability of a radical transformation of all existing political societies at least in some respects in order to maximize learning capacity. Second, it prescribes a form of politics within which constant revolutionary change would be possible, the only principle of limitation being the basic form itself. This is what I understand Deutsch to mean by his statement that the normative concern at the heart of the communications point of view is "to preserve for any finite mind or group some open pathway to the infinite, that is, to preserve for it the possibility of communication with a potentially inexhaustible environment and a potentially infinite future."[42]

III.

One of the consequences of this discussion is that, on the elemental level of normative theory with which this essay has been concerned, *jurisdictio* and *gubernaculum* are not at enmity, but are rather one and the same in basic pattern, direction, and goal. Moreover, in their common character, they are not alien to a revolutionary age, but instead provide a critical basis for interpreting, evaluating, and directing revolutionary effort whether in long-established political systems or in the newly developing Third World.

[42] *Ibid.*, p. xiv.

It might be instructive, as a concluding note, to interpret the common logic of the dynamic concept of Rule of Law and the politics of growth as a mode of conjoining two sets of qualities which are often contrasted as antithetical, but which are more properly understood as problematically related in the actual patterns (and ideals) of human existence. One set includes continuity (or orderliness) and change. The other set includes relatedness and individuality.

As already stated, the dynamic concept of the Rule of Law is not antithetical to change, novelty or radically innovative action. Rather it proposes a general pattern for change, a pattern that provides for maximal participation in changes that affect the public order and that provides for innovation and experimentation by individuals and associations in the private sphere.

The continuity of this pattern is thus a type of continuity that permits— indeed is productive of—change. It is a continuity that is fitting for an age in which change in the order of the day. More profoundly, it is a pattern that permits the fullest expression of the human person understood as one who is essentially open, creative, unfinished, incomplete, as one who makes and remakes himself, as one whose identity is not totally given but formed by his own act.

Further the dynamic concept of the Rule of Law includes both relatedness and individuality. The individualistic quality is expressed in its stress on the individual human personality as the ultimate aim and purpose all all organization and thus on the free society as its most fundamental constitutive value.

But the rights and the operations of Rule of Law are indicative also of the relatedness of individual persons and groups. For one thing, rights are, after all, claims upon others; they are the correlatives of duties. The actualization of these rights and operations, whether in full or in part, rests upon the coordination and cooperation of human effort. Moreover, the constructive actions that eventuate from the employment and exploitation of these rights and operations result in a constant interflow and interchange of diverse human creations. Thus Rule of Law involves a kind of relatedness in which there is both a high degree of flexibility in individual action and plasticity in the more concrete determinations of the content of human relations.

These general comments on continuity and change, relatedness and individuality apply equally to the communications and control model of political systems and the notion of a politics of growth. Briefly, the continuity of a "healthy" system is located in all those factors needed for self-preservation and autonomy— that is, the kinds of receptors of information effectors of action, and feedback mechanisms that provide a high degree of learning capacity and performance. But that form of continuity includes the ability for radical rearrangement of the system itself and for effective action in and on its environment. Thus it is a form of continuity that constitutes the structure of the possibility of change.

Moreover, a healthy political system is a structure through which the members of a social system may participate in cooperative effort in the attainment of common goals. Yet, at the same time, it is pluralistic, it maximizes the possibility for dissent and individual action. In Deutsch's words there is an essential "interplay between the dimensions of growth of the organization and the growth of the individuals and of the more or less autonomous subgroups that compose it. In this sense, the growth of human organizations is always the growth of several levels of autonomous systems, and the autonomous growth and enhanced self-determination of individuals is one of its touchstones."[43]

\*        \*        \*        \*

In sum, within the framework of this essay, the basic professional responsibility of the jurist and the basic task of the politician devoted to the survival of the political system are one and the same—to make the principles of constitutionalism universally concrete in institutional form and in cultural ethos—and that, if I may say so, is a revolutionary venture of the profoundest dimensions.

[43] *Ibid.,* p. 253.

# CHAPTER VII

# JUDICIAL REASONING

In every legal system a large and important field is left open for the exercise of discretion by courts and other officials in rendering initially vague standards determinate, in resolving the uncertainties of statutes, or in developing and qualifying rules only broadly communicated by authoritative precedents. None the less these activities, important and insufficiently studied though they are, must not disguise the fact that both the framework within which they take place and their chief end-product is one of general rules.

H. L. A. Hart, *The Concept of Law*

Constitutional law theorists have brought increasing recognition that older, sharp-line demarcations between executive, legislative, and judicial powers have yielded considerably in the face of the pragmatic necessities of modern political systems (see especially M. J. C. Vile, *Constitutionalism and the Separation of Powers*, Oxford, Clarendon Press, 1967). Administrative agencies both legislate and judge within an extensive range of delegated discretionary powers; legislatures, themselves, serve the function of highest court within some national systems and constitute the executive itself from within their ranks.

It should not, then, be surprising (though it is hotly denied in many quarters) to discover that courts, too, on occasion *legislate*—not just in the restricted sense of clarifying or mediating obscure or conflicting legislative directives, but in setting fundamental policy guidelines when standing as the supreme arbiter of constitutional right and intent.

Much confusion on the topic of judicial 'legislation' has arisen, it is argued here, largely due to fundamental differences in the basic political structures of the American and British governments. As every British schoolchild knows but an American President recently forgot much to his embarrassment (Britons were publically scandalized when a mere Chief Justice of the United States Supreme Court was sent as a major representative to the funeral of Winston Churchill), the 'King (or Queen) acting in Parliament' is the final judicial authority in any conflict between court and Commons. Similarly Americans are aware, if sometimes less accepting of the fact, that our Supreme Court may and on occasion does overrule on Constitutional grounds acts of both President and Congress. Thus H. L. A. Hart's strict interpretation of judicial discretion (of which the above citation is but one of many such usually combined with heavy criticisms of American realism's broad interpretive posture) is only a formally accurate account of the American federal structure, a complete distortion of open-ended legal systems such as that developing in modern India, and perhaps even a misleading description of current practice in the domain of British administrative law where delegated authorities hold discretionary powers far exceeding those of any American court. For instance, the British Land Planning Acts of 1947 passed in the wake of more dramatic nationalization of major industries granted the sole power of decision *and review* of the minutest details of local land and property use (e.g. the color a house could be painted) to a minister of Parliament (see Charles M. Haar, *Land Planning Law in a Free Society*, Cambridge, 1951).

The truth in Hart's assertion is that courts, of course, normally attempt to operate within a general framework of procedural rules. However, due process sets no fixed or necessary limit to decisions of *substance* in a variety of formally structured systems. There have been differences in the *modus operandi* of major traditions: in Civil Code countries (i.e. those following the Roman and Napoleonic models) judges apply legal principles formulated in somewhat more abstract and systematic fashion than, say, the historically developed case precedents of the British common law. The judicial functions of the two systems however, are largely similar and both face certain problems in common:

(1) Alternative sources of law: Normally, statutory emendation supersedes the authoritative precedents of either code or case. However, this rule is not absolute given a certain degree of flexibility in the reasons judges may give for a particular decision (For example, local Canadian courts in one jurisdiction 'got around' a statute calling for stiffer penalties for drunken driving by successively considering an automobile stuck in a snow bank not a 'motor vehicle', an unconscious driver not a 'motor vehicle operator', etc., until the unpopular statute was repealed by an exasperated legislature). Judges may also look to custom, constitution, decisions in other jurisdictions, law journals, or simply general social interests to justify decisions at hand. Such decisions will stand unless overruled by higher authority and are accepted judicial practice.

(2) Open texture of legal rules: In any system of laws necessarily

formulated in abstract language, gaps and overlappings in rule provisions allow a degree of latitude in deciding the 'hard case.' Should the driver of a private automobile be considered a 'public carrier' and subject to special liabilities if he has accepted contributions to travel expenses from a passenger subsequently injured in an accident?

(3) Argument from analogy: The need to extend legal precedents to cover circumstances not anticipated has made the argument from analogy (considered one of the weakest by some professional philosophers) a central tool in legal reasoning (See especially the Cardozo selection below). Should an airplane be considered primarily a 'dangerous object' or a 'mode of transportation' and be treated accordingly in radically differing rule contexts?

(4) Legislative intent or objective rule interpretation: Not infrequently the product of political compromise, the wording of statutes is sometimes vague and so highly abstract as to open them to new interpretations scarcely intended by some or all of their originators. For instance, anti-trust legislation in this country formulated to curb the monopolistic practices of business corporate interests later became a tool for suppressing incipient labor unions. Anti-trust laws to this day are so open-ended in their language and provisions for enforcement that the U.S. Attorney General's Office is obliged to pick and choose its cases almost arbitrarily with little 'basis of expectation' regarding the courts' eventual judgment.

Apart from these traditional areas of uncertainty rapidly changing economic and social conditions have also required modification in accepted assumptions about judicial discretionary powers. Particularly in underdeveloped nations where rapid economic expansion is of a premium, it has been found necessary to grant almost absolute discretionary powers to economic planners and management. Nations as diverse in ideological assumptions as India and the Soviet Union have during the past decade both dramatically moved in this same direction in the face of economic necessities. More flexible and able to move more rapidly and efficiently than the cumbersome mechanisms of standing legislatures, courts have been called upon to render crucial and immediate policy decisions wherever massive social and economic forces operate. The creative interplay of court and legislature in establishing and adjusting policy guidelines has been one of the most healthy signs of a constructive and effective polity in this country during past decades, e.g. the mutual development of civil rights standards following the historic Supreme Court decision on school desegrigation in 1954.

A second major problem demanding greater judicial flexibility at all levels of government is posed by the article of the American legal realist, Harry Jones, reprinted below, namely, the equitable treatment of individuals caught in an increasingly complex and impersonal system of legal and economic communities. Particularly the difficulties involved in protecting the rights and interests of the disadvantaged have led some led some observers to propose the creation of new legal institutions (e.g. special courts attuned to the complexities of such areas as city planning and mental disease) as well as revised legal practices to deal with the inequities produced in special circumstances by otherwise adequate laws. Only recently judges have been empowered to release suspects without bail or to reduce fines of those convicted without funds who might otherwise languish in jail for long periods for want of a few dollars. Law journals abound with studies of the special inequitable effects on the ghetto of otherwise sound laws: the ghetto-dweller today cannot obtain basic fire, theft or liability insurance. He may be obliged to pay double rates for so-called "assigned risk" automobile insurance. By accident of geography he will be denied credit—except at exorbitant rates. Food and other basic necessities cost more; public transportation is less available, police protection, virtually non-existent and the risk of unjust arrest and conviction significantly higher. The courts cannot alone solve these and other problems. However, as the selections in this chapter reveal American jurists have pioneered both in attempting to achieve greater understanding of the uses and abuses of judicial discretionary powers and in the effective employment of judicial powers in the larger social interest.

# 28

# Benjamin Nathan Cardozo

Benjamin Cardozo (1870–1938), noted legal scholar and Associate Justice of the United States Supreme Court, both in his person and in his writings established new standards for the development of the judicial process.

# THE NATURE OF THE JUDICIAL PROCESS*

LECTURE I

## INTRODUCTION. THE METHOD OF PHILOSOPHY

The work of deciding cases goes on every day in hundreds of courts throughout the land. Any judge, one might suppose, would find it easy to describe the process which he had followed a thousand times and more. Nothing could be farther from the truth. Let some intelligent layman ask him to explain: he will not go very far before taking refuge in the excuse that the language of craftsmen is unintelligible to those untutored in the craft. Such an excuse may cover with a semblance of respectability an otherwise ignominious retreat. It will hardly serve to still the pricks of curiosity and conscience. In moments of introspection, when there is no longer a necessity of putting off with a show of wisdom the uninitiated interlocutor, the troublesome problem will recur, and press for a solution. What is it that I do when I decide a case? To what sources of information do I appeal for guidance? In what proportions do I permit them to contribute to the the result? In what proportions ought they to contribute? If a precedent is applicable, when do I refuse to follow it? If no precedent is applicable, how do I reach the rule that will make a precedent for the future? If I am seeking logical consistency, the symmetry of the legal structure, how far shall I seek it? At what point shall the quest be halted by some discrepant custom, by some consideration of the social welfare, by my own or the common standards of justice and morals? Into that strange compound which is brewed daily in the caldron of the courts, all these ingredients enter in varying proportions. I am not concerned to inquire whether judges ought to be allowed to brew such a compound at all. I take judge-made law as one of the existing realities of life. There, before us, is the brew. Not a judge on the bench but has had a hand in the making. The elements have not come together by chance. *Some* principle, however unavowed and inarticulate and subconscious, has regulated the infusion. It may not have been the same

*Benjamin Cardozo, *The Nature of the Judicial Process*, Lecture I. "Introduction. The Method of Philosophy." New Haven, 1921. Copyright © 1921 by Yale University Press.

principle for all judges at any time, nor the same principle for any judge at all times. But a choice there has been, not a submission to the decree of Fate; and the considerations and motives determining the choice, even if often obscure, do not utterly resist analysis. In such attempt at analysis as I shall make, there will be need to distinguish between the conscious and the subconscious. I do not mean that even those considerations and motives which I shall class under the first head are always in consciousness distinctly, so that they will be recognized and named at sight. Not infrequently they hover near the surface. They may, however, with comparative readiness be isolated and tagged, and when thus labeled, are quickly acknowledged as guiding principles of conduct. More subtle are the forces so far beneath the surface that they cannot reasonably be classified as other than subconscious. It is often through these subconscious forces that judges are kept consistent with themselves, and inconsistent with one another. We are reminded by William James in a telling page of his lectures on Pragmatism that every one of us has in truth an underlying philosophy of life, even those of us to whom the names and the notions of philosophy are unknown or anathema. There is in each of us a stream of tendency, whether you choose to call it philosophy or not,[1] which gives coherence and direction to thought and action. Judges cannot escape that current any more than other mortals. All their lives, forces which they do not recognize and cannot name, have been tugging at them—inherited instincts, traditional beliefs, acquired convictions; and the resultant is an outlook on life, a conception of social needs, a sense in James's phrase of "the total push and pressure of the cosmos," which, when reasons are nicely balanced, must determine where choice shall fall. In this mental background every problem finds its setting. We may try to see things as objectively as we please. None the less, we can never see them with any eyes except our own. To that test they are all brought—a form of pleading or an act of parliament, the wrongs of paupers or the rights of princes, a village ordinance or a nation's charter.

I have little hope that I shall be able to state the formula which will rationalize this process for myself, much less for others. We must apply to the study of judge-made law that method of quantitative analysis which Mr. Wallas has applied with such fine results to the study of politics.[2] A richer scholarship than mine is requisite to do the work aright. But until that scholarship is found and enlists itself in the task, there may be a passing interest in an attempt to uncover the nature of the process by one who is himself an active agent, day by day, in keeping the process alive. That must be my apology for these introspective searchings of the spirit.

Before we can determine the proportions of a blend, we must know the ingredients to be blended. Our first inquiry should therefore be: Where does the judge find the law which he embodies in his judgment? There are times when the source is obvious. The rule that fits the case may be supplied by the

---

[1] Cf. N. M. Butler, "Philosophy," pp. 18, 43.
[2] "Human Nature in Politics," p. 138.

constitution or by statute. If that is so, the judge looks no farther. The correspondence ascertained, his duty is to obey. The constitution overrides a statute, but a statute, if consistent with the constitution, overrides the law of judges. In this sense, judge-made law is secondary and subordinate to the law that is made by legislators. It is true that codes and statutes do not render the judge superfluous, nor his work perfunctory and mechanical. There are gaps to be filled. There are doubts and ambiguities to be cleared. There are hardships and wrongs to be mitigated if not avoided. Interpretation is often spoken of as if it were nothing but the search and the discovery of a meaning which, however obscure and latent, had none the less a real and ascertainable pre-existence in the legislator's mind. The process is, indeed, that at times, but it is often something more. The ascertainment of intention may be the least of a judge's troubles in ascribing meaning to a statute. "The fact is," says Gray in his lectures on the "Nature and Sources of the Law,"[3] "that the difficulties of so-called interpretation arise when the legislature has had no meaning at all; when the question which is raised on the statute never occurred to it; when what the judges have to do is, not to determine what the legislature did mean on a point which was present to its mind, but to guess what it would have intended on a point not present to its mind, if the point had been present."[4] So Brütt:[5] "One weighty task of the system of the application of law consists then in this, to make more profound the discovery of the latent meaning of positive law. Much more important, however, is the second task which the system serves, namely the filling of the gaps which are found in every positive law in greater or less measure." You may call this process legislation, if you will. In any event, no system of *jus scriptum* has been able to escape the need of it. Today a great school of continental jurists is pleading for a still wider freedom of adaptation and construction. The statute, they say, is often fragmentary and illconsidered and unjust. The judge as the interpreter for the community of its sense of law and order must supply omissions, correct uncertainties, and harmonize results with justice through a method of free decision—"libre recherche scientifique." That is the view of Gény and Ehrlich and Gmelin and others.[6] Courts are to "search for light among the social elments of every kind that are the living force behind the facts they deal with."[7] The power thus put in their hands is great, and subject, like all power, to abuse; but we are not to flinch from granting it. In the long run "there is no guaranty of justice," says Ehrlich,[8] "except the personality of the judge."[9] The same pro-

---

[3] Sec. 370, p. 165.
[4] Cf. Pound, "Courts and Legislation," 9 Modern Legal Philosophy Series, p. 226.
[5] "Die Kunst der Rechtsanwendung," p. 72.
[6] "Science of Legal Method," 9 Modern Legal Philosophy Series, pp. 4, 45, 65, 72, 124, 130, 159.
[7] Gény, "Méthode d'Interprétation et Sources en droit privé positif," vol. II, p. 180, sec. 176, ed. 1919; transl. 9 Modern Legal Philosophy Series, p. 45.
[8] P. 65, *supra;* "Freie Rechtsfindung und freie Rechtswissenschaft," 9 Modern Legal Philosophy Series.
[9] Cf. Gnaeus Flavius (Kantorowicz), "Der Kampf um Rechtswissenschaft," p. 48: "Von der Kultur des Richters hängt im letzten Grunde aller Fortschritt der Rechtsentwicklung ab."

blems of method, the same contrasts between the letter and the spirit, are living problems in our own land and law. Above all in the field of constitutional law, the method of free decision has become, I think, the dominant one today. The great generalities of the constitution have a content and a significance that vary from age to age. The method of free decision sees through the transitory particulars and reaches what is permanent behind them. Interpretation, thus enlarged, becomes more than the ascertainment of the meaning and intent of lawmakers whose collective will has been declared. It supplements the declaration, and fills the vacant spaces, by the same processes and methods that have built up the customary law. Codes and other statutes may threaten the judicial function with repression and disuse and atrophy. The function flourishes and persists by virtue of the human need to which it steadfastly responds. Justinian's prohibition of any commentary on the product of his codifiers is remembered only for its futility.[10]

I will dwell no further for the moment upon the significance of constitution and statute as sources of the law. The work of a judge in interpreting and developing them has indeed its problems and its difficulties, but they are problems and difficulties not different in kind or measure from those besetting him in other fields. I think they can be better studied when those fields have been explored. Sometimes the rule of constitution or of statute is clear, and then the difficulties vanish. Even when they are present, they lack at times some of that element of mystery which accompanies creative energy. We reach the land of mystery when constitution and statute are silent, and the judge must look to the common law for the rule that fits the case. He is the "living oracle of the law" in Blackstone's vivid phrase. Looking at Sir Oracle in action, viewing his work in the dry light of realism, how does he set about his task?

The first thing he does is to compare the case before him with the precedents, whether stored in his mind or hidden in the books. I do not mean that precedents are ultimate sources of the law, supplying the sole equipment that is needed for the legal armory, the sole tools, to borrow Maitland's phrase,[11] "in the legal smithy." Back of precedents are the basic juridical conceptions which are the postulates of judicial reasoning, and farther back are the habits of life, the institutions of society, in which those conceptions had their origin, and which, by a process of interaction, they have modified in turn.[12] None the less, in a system so highly developed as our own, precedents have so covered the ground that they fix the point of departure from which the labor of the judge begins. Almost invariably, his first step is to examine and compare them. If they are plain and to the point, there may be need of nothing more. *Stare decisis* is at least the everyday working rule of our law. I shall have something to say later about the propriety of relaxing the rule in exceptional conditions.

---

[10] Gray, "Nature and Sources of the Law," sec. 395; Muirhead, "Roman Law," pp. 39, 4900.
[11] Introduction to Gierke's "Political Theories of the Middle Age," p. viii.
[12] Saleilles, "De la Personnalité Juridique," p. 45; Ehrlich, "Grundlegung der Soziologie des Rechts," pp. 34, 35; Pound, "Proceedings of American Bar Assn. 1919," p. 455.

But unless those conditions are present, the work of deciding cases in accordance with precedents that plainly fit them is a process similar in its nature to that of deciding cases in accordance with a statute. It is a process of search, comparison, and little more. Some judges seldom get beyond that process in any case. Their notion of their duty is to match the colors of the case at hand against the colors of many sample cases spread out upon their desk. The sample nearest in shade supplies the applicable rule. But, of course, no system of living law can be evolved by such a process, and no judge of a high court, worthy of his office, views the function of his place so narrowly. If that were all there was to our calling, there would be little of intellectual interest about it. The man who had the best card index of the cases would also be the wisest judge. It is when the colors do not match, when the references in the index fail, when there is no decisive precedent, that the serious business of the judge begins. He must then fashion law for the litigants before him. In fashioning it for them he will be fashioning it for others. The classic statement is Bacon's: "For many times, the things deduced to judgment may be meum and tuum, when the reason and consequence thereof may trench to point of estate."[13] The sentence of today will make the right and wrong of tomorrow. If the judge is to pronounce it wisely, some principles of selection there must be to guide him among all the potential judgments that compete for recognition.

In the life of the mind as in life elsewhere, there is a tendency toward the reproduction of kind. Every judgment has a generative power. It begets in its own image. Every precedent, in the words of Redlich, has a "directive force for future cases of the same or similar nature."[14] Until the sentence was pronounced, it was as yet in equilibrium. Its form and content were uncertain. Any one of many principles might lay hold of it and shape it. Once declared, it is a new stock of descent. It is charged with vital power. It is the source from which new principles or norms may spring to shape sentences thereafter. If we seek the psychological basis of this tendency, we shall find it, I suppose, in habit.[15] Whatever its psychological basis, it is one of the living forces of our law. Not all the progeny of principles begotten of a judgment survive, however, to maturity. Those that cannot prove their worth and strength by the test of experience, are sacrificed mercilessly and thrown into the void. The common law does not work from pre-established truths of universal and inflexible validity to conclusions derived from them deductively. Its method is inductive, and its draws its generalizations from particulars. The process has been admirably stated by Munroe Smith: "In their effort to give to the social sense of justice articulate expression in rules and in principles, the method of the lawfinding experts has always been experimental. The rules and principles of cases law have never been treated as final truths, but as working hypotheses,

13 "Essay on Judicature."
14 Redlich, "The Case Method in American Law Schools," Bulletin No. 8, Carnegie Foundation, p. 37.
15 McDougall, "Social Psychology," p. 354; J. C. Gray, "Judicial Precedents," 9 Harvard L. R. 27.

continually retested in those great laboratories of the law, the courts of justice. Every new case is an experiment; and if the accepted rule which seems applicable yields a result which is felt to be unjust, the rule is reconsidered. It may not be modified at once, for the attempt to do absolute justice in every single case would make the development and maintenance of general rules impossible;. but if a rule continues to work injustice, it will eventually be reformulated The principles themselves are continually retested; for if the rules derived from a principle do not work well, the principle itself must ultimately be re-examined."[16]

The way in which this process of retesting and reformulating works, may be followed in an example. Fifty years ago, I think it would have been stated as a general principle that A. may conduct his business as he pleases, even though the purpose is to cause loss to B., unless the act involves the creation of a nuisance.[17] Spite fences were the stock illustration, and the exemption from liability in such circumstances was supposed to illustrate not the exception, but the rule.[18] Such a rule may have been an adequate working principle to regulate the relations between individuals or classes in a simple or homogeneous community. With the growing complexity of social relations, its inadequacy was revealed. As particular controversies multiplied and the attempt was made to test them by the old principle, it was found that there was something wrong in the results, and this led to a reformulation of the principle itself. Today, most judges are inclined to say that what was once thought to be the exception is the rule, and what was the rule is the exception. A. may never do anything in his business for the purpose of injuring another without reasonable and just excuse.[19] There has been a new generalization which, applied to new particulars, yields results more in harmony with past particulars, and, what is still more important, more consistent with the social welfare. This work of modification is gradual. It goes on inch by inch. Its effects must be measured by decades and even centuries. Thus measured, they are seen to have behind them the power and the pressure of the moving glacier.

We are not likely to underrate the force that has been exerted if we look back upon its work. "There is not a creed which is not shaken, not an accredited dogma which is not shown to be questionable, not a received tradition which does not threaten to dissolve."[20] Those are the words of a critic of life and letters writing forty years ago, and watching the growing scepticism of his day. I am tempted to apply his words to the history of the law. Hardly a rule of today but may be matched by its opposite of yesterday. Absolute liability for

---

[16] Munroe Smith, "Jurisprudence," Columbia University Press, 1909, p. 21; cf. Pound, "Courts and Legislation," 7 Am. Pol. Science Rev. 361; 9 Modern Legal Philosophy Series, p. 214; Pollock, "Essays in Jurisprudence and Ethics," p. 246.

[17] Cooley, "Torts," 1st ed., p. 93; Pollock, "Torts," 10th ed., p. 21.

[18] Phelps v. Nowlen, 72 N. Y. 39; Rideout v. Knox, 148 Mass. 368.

[19] Lamb v. Cheney, 227 N. Y. 418; Aikens v. Wisconsin, 195 U. S. 194, 204; Pollock, "Torts," *supra*.

[20] Arnold, "Essays in Criticism," second series, p. 1.

one's acts is today the exception; there must commonly be some tinge of fault, whether willful or negligent. Time was, however, when absolute liability was the rule.[21] Occasional reversions to the earlier type may be found in recent legislation.[22] Mutual promises give rise to an obligation, and their breach to a right of action for damages. Time was when the obligation and the remedy were unknown unless the promise was under seal.[23] Rights of action may be assigned, and the buyer prosecute them to judgment though he bought for purposes of suit. Time was when the assignment was impossible, and the maintenance of the suit a crime. It is no basis today for an action of deceit to show, without more, that there has been the breach of an executory promise; yet the breach of an executory promise came to have a remedy in our law because it was held to be a deceit.[24] These changes or most of them have been wrought by judges. The men who wrought them used the same tools as the judges of today. The changes, as they were made in this case or that, may not have seemed momentous in the making. The result, however, when the process was prolonged throughout the years, has been not merely to supplement or modify; it has been to revolutionize and transform. For every tendency, one seems to see a counter-tendency; for every rule its antinomy. Nothing is stable. Nothing absolute. All is fluid and changeable. There is an endless "becoming." We are back with Heraclitus. That, I mean, is the average or aggregate impression which the picture leaves upon the mind. Doubtless in the last three centuries, some lines, once wavering, have become rigid. We leave more to legislatures today, and less perhaps to judges.[25] Yet even now there is change from decade to decade. The glacier still moves.

In this perpetual flux, the problem which confronts the judge is in reality a twofold one: he must first extract from the precedents the underlying principle, the *ratio decidendi;* he must then determine the path or direction along which the principle is to move and develop, if it is not to wither and die.

The first branch of the problem is the one to which we are accustomed to address ourselves more consciously than to the other. Cases do not unfold their principles for the asking. They yield up their kernel slowly and painfully. The instance cannot lead to a generalization till we know it as it is. That in itself is no easy task. For the thing adjudged comes to us oftentimes swathed in obscuring dicta, which must be stripped off and cast aside. Judges differ greatly in their reverence for the illustrations and comments and side-remarks

[21] Holdsworth, "History of English Law," 2, p. 41; Wigmore, "Responsibility for Tortious Acts," 7 Harvard L. R. 315, 383, 441; 3 Anglo-Am. Legal Essays 474; Smith, "Liability for Damage to Land," 33 Harvard L. R. 551; Ames, "Law and Morals," 22 Harvard L. R. 97, 99; Isaacs, "Fault and Liability," 31 Harvard L. R. 954.
[22] Cf. Duguit, "Les Transformations générales du droit privé depuis le Code Napoléon,' Continental Legal Hist. Series, vol. XI, pp. 125, 126, secs. 40, 42.
[23] Holdsworth, *supra,* 2, p. 72; Ames, "History of Parol Contracts prior to Assumpsit," 3 Anglo-Am. Legal Essays 304.
[24] Holdsworth, *supra,* 3, pp. 330, 336; Ames, "History of Assumpsit," 3 Anglo-Am. Legal Essays 275, 276.
[25] F. C. Montague in "A Sketch of Legal History," Maitland and Montague, p. 161.

of their predecessors, to make no mention of their own. All agree that there may be dissent when the opinion is filed. Some would seem to hold that there must be none a moment thereafter. Plenary inspiration has then descended upon the work of the majority. No one, of course, avows such a belief, and yet sometimes there is an approach to it in conduct. I own that it is a good deal of a mystery to me how judges, of all persons in the world, should put their faith in dicta. A brief experience on the bench was enough to reveal to me all sorts of cracks and crevices and loopholes in my own opinions when picked up a few months after delivery, and reread with due contrition. The persuasion that one's own infallibility is a myth leads by easy stages and with somewhat greater satisfaction to a refusal to ascribe infallibility to others. But dicta are not always ticketed as such, and one does not recognize them always at a glance. There is the constant need, as every law student knows, to separate the accidental and the non-essential from the essential and inherent. Let us assume, however, that this task has been achieved, and that the precedent is known as it really is. Let us assume too that the principle, latent within it, has been skillfully extracted and accurately stated. Only half or less than half of the work has yet been done. The problem remains to fix the bounds and the tendencies of development and growth, to set the directive force in motion along the right path at the parting of the ways.

The directive force of a principle may be exerted along the line of logical progression; this I will call the rule of analogy or the method of philosophy; along the line of historical development; this I will call the method of evolution; along the line of the customs of the community; this I will call the method of tradition; along the lines of justice, morals and social welfare, the *mores* of the day; and this I will call the method of sociology.

I have put first among the principles of selection to guide our choice of paths, the rule of analogy or the method of philosophy. In putting it first, I do not mean to rate it as most important. On the contrary, it is often sacrificed to others. I have put it first because it has, I think, a certain presumption in its favor. Given a mass of particulars, a congeries of judgments on related topics, the principle that unifies and rationalizes them has a tendency, and a legitimate one, to project and extend itself to unify and rationalize. It has the primacy that comes from natural and orderly and logical succession. Homage is due to it over every competing principle that is unable by appeal to history or tradition or policy or justice to make out a better right. All sorts of deflecting forces may appear to contest its sway and absorb its power. At least, it is the heir presumptive. A pretender to the title will have to fight his way.

Great judges have sometimes spoken as if the principle of philosophy, i.e., of logical development, meant little or nothing in our law. Probably none of them in conduct was ever true to such a faith. Lord Halsbury said in Quinn v. Leathem, 1901, A.C. 495, 506: "A case is only an authority for what it actually decides. I entirely deny that it can be quoted for a proposition that may seem to follow logically from it. Such a mode of reasoning assumes that the law is necessarily a logical code, whereas every lawyer must acknowledge that the law is not always logical at all." [26] All this may be true, but we must not press the truth too far. Logical consistency does not cease to be a good because it is not supreme good. Holmes has told us in a sentence which is now classic that "the life of the law has not been logic; it has been experience." [27] But Homes did not tell us that logic is to be ignored when experience is silent. I am not to mar the symmetry of the legal structure by the introduction of inconsistencies and irrelevancies and artificial exceptions unless for some sufficient reason, which will commonly be some consideration of history or custom or policy or justice. Lacking such a reason, I must be logical, just as I must be impartial, and upon like grounds. It will not do to decide the same question one way between one set of litigants and the opposite way between another. "If a group of cases involves the same point, the parties expect the same decision. It would be a gross injustice to decide alternate cases on opposite principles. If a case was decided against me yesterday when I was defendant, I shall look for the same judgment today if I am plaintiff. To decide differently would raise a feeling of resentment and wrong in my breast; it would be an infringement, material and moral, of my rights." [28] Everyone feels the force of this sentiment when two cases are the same. Adherence to precedent must then be the rule rather than the exception if litigants are to have faith in the even-handed administration of justice in the courts. A sentiment like in kind, though different in degree, is at the root of the tendency of precedent to extend itself along the lines of logical development.[29] No doubt the sentiment is powerfully reinforced by what is often nothing but an intellectual passion for *elegantia juris*, for symmetry of form and substance.[30] That is an ideal which can never fail to exert some measure of attraction upon the professional experts who make up the lawyer class. To the Roman lawyers, it meant much, more than it has meant to English lawyers or to ours, certainly more than it has meant to clients. "The client," says Miller in his "Data of Jurisprudence," [31] "cares little for a 'beautiful' case! He wishes it settled somehow on the most favorable terms he can obtain," Even that is not always true. But as a system of case law develops, the sordid controversies of litigants are the stuff out of which great and shining truths will ultimately be shaped. The accidental and the transitory will yield the essential and the permanent. The judge who moulds the law by the method of philosophy may be satisfying an intellectual craving for symmetry of form and substance. But he is doing something more. He is keeping the law true in its response to a deep-seated and imperious sentiment. Only experts perhaps may be able to gauge the quality of his work and appraise its significance. But their judgment, the judgment of the lawyer class, will spread to others, and tinge the common

---

[26] Cf. Bailhache, J., in Belfast Ropewalk Co. v. Bushell, 1918, 1 K. B. 210, 213: "Unfortunately or fortunately, I am not sure which, our law is not a science."
[27] "The Common Law," p. 1.
[28] W. G. Miller, "The Data of Jurisprudence," p. 335; cf. Gray, "Nature and Sources of the Law," sec. 420; Salmond, "Jurisprudence," p. 170.
[29] Cf. Gény, "Méthode d'Interprétation et Sources en droit privé positif," vol. II, p. 119.
[30] W. G. Miller, *supra*, p. 281; Bryce, "Studies in History and Jurisprudence," vol. II, p. 629.
[31] P. 1.

consciousness and the common faith. In default of other tests, the method of philosophy must remain the organon of the courts if chance and favor are to be excluded, and the affairs of men are to be governed with the serene and impartial uniformity which is of the essence of the idea of law.

You will say that there is an intolerable vagueness in all this. If the method of philosophy is to be employed in the absence of a better one, some test of comparative fitness should be furnished. I hope, before I have ended, to sketch, though only in the broadest outline, the fundamental considerations by which the choice of methods should be governed. In the nature of things they can never be catalogued with precision. Much must be left to that deftness in the use of tools which the practice of an art develops. A few hints, a few suggestions, the rest must be trusted to the feeling of the artist. But for the moment, I am satisfied to establish the method of philosophy as one organon among several, leaving the choice of one or the other to be talked of later. Very likely I have labored unduly to establish its title to a place so modest. Above all, in the Law School of Yale University, the title will not be challenged. I say that because in the work of a brilliant teacher of this school, the late Wesley Newcomb Hohfeld I find impressive recognition of the importance of this method, when kept within due limits, and some of the happiest illustrations of its legitimate employment. His treatise on "Fundamental Conceptions Applied in Judicial Reasoning" is in reality a plea that fundamental conceptions be analyzed more clearly, and their philosophical implications, their logical conclusions, developed more consistently. I do not mean to represent him as holding to the view that logical conclusions must always follow the conceptions developed by analysis. "No one saw more clearly than he that while the analytical matter is an indispensable tool, it is not an all-sufficient one for the lawyer." [32] "He emphasized over and over again" that "analytical work merely paves the way for other branches of jurisprudence, and that without the aid of the latter, satisfactory solutions of legal problems cannot be reached." [33] We must know where logic and philosophy lead even though we may determine to abandon them for other guides. The times will be many when we can do no better than follow where they point.

Example, if not better than precept, may at least prove to be easier. We may get some sense of the class of questions to which a method is adapted when we have studied the class of questions to which it has been applied. Let me give some haphazard illustrations of conclusions adopted by our law through the development of legal conceptions to logical conclusions. A. agrees to sell a chattel to B. Before title passes, the chattel is destroyed. The loss falls on the seller who has sued at law for the price. [34] A. agrees to sell a house and lot. Before title passes, the house is destroyed. The seller sues in equity for specific performance. The loss falls upon the buyer. [35] That is probably the prevailing view,

[32] Introduction to Hohfeld's Treatise by W. W. Cook.
[33] Professor Cook's Introduction.
[34] Higgins v. Murray, 73 N. Y. 252, 254; 2 Williston on Contracts, sec. 962; N. Y. Personal Prop. Law, sec. 103a.
[35] Paine v. Meller, 6 Ves. 349, 352; Sewell v. Underhill, 197 N. Y. 168; 2 Williston on Contracts, sec. 931.

though its wisdom has been sharply criticized.[36] These variant conclusions are not dictated by variant considerations of policy or justice. They are projections of a principle to its logical outcome, or the outcome supposed to be logical. Equity treats that as done which ought to be done. Contracts for the sale of land, unlike most contracts for the sale of chattels, are within the jurisprudence of equity. The vendee is in equity the owner from the beginning. Therefore, the burdens as well as the benefits of ownership shall be his. Let me take as another illustration of my meaning the cases which define the rights of assignees of choses in action. In the discussion of these cases, you will find much conflict of opinion about fundamental conceptions. Some tell us that the assignee has a legal ownership.[37] Others say that his right is purely equitable.[38] Given, however, the fundamental conception, all agree in deducting its consequences by methods in which the preponderating element is the method of philosophy. We may find kindred illustrations in the law of trusts and contracts and in many other fields. It would be wearisome to accumulate them.

The directive force of logic does not always exert itself, however, along a single and unobstructed path. One principle or precedent, pushed to the limit of its logic, may point to one conclusion; another principle or precedent, followed with like logic, may point with equal certainty to another. In this conflict, we must choose between the two paths, selecting one or other, or perhaps striking out upon a third, which will be the resultant of the two forces in combination, or will represent the mean between extremes. Let me take as an illustration of such conflict the famous case of Riggs v. Palmer, 115 N. Y. 506. That case decided that a legatee who has murdered his testator would not be permitted by a court of equity to enjoy the benefits of the will. Conflicting principles were there in competition for the mastery. One of them prevailed, and vanquished all the others. There was the principle of the binding force of a will disposing of the estate of a testator in conformity with law. That principle, pushed to the limit of its logic, seemed to uphold the title of the murderer. There was the principle that civil courts may not add to the pains and penalties of crimes. That, pushed to the limit of its logic, seemed again to uphold his title. But over against these was another principle, of greater generality, its roots deeply fastened in universal sentiments of justice, the principle that no man should profit from his own inequity or take advantage of his own wrong. The logic of this principle prevailed over the logic of the others. I say its logic prevailed. The thing which really interests us, however, is why and how the choice was made between one logic and another. In this instance, the reason is not obscure. One path was followed, another closed, because of the conviction in the judicial mind that the one selected led to justice. Analogies and precedents and the principles behind them were brought together as rivals for precedence; in the end, the principle that was thought to be most fundamental, to represent the larger and deeper social interests, put its competitors

[36] 2 Williston on Contracts, sec. 940.
[37] Cook, 29 Harvard L. R. 816, 836.
[38] Williston, 30 Harvard L. R. 97; 31 ibid. 822.

to flight. I am not greatly concerned about the particular formula through which justice was attained. Consistency was preserved, logic received its tribute, by holding that the legal title passed, but that it was subjected to a constructive trust.[39] A constructive trust is nothing but "the formula through which the conscience of equity finds expression."[40] Property is acquired in such circumstances that the holder of the legal title may not in good conscience retain the beneficial interest. Equity, to express its disapproval of his conduct, converts him into a trustee.[41] Such formulas are merely the remedial devices by which a result conceived of as right and just is made to square with principle and with the symmetry of the legal system. What concerns me now is not the remedial device, but rather the underlying motive, the indwelling, creative energy, which brings such devices into play. The murderer lost the legacy for which the murder was committed because the social interest served by refusing to permit the criminal to profit by his crime is greater than that served by the preservation and enforcement of legal rights of ownership. My illustration, indeed, has brought me ahead of my story. The judicial process is there in miscrocosm. We go forward with our logic, with our analogies, with our philosophies, till we reach a certain point. At first, we have no trouble with the paths; they follow the same lines. Then they begin to diverge, and we must make a choice between them. History or custom or social utility or some compelling sentiment of justice or sometimes perhaps a semi-intuitive apprehension of the pervading spirit of our law, must come to the rescue of the anxious judge, and tell him where to go.

It is easy to accumulate examples of the process—of the constant checking and testing of philosophy by justice, and of justice by philosophy. Take the rule which permits recovery with compensation for defects in cases of substantial though incomplete performance. We have often applied it for the protection of builders who in trifling details and without evil purpose have departed from their contracts. The courts had some trouble for a time, when they were deciding such cases, to square their justice with their logic. Even now, an uneasy feeling betrays itself in treatise and decision that the two fabrics do not fit. As I had occasion to say in a recent case: "Those who think more of symmetry and logic in the development of legal rules than of practical adaption to the attainment of a just result" remain "troubled by a classification where the lines of division are so wavering and blurred."[42] I have no doubt that the inspiration of the rule is a mere sentiment of justice. That sentiment asserting itself, we have proceeded to surround it with the halo of conformity to precedent. Some judges saw the unifying principle in the law of quasi-contracts. Others saw it in the distinction between dependent and independent promises, or between promises and conditions. All found, however, in the end that there *was* a principle in the legal armory which, when taken down from the wall where it

---

[39] Ellerson v. Westcott, 148 N. Y. 149, 154; Ames, "Lectures on Legal History," pp. 313m 314.
[40] Beatty v. Guggenheim Exploration Co., 225 N. Y. 380, 386.
[41] Beatty v. Guggenheim Exploration Co., *supra;* Ames, *supra.*
[42] Jacobs & Youngs, Inc. v. Kent, 230 N. Y. 239.

was rusting, was capable of furnishing a weapon for the fight and of hewing a path to justice. Justice reacted upon logic, sentiment upon reason, by guiding the choice to be made between one logic and another. Reason in its turn reacted upon sentiment by purging it of what is arbitrary, by checking it when it might otherwise have been extravagant, by relating it to method and order and coherence and tradition.[43]

In this conception of the method of logic or philosophy as one organon among several, I find nothing hostile to the teachings of continental jurists who would dethrone it from its place and power in systems of jurisprudence other than our own. They have combated an evil which has touched the common law only here and there, and lightly. I do not mean that there are not fields where we have stood in need of the same lesson. In some part, however, we have been saved by the inductive process through which our case law has developed from evils and dangers inseparable from the development of law, upon the basis of the *jus scriptum*, by a process of deduction.[44] Yet even continental jurists who emphasize the need of other methods, do not ask us to abstract from legal principles all their fructifying power. The misuse of logic or philosophy begins when its method and its ends are treated as supreme and final. They can never be banished altogether. "Assuredly," says François Gény,[45] "there should be no question of banishing ratiocination and logical methods from the science of positive law." Even general principles may sometimes be followed rigorously in the deduction of their consequences. "The abuse," he says, "consists, if I do not mistake, in envisaging ideal conceptions, provisional and purely subjective in their nature, as endowed with a permanent objective reality. And this false point of view, which, to my thinking, is a vestige of the absolute realism of the middle ages, ends in confining the entire system of positive law, *a priori*, within a limited number of logical categories, which are predetermined in essence, immovable in basis, governed by inflexible dogmas, and thus incapable of adapting themselves to the ever varied and changing exigencies of life."

In law, as in every other branch of knowledge, the truths given by induction tend to form the premises for new dedutions. The lawyers and the judges of successive generations do not repeat for themselves the process of verification, any more than most of us repeat the demonstrations of the truths of astronomy or physics. A stock of juridical conceptions and formulas is developed, and we take them, so to speak, ready-made. Such fundamental conceptions as contract and possession and ownership and testament and many others, are there, ready for use. How they came to be there, I do not need to inquire. I am writing, not a history of the evolution of law, but a sketch of the judicial process applied to law full grown. These fundamental conceptions once attained form the starting point from which are derived new consequences, which, at first tentative and

---

[43] Cf. Hynes v. N. Y. Central R. R. Co. (231 N. Y. 229, 235).
[44] "Notre droit public, comme notre droit privé, est un *jus scriptum*" (Michoud, "La Responsibilité de l'état à raison des fautes de ses agents," Revue du droit public, 1895, p. 273, quoted by Gény, vol. I, p. 40, sec. 19).
[45] *OP. cit.*, vol. I, p. 127, sec. 61.

groping, gain by reiteration a new permanence and certainty. In the end, they become accepted themselves as fundamental and axiomatic. So it is with the growth from precendent to precendent. The implications of a decision may in the beginning be equivocal. New cases by commentary and exposition extract the essence. At least there emerges a rule or principle which becomes a datum, a point of departure, from which new lines will be run, from which new courses will be measured. Sometimes the rule or principle is found to have been formulated too narrowly or too broadly, and has to be reframed. Sometimes it is accepted as a postulate of later reasoning, its origins are forgotten, it becomes a new stock of descent, its issue unite with other strains, and persisting permeate the law. You may call the process one of analogy or of logic or of philosophy as you please. Its essence in any event is the derivation of a consequence from a rule or a principle or a precedent which, accepted as a datum, contains implicitly within itself the germ of the conclusion. In all this, I do not use the word philosophy in any strict or formal sense. The method tapers down from the syllogism at one end to mere analogy at the other. Sometimes the extension of a precedent goes to the limit of its logic. Sometimes it does not go so far. Sometimes by a process of analogy it is carried even farther. That is a tool which no system of jurisprudence has been able to discard.[46] A rule which has worked well in one field, or which, in any event, is there whether its workings have been revealed or not, is carried over into another. Instances of such a process I group under the same heading as those where the nexus of logic is closer and more binding.[47] At bottom and in their underlying motives, they are phases of the same method. They are inspired by the same yearning for consistency, for certainty, for uniformity of plan and structure. They have their roots in the constant striving of the mind for a larger and more inclusive unity, in which differences will be reconciled, and abnormalities will vanish.

[46] Ehrlich, "Die Juristische Logik," pp. 225, 227.
[47] Cf. Gény, *op. cit.*, vol. II, p. 121, sec. 165; also vol. I, p. 304, sec. 107.

# 29

# Joseph C. Hutcheson, Jr.

Joseph C. Hutcheson (1879–    ), author of one of the most candid appraisals of the judicial function, has served since 1918 as United States District and later Circuit Judge, based in his native city of Houston.

# THE JUDGMENT INTUITIVE*

Many years ago, at the conclusion of a particularly difficult case both in point of law and of fact, tried to a court without a jury, the judge, a man of great learning and ability, announced from the Bench that since the narrow and prejudiced modern view of the obligations of a judge in the decision of causes prevented his resort to the judgment aleatory by the use of his "little, small dice" he would take the case under advisement, and, brooding over it, wait for his hunch. [1]

To me, a young, indeed a very young lawyer, picked, while yet the dew was on me and I had just begun to sprout, from the classic gardens of a University, where I had been trained to regard the law as a system of rules and precedents, of categories and concepts, and the judge had been spoken of as an administrator, austere, remote, "his intellect a cold logic engine," who, in that rarified atmosphere in which he lived coldly and logically determined the relation of the facts of a particular case to some of these established precedents, it appeared that the judge was making a jest, and a very poor one, at that.

I had been trained to expect inexactitude from juries, but from the judge quite the reverse. I exalted in the law its tendency to formulize. I had a slot machine mind. I searched out categories and concepts and, having found them, worshiped them.

I paid homage to the law's supposed logical rigidity and exactitude. A logomachist, I believed in and practiced logomancy. I felt a sense of real pain when some legal concept in which I had put my faith as permanent, constructive and all-embracing opened like a broken net, allowing my fish to fall back into the legal sea. Paraphrasing Huxley, I believe that the great tragedy of the law was the slaying of a beautiful concept by an ugly fact. Always I looked for perfect formulas, fact proof, concepts so general, so flexible, that in their terms

---

*Joseph C. Hutcheson, Jr., "The Judgment Intuitive: The Function of the 'Hunch' in Judicial Decision," *Cornell Law Quarterly*, XIV (1928), pp. 274–288. Reprinted by permission of the author and publisher. Copyright © 1929 by Cornell University.
[1] "A strong, intuitive impression that something is about to happen." WEBSTER, INTERNATIONAL DICTIONARY.

the jural relations of mankind could be stated, and I rejected most vigorously the suggestion that there was, or should be, anything fortuitous or by chance in the law. Like Jurgen I had been to the Master Philologist and with words he had conquered me.

I had studied the law in fragments and segments, in sections and compartments, and in my mind each compartment was nicely and logically arranged so that every case presented to me only the problem of arranging and re-arranging its facts until I could slip it into the compartment to which it belonged. The relation of landlord and tenant, or principal and agent, of bailor and bailee, of master and servant, these and a hundred others controlled my thinking and directed its processes.

Perceiving the law as a thing fullgrown, I believed that all of its processes were embraced in established categories, and I rejected most vigorously the suggestion that it still had life and growth, and if anyone had suggested that the judge had a right to feel, or hunch out a new category into which to place relations under his investigation, I should have repudiated the suggestion as unscientific and unsound, while as to the judge who dared to do it. I should have cried "Away with him! Away with him!"

I was too much influenced by the codifiers, by John Austin and Bentham, and by their passion for exactitude. I knew that in times past the law had grown through judicial action; that rights and processes had been invented by the judges, and that under their creative hand new remedies and new rights had flowered.

I knew that judges "are the depositories of the laws like the oracles, who must decide in all cases of doubt and are bound by an oath to decide according to the law of the land",[2] but I believed that creation and evolution were at an end, that in modern law only deduction had place, and that the judges must decide "through being long personally accustomed to and acquainted with the judicial decisions of their predecessors".[3]

I recognized, of course, that in the preparation of the facts of a case there was room for intuition, for feeling; that there was a sixth sense which must be employed in searching out the evidence for clues, in order to assemble facts and more facts, but all of this before the evidence was in. I regarded the solution of the problem when the evidence was all in as a matter for determination by the judge by pure reason and reflection, and while I knew that juries might and did arrive at their verdicts by feeling, I repudiated as impossible the idea that good judges did the same.

I knew, of course, that some judges did follow "hunches"—"guesses" I indignantly called them. I knew my Rabelais, and had laughed over without catching the true philosophy of old Judge Bridlegoose's trial, and roughly, in my youthful, scornful way, I recognized four kinds of judgments; first the cogitative, of and by reflection and logomancy; second, aleatory, of and by the dice; third, intuitive, of and by feeling or "hunching"; and fourth, asinine,

2 BL. COMM. 169.
3 *Ibid.*

of and by an ass; and in that same youthful, scornful way I regarded the last three as only variants of each other, the results of processes all alien to good judges.

As I grew older, however, and knew and understood better the judge to whom I have in this opening referred; as I associated more with real lawyers, whose intuitive faculties were developed and made acute by the use of a trained and cultivated imagination; as I read more after and came more under the spell of those great lawyers and judges whose thesis is that "modification is the life of the law",[4] I came to see that "as long as the matter to be considered is debated in artificial terms, there is danger of being led by a technical definition to apply a certain name and then to deduce consequences which have no relation to the grounds on which the name was applied";[5] that "the process of inclusion and exclusion so often applied in developing a rule, cannot end with its first enunciation. The rule announced must be deemed tentative. For the many and varying facts to which it will be applied cannot be foreseen."[6]

I came to see that "every opinion tends to become a law."[7] That "regulations, the wisdom, necessity and validity of which as applied to, existing conditions, are so apparent that they are now uniformly sustained, a century ago, or even half a century ago, would probably have been rejected as arbitrary and oppressive, . . . and that in a changing world it is impossible that it should be otherwise."[8]

I came to see that "resort to first principles is, in the last analysis, the only safe way to a solution of litigated matters".[9]

I came to see that instinct in the very nature of law itself is change, adaptation, conformity, and that the instrument for all of this change, this adaptation, this conformity, for the making and the nurturing of the law as a thing of life, is the power of the brooding mind, which in its very brooding makes, creates and changes jural relations, establishes philosophy, and drawing away from the outworn past, here a little, there a little, line upon line, precept upon precept, safely and firmly, bridges for the judicial mind to pass the abysses between that past and the new future."[10]

So, long before I came to the Bench, and while I was still uncertain as to the function of the judge, his office seeming pale and cold to me, too much

---

[4] CARTER, LAW, ITS ORIGIN, GROWTH AND FUNCTION (1907). "Modification implies growth. It is the life of the law." Washington v. Dawson, 264 U. S. 219, 236, 44 Sup. Ct. 302 (1924), Brandeis, J., dissenting.

[5] Guy v. Donald, 203 U. S. 399, 406, 27 Sup. Ct. 63 (1926).

[6] Washington v. Dawson, *supra* note 4.

[7] Lochner v. New York, 198 U. S. 45, 76, 25 Sup. Ct. 539 (1905).

[8] Euclid Valley v. Ambler, 272 U. S. 365, 47 Sup. Ct. 114 (1926).

[9] Old Colony Trust Co. v. Sugarland Industries, 296 Fed. 129, 138 (S. D. Tex. 1924).

[10] "Judges do and must legislate, but they can do so only interstitially. They are confined from Molar to molecular motions. A common law judge could not say, I think the doctrine of consideration a bit of historical nonsense, and shall not enforce it in my court. No more could a judge exercising the limited jurisdiction of admiralty say I think well of the common law rules of master and servant, and propose to introduce them here *en bloc*." Southern Pacific v. Jensen, 244 U.S. 205, 221, 37 Sup. Ct. 524 (1917), Holmes, J., dissenting.

concerned with logomachy; too much ruled by logomancy, I loved jury trials, for there, without any body of precedent to guide them, any established judicial recognition of their right so to do, nay, in the face of its denial to them, I could see those twelve men bringing equity, "the correction of that wherein by reason of its universality the law is deficient," into the law.

There they would sit, and hearing sometimes the "still, sad music of humanity," sometimes "catching sight through the darkness of the fateful threads of woven fire which connect error with its retribution," wrestling in civil cases with that legal Robot, "the reasonably prudent man," in criminal cases with that legal paradox, "beyond a reasonable doubt," would hunch out, just verdict after verdict by the use of that sixth sense, that feeling, which flooding the mind with light, gives the intuitional flash necessary for the just decision.

Later, when I became more familiar with the practices in admiralty and in equity, more especially when, a judge in such cases, I felt the restless, eager ranging of the mind to overcome the confusion and the perplexities of the evidence, or of constricting and outworn concepts, and so to find the hidden truth, I knew that not only was it the practice of good judges to "feel" their way to a decision of a close and difficult case, but that in such cases any other practice was unsound. "For it is no paradox to say that in our most theoretical moods we may be nearest to our most practical applications."

I knew that "general propositions do not decide concrete cases. The decision will depend on a judgment or intuition more subtle than any articulate major premise."[11]

And so, after eleven years on the Bench following eighteen at the Bar, I, being well advised by observation and experience of what I am about to set down, have thought it both wise and decorous to now boldly affirm that "having well and exactly seen, surveyed, overlooked, reviewed, recognized, read and read over again, turned and tossed about, seriously perused and examined the preparitories, productions, evidence, proofs, allegations, depositions, cross speeches, contradictions . . . and other such like confects and spiceries, both at the one and the other side, as a good judge ought to do, I posit on the end of the table in my closet all the pokes and bags of the defendants—that being done I thereafter lay down upon the other end of the same table the bags and satchels of the plaintiff."[12]

Thereafter I proceed "to understand and resolve the obscurities of these various and seeming contrary passages in the law, which are laid claim to by the suitors and pleading parties", even just as Judge Bridlegoose did, with one difference only. "That when the matter is more plain, clear and liquid, that is to say, when there are fewer bags," and he would have used his "other large great dice, fair and goodly ones," I decide the case more or less off hand and by rule of thumb. While when the case is difficult or involved, and turns upon

---

[11] *Ibid.*
[12] RABELAIS, BOOK 111, c. 39.

a hairsbreadth of law or of fact, that is to say, "when there are many bags on the one side and on the other" and Judge Bridlegoose would have used his "little small dice," I, after canvassing all the available material at my command, and duly cogitating upon it, give my imagination play, and brooding over the cause, wait for the feeling, the hunch—that intuitive flash of understanding which makes the jump-spark connection between question and decision, and at the point where the path is darkest for the judicial feet, sheds its light along the way.

And more, "lest I be stoned in the street" for this admission, let me hasten to say to my brothers of the Bench and of the Bar, "my practice is therein the same with that of your other worships." [13]

For let me premise here, that in feeling or "hunching" out his decisions, the judge acts not differently from, but precisely as the lawyers do in working on their cases, with only this exception; that the lawyer, having a predetermined destination in view—to win his law suit for his client—looks for and regards only those hunches which keep him in the path that he has chosen, while the judge, being merely on his way with a roving commission to find the just solution, will follow his hunch wherever it leads him, and when, following it, he meets the right solution face to face, he can cease his labors and blithely say to his troubled mind—"Trip no farther, pretty sweeting, journeys end in lovers meeting, as every wise man's son doth know."

Further, at the outset, I must premise that I speak now of the judgment or decision, the solution itself, as opposed to the apologia for that decision; the decree, as opposed to the logomachy, the effusion of the judge by which that decree is explained or excused. I speak of the judgment pronounced, as opposed to the rationalization by the judge on that pronouncement.

I speak, in short, of that act of definitive sentence of which Trinquamelle and Bridlegoose discoursed.

"But when you do these fine things" quoth Trinquamelle, "how do you, my fine friend, award your decrees and pronounce judgment?" "Even as your other worships," quoth Bridlegoose, "for I give out sentence in his favor unto whom hath befallen the best chance by the dice, judiciary, tribunian, pretorial, which comes first. So doth the law command." [14]

And not only do I set down boldly that I, "even as your other worships do," invoke and employ hunches in decisions, but I do affirm, and will preesntly show, that it is that tiptoe faculty of the mind which can feel and follow a hunch which makes not only the best gamblers, the best detectives, the best lawyers, the best judges, the materials of whose trades are the most chancey because most human, and the results of whose activities are for the same cause the most subject to uncertainty and the best attained by approximation, but it is that same faculty which has guided and will continue to guide the great scientists of the world, [15] and even those august dealers in certitude, the

[13] *Ibid.*
[14] *Ibid.*

mathematicians themselves, to their most difficult solutions, which have opened and will continue to open hidden doors; which have widened and will ever widen man's horizon.

"For facts are sterile until there are minds capable of choosing between them and discerning those which conceal something, and recognizing that which is concealed. Minds which under the bare fact see the soul of the fact." [16]

I shall further affirm, and I think maintain, that the judge is, in the exercise of this faculty, popularly considered to be an attribute of only the gambler and the short story detective, in the most gallant of gallant companies; a philosopher among philosophers, and I shall not fear to stand, unrebuked and unashamed before my brothers of the Bench and Bar.

I remember once, in the trial of a patent case, where it was contended with great vigor on the one side that the patent evidenced invention of the highest order, and with equal vigor on the other that the device in question was merely a mechical advance, I announced, almost without any sense of incongruity, that I would take the case under advisement, and after "having well and exactly seen and surveyed, overlooked, reviewed, read and read over again" etc., all of the briefs, authorities and the record, would wait awhile before deciding to give my mind a chance to hunch it out, for if there was the flash of invention in the device my mind would give back an answering flash; while if there were none, my mind would, in a dully cogitative way, find only mechanical advance.

One of the lawyers, himself a "huncher," smiled and said—"Well, Your Honor, I am very grateful to you for having stated from the Bench what I have long believed, but have hesitated to avow, that next to the pure arbitrament of the dice in judicial decisions, the best chance for justice comes through the hunch." The other lawyer, with a different type of mind, only looked on as though impatient of such foolery.

But I, proceeding according to custom, got my hunch, found invention and infringement, and by the practice of logomachy so bewordled my opinion in support of my hunch that I found myself in the happy situation of having so satisfied the intuitive lawyer by the correctness of the hunch, and the logomachic lawyer by the spell of my logomancy, that both sides accepted the result and the cause was ended.

Now, what is this faculty? What are its springs, what its uses? Many men have spoken of it most beautifully. Some call it "intuition"—some, "imagination," this sensitiveness to new ideas, this power to range when the track is cold, this power to cast in ever widening circles to find a fresh scent, instead of standing baying where the track was lost.

"Imagination, that wondrous faculty, which properly controlled by

[15] "The method of science indeed is the method of the Chancery Court—it involves the collection of all available evidence and the subjection of all such evidence to the most searching examination and cross examination." GREGORY, DISCOVERY, THE SPIRIT AND SERVICE OF SCIENCE 166, quoting H. E. Armstrong.

[16] *Ibid.*, at 170, quoting Henri Poincare.

experience and reflection, becomes the noblest attribute of man, the source of poetic genius, the instrument of discovery in science." [17]

"With accurate experiment and observation to work upon, imagination becomes the architect of physical theory. Newton's passage from a falling apple to a falling moon was an act of the prepared imagination without which the laws of Kepler could never have been traced to their foundations.

"Out of the facts of chemistry the constructive imagination of Dalton formed the atomic theory. Scientific men fight shy of the word because of its ultra-scientific connotations, but the fact is that without the exercise of this power our knowledge of nature would be a mere tabulation of co-existences and sequences." [18]

Again—"There is in the human intellect a power of expansion, I might almost call it a power of creation, which is brought into play by the simple brooding upon facts. The legend of the spirit brooding over chaos may have originated in experience of this power." [19]

It is imagination which, from assembled facts, strikes out conclusions and establishes philosophies. "Science is analytical description. Philosophy is synthetic interpretation. The philosopher is not content to describe the fact; he wishes to ascertain its relation to experience in general, and thereby to get at its meaning and its worth. He combines things in interpretative synthesis. To observe processes and to construct means is science. To criticize and co-ordinate ends is philosophy. For a fact is nothing except in relation to desire; it is not complete except in relation to a purpose and a whole. Science, without philosophy, facts without perspective and valuation cannot save us from havoc and despair. Science gives us knowledge, but only philosophy can give us wisdom." [20] Cardozo expresses it most beautifully.

"Repeatedly, when one is hard beset, there are principles and precedents and analogies which may be pressed into the service of justice, if one has the perceiving eye to use them. It is not unlike the divinations of the scientist. His experiments must be made significant by the flash of a luminous hypothesis. For the creative process in law, and indeed in science generally, has a kinship to the creative process in art. Imagination, whether you call it scientific or artistic, is for each the faculty that creates."

"Learning is indeed necessary, but learning is the springboard by which imagination leaps to truth. The law has its piercing intuitions, its tense, apocalyptic moments. We gather together our principles and precedents and analogies, even at times our fictions, and summon them to yield the energy that will best attain the jural end. If our wand has the divining touch, it will seldom knock in vain. So it is that the conclusion, however deliberate and labored, has often the aspect of a lucky find."

[17] Address to the Royal Society of England, November 3, 1859, Sir Benjamin Brodie, quoted from FRAGMENTS OF SCIENCE, 109.
[18] "Scientific Use of the Imagination" Address delivered before the British Association at Liverpool, Sept. 16, 1860 by Tyndall, quoted from FRAGMENTS OF SCIENCE, 111.
[19] Ibid., at 114.
[20] DURANT, STORY OF PHILOSOPHY.

" 'When I once asked the best administrator whom I knew,' writes Mr. Wallas, 'how he formed his decisions, he laughed, and with the air of letting out for the first time a guilty secret, said: "Oh, I always decide by feeling. So and so always decides by calculation, and that is no good." When again I asked an American judge, who is widely admired both for his skill and for his impartiality, how he and his fellows formed their conclusions, he also laughed, and said that he would be stoned in the street if it were known that, after listening with full consciousness to all the evidence, and following as carefully as he could all the arguments, he waited until he "felt" one way or the other. He had elided the preparation and the brooding, or at least had come to think of them as processes of faint kinship with the state of mind that followed.' 'When the conclusion is there', says William James, 'we have already forgotten most of the steps preceding its attainment.' " [21]

Collision cases in admiralty furnish excellent illustrations of the difficulty of arriving at a sound fact conclusion by mere reasoning upon objective data. In these cases, as every trier knows, the adherents of the respective ships swear most lustily in true seagoing fashion for their side, and if a judge were compelled to decide the case by observing the demeanor of the witnesses alone, he would be in sad plight, for at the end of eleven years upon the Bench I am more convinced than ever that the shrewdest, smartest liars often make the most plausible and satisfactory witnesses, while the humblest and most honest fellows often, upon the witness stand, acquit themselves most badly.

Now, in such circumstances, deprived of the hunch which is the clue to judgment, "the intuition more subtle than any major premise," it would be better for the judge either to resort to the device of summoning the litigants "to personally compear before him a precise hundred years thereafter to answer to some interrogatories touching certain points which were not contained in the verbal defense" [22] or to use the "little small dice" in which Judge Bridlegoose placed so much confidence in tight cases, than to try to decide the case by rule of thumb upon the number of witnesses, or the strength of their asseverations.

Fortunately, however, in these cases the judge may, reconciling all the testimony reconcilable, and coming to the crux of the conflict, having a full and complete picture of the scene itself furnished by the actors, re-enact the drama and as the scene unfolds with the actors each in the place assigned by his own testimony, play the piece out, watching for the joints in the armor of proof, the crevices in the structure of the case or its defense. If the first run fails, the piece may be played over and over until finally, when it seems perhaps impossible to work any consistent truth out of it, the hunch comes, the scenes and the players are rearranged in accordance with it, and lo, it works successfully and in order.

If in other causes this faculty of "feeling" the correct decision is important

[21] CARDOZO, PARADOXES OF LEGAL SCIENCE (1928) 59, 60.
[22] RABELAIS, BOOK III, c. 44.

to the successful trier of facts, it is doubly so in patent cases for "it is not easy to draw the line which separates the ordinary skill of a mechanic versed in his art, from the exercise of patentable invention, and the difficulty is especially great in the mechanic arts, where the successive steps in improvements are numerous, and where the changes and modifications are introduced by practical mechanics."[23]

Mr. Roberts, in his scholarly and exhaustive treatise on *Patentability and Patent Interpretation,* has this to say of the Krementz case:

> "How the court could have arrived at the conclusion that this case furnished an instance of patentable invention is very difficult to understand in view of its attitude toward many other cases. . . . The explanation must be sought in the fact that no objective criteria has ever been recognized as decisive of the question of patentability, and that accordingly each case has had to be decided upon consideration of what the judicial mind could determine to be, on the whole, just and fair under the particular circumstances which happened to be present."[24]

Nevertheless, says Roberts, "There have frequently been unmistakable indications of perplexity on the part of the judges when endeavoring to assign reasons for their decision one way or another in cases where patentable invention was doubtful" and commenting further on the remarks of Mr. Justice Shiras in the Krementz case at page 559, parts of which are quoted herein, he concludes:

> "This was not a logical conclusion founded upon well established premises; it was only a confession of doubt, and a guess induced by special considerations which could not furnish a rule for the determination of any other question of a similar kind."[25]

To relieve this "perplexity" and to avoid these "confessions of doubt" and "guesses induced by special considerations" Mr. Roberts proposes to substitute for the subjective determination which breeds these undesirable conditions, decisions upon purely objective criteria, wholly dependent upon objective evidence, and wholly free from the influence of subjective bias.

"In short," says Roberts, "it is utterly futile to attempt to settle questions of patentability by resorting to merely subjective tests. All changes effected in the industrial arts are the production of thought, but it is impossible to discover any certain gauge for their rank in the inventive scale by simply contemplating the mental processes which have accomplished their origination." [26]

Mr. Roberts' effort, while vigorous and sustained, and supported by a wealth of learning, leaves me, as to the proposition that questions of invention may in all cases be decided upon purely objective criteria, without "the intuition more subtle than any major premise," cold.

---

[23] Krementz v. S. Cottle Co., 148 U.S. 559.
[24] ROBERTS, PATENTABILITY, AND PATENT INTERPRETATION 181.
[25] *Ibid.,* at 181.
[26] *Ibid.,* at 247.

Judges who have tried many patent cases, who have heard the testimony of experts, the one affirming the matter to be merely an advance in mechanical steps, the other to be invention of the highest order; the one affirming prior use, the other denying it; the one affirming it to be the flight of genius into new fields, the other, the mere dull trudging of an artisan, knowing that for a just decision of such causes no objective criteria can be relied on. They well know that there must be in the trier something of the same imaginative response to an idea, something of that same flash of genius that there is in the inventor, which all great patent judges have had, that intuitive brilliance of the imagination, that luminous quality of the mind, that can give back, where there is invention, an answering flash for flash.

Time was when judges, lawyers, law writers and teachers of the law refused to recognize in the judge this right and power of intuitive decision. It is true that the trial judge was always supposed to have superior facilities for decision, but these were objectivized in formulas, such as—the trial judge has the best opportunity of observing the witnesses, their demeanor—the trial judge can see the play and interplay of forces as they operate in the actual clash of the trial.

Under the influence of this kind of logomachy, this sticking in the "skin" of thought, the trial judge's superior opportunity was granted, but the real reason for that superior position, that the trial creates an atmosphere springing from but more than the facts themselves, in which and out of which the judge may get the feeling which takes him to the desired end, was deliberately suppressed.

Later writers, however, not only recognize but emphasize this faculty, nowhere more attractively than in Judge Cardozo's lectures before the law schools of Yale University, in 1921 [27] and Columbia University in 1927,[28] while Max Radin, in 1925, in a most sympathetic and charming way, takes the judge's works apart, and shows us how his wheels go round.[29]

He tells us, first, that the judge is a human being; that therefore he does not decide causes by the abstract application of rules of justice or of right, but having heard the cause and determined that the decision ought to go this way or that way, he then takes up his search for some category of the law into which the case will fit.

He tells us that the judge really feels or thinks that a certain result seems desirable, and he then tries to make his decision accomplish that result. "What makes certain results seem desirable to a judge?" he asks, and answers his question that that seems desirable to the judge which, according to his training, his experience, and his general point of view, strikes him as the jural consequence that ought to flow from the facts, and he advises us that what gives the judge the struggle in the case is the effort so to state the reasons for his judgment that they will pass muster.

[27] CARDOZO, THE NATURE OF THE JUDICIAL PROCESS (1921).
[28] *Supra* note 21.
[29] Radin, *Theory of Judical Decision* (1925) 2 AM. B. A. J. 359.

Now what is he saying except that the judge really decides by feeling, and not by judgment; by "hunching" and not by a ratiocination, and that the ratiocination appears only in the opinion?

Now what is he saying but that the vital, motivating impulse for the decision is an intuitive sense of what is right or wrong for that cause, and that the astute judge, having so decided, enlists his every faculty and belabors his laggard mind, not only to justify that intuition to himself, but to make it pass muster with his critics?

There is nothing unreal or untrue about this picture of the judge, nor is there anything in it from which a just judge should turn away. It is true, and right that it is true, that judges really do try to select categories or concepts into which to place a particular case so as to produce what the judge regards as a righteous result, or, to avoid any confusion in the matter of morals, I will say a "proper result."

This is true. I think we should go further, and say it ought to be true. No reasoning applied to practical matters is ever really effective unless motivated by some impulse.

"Occasionally and frequently, the exercise of the judgment ought to end in absolute reservation. We are not infallible, so we ought to be cautious." [30] "Sometimes," however, "if we would guide by the light of reason, we must let our minds be bold." [31]

The purely contemplative philosopher may project himself into an abstract field of contemplation where he reasons, but practical men, and in that judges must be included, must have impulses. The lawyer has them, and because he has them his work is tremendously important. If a lawyer merely reasoned abstractly and without motive he would do the judge no good. But the driving impulse to bring about this client's success not only makes him burrow industriously for precedents, and as industriously bring them forth, but also makes him belabor and cudgel the brains of the listening judge to bring him into agreement.

It is this factor in our jurisprudence, and only this, that clients have lawyers and that lawyers are advocates, which has made and will continue to make it safe for judges not only to state, but sometimes to make the law. "A thorough advocate in a just cause,—a penetrating mathematician facing the starry heavens, alike bear the semblance of divinity."

If the judge sat upon the Bench in a purely abstract relation to the cause, his opinion in difficult cases would be worth nothing. He must have some motive to fire his brains, to "let his mind be bold."

By the nature of his occupation he cannot have advocacy for either side of the case as such, so he becomes an advocate, an earnest one, for the—in a way—abstract solution. Having become such advocate, his mind reaches and strains and feels for that result. He says with Elihu, the son of Barachel, the

---

[30] Op. cit. supra note 15, at 36, quoting Faraday.
[31] Burns v. Bryan, 264 U.S. 504, 520, 44 Sup. Ct. 412 (1923), Brandies, J., dissenting.

Buzite, of the family of Ram—"There is a spirit in man, and the breath of the Almighty giveth him understanding. It is not the great that are wise, nor the aged that understand justice.——Hearken to me; I also will show mine opinion. For I am full of matter; the spirit within me constraineth me. Behold my belly is as wine which hath no vent. Like new wineskins it is ready to burst."[32]

And having travailed and reached his judgment, he struggles to bring up and pass in review before his eager mind all of the categories and concepts which he may find useful directly or by analogy, so as to select from them that which in his opinion will support his desired result.

For while the judge may be, he cannot appear to be, arbitrary. He must at least appear reasonable, and unless he can find a category which will at least "semblably" support his view, he will feel uncomfortable.

Sometimes he must almost invent a category, but he can never do quite that thing, for as we have seen, the growth of the law is interstitial, and the new category cannot be new enough wholly to avoid contact and placement in the midst of prior related categories.

But whether or not the judge is able in his opinion to present reasons for his hunch which will pass jural muster, he does and should decide difficult and complicated cases only when he has the feeling of the decision, which accounts for the beauty and the fire of some, and the labored dullness of many dissenting opinions.

All of us have known judges who can make the soundest judgments and write the dullest opinions on them; whose decisions were hardly ever affirmed for the reasons which they gave. Their difficulty was that while they had the flash, the intuitive power of judgment, they could not show it forth. While they could by an intuitive flash leap to a conclusion, just as an inventor can leap to his invention, just as often as an inventor cannot explain the result or fully understand it, so cannot and do not they.

There is not one among us but knows that while too often cases must be decided without that "feeling" which is the triumphant precursor of the just judgment, that just as "sometimes a light surprises the Christian while he sings," so sometimes, after long travail and struggle of the mind, there does come to the dullest of us, flooding the brain with the vigorous blood of decision, the hunch that there is, or is not invention; that there is or is not, anticipation; that the plaintiff should be protected by a decree, or should be denied protection. This hunch, sweeping aside hesitancy and doubt, takes the judge vigorously on to his decision; and yet, the cause decided, the way thither, which was for the blinding moment a blazing trail, becomes wholly lost to view.

Sometimes again that same intuition of hunch, which warming his brain and lighting his feet produced the decision, abides with the decider "while working his judgment backward" as he blazes his trail "from a desirable conclusion back to one or another of a stock of logical premises".[33]

[32] JOB, CHAPTER 32, verses 9, 10, 18, 19.
[33] *Supra* note 29.

It is such judicial intuitions, and the opinions lighted and warmed by the feeling which produced them, that not only give justice in the cause, but like a great white way, make plain in the wilderness the way of the Lord for judicial feet to follow.

If these views are even partly sound, and if to great advocacy and great judging the imaginative, the intuitional faculty is essential, should there not be some change in the methods of the study and of the teaching of the law in our great law schools? Should there not go along with the plain and severely logical study of jural relations study and reflection upon, and an endeavor to discover and develop, those processes of the mind by which such decisions are reached, those processes and faculties which, lifting the mind above the mass of constricting matter whether of confused fact or precedent that stands in the way of just decision, enable it by a kind of apocalyptic vision to "trace the hidden equities of divine reward, and to catch sight through the darkness, of the fateful threads of woven fire which connect error with its retribution?" 34

34 Ruskin, Sesame and Lilies.

# 30

## Jerome N. Frank

Jerome Frank (1889–1957), leading American legal realist and 'fact sceptic', questioned the myth of law determined by rule apart from the personal and even psychoanalytic peculiarities of judges and juries.

# LAW AND THE MODERN MIND*

FROM THE PREFACE

Actually, these so-called realists have but one common bond, a negative characteristic already noted: skepticism as to some of the conventional legal theories, a skepticism stimulated by a zeal to reform, in the interest of justice, some court-house ways. Despite the lack of any homogeneity in their positive views, these "constructive skeptics," roughly speaking, do divide into two groups; however, there are marked differences, ignored by the critics, between the two groups.

The first group, of whom Llewellyn is perhaps the outstanding representative, I would call "rule skeptics." They aim at greater legal certainty. That is, they consider it socially desirable that lawyers should be able to predict to their clients the decisions in most lawsuits not yet commenced. They feel that, in too many instances, the layman cannot act with assurance as to how, if his acts become involved in a suit, the court will decide. As these skeptics see it, the trouble that the formal legal rules enunciated in courts' opinions—sometimes called "paper rules"—too often prove unreliable as guides in the prediction of decisions. They believe that they can discover, behind the "paper rules" some "real rules" descriptive of uniformities or regularities in actual judicial behavior, and that those "real rules" will serve as more reliable prediction-instruments, yielding a large measure of workable predictability of the outcome of future suits. In this undertaking, the rule skeptics concentrate almost exclusively on upper-court opinions. They do not ask themselves whether their own or any other prediction-device will render it possible for a lawyer or layman to prophesy, before an ordinary suit is instituted or comes to trial in a trial court, how it will be decided. In other words, these rule skeptics seek means for making accurate guesses, not about decisions of trial courts, but about decisions of upper courts when trial-court decisions are appealed. These skeptics cold-shoulder the trial courts. Yet, in most instances, these skeptics do not inform their readers that they are writing chiefly of upper courts.

The second group I would call "fact skeptics." They, too, engaging in "rule skepticism," peer behind the "paper rules." Together with the rule skeptics, they have stimulated interest in factors, influencing upper-court decisions, of which, often, the opinions of those courts give not hint. But the fact skeptics go much further. Their primary interest is in the trial courts. No matter how precise or definite may be the formal legal rules, say these fact skeptics, no matter what the discoverable uniformities behind these formal rules, nevertheless it is impossible, and will always be impossible, because of the elusiveness of the facts on which decisions turn, to predict future decisions in most (not all) law suits, not yet begun or not yet tried. The fact skeptics, thinking that therefore the pursuit of greatly increased legal certainty is, for the most part, futile—and that its pursuit, indeed, may well work injustice—aim rather at increased judicial justice. This group of fact skeptics includes, among others, Dean Leon Green, Max Radin, Thurman Arnold, William O. Dougals (now Mr. Justice Douglas), and perhaps E. M. Morgan.

CHAPTER XVI

THE BASIC MYTH AND THE JURY

The demand for excessive legal certainty produces, it has been seen, a violent prejudice against a recognition of the practical need for flexible adaption and individualization of law based upon the unique facts of particular cases. Yet the life and growth of society make imperative such flexible individualization of the rules. Not allowed to operate in the open, such individualization has been worked out by surreptitious methods. Notable among such surreptitious methods is our amazing use of the jury.

The function of the jury is supposed to be fact-finding. According to the official or naïve theory, when a case is tried before a judge and jury, there is a nicely divided tribunal: to the judge is left the determination of the rules of law; to the jury is left solely the ascertaining of facts. The jury, so the story goes, must in no manner encroach upon the powers of the judge. It must not concern itself in any manner with the authority or widsom of the law. What the judge announces as law must be taken by the jury as completely authoritative.[1]

If practice followed theory, the judge would ask the jury to determine, from the evidence, specific facts. "Do you believe from the evidence that Jones fell through the elevator shaft and broke his leg?" "Do you believe from the evidence that Smith represented to McCarthy that there was an oil well on the premises?" "Do you believe from the evidence that Robinson agreed to

---

[1] See Appendix V for a discussion of the "naive," the "sophisticated" and the "realistic" views of the function of the jury.

marry Miss Brown?" After the jury had reported its specific "findings," the judge would then decide, in the light of these findings, the respective legal rights and liabilities of the parties.

But seldom is anything approximating such a plan followed. In the great run of cases the "general verdict" is used. Briefly described, the usual process is this: After the evidence has been heard, the judge gives the jury what are known as "instructions on the law" which in effect tell the jury that, if they believe from the evidence that facts A and B exist, then the law requires them to bring in a verdict for the plaintiff, but if they believe facts C and D exist, then the rules of law are thus and so, and require them to find for the defendant. Thus they are told that, if they believe that Smith did not represent to McCarthy that there was an oil well on the premises, they must, as a matter of law, bring in a verdict for Smith and against McCarthy.[2]

The jury then retire and later report back to the judge—what? That they believe from the evidence that Smith did represent there was an oil well and that, therefore, they have found for McCarthy? Not at all. They bring in a "general" verdict; they report simply that their verdict is for McCarthy. No details are given. No one knows and no one is permitted to ask the jury how they arrived at this verdict. It may be, indeed, that their verdict would have been against McCarthy and for Smith, had they applied the legal rules, contained in the judge's instructions, to what they honestly believed to be the facts. But their beliefs on the question of fact are not disclosed. Whether they applied or disregarded the rules of law cannot be ascertained.[3]

The truth is (as anyone can discover by questioning the average man who has served as a juror) that usually the jury are neither able to, nor do they attempt to, apply the instructions of the court. The jury are more brutally direct. They determine that they want Jones to collect $5000 from the railroad company or that they don't want pretty Nellie Brown to go to jail for killing her husband, and they bring in their general verdict accordingly. Ordinarily, to all practical intents and purposes, the judge's views of the law might never have been expressed.

In most jury cases, then, the jury determine not the "facts" but the legal rights and obligations of the parties to the suit. For the judgment of the court follows the general verdict of the jury, so that the verdict, since it produces a judgment which determined the respective rights and obligations, decides the

---

[2] Of course, the instructions are often more intricate and state rules largely unintelligible to the jury.

[3] "In a vast majority of cases, the verdict is a complete mystery, throwing a mantle of impenetrable darkness over the operations of the jury. Whether the jurors deliberately and openly threw the law into the discard, and rendered a verdict out of their own heads, or whether they tried to apply it properly but failed for lack of understanding—these are questions respecting which the verdict discloses nothing. . . . No one but the jurors can tell what was put into it and the jurors will not be heard to say. The general verdict is as inscrutable and essentially mysterious as the judgment which issued from the ancient oracle of Delphi. Both stand on the same foundation—a presumption of wisdom. The court protects the jury from all investigation and inquiry as fully as the temple authorities protected the priestess who spoke to the suppliant votary at the shrine." Sunderland, "Verdicts, General and Special," 29 Yale Law Journal, 253, 258.

law of the particular case.[4] But this decision is made by persons with little understanding of the pre-existing "rules of law" and scant will to adhere to or employ these rules even so far as they are comprehended.

The general-verdict jury trial, in practice, negates that which the dogma of precise legal predictability maintains to be the nature of law. A better instrument could scarcely be imagined for achieving uncertainty, capriciousness, lack of uniformity, disregard of former decisions—utter unpredictability. A wise lawyer will hesitate to guarantee, although he may venture to surmise, what decision will be rendered in a case heard and decided by a judge alone. Only a very foolish lawyer will dare guess the outcome of a jury trial.[5]

Why, then, has the general-verdict jury system developed? In large part, it would seem, because it serves two purposes: It preserves the basic legal dogma in appearance and at the same time (albeit crudely and bunglingly) circumvents it in fact, to the end of permitting that pliancy and elasticity which is impossible according to the dogma, but which life demands.[6]

An English judge, Mr. Justice Chalmers, not at all satirically, but with delightful simplicity and naïveté, has lauded the jury system because it leads to just such results:

"Again," he writes, "there is an old saying that hard cases make bad law. So they do when there is no jury. The Judge is anxious to do justice to the particular parties before him. To meet a particularly hard case he is tempted to qualify or engraft an exception upon a sound general principle. When a judge once leaves the straight and narrow path of law, and wanders into the wide fields of substantial justice, he is soon irretrievably lost. . . . *But hard cases tried with a jury do not make bad law, for they make no law at all, as far as the findings of the jury are concerned. The principle is kept intact while the jury do justice in the particular case by not applying it.*"[7]

The courts usually hold that no evidence can be introduced to show that the jury misunderstood the judge's instructions; or that they so understood the facts that, in the light of the judge's instructions, they should have brought in a different verdict; or that they reached their verdict without deliberation, or by lot or some other gaming device.

[4] In criminal cases the verdict, if for the accused, is conclusive and, therefore, there should be little doubt that the jury, in such cases, decides the law. See Appendix V, "Notes on the Jury."

In civil jury cases, the judge has a limited power to set aside the verdict. This is at best however, a negative power—a power to veto but not to decide. It is a veto based upon a guess. Even this limited power can be exhausted. See Appendix V.

[5] See where the jury leaves the "art of prediction." The lawyer must guess, at a minimum, what the judge will say to the jury; what heed the jury will pay to what the judge says; what elements in the evidence the jury will consider; what factors not in the record (their feelings about the judge, the lawyers, the clients, the witnesses) the jury may consider; what the attitude of the jurors may be to one another. . . .

Surely, if any law is retroactive—unknowable at the time of action—it is jury law. As long as the jury flourishes it will be peculiarly absurd to say that any man warrantably acted with reference to a known state of law.

[6] Probably because this use of the jury seems to square the legal circle, it has been said that "the whole machinery of the state, all the apparatus of the system and its varied workings, end in simply bringing twelve good men into a box."

[7] That juries decide the law is a statement which does not satisfy the Realist. For he thinks of the law as expressed in rules, generalizations, principles. But the law of a particular case issues in a decision as between the contestants. To them the law of their case has its value and significance

By such use of the jury, you can eat your cake and have it too. You can preserve your rules and principles unswerving and unyielding—in the form of the judge's instructions—and you can have a jury's decision (which determines the rights of the parties to the case) that is based upon scant respect for those abstractions as against emotional appeals. The rules and principles remain pure and unsullied—because, while clearly enunciated, they are not applied. . . .

We have thus arrived at an almost unbelievable result. The dogma of precise legal predictability requires the denial of any large measure of discretion in the judge adequately to vary and adjust the abstract legal formulations to meet the unique and novel aspects of particular cases. This dogmatic denial of novelty and creativeness in the making and adjustment of law in turn traces back, as we have seen, to an unsatisfiable childish longing for certainty, finality and predictability. In jury trials this longing is largely satisfied—in appearance —and hopelessly thwarted in practice. The result is that, to preserve the self-delusion of legal fixity, certainty and impartiliaty, in many cases we hand over the determination of legal rights and liabilities to the whims of twelve men casually gathered together. Seeking to escape judge-made law, we have evolved jury-made law.

The jury, and not the judge, determine the rights of the respective parties and the jury's determination of these rights is guided by no real regard for "rules," abstract or otherwise. The decisions of many cases are products of irresponsible jury caprice and prejudice. That the defendant is a wealthy corporation and the plaintiff is a poor boy; that the principal witness for one of the parties is a Mason or a Catholic; that the attorney for the accused is a brilliant orator—such facts often determine who will win or lose.

The jury system means that the illusion of the existence of an inflexible body of rules ostensibly has been maintained, whereas, in fact, uniformity and in-flexibility are negated. Proclaiming that we have a government of laws, we have, in jury cases, created a government of often ignorant and prejudiced men. . . .

solely in the determination of their respective rights and liabilities. If Jones, as a result of a jury verdict, at the end of a lawsuit collects $5,000 from Smith, he cares little about the general legal principles which may have been involved.

Jury-made law, as compared with judge-made law, is peculiar in form. It does not issue general pronouncements. You will not find it set forth in the law reports or in text-books. It does not become embodied in a series of precedents. It is nowhere codified. For each jury makes its own law in each case with little or no knowledge of or reference to what has been done before or regard to what will be done thereafter in similar cases. Yet jury law, although not referred to as law, is real law none the less. If all cases were general-verdict jury cases and if judges never directed a verdict, the law of all decided cases would be jury law.

# 31

# Harry W. Jones

Harry Jones (1911–    ), Cardozo Professor of Jurisprudence at Columbia University and an American legal realist, defends judicial individualisation and the case method as essential instruments in the equitable implementation of abstract legal rules.

# THE PRACTICE OF JUSTICE*

Thirty-five years ago, I studied Contracts at the feet of the great teacher whose memory honors this series of annual lectures. I could not now recite a single rule I learned from Tyrrell Williams or state the facts of any case we covered in his course. What I retain from Professor Williams' teaching is something incomparably more important, his insistence that the administration of law is not a closed system but a social process and that legal reasoning requires not only powers of abstraction and logical inference, but also continuing acts of imaginative perception and ethical judgment. Best of all I remember a morning in the fall of 1931 when I began to put away childish things and understand what law in life is all about.

Professor Williams began his Contracts class that day by expounding one of his wonderful hypothetical cases and inviting volunteers. Angels would have feared to tread there, but I rushed in with a confident and categorical answer. Professor Williams looked over his glasses quizzically, shook his head to brush me off, and called on someone else. Strong in valor of ignorance I took up the argument with him after class. To be sure, his analysis of the problem case had made it plain that the result for which I was contending would be unfair as between the parties to the supposed controversy. But what of that? I was relying on an impeccable general proposition of law, and the syllogism in which my argument moved from major premise to conclusion was steady and remorseless, or so it seemed to me. "And so, sir," I concluded, "isn't that the way your case would have to go?"

Tyrrell Williams was kind, but his vast kindness was tempered with intellectual toughness as every great teacher's must be. "You are losing sight of the merits of the case," he said. "That decision would be terribly unjust on the facts I gave you. You know—or ought to by now—that no decent judge would reach that result in my case."

"But, sir," I persisted, "that is how he would have to decide it, whether he wanted to or not."

*Harry W. Jones, "The Practice of Justice," *Washington University Law Quarterly*, (1966), pp. 133-146. Reprinted by permission of the author and the *Washington University Law Quarterly*.

*"Have to,* my eye!" replied my master. "It isn't very often that a judge has to decide a case unjustly. He'd find a way to decide it right—and so would you if you could get it through your head this is a *case,* not an exercise in algebra."

This was the greatest of the countless lessons I learned from Tyrrell Williams during the three years I was his student and the three additional years, here at Washington University, when I was his colleague on the law faculty but his student still. It is appropriate, I think, that I make this crucial lesson the subject of our 1966 Tyrrell Williams Lecture. Individual case "merits" are fully as influential as general legal rules as factors in how cases actually get decided. It is only rarely in our legal order that the justness of a claim is not the strongest argument that can be made in support of its recognition. Jurisprudential theory is remote from the reality of law in action unless it takes full and sufficient account of this element of individual justice in the administration of law. The practicing lawyer who ignores this fact of legal life does so at his peril.

### I. THE BINOCULAR VISION OF JUSTICE

"A *case,* not an exercise in algebra[3]" Professor Williams' crisp reminder of the primacy of the case for the practice of justice came back to me many years later at a university seminar on the professions, when I heard a great internist[1] describe the practice of his profession. There are, he said, two equally important elements in medical practice, the science of medicine and the art of healing. The art without the science is at best benevolent quackery, the science without the art cold and limited in therapeutic effectiveness. The great physician is master of them both, learned in the science of his profession and, at the same time, possessed of a sympathetic vision that sees the patient before him not just as a more or less standard example of encephalitis or Parkinsonism but as a unique and complex individual, a whole man of personal dignity and inalienable singularity.

Similarly, I suggest, there are two equally important elements in the administration of justice, the science of law—for legal precepts and legal reasoning have at least some of the attributes of a science—and what I will call the art of the lawyer. Every case that comes to a court for decision—or to a lawyer's office for counseling or advocacy—is, on the scientific view of things, an item for conceptual analysis and classification. *Doe v. Roe* is, we say, an equal protection case or a third party beneficiary case or a constructive trust case, and this classification brings the applicable rules and precedents into play for analysis, argument, and judicial explanation. But *Doe v. Roe* is more than a

---

[1] Dr. Dana W. Atchley, Professor Emeritus of Clinical Medicine, College of Physicians and Surgeons, Columbia University. The University Seminar on the Professions, which met at Columbia from 1950 to 1953 under the chairmanship of the distinguished sociologist, Robert K. Merton, was supported by a grant from the Russell Sage Foundation. The Seminar was composed of members representing eight professions: medicine, law, architecture, engineering, social work, the ministry, nursing, and education.

specimen for classification; it has its further reality as a concrete dispute between living claimants and calls for fair and just disposition between them.

Which is the ultimate reality, the general rule or the concrete case? To ask this is to enter a battleground over which philosophers have fought for many centuries. Are we to associate ourselves with the philosophical "realists" and to locate ultimate legal reality in the area of the universal, the general legal proposition or concept? Or are we to join forces with the philisophocal "nominalists" and assert that only concrete cases are real and general legal concepts but names devised for convenient groupings of singular reality? In law, no such hard choice is forced on us. Realism and nominalism are two ways of seeing, and our adjudicative tradition makes use of them both.

Consider, as our analogy, the following passage from Ernst Cassirer's *Essay on Man:*

> In science we try to trace phenomena back to their first causes, and to general laws and principles. In art we are absorbed in their immediate appearance, and we enjoy this appearance to the fullest extent in all its richness and variety. . . . The two views of truth are in contrast with one another, but not in conflict or contradiction. . . . The psychology of sense perception has taught us that without the use of both eyes, without a binocular vision, there would be no awareness of the third dimension of space. The depth of human experience in the same sense depends on the fact that we are able to vary our modes of seeing, that we can alternate our views of reality.[2]

This is the heart of what I have to say in this Tyrrell Williams Lecture. Legal reality has a twofold aspect. There is a "science" of law in which every case is, in truth, an illustration of a general rule. There is an "art" of law in which the focus of perception is on the individual case, in all its immediacy and singularity. "The particular in isolation," Felix Frankfurter once wrote, "is meaningless: the generalization without concreteness, sterile."[3] Without binocular vision, without the use of both eyes, there can be no true understanding of the problem of justice as it exists in law in life.

Here, I suggest, is the middle ground between a jurisprudence of conceptions, in which legal rules are primary and particular cases seen as generalization fodder, and an equally unacceptable legal nominalism which looks only to "fireside equities"[4] and dismisses legal rules as mere grounds for rationalization of decisions reached *ad hoc.* Conceptualist and nominalist theories of the decisional process are equally misdescriptive of the practice of justice as it goes on from day to day in the real world of courts, law enforcement agencies, and law offices. Each, the conceptualist and the nominalist, has hold of a part of the truth, but

---

[2] CASSIRER, AN ESSAY ON MAN 1969-70 (Yale ed. 1962).
[3] FRANKFURTER, *Mr. Justice Holmes and the Constitution,* 41 HARV. L. REV. 121, 157 (1929).
[4] The late Karl N. Llewellyn drew a sharp distinction between "the relevant problem-situation *as a type*" and the "fireside equities" or "other possibly unique attributes of the case in hand." LLEWELLYN, THE COMMON LAW TRADITION—DECIDING APPEALS 268 (1960). (Emphasis added.) The term "fireside equities" is used as the equivalent of "the immediate equities of the controversy." *Id.* at 443.

each asserts a profoundly false *either/or* relation between the demand of the general legal principle and the appeal of the concrete situation embodied in a particular controversy. For it is not *either/or* in the practice of justice. A legal order like ours is at once mindful of the values of consistency and predictability in the application of principles and sensitive to the variety, the intractable singularity, of the controversies that arise between men in society.

My emphasis, in the next part of this discussion, will be on the many ways in which the legal order, as it exists, manifests its sensitivity and responsiveness to the individual merits of particular cases. Do not infer from this emphasis that I am subscribing to the full nominalist thesis and forgetting the "law as rule" side of the binocular vision of justice. If I were forced, as I am not, to choose between the schools and become either a card-carrying nominalist or a card-carrying conceptualist, I would, I suppose, say that the nominalists are rather closer to legal reality, at least as it exists in trial courts and in law offices, than their rule-minded adversaries are, but that is not the explanation of my emphasis. My point is rather that the "scientific" view—rules as primary and cases as incidental and secondary—is vastly over-represented in the literature of jurisprudence and legal scholarship, and I hope to contribute towards some restoration of the balance by emphasizing, perhaps over-emphasizing, the aspect of case-mindedness and individualization in the practice of justice. A little skeptical nominalism is good for legal analysis, and long overdue. For, and this will be one conclusion of this Lecture, the exaltation of general rule over concrete case in formal professional discourse, in discussions of law and legal institutions by scholars in other fields, and in the understanding of citizens generally, has gravely undesirable consequences for law administration and law practice, and for law itself.

## II. THE WAYS AND MEANS OF INDIVIDUALIZATION

The "scientific" element in the practice of justice is related to the basic requirement that law's precepts be general in statement and application. Without generality in law, there would be no equality in the legal order, no impersonality or formal rationality in the operation of adjudicative institutions, no predictability in the planning of future conduct. "On the whole," wrote the late Edwin W. Patterson, "the generality of law is its most important character-istic."[5] Indeed, the idea of the legal precept as a measure, a norm, a general rule, is so deeply ingrained in our legal philosophy that most definitions of "law" list generality as an essential attribute and exclude the particular command, order or judgment.

Yet we know that there is another side to law's formal generality. To be general, a precept must be abstract, and the inclusiveness of any abstract formulation is achieved only by sacrificing something of concrete reality. We are mindful of Alfred North Whitehead's warning that "No code of verbal

---

[5] PATTERSON, JURISPRUDENCE—MEN AND IDEAS OF THE LAW 97 (1953).

statement can ever exhaust the shifting background of presupposed fact,"[6] and of Justice Holmes' astringent observation that "General propositions do not decide concrete cases."[7] But the classic statement of this aspect of the problem of justice is much older and comes, curiously enough, from Aristotle, a thinker far more inclined in his general world view to universals than to singulars:

> Law is always a general statement, yet there are cases which it is not possible to cover in a general statement. In matters therefore, while it is necessary to speak in general terms, it is not possible to do so correctly, the law takes into consideration the majority of cases, although it is not unaware of the error this involves. And this does not make it a wrong law; for the error is not in the law nor in the lawgiver, but in the nature of the case: the material of conduct is essentially irregular. . . . This is the essential nature of the equitable: it is a rectification of law where law is defective because of its generality.[8]

Aristotle's definition of the "equitable" is a prophetic and wonderfully apt description of the historic role of the English courts of chancery during the sixteenth and seventeenth centuries, when the common law, for a time, lost its traditional sensitivity to the merits of individual cases and became rigid and rule-bound. Equity has disappeared since then as a separate system of courts, but the idea of the equitable survives in full vitality and invigorates the common law judicial process. Consider, as a manifest example, the extent to which our law's central working policy, the doctrine of precedent, reflects this pervasive inclination to concrete and singular cases rather than to abstract and general rules. To say that a court follows the principle of *stare decisis* does not mean that it applies, in a mechanical and undiscriminating way, the general propositions of law stated in past judicial opinions. In the use of case-law precedents there is always room for necessary case-to-case individualization, always leeway for Aristotle's "rectification of law where law is defective becuase of its generality."

The common law doctrine of precedent is grossly misunderstood if seen only as a device for insuring certainty and generality in the application of established case-law principles. To be sure, it has that function: as a general matter, like cases are to be decided alike. But common law method is intractably case-minded, fully as sensitive to factual differences in cases as to their factual similarities. Rules stated in past judicial opinions are mere *dicta*—"persuasive" but not "controlling" as statements of legal principle—if they go beyond the material facts of the cases that were then before the court for decision. Yesterday's precedent is "binding" on the court in today's controversy only if the two cases involve the same material facts. And it is today's court, confronted with

---

[6] WHITEHEAD, ADVENTURES OF IDEAS 71 (Mentor ed. 1933).

[7] Lochner v. New York, 198 U.S. 45, 76 (1905) (dissenting opinion). Shortly before the *Lochner* decision, Holmes had written the following to tis friend, Sir Frederick Pollock: "My intellectual furniture consists of an assortment of general propositions which grow fewer and more general as I grow older. I always say that the chief end of man is to frame them and that no general proposition is worth a damn." 1 HOLMES-POLLOCK LETTERS 118 (Howe ed. 1941).

[8] NICOMACHEAN ETHICS, Book 5, reprinted in MORRIS, THE GREAT LEGAL PHILOSOPHERS 25 (1959). The quotation is from the Rackham translation in the Loeb Classical Library. Compare the same text, in the Ross translation, in McKEON, INTRODUCTION TO ARISTOTLE 421 (1947).

today's concrete and singular controversy, that determines what the material facts of yesterday's case were—and so whether yesterday's decision is a binding precedent for the disposition of today's controversy.

It is quite true, as exponents of one or another version of slot-machine jurisprudence enjoy pointing out, that flat overrulings are few and far between, except perhaps in the Supreme Court of the United States, where special considerations and special ground rules apply. A typical state court of last resort —the Supreme Court of Missouri or the Court of Appeals of New York—will, in the course of a working year, explicitly overrule at most two or three of its established case-precedents. But to stress this is to miss the point of the common law tradition. Out-and-out overruling of precedents is rarely necessary, because, in most situations, a just and sensible decision for today's case can be reached by distinguishing any embarrassing precedents away as somehow different in material facts from the concrete case now before the court. As this selective process continues over the years—this helpful precedent extended to justify sought results in new situations, that awkward one limited or distinguished away —we are likely to see the emergence of competing lines of precedent, so that a conscientious trial judge, called on to decide a close and difficult controversy, can decide that new case either way and support his chosen decision with all conventional legal proprieties.

What I have said about the room for case-by-case individualization within the policy of *stare decisis* is not to be taken as a cynical account of the judicial process. To me, as I think to most lawyers, this flexibility and responsiveness to the particular merits of particular cases is the essential genius of the common law system. My present point is the narrower but, I think, more important one that the workings of our method of precedent exhibit dramatically the interplay of science and art, general rule and concrete case, in the practice of justice.

What does this mean for the work of counselors, advocates and judges in the world of law in action? All the implications could not be exhausted in a lecture ten times longer than this one, but a few should suffice for our present purposes. If the counselor is to make an accurate prediction of "what the courts will do in fact"[9] in a given problem situation, he must be as sensitive to the factual singularity and intrinsic equity of the concrete case on which his professional advice is sought as he is knowledgeable about the general "state of the law" embodied in the precedents. If the advocate is to make an effective presentation of a case committed to his charge, he cannot proceed, as too many do, by offering the court a formless and unfocussed collection of past judicial statements and holdings; what matters most is not past cases but *the case he has now*, and the factual merits of that case must shine through if his argument is ever to engage the serious attention of the court.

---

[9] "The prophecies of what the courts will do in fact, and nothing more pretentious, are what I mean by the law." HOLMES, *The Path of the Law* in COLLECTED LEGAL PAPERS 173 (1920). *The Path of the Law*, the most influential piece of writing in the history of American jurisprudence was originally delivered as an address to law students at Boston University and first published in 10 HARV. L. REV. 457 (1897).

To be sure, the judge presiding over any argument is doing his best to apply the law; he is bound by his judicial oath to do precisely that. But he wants, too, to reach a just result in the particular case before him. More often than not, if the judge gets proper assistance from counsel in a case, he can accomplish both of his sought objectives. There is no paradox in this; it is a consequence of our legal system's built-in responsiveness to the appeal of justice in concrete situations. In the binocular vision of justice, fidelity to general law and fairness in the disposition of particular cases are contrasting but not contradictory objectives.

Thus far I have been dealing almost exclusively with the realities of our common law method of precedent. *Stare decisis* is, after all, the distinctive policy of Anglo-American law and the one most often misunderstood by critics within and without the fraternity of legal scholarship. But I do not mean to suggest that the process of discrimintating individualization is found uniquely in the use of case precedents as decisional sources. Established techniques of statutory construction in the federal and state courts reflect the same inclination to take due account of the particular facts of concrete cases, and there is as much room for responsible case-by-case individualization in the judicial application of statutes as in the decision of controversies by reference to case-law precedents.

To say this is not to affix a general endorsement to Bishop Hoadley's famous pronouncement, so often quoted by John Chipman Gray, that "Whoever hath an absolute authority to interpret any written or spoken laws, it is he who is truly the Law-giver to all intents and purposes, and not the person who first wrote of spoke them."[10] Whatever the scope of judicial discretion, the judicial process in the interpretation of statutes is not as free-wheelling as all that! But there are ways and means, accepted and legitimate ones, of case-to-case "rectification" of statutory generality. If the words of a statute, read alone, point to what a court deems the fair result in a concrete case, the court can invoke the familiar plain meaning rule and refuse to go beyond the text of the statute. If the same statute, literally applied, would lead to an unjust result on the facts of the next case, the court is likely to take another look into its bag of clubs and pull out the equally respectable principle that statutes are to be applied not literally but in accordance with the intention of the legislature. If neither of these approaches accomplishes the sensible result, there is a whole armory of devices to be drawn on: canons of strict construction, presumptions against retroactive application, maxims like *ejusdem generis* and *expressio unius,* and many more.

Orderly minded, scholarly critics are likely to find nothing but rampant confusion and inconsistency in the decisional literature of statutory construction. They should dig deeper, because much of the inconsistency vanishes, or take on

---

[10] Gray uses the quotation three times in THE NATURE AND SOURCES OF THE LAW 102, 125, 172 (Beacon Press ed. 1963). Gray's views on the interpretation of statutes are sharply criticized as "atomistic" in FULLER, THE MORALITY OF LAW 84 (1964).

a different appearance, if we borrow a clue from Holmes[11] and address our inquiry not to "What rule of construction was employed by the court in this case?" but to "*Why* did the court in this case use this rule of construction rather than one of the others at hand?" Try this little exercise on the next ten cases you read that involve questions of statutory construction. I warrant that you will find, in at least nine of them, that the court chose the rule of construction it did because that was the one that led to a sensible and just decision in the concrete case at hand. In statutory cases, too, accurate prediction and effective counseling depend not only on the lawyer's understanding of what the statute says but also and equally on his sensitivity to and ability to convey the intrinsic merits of the case he has now.

Law's responsiveness to the variety and case-to-case singularity of the controversies that can arise between men in society finds expression not only in our accepted techniques for the use of legal sources but also, and perhaps more obviously, in the form of the sources themselves. Outsiders, even philosophers and social scientists who should know better, tend to think of the law as a body of quite specific rules, an aggregate of precise and narrowly worded propositions like "don't start until the light turns green," "a will is invalid unless witnessed by two persons," or "a bid at an auction sale is not an offer." There are many cut-and-dried directions like these: one finds them, for example, in real property, where certainty of record is a value of top-priority importance; in criminal law, where our tradition requires that explicit warning be given to possible offenders; and in income taxation, where the administrative efficiency of a mass-production operation is a dominant consideration. In most areas of the law, however, the crucial precepts are formulated in terms of far wider connotation. As Cardozo wrote almost fifty years ago: "We are tending more and more towards an appreciation of the truth that, after all, there are few rules; there are chiefly standards and degrees."[12]

Thus in the law of contracts—a course I teach as everyone who ever took Contracts from Tyrrell Williams must long to do—a right to restitution for a benefit conferred on another person exists "if as between the two persons it is unjust for the recipient to retain it,"[13] and an unbargained-for promise that has induced action by the promisee is binding on the promisor "if injustice can be avoided only be enforcement of the promise."[14] There is no tension here between the demand of general legal policy and the claim of justice in the concrete case; the legal principle itself incorporates individual justice as the governing test.

---

[11] "You can give any conclusion a logical form. You always can imply a condition in a contract But why do you imply it? . . . Such matters really are battlegrounds . . . where the decision can do no more than embody the preference of a given body in a given time and place." HOLMES *supra* note 9, at 181.

[12] CARDOZO, THE NATURE OF THE JUDICIAL PROCESS 161 (1921).

[13] RESTATEMENT, RESTITUTION § 1 and comment *c* (1937), summarized in JONES, FARNSWORTH & YOUNG, CASES AND MATERIALS ON CONTRACTS 195 (1965).

[14] RESTATEMENT, CONTRACTS § 90 (1932).

Broad standards like these are not unique to the law of contracts; indeed, contracts is a "reliance" area of law, and its precepts are probably less wide in formulation than in many other fields. The law of torts has its standard of the "reasonably prudent man," the law of trusts its sweeping concept of "fiduciary obligation," and constitutional law its standard of "due process of law" and others expressed in terms so broad that Learned Hand characterized them as "empty vessels into which [the judge] can pour nearly anything he will."[15]

The use of broadly formulated standards is not, we must note, a survival from more primitive stages of law's development but a phenomenon of law's maturity. As law becomes more sophisticated about the efficacy of detailed rules and more sensitive to the varieties of human controversy, less faith is put in narrow commands as instruments of justice and more faith in case-by-case discretion and judicial judgment. Roscoe Pound recorded this prevailing movement in legislative and judicial lawmaking in words that would be hard to improve on:

> [Standards] are general limits of permissible conduct to be applied according to the circumstances of each case. They are the chief reliance of modern law for individualization of application and are coming to be applied to conduct and conduct of enterprises over a very wide domain. . . . It may be said that in each case there is a rule (in the narrower sense) prescribing adherence to the standard and imposing consequences if the standard is not lived up to. This is true. But no definite, detailed state of facts is provided for. No definite pattern is laid down. No threat is attached to any defined situation. The significant thing is the standard, to be applied, not absolutely as in case of a rule, but in view of the facts of each case.[16]

Statutes and case-law principles expressed in standards like these do more than authorize case-by-case judgment in the decisional process. They invite and command it, and, for the counselor, the advocate and the judge, everything turns again on the singular factual merits of the concrete case at hand.

Institutions for case-by-case individualization in the handling of concrete human controversies are encountered everywhere in the practice of justice. If we were not as preoccupied as we are with the idea of law as a body of rules, explicit commands, we would see these institutions for what they are and so be able to appraise them in terms of their actual, not their formal, function. The jury system, seen in this perspective, is far less a device for the finding of facts than an agency—perhaps, to be sure, an outmoded one—for individualization in the application of law. When a jury brings in a verdict that seems against the weight of the evidence, it is an incomplete explanation to say that it has made an erroneous finding of the facts. The jurymen may have known perfectly well what the out-of-court facts were but made their decision, against their instructions and in the teeth of the facts, because of their shared conviction that the essential justice of the case was with one party rather than the other.

---

[15] *Sources of Tolerance*, address by Learned Hand, June 1930, in THE SPIRIT OF LIBERTY 81 (Dillard ed. 1952).
[16] Pound, *Hierarchy of Sources and Forms in Different Systems of Law*, 7 TUL. L. REV. 475, 485 (1933).

Decisions like these, turning on the decision-maker's impression as to the essential justice of a matter, are made every day in the enforcement of the criminal law, and it is in prosecutors' offices, rather than in courts, that most of these decisions are arrived at. Shall an accused person be charged, and, if so, with how grave a crime? Shall he be given the opportunity to plead guilty to a lesser offense, or shall he be prosecuted for the most serious crime that the evidence will support? Twenty-five years ago, I had responsibility for the direction of a massive law enforcement program,[17] and I have believed ever since that the discretion of the prosecutor is the most important single element in a state's criminal law. The Model Penal Code prepared under the leadership of my colleague, Herbert Wechsler, is a towering achievement in legal scholarship and law reform, but I rejoice equally in the growing increase of our knowledge, to which Professor Miller and Professor Gerard of this law faculty have made substantial contributions, concerning the ways in which police officials and prosecuting officers exercise their discretion and inevitable dispensing power in the individualization of criminal prosecution and punishment.[18]

On an occasion like this one, I could not possibly undertake a complete and encyclopedic inventory of the agencies of individualization that abound in our legal order. It must be noted, however, that the task of case-by-case individualization is performed not only by judges and other public ministers of the law but also be practicing lawyers. The lawyer's distinctive art, adaptation of law's general rules to the merits and necessities of concrete situations, is called for at every stage of the profession's work: in the drafting of wills, agreements, and other documents, in the structuring of transactions, in the arbitration of disputes, and in the negotiation and arrangement of out-of-court settlements.

Anyone with a little legal training can consult the law books and tell a client what he cannot do. The lawyer—the honest-to-God lawyer—has the imagination and intellectual resourcefulness necessary to tell his client *how* he can do, legally and fairly, the things that a concrete situation requires be done. This necessitates not only knowledge of the state of the law but also—and this is far harder—deep and perceptive understanding of what I have been calling "the case you have now." In the lawyer's office, as in the courtroom, there is need for a binocular vision that is, at once, mindful of the demands of the general rule and sensitive to the merits and necessities of the concrete situation.

### III. LEGAL REALITY: THE NEED FOR CANDOR

"A *case,* not an exercise in algebra!" Why have I made this the essential theme of today's lecture? One reason, and a sufficient one, is that it is something I learned from my great teacher, Tyrrell Williams. The other and closely

[17] Director of Food Enforcement, Office of Price Administration.
[18] LAFAVE, ARREST—THE DECISION TO TAKE A SUSPECT INTO CUSTODY (1965) is the first of a series of monographs on the administration of criminal justice in the United States being brought out by the American Bar Foundation under the general editorship of Professor Frank J. Remington. The volume on prosecution for this important series is being written by Professor Frank W. Miller of the Washington University School of Law.

related reason is that I consider it the most important single thing that can be said to law students, or to scholars in any field who want to have a grasp of legal reality.

We are always hearing about a supposed "gap between law school and law practice." This, I suggest, is not a matter of knowing where the clerk's office is or how to prepare an affidavit. Law graduates are brighter than they were in my day, and they catch on to workaday details with astonishing ease and speed. The true gap is that students—and here they are like scholars in any field—leave law school almost too well informed about general legal principles and insufficiently aware of law's pervasive occasions for case-by-case individualization. A few years practice of the lawyer's art corrects this imbalance in most instances, but it is a gap that many lawyers never manage to get across, to the lasting damage of their professional careers and the profound disservice of their unhappy clients.

In university legal education, it is the case method of instruction on which we rely to give our students an awareness of the continuing interplay of legal science and the lawyer's art.[19] The founder of the case method, Christopher Columbus Langdell, built better than he knew. We have abandoned Dean Langdell's notion of the case method as a "scientific" procedure, but we have retained it as the way to develop the qualities of what we like to call the "legal mind": precision in the understanding and statement of facts, distrust of easy generalizations, and capacity for original and constructive thought.

There is need for a continuing rear-guard action to maintain the integrity of the law school case method. We law teachers are too much inclined toward the use of cases not as exercises in the practice of the lawyer's art but as mere illustrations of general rules and principles. With the vast extension of government regulation and the proliferation of legal materials, we are under increasing pressures to cover more ground, offer more courses, give law students more and more legal information. Like our brothers of the judiciary and the practicing bar, we academic lawyers are unduly preoccupied with the appellate courts— where the distinctive task is that of clarifying the general law—and give insufficient attention to the trial courts, where the task of fair individual decision is central. At the risk of sounding like the Ancient Mariner, I would have us stand by the case method. It is a painfully slow way of covering substantive ground, but it is the best device I know for communicating the realities of the binocular vision of justice.

When one moves outside the universe of the law schools and the legal profession, he becomes conscious of other damage done by the undue concentration of our professional discourse on law as general rule. Social scientists are becoming more interested in legal institutions and far more willing than they used to be to work in collaboration with lawyers for better understanding and

---

[19] See Jones, *Objectives and Insights in University Legal Education*, 11 Ohio St. L. J. 4, 5-7 (1950) Patterson, *The Case Method in American Legal Education: Its Origins and Objectives*, 4 J. Legal Ed 1 (1951).

practical improvement of the legal order. But, by and large, the scholarly and pragmatic value of the work done so far in law-related fields by sociologists, economists, social psychologists, political scientists and others has been gravely reduced by their failure to apprehend the primacy of the case in the practice of justice. It is painful to see how a social scientist, wonderfully sophisticated in his own field, can adopt a slot machine theory of justice and remain oblivious to the occasions for case-to-case discretion that characterize present-day American law.

But there are even more serious consequences. Widespread public mis-apprehensions concerning the realities of law in action have contributed almost everywhere to a serious underrating of the importance of judicial personnel and judicial selection.[20] The Missouri Plan of merit selection of judges is, I am confident, the wave of the future, but it is not state-wide even in Missouri, and it is a long way off in most jurisdictions. We will not have a sound system of judicial selection throughout the United States until informed citizens generally are made conscious of the interplay of law as science and law as art in the administration of justice.

Too many people, unaware that law has its aspect of discriminating indivi-dualization as well as its aspect of generality, conclude that it makes little differ-ence who occupies the bench. Assuming elementary probity, they ask, will not any two judges decide a case the same way? Other laymen, a bit better informed, but not much, make the frightful assumption that a lawyer is best qualified to be a judge if he is a walking encyclopedia of legal rules and principles. I hardly need to add that everything I have just said applies equally to the selection of district attorneys and other prosecuting officials. If, as I believe, the most important thing about a jurisdiction's criminal law is who its district attorney is, it is urgent that citizens generally be made aware of the fact that prosecuting attorneys, informally, and largely on their impressions of offenses and offenders, decide the fate of far more accused persons than ever appear in the courts for trial.

But I would not rest my case entirely on pragmatic considerations. The rule of law is central to our society, and it should be known, discussed and venerated for what it is. Public awareness of the binocular vision of justice will not, as the conceptualists fear, reduce respect for legal institutions. For there is surely nothing discreditable about a legal order that pursues, at once, the goal of equality before the law and the contrasting but not, in our system, contra-dictory goal of justice in the individual case.

---

[20] Winters & Allard, *Judicial Selection and Tenure in the United States* in THE COURTS, THE PUBLIC AND THE LAW EXPLOSION 147 (Jones ed. 1965).

# 32

# Martin P. Golding

Martin Golding (1930–    ) of Columbia University has been a contributor to the contemporary dialogue in rights theory and is working on a major study of procedural justice.

# PRINCIPLED JUDICIAL DECISION-MAKING*

## I

The purpose of this paper is to answer in outline the question: What are the distinguishing characteristics of principled judicial decision-making?[1] My discussion is inevitably programmatic. The broader subject into which my topic falls is that of casuistry, and a more thorough delineation of the characteristics of principled judicial decision must await, among other things, an extensive development of that subject matter. Unfortunately, the term "casuistry" has acquired rather negative connotations, but any study of the relationship between principle and practice falls under this general heading. Typically, this has long been the province of the moral philosopher, but it is not at all improper to suggest that moral philosophy may itself be enriched by attention to casuistry as it occurs in other areas. One such area is obviously the law, which provides in this connection a veritably inexhaustible fund of materials.

The law, especially in its adjudicative aspects, is, of course, a social institution imbedded in the framework of other social institutions. Undoubtedly, these are among the "other things" that must also be understood for a full delineation of the characteristics of principled judicial decision-making. The complexities of the inquiry ought not be minimized. Ultimately they may embrace a whole philosophy of government.

## II

In answering the above question it is useful to recognize that its analogs may be found in moral philosophy. Morally we admire a principled person.

*Martin P. Golding, "Principled Judicial Decision-Making," Ethics, Vol. LXXIII, No. 4 (1963), pp. 247ff. Reprinted by permission of the publisher and author. © Copyright 1963 by the University of Chicago.
[1] This topic has been lately discussed with respect to the constitutional decision-making of the Supreme Court. See my "Principled Decision-making and the Supreme Court," Columbia Law Review, LXIII (1963), 35, and references cited therein, especially H. Wechsler, "Towards Neutral Principles of Constitutional Law," Harvard Law Review, LXXIII (1959), 1.

Morally we deplore an *ad hoc* judgment, and the very possibility of discussion over moral matters seems to presuppose appeal to principle. Principle and principles: how are they related? This is an important question, for it is the thesis of this paper that a principled judicial decision is one that is based on a principle, but a principle that is able to withstand a certain type of criticism.

A. Bentham and Kant, who must always seem strange bedfellows, are instructive here. Thus, the "principle of sympathy and antipathy," namely, "that principle which approves or disapproves of certain actions . . . merely because a man finds himself disposed to approve or disapprove of them," is rejected by Bentham. This alleged "principle" (the "principle of caprice," as he came to call it), he says, is in reality a "term employed to signify the negation of all principle. What one expects to find in a principle is something that points out some external consideration, as a means of warranting and guiding the internal sentiments of approbation and disapprobation."[2] The key notion here is that of an "external consideration" that controls the judgment of approval (of disapproval) in a particular case. This I regard as an element of the concept of principle that must be satisfied by a putative "principle" in order that it function as a principle of judgment or decision.

B. Of course, for Bentham it is the Principle of Utility that ought to be the ultimate arbiter of moral judgment, all others being either "despotical" or "anarchical." Now in operating the hedonic calculus it is clear that another element of the concept of principle comes into play. That is, in calculating which of two alternative actions maximizes the greatest good of the greatest number, the happiness of members of the nobility, for example, is given no greater weighting than the happiness of members of the laboring class, or vice versa. But that this must be so is hardly itself deducible from the Principle of Utility. It is, rather, that impartiality in respect of persons is an element of the concept of principle.

C. Kant's moral theory is notorious for its emphasis on principles. The "moral value of an act," says Kant, depends "on the principle of volition by which the action is done without any regard to the objects of the faculty of desire."[3] The manner in which Kant works this out and the difficulties that he encounters are familiar. But Kant's main insights are not to be rejected lightly, for he is attempting to take into account yet another component of the concept of principle, namely, consistency, in one of its modes. Every moral decision makes a universal claim: If an act is right for me, it must be right for every similarly situated person.[4] To distinguish arbitrarily some individual (oneself included) or some class of individuals, and thus claim that it is right for me to treat him, or them, differently from the way in which I treat others is to not act on principle or in accordance with principle, and to decide to act in such ways is to not make a principled decision. Whenever we appeal to principle

---

[2] *An Introduction to the Principles of Morals and Legislation,* chap. ii, secs. xi and xii.
[3] *Foundations of the Metaphysics of Morals,* sec. 1.
[4] See Singer's discussion of the "generalization principle" in his *Generalization in Ethics,* pp. 13–33.

we mean to shut out at least an accusation of arbitrariness. When we do this we are claiming that our decision or judgment in this situation falls under a more general class of cases for which we regard the given treatment or disposition as appropriate. That is, the instant case is disposed of in a manner that is consistent with the way cases of its type ought to be disposed of. The notion of consistency as an element of the concept of principle, then, goes beyond impartiality in respect of persons but includes circumstances or situations as well.

III

This brief foray into moral philosophy prepares the ground for a discussion of principled judicial decision. It hardly needs saying that the concept of principle is richer than the elements that have been delineated here. Moreover, much remains to be said about each of these items in themselves. The ideas of an "external consideration," impartiality, and consistency are all, at a bare minimum, involved in the functioning of a principle as a principle of decision. Yet it is not at all unlikely that a finer analysis of these elements will reveal that they are at bottom the same, or are at most different sides of the same coin; for each leads to the elimination of *ad hoc* decision in a particular case by requiring in a sense that the particular case be viewed in terms of a wider perspective. This parallels the way in which *ad hoc* explanations of natural occurrences are eliminated, namely, by requiring that an explanation have a richness of content or a range that, of course, includes but also goes beyond the particular happening that is to be explained.

These elements of principle combine to eliminate the *ad hoc* in a given decision-making context by providing, also, certain stable factors in reference to which the principled character of a decision may be tested. This is to be seen, for example, in connection with the idea of "relevance." A decision is arbitrary, or at least faulty, if the decision-maker fails to take into account every relevant feature of the case.[5] What features are relevant depends on matters of principle and the demands of particular principles. Moreover, any putative difference between two similar cases can justify a difference in disposition only if the difference is a relevant one. This observation is trite, but it raises one of the most intricate issues in moral philosophy. Questions of relevance are often settled by reference to causal connections. Thus, the color of one's eyes is not relevant to one's fitness to receive a driver's license in a way that one's eyesight is. Color of eyes does not affect one's ability to handle a car safely, but quality of eyesight does. On the other hand, sometimes the requisite causal connections in the given context are rather indirect or tenuous, and yet we still regard certain

---

[5] Of course, it is one thing to characterize a decision as arbitrary (or not principled) and quite another to characterize a decision-maker as arbitrary (or unprincipled). If a decision-maker, through lack of intelligence, fails to take into account every relevant feature of a case, his decision is certainly faulty in an important sense, although it would be unfair to call the man arbitrary. On the other hand, there is an important sense in which a "right" decision rendered for the "wrong" reasons is faulty.

distinctions as justifying difference of treatment; as, for example, between male and female, or adult and child in some situations. At one time being propertied was necessary to qualify to vote. It was thought that possession or lack of possession of property affected the state of mind of the prospective voter in an important way. Is it because we no longer believe that there is any such causal connection that we no longer require that a voter be propertied? Or is it rather that whatever the connection, we, as a matter of principle, do not believe that it *ought* to count?

Questions of relevance are clearly issues over which men may disagree, and it is a nice problem to delimit the ways such disagreements can be said to have any rational character. Moreover, one may come to change one's own views on what differences are or are not relevant for certain purposes. How can such a situation be described? Here we seem to have the subtle interplay of principle and principles, together with their refinement, revision, and elaboration. We have also to take into account a time factor, the occurrence of change, and the brute fact that things that were better left undone were done. All these have implications for our notions of maturation, on the one hand, and of adherence to principle that resists forces from without, on the other. And, again, the moral philosopher may learn much from an examination of the judicial process, which faces the need for both stability and change and must also contend constantly with high questions of relevance. The interesting thing to notice is how the elements of principle, which are required for the functioning of a principle as a principle of decision in a praticular case, are transformed, in a sense, in the legal context. They are partially given a specific material content.

## IV

An important contrast between moral and judicial decision arises from the fact that a legal system may, to a large extent, specify in advance the principles that must be employed in decision-making. So also the positive law may lay down what shall count or shall not count as a relevant difference that justifies difference of disposition with respect to certain types of cases. Thus, mere racial difference may be set down as relevant or irrelevant for certain matters. This does raise matters of principle on the legislative side, but, as far as the judiciary is concerned, its hands are tied. Nevertheless, it would be a serious mistake to suppose that judges are always so bound. Judicial decision-making takes place on three levels, and a discretionary element enters into all three of them.

A. The first level is that of the standard case of a "finite rule of law." Here we think of relatively simple statutes, for example, parking ordinances and the like. These give rise to a good deal of the inconveniences of modern living, but we do not ordinarily think of many of these as presenting judicial problems. The plain citizen is capable of understanding them on his own and behaves accordingly. This category includes, also, more complicated pieces of legislation that require the skills of the tax lawyer or accountant. The point of connection is that for items included in this level there is always a standard-case area of application.

B. The second level is that of cases of "first impression." I refer here to cases for which there pre-exists no relevant law, statutory or otherwise. They clearly call for judicial legislation. The occurrence of such cases in a pristine form is surely rare. Thus, although Lord Abinger characterizes the issue in the famous case of *Priestly* versus *Fowler* (whether an employer is liable to his employee for injury caused in the course of work by a fellow employee) [6] as one for which "it is admitted there is no precedent," it is at least arguable that it was not so remote to preclude it from falling under the prevailing common-law tort doctrine.

C. The third level comprises cases of "institutional values," for want of a better name. The deciding of such cases involves the invocation of broad interests and values, such as are embodied in the Constitution: national security, due process, and the free exercise of religion, for example. The judge must juggle concepts that may be both ambiguous and vague.

It may be possible to distinguish other levels of judicial decision-making, but three are enough here. I do not wish to assert that there is a hard and fast line that clearly separates them from one another. Certainly, many cases that come before the courts are complex enough to exhibit characteristics of all three levels. The important point is the recognition of the wide scope of judicial discretion, no matter how finely legislation is drafted or how craftsman-like judicial opinions are written.[7] Consider even the "finite rule of law." If it has a clear-cut area of application, it also has what Hart has called the area of the "penumbra."[8] If Cadillacs and Fords are vehicles, are horses and kiddy cars also vehicles? Rules of law are "open-textured," and they inevitably leave open for the judge a sphere of decision-making that calls for judicial choice. This is obvious in cases of "first impression," if such occur; but it also obtains whenever a case raises questions of legal categorization or classification. Perhaps the most complex cases in which the need for judicial choice arises are those that involve "institutional values," for here we may find the claims of competing interests and problems of constitutional interpretation.[9]

---

[6] Mees. and Wels. III (Exchequer, 1837), 1.

[7] Cf. Cardozo, *The Nature of the Judicial Process*, p. 143: "No doubt the ideal system, if it were attainable, would be a code at once so flexible and so minute, as to supply in advance for every conceivable situation the just and fitting rule. But life is too complex to bring the attainment of this ideal within the compass of human powers."

[8] See Hart, *The Concept of Law*, pp. 121–32, and his "Positivism and the Separation of Law and Morals," *Harvard Law Review*, LXXI (1958), 606–15. While in sympathy with Hart's general position, I find myself in agreement with many of Fuller's criticisms of Hart's view of interpretation of statutes. See Fuller, "Positivism and Fidelity to Law—A Reply to Professor Hart," *Harvard Law Review*, LXXI (1958), 661–69. On the "open" character of legal systems see also my "Kelsen and the Concept of 'Legal System'," *Archiv für Rechts und Sozialphilosophie*, XLVII (1961), 378–83.

[9] For a discussion of the role of principle in constitutional interpretation in cases which present a conflict of values see my "Principled Decision-making . . .," *op. cit.*, pp. 46–49.

It is to the credit of the American legal realists that they appreciated the discretionary factor in judicial decision, that judges play a creative role, that judges make law. But what is not sufficiently appreciated, in my view, is the fact that the existence of judicial discretion does not of itself condemn us to the vagaries of so-called gastronomic jurisprudence.[10] Even if the old declaratory theory of law (both prescriptively and descriptively) obfuscated the nature of judicial decision-making, we need not adopt a no-holds-barred discretionary theory. Aside from the plentiful occurrence of standard-type cases, discretion may be exercised in a principled manner.

V

A principled decision is one that is justified by appeal to a principle for every relevant issue of the case, and the principle to which appeal is made must be able to withstand a certain type of criticism. Any judge may, of course, invoke a "principle" when he decides a case. But it should be clear that there is no way to tell by mere inspection of the putative "principle," in isolation from the context of its application and other broader demands, whether the decision in the case is principled. Questions of the forms," Is such-and-such an acceptable legal principle?" or "Can you give an example of an acceptable legal principle?" cannot be answered *in abstracto*.

In order to approach the kind of criticism that the putative principle must withstand, it is necessary to keep in mind what is involved in the functioning of a principle as a principle of decision in a particular case, what must be satisfied lest the decision be condemned as *ad hoc*. A principled decision implies a claim of right in the sense that the instant case is so decided because cases of its type ought to be treated in that way. This immediately raises questions of relevance and classification, and these depend on the total framework of principles and their implications for practice. Many of these principles will be stipulated in advance by the legal system itself. Thus, when the decision-maker offers a principle in justification of a decision and there already exists a principle that requires that the case be decided in a different way, then the decision-maker must either distinguish his case or (failing this) reject his principle. The distinction, if he draws one, must itself be drawn in a principled way.

It follows that the typical kind of argument that will be employed in determining the principled character of a decision is that of *reductio ad absurdum*. Just as a factual proposition is shown to be false if it implies a false proposition, so also a principle of decision is shown to be unacceptable if acting on it would lead to treating some case in a manner in which it may not be treated *ex hypothesi*. Every legal system (and every practical decision making context, too) has its "given,"[11] which constitutes some of the stable factors to which I

---

[10] I do not mean to attribute this view to any American legal realist, living or dead.

[11] So far as I am aware this notion was first introduced by Francois Geny (see his *Science et Technique en Droit Privé Positif*, II [1915], 351–89). It is discussed from various points of view and criticized by Jean Dabin in his *Théorie Générale du Droit* (1944), translated in *The Legal*

alluded above. This is comprised of principles and sets of social values and objectives that are formulated in enactments, constitutions, and perhaps other, less formal, instruments. These supply the substantive criteria of principled judicial decision. Calling them "the given" does not, of course, carry an implication that they are immune to criticism on the legislative level. But judicial decision takes place within the context of a legal system, and a decision is not principled if acting on its principle is incompatible with the demands of given principles, or if it leads to the frustrating of given social values and objectives. But this does not mean that principled judicial decision-making can be identified with mere conformity to existing law; for there is also the inevitable feature of "openness" that legal systems possess. In addition to the "given" a decision-maker also has a fund of principles that he has applied or *would* apply over a wide area of cases. His decision in the instant case is not principled unless it can be squared with the demands of these principles as well.

Involved in this account of principled decision is the important, but difficult, concept of pragmatic consistency, which is crucial to the analysis of moral and legal reasoning. Its difficulties are compounded in law whenever judges must deal with conflicting interests, values, objectives, or principles. Implicated in its complexities is also the "time factor" to which I alluded previously. The theoretical resolution of these difficulties awaits a more comprehensive study of casuistry.

VI

The reference made above to the principles that the decision-maker has applied and, especially, is willing to apply in other cases bears on a number of important points, which can be touched on only briefly here.

A. First and foremost is our old friend "relevance." Obviously, the kind of distinctions that justify difference of treatment will depend upon what the judge is willing to do in other similar cases, for such distinctions must be principled. This is tested by the *reductio ad absurdum* form of argument. This type of argument can be employed to show that a given principle is either unacceptable, or too broad, or too narrow. But it is entirely consistent with this account of principled judicial decision that two judges should disagree in their judgments in a particular case and yet both be principled.

B. It will always be tempting to the decision-maker, in order to avoid the incidence of conflicting principles and pragmatic inconsistencies, to justify a decision in terms of the narrowest possible principle. For all its plausibility, the wisdom of this procedure is at least debatable. Two of the functions of principles are, first, to simplify problems of conduct by the putting of principles of action into broad terms, and, second, to get us to structure our conduct into a coherent pattern, which may also be accomplished through framing our principles

---

*Philosophies of Lask, Radbruch, and Dabin* ("20th Century Legal Philosophy Series"), pp. 318–49. Both, however, discuss the question of the *donnée* and the *construée* in law primarily within the context of legislation.

broadly. For the judiciary these considerations are of special importance, because it is through the articulation of principles of decision that they supply guidance to both private citizens and other judges. Principles are commitments with respect to future cases.

C. In the legal context, another important function of justifying decisions in terms of a principle is to secure their public acceptance. For all their truth, I think it misleading to say that the reason why judges write opinions in support of their decisions is to show how learned they are or to conceal the so-called "real" reasons for their decisions. However arbitrary or subjective, in an ultimate analysis, our value choices or our judgments of relevance are shown to be, once the community accepts the underlying principle, it is morally and intellectually bound to accept the decision. In appealing to principles the judge is appealing to the "generalized other," so to speak, and therefore rests his decision on general grounds. This is the result, then, of a recognition of the social setting of judicial decision, and not, as the late Karl Llewellyn once suggested, mere "superstition."[12] Clearly, one of the old chestnuts of moral philosophy, whether egoism can be made a consistent principle of action, is out of place in the judicial context. Judges might do what they like doing, but do not offer their mere likes and dislikes in justification of their decisions.

D. It is a corollary of these considerations, and of the nature of principled decision, that judicial reasoning cannot dispense with the concepts of primary rights and duties. Justice Holmes, in his famous essay "The Path of the Law,"[13] attempted to wash the law clear of moral notions with his "cynical acid." There is much to be said, from the lawyer's point of view, for replacing concepts of primary rights and duties by those of secondary or remedial rights and duties. But the former are indispensable to the judge.

---

[12] *The Bramble Bush* (1951), p. 43.

[13] *Harvard Law Review*, X (1896), 457–78: "The primary rights and duties with which jurisprudence busies itself again are nothing but prophecies. One of the many evil effects of the confusion between legal and moral ideas . . . is that theory is apt to get the cart before the horse, and to consider the right or the duty as something existing apart from and independent of the consequences of the breach, to which certain sanctions are added afterward. But, as I shall try to show, a legal duty so called is nothing but a prediction that if a man does or omits certain things he will be made to suffer in this or that way by judgment of the court" (p.458). "Nowhere is the confusion between legal and moral ideas more manifest than in the law of contract. Among other things, here again the so-called primary rights and duties are invested with a mystic significance beyond what can be assigned and explained. The duty to keep a contract at common law means a prediction that you must pay damages if you do not keep it—and nothing else. If you commit a tort, you are liable to pay a compensatory sum. If you commit a contract, you are liable to pay a compensatory sum unless the promised event comes to pass, and that is all the difference. But such a mode of looking at the matter stinks in the nostrils of those who think it advantageous to get as much ethics into the law as they can. . . . I think it would be better to cease troubling ourselves about primary rights and sanctions altogether, than to describe our prophecies concerning the liabilities commonly imposed by the law in these inappropriate terms" (p. 462). Cf. Buckland, *Some Reflections on Jurisprudence*, pp. 96–97. Holmes's view derives, I think, both from a narrow conception of morality and the "prediction" theory of law. Clearly, whatever the judge is doing when he decides that someone has a right or a duty, the judge is not "prophesying" that someone will be made to suffer in this or that way by judgment of the court.

E. Finally, principled decision-making, which I take to be intimately connected with notions of justice and rationality, and which I regard as a moral and logical feature of both moral and judicial reasoning, seems prima facie to be a purely formal notion. Principled judicial decision, it would seem, is completely compatible with the administration of thoroughly iniquitous laws and an absolutely wicked legal order. I wonder whether this is so. Not the least intriguing question in the study of casuistry, the study of the relationship between principle and practice, is whether and to what degree the purely formal requirements of principle affect the substance of principles. It is the old problem of form and matter transferred to the moral sphere.

I should like to make clear that the outline of principled judicial decision-making that I have presented here comprises *one* type of evaluation that can be applied to a decision of the courts. I have not meant to oppose it to other forms of evaluation, utilitarian, for example. But I think that considerations of principles and principle cannot be escaped even there. They are involved whenever we must balance long-term against short-term utilities, as the judicial process inevitably must. Not the least significance would emerge for moral philosophy from the study of casuistry generally, and the judicial process in particular, if it reveals just those areas in which, in opposition to the situation in the context of judicial decision and adjudication, appeal to principles and principle is entirely inappropriate—if such exist.

# 33

# Ronald G. Dworkin

Ronald Dworkin (1931–    ), Professor of Jurisprudence at Oxford University and formerly Professor of Law at Yale, develops the distinction between legal rules, principles and policies in the wider context of a critique of contemporary legal positivism.

# THE MODEL OF RULES*

### III. Rules, Principles, and policies

I want to make a general attack on positivism, and I shall use H. L. A. Hart's version as a target, when a particular target is needed. My strategy will be organized around the fact that when lawyers reason or dispute about legal rights and obligations, particularly in those hard cases when our problems with these concepts seem most acute, they make use of standards that do not function as rules, but operate differently as principles, policies, and other sorts of standards. Positivism, I shall argue, is a model of and for a system of rules, and its central notion of a single fundamental test for law forces us to miss the important roles of these standards that are not rules.

I just spoke of "principles, policies, and other sorts of standards." Most often I shall use the term "principle" generically, to refer to the whole set of these standards other than rules; occasionally, however, I shall be more precise, and distinguish between principles and policies. Although nothing in the present argument will turn on the distinction, I should state how I draw it. I call a "policy" that kind of standard that sets out a goal to be reached, generally an improvement in some economic, political, or social feature of the community (though some goals are negative, in that they stipulate that some present feature is to be protected from adverse change). I call a "principle" a standard that is to be observed, not because it will advance or secure an economic, political, or social situation deemed desirable, but because it is a requirement of justice or fairness or some other dimension of morality. Thus the standard that automobile accidents are to be decreased is a policy, and the standard that no man may profit by his own wrong a principle. The distinction can be collapsed by construing a principle as stating a social goal (*i.e.*, the goal of a society in which no man profits by his own wrong), or by construing a policy as stating a

*Ronald G. Dworkin, From "The Model of Rules," *University of Chicago Law Review*, 35 (1967), pp. 22–40. Copyright © 1967 by the author. This article is adopted from a chapter in a forthcoming book. Footnotes have been renumbered.

principle (*i.e.*, the principle that the goal the policy embraces is a worthy one) or by adopting the utilitarian thesis that principles of justice are disguised statements of goals (securing the greatest happiness of the greatest number). In some contexts the distinction has uses which are lost if it is thus collapsed.[1]

My immediate purpose, however, is to distinguish principles in the generic sense from rules, and I shall start by collecting some examples of the former. The examples I offer are chosen haphazardly; almost any case in a law school casebook would provide examples that would serve as well. In 1889 a New York court, in the famous case of *Riggs v. Palmer*,[2] had to decide whether an heir named in the will of his grandfather could inherit under that will, even though he had murdered his grandfather to do so. The court began its reasoning with this admission: "It is quite true that statutes regulating the making, proof and effect of wills, and the devolution of property, if literally construed, and if their force and effect can in no way and under no circumstances be controlled or modified, give this property to the murderer."[3] But the court continued to note that "all laws as well as all contracts may be controlled in their operation and effect by general, fundamental maxims of the common law. No one shall be permitted to profit by his own fraud, or to take advantage of his own wrong, or to found any claim upon his own iniquity, or to acquire property by his own crime."[4] The murderer did not recieve his inheritance.

In 1960, a New Jersey court was faced, in *Henningsen v. Bloomfield Motors, Inc.*,[5] with the important question of whether (or how much) an automobile manufacturer may limit his liability in case the automobile is defective. Henningsen had bought a car, and signed a contract which said that the manufacturer's liability for defects was limited to "making good" defective parts—"this warranty being expressly in lieu of all other warranties, obligations or liabilities." Henningsen argued that, at least in the circumstances of his case, the manufacturer ought not to be protected by this limitation, and ought to be liable for the medical and other expenses of persons injured in a crash. He was not able to point to any statute, or to any established rule of law, that prevented the manufacturer from standing on the contract. The court nevertheless agreed with Henningsen. At various points in the court's argument the following appeals to standards are made: (a) "[We] must keep in mind the general principle that, in the absence of fraud, one who does not choose to read a contract before signing it cannot later relieve himself of its burdens."[6] (b) "In applying that principle, the basic tenet of freedom of competent parties to contract is a factor of importance."[7] (c) "Freedom of contract is not such an immutable doctrine as to admit of no qualification in the area in which we are

---

[1] *See* Dworkin, *Wasserstrom: The Judicial Decision*, 75 ETHICS 47 (1964), reprinted as *Does Law Have a Function?*, 74 YALE L.J. 640 (1965).
[2] 115 N. Y. 506, 22 N.E. 188 (1889).
[3] *Id.* at 509, 22 N.E. at 189.
[4] *Id.* at 511, 22 N.E. at 190.
[5] 32 N.J. 358, 161 A.2d 69 (1960).
[6] *Id.* at 386, 161 A.2d at 84.
[7] *Id.*

concerned." [8] (d) "In a society such as ours, where the automobile is a common and necessary adjunct of daily life, and where its use is so fraught with danger to the driver, passengers and the public, the manufacturer is under a special obligation in connection with the construction, promotion and sale of his cars. Consequently, the courts must examine purchase agreements closely to see if consumer and public interests are treated fairly." [9] (e) " '[I]s there any principle which is more familiar or more firmly embedded in the history of Anglo-American law than the basic doctrine that the courts will not permit themselves to be used as instruments of inequity and injustice?' " [10] (f) " 'More specifically, the courts generally refuse to lend themselves to the enforcement of a "bargain" in which one party has unjustly taken advantage of the economic necessities of other . . . .' " [11]

The standard set out in these quotations are not the sort we think of as legal rules. They seem very different from propositions like "The maximum legal speed on the turnpike is sixty miles an hour" or "A will is invalid unless signed by three witnesses." They are different because they are legal principles rather than legal rules.

The difference between legal principles and legal rules is a logical distinction. Both sets of standards point to particular decisions about legal obligation in particular circumstances, but they differ in the character of the direction they give. Rules are applicable in an all-or-nothing fashion. If the facts a rule stipulates are given, then either the rule is valid, in which case the answer it supplies must be accepted, or it is not, in which case it contributes nothing to the decision.

This all-or-nothing is seen most plainly if we look at the way rules operate, not in law, but in some enterprise they dominate—a game, for example. In baseball a rule provides that if the batter has had three strikes, he is out. An official cannot consistently acknowledge that this is an accurate statement of a baseball rule, and decide that a batter who has had three strikes is not out. Of course, a rule may have exceptions (the batter who has taken three strikes is not out if the catcher drops the third strike). However, an accurate statement of the rule would take this exception into account, and any that did not would be incomplete. If the list of exceptions is very large, it would be too clumsy to repeat them each time the rule is cited; there is, however, no reason in theory why they could not all be added on, and the more that are, the more accurate is the statement of the rule.

If we take baseball rules as a model, we find that rules of law, like the rule that a will is invalid unless signed by three witnesses, fit the model well. If the requirement of three witnesses is a valid legal rule, then it cannot be that a will has been signed by only two witnesses and is valid. The rule might have excep-

---

[8] *Id.* at 388, 161 A.2d at 86.
[9] *Id.* at 387, 161 A.2d at 85.
[10] *Id.* at 389, 161 A.2d at 86 (quoting Frankfurter, J., in United States v. Bethlehem Steel, 315 U.S. 289, 326 (1942)).
[11] *Id.*

tions, but if it does then it is inaccurate and incomplete to state the rule so simply, without enumerating the exceptions. In theory, at least, the exceptions could all be listed, and the more of them that are, the more complete is the statement of the rule.

But this is not the way the sample principles in the quotations operate. Even those which look most like rules do not set out legal consequences that follow automatically when the conditions provided are met. We say that our law respects the principle that no man may profit from his own wrong, but we do not mean that the law never permits a man to profit from wrongs he commits. In fact, people often profit, perfectly legally, from their legal wrongs. The most notorious case is adverse possession—if I trespass on your land long enough, some day I will gain a right to cross your land whenever I please. There are many less dramatic examples. If a man leaves one job, breaking a contract, to take a much higher paying job, he may have to pay damages to his first employer, but he is usually entitled to keep his new salary. If a man jumps bail and crosses state lines to make a brilliant investment in another state, he may be sent back to jail, but he will keep his profits.

We do not treat these—and countless other counter-instances that can easily be imagined—as showing that the principle about profiting from one's wrongs is not a pinciple of our legal system, or that it is incomplete and needs qualifying exceptions. We do not treat counter-instances as exceptions (at least not exceptions in the way in which a catcher's dropping the third strike is an exception) because we could not hope to capture these counter-instances simply by a more extended statement of the principle. They are not, even in theory, subject to enumeration, because we would have to include not only these cases (like adverse possession) in which some institution has already provided that profit can be gained through a wrong, but also those numberless imaginary cases in which we know in advance that the principle would not hold. Listing some of these might sharpen our sense of the principle's weight (I shall mention that dimension in a moment), but it would not make for a more accurate or complete statement of the principle.

A principle like "No man may profit from his own wrong" does not even purport to set out conditions that make its application necessary. Rather, it states a reason that argues in one direction, but does not necessitate a particular decision. I a man has or is about to receive something, as a direct result of something illegal he did to get it, then that is a reason which the law will take into account in deciding whether he should keep it. There may be other principles or policies arguing in the other direction—a policy of securing title, for example, or a principle limiting punishment to what the legislature has stipulated. If so, our principle may not prevail, but that does not mean that it is not a principle of our legal system, because in the next case, when these contravening considerations are absent or less weighty, the principle may be decisive. All that is meant, when we say that a particular principle is a principle of our law, is that the principle is one which officials must take into account, if it is relevant, as a consideration inclining in one direction or another.

The logical distinction between rules and principles appears more clearly when we consider principles that do not even look like rules. Consider the proposition, set out under "(d)" in the excerpts from the *Henningsen* opinion, that "the manufacturer is under a special obligation in connection with the construction, promotion and sale of his cars." This does not even purport to define the specific duties such a special obligation entails, or to tell us what rights automobile consumers acquire as a result. It merely states—and this is an essential link in the *Henningsen* argument—that automobile manufacturers must be held to higher standards than other manufacturers, and are less entitled to rely on the competing principle of freedom of contract. It does not mean that they may never rely on that principle, or that courts may rewrite automobile purchase contracts at will; it means only that if a particular clause seems unfair or burdensome, courts have less reason to enforce the clause than if it were for the purchase of neckties. The "special obligation" counts in favor, but does not in itself necessitate, a decision refusing to enforce the terms of an automobile purchase contract.

This first difference between rules and principles entails another. Principles have a dimension that rules do not—the dimension of weight or importance. When principles intersect (the policy of protecting automobile consumers intersecting with principles of freedom of contract, for example), one who must resolve the conflict has to take into account the relative weight of each. This cannot be, of course, an exact measurement, and the judgment that a particular principle or policy is more important than another will often be a controversial one. Nevertheless, it is an integral part of the concept of a principle that it has this dimension, that it makes sense to ask how important or how weighty it is.

Rules do not have this dimension. We can speak of rules as being *functionally* important or unimportant (the baseball rule that three strikes are out is more important than the rule that runners may advance on a balk, because the game would be much more changed with the first rule altered than the second). In this sense, one legal rule may be more important than another because it has a greater or more important role in regulating behavior. But we cannot say that one rule is more important than another within the system of rules, so that when two rules conflict one supercedes the other by virtue of its greater weight. If two rules conflict, one of them cannot be a valid rule. The decision as to which is valid, and which must be abandoned or recast, must be made by appealing to considerations beyond the rules themselves. A legal system might regulate such conflicts by other rules, which prefer the rule enacted by the higher authority, or the rule enacted later, or the more specific rule, or something of that sort. A legal system may also prefer the rule supported by the more important principles. (Our own legal system uses both of these techniques.)

It is not always clear from the form of a standard whether it is a rule or a principle. "A will is invalid unless signed by three witnesses" is not very different in form from "A man may not profit from his own wrong," but one who knows something of American law knows that he must take the first as stating a rule and the second as stating a principle. In many cases the distinction is difficult to make—it may not have been settled how the standard should operate, and this issue may itself be a focus of controversy. The first amendment to the United States Constitution contains the provision that Congress shall not abridge freedom of speech. Is this a rule, so that if a particular law does abridge freedom of speech, it follows that it is unconstitutional? Those who claim that the first amendment is "an absolute" say that it must be taken in this way, that is, as a rule. Or does it merely state a principle, so that when an abridgement of speech is discovered, it is unconstitutional unless the context presents some other policy or principle which in the circumstances is weighty enough to permit the abridgement? That is the position of those who argue for what is called the "clear and present danger" test or some other form of "balancing."

Sometimes a rule and a principle can play much the same role, and the difference between them is almost a matter of form alone. The first section of the Sherman Act states that every contract in restraint of trade shall be void. The Supreme Court had to make the decision whether this provision should be treated as a rule in its own terms (striking down every contract "which restrains trade," which almost any contract does) or as a principle, providing a reason for striking down a contract in the absence of effective contrary policies. The Court construed the provision as a rule, but treated that rule as containing the word "unreasonable," and as prohibiting only "unreasonable" restraints of trade.[12] This allowed the provision to function logically as a rule (whenever a court finds that the restraint is "unreasonable" it is bound to hold the contract invalid) and substantially as a principle (a court must take into account a variety of other principles and policies in determining whether a particular restraint in particular economic circumstances is "unreasonable").

Words like "reasonable," "negligent," "unjust," and "significant" often perform just this function. Each of these terms makes the application of the rule which contains it depend to some extent upon principles or policies lying beyond the rule, and in this way makes that rule itself more like a principle. But they do not quite turn the rule into a principle, because even the least confining of these terms restricts the *kind* of other principles and policies on which the rule depends. If we are bound by a rule that says that "unreasonable" contracts are void, or that grossly "unfair" contracts will not be enforced, much more judgment is required than if the quoted terms were omitted. But suppose a case in which some consideration of policy or principle suggests that a contract should be enforced even though its restraint is not reasonable, or even though it it grossly unfair. Enforcing these contracts would be forbidden by our rules, and thus permitted only if these rules were abandoned or modified. If we were dealing, however, not with a rule but with a policy against enforcing unreasonable contracts, or a principle that unfair contracts ought not to be enforced, the contracts could be enforced without alteration of the law.

---

[12] Standard Oil v. United States, 221 U.S. 1, 60 (1911); United States v. American Tobacco Co., 221 U.S. 106, 180 (1911).

## IV. Principles and the Concept of Law

Once we identify legal principles as separate sorts of standards, different from legal rules, we are suddenly aware of them all around us. Law teachers teach them, lawbooks cite them, legal historians celebrate them. But they seem most energetically at work, carrying most weight, in difficult lawsuits like *Riggs* and *Henningsen*. In cases like these, principles play an essential part in arguments supporting judgments about particular legal rights and obligations. After the case is decided, we may say that the case stands for a particular rule (*e.g.*, the rule that one who murders is not eligible to take under the will of his victim). But the rule does not exist before the case is decided; the court cites principles as its justification for adopting and applying a new rule. In *Riggs,* the court cited the principle that no man may profit from his own wrong as a background standard against which to read the statute of wills and in this way justified a new interpretation of that statute. In *Henningsen,* the court cited a variety of intersecting principles and policies as authority for a new rule respecting manufacturer's liability for automobile defects.

An analysis of the concept of legal obligation must therefore account for the important role of principles in reaching particular decisions of law. There are two very different tacks we might take.

(a) We might treat legal principles the way we treat legal rules and say that some principles are binding as law and must be taken into account by judges and lawyers who make decisions of legal obligation. If we took this tack, we should say that in the United States, at least, the "law" includes principles as well as rules.

(b) We might, on the other hand, deny that principles can be binding the way some rules are. We would say, instead, that in cases like *Riggs* or *Henningsen* the judge reaches beyond the rules that he is bound to apply (reaches, that is, beyond the "law") for extra-legal principles he is free to follow if he wishes.

One might think that there is not much difference between these two lines of attack, that it is only a verbal question of how one wants to use the word "law." But that is a mistake, because the choice between these two accounts has the greatest consequences for an analysis of legal obligation. It is a choice between two *concepts* of a legal principle, a choice we can clarify by comparing it to a choice we might make between two concepts of a legal rule. We sometimes say of someone that he "makes it a rule" to do something, when we mean that he has chosen to follow a certain practice. We might say that someone has made it a rule, for example, to run a mile before breakfast because he wants to be healthy and believes in a regimen. We do not mean, when we say this, that he is *bound* by the rule that he must run a mile before breakfast, or even that he regards it as binding upon him. Accepting a rule as binding is something different from making it a rule to do something. If we use Hart's example again, there is a difference between saying that Englishmen make it a rule to see a movie once a week, and saying that the English have a rule that one must see a movie once a week. The second implies that if an Englishman does not follow the rule, he is subject to criticism or censure, but the first does not. The first does not exclude the possibility of a *sort* of criticism—we can say that one who does not see movies is neglecting his education—but we do not suggest that he is doing something wrong *just* in not following the rule.[13]

If we think of the judges of a community as a group, we could describe the rules of law they follow in these two different ways. We could say, for instance, that in a certain state the judges make it a rule not to enforce wills unless there are three witnesses. This would not imply that the rare judge who enforces such a rule is doing anything wrong just for that reason. On the other hand we can say that in that state a rule of law requires judges not to enforce such wills; this does imply that a judge who enforces them is doing something wrong. Hart, Austin and other positivists, of course, would insist on this latter account of legal rules; they would not at all be satisfied with the "make it a rule" account. It is not a verbal question of which account is right. It is a question of which describes the social situation more accurately. Other important issues turn on which description we accept. If judges simply "make it a rule" not to enforce certain contracts, for example, then we cannot say, before the decision, that anyone is "entitled" to that result, and that proposition cannot enter into any justification we might offer for the decision.

The two lines of attack on principles parallel these two accounts of rules. The first tack treats principles as binding upon judges, so that they are wrong not to apply the principles when they are pertinent. The second tack treats principles as summaries of what most judges "make it a principle" to do when forced to go beyond the standards that bind them. The choice between these approaches will affect, perhaps even determine, the answer we can give to the question whether the judge in a hard case like *Riggs* or *Henningsen* is attempting to enforce pre-existing legal rights and obligations. If we take the first tack, we are still free to argue that because such judges are applying binding legal standards they are enforcing legal rights and obligations. But if we take the second, we are out of court on that issue, and we must acknowledge that the murderer's family in *Riggs* and the manufacturer in *Henningsen* were deprived of their property by an act of judicial discretion applied *ex post facto*. This may not shock many readers—the notion of judicial discretion has percolated through the legal community—but it does illustrate one of the most nettlesome of the puzzles that drive philosophers to worry about legal obligation. If taking property away in cases like these cannot be justified by appealing to an established obligation, another justification must be found, and nothing satisfactory has yet been supplied.

In my skeleton diagram of positivism, previously set out, I listed the doctrine of judicial discretion as the second tenet. Positivists hold that when a case is not covered by a clear rule, a judge must exercise his discretion to decide that case by what amounts to a fresh piece of legislation. There may be an important

---

[13] The distinction is in substance the same as that made by Rawls, *Two Concepts of Rules*, 64 PHILOSOPHICAL REV. 3 (1955).

connection between this doctine and the question of which of the two approaches to legal principles we must take. We shall therefore want to ask whether the doctrine is correct, and whether it implies the second approach, as it seems on its face to do. En route to these issues, however, we shall have to polish our understanding of the concept of discretion. I shall try to show how certain confusions about that concept, and in particular a failure to discriminate different senses in which it is used, account for the popularity of the doctrine of discretion. I shall argue that in the sense in which the doctrine does have a bearing on our treatment of principles, it is entirely unsupported by the arguments the positivists use to defend it.

## V. DISCRETION

The concept of discretion was lifted by the positivists from ordinary language, and to understand it we must put it back *in habitat* for a moment. What does it mean, in ordinary life, to say that someone "has discretion"? The first thing to notice is that the concept is out of place in all but very special contexts. For example, you would not say that I either do or do not have discretion to choose a house for my family. It is not true that I have "no discretion" in making that choice, and yet it would be almost equally misleading to say that I do have discretion. The concept of discretion is at home in only one sort of context: when someone is in general charged with making decisions subject to standards set by a particular authority. It makes sense to speak of the discretion of a sergeant who is subject to orders of superiors, or the discretion of a sports official or contest judge who is governed by a rule book or the terms of the contest. Discretion, like the hole in a doughnut, does not exist as an area left open by a surrounding belt of restriction. It is therefore a relative concept. It always makes sense to ask, "Discretion under which standards?" or "Discretion as to which authority?" Generally the context will make the answer to this plain, but in some cases the official may have discretion from one standpoint though not from another.

Like almost all terms, the precise meaning of "discretion" is affected by features of the context. The term is always colored by the background of understood information against which it is used. Although the shadings are many, it will be helpful for us to recognize some gross distinctions.

Sometimes we use "discretion" in a weak sense, simply to say that for some reason the standards an official must apply cannot be applied mechanically but demand the use of judgment. We use this weak sense when the context does not already make that clear, when the background our audience assumes does not contain that piece of information. Thus we might say, "The sergeant's orders left him a great deal of discretion," to those who do not know what the sergeant's orders were or who do not know something that made those orders vague or hard to carry out. It would make perfect sense to add, by way of amplification, that the lieutenant had ordered the sergeant to take his five most experienced men on patrol but that it was hard to determine which were the most experienced.

Sometimes we use the term in a different weak sense, to say only that some official has final authority to make a decision and cannot be reviewed and reversed by any other official. We speak this way when the official is part of a hierarchy of officials structured so that some have higher authority but in which the patterns of authority are different for different classes of decision. Thus we might say that in baseball certain decisions, like the decision whether the ball or the runner reached second base first, are left to the discretion of the second base umpire, if we mean that on this issue the head umpire has no power to substitute his own judgment if he disagrees.

I call both of these senses weak to distinguish them from a stronger sense. We use "discretion" sometimes not merely to say that an official must use judgment in applying the standards set him by authority, or that no one will review that exercise of judgment, but to say that on some issue he is simply not bound by standards set by the authority in question. In this sense we say that a sergeant has discretion who has been told to pick any five men for patrol he chooses or that a judge in a dog show has discretion to judge airedales before boxers if the rules do not stipulate an order of events. We use this sense not to comment on the vagueness or difficulty of the standards, or on who has the final word in applying them, but on their range and the decisions they purport to control. If the sergeant is told to take the five most experienced men, he does not have discretion in this strong sense because that order purports to govern his decision. The boxing referee who must decide which fighter has been the more aggressive does not have discretion, in the strong sense, for the same reason.[14]

If anyone said that the sergeant of the referee had discretion in these cases, we should have to understand him, if the context permitted, as using the term in one of the weak senses. Suppose, for example, the lieutenant ordered the sergeant to select the five men he deemed most experienced, and then added that the sergeant had discretion to choose them. Or the rules provided that the referee should award the round to the more aggressive fighter, with discretion in selecting him. We should have to understand these statements in the seond weak sense, as speaking to the question of review of the decision. The first weak sense—that the decisions take judgment—would be otiose, and the third, strong sense is excluded by the statements themselves.

We must avoid one tempting confusion. The strong sense of discretion is not tantamount to license, and does not exclude criticism. Almost any situation in which a person acts (including those in which there is no question of decision under special authority, and so no question of discretion) makes relevant certain standards of rationality, fairness, and effectiveness. We criticize each other's acts in terms of these standards, and there is no reason not to do so when the

---

[14] I have not spoken of that jurisprudential favorite, "limited" discretion, because that concept presents no special difficulties if we remember the relativity of discretion. Suppose the sergeant is told to choose from "amongst" experienced men, or to "take experience into account." We might say either that he has (limited) discretion in picking his patrol, or (full) discretion to either pick amongst experienced men or decide what else to take into account.

acts are within the center rather than beyond the perimeter of the doughnut of special authority. So we can say that the sergeant who was given discretion (in the strong sense) to pick a patrol did so stupidly or maliciously or carelessly, or that the judge who had discretion in the order of viewing dogs made a mistake because he took boxers first although there were only three airedales and many more boxers. An official's discretion means not that he is free to decide without recourse to standards of sense and fairness, but only that his decision is not controlled by a standard furnished by the particular authority we have in mind when we raise the question of discretion. Of course this latter sort of freedom is important; that is why we have the strong sense of discretion. Someone who has discretion in this third sense can be criticized, but not for being disobedient, as in the case of the soldier. He can be said to have made a mistake, but not to have deprived a participant of a decision to which he was entitled, as in the case of a sports official or contest judge.

We may now return, with these observations in hand, to the positivists' doctrine of judicial discretion. That doctrine argues that if a case is not controlled by an established rule, the judge must decide it by exercising discretion. We want to examine this doctrine and to test its bearing on our treatment of principles; but first we must ask in which sense of discretion we are to understand it.

Some nominalists argue that judges always have discretion, even when a clear rule is in point, because judges are ultimately the final arbiters of the law. This doctrine of discretion uses the second weak sense of that term. because it makes the point that no higher authority reviews the decisions of the highest court. It therefore has no bearing on the issue of how we account for principles, any more than it bears on how we account for rules.

The positivists do not mean their doctrine this way, because they say that a judge has no discretion when a clear and established rule is available. If we attend to the positivists' arguments for the doctrine we may suspect that they use discretion in the first weak sense to mean only that judges must sometimes exercise judgment in applying legal standards. Their arguments call attention to the fact that some rules of law are vague (Professor Hart, for example, says that all rules of law have "open texture"), and that some cases arise (like *Henningsen*) in which no established rule seems to be suitable. They emphasize that judges must sometimes agonize over points of law, and that two equally trained and intelligent judges will often disagree.

These points are easily made; they are commonplace to anyone who has any familiarity with law. Indeed, that is the difficulty with assuming that positivists mean to use "discretion" in this weak sense. The proposition that when no clear rule is available discretion in the sense of judgment must be used is a tautology. It has no bearing, moreover, on the problem of how to account for legal principles. It is perfectly consistent to say that the judge in *Riggs*, for example, had to use judgement, and that he was bound to follow the principle that no man may profit from his own wrong. The positivists speak as if their doctrine of judicial discretion is an insight rather than a tautology, and as if it does have a bearing on the treatment of principles. Hart, for example, says that when the judge's discretion is in play, we can no longer speak of his being bound by standards, but must speak rather of what standards he "characteristically uses." 15 Hart thinks that when judges have discretion, the principles they cite must be treated on our second approach, as what courts "make it a principle" to do.

It therefore seems that positivists, at least sometimes, take their doctrine in the third, strong sense of discretion. In that sense it does bear on the treatment of principles; indeed, in that sense it is nothing less than a restatement of our second approach. It is the same thing to say that when a judge runs out of rules he has discretion, in the sense that he is not bound by any standards from the authority of law, as to say that the legal standards judges cite other than rules are not binding on them.

So we must examine the doctrine of judicial discretion in the strong sense. (I shall henceforth use the term "discretion" in that sense.) Do the principles judges cite in cases like *Riggs* or *Henningsen* control their decisions, as the sergeant's orders to take the most experienced men or the referee's duty to choose the more aggressive fighter control the decisions of these officials? What arguments could a positivist supply to show that they do not?

(1) A positivist might argue that principles cannot be binding or obligatory. That would be a mistake. It is always a question, of course, whether any particular principle is *in fact* binding upon some legal official. But there is nothing in the logical character of a principle that renders it incapable of binding him. Suppose that the judge in *Henningsen* had failed to take any account of the principle that automobile manufacturers have a special obligation to their consumers, or the principle that the courts seek to protect those whose bargaining position is weak, but had simply decided for the defendant by citing the principle of freedom of contract without more. His critics would not have been content to point out that he had not taken account of considerations that other judges have been attending to for some time. Most would have said that it was his duty to take the measure of these principles and that the plaintiff was entitled to have him do so. We mean no more, when we say that a *rule* is binding upon a judge, than that he must follow it if it applies, and that if he does not he will on that account have made a mistake.

It will not do to say that in a case like *Henningsen* the court is only "morally" obligated to take particular principles into account, or that it is "institutionally" obligated, or obligated as a matter of judicial "craft," or something of that sort. The question will still remain why this type of obligation (whatever we call it) is different from the obligation that rules impose upon judges, and why it entitles us to say that principles and policies are not part of the law but are merely extra-legal standards "courts characteristically use."

(2) A positivist might argue that even though some principles are binding, in the sense that the judge must take them into account, they cannot determine a particular result. This is a harder argument to assess because it is not clear what it means for a standard to "determine" a result. Perhaps it means that the

---

15 H.L.A. HART, THE CONCEPT OF LAW 144 (1961).

standard *dictates* the result whenever it applies so that nothing else counts. If so, then it is certainly true that individual principles do not determine results, but that is only another way of saying that principles are not rules. Only rules dictate results, come what may. When a contrary result has been reached, the rule has been abandoned or changed. Principles do not work that way; they incline a decision one way, though not conclusively, and they survive intact when they do not prevail. This seems no reason for concluding that judges who must reckon with principles have discretion because a set of principles *can* dictate a result. If a judge believes that principles he is bound to recognize point in one direction and that principles pointing in the other direction, if any, are not of equal weight, then he must decide accordingly, just as he must follow what he believes to be a binding rule. He may, of course, be wrong in his assessment of the principles, but he may also be wrong in his judgment that the rule is binding. The sergeant and the referee, we might add, are often in the same boat. No one factor dictates which soldiers are the most experienced or which fighter the more aggressive. These officials must make judgments of the relative weights of these various factors; they do not on that account have discretion.

(3) A positivist might argue that principles cannot count as law because their authority, and even more so their weight, are congenitally *controversial*. It is true that generally we cannot *demonstrate* the authority or weight of a particular principle as we can sometimes demonstrate the validity of a rule by locating it in an act of Congress or in the opinion of an authoritive court. Instead, we make a case for a principle, and for its weight, by appealing to an amalgam of practice and other principles in which the implications of legislative and judicial history figure along with appeals to community practices and understandings. There is no litmus paper for testing the soundness of such a case—it is a matter of judgment, and reasonable men may disagree. But again this does not distinguish the judge from other officials who do not have discretion. The sergeant has no litmus paper for experience, the referee none for agressiveness. Neither of these has discretion, because he is bound to reach an understanding, controversial or not, of what his orders or the rules require, and to act on that understanding. That is the judge's duty as well.

Of course, if the positivists are right in another of their doctrines—the theory that in each legal system there is an ultimate *test* for binding law like Professor Hart's rule of recognition—it follows that principles are not binding law. But the incompatibility of principles with the positivists' theory can hardly be taken as an argument that principles must be treated any particular way. That begs the question; we are interested in the status of principles because we want to evaluate the positivists' model. The positivist cannot defend his theory of a rule of recognition by fiat; if principles are not amenable to a test he must show some other reason why they cannot count as law. Since principles seem to play a role in arguments about legal obligation (witness, again, *Riggs* and *Henningsen*), a model that provides for that role has some initial advantage over one that excludes it, and the latter cannot properly be inveighed in its own support.

These are the most obvious of the arguments a positivist might use for the doctrine of discretion in the strong sense, and for the second approach to principles. I shall mention one strong counter-argument against that doctrine and in favor of the first approach. Unless at least some principles are acknowledged to be binding upon judges, requiring them as a set to reach particular decisions, then no rules, or very few rules, can be said to be binding upon them either.

In most American jurisdictions, and now in England also, the higher courts not infrequently reject established rules. Common law rules—those developed by earlier court decisions—are sometimes over-ruled directly, and sometimes radically altered by further development. Statutory rules are subjected to interpretation and reinterpretation, sometimes even when the result is not to carry out what is called the "legislative intent." [16] If courts had discretion to change established rules, then these rules would of course not be binding upon them, and so would not be law on the positivists' model. The positivist must therefore argue that there are standards, themselves binding upon judges, that determine when a judge may overrule or alter an established rule, and when he may not.

When, then, is a judge permitted to change an existing rule of law? Principles figure in the answer in two ways. First, it is necessary, though not sufficient, that the judge find that the change would advance some policy or serve some principle, which policy or principle thus justifies the change. In *Riggs* the change (a new interpretation of the statute of wills) was justified by the principle that no man should profit from his own wrong; in *Henningsen* certain rules about automobile manufacturer's liability were altered on the basis of the principles and policies I quoted from the opinion of the court.

But not any principle will do to justify a change, or no rule would ever be safe. There must be some principles that count and others that do not, and there must be some principles that count for more than others. It could not depend on the judge's own preferences amongst a sea of respectable extra-legal standards, any one in principle eligible, because if that were the case we could not say that any rules were binding. We could always imagine a judge whose preferences amongst extra-legal standards were such as would justify a shift or radical reinterpretation of even the most entrenched rule.

Second, any judge who proposes to change existing doctrine must take account of some important standards that argue against departures from established doctrine, and these standards are also for the most part principles. They include the doctrine of "legislative supremacy," a set of principles and policies that require the courts to pay a qualified deference to the acts of the legislature. They also include the doctrine of precedent, another set of principles and policies reflecting the equities and efficiencies of consistency. The doctrines of legislative supremacy and precedent incline toward the *status quo*, each within its sphere, but they do not command it. Judges are not free, however, to pick

---

[16] *See* Wellington & Albert, *Statutory Interpretation and the Political Process: A Comment on Sinclair v. Atkinson,* 72 YALE L. J. 1547 (1963).

and choose amongst the principles and policies that make up these doctrines—if they were, again, no rule could be said to be binding.

Consider, therefore, what someone implies who says that a particular rule is binding. He may imply that the rule is affirmatively supported by principles the court is not free to disregard, and which are collectively more weighty than other principles that argue for a change. If not, he implies that any change would be condemned by a combination of conservative principles of legislative supremacy and precedent that the court is not free to ignore. Very often, he will imply both, for the conservative principles, being principles and not rules, are usually not powerful enough to save a common law rule or an aging statute that is entirely unsupported by substantive principles the court is bound to respect. Either of these implications, of course, treats a body of principles and policies as law in the sense that rules are; it treats them as standards binding upon the officials of a community, controlling their decisions of legal right and obligation.

We are left with this issue. If the positivist's theory of judicial discretion is either trivial because it uses "discretion" in a weak sense, or unsupported because the various arguments we can supply in its defense fall short, why have so many careful and intelligent lawyers embraced it? We can have no confidence in our treatment of that theory unless we can deal with that question. It is not enough to note (although perhaps it contributes to the explanation) that "discretion" has different senses that may be confused. We do not confuse these senses when we are not thinking about law.

Part of the explanation, at least, lies in a lawyer's natural tendency to associate laws and rules, and to think of "the law" as a collection or system of rules. Roscoe Pound, who diagnosed this tendency long ago, thought that English speaking lawyers were tricked into it by the fact that English uses the same word, changing only the article, for "a law" and "the law." [17] (Other languages, on the contrary, use two words: "loi" and "droit," for example, and "Gesetz" and "Recht.") This may have had its effect, with the English speaking positivists, because the expression "a law" certainly does suggest a rule. But the principal reason for associating law with rules runs deeper, and lies, I think, in the fact that legal education has for a long time consisted of teaching and examining those established rules that form the cutting edge of law.

In any event, if a lawyer thinks of law as a system of rules, and yet recognizes, as he must, that judges change old rules and introduce new ones, he will come naturally to the theory of judicial discretion in the strong sense. In those other systems of rules with which he has experience (like games), the rules are the only special authority that govern official decisions, so that if an umpire could change a rule, he would have discretion as to the subject matter of that rule. Any principles umpires might mention when changing the rules would represent only their "characteristic" preferences. Positivists treat law like baseball revised in this way.

---

[17] R. Pound, An Introduction to the Philosophy of Law 56 (rev. ed. 1954).

There is another, more subtle consequence of this initial assumption that law is a system of rules. When the positivists do attend to principles and policies, they treat them as rules *manque*. They assume that *if* they are standards of law they must be rules, and so they read them as standards that are trying to be rules. When a positivist hears someone argue that legal principles are part of the law, he understands this to be an argument for what he calls the "higher law" theory, that these principles are the rules of a law above the law.[18] He refutes this theory by pointing out that these "rules" are sometimes followed and sometimes not, that for every "rule" like "no man shall profit from his own wrong" there is another competing "rule" like "the law favors security of title", and that there is no way to test the validity of "rules" like these. He concludes that these principles and policies are not valid rules of a law above the law, which is true, because they are not rules at all. He also concludes that they are extra-legal standards which each judge selects according to his own lights in the exercise of his discretion, which is false. It is as if a zoologist had proved that fish are not mammals, and then concluded that they are really only plants.

[18] *See, e.g.,* Dickinson, *The Law Behind Law* (pts. 1 & 2), 29 Colum. L. Rev. 112, 254 (1929).

CHAPTER VIII

# JUSTICE

Now 'justice' and 'injustice' seem to be ambiguous, but because their different
meanings approach near to one another the ambiguity escapes notice and is not obvious
Aristotle, *Nicomachean Ethics*

Undoubtedly more energies for a longer period of time have been mobilized
behind the attempt to establish a universal definition of justice than any other
concept intimately connected with law. As the infinite variety in popular and
professional usage is all too evident witness ("An unjust law is no law. . . ",
"Justice is swift in Spain. . . ", "Law and order, but justice"), Aristotle's caution
regarding the ambiguity of the concept still stands. As Chaim Perelman makes
manifestly clear in the selection printed below, there has never existed in the
Western tradition any single pre-eminent universal standard of positive justice.
Common criteria, perhaps, are shared by most major formulations (e.g. formal
equality) but substantial elucidations of justice have been supplemented by one
or another of several possible social ideals—merit, works, need, rank, legal
entitlement and others.

Inner tensions within the concept are apparent even from the format in
which most definitions are framed—a set of one or more general principles
bolstered by a variable list of qualifications and exceptions to the general rule.
The complimentary concept, equity, in fact has been defined as the corrective
to formal legal rule. Justice seems to entail the conflict of competing claims and
not infrequently the clash of powerful social interests with the rights of individuals
ensnared from time to time in the mechanism of *raison d'Etat*.

Natural law theorists and positivists have tended to stress respectively the

'fair' and the 'lawful' of Aristotle's breakdown of the generic concept. Austin
and his followers, for instance, defended the separation of law and morals;
argued that a law was just if properly promulgated (i.e. by sovereign authority
in clear language, publicized and with specified sanctions). Aquinas and
natural law theorists generally have added welfare or natural rights corollaries
to the stipulation of due process. Theorists have differed widely both over the
proper distribution of social goods and the rectification of civil and criminal
injuries.

Recently John Rawls, in a series of articles, has attempted to reformulate
the principle of equality as a new basis for the social contract. Wary of the potential oppression of minorities entailed by the utilitarian 'greatest happiness'
principle, Rawls argues that departure from strict equality can only be justified
by the individual and collective advantage of each member of society. Rawls'
elaboration has been criticized in turn for its formalism and assumption of a
simple scale of social goods which neglects the actual hard conflict of competing
social interests.

The legal fraternity on its side is generally sceptical of abstract definitions
of justice. The beginning law student is quickly disabused of prior notions of
'justice' that challenge allegiance to due process and the adversary system. Its
attitude was characteristically expressed by William Maitland, who commem-
orated the decline of ancient Chancery courts once charged with the equitable
protection of weaker interests against the rigidities of the common law system:

> And the first thing we have to observe is that this relation was not one of conflict.
> Equity had come not to destroy the law but to fulfil it. Every jot and every tittle of the
> law was to be obeyed, but when all this had been done something might yet be needful,
> something that equity would require. Of course, now and again there had been conflicts:
> there was an open conflict, for example, when Coke was for indicting a man who sued
> for an injunction. But such conflicts as this belong to old days, and for two centuries
> before the year 1875 the two systems had been working together harmoniously.
>
> Maitland, *Equity*, 1913.

It should not be surprizing, then, to discover a sharp divergence between
legal theorists and other 'moralists' in the application of the terms, 'just,' 'equitable', 'unjust.' For the legal profession justice largely connotes due process,
impartial judgment, fair trial by constituted authority. Thus, H.L.A. Hart, for
instance, has been reluctant to consider 'valid' Nazi laws 'unjust'; rather he
considers them "iniquitous," a term he reserves for moral as opposed to legal
disapprobation. To the legal practitioner, civil disobedients are justly punished
no matter how morally justified their cause. Only recently have younger
theorists, in response to new claims such as that of the civil rights movement,
begun to re-examine the concept and reformulate new criteria which may yet
make it a useful tool for the redress of inequitable effects of established rule.
Here again another of Aristotle's admonitions seems appropriate: "All law is
universal but about some things it is not possible to make a universal statement
which shall be correct."

# 34

# Aristotle

Aristotle's analysis suggests many complex subdivisions in the generic
concept of justice.

# JUSTICE*

### I

With regard to justice and injustice we must consider (1) what kind of
actions they are concerned with, (2) what sort of mean justice is, and (3) between
what extremes the just act is intermediate. Our investigation shall follow the
same course as the preceding discussions.

We see that all men mean by justice that kind of state of character which
makes people disposed to do what is just and makes them act justly and wish
for what is just; and similarly by injustice that state which makes them act
unjustly and wish for what is unjust. Let us too, then, lay this down as a general
basis. For the same is not true of the sciences and the faculties as of states of
character. A faculty or a science which is one and the same is held to relate to
contrary objects, but a state of character which is one of two contraries does *not*
produce the contrary results; e.g. as a result of health we do not do what is the
opposite of healthy, but only what is healthy; for we say a man walks healthily,
when he walks as a healthy man would.

Now often one contrary state is recognized from its contrary, and often states
are recognized from the subjects that exhibit them; for (A) if good condition is
known, bad condition also becomes known, and (B) good condition is known
from the things that are in good condition, and they from it. If good condition
is firmness of flesh, it is necessary both that bad condition should be flabbiness
of flesh and that the wholesome should be that which causes firmness in flesh.
And it follows for the most part that if one contrary is ambiguous the other also
will be ambiguous; e.g. if 'just' is so, that 'unjust' will be so too.

Now 'justice' and 'injustice' seem to be ambiguous, but because their
different meanings approach near to one another the ambiguity escapes notice
and is not obvious as it is, comparatively, when the meanings are far apart, e.g.
(for here the difference in outward form is great) as the ambiguity in the use of

---

*Aristotle, *Nicomachean Ethics*, V, 1129al–1131a32, 1131b15–1132a19, 1132b11–29, 1133b30–
1134a16, 1134b18–1135a7, 1137a31–1138b14, reprinted by permission of the publisher from
*The Oxford Translation of Aristotle*, Clarendon Press, Oxford, edited by W. D. Ross. (Also see V, 8
reprinted in Chapter IV above).

κλείς for the collar-bone of an animal and for that with which we lock a door. Let us take as a starting-point, then, the various meanings of 'an unjust man'. Both the lawless man and the grasping and unfair man are thought to be unjust, so that evidently both the law-abiding and the fair man will be just. The just, then, is the lawful and the fair, the unjust the unlawful and the unfair.

Since the unjust man is grasping, he must be concerned with goods—not all goods, but those with which prosperity and adversity have to do, which taken absolutely are always good, but for a particular person are not always good. Now men pray for and pursue these things; but they should not, but should pray that the things that are good absolutely may also be good for them, and should choose the things that *are* good for them. The unjust man does not always choose the greater, but also the less—in the case of things bad absolutely; but because the lesser evil is itself thought to be in a sense good, and graspingness is directed at the good, therefore he is thought to be grasping. And he is unfair; for this contains and is common to both.

Since the lawless man was seen to be unjust and the law-abiding man just, evidently all lawful acts are in a sense just acts; for the acts laid down by the legislative art are lawful, and each of these, we say, is just. Now the laws in their enactments on all subjects aim at the common advantage either of all or of the best or of those who hold power, or something of the sort; so that in one sense we call those acts just that tend to produce and preserve happiness and its components for the political society. And the law bids us do both the acts of a brave man (e.g. not to desert our post nor take to flight nor throw away our arms), and those of a temperate man (e.g. not to commit adultery nor to gratify one's lust), and those of a good-tempered man (e.g. not to strike another nor to speak evil), and similarly with regard to the other virtues and forms of wickedness, commanding some acts and forbidding others; and the rightly-framed law does this rightly, and the hastily conceived one less well.

This form of justice, then, is complete virtue, but not absolutely, but in relation to our neighbour. And therefore justice is often thought to be the greatest of virtues, and 'neither evening nor morning star' is so wonderful; and proverbially 'in justice is every virtue comprehended'. And it is complete virtue in its fullest sense, because it is the actual exercise of complete virtue. It is complete because he who possesses it can exercise his virtue not only in himself but towards his neighbour also; for many men can exercise virtue in their own affairs, but not in their relations to their neighbour. This is why the saying of Bias is thought to be true, that 'rule will show the man'; for a ruler is necessarily in relation to other men and a member of a society. For this same reason justice, alone of the virtues, is thought to be 'another's good', because it is related to our neighbour; for it does what is advantageous to another, either a ruler or a copartner. Now the worst man is he who exercises his wickedness both towards himself and towards his friends, and the best man is not he who exercises his virtue towards himself but he who exercises it towards another; for this is a difficult task. Justice in this sense, then, is not part of virtue but virtue entire, nor is the contrary injustice a part of vice but vice entire. What the difference is between virtue and justice in this sense is plain from what we have said; they are the same but their essence is not the same; what, as a relation to one's neighbour, is justice is, as a certain kind of state without qualification, virtue.

2

But at all events what we are investigating is the justice which is a *part* of virtue; for there is a justice of this kind, as we maintain. Similarly it is with injustice in the particular sense that we are concerned.

That there is such a thing is indicated by the fact that while the man who exhibits in action the other forms of wickedness acts wrongly indeed, but not graspingly (e.g. the man who throws away his shield through cowardice or speaks harshly through bad temper or fails to help a friend with money through meanness), when a man acts graspingly he often exhibits none of these vices,— no, nor all together, but certainly wickedness of some kind (for we blame him) and injustice. There is, then, another kind of injustice which is a part of injustice in the wide sense, and a use of the word 'unjust' which answers to a part of what is unjust in the wide sense of 'contrary to the law'. Again, if one man commits adultery for the sake of gain and makes money by it, while another does so at the bidding of appetite though he loses money and is penalized for it, the latter would be held to be self-indulgent rather than grasping, but the former is unjust, but not self-indulgent; evidently, therefore, he is unjust by reason of his making gain by his act. Again, all other unjust acts are ascribed invariably to some particular kind of wickedness, e.g. adultery to self-indulgence, the desertion of a comrade in battle to cowardice, physical violence to anger; but if a man makes gain, his action is ascribed to no form of wickedness but injustice. Evidently, therefore, there is apart from injustice in the wide sense another, 'particular', injustice which shares the name and nature of the first, because its definition falls within the same genus; for the significance of both consists in a relation to one's neighbour, but the one is concerned with honour or money or safety—cr that which includes all these, if we had a single name for it—and its motive is the pleasure that arises from gain; while the other is concerned with all the objects with which the good man is concerned.

It is clear, then, that there is more than one kind of justice, and that there is one which is distinct from virtue entire; we must try to grasp its genus and differentia.

The unjust has been divided into the unlawful and the unfair, and the just into the lawful and the fair. To the unlawful answers the afore-mentioned sense of injustice. But since the unfair and the unlawful are not the same, but are different as a part is from its whole (for all that is unfair is unlawful, but not all that is unlawful is unfair), the unjust and injustice in the sense of the unfair are not the same as but different from the former kind, as part from whole, for injustice in this sense is a part of injustice in the wide sense, and similarly justice in the one sense of justice in the other. Therefore we must speak also about particular justice and particular injustice, and similarly about the just and the unjust. The justice, then, which answers to the whole of virtue, and the corresponding injustice, one being the exercise of virtue as a whole, and the other that of vice as a whole, towards one's neighbor, we may leave on one side. And how the meanings of 'just' and 'unjust' which answer to these are to be distinguished is evident; for practically the majority of the acts commanded by the law are those which are prescribed from the point of view of virtue taken as a whole; for the law bids us practise every virtue and forbids us to practise any vice. And the things that tend to produce virtue taken as a whole are those of the acts prescribed by the law which have been prescribed with a view to education for the common good. But with regard to the education of the individual as such, which makes him without qualification a good *man*, we must determine later whether this is the function of the political art or of another; for perhaps it is not the same to be a good man and a good citizen of any state taken at random.

Of particular justice and that which is just in the corresponding sense, (A) one kind is that which is manifested in distributions of honor or money or the other things that fall to be divided among those who have a share in the constitution (for in these it is possible for one man to have a share either unequal or equal to that of another), and (B) one is that which plays a rectifying part in transactions between man and man. Of this there are two divisions; of transactions (1) some are voluntary and (2) others involuntary—voluntary such transactions as sale, purchase, loan for consumption, pledging, loan for use, depositing, letting (they are called voluntary because the origin of these transactions is voluntary), while of the involuntary (a) some are clandestine, such as theft, adultery, poisoning, procuring, enticement of slaves, assassination, false witness, and (b) others are violent, such as assault, imprisonment, murder, robbery with violence, mutilation, abuse , insult.

### 3

(A) We have shown that both the unjust man and the unjust act are unfair or unequal; now it is clear that there is also an intermediate between the two unequals involved in either case. And this is the equal; for in any kind of action in which there is a more and a less there is also what is equal. If, then, the unjust is unequal, the just is equal, as all men suppose it to be, even apart from argument, And since the equal is intermediate, the just will be an intermediate. Now equality implies at least two things. The just, then, must be both intermediate and equal and relative (i.e. for certain persons). And *qua* intermediate it must be between certain things (which are respectively greater and less); *qua* equal, it involves *two* things; *qua* just, it is for certain people. The just, therefore, involves at least four terms; for the persons for whom it is in fact just are two, and the things in which it is manifested, the objects distributed, are two. And the same equality will exist between the persons and between the things concerned; for as the latter—the things concerned—are related, so are the former; if they are not equal, they will not have what is equal, but this is the origin of quarrels and complaints—when either equals have and are awarded unequal shares, or unequals equal shares. Further, this is plain from the fact that awards should be 'according to merit'; for all men agree that what is just in distribution must be according to merit in some sense, though they do not all specify the same sort of merit, but democrats identify it with the status of freeman, supporters of oligarchy with wealth (or with noble birth), and supporters of aristocracy with excellence.

The just, then, is a species of the proportionate (proportion being not a property only of the kind of number which consists of abstract units, but of number in general). . . . This proportion is not continuous; for we cannot get a single term standing for a person and a thing.

This, then, is what the just is—the proportional; the unjust is what violates the proportion. Hence one term becomes too great, the other too small, as indeed happens in practice; for the man who acts unjustly has too much, and the man who is unjustly treated too little, of what is good. In the case of evil the reverse is true; for the lesser evil is reckoned a good in comparison with the greater evil, since the lesser evil is rather to be chosen than the greater, and what is worthy of choice is good, and what is worthier of choice a greater good.

This, then, is one species of the just.

4

(B) The remaining one is the rectificatory, which arises in connexion with transactions both voluntary and involuntary. This form of the just has a different specific character from the former. For the justice which distributes common possessions is always in accordance with the kind of proportion mentioned above (for in the case also in which the distribution is made from the common funds of a partnership it will be according to the same ratio which the funds put into the business by the partners bear to one another); and the injustice opposed to this kind of justice is that which violates the proportion. But the justice in transactions between man and man is a sort of equality indeed, and the injustice a sort of inequality; not according to that kind of proportion, however, but according to arithmetical proportion. For it makes no difference whether a good man has defrauded a bad man or a bad man a good one, nor whether it is a good or a bad man that has committed adultery; the law looks only to the distinctive character of the injury, and treats the parties as equal, if one is in the wrong and the other is being wronged, and if one inflicted injury and the other has received it. Therefore, this kind of injustice being an inequality, the judge tries to equalize it; for in the case also in which one has received and the other has inflicted a wound, or one has slain and the other been slain, the suffering and the action have been unequally distributed; but the judge tries to equalize things by means of the penalty, taking away from the gain of the assailant. For the term 'gain' is applied generally to such cases, even if it be not a term appropriate to certain cases, e.g. to the person who inflicts a wound—and 'loss' to the sufferer; at all events when the suffering has been estimated, the one is called loss and the other gain. Therefore the equal is intermediate between the greater and the less, but the gain and the loss are respectively greater and less in contrary ways; more of the good and less of the evil are gain, and the contrary is loss; intermediate between them is, as we saw, the equal, which we say is just; therefore corrective justice will be the intermediate between loss and gain. . . . These names, both loss and gain, have come from voluntary exchange; for to have more than one's own is called gaining, and to have less than one's original share is called losing, e.g. in buying and selling and in all other matters in which the law has left people free to make their own terms; but when they get neither more nor less but just what belongs to themselves, they say that they have their own and that they neither lose nor gain.

Therefore the just is intermediate between a sort of gain and a sort of loss, viz. those which are involuntary; it consists in having an equal amount before and after the transaction.

5

Some think that *reciprocity* is without qualification just, as the Pythagoreans said; for they defined justice without qualification as reciprocity. Now 'reciprocity' fits neither distributive nor rectificatory justice—yet people *want* even the justice of Rhadamanthus to mean this:

Should a man suffer what he did, right justice would be done.

—for in many cases reciprocity and rectificatory justice are not in accord; e.g. (1) if an official has inflicted a wound, he should not be wounded in return, and if some one has wounded an official, he ought not to be wounded only but punished in addition. . . .

We have now defined the unjust and the just. These having been marked off from each other, it is plain that just action is intermediate between acting unjustly and being unjustly treated; for the one is to have too much and the other to have too little. Justice is a kind of mean, but not in the same way as the other virtues, but because it relates to an intermediate amount, while injustice relates to the extremes. And justice is that in virtue of which the just man is said to be a doer, by choice, of that which is just, and one who will distribute either between himself and another or between two others not so as to give more of what is desirable to himself and less to his neighbor (and conversely with what is harmful), but so as to give what is equal in accordance with proportion; and similarly in distributing between two other persons. Injustice on the other hand is similarly related to the unjust, which is excess and defect, contrary to proportion, of the useful or hurtful. For which reason injustice is excess and defect, viz. because it is productive of excess and defect—in one's own case excess of what is in its own nature useful and defect of what is hurtful, while in the case of others it is as a whole like what it is in one's own case, but proportion may be violated in either direction. In the unjust act to have too little is to be unjustly treated; to have too much is to act unjustly.

Let this be taken as our account of the nature of justice and injustice, and similarly of the just and the unjust in general. . . .

## 7

Of political justice part is natural, part legal,—natural, that which everywhere has the same force and does not exist by people's thinking this or that; legal, that which is originally indifferent, but when it has been laid down is not indifferent, e.g. that a prisoner's ransom shall be a mina, or that a goat and not two sheep shall be sacrificed, and again all the laws that are passed for particular cases, e.g. that sacrifice shall be made in honor of Brasidas, and the provisions of decrees. Now some think that all justice is of this sort, because that which is by nature is unchangeable and has everywhere the same force (as fire burns both here and in Persia), while they see change in the things recognized as just. This, however, is not true in this unqualified way, but is true in a sense; or rather, with the gods it is perhaps not true at all, while with us there is something that is just even by nature, yet all of it is changeable; but still some is by nature, some not by nature. It is evident which sort of thing, among things capable of being otherwise, is by nature; and which is not but is legal and conventional, assuming that both are equally changeable. And in all other things the same distinction will apply; by nature the right hand is stronger, yet it is possible that all men should come to be ambidextrous. The things which are just by virtue of convention and expediency are like measures; for wine and corn measures are not everywhere equal, but larger in wholesale and smaller in retail markets. Similarly, the things which are just not by nature but by human enactment are not everywhere the same, since constitutions also are not the same, though there is but one which is everywhere by nature the best.

Of things just and lawful each is related as the universal to its particulars; for the things that are done are many, but of *them* each is one, since it is universal. . . .

## 10

Our next subject is equity and the equitable (τὸ ἐπιεικές), and their respective relations to justice and the just. For on examination they appear to be neither absolutely the same nor generaically different; and while we sometimes praise what is equitable and the equitable man (so that we apply the name by way of praise even to instances of the other virtues, instead of 'good', meaning by ἐπιεικέστερον that a thing is better), at other times, when we reason it out, it seems strange if the equitable, being something different from the just, is yet praiseworthy; for either the just or the equitable is not good, if they are different; or, if both are good, they are the same.

These, then, are pretty much the considerations that give rise to the problem about the equitable; they are all in a sense correct and not opposed to one another; for the equitable, though it is better than one kind of justice, yet is just, and it is not as being a different class of thing that it is better than the just. The same thing, then, is just and equitable, and while both are good the equitable is superior. What creates the problem is that the equitable is just, but not the legally just but a correction of legal justice. The reason is that all law is universal but about some things it is not possible to make a universal statement which shall be correct. In those cases, then, in which it is necessary to speak universally, but not possible to do so correctly, the law takes the usual case, though it is not ignorant of the possibility of error. And it is none the less correct; for the error is not in the law nor in the legislator but in the nature of the thing, since the matter of practical affairs is of this kind from the start. When the law speaks universally, then, and a case arises on it which is not covered by the universal statement, then it is right, where the legislator fails us and has erred by over-simplicity, to correct the omission—to say what the legislator himself would have said had he been present, and would have put into his law if he had known. Hence the equitable is just, and better than one kind of justice—not better than absolute justice but better than the error that arises from the absoluteness of the statement. And this is the nature of the equitable, a correction of law where it is defective owing to its universality. In fact this is the reason why all things are not determined by law, viz. that about some things it is impossible to lay down a law, so that a decree is needed. For when the thing is indefinite the rule also is indefinite, like the leaden rule used in making the Lesbian moulding; the rule adapts itself to the shape of the stone and is not rigid, and so too the decree is adapted to the facts.

It is plain, then, what the equitable is, and that it is just and is better than one kind of justice. It is evident also from this who the equitable man is; the man who chooses and does such acts, and is no stickler for his rights in a bad sense but tends to take less than his share though he has the law on his side, is equitable, and this state of character is equity, which is a sort of justice and not a different state of character.


## 11

Whether a man can treat himself unjustly or not, is evident from what has been said. For (a) one class of just acts are those acts in accordance with any virtue which are prescribed by the law; e.g. the law does not expressly permit suicide, and what it does not expressly permit it forbids. Again, when a man in violation of the law harms another (otherwise than in retaliation) voluntarily, he acts unjustly, and a voluntary agent is one who knows both the person he is affecting by his action and the instrument he is using; and he who through anger voluntarily stabs himself does this contrary to the right rule of life, and this the law does not allow; therefore he is acting unjustly. But towards whom? Surely towards the state, not towards himself. For he suffers voluntarily, but no one is voluntarily treated unjustly. This is also the reason why the state punishes; a certain loss of civil rights attaches to the man who destroys himself, on the ground that he is treating the state unjustly.

Further (*b*) in that sense of 'acting unjustly' in which the man who 'acts unjustly' is unjust only and not bad all round, it is not possible to treat oneself unjustly (this is different from the former sense; the unjust man in one sense of the term is wicked in a particularized way just as the coward is, not in the sense of being wicked all round, so that his 'unjust act' does not manifest wickedness in general). For (i) that would imply the possibility of the same thing's having been subtracted from and added to the same thing at the same time; but this is impossible—the just and the unjust always involve more than one person. Further, (ii) unjust action is voluntary and done by choice, and *takes the initiative* (for the man who because he has suffered does the same in return is not thought to act unjustly); but if a man harms himself he suffers and does the same things *at the same time*. Further, (iii) if a man could treat himself unjustly, he could be voluntarily treated unjustly. Besides, (iv) no one acts unjustly without committing particular acts of injustice; but no one can commit adultery with his own wife or housebreaking on his own house or theft on his own property.

In general, the question 'can a man treat himself unjustly?' is solved also by the distinction we applied to the question 'can a man be voluntarily treated unjustly?'

(It is evident too that both are bad, being unjustly treated and acting unjustly; for the one means having less and the other having more than the intermediate amount, which plays the part here that the healthy does in the medical art, and that good condition does in the art of bodily training. But still acting unjustly is the worse, for it involves vice and is blameworthy—involves vice which is either of the complete and unqualified kind or almost so (we must admit the latter alternative, because not all voluntary unjust action implies injustice as a state of character), while being unjustly treated does not involve vice and injustice in oneself. In itself, then, being unjustly treated is less bad, but there is nothing to prevent its being incidentally a greater evil. But theory cares nothing for this; it calls pleurisy a more serious mischief than a stumble; yet the latter may become incidentally the more serious, if the fall due to it leads to your being taken prisoner or put to death by the enemy.)

Metaphorically and in virtue of a certain resemblance there is a justice, not indeed between a man and himself, but between certain parts of him; yet not every kind of justice but that of master and servant or that of husband and wife. For these are the ratios in which the part of the soul that has a rational principle stands to the irrational part; and it is with a view to these parts that people also think a man can be unjust to himself, viz. because these parts are liable to suffer something contrary to their respective desires; there is therefore thought to be a mutual justice between them as between ruler and ruled.

Let this be taken as our account of justice and the other, i.e. the other moral, virtues.

## 35

# Chaim Perelman

Chaim Perelman (1912–    ), Professor of Philosophy at the University of Brussles, has made a significant contribution to the logic of argument in law as well as to the concept of justice.

# CONCERNING JUSTICE*

It is vain to try to enumerate all the possible meanings of the idea of justice. Let us, however, give a few examples which constitute the most current conceptions of justice, and whose irreconcilable character is at once obvious:

1. To each the same thing.
2. To each according to his merits.
3. To each according to his works.
4. To each according to his needs.
5. To each according to his rank.
6. To each according to his legal entitlement.

Let us take a closer and more precise look at each of these conceptions.

### 1. *To Each The Same Thing*

According to this conception, all the people taken into account must be treated in the same way, without regard to any of their distinguishing particularities. Young or old, well or sick, rich or poor, virtuous or criminal, aristocrat or boor, white or black, guilty or innocent—it is just that all should be treated in the same way, without any discrimination or differentiation. In popular imagery the perfectly just being is death, which touches every man on the shoulder regardless of any of his privileges.

### 2. *To Each According To His Merits*

Here we have a conception of justice that no longer demands universal equality, but treatment proportional to an intrinsic quality —the merit of the human person. How are we to define this merit? What common measure are we to find between the merit or demerits of different beings? Is there, generally speaking, such a common measure? What are the criteria we must have regard to in establishing this merit? Should we have regard to the result of the action,

*Chaim Perelman, from "Concerning Justice" in *The Idea of Justice and the Problem of Argument,* New York, Humanities Press, 1963, pp. 6–26. Reprinted by permission of Humanities Press Inc. and Routledge & Kegan Paul Ltd., London.

to the intention behind it, to the sacrifice made, and, if so, how far? Ordinarily we do not answer all these questions: indeed, we do not even put them to ourselves. If we are driven into a corner we tell ourselves that it is after death that all beings will be treated in accordance with their merits; that their 'weight' of merit and demerit will be established by means of a balance; and that the result of this 'weighing' will indicate automatically, so to speak, the fate in store for them. Life beyond the grave, heaven and hell, constitute the just recompense or the just punishment for life on earth. The intrinsic moral worth of the individual will be the sole criterion of the judge, who will be blind to all other considerations.

### 3. To Each According To His Works

This conception of justice also does not call for equal treatment, but for proportional treatment. Only the criterion is no longer ethical, for regard is no longer had either to intention or to sacrifices made, but solely to the result of action.

This criterion, in that it ceases to make demands relative to the agent, we find less satisfying from the ethical point of view. But it becomes infinitely easier to apply in practice, and, instead of constituting an ideal practically impossible of realisation, this formula of justice makes it possible to take account, for the most part, only of elements which can be reckoned up, weighed and measured. It is this conception—of which incidentally several variants are possible—that underlies the payment of workers' wages, whether at time-rates or at piece-rates, and which also underlies examinations and competitions in which, regardless of the effort exerted, account is taken only of the result—the candidate's answers and the work he has shown up.

### 4. To Each According To His Needs

This formula of justice, instead of having regard to the merits of the man or of his output, seeks above all to lessen the sufferings which result from the impossibility in which he finds himself of satisfying his essential needs. It is in that respect that this formula of justice comes nearest to our conception of charity.

It goes without saying that this formula, if it is to be socially applicable, must be based on formal criteria of the needs of each person, the divergence between these criteria giving rise to the differing variants of the formula. Thus regard will be had to a basic minimum of which each man must be assured, to his family responsibilities, to the more or less precarious state of his health, to the care and attention required in his youth or his old age, etc., etc. It is this formula of justice which, making itself felt more and more in contemporary social legislation, has reversed the liberal economy in which labour, treated as though it were an article of sale, was subject to the fluctuations resulting from the law of supply and demand. Protection of labour and the worker, all the laws on the minimum wage, the limitation of hours of work, insurance against unemployment, sickness and old age, family allowances and so on—all these spring from the desire to assure to each human being the satisfaction of his most essential needs.

### 5. *To Each According To His Rank*

Here we have an aristocratic formula of justice, It consists in treating human beings, not in accordance with criteria intrinsic to the individual, but according as they belong to such or such a determined category of beings. *Quod licet Jovi non licet bovi,* says an old Latin saw. The same rules of justice do not apply to beings springing from categories which are too widely separated. Thus it is that the formula 'to each according to his rank' differs from the other formulas in that, instead of being universalist, it divides men into various categories which will be treated differently.

In antiquity different treatment was reserved for the native and the foreigner, for the free man and the slave. At the beginning of the Middle Ages the Frankish masters were treated differently from the native Gallo-Romans. Later, distinction was made between the nobles, the bourgeoisie, the clergy and the serfs bound to the soil.

At the present day white and black are treated differently in the colonies. In the army there are different rules for officers, non-commissioned officers and private soldiers. There are well-known distinctions based on criteria of race, religion, wealth, etc., etc. The characteristic which acts as a criterion is of a social nature and, for the most part, hereditary, and so independent of the will of the individual.

If we regard this formula of justice as aristocratic it is because it is always maintained and bitterly defended by its beneficiaries, who demand or enforce favourable treatment for the categories of beings whom they put forward as being superior. And this claim is normally sustained by force, whether by force of arms, or by the fact of being a majority as against a defenceless minority.

### 6. *To Each According To His Legal Entitlement*

This formula is the paraphrase of the celebrated *cuique suum* of the Romans. If to be just means to attribute to each what is his own, then, if a vicious circle is to be avoided, it is necessary to be able to determine what each man's own is. If we allow a juridical meaning to the phrase 'that which is each man's own' we arrive at the conclusion that to be just means to accord to each person what the law entitles him to.

This conception enables us to say that a judge is just, that is, impartial and uncorrupt, when he applies the same laws to the same situations (*in paribus causis paria jura*). To be just is to apply the laws of the country. This conception of justice, unlike all the previous ones, does not set itself up a judge of positive law, but limits itself to applying it.

This formula in practice naturally admits of as many variants as there are different codes of law. Each system of law assumes a justice relative to that law. What may be just under one code may not be so under another. In effect, to be just is to apply the rules of a given juridical system, and to be unjust is to misapply them.

Professor Dupréel contrasts this conception with all the others.[1] He characterises it as 'static justice', because it is based on the maintenance of the established order; and he contrasts with it all the others which are considered as forms of 'dynamic justice' because they are capable of modifying that order and the rules which define it. 'Dynamic justice is a factor of change, and appears as an instrument of the reforming or, to take its self-given name, the *progressivist* spirit. Static justice, essentially conservative, is a factor of rigidity.'[2]

This summary analysis of the most prevalent conceptions of the idea of justice has demonstrated to us the existence of at least six formulas of justice, most of them admitting numerous variants, and all of them normally irreconcilable. True, by recourse to more or less forced interpretations and to more or less arbitrary assertions one can attempt to bring one of these different formulas into line with another. Nevertheless, they present aspects of justice which are quite distinct and are for the most part mutually opposed.

Given this state of affairs, there are three possible standpoints.

The first would consist in declaring that these differing conceptions of justice have absolutely nothing in common; that characterising them in one and the same manner is improper and creates hopeless confusion; and that the only possible analysis would consist in distinguishing the different meanings, it being accepted that these meanings are not united by any conceptual link.

If this is the case we shall, if all misunderstanding is to be avoided, be driven to characterise in different fashion each one of these six conceptions. Either we shall deny the name of justice to any of them or we shall regard one of them as alone capable of being characterised as just.

This latter mode of action would lead indirectly to the second standpoint. This consists in choosing from among the various formulas of justice only one, and in trying to convince us that that is the only admissible, the only true, the only really and thoroughly just formula.

Now it is precisely this way of reasoning that we would wish to avoid at any cost; it is the one against which we have warned the reader. Whatever our reasons for choosing one formula, antagonists would advance equally valid reasons for choosing another. The debate, far from bringing about agreement, would serve only to provoke a conflict, which would be the more violent in so far as each party was more bitter in defence of his own conception. And anyway the analysis of the idea of justice would be little forwarded thereby.

That is why we give our preference to the third standpoint. This would

---

[1] *Traité de Morale,* Vol. II, pp. 485–496.
[2] *Ibid.,* Vol. II, p. 489.

shoulder the extremely delicate task of seeking out what there is in common between the various conceptions of justice that could be formulated. Or at least—to avoid the impossible requirement of seeking out the element which is common to an indefinite multitude of different conceptions—there would be an attempt to find what there is in common between the conceptions of justice most currently accepted, those, namely, that we have distinguished in the preceding pages.

### (II) FORMAL JUSTICE

For a logical analysis of the idea of justice to constitute an irrefutable step forward in the clarification of this confused notion, that analysis must succeed in giving a precise description of what there is in common between the various formulas of justice and in showing the points in which they differ. This preliminary discrimination will enable us to consider it a formula of justice on which unanimous agreement will be possible—a formula which will retain all that there is in common between the contrasting conceptions of justice.

This does not mean in the least that the disagreement prevailing between the champions of the various conceptions of justice will be reduced to nothing. The logician is not a conjurer, and it is not his job to spirit away that which exists. On the contrary, it is his duty to fix the point at which disagreement arises, bring it out into the light of day and demonstrate the reasons why, setting out from a certain common idea of justice, men nevertheless arrive at formulas that are not merely different but in fact irreconcilable.

To everyone the idea of justice inevitably suggests the notion of a certain equality. From Plato and Aristotle, through St. Thomas Aquinas, down to the jurists, moralists and philosophers of our own day runs a thread of universal agreement on this point. The notion of justice consists in a certain application of the notion of equality. The whole problem is to define this application in such fashion that, while constituting the element common to the various conceptions of justice, it leaves scope for their divergencies. This is possible only if the definition of the idea of justice contains an indeterminate element, a variable, whose various specific applications will produce the most contrasting formulas of justice.

In his treatise on 'The Three Kinds of Justice',[3] de Tourtoulon endeavours to establish a link between the differing conceptions of justice by having recourse to the notion of limit.

For him, perfect justice would consist in the complete equality of all mankind. The ideal of justice would correspond to the first of our six formulas. But this perfect equality, as everyone at once realises, cannot be achieved in practice. It can, therefore only constitute an ideal towards which we may

---

[3] P. DE TOURTOULON, *Les Trois Justices,* Paris, 1932.

strive, a mathematical limit which we can seek to approach only within the bounds of the possible. On this theory, all other conceptions of justice are no more than imperfect attempts to bring about this equality. Men try at least to bring about a partial equality, which is the easier to attain as it is further removed from the stated ideal of complete equality.

'Logically,' says de Tourtoulon,[4] 'the various conceptions of justice equality, far from being contradictory, are essentially the same. They differ only in their potentialities. Perfect equality being a limit-idea, its potentiality for being realised in practice is nil. The potentialities increase in proportion as the other egalitarian conceptions depart from this point which is set at infinity.'

'One might,' he says,[5] 'call justice charity, or equality charity, when it tries to come to the help of those who are naturally unfortunate and to secure for them the largest possible share of the satisfactions others can enjoy.

'Distributive justice has for object another kind of equality which takes account of individual capacities and efforts in conferring benefits. Its motto is— to each according to his merits. Removed as it is from equality as a mathematical limit, it comes nearer to being something that could be realised in practice.

'Commutative justice, however, is not concerned with individual life taken as a whole. It seeks to establish equality in each and every juridical act, with a view to ensuring that a contract shall not ruin one party while enriching the other. With it we may associate compensatory justice, by means of which an equality prejudiced by the fault of others is redressed . . .

'The fact that the equality contained in the idea of justice appears under so many and so different guises is often employed as a weapon in order to reject all these conceptions *en bloc* as having no logical validity. But this is far too superficial an argument. Between these differing notions of equality there is no contradiction whatever. On the contrary, they are so many points that, taken on an abscissa whose limit is "perfect equality", come nearer and nearer to the ordinate constituted by the "potentiality of being realised".'

This conception undeniably represents a worthy attempt at the understanding of the idea of justice. Two objections may be advanced against it.

The first objection is this. The conception, faced with the various formulas of justice, makes the arbitrary choice of a single one; and this seems, with good reason, quite unacceptable to very many, if not most, consciences. Are all men to be treated in the same fashion without regard to their merits, their deeds, their origin, their needs, their talents or their vices? A great many moralists would be entitled to rise up against this pseudo-justice, of which the most that could be said is that from no point of view does it make itself felt as necessary.

The second objection is decisive from the point of view of logic. It is that the link which de Tourtoulon would like to establish between the different conceptions of justice is quite illusory. In effect, if it were the function of the

4 *Ibid.*, p. 47.
5 P. DE TOURTOULON, *Les Trois Justices*, pp. 48–49.

different formulas of justice to promote partial equalities, then either they ought to have flowed one from another by syllogism, like a part contained in the whole; or else they should have been capable of complementing one another, like two different parts of one and the same whole. Now, whatever de Tourtoulon may say, the different formulas of justice frequently contradict one another. It is usually impossible to reconcile the formulas 'to each according to his merits' and 'to each according to his needs', not to mention the other formulas which ought, taken as a whole, to form a coherent system. In any case, the best proof of the impossibility of resuming all the formulas of justice in the one which advocates the perfect equality of all mankind is this: the champions of the other conceptions of justice rebel against it, regarding it not only as arbitrary but also as utterly opposed to our innate sense of justice.

In contrast to de Tourtoulon's idea (which regards the differing conceptions of justice as resulting from a different interpretation of the expression 'the same thing' in the formula 'to each the same thing') one might try to reduce the divergencies to a differing interpretation of the notion of 'each' in the same formula.

Aristotle observed long since that it was necessary that there should exist a certain likeness between the beings to whom justice is administered. Historically, indeed, it can be stated plausibly enough that justice began by being administered to the members of one and the same family, to be extended later to the members of the tribe, the inhabitants of the city, then of a territory, with, as the final outcome, the notion of a justice for all mankind.

In an interesting article [6] Tisset says, 'There must exist between individuals something in common whereby a partial identity may be established, if there is to be any attempt to realise justice as between them. Where there is no common measure, and therefore no identity, the question of realising justice does not even arise. And it may be noted that to this day the principle, in the human intellect, remains unchanged. There can, for instance, be no question of justice in the relations between men and plants. If today the idea of justice has been more widely extended and applies to all mankind, the reason is that man has come to recognise all his fellows as his fellows: the idea of humanity has little by little emerged . . .'

*A priori,* the field in which justice can and should be applied is not laid down. It is therefore susceptible of variation. Every time we speak of 'each' in a formula of justice we may be thinking of a different group of beings. This variation in the field of application of the idea of 'each' to variable groups will produce variants not only of the formula 'to each the same thing' but also of all the other formulas. But this is not the way in which it will be possible to solve the problem we have set ourselves. Indeed, far from demonstrating the existence of an element common to the different formulas of justice, the foregoing reflections prove, on the contrary, that each one of the formulas can in turn be interpreted in different ways and give rise to a very large number of variants.

[6] TISSET, 'Les Notions de Droit et de Justice', *Revue de Métaphysique et de Morale,* 1930, p. 66.

Let us, then, after these unfruitful attempts, take up our problem again from the very beginning. The question is to find a formula of justice which is common to the different conceptions we have analysed. This formula must contain an indeterminate element—what in mathematics is called a variable— the determination of which will give now one, now another, conception of justice. The common idea will constitute a definition of *formal* or *abstract* justice. Each particular or *concrete* formula of justice will constitute one of the innumerable values of formal justice.

Is it possible to define formal justice? Is there a conceptual element common to all the formulas of justice? Apparently, yes. In effect, we all agree on the fact that to be just is to treat in equal fashion. Unfortunately, difficulties and controversies arise as soon as precision is called for. Must everyone be treated in the same way, or must we draw distinctions? And if distinctions must be drawn, which ones must we take into account in administering justice? Each man puts forward a different answer to these questions. Each man advocates a different system. No system is capable of securing the adherence of all. Some say that regard must be had to the individual's merits. Others that the individual's needs must be taken into consideration. Yet others say it is impossible to disregard origin, rank, etc.

But despite all their differences, they all have something in common in their attitude. He who requires merit to be taken into account wants the same treatment for persons having equal merits. A second wants equal treatment to be provided for persons having the same needs. A third will demand just, that is, equal, treatment for persons of the same social rank and so on. Whatever, then, their disagreement on other points, they are all agreed that to be just is to give the same treatment to those who are equal from some particular point of view, who possess one characteristic, the same, *and the only one to which regard must be had in the adminstration of justice.* Let us qualify this characteristic as *essential.* If the possession of any characteristic whatever always makes it possible to group people in a class or category defined by the fact that its members possess the characteristic in question, people having an essential characteristic in common will form part of one and the same category, the same essential category.

We can, then define formal or abstract justice as *a principle of action in accordance with which beings of one and the same essential category must be treated in the same way.*

Be it noted at once that the definition we have just offered is of a purely formal idea, leaving untouched and entire all the differences that arise in respect of concrete justice. Our definition tells us neither when two beings participate in an essential category nor how they ought to be treated. We know that beings must be treated not in such or such a manner, but equally, so that it is impossible to say that one has been placed at a disadvantage by reference to another. We know, too, that equal treatment must be provided only for beings forming part of the same essential category.

The six formulas of concrete justice, among which we have been seeking as it were a common denominator, differ in as much as each one of them regards a different characteristic as the only one to be taken account of in administering justice. In other words, they determine membership of the same essential category in different ways. Equally, however, they indicate, with more or less precision, how the members of the same essential category ought to be treated.

Our definition of justice is formal for the reason that it does not lay down the categories that are essential for the adminstration of justice. It makes it possible for the differences to come into play at the point of transition from a common formula of formal justice to differing formulas of concrete justice. Disagreement arises as soon as it comes to settling the criteria essential for the administration of justice.

Let us take up again one by one our different formulas of concrete justice and show how they are all differing resolutions of the same conception of formal justice.

### 1. To Each The Same Thing

The conception of justice advanced by this formula is the only purely egalitarian one, in contrast to all the others, which call for a certain degree of proportionality. In effect, all the beings to whom it is desired to administer justice form part of one single and unique essential category. Whether we are concerned with all mankind or merely with a few kinsmen taking part in the sharing of an inheritance, all those brought into consideration when we speak of 'each' have no other distinguishing characteristic. The view is taken that no characteristics other than those that have served to determine the totality of persons to whom the formula 'to each the same thing' must be applied can be taken into account; that the differences between these persons are not, from this point of view, essential.

This leads us, in considering the qualities that differentiate one person from another, to distinguish those qualities that are essential from the secondary qualities which are irrelevant for the administration of justice. Admittedly, the debate on distinguishing essential from secondary qualities could not be settled to everyone's satisfaction. Its solution would bring with it the solution of all other problems concerning values.

The formula 'to each the same thing' may establish an egalitarian conception of justice. It does not necessarily coincide with an egalitarian humanitarianism. Indeed, to make that true, it would be necessary that the class of beings to whom it was desired to apply the formula should consist of all mankind. It is, however, possible for this application to be limited to a much smaller category. Sparta applied this egalitarian formula to none but the 'homoioi', the aristocrats, the superior class of the population. It would never have occurred to the 'homoioi' of Sparta to try to apply this conception of justice to the other strata of the population, with which they felt they had nothing in common.

The same phenomenon is to be found in an analogous institution, notwithstanding that it arose in quite different circumstances of time and space— that of the peers of France and of England. The uppermost stratum of the aristocracy, recognising nothing higher than itself, expects the same treatment for all its members, as being equal one with another and superior to everyone else.

We see, then, that the egalitarian formula of justice, so far from manifesting an attachment to a humanitarian ideal, may constitute nothing better than a means of strengthening the links of solidarity within a class regarding itself as incomparably superior to the other inhabitants of the country.

In so far as we can arbitrarily determine the category of beings to whom egalitarian justice is applicable, we are enabled to show the points in which this formula, rather than the others, appears to give real effect to the ideal of perfect justice.

Indeed, on the basis of the formula we can succeed in framing a second definition of formal justice. All that is necessary is to specify that by 'each one' is meant the members of the same essential category. Thus we get the formula 'to each member of the same essential category, the same thing', which is equivalent in every point to the definition of formal justice we offered earlier. It was, perhaps, this possibility that was unconsciously glimpsed by de Tourtoulon when he thought to make of the egalitarian formula the unattainable ideal of perfect justice.

## 2. *To Each According To His Merits*

This formula of justice requires beings to be treated in proportion with their merits. That is, beings forming part of the same category so far as concerns their merit—and the degrees of merit will serve as criteria for settling the essential categories—are to be treated in the same way.

Let us observe that the application of justice in proportion with the degree of intensity of a quality susceptible of variation, such as merit, raises problems of logic which are elucidated in a striking work by Messrs. Hempel and Oppenheim.[7]

To form part of the same essential category is not merely a matter of possessing one identical given characteristic. It must be possessed in the same *degree*. If two people are to be treated in the same way it is not enough that each should have merit. They must further have that merit to the same degree.

We must, then, have available for the application of this formula a criterion which will enable us either to measure the degree of merit—if we wish the rewards to be numerically comparable—or else to range beings according to the size of their merit, if we want higher merit to receive a higher reward. Naturally, the reward must be capable of varying to the same extent as the merit, if, that is, strict proportionality is desired.

If, in the administration of justice, we are not content with giving rewards but also wish to be able to punish, the idea of merit must be widened so as to take in demerit also.

[7] C. HEMPEL and P. OPPENHEIM, *Der Typusbegriff im Lichte der Neuen Logik*, The Hague, 1937.

In order that two people should have the same conception of concrete justice, it is not enough that they should both wish to apply the formula 'to each according to his merits'. They must also accord the same degree of merit to the same acts, and their system of rewards or penalties must be equivalent.

For two people to judge in the same way when applying the formula 'to each according to his merits', they must not only have the desire to apply the same formula of concrete justice. They must further have the same statement of the facts submitted to their consideration.

A judgment could be characterised as unjust—

1. Because it applied a formula of concrete justice which is not accepted.
2. Because its conception of the same formula of justice was a different one.
3. Because it was founded on an inadequate statement of the facts.
4. Because it infringed the specification of formal justice requiring the same treatment for beings forming part of one and the same essential category.

Let us at once observe that the two first reasons are very often based on an equivocation. In effect, they are valid only in so far as the judge is bound to observe certain rules of justice, which is what happens in law, but never in ethics. In principle, a person cannot be considered unjust simply because he applies a different formula of concrete justice. For example, a man cannot be required to make an equal distribution when, according to him, the distribution ought to be made in proportion with the needs of each of the beneficiaries. Since injustice consists in violating the rules of concrete justice in accordance with which one is supposed to be judging, an act cannot be regarded as unjust if the formula of justice employed to criticise the judgement is not that of the judge.

If the judge violates the rules of concrete justice he has himself accepted, then he is unjust. He is so involuntarily if his judgment proceeds from an inadequate presentation of the facts. He is so voluntarily only when he infringes the specifications of formal justice.

### 3. To Each According To His Works

The formula of concrete justice 'to each according to his works' is arrived at by considering as forming part of the same essential category those whose production or knowledge have equal value in the eyes of the judge. If, from a certain standpoint, certain works or certain pieces of knowledge are regarded as equivalent, the same treatment must be accorded to those who have performed the work or whose knowledge is under examination.

This formula of justice is usually employed when it comes to remunerating workmen or marking candidates in an examination or competition.

Society has invented a tool for the common measure of labor and its products—namely, money. The ideas of 'just wage' and 'just price' are merely applications of the formula 'to each according to his works'. But it is very difficult to determine the just wage and the just price, seeing how disturbing are the effects of the law of supply and demand.

If it is desired to fix wages proportionally to the work carried out, account can be taken of the duration of the work, its output and its quality, this last usually varying with the length of the period of apprenticeship. But acceptable results can be obtained by proceeding in this way only so long as the work in question is such that its performance does not call for special capacity. For, as soon as there is need for a certain degree of talent, not to mention genius, to bring a task to completion, the common measure breaks down. That is why in such a case we usually prefer to judge the task on its own merits, with the help of its intinsic qualities—to take stock of the result of the work rather than use as a basis the time necessary to carry out the task in question. The same applies to examinations and to competitions, where, instead of trying to measure the industry of the candidate, one is content to test his knowledge in the light or the work which he submits.

In all such cases we give up the attempt to establish a common measure for all tasks and remain content with comparing those for which a like criterion is accepted—tasks of the same kind. We will not attempt to compare pictures with works of literature, or symphonies with works of architecture. It may be true that at first sight the price of these works may seem to offer such a common measure, but that can be the case only when we are assured that this price is the just price, that is to say that it corresponds to their value. Now, if the price constitutes the sole element of comparison between works it is impossible to see how to determine their value in order to be able to know whether the price is just or not.

On the other hand, when it comes to comparing not works but knowledge, as in the case of an examination, recourse to money as a standard of measurement is not merely insufficient but quite impossible. The examiner can then judge the candidates only by reference to a purely internal criterion, the requirements which he himself formulates in the matter. The examination will make it possible to establish a relation between these requirements and the candidate's answers.

The examination postulates a kind of convention between the parties. In order to be able to submit to it, the candidate must be in a position to know the requirements of the judge. That is why the judge is accused of injustice every time he fails to observe the rules of the convention and sets a question 'which is not in the syllabus'.

In order to be able to compare candidates judged by different examiners on the basis of different syllabuses, we must be able to establish a relation between those syllabuses and also to assume that the judges evaluate the candidates' failings in the same way. As these comparisons are normally made only on practical and purely formal grounds—equivalence of diplomas, for example— the rival syllabuses ordinarily have reference to knowledge of the same kind, while, in the absence of special reasons, the differences between the examiners are disregarded.

Whereas the formula 'to each according to his merits' has its claims to universality in that it asserts its ability to constitute a common measure applicable to all men, the application of the formula 'to each according to his works' usually makes claims that are more modest and more immediately useful. When it comes to comparing work or knowledge, this latter formula of justice, which is one of the most common in social life, is limited, in the absence of a universal criterion and for purely practical reasons, to the comparison of work and of knowledge of the same kind.

### 4. *To Each According To His Needs*

The application of this formula calls for like treatment of those who form part of the same essential category from the point of view of their needs.

In social life it is only quite exceptionally that the application of this formula will be preceded by a psychological study of the needs of the men under consideration. In effect, we do not wish to take account of the individual's every whim, but only of his most essential needs, those alone that are to be retained in putting the formula into practical effect. The formula ought rather to be enunciated as 'to each according to his essential needs'. This limitation will at once give rise to argument about what is to be understood by 'essential needs', the differing conceptions producing variants of this formula of justice.

Often enough indeed, for the sake of facilitating the application of this formula, there will be a tendency to disregard needs that are considered important but whose existence is difficult either to discover or to check. Usually the attempt will be to determine these needs with the help of purely formal criteria, taking as a basis the requirements of the human organism in general. Only in so far as the application of this formula is restricted to a limited number of persons can the particular needs of each one be brought progressively into account. One of the most delicate problems of statistics in social affairs is to settle the details the inquiry is to concern itself with, given the number of persons to whom it extends. In its application to large numbers, such an inquiry will for preference take account only of numerically measurable elements, such as, for example, the number and ages of the persons in a family, the amount of money available to them, the number of calories in their diet, the cubic footage of air in their dwelling, the number of hours allotted to work, rest, leisure, etc.

Only rarely do we try to apply the formula 'to each according to his needs' to more refined and more individual needs. Indeed—and this is the difference between charity and this formula of justice which comes closest to charity—justice can be applied only to beings considered as elements of a whole, of the essential category. Whereas charity has regard to beings as individuals and takes account of the characteristics proper to them, justice, on the other hand, tends to discount the elements that are not common to a number of beings—their individual peculiarities, in fact. He who seeks out of charity to satisfy the desire of his neighbour will go to more trouble to take into account the individual and psychological factor than will the man moved by his conception of justice.

The man who desires to apply the formula 'to each according to his needs' will have not only to establish a distinction between essential needs and other needs but also to range the essential needs in an order of importance. Thus it will be known which needs call for priority in satisfaction, and the price of that satsifaction will be determined. This operation will lead on to the definition of the idea of the basic minimum.

Everyone knows what bitter controversies have been roused by this notion and all the ideas associated with it. Almost all the differences arising in this connection result from a different conception of the essential needs of man, that is to say, of the needs that ought to be taken into account by a social justice based on the principle 'to each according to his needs'—a justice that works towards settling the obligations of society towards each of its members.

## 5. *To Each According To His Rank*

The application of this formula assumes that the beings in respect of whom one would wish to be just are divided into classes, usually, though not necessarily, ranged in a hierarchical order. This formula regards it as just to adopt a different attitude towards the members of the various classes, provided that the same treatment is given to those who form part of the same class, that is to say, of the same essential category.

This division into classes, in the broad sense, can be effected in various ways. It can be based on the colour of the skin, on language, on religion or on the fact of belonging to a social class, to a caste or to an ethnic group. The subdivision of human beings can also be effected in accordance with their functions, their responsibilities and so on.

It is possible for the classes so distinguished not to be ranged in order. To treat the members of one class in a different way from those of another might not be favorable in all respects to a given category. Most often, however, the various classes are ranged in order. The upper classes, the privileged classes, enjoy more rights than the others. But ordered societies, according as they are in full flower or decadent, will impose greater burdens of duty on their élites or else will establish no correspondence between the rights accorded and the duties or responsibilities. The saying *noblesse oblige* is the expression of an aristocracy conscious of its specific duties and realising that it is only by paying that price that it will succeed in justifying its privileged situation.

Generally speaking, a régime is workable only if each member of its upper class is made to face his responsibilities, and if the rights accorded to him flow from the burdens laid on him. Where specific rights do not coincide with special responsibilities, the régime, thanks to the generalising of the factor of the arbitrary, will soon degenerate into a system of calculated favouritism—an 'old boy network'.

These reflections are applicable not only to régimes in which superior status goes by birth but also to quite different régimes, such as the democratic.

In effect, in every régime there exists a superior class, the class which has at its disposal power and force in the state. A régime will be workable in the long run only if the demands laid on this class are quite specific and if the severity exercised in calling each individual's management to account is proportional to the responsibilities he has undertaken.

### 6. *To Each According To His Legal Entitlement*

This formula of justice is to be distinguished from all the others in that the judge, the person made responsible for applying it, is not now free to choose the conception of justice he prefers: he is bound to observe the established rules. Classification, division into essential categories—these are laid down for him, and he must, as a matter of obligation, take account of them. Here we have the fundamental distinction between the ethical and the juridical conceptions of justice.

In ethics, there is freedom to choose the formula of justice that one intends to apply and the interpretation that one desires to give it. In law, the formula of justice is laid down, and its interpretation is made subject to the control of the highest court of the state. In ethics, the rule adopted is the result of the free adherence of the conscience. In law, it is necessary to consult the established order. In ethics, he who judges has first to settle the categories in accordance with which he will judge, then to see which are the categories applicable to the facts. In law, the sole problem to be entertained is that of knowing how the facts under consideration fit into the established juridical system, and how they are to be characterised. In modern law the two authorities—the one which settles the categories and the one which applies them—are rigously kept apart. In ethics, they are united in the same conscience.

In law, how far has the judge, in the exercise of his functions, the means of bringing to bear his own particular conception of justice? How far is the law influenced by ethical conceptions?

The answer to the first question will be different according as by judge is meant any individual official whatever having the responsibility of administering justice, or jurisprudence as a whole. Even in the case of a judge who rests content with following the beaten tracks of jurisprudence and has no desire for innovation, his role is not entirely passive. Indeed, since every vision of reality is to some extent subjective—the more so in that it is a question of a reconstruction rather than of a direct vision—the upright judge will, even involuntarily, be led, in his evaluation of the facts, to make the law and his own inner feeling for justice coincide. By taking his stand on certain evidence or by denying its importance, by having regard to certain facts or by so interpreting them as to deprive them of all meaning, the judge is able to produce a different picture of reality and to deduce from it a different application of the rules of justice.

As for jurisprudence, in so far as it interprets the laws, it can even go farther. On it depends the definition of all the confused ideas, all the equivocal expressions, of the law. It will be for it an easy matter to define those ideas and to interpret those expressions in such fashion that the judge's feeling of justice and the exigencies of the law shall not clash too violently. In some cases, when laws were in question whose meaning was difficult to distort, jurisprudence has even been content quite simply to forget their existence, and by dint of not administering them has caused them to fall into desuetude. In Roman law the *praetor* could allow himself to take advantage of fictions so as to modify the application of the categories established by the law, whereas now the determination of those categories is the work of the legislator. He will make it his business to give legal force to the conception of justice of those who hold power in the state.

*A priori,* nothing can be said of the ethical character of the law, of the way in which the categories established by the legislator coincide with those of the mass of the population. Everything depends on the relation between that mass and those who hold power. According as these latter are or are not the true reflection of the majority of the nation, the juridical categories laid down will coincide more or less with popular feeling. In any democratic régime the law, albeit with some delay, follows the evolution undergone by the conception of justice in the minds of the majority of the citizens. During the period for which there is failure to correspond, jurisprudence makes it is business, as best it may, to reduce to a minimum the disadvantages due to the inevitable slowness of the legislative power.

Can justice conflict with law? Is there an unjust law? The question can be put in this way only if no account is taken of the distinction we have established between formal justice and concrete justice. Indeed, an attempt to judge law in the name of justice is possible only by means of a confusion. Law will be judged by means, not of formal justice, but of concrete justice, that is of a particular conception of justice which assumes a settled scale of values. In effect, we shall not condemn or reform in the name of justice, but in the name of a vision of the universe—sublime perhaps, but in any case regarded arbitrarily as the only just one. Whereas one conception of the world is condemned by means of another, we must not say that law is condemned in the name of justice, unless, that is, we want to create confusions advantageous only to the sophists. Indeed, positive law can never enter into conflict with formal justice, seeing that all it does is to establish the categories of which formal justice speaks, and without whose establishment the administration of justice is quite impossible.

## 36

## John Rawls

John Rawls' article reprinted here represents an early version of a modern social contract theory still in the process of being formulated.

## JUSTICE AS FAIRNESS*[1]

The fundamental idea in the concept of justice is that of fairness. It is this aspect of justice for which utilitarianism, in its classical form, is unable to account, but which is represented, even if misleadingly so, in the idea of the social contract. To establish these propositions I shall develop, but of necessity only very briefly, a particular conception of justice by stating two principles which specify it and by considering how they may be thought to arise. The parts of this conception are familiar; but perhaps it is possible by using the notion of fairness as a framework to assemble and to look at them in a new way.

1. Throughout I discuss justice as a virtue of institutions constituting restrictions as to how they may define offices and powers, and assign rights and duties; and not as a virtue of particular actions, or persons. Justice is but one of many virtues of institutions, for these may be inefficient, or degrading, or any of a number of things, without being unjust. Essentially justice is the elimination of arbitrary distinctions and the establishment, within the structure of a practice, of a proper balance between competing claims. I do not argue that the principles given below are *the* principles of justice. It is sufficient for my purposes that they be typical of the family of principles which might reasonably be called principles of justice as shown by the background against which they may be thought to arise.

The first principle is that each person participating in a practice, or affected by it, has an equal right to the most extensive liberty compatible with a like liberty for all; and the second is that inequalities are arbitrary unless it is reasonable to expect that they will work out for everyone's advantage and unless the offices to which they attach, or from which they may be gained, are open to all. These principles express justice as a complex of three ideas: liberty, equality, and reward for contributions to the common advantage.

*John Rawls, "Justice as Fairness," *The Journal of Philosophy*, LIV (1957), pp. 653–662. Reprinted be permission of the author and the editors of *The Journal of Philosophy*. In as yet unpublished and widely circulated manuscripts Professor Rawls has extensively modified and expanded upon this early statement of the 'justice as fairness' thesis.
[1] Considerations of space have made it impossible to give appropriate references. I must, however, mention that in the second paragraph of section 3 I am indebted to H. L. A. Hart. See his paper "Are There Any Natural Rights?", *Philosophical Review*, LXIV (1955), pp. 185 f.

The first principle holds, of course, only *ceteris paribus:* while there must always be a justification for departing from the initial position of equal liberty (which is defined by the pattern of rights and duties), and the burden of proof is placed upon him who would depart from it, nevertheless, there can be, and often there is, a justification for doing so. One can view this principle as containing the principle that similar cases be judged similarly, or if distinctions are made in the handling of cases, there must be some relevant difference between them (a principle which follows from the concept of a judgement of any kind). It could be argued that justice requires only an equal liberty; but if a greater liberty were possible for all without loss or conflict, then it would be irrational to settle on a lesser liberty. There is no reason for circumscribing rights until they mutually interfere with one another. Therefore no serious distortion of the concept of justice is likely to follow from including within it the concept of the greatest equal liberty instead of simply equal liberty.

The second principle specifies what sorts of inequalities are permissible, where by inequalities it seems best to understand not any difference between offices and positions, since structural differences are not usually an issue (people do not object to there being different offices as such, and so to there being the offices of president, senator, governor, judge, and so on), but differences in the benefits and burdens attached to them either directly or indirectly, such as prestige and wealth, or liability to taxation and compulsory service. An inequality is allowed only if there is reason to believe that the practice with the inequality will work to the advantage of *every* party. This is interpreted to require, first, that there must normally be evidence acceptable to common sense and based on a common fund of knowledge and belief which shows that this is in fact likely to be the case. The principle does not rule out, however, arguments of a theological or metaphysical kind to justify inequalities (e.g., a religious basis for a caste system) provided they belong to common belief and are freely acknowledged by people who may be presumed to know what they are doing.

Second, an inequality must work for the common advantage; and since the principle applies to practices, this implies that the representative man in *every* office or position of the practice, when he views it as a going institution, must find it reasonable to prefer his condition and prospects with the inequality to what they would be without it. And finally, the various offices to which special benefits and burdens attach are required to be open to all; and so if, for example, it is to the common advantage to attach benefits to offices (because by doing so not only is the requisite talent attracted to them, but encouraged to give its best efforts once there), they must be won in a fair competition in which contestants are judged on their merits. If some offices were not open, those excluded would normally be justified in feeling wronged, even if they benefited from the greater efforts of those who were allowed to compete for them. Assuming that offices are open, it is necessary only to consider the design of the practices themselves and how they jointly, as a system, work together. It is a mistake to fix attention on the varying relative positions of particular persons and to think that each such change, as a once-for-all transaction, must be in itself just. The system must be judged from a general point of view: unless one is prepared to criticize it from the standpoint of a representative man holding some particular office, one has no complaint against it.

2. Given these principles, one might try to derive them from *a priori* principles of reason, or offer them as known by intuition. These are familiar steps, and, at least in the case of the first principle, might be made with some success. I wish, however, to look at the principles in a different way.

Consider a society where certain practices are already established, and whose members are mutually self-interested: their allegiance to the established practices is founded on the prospect of self-advantage. It need not be supposed that they are incapable of acting from any other motive: if one thinks of the members of this society as families, the individuals thereof may be bound by ties of sentiment and affection. Nor must they be mutually self-interested under all circumstances, but only under those circumstances in which they ordinarily participate in their common practices. Imagine also that the persons in this society are rational: they know their own interests more or less accurately; they are capable of tracing out the likely consequences of adopting one practice rather than another and of adhering to a decision once made; they can resist present temptations and attractions of immediate gain; and the knowledge, or the perception, of the difference between their condition and that of others is not, in itself, a source of great dissatisfaction. Finally, they have roughly similar needs and interests and are sufficiently equal in power and ability to assure that in normal circumstances none is able to dominate the others.

Now suppose that on some particular occasion several members of this society come together to discuss whether any of them has a legitimate complaint against their established institutions. They try first to arrive at the prinicples by which complaints, and so practices themselves, are to be judged. Their procedure for this is the following: each is to propose the principles upon which he wishes his complaints to be tried with the understanding that, if acknowledged, the complaints of others will be similarly tried, and that no complaints will be heard at all until everyone is roughly of one mind as to how complaints are to be judged. They understand further that the principles proposed and acknowledged on this occasion are to be binding on future occasions. Thus each will be wary of proposing principles which give him a peculiar advantage, supposing them to be accepted, in his present circumstances, since he will be bound by it in future cases the circumstances of which are unknown and in which the principle might well be to his detriment. Everyone is, then, forced to make in advance a firm commitment, which others also may reasonably be expected to make, and no one is able to tailor the canons of a legitimate complaint to fit his own special condition. Therefore each person will propose principles of a general kind which will, to a large degree, gain their sense from the various applications to be made of them. These principles will express the conditions in accordance with which each is least unwilling to have his interests limited in the design of practices on the supposition that the interests of others will be limited likewise.

The restrictions which would so arise might be thought of as those a person would keep in mind if he were designing a practice in which the enemy were to assign him his place.

In this account of a hypothetical society the character and respective situations of the parties reflect the circumstances in which questions of justice may be said to arise, and the procedure whereby principles are proposed and acknowledged represents constraints, analogous to those of having a morality, whereby rational and mutually self-interested parties are brought to act reasonably. Given all conditions as described, it would be natural to accept the two principles of justice. Since there is no way for anyone to win special advantage for himself, each might consider it reasonable to acknowledge equality as an initial principle. There is, however, no reason why they should regard this position as final; for if there are inequalities which satisfy the second principle, the immediate gain which equality would allow can be considered as intelligently invested in view of its future return. If, as is quite likely, these inequalities work as incentives to draw out better efforts, the members of this society may look upon them as concessions to human nature: they, like us, may think that people ideally should want to serve one another. But as they are mutually self-interested, their acceptance of these inequalities is merely the acceptance of the relations in which they actually stand. They have no title to complain of one another. And so, provided the conditions of the principle are met, there is no reason why they should reject such inequalities in the design of their social practices. Indeed, it would be short-sighted of them to do so, and could result, it seems, only from their being dejected by the bare knowledge, or perceptions, that others are better situated. Each person will, however, insist on a common advantage, for none is willing to sacrifice anything for the others.

These remarks are not, of course, offered as a proof that persons so circumstanced would settle upon the two principles, but only to show that the principles of justice could have such a background; and so can be viewed as those principles which mutually self-interested and rational persons, when similarly situated and required to make in advance a firm commitment, could acknowledge as restrictions governing the assignment of rights and duties in their common practices, and thereby accept as limiting their rights against one another.

3. That the principles of justice can be regarded in this way is an important fact about them. It brings out the idea that fundamental to justice is the concept of fairness which relates to right dealing between persons who are cooperating with or competing against one another, as when one speaks of fair games, fair competition, and fair bargains. The question of fairness arises when free persons, who have no authority over one another, are engaging in a joint activity and amongst themselves settling or acknowledging the rules which define it and which determine the respective shares in its benefits and burdens. A practice will strike the parties as fair if none feels that, by participating in it, he, or any of the others, is taken advantage of, or forced to give in to claims which he does not regard as legitimate. This implies that each has a conception of legitimate claims which he thinks it reasonable that others as well as himself should acknow-

ledge. If one thinks of the principles of justice as arising in the way described, then they do define this sort of conception. A practice is just, then, when it satisfies the principles which those who participate in it could propose to one another for mutual acceptance under the aforementioned circumstances. Persons engaged in a just, or fair, practice can face one another honestly, and support their respective positions, should they appear questionable, by reference to principles which it is reasonable to expect each to accept. It is this notion of the possibility of mutual acknowledgment which makes the concept of fairness fundamental to justice. Only if such acknowledgment is possible, can there be true community between persons in their common practices; otherwise their relations will appear to them as founded to some extent on force and violence. If, in ordinary speech, fairness applies more particularly to practices in which there is a choice whether to engage or not, and justice to practices in which there is no choice and one must play, the element of necessity does not alter the basic conception of the possibility of mutual acceptance, although it may make it much more urgent to change unjust that unfair institutions.

Now if the participants in a practice accept its rules as fair, and so have no complaint to lodge against it, there arises a prima facie duty (and a corresponding prima facie right) of the parties to each other to act in accordance with the practice when it falls upon them to comply. When any number of persons engage in a practice, or conduct a joint undertaking, according to rules, and thus restrict their liberty, those who have submitted to these restrictions when required have a right to a similar acquiesence on the part of those who have benefited by their submission. These conditions will, of course, obtain if a practice is correctly acknowledged to be fair, for in this case, all who participate in it will benefit from it. The rights and duties so arising are special rights and duties in that they depend on previous voluntary actions—in this case, on the parties' having engaged in a common practice and accepted its benefits. It is not, however, an obligation which presupposes a deliberate performative act in the sense of a promise, or contract, and the like. It is sufficient that one has knowingly participated in a practice acknowledged to be fair and accepted the resulting benefits. This prima facie obligation may, of course, be overridden: it may happen, when it comes one's turn to follow a rule, that other considerations will justify not doing so. But one cannot, in general, be released from this obligation by denying the justice of the practice only when it falls on one to obey. If a person rejects a practice, he should, as far as possible, declare his intention in advance, and avoid participating in it or accepting its benefits.

This duty may be called that of fair play, which is, perhaps, to extend the ordinary notion; for acting unfairly is usually not so much the breaking of any particular rule, even if the infraction is difficult to detect (cheating), but taking advantage of loopholes or ambiguities in rules, availing oneself of unexpected or special circumstances which make it impossible to enforce them, insisting that rules be enforced when they should be suspended, and, more generally, acting contrary to the intention of a practice .(Thus one speaks of the sense of fair play: acting fairly is not simply following rules; what is fair must be felt or perceived.) Nevertheless, it is not an unnatural extension of the duty of fair play to have it include the obligation which participants in a common practice owe to each other to act in accordance with it when their performance falls due. Consider the tax dodger, or the free rider.

The duty of fair play stands beside those of fidelity and gratitude as a fundamental moral notion; and like them it implies a constraint on self-interest in particular cases. I make this point to avoid a misunderstanding: the conception of the mutual acknowledgment of principles under special circumstances is used to analyze the concept of justice. I do not wish to imply that the acceptance of justice in actual conduct depends solely on an existing equality of conditions. My own view, which is perhaps but one of several compatible with the preceding analysis, and which I can only suggest here, is that the acknowledgment of the duty of fair play, as shown in acting on it, and wishing to make amends and the like when one has been at fault, is one of the forms of conduct in which participants in a common practice show their recognition of one another as persons. In the same way that, failing a special explanation, the criterion for the recognition of suffering is helping him who suffers, acknowledging the duty of fair play is the criterion for recognizing another as a person with similar capacities, interests, and feelings as oneself. The acceptance by participants in a common practice of this duty is a reflection in each of the recognition of the aspirations of the others to be realized by their joint activity. Without this acceptance they would recognize one another as but complicated objects in a complicated routine. To recognize another as a person one must respond to him and act towards him as one; and these forms of action and response include, among other things, acknowledging the duty of fair play. These remarks are unhappily obscure; their purpose here is to forestall the misunderstanding mentioned above.

The conception at which we have arrived, then, it that the principles of justice may be thought of as arising once the constraints of having a morality are imposed upon rational and mutually self-interested parties who are related and situated in a special way. A practice is just if it is in accordance with the principles which all who participate in it might reasonably be expected to propose or to acknowledge before one another when they are similarly circumstanced and required to make a firm commitment in advance; and thus when it meets standards which the parties could accept as fair should occasion arise for them to debate its merits. Once persons knowingly engage in a practice which they acknowledge to be fair and accept the benefits of doing so, they are bound by the duty of fair play which implies a limitation on self-interest in particular cases.

Now if a claim fails to meet this conception of justice there is no moral value in granting it, since it violates the conditions of reciprocity and community amongst persons: he who presses it, not being willing to acknowledge it when pressed by another, has no grounds for complaint when it is denied; whereas him against whom it is pressed can complain. As it cannot be mutually acknowledged, it is a resort to coercion: granting the claim is only possible of one party can compel what the other will not admit. Thus in deciding on the justice of a practice it is not enough to ascertain that it answers to wants and interest in the fullest and most effective manner. For if any of these be such that they conflict with justice, they should not be counted; their satisfaction is no reason for having a practice. It makes no sense to concede claims the denial of which gives rise to no complaint in preference to claims the denial of which can be objected to. It would be irrelevant to say, even if true, that it resulted in the greatest satisfaction of desire.

4. This conception of justice differs from that of the stricter form of utilitarianism (Bentham and Sidgwick), and its counterpart in welfare economics, which assimilates justice to benevolence and the latter in turn to the most efficient design of institutions to promote the general welfare. Now it is said occasionally that this form of utilitarianism puts no restrictions on what might be a just assignment of rights and duties. But this is not so. Beginning with the notion that the general happiness can be represented by a social utility function consisting of the sum of individual utility functions with identical weights (this being the meaning of the maxim that each counts for one and no more than one), it is commonly assumed that the utility functions of individuals are similar in all essential respects. Differences are laid to accidents of education and upbringing, and should not be taken into account; and this assumption, coupled with that of diminishing marginal utility, results in a prima facie case for equality. But even if such restrictions are built into the utility function, and have, in practice, much the same results as the application of the principles of justice (and appear, perhaps, to be ways of expressing these principles in the language of mathematics and psychology), the fundamental idea is very different from the conception of justice as reciprocity. Justice is interpreted as the contingent result of a higher order administrative decision whose form is similar to that of an entrepreneur deciding how much to produce of this or that commodity in view of its marginal revenue, or to that of someone distributing goods to needy persons according to the relative urgency of their wants. The choice between practices is thought of as being made on the basis of the allocation of benefits and burdens to individuals (measured by the present capitalized value of the utility of these benefits over the full period of the practice's existence) which results from the distribution of rights and duties established by a practice. The individuals receiving the benefits are not thought of as related in any way: they represent so many different directions in which limited resources may be allocated. Preferences and interest are taken as given; and their satisfaction has value irrespective of the relations between persons which they represent and the claims which the parties are prepared to make on one another. This value is properly taken into account by the (ideal) legislator who is conceived as adjusting the rules of the system from the center so as to maximize the present capitalized value of the social utility function. The principles of justice will not be violated by a legal system so conceived provided these executive decisions are correctly made; and in this fact the principles of justice are said to find their derivation and explanation.

Some social decisions are, of course, of an administrative sort; namely, when the decision turns on social utility in the ordinary sense: on the efficient use of common means for common ends whose benefits are impartially distributed, or in connection with which the question of distribution is misplaced, as in the case of maintaining public order, or national defense. But as an interpretation of the basis of the principles of justice the utilitarian conception is mistaken. It can lead one to argue against slavery on the grounds that the advantages the slaveholder do not counterbalance the disadvantages to the slave and to society at large burdened by a comparatively inefficient system of labor. The conception of justice as fairness, when applied to the offices of slaveholder and slave, would forbid counting the advantages of the slaveholder at all. These offices could not be founded on principles which could be mutually acknowledged, so the question whether the slaveholder's gains are great enough to counterbalance the losses to the slave and society cannot arise in the first place.

The difference between the two conceptions is whether justice is a fundamental moral concept arising directly from the reciprocal relations of persons engaging in common practices, and its principles those which persons similarly circumstanced could mutually acknowledge; or whether justice is derivative from a kind of higher order executive decision as to the most efficient design of institutions conceived as general devices for distributing benefits to individuals the worth of whose interests is defined independently of their relations to each other. Now even if the social utility function is constructed so that the practices chosen by it would be just, at least under normal circumstances, there is still the further argument against the utilitarian conception that the various restrictions on the utility function needed to get this result are borrowed from the conception of justice as fairness. The notion that individuals have similar utility functions, for example, is really the first principle of justice under the guise of a psychological law. It is assumed not in the manner of an empirical hypothesis concerning actual desires and interests, but from sensing what must be laid down if justice is not to be violated. There is, indeed, irony in this conclusion; for utilitarians attacked the notion of the original contract not only as a historical fiction but as a superfluous hypothesis: they thought that utility alone provides sufficient grounds for all social obligations, and is in any case the real basis of contractual obligations. But this is not so unless one's conception of social utility embodies within it restrictions whose basis can be understood only if one makes reference to one of the ideas of contractarian thought: that persons must be regarded as possessing an original and equal liberty, and their common practices are unjust unless they accord with principles which persons so circumstanced and related could freely accept.

CHAPTER IX

# PROPERTY

'Private property is theft.'

Proudhon, What is Property?, 1840

Perhaps because of the very massiveness of Karl Marx's attack on private production and distribution of economic resources and the resulting polemical struggles within that context, little has been done in the twentieth century in the way of formulating a general theory of property accountable both to pragmatic necessities and to divergent ideological persuasions. Ironically, while Marx set new standards for historical analysis, he was a notoriously bad technical economist. And even more significant for contemporary property analysis, he really said very little about the future of property in the perfected Communist society. We know at least from his early *Economic and Philosophic Manuscripts of 1844* (published only in 1961 by the Foreign Language Publishing House in Moscow) that Marx had strong reservations about the notion of 'common' property so frequently identified with his name. A scathing comment from that document is worth quoting at length:

> Finally, communism is the positive expression of annulled private property—at first as universal private property . . . It may be said that [the] idea of the community of women gives away the secret of this as yet completely crude and thoughtless communism. Just as the woman passes from marriage to general prostitution, so the entire world of wealth (that is, of man's objective substance) passes from the relationship of exclusive marriage with the owner of private property to a state of universal prostitution with the community . . . How little this annulment of private property is

really an appropriation is in fact proved by the abstract negation of the entire world of culture and civilization, the regression to the unnatural simplicity of the poor and undemanding man who has not only failed to go beyond private property, but has not yet even attained to it.

Whatever property ideal may someday be adopted by the several Communist regimes, none to date has fully abolished the rules, practices, and effects of traditional private ownership. In the heat of revolutionary change in 1921, for instance, the Soviet government borrowed 'temporarily' the private property provisions of the French Civil Code with only a qualifying clause precluding excessive capitalist profit-making — the code is still in effect with, if anything, some liberalization of the profit clause. In the conclusion of his article, "Ownership" (reprinted in part below), A. M. Honoré compares at large the working operation of liberal and socialist property models:

> In practice the two overlap, and operate side by side, together with various types of split ownership and ownership of funds which diverge, to a greater or less extent, from the standard instances depicted in the first section. The final picture is that of a set of related institutions of great complexity which are best studied against the background of the basic model—a single human being owning, in the full liberal sense, a single material thing.

The fundamental problem of property is analogous to that of civil liberties. As freedoms of speech, press, and demonstration are diminished in times of national crisis, so, too, are individual property claims balanced against larger social interests and general needs. The one certainty that seems to have emerged in this sphere is that neither absolute state control nor absolute private property right can operate effectively in modern society. At the very minimum, authoritarian regimes must delegate considerable discretionary powers both to management of large economic enterprizes and to a wide spectrum of private individuals, simply to maintain efficient production and distribution of economic resources (Soviet planners have made radical departures in this direction during the past five years).

Again, no private enterprise system has been so radical as to abolish taxes or the obligations of private contract, which, of course, significantly define and limit property use. Property analysis in most non-communist countries today shares the concerns enunciated years ago by the Austrian socialist, Karl Renner: which types of property, must be controlled, and how, so as to maintain acceptable standards of human welfare.

Classical apologists for private property have generally recognized that precisely an 'apology' is called for: St. Thomas acknowledged that "the common possession of things is attributed to natural law;" Locke, that "God... 'has given the earth to the children of men,' given it to mankind in common". Both agreed that private property was the invention of 'human agreement.' Subsequent theorists have argued, as the Morris Cohen selection recounts, a wide variety of private property 'justifications'. Of these, perhaps, the argument from utility and the claim of personality are implicitly dominant today. Apart from his theory of politics even Marx praised the humane, family-centered guild system of early capitalism and hinted that utopian communism might recapture something of its spirit; comparison of 'gross national product' is a favorite game of contemporary statesmen.

Ideology aside, new economic institutions have shattered the simplicities of the liberal (one man) model of ownership which briefly displaced late feudal structures of overlapping rights and responsibilities. No single incident of ownership can adequately account for the variety of types of control, particularly of productive resources. In their classic study, *The Modern Corporation and Private Property* (1933), Adolf Berle and Gardiner Means demonstrated conclusively that corporate properties with their divided incidence of ownership, use, management and control have much more in common with feudal patterns of multiple obligation than the simple liberal model. It is now generally acknowledged by legal theorists that property ownership is a complex relationship, involving 'no-rights' and 'duties' of members of society at large as well as rights and privileges of individual owners. The limiting identification of property with material goods has given way to recognition of numerous intangible elements (e.g. business 'goodwill', the right to practice a profession at a particular place and time, the right to receive dividends on corporate stock).

One of the special problems which has undoubtedly delayed the development of an explicit general theory of property relevant to the contemporary scene has been the sharp and almost mutually exclusive division of labor amongst the various professional and academic disciplines which treat essential aspects of property analysis. Modern economists, for instance, have virtually abandoned all responsibility for humane values in their analyses of technical economic models. The new normative school of economists has thus far settled for the crudest reduction of values in general to statistically manageable evidence of economic preferences (see *Human Values and Economic Policy*, edited by Sidney Hook, New York, 1967). Radical and liberal sociologists seem sadly out of touch with actual and potential property reforms within the existing legal 'establishment'. Still largely trained by architecture schools and lacking in economic sophistication, city planners have produced a record of utopian failures that in all too many cases could have been anticipated and avoided by slight changes in timing and structure. For example, the byword of British planners of recent decades—a 'green belt' of agricultural and recreational lands surrounding London— is rapidly becoming a gray wasteland which serves neither of two proposed uses through lack of positive development. In this country the fragmentation of strong local jurisdictions has made nonsense of ambitious regional schemes (e.g. *The Case for Regional Planning with Special Reference to New England*, New Haven, Yale University Press, 1947) and in the meantime special interest groups do business as usual to the general detriment of the public interest (one is saddened, but scarcely surprized, as successive communities bordering the Great Lakes wake up to the permanent pollution of their favored recreational shorefronts).

General property theory today is in a shambles because no single body of epperts is either trained or responsible for all dimensions of the property xroblem. Intelligent concern has been for all practical purposes divorced from technical proficiency in this subject, perhaps the most crucial of all affecting the long range welfare of men.

# 37

# Saint Thomas Aquinas

St. Thomas' theory of property expresses characteristic medieval welfare concerns and distaste for commercial enterprise.

# THE RIGHT TO PROPERTY*

## 21. THE RIGHT TO PROPERTY. (QU. 66.)

### *Man's Control Over Nature. (Art. 1, concl.)*

Material things may be considered under two aspects. First, as to their nature: and this in no way lies within human power, but only within the divine power whose wish all things obey. Secondly, as to the use of such things. And in this respect, man has a natural control over material things; for he can, in virtue of his reason and will, make use of material things for his own benefit, as though they were created for this purpose: for imperfect things exist to serve the advantage of the more perfect as we have already seen. On this principle the Philosopher proves (I, *Politics*), that the possession of material things is natural to man. And this natural dominion which man has over other creatures, in virtue of reason which makes him the image of God, is clearly shown in the creation of man (*Genesis* I) where it is said: 'Let us make man to our own image and likeness, and he shall rule over the fish of the sea' etc.

### *The Limits of Private Property. (Art. 2, concl.)*

With respect to material things there are two points which man must consider. First, concerning the power of acquisition and disposal: and in this respect private possession is permissible. It is also necessary to human life for three reasons. First, because every one is more concerned with the obtaining of what concerns himself alone than with the common affairs of all or of many others: for each one, avoiding extra labour, leaves the common task to the next man; as we see when there are too many officials. Secondly, because human affairs are dealt with in a more orderly manner when each has his own business to go about: there would be complete confusion if every one tried to do everything. Thirdly, because this leads to a more peaceful condition of man; provided

*Saint Thomas Aquinas, from the *Summa Theologica*, reprinted by permission of the publisher from *Thomas Aquinas: Selected Political Writings* (edited by A. P. d'Entreves and translated by J. G. Dawson), Basil Blackwell, Oxford, 1948, pp. 167–173. Latin text omitted.

each is content with his own. So we see that it is among those who possess something jointly and in common that disputes most frequently arise.

The other point which concerns man with regard to material things is their use. As to this, men should not hold material things as their own but to the common benefit: each readily sharing them with others in their necessity. So the Apostle says (I *Tim.*, ult.): 'Charge the rich of this world to give easily, to communicate to others.'

*The Right to Private Property Derives From Human Law. (Ibid. ad 1um.)*

The common possession of things is to be attributed to natural law, not in the sense that natural law decrees that all things are to be held in common and that there is to be no private possession: but in the sense that there is no distinction of property on grounds of natural law, but only by human agreement; and this pertains to positive law, as we have already shown. Thus private property is not opposed to natural law, but is an addition to it, devised by the human reason.

### *The Duty of Charity. (Art. 7 concl.)*

What pertains to human law can in no way detract from what pertains to natural law or to divine law. Now according to the natural order, instituted by divine providence, material goods are provided for the satisfaction of human needs. Therefore the division and appropriation of property, which proceeds from human law, must not hinder the satisfaction of man's necessity from such goods. Equally, whatever a man has in superabundance is owed, of natural right, to the poor for their sustenance. So Ambrosius says, and it is also to be found in the *Decretum Gratiani* (Dist. XLVII): 'The bread which you withhold belongs to the hungry; the clothing you shut away, to the naked; and the money you bury in the earth is the redemption and freedom of the penniless.' But because there are many in necessity, and they cannot all be helped from the same source, it is left to the initiative of individuals to make provision from their own wealth, for the assistance of those who are in need. If, however, there is such urgent and evident necessity that there is clearly an immediate need of necessary sustenance,—if, for example, a person is in immediate danger of physical privation, and there is no other way of satisfying his need,—then he may take what is necessary from another person's goods, either openly or by stealth. Nor is this, strictly speaking, fraud or robbery.

### 22. USURY

### *The Profit Motive. (Qu. 77, Art. 4, concl.)*

Traders are those who apply themselves to the exchange of goods. But as the Philosopher says (I *Politics*, ch. 3) there are two reasons for the exchange of things. The first may be called natural and necessary; and obtains when exchange is made either of goods against goods, or of goods against money, to meet the necessities of life. Such exchange is not, strictly speaking, the business of traders; but is rather the province of the steward or politician whose duty it is to see that the household or the state obtain the necessities of life. The other form of exchange, either of money against money or of any sort of goods against money, is carried on not for the necessary business of life, but for the sake of profit. And it is this form of exhange which would seem, strictly speaking, to be the business of traders. Now, according to the Philosopher, the first form of exchange, because it serves natural necessity, is praiseworthy. But the second form is rightly condemned; for of itself it serves only the desire for gain, which knows no bounds but spreads always further. Therefore trading, considered in itself, always implies a certain baseness, in that it has not of itself any honest or necessary object.

Though profit, which is the object of trading does not of itself imply any honest or necessary aim, neither does it imply anything vicious or contrary to virtue. So there is nothing to prevent its being turned to some honest or necessary object. In this way trading is made lawful. As, for example, when a person uses a moderate profit, which he seeks from trading, for the upkeep of his household, or for assisting the poor, or again, when a person carries on trade for the public welfare, and to provide the country with the necessities of life: and when he seeks profit, not for its own sake, but as a reward for his labor.

## 38

# John Locke

John Locke offers separate justifications of private property (an ambiguous concept in his usage, referring sometimes to private goods, and at other times to "life, liberty and estate") in the state of nature and in civil society.

# OF PROPERTY*

Whether we consider natural reason, which tells us that men being once born have a right to their preservation, and consequently to meat and drink and such other things as nature affords for their subsistence; or Revelation, which gives us an account of those grants God made of the world to Adam, and to Noah and his sons, 'tis very clear that God, as King David says, Psalm cxv. 16, "has given the earth to the children of men," given it to mankind in common. But this being supposed, it seems to some a very great difficulty how any one should ever come to have a property in anything. I will not content myself to answer that if it be difficult to make out property upon a supposition that God gave the world to Adam and his posterity in common, it is impossible that any man but one universal monarch should have any property upon a supposition that God gave the world to Adam and his heirs in succession, exclusive of all the rest of his posterity. But I shall endeavor to show how men might come to have a property in several parts of that which God gave to mankind in common, and that without any express compact of all the commoners.

God, who hath given the world to men in common, hath also given them reason to make use of it to the best advantage of life and convenience. The earth and all that is therein is given to men for the support and comfort of their being. And though all the fruits it naturally produces, and beasts it feeds, belong to mankind in common, as they are produced by the spontaneous hand of nature; and nobody has orginally a private dominion exclusive of the rest of mankind in any of them as they are thus in their natural state; yet being given for the use of men, there must of necessity be a means to appropriate them some way or other before they can be of any use or at all beneficial to any particular man. The fruit or venison which nourishes the wild Indian, who knows no enclosure, and is still a tenant in common, must be his, and so his, *i.e.*, a part of him, that another can no longer have any right to it, before it can do any good for the support of his life.

*John Locke, *Second Treatise of Civil Government,* Chap. V.

Though the earth and all inferior creatures be common to all men, yet every man has a property in his own person; this nobody has any right to but himself. The labor of his body and the work of his hands we may say are properly his. Whatsoever, then, he removes out of the state that nature hath provided and left it in, he hath mixed his labor with, and joined to it something that is his own, and thereby makes it his property. It being by him removed from the common state nature placed it in, it hath by this labor something annexed to it that excludes the common right of other men. For this labor being the unquestionable property of the laborer, no man but he can have a right to what that is once joined to, at least where there is enough and as good left in common for others.

He that is nourished by the acorns he picked up under an oak, or the apples he gathered from the trees in the wood, has certainly appropriated them to himself. Nobody can deny but the nourishment is his. I ask, then, When did they begin to be his? when he digested? or when he ate? or when he boiled? or when he brought them home? or when he picked them up? And 'tis plain, if the first gathering made them not his, nothing else could. That labor put a distinction between them and common; that added something to them more than nature, the common mother of all, had done, and so they became his private right. And will any one say he had no right to those acorns or apples he thus appropriated, because he had not the consent of all mankind to make them his? Was it a robbery thus to assume to himself what belonged to all in common? If such a consent as that was necessary, man had starved, notwithstanding the plenty God had given him. We see in commons which remain so by compact that 'tis the taking any part of what is common and removing it out of the state nature leaves it in, which begins the property; without which the common is of no use. And the taking of this or that part does not depend on the express consent of all the commoners. Thus the grass my horse has bit, the turfs my servant has cut, and the ore I have dug in any place where I have a right to them in common with others, become my property without the assignation or consent of anybody. The labor that was mine removing them out of that common state they were in, hath fixed my property in them.

By making an explicit consent of every commoner necessary to any one's appropriating to himself any part of what is given in common, children or servants could not cut the meat which their father or master had provided for them in common without assigning to every one his peculiar part. Though the water running in the fountain be every one's, yet who can doubt but that in the pitcher is his only who drew it out? His labor hath taken it out of the hands of nature, where it was common, and belonged equally to all her children, and hath thereby appropriated it to himself.

Thus this law of reason makes the deer that Indian's who hath killed it; 'tis allowed to be his goods who hath bestowed his labor upon it, though before it was the common right of every one. And amongst those who are counted the civilised part of mankind, who have made and multiplied positive laws to determine property, this original law of nature, for the beginning of property in what was before common, still takes place; and by virtue thereof, what fish any one catches in the ocean, that great and still remaining common of mankind, or what ambergris any one takes up here, is, by the labor that removes it out of that common state nature left it in, made his property who takes that pains about it. And even amongst us, the hare that any one is hunting is thought his who pursues her during the chase. For being a beast that is still looked upon as common, and no man's private possession, whoever has employed so much labor about any of that kind as to find and pursue her has thereby removed her from the state of nature wherein she was common, and hath begun a property.

It will perhaps be objected to this, that if gathering the acorns, or other fruits of the earth, etc., makes a right to them, then any one may engross as much as he will. To which I answer, Not so. The same law of nature that does by this means give us property, does also bound that property too. "God has given us all things richly" (1 Tim. vi. 17), is the voice of reason confirmed by inspiration. But how far has he given it us? To enjoy. As much as any one can make use of to any advantage of life before it spoils, so much he may by his labor fix a property in; whatever is beyond this is more than his share, and belongs to others. Nothing was made by God for man to spoil or destroy. And thus considering the plenty of natural provisions there was a long time in the world, and the few spenders, and to how small a part of that provision the industry of one man could extend itself, and engross it to the prejudice of others—especially keeping within the bounds, set by reason, of what might serve for his use—there could be then little room for quarrels or contentions about property so established.

But the chief matter of property being now not the fruits of the earth, and the beasts that subsist on it, but the earth itself, as that which takes in and carries with it all the rest, I think it is plain that property in that, too, is acquired as the former. As much land as a man tills, plants, improves, cultivates, and can use the product of, so much is his property. He by his labor does as it were enclose it from the common. Nor will it invalidate his right to say, everybody else has an equal title to it; and therefore he cannot appropriate, he cannot enclose, without the consent of all his fellow-commoners, all mankind. God, when he gave the world in common to all mankind, commanded man also to labor, and the penury of his condition required it of him. God and his reason commanded him to subdue the earth, *i.e.,* improve it for the benefit of life, and therein lay out something upon it that was his own, his labor. He that, in obedience to his command of God, subdued, tilled, and sowed any part of it, thereby annexed to it something that was his property, which another had no title to, nor could without injury take from him.

Nor was this appropriation of any parcel of land, by improving it, any prejudice to any other man, since there was still enough and as good left; and more than the yet unprovided could use. So that in effect there was never the less left for others because of his enclosure for himself. For he that leaves as much as another can make use of, does as good as take nothing at all.

Nobody could think himself injured by the drinking of another man, though he took a good draught, who had a whole river of the same water left him to quench his thirst; and the case of land and water, where there is enough of both, is perfectly the same.

God gave the world to men in common; but since he gave it them for their benefit, and the greatest conveniences of life they were capable to draw from it, it cannot be supposed he meant it should always remain common and uncultivated. He gave it to the use of the industrious and rational (and labor was to be his title to it), not to the fancy or covetousness of the quarrelsome and contentious. He that had as good left for his improvement as was already taken up, needed not complain, ought not to meddle with what was already improved by another's labor; if he did, it is plain he desired the benefit of another's pains, which he had no right to, and not the ground which God had given him in common with others to labor on, and whereof there was as good left as that already possessed, and more than he knew what to do with, or his industry could reach to.

It is true, in land that is common in England, or any other country where there is plenty of people under government, who have money and commerce, no one can enclose or appropriate any part without the consent of all his fellow-commoners: because this is left common by compact, *i.e.,* by the law of the land, which is not to be violated. And though it be common in respect of some men, it is not so to all mankind; but is the joint property of this country, or this parish. Besides, the remainder, after such enclosure, would not be as good to the rest of the commoners as the whole was, when they could all make use of the whole; whereas in the beginning and first peopling of the great common of the world it was quite otherwise. The law man was under was rather for appropriating. God commanded, and his wants forced him, to labor. That was his property, which could not be taken from him wherever he had fixed it. And hence subduing or cultivating the earth, and having dominion, we see are joined together. The one gave title to the other. So that God, by commanding to subdue, gave authority so far to appropriate. And the condition of human life, which requires labor and materials to work on, necessarily introduces private possessions.

The measure of property nature has well set by the extent of men's labor and the convenience of life. No man's labor could subdue or appropriate all; nor could his enjoyment consume more than a small part; so that it was impossible for any man, this way, to intrench upon the right of another, or acquire to himself a property to the prejudice of his neighbor, who would still have room for as good and as large a possession (after the other had taken out his) as before it was appropriated. This measure did confine every man's possession to a very moderate proportion, and such as he might appropriate to himself without injury to anybody, in the first ages of the world, when men were more in danger to be lost by wandering from their company in the then vast wilderness of the earth than to be straitened for want of room to plant in. And the same measure may be allowed still without prejudice to anybody, as full as the world seems. For supposing a man or family in the state they were at first peopling of the world by the children of Adam or Noah; let him plant in some inland vacant places of America, we shall find that the possessions he could make himself, upon the measures we have given, would not be very large, nor, even to this day, prejudice the rest of mankind, or give them reason to complain or think themselves injured by this man's encroachment, though the race of men have now spread themselves to all the corners of the world, and do infinitely exceed the small number that was at the beginning. Nay, the extent of ground is of so little value without labor, that I have heard it affirmed that in Spain itself a man may be permitted to plough, sow, and reap, without being disturbed, upon land he has no other title to but only his making use of it. But, on the contrary, the inhabitants think themselves beholden to him who by his industry on neglected and consequently waste land has increased the stock of corn which they wanted. But be this as it will, which I lay no stress on, this I dare boldly affirm—that the same rule of propriety, *viz.*, that every man should have as much as he could make use of, would hold still in the world without straitening anybody, since there is land enough in the world to suffice double the inhabitants, had not the invention of money, and the tacit agreement of men to put a value on it, introduced (by consent) larger possessions and a right to them; which how it has done I shall by-and-bye show more at large.

This is certain, that in the beginning, before the desire of having more than man needed had altered the intrinsic value of things, which depends only on their usefulness to the life of man; or had agreed that a little piece of yellow metal which would keep without wasting or decay should be worth a great piece of flesh or a whole heap of corn, though man had a right to appropriate by their labor, each one to himself, as much of the things of nature as he could use, yet this could not be much, not to the prejudice of others, where the same plenty was still left to those who would use the same industry. To which let me add, that he who appropriates land to himself by his labor does not lessen but increase the common stock of mankind. For the provisions serving to the support of human life produced by one acre of enclosed and cultivated land are (to speak much within compass) ten times more than those which are yielded by an acre of land of an equal richness lying waste in common. And therefore he that encloses land, and has a greater plenty of the conveniences of life from ten acres than he could have from a hundred left to nature, may truly be said to give ninety acres to mankind: for his labor now supplies him with provisions out of ten acres, which were but the product of a hundred lying in common. I have here rated the improved land very low, in making its product but as ten to one, when it is much nearer a hundred to one. For I ask, whether in the wild woods and uncultivated waste of America, left to nature without any improvement, tillage, or husbandry, a thousand acres yield the needy and wretched inhabitants as many conveniences of life as ten acres of equally fertile land do in Devonshire, where they are well cultivated?

Before the appropriation of land, he who gathered as much of the wild fruit, killed, caught, or tamed as many of the beasts as he could; he that so employed his pains about any of the spontaneous products of nature as any way to alter them from the state which nature put them in, by placing any of his labor on them, did thereby acquire a propriety in them. But if they perished in his possession without their due use; if the fruits rotted, or the venison putrefied before he could spend it, he offended against the common law of nature, and was liable to be punished; he invaded his neighbor's share, for he had no right further than his use called for any of them and they might serve to afford him conveniences of life.

The same measures governed the possessions of land, too. Whatsoever he tilled and reaped, laid up, and made use of before it spoiled, that was his peculiar right; whatsoever he enclosed and could feed and make use of, the cattle and product was also his. But if either the grass of his enclosure rotted on the ground, or the fruit of his planting perished without gathering and laying up, this part of the earth, notwithstanding his enclosure, was still to be looked on as waste, and might be the possession of any other. Thus, at the beginning, Cain might take as much ground as he could till and make it his own land, and yet leave enough for Abel's sheep to feed on; a few acres would serve for both their possessions. But as families increased, and industry enlarged their stocks, their possessions enlarged with the need of them; but yet it was commonly without any fixed property in the ground they made use of, till they incorporated, settled themselves together, and built cities; and then, by consent, they came in time to set out the bounds of their distinct territories, and agree on limits between them and their neighbors, and, by laws within themselves, settled the properties of those of the same society. For we see that in that part of the world which was first inhabited, and therefore like to be the best peopled, even as low down as Abraham's time they wandered with their flocks and their herds, which were their substance, freely up and down; and this Abraham did in a country where he was a stranger: whence it is plain that at least a great part of the land lay in common; that the inhabitants valued it not, nor claimed property in any more than they made use of. But when there was not room enough in the same place for their herds to feed together, they by consent, as Abraham and Lot did (Gen. xiii. 5), separated and enlarged their pasture where it best liked them. And for the same reason Esau went from his father and his brother, and planted in Mount Seir (Gen. xxxvi. 6).

And thus, without supposing any private dominion and property in Adam over all the world, exclusive of all other men, which can no way be proved, nor any one's property be made out from it; but supposing the world given as it was to the children of men in common, we see how labor could make men distinct titles to several parcels of it for their private uses, wherein there could be no doubt of right, no room for quarrel.

Nor is it so strange, as perhaps before consideration it may appear, that the property of labor should be able to overbalance the community of land. For it is labor indeed that puts the difference of value on everything; and let any one consider what the difference is between an acre of land planted with tobacco or sugar, sown with wheat or barley, and an acre of the same land lying in common without any husbandry upon it, and he will find that the improvement of labor makes the far greater part of the value. I think it will be but a very modest computation to say that of the products of the earth useful to the life of man nine-tenths are the effects of labor; nay, if we will rightly estimate things as they come to our use, and cast up the several expenses about them—what in them is purely owing to nature, and what to labor— we shall find that in most of them ninety-nine hundredths are wholly to be put on the account of labor.

There cannot be a clearer demonstration of anything than several nations of the Americans are of this, who are rich in land and poor in all the comforts of life, whom nature having furnished as liberally as any other people with the materials of plenty—*i.e.,* a fruitful soil, apt to produce in abundance what might serve for food, raiment, and delight—yet, for want of improving it by labor, have not one-hundredth part of the conveniences we enjoy. And a king of a large and fruitful territory there, feeds, lodges, and is clad worse than a day-laborer in England.

To make this a little clearer, let us but trace some of the ordinary provisions of life through their several progresses before they come to our use, and see how much they receive of their value from human industry. Bread, wine, and cloth are things of daily use and great plenty; yet, notwithstanding, acorns, water, and leaves or skins must be our bread, drink, and clothing, did not labor furnish us with these more useful commodities. For whatever bread is more worth than acorns, wine than water, and cloth or silk than leaves, skins, or moss, that is wholly owing to labor and industry: the one of these being the food and raiment which unassisted nature furnishes us with; the other, provisions which our industry and pains prepare for us; which how much they exceed the other in value when any one hath computed, he will then see how much labor makes the far greatest part of the value of things we enjoy in this world. And the ground which produces the materials is scarce to be reckoned in as any, or at most but a very small, part of it; so little that even amongst us land that is left wholly to nature, that hath no improvement of pasturage, tillage, or planting, is called, as indeed it is, "waste," and we shall find the benefit of it amount to little more than nothing.

This shows how much numbers of men are to be preferred to largeness of dominions; and that the increase of lands and the right employing of them is the great art of government: and that prince, who shall be so wise and godlike as by established laws of liberty to secure protection and encouragement to the honest industry of mankind, against the oppression of power and narrowness of party, will quickly be too hard for his neighbours: but this by the by.

To return to the argument in hand.

An acre of land that bears here twenty bushels of wheat, and another in America which, with the same husbandry, would do the like, are without doubt of the same natural intrinsic value; but yet the benefit mankind receives from the one in a year is worth £5, and from the other possibly not worth a penny, if all the profit an Indian received from it were to be valued and sold here; at least, I may truly say, not one-thousandth. 'Tis labor, then, which puts the greatest part of value upon land, without which it would scarcely be worth anything; 'tis to that we owe the greatest part of all its useful products, for all that the straw, bran, bread of that acre of wheat is more worth than the product of an acre of as good land which lies waste, is all the effect of labor. For 'tis not barely the ploughman's pains, the reaper's and thresher's toil, and the baker's sweat, is to be counted into the bread we eat; the labor of those who broke the oxen, who dug and wrought the iron and stones, who felled and framed the timber employed about the plough, mill, oven, or any other utensils, which are a vast number, requisite to this corn, from its being seed to be sown to its being made bread, must all be charged on the account of labor, and received as an effect of that. Nature and the earth furnished only the almost worthless materials as in themselves. 'Twould be a strange catalogue of things that industry provided and made use of, about every loaf of bread before it came to our use, if we could trace them—iron, wood, leather, bark, timber, stone, bricks, coals, lime, cloth, dyeing drugs, pitch, tar, masts, ropes, and all the materials made use of in the ship that brought any of the com- modities made use of by any of the workmen to any part of the work, all which it would be almost impossible—at least, too long—to reckon up.

From all which it is evident that, though the things of nature are given in common, yet man, by being master of himself and proprietor of his own person and the actions or labor of it, had still in himself the great foundation of property; and that which made up the great part of what he applied to the support or comfort of his being, when invention and arts had improved the conveniences of life, was perfectly his own, and did not belong in common to others.

Thus labor, in the beginning, gave a right of property, wherever any one was pleased to employ it upon what was common, which remained a long while the far greater part, and is yet more than mankind makes use of. Men at first, for the most part, contented themselves with what unassisted nature offered to their necessities; and though afterwards, in some parts of the world (where the increase of people and stock, with the use of money, had made land scarce, and so of some value), the several communities settled the bounds of their distinct territories, and, by laws within themselves, regulated the properties of the private men of their society, and so, by compact and agreement, settled the property which labour and industry began—and the leagues that have been made between several states and kingdoms, either expressly or tacitly disowning all claim and right to the land in the other's possession, have, by common consent, given up their pretences to their natural common right, which originally they had to those countries; and so have, by positive agreement, settled a property amongst themselves in distinct parts and parcels of the earth—yet there are still great tracts of ground to be found which, the inhabitants thereof not having joined with the rest of mankind in the consent of the use of their common money, lie waste, and are more than the people who dwell on it do or can make use of, and so still lie in common; though this can scarce happen amongst that part of mankind that have consented to the use of money.

The greatest part of things really useful to the life of man, and such as the necessity of subsisting made the first commoners of the world look after, as it doth the Americans now, are generally things of short duration, such as, if they are not consumed by use, will decay and perish of themselves: gold, silver, and diamonds are things that fancy or agreement have put the value on more than real use and the necessary support of life. Now, of those good things which nature hath provided in common, every one had a right, as hath been said, to as much as he could use, and property in all he could effect with his labor; all that his industry could extend to, to alter from the state nature had put it in, was his. He that gathered a hundred bushels of acorns or apples had thereby a property in them; they were his goods as soon as gathered. He was only to look that he used them before they spoiled, else he took more than his share, and robbed others; and, indeed, it was foolish thing, as well as dishonest, to hoard up more than he could make use of. If he gave away part to anybody else, so that it perished not uselessly in his possession, these he also made use of; and if he also bartered away plums that would have rotted in a week, for nuts that would last good for his eating a whole year, he did no injury; he wasted not the common stock, destroyed no part of the portion of goods that belonged to others, so long as nothing perished uselessly in his hands. Again, if he would give his nuts for a piece of metal, pleased with its color, or exchange his sheep for shells, or wool for a sparkling pebble or a diamond, and keep those by him all his life, he invaded not the right of others; he might heap up as much of these durable things as he pleased, the exceeding of the bounds of his just property not lying in the largeness of his possessions, but perishing of anything uselessly in it.

And thus came in the use of money—some lasting thing that men might keep without spoiling, and that, by mutual consent, men would take in exchange for the truly useful but perishable supports of life.

And as different degrees of industry were apt to give men possessions in different proportions, so this invention of money gave them the opportunity to continue and enlarge them; for supposing an island, separate from all possible commerce with the rest of the world, wherein there were but a hundred families—but there were sheep, horses, and cows, with other useful animals, wholesome fruits, and land enough for corn for a hundred thousand times as many, but nothing in the island, either because of its commonness or perishableness, fit to supply the place of money—what reason could any one have there to enlarge his possessions beyond the use of his family and a plentiful supply to its consumption, either in what their own industry produced, or they could barter for like perishable useful commodities with others? Where there is not something both lasting and scarce, and so valuable to be hoarded up, there men will not be apt to enlarge their possessions of land, were it never so rich, never so free for them to take; for I ask, what would a man value ten thousand or a hundred thousand acres of excellent land, ready cultivated, and well stocked too with cattle, in the middle of the inland parts of America, where he had no hopes of commerce with other parts of the world, to draw money to him by the sale of the product? It would not be worth the enclosing, and we should see him give up again to the wild common of nature whatever was more than would supply the conveniences of life to be had there for him and his family.

Thus in the beginning all the world was America, and more so than that is now, for no such thing as money was anywhere known. Find out something that hath the use and value of money amongst his neighbors, you shall see the same man will begin presently to enlarge his possessions.

But since gold and silver, being little useful to the life of man in proportion to food, raiment, and carriage, has its value only from the consent of men, whereof labor yet makes, in great part, the measure, it is plain that the consent of men have agreed to a disproportionate and unequal possession of the earth; they having, by a tacit and voluntary consent, found out a way how a man may fairly possess more land than he himself can use the product of, by receiving in exchange for the overplus, gold and silver, which may be hoarded up without injury to any one; these metals not spoiling or decaying in the hands of the possessor. This partage of things in an equality of private possessions men have made practicable, out of the bounds of society, and without compact, only by putting a value on gold and silver, and tacitly agreeing in the use of money. For in governments the laws regulate the right of property, and the possession of land is determined by positive constitutions.

And thus, I think, it is very easy to conceive without any difficulty how labor could at first begin a title of property in the common things of nature, and how the spending it upon our uses bounded it; so that there could then be no reason of quarrelling about title, nor any doubt about the largeness of possession it gave. Right and conveniency went together; for as a man had a right to all he could employ his labor upon, so he had no temptation to labor for more than he could make use of. This left no room for controversy about the title, nor for encroachment on the right of others; what portion a man carved to himself was easily seen, and it was useless, as well as dishonest, to carve himself too much, or take more than he needed.

## 39

# Karl Renner

Karl Renner (1870–1950), first Chancellor of the Austrian Republic
(1918) and later elected President of the liberated Austrian Republic
(1945), was one of the first Marxists to develop an extensive and
positive theory of law.

# THE INSTITUTIONS OF PRIVATE LAW*

SECTION V. MODERN POSSESSIONS. THE AGGREGATE OF ASSETS AND LIABILITIES

The change of functions is most strikingly revealed, if now, at the end of the
development of property, we compare norm and substratum, as we did before
(chapter i. 2) with regard to patrimonial property.

Property is an individual right to an object, its exclusive subjection to the
individual will of the owner. But is there any individual disposition of his property on the part of the bank customer of a bank, of the share-holder or
of the member of an association? Is it not the market which rules the most
independent factory owner as well as the isolated peasant who lives alone on
his solitary farm? The right of ownership is absolute: this means that it requires
all other subjects of the norm to refrain from interference with the object.
But the house-owner exercises his absolute right by taking in strangers from
the street and setting them up in his so-called "own"; the landlord, by surrendering his possession completely to a tenant with his army of labourers, for ten or
even for 99 years. The urban or agricultural tenant is protected in his possession:
he can, with the help of the authorities, send away the interfering owner who
enters uninvited. The owners of a railway even invite all and sundry to roam
over their property, the more the merrier. Property establishes complete power
of the individual over the object; but an economic object, the substratum of the
right, is not an aggregate of objects, not an independent microcosm, it is merely
a particle of the whole of society's working order, admitting of one special
manner of disposal only. Even the number of revolutions performed by a
spinning wheel is prescribed by the requirements of industrial technique. The
universal power of disposal given by the law is confronted, in economic reality,
by a most limited scope for the exercise of this power. Property is univeral
with regard to subject and object, any individual may own any kind of object,
and this was actually so in the period of simple commodity production, when

*Karl Renner, From *The Institutions of Private Law and Their Social Functions,* first published in
German in 1928, London, Routledge & Kegan Paul Ltd., 1949, p.p. 289-300. Edited by
O. Kahn-Freund. Reprinted by permission of the publisher.

every individual[1] of full age had disposal of a microcosm which was made up of objects of every description. Now one part of the population, the great majority, owns nothing but a week's provisions, another part nothing but houses, another part nothing but machines and the raw materials to feed them, and still others nothing but printed paper. Modern possessions no longer form a cosmos, large or small, they are neither microcosm nor macrocosm. They are an amorphous agglomeration of possessions for the purposes of consumption and production, and in part they are mere "paper-possessions". These latter comprise shares in various railway undertakings at home and abroad, and in various manufacturing enterprises, government bonds and so forth: a loose pile of shavings which derives its unity only from its purpose, the purpose of securing average profits. These possessions represented by documents are in no way connected with the individuality of the owner, they can be increased as convenient. The legal character mask of a monarch is compatible with the economic mask of a distiller of spirits, the legal mask of a state minister is compatible with the economic mask of a gambler on the stock exchange, the ecclesiastic mask of an Archbishop is compatible with the economic mask of an employer of sweated labour. Such unity as modern possessions have, is a mere consequence of the legal abstraction which does not require a unitary substratum; their unity is artificial, easily permitting of arithmetical division by 2, 3, or 4 in cases of inheritance. Modern possessions form no material whole, only a mathematical sum.

Norm and substratum have become so dissimilar, so incommensurable, that the working of property, the way in which it functions, is no longer explained and made intelligible by the property-norm; to-day we must look to the complementary institutions of property. The lives of most of the people, even of the capitalists, are regulated by the law relating to landlord and tenant, their food is controlled by the law of the market, and their clothing, expenditure and pleasures are controlled by the law of wages. Property remains only in the background as a general legal presupposition for the special law that comes into operation, an institution of which we are dimly aware as the necessary consequence of the regrettable fact that there must be someone who is in the last resort responsible for the disposal of any object. But primarily disposal rests with the labourer in the case of the machine, the tool or the plough, with the tenant in the case of the house, and in general with the non-owner. The subjective, absolute, and all-embracing power of disposal seems to the casual observer to be completely eliminated; yet it is perpetuated as the subjective, absolute, and all-embracing power of the capitalist class to dispose of the whole of society, of man and matter and their annual surplus product.

But this fact is hidden from a merely legal interpretation; it is not intended, not expressed nor reflected by the norm. Norm and substratum can scarcely be said to correspond, they are no longer similar, and the present function of the norm is the result of a process in the course of which the relations of

---

[1] In the case of journeymen and apprentices somewhat later.

production and the relations of the law entered on a disparate development. The conflict between a growing (and partly completed) social working order which is conscious of its own unity, and a law which is still in existence although adapted to a previous system of private enterprise based upon economic microcosms, results in property assuming the function of capital. As the conflict increases, the functions of modern property become more and more distinct and differentiated. An increasing number of complementary institutions is developed, and it becomes more and more obvious that property itself has withdrawn into a position where it is solely concerned with disposal over, and acquisition of, values.

### SECTION VI. THE DEVELOPMENT OF THE LAW

I maintain that Karl Marx deliberately set out to observe and describe each and every phenomenon of the capitalist epoch, correlating these to a continuous development of human society on the basis of an inherited legal system, rigid, retarded and fossilised. Those who expect from his critique of political economy a guide for economic behaviour, or an analysis of subjective valuations, or something similar, are therefore bound to misunderstand him. Only if the great historical drama is approached as he approached it, only then is it revealed in a true light: a society of small commodity producers has overcome feudal restrictions by dint of hard struggle, and at last establishes a system wherein the producer freely disposes over his means of production. It is now declared that everyone shall own his means of production, that everyone shall be free to exchange the fruits of his labours for those of everyone else, it is ordained that everybody shall peacefully enjoy and keep his own as he has saved it from the ruins of the feudal system. The law leaves to every individual the use of his means of production, permitting him to work as he finds expedient. As the product of everybody's labours automatically becomes his property, the law may safely do so. The law also leaves it to every individual to provide for his descendants, and it may safely do so: for the father's property forms a fund of subsistence for the inheriting children. This plain and simple regulation of property merely attempts legally to stabilise[2] the existing living conditions of society.

### 1. *Change of Functions and Change of Norms*

But now we find the peaceful enjoyment of one's own property developing into the draconic control of alien labour-power, and giving rise to a new regulation of labour, more severe and in its initial stages more cruel than any regula-

---

[2] The bourgeois revolution was so much easier because there was no necessity to form new social groups or to redistribute possessions, apart from the liberation of the peasants. Fundamentally it proclaimed only two commandments: a material one, that everyone should keep what he had, and a personal one, that everyone should mind his own business.

tion of feudal times or of the time of the pharaos—we need only mention child labour. Thus peaceful enjoyment of one's own object becomes constant appropriation of the proceeds of the labour of others; it becomes title to surplus value, distributing the whole of the social product as profit, interest and rent among an idle class, and limiting the working class to the mere necessities of existence and procreation. In the end it reverses all its original functions. The owner has now no longer even detention of his property; it is deposited at some bank, and whether he is labourer or working capitalist, the owner cannot dispose of his own. He may not even be acquainted with the locality of the concern in which he has invested his property. Yet one function of capital is indestructibly linked up with his person, the function of appropriating the products of alien labour; and month by month the bank messenger delivers to the owner the revenue of his economic property.

This vast process of change, with all its accompanying phenomena, is unfolded before the eyes of Karl Marx; he exposes it as the problem of our time, as the vital question of the whole of human society in our present era. His thoughts cover the whole of human society and at the same time they concentrate upon the inherent and most secret principles of its existence; in his thoughts he is in advance of the overwhelming majority of our generation.

He has made it clear to us that property in the capitalist epoch fulfils functions quite different from those which it fulfilled in the era of simple commodity production, and partly opposed to these. He has made it clear that property has become antisocial, intrinsically opposed to the real interests of society. Yet all property is conferred by the law, by a conscious exercise of the power of society. When society was in control it endowed the individual with the power of disposal over corporeal things; but now the corporeal object controls the individuals, labour-power, even society itself—it regulates the hierarchy of power and labour, the maintenance and procreation of society. Mankind has become tributary to its own creation.

The norm is the result of free action on the part of a society that has become conscious of its own existence. The society of simple commodity producers attempts to stabilise its own conditions of existence, the substratum of its existence, by means of the norm. But in spite of the norm, the substratum changes, yet this change of the substratum takes place within the forms of the law; the legal institutions automatically change their functions which turn into their very opposite, yet this change is scarcely noticed and is not understood. In view of all this the problem arises whether society is not bound to change the norm as soon as it has become conscious of the change in its functions.

## 2. *Complementary Institutions Displace the Principal Institution*

An urgent demand for a human society that acts in freedom and in full consciousness, that creates its norms in complete independence: this is socialism. The very word expresses this. The passing of man from the realm of necessity to the realm of freedom cannot be conceived otherwise than as a marshalling of the organised will of society against the paltry presumptuousness of the individual, so that the object that has become the master of man may again be subjected to the control of society. Common will can achieve this only by a direct, controlled and well-aimed regulation of the relations among men and between man and nature, so that every person and every object may have its functions openly established and may fulfil them in a straightforward manner.

Utopians indulged in dreams and speculations as to how this could be achieved, fanatics of law and philosophy felt themselves obliged to preach fantastic remedies. It was thought that completely new legal institutions would have to be fashioned and the old ones abolished by decree, in order to bring about something that man had never known before. The socialists of this period, the Messianic era of socialism, failed to recognise that it is above all the way of experience which can lead to the new, that even the state of the future is conditioned by the past and that it cannot be otherwise. This era has long since passed away, nowadays we rely on empirical fact, and rightly so. But the socialists, and also unfortunately their leading group, the Marxists, disdain to apply this experience in the realm of the law and the state. They fail to comprehend and to investigate scientifically, how far it is true that the new society is already pre-formed in the womb of the old, even in the field of the law. May it not be true that here also new life is already completely developed in the mother's womb, waiting only for the liberating act of birth?

Some vista of the future, some answers to the questions which we have raised, must have occurred to anyone who has accompanied us on our journey through economics, who has joined in our study with critical regard to the sufferings of mankind. Every society requires a regulation of power and labour. Why do we not set out to create it directly? Why do we not appoint skilled teachers to be masters of our apprentices, why does society accept blindly everyone who takes over an enterprise by the chance of birth or inheritance, although he may be totally unfit to instruct? Why does not society select the best-qualified agriculturist to succeed into a farm that has become vacant, instead of the rich city man who buys it as a hobby, or instead of the fortuitous heir who may be no good? If hereditary appointments are now abolished as insufferable in the case of the most unimportant public office, why is it that the fortuitous heir may still succeed into an important economic enterprise which is responsible for the good or bad fortune of a thousand workers, and, maybe, for the adequate supply of certain goods the whole of society? Anyone can see that society is in immediate need of a regulation of appointments. Our expositions have shown that the real successor who serves the economic functions of a concern is appointed by contract of employment, so that the heir need only play the part of possessor of a title to surplus value without performing any function. We have seen that even to-day property is supplemented by complementary institutions which take over its real functions. Should we not come to the conclusion that the process of change towards a new legal order has already begun, that the complementary institutions already pre-shaped in the framework of the old order will become the principal institutions so that the institution which has previously played the principal part can be abolished, without any disturbance of the economic process, in so far as it no longer serves a useful social purpose?

Feasible as this idea seems, it nevertheless comes up against the most rampant prejudices. It would mean that the contract of employment would become the principal institution of the social regulation of labour, but this institution was during the last century denounced as the source of all social suffering. We are asked to revolutionise our conceptions completely. But we have already met two decisive reasons for changing this opinion. We have seen that the contract of employment, like all legal forms, is in itself neither good nor evil, that the value of the legal form is solely determined by the social function fulfilled by the legal institution. We have seen that it is not the legal form of the contract of employment but its connection with the institution of property which makes the former an instrument of exploitation. Secondly, experience has shown us that the contract of employment even to-day has developed into the established "position" and has to a large extent become socialised and made secure by means of manifold social rights.

### 3. Complementary Institutions of Public Law Force The Private Law Institutions into the Background

A second and probably even more important phenomenon becomes apparent and must be considered by the intelligent observer.

Property is a matter of private law. The whole body of our legal doctrine is based upon this fact. We distinguish between private and public law as the two principal branches of our legal analysis, as we understand it. The normative content of our existing laws fully justifies this division and we cannot avoid making this distinction. Our observations, however, have led us to recognise that every legal order must grant to everybody a private sphere into which the common will does not intrude. After the victory of a liberalist philosophy with its concepts of natural rights, to which the victory of the bourgeoisie over the feudal system corresponded in practice, a theory of constitutional law was evolved which set limits to the powers of the state, affecting even the public law. Public law may not transgress these limits; within them the individual is free and not subject to the control of the state. Here he is no longer a citizen of the state but simply a human being who enjoys freedom of thought and religion, freedom of convictions which the state may not touch. We hold this freedom of the individual in high esteem. It is not a present of nature and it was gained as a precious good of civilisation only after severe social and political struggle; and no thinking socialist would dream of surrendering it.[3] As far

---

[3] This has not prevented Bolshevism from again establishing the omnipotence of the state, from stringently curtailing human freedom in the spiritual sphere. I think this is a disastrous retrogression. It is not justifiable to surrender achievements of civilisation even if they are branded as introductions of the enemy, the hated bourgeoisie.

as we can judge looking into the future, material goods will also belong to this sphere, not only family portraits and other articles of sentimental value, but also the bulk of goods intended for consumption, household utensils, perhaps even the home itself. There will always be a private *"suum"*, a sphere of one's "legal own", even with regard to rights *in rem*, no matter what social order men may give themselves.

But contemporary property, capital as the object of property, though *de jure* private, has in fact ceased altogether to be private. No longer does the owner make use of property in a technical way; the tenement house serves a number of strangers and the railway serves all and sundry. Property in its technical aspect has been completely estranged from the owner. The Roman civil lawyer believed that *dominus rei suae legem dicit*. As far as ownership of capital is concerned, this pronouncement is no longer true: it is society that disposes of capital and prescribes the laws for its use. It may be maintained at least that the object has ceased to be private and is becoming social. An army of a thousand miners, an army with its own generals, commissioned and non-commissioned officers, all of them employees, have complete technical control of the mine; they search its depths and bring its treasures to light, securing not only its continuity but also its very existence; and they stake their own lives for this purpose. Evidently it is a mere provocative fiction that this army should be regarded as a disconnected crowd of strangers, and the shareholders, who may not even know where their property is situated, as the real owners. Language, indeed, revolts against such abuse.

What is it that makes this abuse nevertheless apparently tolerable? Public law has for a long time recognised that where the whole of society is in principle concerned with an object, it can no longer be treated as a matter that is merely private. So it comes about that private law is supplemented by rules of public law relating to the object; a process that was cautious and tentative in the beginning but soon became more decided and in the end was developed in full consciousness.

In the liberal epoch the state considered every interference with the economic system and therefore with private law as contrary to reason and natural law; accordingly it refrained from it completely and merely exercised the restricted functions of protection and administration of justice. But since the middle of the last century the state is no longer content merely to hold the mace and the scales, it begins to take an active part in administration. New norms are made year by year in increasing numbers in the form of statutes, orders and instructions of the administrators of the state. Administrative law develops into a special branch of legal analysis, and economic administration soon becomes the most extensive part within this branch. Grievances arise out of the application of the law of property and the contract of employment to the factory, and therefore administrative law must step in. Regulations relating to the normal working day, factory inspection, and protection of women and children are institutions of public law which increasingly supplement these institutions of private law. Insurance against sickness, accident and old age follow suit, public labour exchanges replace the private labour market, and so on. In the end the relations of labour are as to nine parts regulated by public law, and the field of influence of private law is restricted to the remaining tenth.

When we were dealing with the functions of capital, we nearly always had occasion to refer to complementary institutions of public law and to emphasise that these are new creations; in the main they were introduced or at least perfected only after the death of Karl Marx.

Thus we are led to surmise that a two-fold development is taking place: first, that the complementary institutions of private law have deprived the owners of their technical disposal over their property; and secondly, that the common will has subjected property to its direct control, at least from the point of view of the law. Elements of a new order have been developed within the framework of an old society. So it may not be necessary to clamour for prophets whose predictions of the future will flow from esoteric qualities of the soul. It may well be that there is no need to proclaim premiums for those who would draft the new legal constitution of a reasonable social order: perhaps the truth is that we can simply deduce the law of the future from the data supplied by our experience of to-day and yesterday.

Should this be so, and we have good reason to believe it, our only problem would be to burst the shell which still obstructs the new development; to set free the complementary and supplementary institutions and to use them straightforwardly in accordance with their present and real functions, freed from restriction; to elevate them, the previous handmaidens of property, into the principal institutions; and to liberate them from the fetters of traditional property, which has lost its functions and has itself become a restrictive force.

Our observations have shown, however, that this cannot be the automatic result of a change of functions, that new norms are required to achieve it. For there can be no doubt that only a norm can break another norm. The norm, however, is a conscious act of will performed by society.

## 4. *Legal Doctrine and the Tasks of Society*

If society has become conscious of the changes in the functions of property and its contradictory effects, the question arises whether it must not change the norm. If it has surrounded property with so many barriers that these have gained the specific and paramount importance of a legal construction *sui generis*, should it not set free this new construction from the obstructions caused by its origin? Or has it surrendered so much of its autonomy that it can no longer perform this last step or dare not do so? Does society still enjoy freedom of will, the power to create new norms?[4] Even if it disposes of the instruments

---

[4] The law relating to labour and the law relating to economics are, as branches of legal analysis, to-day overshadowed by the law of obligations on the one hand and the law of administration on the other: these latter belong to a sphere where public law and private law merge into one another. The trend of development indicates, however, that these two latter branches will eventually be the basis of a new regulation of labour and of society.

of legislation, if its legal title to free legislation is beyond dispute, the question still remains: is society still able to control technically the forces of development which have been set free? Society is sovereign as the legislator, but is it equally sovereign in practice? Or can it achieve in practical life only what it must? We have already become acquainted with the external limits which restrict the efficacy of the norm. If the law changes its functions, does this enforce a change of norms as well? Why do the norms not change equally automatically? If a change in functions is always also the cause of a change in norms, why is it that this cause cannot equally take effect in the quiet way of facts? How is the law determined by economics?

We have seen that the economic substratum dislocates the functions of the norm, that it reverses them; but the norm itself remains indestructible. The capital function also remains indestructible, and all development serves only its perfection. Therefore it may seem as if the crudest change of function does not react on this nebulous creation, this immaterial formula, those imperatives which apparently have no existence or only modestly vegetate in the documents of the statutes. Does it mean that the norms are indestructible, eternal, changeless, or at least determined by no other power than their own?

Given that, like all else under the sun, norms have their causes, wherein do these lie? Given that they enjoy a real existence, what are its characteristics, what is the mode of their existence and how do they change? Given that their origin lies in the conditions of life of the human race, that they are nothing more than a means of preserving human society, what part do they actually play in the existence and development of our own generation?

These are open questions of jurisprudence. The time has come to engage in an attempt at their solution.

# 40

# Morris Raphael Cohen

Morris R. Cohen (1880–1947), Professor of Philosophy at the City College of New York, almost alone sustained dialogue between law and philosophy during the first half of the twentieth century and sought clarification of legal problems along lines of logico-scientific analysis.

# PROPERTY AND SOVEREIGNTY*

## I. PROPERTY AS POWER

Any one who frees himself from the crudest materialism readily recognizes that as a legal term "property" denotes not material things but certain rights. In the world of nature apart from more or less organized society, there are things but clearly no property rights.

Further reflection shows that a property right is not to be identified with the fact of physical possession. Whatever technical definition of property we may prefer, we must recognize that a property right is a relation not between an owner and a thing, but between the owner and other individuals in reference to things. A right is always against one or more individuals. This becomes unmistakably clear if we take specifically modern forms of property such as franchises, patents, goodwill, etc., which constitute such a large part of the capitalized assets of our industrial and commercial enterprises.

The classical view of property as a right over things resolves it into component rights such as the *jus utendi, jus disponendi*, etc. But the essence of private property is always the right to exclude others. The law does not guarantee me the physical or social ability of actually using what it calls mine. By public regulations it may indirectly aid me by removing certain general hindrances to the enjoyment of property. But the law of property helps me directly only to exclude others from using the things that it assigns to me. If, then, somebody else wants to use the food, the house, the land, or the plough that the law calls mine, he has to get my consent. To the extent that these things are necessary to the life of my neighbor, the law thus confers on me a power, limited but real, to make him do what I want. If Laban has the sole disposal of his daughters and his cattle, Jacob must serve him if he desires to possess them. In a régime

*Morris R. Cohen, from "Property and Sovereignty" in *Law and the Social Order*, New York, Harcourt Brace & World, Inc., 1933. The essay was first delivered as an Irvine Lecture at Cornell University in 1926 and was published in 13 *Cornell L.Q.* 8 (1927). Reprinted by permission of Harry N. Rosenfield, Administrator, Estate of M. R. Cohen.

where land is the principal source of obtaining a livelihood, he who has the legal right over the land receives homage and service from those who wish to live on it.

The character of property as sovereign power compelling service and obedience may be obscured for us in a commercial economy by the fiction of the so-called labor contract as a free bargain and by the frequency with which service is rendered indirectly through a money payment. But not only is there actually little freedom to bargain on the part of the steel-worker or miner who needs a job, but in some cases the medieval subject had as much power to bargain when he accepted the sovereignty of his lord. Today I do not directly serve my landlord if I wish to live in the city with a roof over my head, but I must work for others to pay him rent with which he obtains the personal services of others. The money needed for purchasing things must for the vast majority be acquired by hard labor and disagreeable service to those to whom the law has accorded dominion over the things necessary for subsistence.

To a philosopher this is of course not at all an argument against private property. It may well be that compulsion in the economic as well as the political realm is necessary for civilized life. But we must not overlook the actual fact that dominion over things is also *imperium* over our fellow human beings.

The extent of the power over the life of others which the legal order confers on those called owners is not fully appreciated by those who think of the law as merely protecting men in their possession. Property law does more. It determines what men shall acquire. Thus, protecting the property rights of a landlord means giving him the right to collect rent, protecting the property of a railroad or a public-service corporation means giving it the right to make certain charges. Hence the ownership of land and machinery, with the rights of drawing rent, interest, etc., determines the future distribution of the goods that will come into being—determines what share of such goods various individuals shall acquire. The average life of goods that are either consumable or used for production of other goods is very short. Hence a law that merely protected men in their possession and did not also regulate the acquisition of new goods would be of little use.

From this point of view it can readily be seen that when a court rules that a gas company is entitled to a return of 6 per cent on its investment, it is not merely protecting property already possessed, it is also determining that a portion of the future social produce shall under certain conditions go to that company. Thus not only medieval landlords but the owners of all revenue-producing property are in fact granted by the law certain powers to tax the future social product. When to this power of taxation there is added the power to command the services of large numbers who are not economically independent, we have the essence of what historically has constituted political sovereignty.

Though the sovereign power possessed by the modern large property owners assumes a somewhat different form from that formerly possessed by the lord of the land, they are not less real and no less extensive. Thus the ancient lord had a limited power to control the modes of expenditure of his subjects by direct sumptuary legislation. The modern captain of industry and of finance has no such direct power himself, though his direct or indirect influence with the legislation may in that respect be considerable. But those who have the power to standardize and advertise certain products do determine what we may buy and use. We cannot well wear clothes except within lines decreed by their manufacturers, and our food is becoming more and more restricted to the kinds that are branded and standardized.

This power of the modern owner of capital to make us feel the necessity of buying more and more of his material goods (that may be more profitable to produce than economical to use) is a phenomenon of the utmost significance to the moral philosopher. The moral philosopher must also note that the modern captain of industry of finance exercises great influence in setting the fashion of expenditure by his personal example. Between a landed aristocracy and the tenantry, the difference is sharp and fixed, so that imitation of the former's mode of life by the latter is regarded as absurd and even immoral. In a money or commercial economy differences of income and mode of life are more gradual and readily hidden, so that there is great pressure to engage in lavish expenditure in order to appear in a higher class than one's income really allows. Such expenditure may even advance one's business credit. This puts pressure not merely on ever greater expenditure but more specifically on expenditure for ostentation rather than for comfort. Though a landed aristocracy may be wasteful in keeping large tracts of land for hunting purposes, the need for discipline to keep in power compels the cultivation of a certain hardihood that the modern wealthy man can ignore. An aristocracy assured of its recognized superiority need not engage in the race of lavish expenditure regardless of enjoyment.

In addition to these indirect ways in which the wealthy few determine the mode of life of the many, there is the somewhat more direct mode that bankers and financiers exercise when they determine the flow of investment, e.g., when they influence building operations by the amount that they will lend on mortgages. This power becomes explicit and obvious when a needy country has to borrow foreign capital to develop its resources.

I have already mentioned that the recognition of private property as a form of sovereignty is not itself an argument against it. Some form of government we must always have. For the most part men prefer to obey and let others take the trouble to think out rules, regulations, and orders. That is why we are always setting up authorities; and when we cannot find any we write to the newspaper as the final arbiter. But although government is a necessity, not all forms of it are of equal value. At any rate it is necessary to apply to the law of property all those considerations of social ethics and enlightened public policy which ought to be brought to the discussion of any just form of government.

To do this, let us begin with a consideration of the usual justifications of private property.

## II. THE JUSTIFICATION OF PROPERTY

### 1. *The Occupation Theory*

The oldest and until recently the most influential defence of private property was based on the assumed right of the original discoverer and occupant to dispose of that which thus became his. This view dominated the thought of Roman jurists and of modern philosophers—from Grotius to Kant—so much so that the right of the laborer to the produce of his work was sometimes defended on the ground that the laborer "occupied" the material that he fashioned into the finished product.

It is rather eays to find fatal flaws in this view. Few accumulations of great wealth were ever simply found. Rather were they acquired by the labor of many, by conquest, by business manipulation, and by other means. It is obvious that today at any rate few economic goods can be acquired by discovery and first occupancy. Even in the few cases when they are, as in fishing and trapping, we are apt rather to think of the labor involved as the proper basis of the property acquired. Indeed, there seems nothing ethically self-evident in the motto "Findings is keepings." There seems nothing wrong in a law that a treasure trove shall belong to the king or the state rather than to the finder. Shall the finder of a river be entitled to all the water in it?

Moreover, even if we were to grant that the original finder or occupier should have possession as against any one else, it by no means follows that he may use it arbitrarily or that his rule shall prevail indefinitely after his death. The right of others to acquire the property from him, by bargain, by inheritance, or by testamentary disposition, is not determined by the principle of occupation.

Despite all these objections, however, there is a kernel of positive value in this principle. Protecting the discoverer or first occupant is really part of the more general principle that possession as such should be protected. There is real human economy in doing so until somebody shows a better claim than the possessor. It makes for certainty and security of transaction as well as for public peace—provided the law is ready to set aside possession acquired in ways that are inimical to public order. Various principles of justice may determine the distribution of goods and the retribution to be made for acts of injustice. But the law must not ignore the principle of inertia in human affairs. Continued possession creates expectations in the possessor and in others, and only a very poor morality would ignore the hardship of frustrating these expectations and rendering human relations insecure, even to correct some old flaws in the original acquisition. Suppose some remote ancestor of yours did acquire your property by fraud, robbery, or conquest, e.g., in the days of William of Normandy. Would it be just to take it away from you and your dependents who have held it in good faith? Reflection on the general insecurity that would result from such procedure leads us to see that as habit is the basis of individual life, continued practice must be the basis of social procedure. Any form of property that exists has therefore a claim to continue until it can be shown that the effort to change it is worth while. Continual changes in property laws would certainly discourage enterprise.

Nevertheless, it would be as absurd to argue that the distribution of property must never be modified by law as it would be to argue that the distribution of political power must never be changed. No less a philosopher than Aristotle argued against changing even bad laws, lest the habit of obedience be thereby impaired. There is something to be said for this, but only so long as we are in the realm of merely mechanical obedience. When we introduce the notion of free or rational obedience. Aristotle's argument loses its force in the political realm; and similar considerations apply to any property system that can claim the respect of rational beings.

## 2. *The Labour Theory*

That every one is entitled to the full produce of his labor is assumed as self-evident both by socialists and by conservatives who believe that capital is the result of the savings of labor. However, as economic goods are never the result of any one man's unaided labor, our maxim is altogether inapplicable. How shall we determine what part of the value of a table should belong to the carpenter, to the lumberman, to the transport worker, to the policeman who guarded the peace while the work was being done, and to the indefinitely large numbers of others whose co-operation was necessary? Moreover, even if we could tell what any one individual has produced—let us imagine a Robinson Crusoe growing up all alone on an island and in no way indebted to any community—it would still be highly questionable whether he has a right to keep the full produce of his labor when some shipwrecked mariner needs his surplus food to keep from starving.

In actual society no one ever thinks it unjust that a wealthy old bachelor should have part of his presumably just earnings taken away in the form of a tax for the benefit of other people's children, or that one immune to certain diseases should be taxed to support hospitals, etc. We do not think there is any injustice involved in such cases because social interdependence is so intimate that no man can justly say: "This wealth is entirely and absolutely mine as the result of my own unaided effort."

The degree of social solidarity varies, of course; and it is easy to conceive of a sparsely settled community, such as Missouri at the beginning of the nineteenth century, where a family of hunters or isolated cultivators of the soil might regard everything that it acquired as the product of its own labor. Generally, however, human beings start with a stock of tools or information acquired from others and they are more or less dependent upon some government for protection against foreign aggression, etc.

Yet despite these and other criticisms, the labor theory contains too much substantial truth to be brushed aside. The essential truth is that labor has to be encouraged and that property must be distributed in such a way as to encourage ever greater efforts at productivity.

As not all things produced are ultimately good, as even good things may be produced at an unjustified expense in human life and worth, it is obvious that other principles besides that of labor or productivity are needed for an adequate basis or justification of any system of property law. We can only say dialectically that all other things being equal, property should be distributed with due regard to the productive needs of the community. We must, however, recognize that a good deal of property accrues to those who are not productive, and a good deal of productivity does not and perhaps should not receive its reward in property. Nor should we leave this theme without recalling the Hebrew-Christian view—and for that matter, the specifically religious view— that the first claim on property is by the man who needs it rather than the man who has created it. Indeed, the only way of justifying the principle of distribution of property according to labor is to show that it serves the larger social need.

The occupation theory has shown us the necessity for security of possession, and the labor theory the need for encouraging enterprise. These two needs are mutually dependent. Anything that discourages enterprise makes our possessions less valuable, and it is obvious that it is not worth while engaging in economic enterprise if there is no prospect of securely possessing the fruit of it. Yet there is also a conflict between these two needs. The owners of land, wishing to secure the continued possession by the family, oppose laws that make it subject to free financial transactions or make it possible that land should be taken away from one's heirs by a judgment creditor for personal debts. In an agricultural economy security of possession demands that the owner of a horse should be able to reclaim it no matter into whose hands it has fallen. But in order that markets should be possible, it becomes necessary that the innocent purchaser should have a good title. This conflict between static and dynamic security has been treated most suggestively by Demogue.

### 3. *Property and Personality*

Hegels, Ahrens, Lorimer, and other idealists have tried to deduce the right of property from the individual's right to act as a free personality. To be free one must have a sphere of self-assertion in the external world. One's private property provides such an opportunity.

Waiving all traditional difficulties in applying the metaphysical idea of freedom to empirical legal acts, we may still object that the notion of personality is too vague to enable us to deduce definite legal consequences by means of it. How, for example, can the principle of personality help us to decide to what extent there shall be private rather than public property in railroads, mines, gas-works, and other public necessities?

Not the extremest communist would deny that in the interest of privacy certain personal belongings such as are typified by the toothbrush must be under the dominion of the individual owner, to the absolute exclusion of every one else. This, however, will not carry us far if we recall that the major effect of property in land, in the machinery of production, in capital goods, etc., is to enable the owner to exclude others from *their necessities,* and thus to compel them to serve him. Ahrens, one of the chief expounders of the personality theory, argues: "It is undoubtedly contrary to the right of personality to have persons dependent on others on account of material goods." But if this is so, the primary effect of property on a large scale is to limit freedom, since the one thing that private property law does not do is to guarantee a minimum of subsistence or the necessary tools of freedom to every one. So far as a régime of private property fails to do the latter it rather compels people to part with their freedom.

It may well be argued in reply that just as restraining traffic rules in the end give us greater freedom of motion, so, by giving control over things to individual property owners, greater economic freedom is in the end assured to all. This is a strong argument, as can be seen by comparing the different degrees of economic freedom that prevail in lawless and in law-abiding communities. It is, however, an argument for legal order rather than for any particular form of government or private property. It argues for a régime where every one has a definite sphere of rights and duties, but it does not tell us where these lines should be drawn. The principle of freedom of personality certainly cannot justify a legal order wherein a few can, by virtue of their legal monopoly over necessities, compel others to work under degrading and brutalizing conditions. A government that limits the right of large landholders limits the rights of property, and yet may promote real freedom. Property owners, like other individuals, are members of a community and must subordinate their ambition to the larger whole of which they are a part. They may find their compensation in spiritually identifying their good with that of the larger life.

## 4. *The Economic Theory*

The economic justification of private property is that by means of it a maximum of productivity is promoted. The classical economic argument may be put thus: The successful business man, the one who makes the greatest profit, is the one who has the greatest power to foresee effective demand. If he has not that power his enterprise fails. He is therefore, in fact, the best director of economic activities.

There can be little doubt that if we take the whole history of agriculture and industry, or compare the economic output in Russia under the *mir* system with that in the United States, there is a strong *prima facie* case for the contention that more intensive cultivation of the soil and greater productiveness of industry prevail under individual ownership. Many *a priori* psychologic and economic reasons can also be brought to explain why this must be so, why the individual cultivator will take greater care not to exhaust the soil, etc. All this, however, is so familiar that we may take it for granted and look at the other side of the case, at the considerations which show that there is a difference between socially desirable productivity and the desire for individual profits.

In the first place, let us note that of many things the supply is not increased by making them private property. This is obviously true of land in cities and of other monopoly or limited goods. Private ownership of land does not increase the amount of rainfall, and irrigation works to make the land more fruitful have been carried through by governments more than by private initiative. Nor was the productivity of French or Irish lands reduced when the property of their landlords in rent charges and other incidents of seigniorage was reduced or even abolished. In our own days, we frequently see tobacco, cotton, or wheat farmers in distress because they have succeeded in raising too plentiful crops; and manufacturers who are well informed know when greater profit is to be made by a decreased output. Patents for processes that would cheapen the product are often bought up by manufacturers and never used. Durable goods that are more economic to the consumer are very frequently crowded out of the market by shoddier goods which are more profitable to produce because of the larger turnover. Advertising campaigns often persuade people to buy the less economical goods and to pay the cost of the uneconomic advice.

In the second place, there are inherent sources of waste in a régime of private enterprise and free competition. If the biologic analogy of the struggle for existence were taken seriously, we should see that the natural survival of the economically fittest is attended, as in the biologic field, with frightful wastefulness. The elimination of the unsuccessful competitor may be a gain to the survivor, but all business failures are losses to the community.

Finally, a régime of private ownership in industry is too apt to sacrifice social interests to immediate monetary profits. This shows itself in speeding up industry to such a pitch that men are exhausted in a relatively few years, whereas a slower expenditure of their energy would prolong their useful years. It shows itself in the way in which private enterprise has wasted a good deal of the natural resources of the United States to obtain immediate profits. Even when the directors of a modern industrial enterprise see the uneconomic consequences of immediate profits, the demand of shareholders for immediate dividends, and the ease with which men can desert a business and leave it to others to stand the coming losses, tend to encourage ultimately wasteful and uneconomic activity. Possibly the best illustration of this is child labor, which by lowering wages increases immediate profits, but in the end is really wasteful of the most precious wealth of the country, its future manhood and womanhood.

Surveying our arguments thus far: We have seen the roots of property in custom, in the need for economic productivity, and in individual needs of privacy. But we have also noted that property, being only one among other human interests, cannot be pursued absolutely without detriment to human life. Hence we can no longer maintain Montesquieu's view that private property is sacrosanct and that the general government must in no way interfere with or retrench its domain. The issue before thoughtful people is therefore not the maintenance or abolition of private property, but the determination of the precise lines along which private enterprise must be given free scope and where it must be restricted in the interests of the common good.

# 41

# A. M. Honore

A. M. Honoré (1921–    ), Rhodes Reader in Roman and Dutch law at Oxford University, is schooled in both classical and comparative law, and co-authored with H. L. A. Hart a significant study, *Causation in the Law*.

# OWNERSHIP*

Ownership is one of the characteristic institutions of human society. A people to whom ownership was unknown, or who accorded it a minor place in their arrangements, who meant by *meum* and *tuum* no more than 'what I (or you) presently hold' would live in a world that is not our world. Yet to see why their world would be different, and to assess the plausibility of vaguely conceived schemes to replace 'ownership' by 'public administration', or of vaguely stated claims that the importance of ownership has declined or its character changed in the twentieth century, we need first to have a clear idea of what ownership is.

I propose, therefore, to begin by giving an account of the standard incidents of ownership: *i.e.* those legal rights, duties and other incidents which apply, in the ordinary case, to the person who has the greatest interest in a thing admitted by a mature legal system. To do so will be to analyse the concept of ownership, by which I mean the 'liberal' concept of 'full' individual ownership, rather than any more restricted notion to which the same label may be attached in certain contexts . . .

## 1. THE LIBERAL CONCEPT OF OWNERSHIP

If ownership is provisionally defined as the *greatest possible interest in a thing which a mature system of law recognizes*, then it follows that, since all mature systems admit the existence of 'interests' in 'things', all mature systems have, in a sense, a concept of ownership. Indeed, even primitive systems, like that of the Trobriand islanders, have rules by which certain persons, such as the 'owners' of canoes, have greater interests in certain things than anyone else.[1]

For mature legal systems it is possible to make a larger claim. In them certain important legal incidents are found, which are common to different

---

*A. M. Honore, from "Ownership" in *Oxford Essays in Jurisprudence* (edited by A. G. Guest),, Oxford, The Clarendon Press, 1961, pp. 107, 108–128. Reprinted by permission of the publisher.
[1] Malinowsky, *Crime and Custom in Savage Society*, p. 18.

systems. If it were not so, 'He owns that umbrella', said in a purely English context, would mean something different from 'He owns that umbrella', proferred as a translation of 'Ce parapluie est à lui'. Yet, as we know, they mean the same. There is indeed, a substantial similarity in the position of one who 'owns' an umbrella in England, France, Russia, China, and any other modern country one may care to mention. Everywhere the 'owner' can, in the simple uncomplicated case, in which no other person has an interest in the thing, use it, stop others using it, lend it, sell it or leave it by will. Nowhere may he use it to poke his neighbour in the ribs or to knock over his vase. Ownership, *dominium, propriété, Eigentum* and similar words stand not merely for the greatest interest in things in particular systems but for a type of interest with common features transcending particular systems. It must surely be important to know what these common features are?

In stressing the importance of such common features, I do not wish to go beyond the claim that these resemblances exist *de facto* and can be explained by the common needs of mankind and the common conditions of human life. It would be rash to assert that the features discussed are *necessarily* common to different mature systems, or that their range and ubiquity proves that what is called 'general jurisprudence' is a reputable pursuit. These assertions may indeed be true, but for my purposes it is enough to show that the standard incidents of ownership do not vary from system to system in the erratic, unpredictable way implied by some writers but, on the contrary, have a tendency to remain constant from place to place and age to age.

Nor must the present thesis be confused with the claim that all systems attach an equal importance to ownership (in the full, liberal sense) or regard the same things as capable of being owned. The latter claim would be patently false. In the Soviet Union, for instance, important assets such as land, businesses and collective farms are in general withdrawn from 'personal ownership' (*viz.* the liberal type of ownership) and subjected to 'government' or 'collective' ownership, which is a different, though related institution.[2] The notion of things 'outside commerce', not subject to private ownership but to special regulation by the state or public authorities, is an ancient one and has retained its importance in modern continental law.[3] Again, there is a case for saying that, in the early middle ages, land in England could not plausibly be said to be 'owned' because the standard incidents of which I shall speak were so divided between lord and tenant that the position of neither presented a sufficient analogy with the paradigm case of owning a thing.[4]

Indeed, in nearly all systems there will be some things to which not all the standard incidents apply, some things which cannot be sold or left by will, some interests which cannot endure beyond a lifetime, some things (flick knives, Colorado beetles) which it is forbidden to use or to use in certain

---

[2] Gsovski, *Soviet Civil Law*, p. 569.
[3] Vegting, *Domaine public et res extra commercium*.
[4] Pollock and Maitland, *History of English Law to* 1290, Vol. II, p.4.

ways. If the differences between these cases and the paradigm case are striking enough, we shall be tempted to say that the things in question are not or cannot be owned, but it would be a mistake to conclude that the legal systems in which these cases occur do not recognize ownership. Whether a system recognizes ownership, and to what extent it permits ownership (who may own, what may be owned), are widely differing questions. No doubt liberal societies are more inclined than socialist societies to extend the list of items that can be owned, but it does not follow that, when a socialist system permits ownership, or 'personal ownership', it is permitting something different from what is permitted in the corresponding case in a liberal society. It may well be—and all the evidence indeed supports the view—that socialist societies recognize the 'liberal' notion of 'full' ownership, but limit the range of things that can be owned. Perhaps definitions of ownership contained in codes are not a safe guide. Still, it is striking that the French civil code, enacted in an atmosphere of liberal individualism, defines ownership as 'the right of enjoying and disposing of things in the most absolute manner, provided that one abstains from any use forbidden by statute or subordinate legislation';[5] while the Soviet civil code, framed in a socialist context, provides, in very similar language, that 'within the limits laid down by law, the owner has the right to possess, to use and to dispose of his property'.[6] Obviously much here depends on what limits are laid down by law in each system; in fact, so far as articles subject to 'personal ownership' are concerned, the limits in the two systems hardly differ.

One further *caveat*. I set out to describe the incidents of ownership in the simple cases in which one would not hesitate to say '$X$ owns that thing, that is $X$'s book or house', even though $Y$ may have borrowed it, or $Y$ may be $X$'s tenant. In doing this I do not lose sight of the existence of more complicated cases in which layman and lawyer alike may be puzzled to know which, of two or more persons interested in a thing, to call owner, or whether to say, on the other hand, that neither or none is owner. Just as the rules of a system may so restrict the permissible ways of dealing with certain types of thing that we are inclined to say that such things are not capable of being owned in that system, or can be owned only a sense different from the full, liberal sense we are to investigate, so the rules of a system may provide for the splitting of interests in a type of thing which, in general, is admittedly capable of being owned. Houses can be owned, and there is no conceptual difficulty in locating the ownership of a house let on a short lease. But if $A$ lets $B$ a house on a lease for 2,000 years it may be very unclear, at least to the layman, whether $A$ or $B$ or neither should be called owner. (In this case, legal usage designates $A$ owner despite the tenuous character of his reversionary right.) Again, can a mortgagor be said to 'own' a house which is mortgaged? (Legal usage here refuses to designate the mortgagee owner despite the potentially indeterminate character of his interest.) No obvious linguistic convention governs the answer to such

[5] *Code Civil*, art. 544.
[6] Soviet civil code, art. 58.

problems, and, if the rules of a legal system demand an answer, it must be sought in positive law, in the comparative strength of competing analogies with the paradigm case and in the light shed on the problem by the social context.

The fact that there are such cases of split ownership and that they present baffling problems to one who is compelled to fix on one interested person as *the* owner of the thing, does not make it worthless to try to delineate the incidents present in the ordinary, uncomplicated case. On the contrary, such a delineation is essential in order that it may be possible to assess the strength of the analogies in the peripheral cases. What must, however, be recognized at the outset, is that the actual use of 'owner' and 'ownership' extends beyond the standard case now to be described and that to delineate the standard case is here, as with most legal notions, not to provide a code for the use of the word. For instance, the sixteen or so pages of Burrows' *Words and Phrases Judicially Defined,*[7] concerned with the interpretation of the word 'owner' in various statutes, amply reveal how the courts have wrestled with provisions extending the legal meaning of 'owner' beyond the standard cases. But it is important to see that the very existence of such problems of statutory interpretation presupposes that there are paradigm cases in which the interpretation of 'owner' is clear.

Thus where a statute provided[8] that ' "owner" in relation to land, includes every person who jointly or severally whether at law or in equity, is entitled' to the profits of the land etc., Griffith C.J. pointed out that the term 'owner' '*Prima facie* connotes entire dominion. Section 3 [the definition section] extends the meaning so as to take in certain persons who possess some, but not all, of the rights of absolute owners. Although, therefore, the launguage of the definition is in form inclusive, and not exhaustive, it must be read as if the words "besides the absolute owner" were inserted after "includes".'[9] This presupposes that we know, without the help of an interpretation clause, what is meant by 'absolute owner'. Again, when Jessel M.R. said in a case on the interpretation of the Highways Act, 1835, 'I am clearly of the opinion that the term "owner" means the man in occupation, who may be either the actual owner or else only the occupying tenant',[10] he could not meaningfully have said this unless there were available criteria for the identification of the interest called 'ownership' and so of the 'actual owner' in the majority of cases.

### THE STANDARD INCIDENTS

I now list what appear to be the standard incidents of ownership. They may be regarded as necessary ingredients in the notion of ownership, in the

---

[7] (1934), Vol. IV, pp. 130–146.
[8] Land Tax Assessment Act, 1910, s. 3.
[9] *Union Trustee Co. of Australia, Ltd.* v. *Land Tax Federal Commission* (1915), 20 C.L.R. 526, at p. 531.
[10] *Woodard v. Billericay Harbour Board* (1879), 11 Ch. D.214, at p. 217.

sense that, if a system did not admit them, and did not provide for them to be united in a single person, we would conclude that it did not know the liberal concept of ownership, though it might still have a modified version of owner-ship, either of a primitive or sophisticated sort. But the listed incidents are not individually necessary, though they may be together sufficient, conditions for the person of inherence to be designated 'owner' of a particular thing in a given system. As we have seen, the use of 'owner' will extend to cases in which not all the listed incidents are present.

Ownership comprises the right to possess, the right to use, the right to manage, the right to the income of the thing, the right to the capital, the right to security, the rights or incidents of transmissibility and absence of term, the prohibition of harmful use, liability to execution, and the incident of residuarity: this makes eleven leading incidents. Obviously, there are alternative ways of classifying the incidents; moreover, it is fashionable to speak of ownership as if it were just a bundle of rights, in which case at least two items in the list would have to be omitted.

No doubt the concentration in the same person of the right (liberty)[11] of using as one wishes, the right to exclude others, the power of alienating and an immunity from expropriation is a cardinal feature of the institution. Yet it would be a distortion—and one of which the eighteenth century, with its overemphasis on subjective rights, was patently guilty—to speak as if this concentration of patiently garnered rights was the only legally or socially important characteristic of the owner's position. The present analysis, by emphasizing that the owner is subject to characteristic prohibitions and limitations, and that ownership comprises at least one important incident independent of the owner's choice, is an attempt to redress the balance.

### (1) *The Right to Possess*

The right to possess, *viz.* to have exclusive physical control of a thing, or to have such control as the nature of the thing admits, is the foundation on which the whole superstructure of ownership rests. It may be divided into two aspects, the right (claim) to be put in exclusive control of a thing and the right to remain in control, *viz.* the claim that others should not without permission, interfere. Unless a legal system provides some rules and procedures for attaining these ends it cannot be said to protect ownership.

It is of the essence of the right to possess that it is *in rem* in the sense of availing against persons generally. This does not, of course, mean that an owner is necessarily entitled to exclude everyone from his property. We happily speak of the ownership of land, yet a largish number of officials have the right of entering on private land without the owner's consent, for some limited period and purpose. On the other hand, a general licence so to enter on the

---

[11] In this article I identify rights with claims, liberties etc. For a criticism of this identification see (1960), 34 Tulane L.R. 453.

'property' of others would put an end to the institution of landowning as we now know it.

The protection of the right to possess (still using 'possess' in the convenient, though over-simple, sense of 'have exclusive physical control') should be sharply marked off from the protection of mere present possession. To exclude others from what one presently holds is an instinct found in babies and even, as Holmes points out,[12] in animals, of which the seal gives a striking example. To sustain this instinct by legal rules is to protect possession but not, as such, to protect the right to possess and so not to protect ownership. If dispossession without the possessor's consent is, in general, forbidden, the possessor is given a right *in rem*, valid against persons generally, to remain undisturbed, but he has no *right to possess in rem* unless he is entitled to recover from persons generally what he has lost or had taken from him, and to obtain from them what is due to him but not yet handed over. Admittedly there may be borderline cases in which the right to possess is partially recognized, *e.g.* where a thief is entitled to recover from those who oust him and all claiming under them, but not from others.

The protection of the right to possess, and so of one essential element in ownership, is achieved only when there are rules allotting exclusive physical control to one person rather than another, and that not merely on the basis that the person who has such control at the moment is entitled to continue in control. When children understand that Christmas presents go not to the finder but to the child whose name is written on the outside of the parcel, when a primitive tribe has a rule that a dead man's things go not to the first taker but to his son or his sister's son, we know that they have at least an embryonic idea of ownership.

To have worked out the notion of 'having a right to' as distinct from merely 'having', or, if that is too subjective a way of putting it, of rules allocating things to people as opposed to rules merely forbidding forcible taking, was a major intellectual achievement. Without it society would have been impossible. Yet the distinction is apt to be overlooked by English lawyers, who are accustomed to the rule that every adverse possession is a root of title, *i.e.* gives rise to a right to possess,[13] or at least that '*de facto* possession is *prima facie* evidence of seisin in fee and right to possession'.[14]

The owner, then, has characteristically a battery of remedies in order to obtain, keep and, if necessary, get back the thing owned. Remedies such as the actions for ojectment and wrongful detention and the *vindicatio* are designed to enable the plaintiff either to obtain or to get back a thing, or at least to put some pressure on the defendant to hand it over. Others, such as the actions for trespass to land and goods, the Roman possessory interdicts and

---

[12] *The Common Law*, p. 213.
[13] Pollock & Wright, *Possession in the Common Law* (1888), pp. 91, 95; Wade and Megarry, *The Law of Real Property* (2nd ed.), p. 955.
[14] *N.R.M.A. Insurance, Ltd.* v. *B. & B. Shipping and Marine Salvage Co. (Pty.), Ltd.* (1947), 47 S.C.R. (N.S.W.) 273.

their modern counterparts are primarily directed towards enabling a present possessor to keep possession. Few of the remedies mentioned are confined to the owner; most of them are available also to persons with a right to possess falling short of ownership, and some to mere possessors. Conversely, there will be cases in which they are not available to the owner, for instance because he has voluntarily parted with possession for a temporary purpose, as by hiring the thing out. The availability of such remedies is clearly not a necessary and sufficient condition of owning a thing; what is necessary, in order that there may be ownership of things at all, is that such remedies shall be available to the owner in the usual case in which no other person has a right to exclude him from the thing.

### (2) *The Right to Use*

The present incident and the next two overlap. On a wide interpretation of 'use', management and income fall within use. On a narrow interpretation, 'use' refers to the owner's personal use and enjoyment of the thing owned. On this interpretation it excludes management and income.

The right (liberty) to use at one's discretion has rightly been recognized as a cardinal feature of ownership, and the fact that, as we shall see, certain limitations on use also fall within the standard incidents of ownership does not detract from its importance, since the standard limitations are, in general, rather precisely defined, while the permissible types of use constitute an open list.

### (3) *The Right to Manage*

The right to manage is the right to decide how and by whom the thing owned shall be used. This right depends, legally, on a cluster of powers, chiefly powers of licensing acts which would otherwise be unlawful and powers of contracting: the power to admit others to one's land, to permit others to use one's things, to define the limits of such permission, and to contract effectively in regard to the use (in the literal sense) and exploitation of the thing owned. An owner may not merely sit in his own deck chair but may validly license others to sit in it, lend it, impose conditions on the borrower, direct how it is to be painted or cleaned, contract for it to be mended in a particular way. This is the sphere of management in relation to a simple object like a deck chair. When we consider more complex cases, like the ownership of a business, the complex of powers which make up the right to manage seems still more prominent. The power to direct how resources are to be used and exploited is one of the cardinal types of economic and political power; the owner's legal powers of management are one, but only one possible basis for it. Many observers have drawn attention to the growth of managerial power divorced from legal ownership; in such cases it may be that we should speak of split ownership or redefine our notion of the thing owned. This does not affect the fact that the right to manage is an important element in the notion of ownership; indeed, the fact that we feel doubts in these cases whether the 'legal owner' *really* owns is a testimony to its importance.

Management often takes the form of making contracts relating to the thing owned, whether with servants or agents or independent contractors. This fact, and the growing relative importance of management in comparison with personal use, at least in regard to some types of thing such as businesses, has led some observers to the neat conclusion that, over a wide sphere, *obligatio* has swallowed up *res*.[15] Even if the contrast were an apt one (and, after all, an *obligatio* is a *res*, a chose in action a chose) the sentiment would be exaggerated because many powers of management are exercised otherwise than by way of contract, not to mention powers of alienation. The point would be better made by saying that, in the owner's battery of rights, powers have increased in calibre while liberties have declined.

### (4) *The Right to the Income*

To use or occupy a thing may be regarded as the simplest way of deriving an income from it, of enjoying it. It is, for instance, expressly contemplated by the English income tax legislation that the rent-free use or occupation of a house is a form of income, and only the inconvenience of assessing and collecting the tax presumably prevents the extension of this principle to movables.

Income in the more ordinary sense (fruits, rents, profits) may be thought of as a surrogate of use, a benefit derived from forgoing personal use of a thing and allowing others to use it for reward; as a reward for work done in exploiting the thing; or as the brute product of a thing, made by nature or by other persons. Obviously the line to be drawn between the earned and unearned income from a thing cannot be firmly drawn.

The owner's right to the income, which has always, under one name or another, bulked large in an analysis of his rights, has assumed still greater significance with the increased importance of income relative to capital. Legally it takes the form of a claim sometimes *in rem,* sometimes *in personam* to the income. When the latter is in the form of money, the claim before receipt of the money is *in personam;* and since the income from many forms of property, such as shares and trust funds, is in this form, there is another opportunity for introducing the apophthegm that *obligatio* has swallowed up *res*.

### (5) *The Right to the Capital*

The right to the capital consists in the power to alienate the thing and the liberty to consume, waste or destroy the whole or part of it: clearly it has an important economic aspect. The latter liberty need not be regarded as unrestricted; but a general provision requiring things to be conserved in the public

---

[15] J. W. Jones, *Forms of Ownership* (1947), 22 Tulane L.R. 83, 93.

interest, so far as not consumed by use in the ordinary way, would perhaps be inconsistent with the liberal idea of ownership.

Most people do not wilfully destroy permanent assets; hence the power of alienation is the more important aspect of the owner's right to the capital of the thing owned. This comprises the power to alienate during life or on death, by way of sale, mortgage, gift or other mode, to alienate a part of the thing and partially to alienate it. The power to alienate may be subdivided into the power to make a valid disposition of the thing and the power to transfer the holder's title (or occasionally a better title) to it. The two usually concur but may be separated, as when *A* has a power of appointment over property held by *B* in trust.[16] Again, in some systems, a sale, mortgage, bequest, etc. may be regarded as valid though the seller or mortgagor cannot give a good title. By giving a good title is meant transferring to the transferee the rights of the owner including his power of alienation.

An owner normally has both the power of disposition and the power of transferring title. Disposition on death is not permitted in many primitive societies but seems to form an essential element in the mature notion of ownership. The tenacity of the right of testation once it has been recognized is shown by the Soviet experience. The earliest writers were hostile to inheritance, but gradually Soviet law has come to admit that citizens may dispose freely of their 'personal property' on death, subject to limits not unlike those known elsewhere.[17]

## (6) *The Right to Security*

An important aspect of the owner's position is that he should be able to look forward to remaining owner indefinitely if he so chooses and he remains solvent. His right to do so may be called the right to security. Legally, this is in effect an immunity from expropriation, based on rules which provide that, apart from bankruptcy and execution for debt, the transmission of ownership is consensual.

However, a general right to security, availing against others, is consistent with the existence of a power to expropriate or divest in the state or public authorities. From the point of view of security of property, it is important that when expropriation takes place, adequate compensation should be paid; but a general power to expropriate subject to paying compensation would be fatal to the institution of ownership as we know it. Holmes' paradox, that where specific restitution of goods is not a normal remedy,[18] expropriation and wrongful conversion are equivalent, obscures the vital distinction between acts which a legal system permits as rightful and those which it reprobates as wrongful: but if wrongful conversion were general and went unchecked, ownership as we know it would disappear, though damages were regularly paid.

---

[16] Hanbury, *Modern Equity* (1952), p.114.
[17] Constitution of the U.S.S.R., 1936, s. 10; Gsovski, *op cit.*, p. 620.
[18] Holmes (1897), 10 Harv. L.R. 457, 461.

In some systems, as *(semble)* English law, a private individual may destroy another's property without compensation when this is necessary in order to protect his own person or property from a greater danger.[19] Such a rule is consistent with security of property only because of its exceptional character. Again, the state's (or local authority's) power of expropriation is usually limited to certain classes of thing and certain limited purposes. A general power to expropriate any property for any purpose would be inconsistent with the institution of ownership. If, under such a system, compensation were regularly paid, we might say either that ownership was not recognized in that system, or that money alone could be owned, 'money' here meaning a strictly fungible claim on the resources on the community. As we shall see, 'ownership' of such claims is not identical with the ownership of material objects and simple claims.

### (7) *The Incident of Transmissibility*

It is often said that one of the main characteristics of the owner's interest is its 'duration'. In England, at least, the doctrine of estates made lawyers familiar with the notion of the 'duration' of an interest and Maitland, in a luminous metaphor, spoke of estates as 'projected upon the plane of time'.[20]

Yet this notion is by no means as simple as it seems. What is called 'unlimited' duration (*perpétuité*)[21] comprises at least two elements (i) that the interest can be transmitted to the holder's successors and so on *ad infinitum* (The fact that in medieval land law all interests were considered 'temporary'[22] is one reason why the terminology of ownership failed to take root, with consequences which have endured long after the cause has disappeared); (ii) that it is not certain to determine at a future date. These two elements may be called 'transmissibility' and 'absence of term' respectively. We are here concerned with the former.

No one, as Austin points out,[23] can enjoy a thing after he is dead (except vicariously) so that, in a sense, no interest can outlast death. But an interest which is transmissible to the holder's successors (persons designated by or closely related to the holder who obtain the property after him) is more valuable than one which stops with his death. This is so both because on alienation the alienee or, if transmissibility is generally recognized, the alienee's successors, are thereby enabled to enjoy the thing after the alienor's death so that a better price can be obtained for the thing, and because, even if alienation were not recognized, the present holder would by the very fact of transmissibility be dispensed *pro tanto* from making provision for his intestate heirs. Hence, for example, the moment when the tenant in fee acquired a heritable (though

---

[19] *Cope* v. *Sharpe*, (1912) 1 K.B. 496; *Cresswell* v. *Sirl*, (1948) 1 K.B. 241.
[20] Pollock & Maitland, *op cit.*, Vol. II, p. 10.
[21] Planiol-Ripert-Esmein, *Traité pratique de droit civil francais* (1952), Vol. II, p. 220.
[22] Hargreaves, *Introduction to the Principles of Land Law* (1952), p. 47.
[23] Austin, *Jurisprudence*, 4th ed., (1873), p. 817.

not yet fully alienable) right was a crucial moment in the evolution of the fee simple. Heritability by the state would not, of course, amount to transmissibility in the present sense: it is assumed that the transmission is in some sense *advantageous* to the transmitter.

Transmissibility can, of course, be admitted, yet stop short at the first, second or third generation of transmittees. The owner's interest is characterized by *indefinite* transmissibility, no limit being placed on the possible number of transmissions, though the nature of the thing may well limit the actual number.

In deference to the conventional view that the exercise of a right must depend on the choice of the holder,[24] I have refrained from calling transmissibility a right. It is, however, clearly something in which the holder has an economic interest, and it may be that the notion of a right requires revision in order to take account of incidents not depending on the holder's choice which are nevertheless of value to him.

## (8) *The Incident of Absence of Term*

This is the second part of what is vaguely called 'duration'. The rules of a legal system usually seem to provide for determinate, indeterminate and determinable interests. The first are certain to determine at a future date or on the occurence of a future event which is certain to occur. In this class come leases for however long a term, copyrights, etc. Indeterminate interests are those, such as ownership and easements, to which no term is set. Should the holder live for ever, he would, in the ordinary way, be able to continue in the enjoyment of them for ever. Since human beings are mortal, he will in practice only be able to enjoy them for a limited period, after which the fate of his interest depends on its transmissibility. Again, since human beings are mortal, interests for life, whether of the holder of another, must be regarded as determinate. The notion of an indeterminate interest, in the full sense, therefore requires the notion of transmissibility, but, if the latter were not recognized, there would still be value to the holder in the fact that his interest was not due to determine on a fixed date or on the occurence of some contingency, like a general election, which is certain to occur sooner or later.

On inspection it will be found that what I have called indeterminate interests are really determinable. The rules of legal systems always provide some contingencies such as bankruptcy, sale in execution, or state expropriation on which the holder of an interest may lose it. It is true that in most of these cases the interest is technically said to be transmitted to a successor *(e.g.,* a trustee in bankruptcy) whereas in the case of determinable interests the interest is not so transmitted. Yet the substance of the matter is that the present holder may lose his interest in certain events. It is never, therefore, certain that, if the present holder and his successors so choose, the interest will never determine as long as the thing remains in existence. The notion of

---

[24] Hart, *Definition and Theory in Jurisprudence* (1953), p. 16; (1954), 70 L.Q.R. 49.

indeterminate interests can only be saved by regarding the purchaser in insolvency or execution, or the state, as succeeding to the same interest as that had by the previous holder. This is an implausible way of looking at the matter, because the expropriability and executability of a thing is not an incident of value to the owner, but a restriction on the owner's rights imposed in the social interest. It seems better, therefore, to deny the existence of indeterminate interests and to classify those which are not determinate according to the number and character of the contingencies on which they will determine. This affords a justification for speaking of a 'determinable fee', of 'fiduciary ownership' etc., for these do not differ essentially from 'full ownership', determinable on bankruptcy or expropriation.

## (9) *The Prohibition of Harmful Use*

An owner's liberty to use and manage the thing owned as he chooses is in mature systems of law, as in primitive systems, subject to the condition that uses harmful to other members of society are forbidden. There may, indeed, be much dispute over what is to count as 'harm' and to what extent give and take demands that minor inconvenience between neighbours shall be tolerated. Nevertheless, at least for material objects, one can always point to abuses which a legal system will not allow.

I may use my car freely but not in order to run my neighbour down, or to demolish his gate, or even to go on his land if he protests; nor may I drive uninsured. I may build on my land as I choose, but not in such a way that my building collapses on my neighbour's land. I may let off fireworks on Guy Fawkes night, but not in such a way as to set fire to my neighbor's house. These and similar limitations on the use of things are so familiar and so obviously essential to the existence of an orderly community that they are not often thought of as incidents of ownership; yet, without them 'ownership' would be a destructive force.

## (10) *Liability to Execution*

Of a somewhat similar character is the liability of the owner's interest to be taken away from him for debt, either by execution of a judgment debt or on insolvency. Without such a general liability the growth of credit would be impeded and ownership would, again, be an instrument by which the owner could defraud his creditors. This incident, therefore, which may be called *executability*, seems to constitute one of the standard ingredients of the liberal idea of ownership.

It is a question whether any other limitations on ownership imposed in the social interest should be regarded as among its standard incidents. A good case can certainly be made for listing *liability to tax* and *expropriability by the state* as such. Although it is often convenient to contrast taxes on property with taxes on persons, all tax must ultimately be taken from something owned, whether a material object or a fund or a chose in action. A general rule exempting the owners of things from paying tax from those things would therefore make taxation impracticable. But it may be thought that to state the matter in this way is to obliterate the useful contrast between taxes on what is owned and taxes on what is earned. Although therefore, a society could not continue to exist without taxation, and although the amount of tax is commonly dependent on what the taxpayer owns or earns, and must be paid from his assets, I should not wish to press the case for the inclusion of liability to tax as a standard incident of ownership. Much the same will hold good of expropriability; for though some state or public expropriation takes place in every society, and though it is not easy to see how administration could continue without it, it tends to be restricted to special classes of property. We are left with the thought that it is, perhaps, a characteristic of ownership that the owner's claims are ultimately postponed to the claims of the public authority, even if only indirectly, in that the thing owned may, within defined limits, be taken from the owner in order to pay the expenses of running the state or to provide it with essential facilities.

## OWNERSHIP AND LESSER INTERESTS

The interest of which the standard incidents have been depicted is usually described as the *greatest* interest in a thing recognized by the law and is contrasted with lesser interests (easements, short leases, licences, special property, mere detention). It is worth while looking a little more closely at this distinction, for it partly depends on a point that the foregoing analysis has not brought to light.

I must emphasize that we are not now concerned with the topic of split ownership—cases where the standard incidents are so divided as to raise a doubt which of two or more persons interested should be called owner. We are dealing with those simpler cases in which the existence of $B$'s interest in a thing, though it restricts $A$'s rights, does not call in question $A$'s ownership of the thing.

The first point that strikes us is that each of the standard incidents of ownership can apply to the holder of a lesser interest in property. The bailee has possession of, and often the right to possess, the goods bailed. The managing director of a company has the right of managing it. The life tenant or usufructuary of a house is entitled to the income from it. The donee of a power of appointment is entitled to dispose of the capital subject to the power. The holder of an easement has a transmissible and non-determinate right in the land subject to the easement. Yet, without more, we feel no temptation to say that the bailee owns the thing, the managing director the company, the life tenant the house, the donee the capital, or the easement holder the land. What criteria do we use in designating these as 'lesser interests'?

One suggested view is that the rights of the holder of a lesser interest can be enumerated while the 'owner's' cannot.[25] This rests on a fallacy about

[25] J. von Gierke, *Sachenrecht* (1948), p. 67. *Cf.*, Markby, *Elements of Law considered with Reference to Principles of General Jurisprudence* (6th ed.), pp. 157–158.

enumeration. The privileges, for instance, exercisable over a thing do not together constitute a finite number of permissible actions. The 'owner' and the lessee alike may do an indefinite number and variety of actions, *viz.* any action not fobidden by a rule of the legal system.

A second view is that the criterion used is the fact that, at least as regards *some* incidents, the holder of the lesser interest has more restricted rights than the owner. The lessee's interest is determinate, the 'owner's' merely determinable, But, converseley, the lessee has the right to possess and manage the property and take its income; in these respects the 'owner's' interest is, for the time being, more restricted than his own. Nor will it help to say that the 'owner's' rights are more extensive than those of the holder of a lesser interest as regards *most* of the incidents listed, for, in such cases as lease, this would lead to the conclusion that the lessee has a much claim to be called owner as the reversioner.

A third suggestion is that some one incident is taken as the criterion. It is possible, however, for all the listed rights, to put examples which would lead to the opposite result from that sanctioned by usage. If *A* lets *B* a car on hire, *B* possesses it but *A* 'owns' it. The holder of a life interest or usufruct manages and takes the income of the thing, but the *dominus* or reversioner 'owns' it. When trust property is subject to a power of appointment, the donee of the power can dispose of it but the trustee 'owns' it. When property is subject to a *fideicommissum*, the fiduciary has no transmissible right (unless the *fideicommissum* fails), yet he is 'owner' while the fideicommissary may, exceptionally, have such a right. A person who holds an interest *in diem* may 'own', while one who has a potentially indeterminate interest *ex die* does not as yet do so.

Besides these examples, where any of the suggested criteria would give a result at variance with actual lay and legal usage, there are many others where the rights in question apply to both or neither of the persons holding an interest in the thing. For instance, some writers appear to treat 'duration'[26] as the criterion for distinguishing between ownership and lesser interests. Yet the holder of an easement, like the 'owner' of land, has a transmissible and indeterminate right over it, while, *per contra*, neither the 'owner' nor the licensee of a copyright has an indeterminate right.

It would be easy but tedious to list examples for the other rights; clearly, if a criterion is to be found, it must be sought elsewhere. A hopeful avenue of inquiry seems to be the following: what happens on the determination of the various interests in the thing under consideration? This brings us to a further standard incident of ownership, *viz.* its residuary character.

## (11) *Residuary Character*

A legal system might recognize interests in things less than ownership and might have a rule that, on the determination of such interests, the rights in question lapsed and could be exercised by no one, or by the first person to

---

26 *Cf.*, Turner, *Some Reflections on Ownership in English Law* (1941), 19 Can. B.R. 342.

exercise them after their lapse. There might be leases and easements; yet, on their extinction, no one would be entitled to exercise rights similar to those of the former lessee or of the holder of the easement. This would be unlike any system known to us and I think we should be driven to say that in such a system the institution of ownership did not extend to any thing in which limited interests existed. In such things there would, paradoxically, be interests less than ownership but no ownership.

This fantasy is intended to bring out the point that it is characteristic of ownership than an owner has a residuary right in the thing owned. In practice, legal systems have rules providing that on the lapse of an interest rights, including liberties, analogous to the rights formerly vested in the holder of the interest, vest in or are exercisable by someone else, who may be said to acquire the 'corresponding rights'. Of course, the 'corresponding rights' are not the same rights as were formerly vested in the holder of the interest. The easement holder had a right to exclude the owner; now the owner has a right to exclude the easement holder. The latter right is not identical with, but corresponds to, the former.

It is true that corresponding rights do not always arise when an interest is determined. Sometimes, when ownership is abandoned, no corresponding right vests in another; the thing is simply *res derelicta*. Sometimes, on the other hand, when ownership is abandoned, a new ownership vests in the state, as is the case in South Africa when land has been abandoned.

It, seems, however, a safe generalization that, whenever an interest less than ownership terminates, legal systems always provide for corresponding rights to vest in another. When easements terminate, the 'owner' can exercise the corresponding rights, and when bailments terminate, the same is true. It looks as if we have found a simple explanation of the usage we are investigating, but this turns out to be but another deceptive short cut. For it is not a sufficient condition of *A*'s being the owner of a thing that, on the determination of *B*'s interest in it, corresponding rights vest in or are exercisable by *A*. On the determination of a sub-lease, the rights in question become exercisable by the lessee, not by the 'owner' of the property.

Can we then say that the 'owner' is the ultimate residuary? When the sub-lessee's interest determines the lessee acquires the corresponding rights; but when the lessee's right determines the 'owner' acquires these rights. Hence the 'owner' appears to be identified as the ultimate residuary. The difficulty is that the series may be continued, for on the determination of the 'owner's' interest the state may acquire the corresponding rights; is the state's interest ownership or a mere expectancy?

A warning is here necessary. We are approaching the troubled waters of split-ownership. Puzzles about the location of ownership are often generated by the fact that an ultimate residuary right is not coupled with present alienability or with the other standard incidents we have listed. Was the feudal lord's right of escheat ownership or merely an expectancy? When land was given in *emphyteusis*, was the *emphyteuta* or the reversioner owner? Other puzzles are created by cases of cross-residuarity. When property is held subject to a *fideicommissum* in the modern law, the fideicommissary benefits from the lapse of the fiduciary's rights and *vice versa;* so which is really residuary?

We are of course here concerned not with the puzzles of split ownership but with simple cases in which the existence of $B$'s lesser interest in a thing is clearly consistent with $A$'s owning it. To explain the usage in such cases it is helpful to point out that it is a necessary but not sufficient condition of $A$'s being owner that, either immediately or ultimately, the extinction of other interests would enure for his benefit. In the end, it turns out that residuarity is merely one of the standard incidents of ownership, important no doubt, but not entitled to any special status.

CHAPTER X

# LAW AND MORALITY

As one might imagine, the multiplication of purported definitions of morality in contemporary philosophic literature has complicated the analysis of the relationship between law and morality. Setting aside for the moment problems of definition, contemporary answers to the normative questions— should morality be enforced by legal sanction and, if so, by what criteria?— largely follow familiar lines of division. Theorists agree that law inescapably must sanction morality, if not directly by positive enforcement then indirectly by what it permits. In Hobbes' words: "In cases where the sovereign has pre-scribed no rule, there the subject has the liberty to do or forbear according to his own discretion. And therefore such liberty is in some places more and in some less. . ." Apart from particular substantial issues, major disagreement arises over the choice of authority appropriate to decide which moral values should or should not be explicitly enforced. Should the decisive voice be that of the dominant power (the sovereign, a democratic majority) or an individual or group selected for superior wisdom and experience (a consensus, the courts, men of special genius)? As well as Thrasymachus, Hobbes and Austin defended the former position with theories of sovereign rule; Bentham deferred to mass public opinion; and recently Lord Devlin (*The Enforcement of Morals,* Oxford Univer-sity Press, New York, 1965) has argued for the 'average man' ("man on the Clapham omnibus") as the proper arbiter of public morality. The criterion of superior reason or experience is proposed by an increasing number of con-temporary ethicists as well as the natural law tradition. Mills's individual who has experienced both higher and lower pleasures and is thus in a position to choose the better *(Utilitarianism)*, as well as his man of genius *(On Liberty)*, seem to fall into the latter camp. Hart follows Mill in his preference for the experienced jurist over the average man *(Law, Liberty, and Morality*. Stanford University Press, Stanford, 1963).

Tensions between these two views are scarcely new to political philosophy: they were fully manifest in Rousseau's ambiguous doctrine of the general will. However, the recent Hart-Devlin debate is perhaps only the last link in a chain of evidence suggesting that the dispute is not to be resolved on formal grounds alone. Positions here seem to reflect deeper historical, and not infrequently ideologically conditioned, concerns; Does an immediate threat of tyranny lie with a majority or minority, a present or anticipated power block? Is civil order (Hobbes) or the free play of genius (Mill and the American Civil Liberties Union) a preferred social interest of the day? Either criterion risks subversion in degenerate political systems: Mill's genius can be translated into Marx's dictatorship of the proletariat; absolute sovereigns and dominant majorities can parade in jackboots. As with most legal-political concepts, either principle alone is incomplete apart from correlation with other concepts, ideals and concrete historical situations which establish standards of legal personality, minimal rights and obligations, hierarchies of social interests.

Other traditional questions have also been revisited by contemporary theorists. Is a moral criterion essential to the definition of law? Natural law theorists have argued for, positivists against, an explicit reference to the common good or community virtue. Positivists obviously have feared the disruption of legal authority by competing moral claims. Yet attempts to define law without some moral reference have been less than satisfactory. Hart finds Austin's sovereign command indistinguishable from the gunman's threat. Hart's own elaboration of law as a system of rules and obligations has been criticized for normative ingenuousness. His proposed "minimum content of natural law" (five basic assumptions: "Human vulnerability", "aproximate equality", "limited altruism", "limited resources", "limited understanding and strength of will", *The Concept of Law*, pp. 190-93) reads from Hobbes and Hume rather than traditional natural law sources. Hart himself does not claim for them the status of moral criteria. Similarly, A. P. d'Entrèves would consider Lon Fuller's "eight ways to fail to make a law", merely "technical imperatives", not moral standards in the full sense of the word (See A. P. d'Entrèves, "The Case for Natural Law Re-examined", *Natural Law Forum*, Vol. 1, 1956, pp. 27-46). Here again competing concepts of morality belie any settled definition of the relation of law and morality. As has been noted in an earlier chapter, the positivist argues that an 'iniquitous' law is still valid so long as it has been formulated according to due process; St. Thomas cautions against the overthrow of unjust government "in the case that it is accompanied by such disorder that the community suffers greater harm from the consequent disturbances than it would from a continuance of the former rule." Both positions imply that prudential considerations may override the moral in determining valid law.

This introduction would not be complete, however, if it did not draw attention to the significant influence of the professional legal code, a largely voluntary ethic, upon the workings of the legal system at large. No institutional system of rules could possibly check abuses by officials inclined to misuse their considerable powers. Presidents and Supreme Courts are only formally curbed by the threat of impeachment; lower officials must necessarily operate with considerable discretionary latitude in the implementation of their respective duties. Throughout this text the ethic of the legal guild—its dedication to the rule of law, impartial judgment, due process and equitable decision—has been more than manifest. The fundamental institution of the jury, the imposing structure of the judicial system, presuppose at their core that justice depends in the last resort upon the individual conscience. No system of punitive sanctions can, therefore be substituted for cautious selection of officials at all levels within the legal-political system—from policeman to President. In the words of Karl Llewellyn, "Our government is not a government of laws, but one of law through men".

## 42

# Saint Thomas Aquinas

Saint Thomas links morality to law but carefully restricts the right to
resist tyrannical government on moral grounds.

# LAW AND THE COMMON GOOD*

*Definition of Law. (Ibid. Art. 4, concl.) (Qu. 90.)*

From the foregoing we may gather the correct definition of law. It is
nothing else than a rational ordering of things which concern the common
good; promulgated by whoever is charged with the care of the community.

### 5. THE VARIOUS TYPES OF LAW. (QU. 91.)

### *The Eternal Law (Art. 1, concl.)*

As we have said above, law is nothing else but a certain dictate of the
practical reason 'in the prince' who rules a perfect community. It is clear, however, supposing the world to be governed by divine providence as we demonstrated in the First Part,[1] that the whole community of the Universe is governed
by the divine reason. Thus the rational guidance of created things on the part
of God, as the Prince of the universe, has the quality of law. . . . This we can call
the eternal law.

### *The Natural Law. (Art. 2, concl.)*

Since all things which are subject to divine providence are measured and
regulated by the eternal law—as we have already shown—it is clear that all
things participate to some degree in the eternal law; in so far as they derive
from it certain inclinations to those actions and aims which are proper to them.
But, of all others, rational creatures are subject to divine providence in a very
special way; being themselves made participators in providence itself, in that
they control their own actions and the actions of others. So they have a certain

*Saint Thomas Aquinas, selections from the *Summa Theologica*, reprinted by permission of the
editor and publisher from *Thomas Aquinas: Selected Political Writings* (edited by A. P. d'Entreves
and translated by J. G. Dawson), Basil Blackwell, Oxford, 1948, pp. 113–21, 161–65. Latin
text omitted.
[1] Ia: q. XXII, Art. 1, 2.

share in the divine reason itself, deriving therefrom a <u>natural inclination</u> to such actions and ends as are fitting. <u>This participation in the eternal law by rational creatures is called the natural law</u>. Thus when the Psalmist said (*Psalm* IV, 6): 'Offer up the sacrifice of justice,' he added, as though being asked the question, what is the sacrifice of justice, 'Many say, who sheweth us good things?', and then replied, saying: 'The light of Thy countenance, O Lord, is signed upon us.' As though the light of natural reason, by which we discern good from evil, and which is the natural law, were nothing else than the impression of the divine light in us. So it is clear that the natural law is nothing else than the participation of the eternal law is rational creatures.

### Human Law. (*Art. 3, concl.*)

Just as in speculative reason we proceed from indemonstrable principles, naturally known, to the conclusions of the various sciences, such conclusions <u>not being innate but arrived at by the use of</u> reason; so also the human reason has to proceed from the precepts of the natural law, as though from certain common and indemonstrable principles, to other more particular dispositions. And such particular dispositions, arrived at by an effort of reason, are called <u>human laws:</u> provided that the other conditions necessary to all law, which we have already noted, are observed. So Cicero says (*De Invent. Rhetor.* II, 53): 'Law springs in its first beginnings from nature: then such standards as are judged to be useful become established by custom: finally reverence and holiness add their sanction to what springs from nature and is established by custom.'

### The Necessity for a Divine Law. (*Art. 4, concl.*)

In addition to natural law and to human law there had of necessity to be also a divine law to direct human life: and this for four reasons. In the first place ① because it is by law that man is directed in his actions with respect to his final end. If, therefore, man were destined to an end which was no more than proportionate to his natural faculties, there would be no need for him to have any directive on the side of reason above the natural law and humanly enacted law which is derived from it. But because man is destined to an end of eternal blessedness, and this exceeds what is proportionate to natural human faculties as we have already shown, it was necessary that he should be directed to this end not merely by natural and human law, but also by a divinely given law.— Secondly: because of the uncertainty of human judgment, particularly in ② matters that are contingent and specific, it is often the case that very differing judgments are passed by various people on human activities; and from these there proceed different, and even contrary laws. In order, therefore, that man should know without any doubt what he is to do and what to avoid, it was necessary that his actions should be directed by a divinely given law, which is known to be incapable of error.—Thirdly: because laws are enacted in respect ③ of what is capable of being judged. But the judgment of man cannot reach to the hidden interior actions of the soul, it can only be about external activities which are apparent. Nevertheless, the perfection of virtue requires that a man should be upright in both classes of actions. Human law being thus insufficient to order and regulate interior actions, it was necessary that for this purpose there should also be a divine law.—Fourthly: because, as Augustine says (I *De Lib. Arb.*), human law can neither punish nor even prohibit all that is evilly done. For in trying to prevent all that is evil it would render impossible also much that is good; and thus would impede much that is useful to the common welfare and therefore necessary to human intercourse. In order, therefore, that no evil should go unforbidden and unpunished it was necessary that there should be a divine law which would prohibit all manner of sin.

## 6. THE EFFECTS OF LAW. (QU. 92.)

### *The Moral Object of Law. (Art. 1, concl.)*

It is clear that the true object of law is to induce those subject to it to seek their own virtue. And since virtue is 'that which makes its possessor good,' it follows that the proper effect of law is the welfare of those for whom it is promulgated: either absolutely or in some certain respect. If the intention of the law-giver is directed to that which is truly good, that is to the common good regulated by divine justice, it will follow that man will, by such a law, be made unconditionally good. If on the other hand the intention of the law-giver is directed, not to that which is absolutely good, but merely to what is useful— in that it is pleasurable to himself or contrary to divine justice— then such a law does not make men good unconditionally, but only in a certain respect; namely, in so far as it has reference to some particular political regime. In this sense good is to be found even in those things which are intrinsically evil: as when a man is termed a good thief, because he is expert in attaining the object he sets before himself.

### *(Ibid. ad 3um.)*

The goodness of any part is to be considered with reference to the whole of which it forms a part: so Augustine says (III *Confess.*, 8): 'All parts are base which are not fittingly adapted to their whole.' So, all men being a part of the city, they cannot be truly good unless they adapt themselves to the common good. Nor can the whole be well constituted if its parts be not properly adapted to it. So it is impossible for the welfare of the community to be in a healthy state unless the citizens are virtuous: or at least such of them as are called to take up the direction of affairs. It would be sufficient for the common well-being if the rest were virtuous to the extent of obeying the commands of the ruler. So the Philosopher says (III *Polit.*, 2): 'A ruler must have the virtue of a truly upright man: but not every citizen is bound to reach a similar degree of uprightness'.

*(Ibid. ad 4um.)*

Tyrannical law, not being according to reason, is not law at all in the true and strict sense, but is rather a perversion of law. It does, however, assume the nature of law to the extent that it provides for the well-being of the citizens. Thus it bears relationship to law in so far as it is the dictate to his subjects of some one in authority; and to the extent that its object is the full obedience of those subjects to the law. For them such obedience is good, not unconditionally, but with respect to the particular regime under which they live.

## 7. THE ETERNAL LAW. (QU. 93.)

### *Its Derivation from the Divine Wisdom. (Art. 1, concl.)*

Just as in the mind of every artist there already exists the idea of what he will create by his art, so in the mind of every ruler there must already exist an ideal of order with respect to what shall be done by those subject to his rule. And just as the ideal of those things that have yet to be produced by any art is known as the exemplar, or actual art of the things so to be produced, the ideal in the mind of the ruler who governs the actions of those subject to him has the quality of law—provided that the conditions we have already mentioned above are also present. Now God, in His wisdom, is the creator of all things, and may be compared to them as the artist is compared to the product of his art; as we have shown in Part I. Moreover he governs all actions and movements of each individual creature, as we also pointed out. So, as the ideal of divine wisdom, in so far as all things are created by it, has the quality of an exemplar or art or idea, so also the ideal of divine wisdom considered as moving all things to their appropriate end has the quality of law. Accordingly, the eternal law is nothing other than the ideal of divine wisdom considered as directing all actions and movements.

### *All Law Derives Ultimately from the Eternal Law. (Ibid. Art. 3, concl.)*

In every case of ruling we see that the design of government is passed from the head of the government to his subordinate governors; just as the scheme of what shall be done in a city derives from the king to his subordinate ministers by statute; or again, in artistic construction, the plan of what is to be made is passed from the architect to the subordinate operators. Since, then, the eternal law is the plan of government in the supreme governor, all schemes of government in those who direct as subordinates must derive from the eternal law. Consequently, all laws, so far as they accord with right reason, derive from the eternal law. For this reason Augustine says (I *De Lib. Arb.*): 'In human law nothing is just or legitimate if it has not been derived by men from the eternal law'.

*(Ibid. ad 2um.)*

Human law has the quality of law only in so far as it proceeds according to right reason: and in this respect it is clear that it derives from the eternal law. In so far as it deviates from reason it is called an unjust law, and has the quality not of law but of violence. Nevertheless, even an unjust law, to the extent that it retains the appearance of law through its relationship to the authority of the law-giver, derives in this respect from the eternal law. 'For all power is from the Lord God' (*Rom.* XIII, 1).

### 16. THE RIGHT TO RESIST TYRANNICAL GOVERNMENT

#### (QU. 42, ART. 2.)

Tyrannical government is unjust government because it is directed not to the common welfare but to the private benefit of the ruler. This is clear from what the Philosopher says in the *Politics,* Book III, and in the *Ethics,* Book VIII. Consequently the overthrowing of such government is not strictly sedition; except perhaps in the case that it is accompanied by such disorder that the community suffers greater harm from the consequent disturbances than it would from a continuance of the former rule. A tyrant himself is, in fact, far more guilty of sedition when he spreads discord and strife among the people subject to him, so hoping to control them more easily. For it is a characteristic of tyranny to order everything to the personal satisfaction of the ruler at the expense of the community.

### 17. POLITICAL PRUDENCE

#### *Its Nature. (Qu. 50, Art. 10.)*

Whoever promotes the common welfare of the community promotes his own welfare at the same time: and this for two reasons. First, because individual well-being cannot exist without the welfare of the family, or city, or realm. Valerius Maximus says of the Romans of old that, 'They preferred rather to be poor men in a rich empire, than rich men in a poor empire,' Secondly, because man, being part of the family, or of the city, it is right that he should consider his personal well-being in the light of what prudence advises with regard to the common welfare. For the good disposition of any part must be determined by its relationship to the whole. For, as St. Augustine says in the *Confessions:* 'All parts are base which do not fit or harmonise with their whole.'

#### *Its Object. (Qu. 50, Art. 1.)*

The object of prudence is government and command. So wherever there is to be found a special form of government and command in human actions, there is to be found also a special form of prudence. But it is clear that in a man whose duty it is to govern, not only himself, but also a perfect community such as a city or realm, there is to be found a special and perfect form of governing. For government is the more perfect the more universal it is, and the further it extends and the higher its aims. Therefore a king, whose duty it is to rule a city or kingdom, must possess prudence of a special and most perfect quality. For this reason we distinguish a species of 'political' prudence.

## 18. NATURAL AND POSITIVE JUSTICE. (QU. 57.)

### The Origin of Positive Justice. (Art. 2, concl.)

Right, or what is just, lies in the due proportion between some exterior action and another according to a certain relationship of equality. Now there are two ways in which such a proportion may be established for man. First, from the nature of the thing itself: as for example when some one gives so much that he may receive equal in return. And this is called natural justice *(ius naturale)*.—Secondly, something may be comparable or commensurate with another by agreement or common consent: as when, for example, some one declares himself content to receive such an amount. This again can happen in two ways. Either by private agreement, as when a pact is reached among a number of private individuals: or by public agreement, when such a proportion or standard of measurement is agreed by the consent of the whole community, or by decree of the ruler who administers and represents the community. And this is called positive justice *(ius positivum)*.

*positive justice*

### The Subordination of Positive to Natural Justice. (Ibid. ad 2um.)

The human will can, by common consent, attribute juridical value to anything which is not in itself contrary to natural justice. And this is precisely the field of positive law. So the Philosopher (V, *Ethics*) defines the legally just as 'that which does not in itself present any difference of values, but which acquires them on being laid down.' But if a thing is in itself contrary to natural justice, it cannot be made just by human volition: if, for example, it were laid down that it is permissible to steal or commit adultery, so it is said in *Isaias* (X, 1): 'Woe to those who make evil laws.' *Yet, paradoxically, an unjust law is a law, although it does not have all the necessary qualities of a law.*

# 43

# John Austin

John Austin distinguished moral rules framed as commands from the moral pressures of public opinion.

# MORAL RULES IMPROPERLY CALLED LAWS*

Now it follows from these premises, that the laws of God, and positive laws, are laws proper, or laws properly so called.

The laws of God are laws proper, inasmuch as they are *commands* express or tacit, and therefore emanate from a *certain* source.

Positive laws, or laws strictly so called, are established directly or immediately by authors of three kinds:—by monarchs, or sovereign bodies, as supreme political superiors: by men in a state of subjection, as subordinate political superiors: by subjects, as private persons, in pursuance of legal rights. But every positive law, or every law strictly so called, is a direct or circuitous command of a monarch or sovereign number in the character of political superior: that is to say, a direct or circuitous command of a monarch or sovereign number to a person or persons in a state of subjection to its author. And being a *command* (and therefore flowing from a *determinate* source), every positive law is a law proper, or a law properly so called.

Besides the human laws which I style positive law, there are human laws which I style positive morality, rules of positive morality, or positive moral rules.

The generic character of laws of the class may be stated briefly in the following negative manner:—No law belonging to the class is a direct or circuitous command of a monarch or sovereign number in the character of political superior. In other words, no law belonging to the class is a direct or circuitous command of a monarch or sovereign number to a person or persons in a state of subjection to its author.

But of positive moral rules, some laws proper or laws properly so called: others are laws improper, or laws improperly so called. Some have all the essential of an *imperative* law or rule: others are deficient in some of those essentials, and are styled *laws* or *rules* by an analogical extension of the term.

The positive moral rules which are laws properly so called, are distinguished from other laws by the union of two marks: 1. They are imperative laws or rules set by men to men. 2. They are not set by men as political superiors,

*John Austin, from Lecture V of *The Province of Jurisprudence Determined*, first published in 1832.

*[handwritten in top margin: are these distinctions necessary?]*

nor are they set by men as private persons, in pursuance of legal rights.

Inasmuch as they bear the latter of these two marks, they are not commands of sovereigns in the character of political superiors. Consequently, they are not positive laws: they are not clothed with legal sanctions, nor do they oblige legally the persons to whom they are set. But being *commands* (and therefore being established by *determinate* individuals or bodies), they are laws properly so called: they are armed with sanctions, and impose duties, in the proper acceptation of the terms.

It will appear from the following distinctions, that positive moral rules which are laws properly so called may be reduced to three kinds.

Of positive moral rules which are laws properly so called, some are established by men who are not subjects, or are not in a state of subjection: Meaning by 'subjects,' or by 'men in a state of subjection,' men in a state of subjection to a monarch or sovereign number.—Of positive moral rules which are laws properly so called, and are not established by men in a state of subjection, some are established by men living in the negative state which is styled a state of nature or a state of anarchy: that is to say, by men who are *not* in the state which is styled a state of government, or are *not* members, sovereign or subject, of any political society.—Of positive moral rules which are laws properly so called, and are not established by men in a state of subjection, others are established by sovereign individuals or bodies, but are not established by sovereigns in the character of political superiors. Or a positive moral rule of this kind may be described in the following manner: It is set by a monarch or sovereign number, but not to a person or persons in a state of subjection to its author.

Of laws properly so called which are set by subjects, some are set by subjects as subordinate political superiors. But of laws properly so called which are set by subjects, others are set by subjects as private persons: Meaning by 'private persons,' subjects not in the class of subordinate political superiors, or subordinate political superiors not considered as such.—Laws set by subjects as subordinate political superiors, are positive laws: they are clothed with legal sanctions, and impose legal duties. They are set by sovereigns or states in the character of political superiors, although they are set by sovereigns circuitously or remotely. Although they are made directly by subject or subordinate authors, they are made through legal rights granted by sovereigns or states, and held by those subject authors as mere trustees for the granters.—Of laws set by subjects as private persons, some are not established by sovereign or supreme authority. And these are rules of positive morality: they are not clothed with legal sanctions, nor do they oblige legally the parties to whom they are set.—But of laws set by subjects as private persons, others are set or established in pursuance of legal rights residing in the subject authors. And these are positive laws or laws strictly so called. Although they are made directly by subject authors, they are made in pursuance of rights granted or conferred by sovereigns in the character of political superiors: they legally oblige the parties to whom they are set, or are clothed with legal sanctions. They are commands

*[handwritten marginal note: Austin has not properly defined what he means by "legal" "system"]*

of sovereigns as political superiors, although they are set by sovereigns circuitously or remotely.[1]

It appears from the foregoing distinctions, that positive moral rules which are laws properly so called are of three kinds: 1. Those which are set by men living in a state of nature. 2. Those which are set by sovereigns, but not by sovereigns as political superiors. 3. Those which are set by subjects as private persons, and are not set by the subject authors in pursuance of legal rights.

To cite an example of rules of the first kind were superfluous labor. A man living in a state of nature may impose an imperative law: though, since the

---

[1] A law set by a subject as a private person, but in pursuance of a legal right residing in the subject author, is either a positive law purely or simply, or is compounded of a positive law and a rule of positive morality. Or (changing the expression) it is either a positive law purely or simply, or it is a positive law as viewed from one aspect, and a rule of positive morality as viewed from another.

The person who makes the law in pursuance of the legal right, is either legally bound to make the law, or he is not. In the first case, the law is positive law purely or simply. In the second case, the law is compounded of a positive law and a positive moral rule.

For example, A guardian may have a right over his pupil or ward, which he is legally bound to exercise, for the benefit of the pupil or ward, in a given or specified manner. In other words, a guardian may be clothed with a right, over his pupil or ward, in trust to exercise the same, for the benefit of the pupil or ward, in a given or specified manner. Now if, in pursuance of his right, and agreeably to his duty or trust, he sets a law or rule to the pupil or ward, the law is a positive law purely or simply. It is properly a law which the state sets to the ward through its minister or instrument the guardian. It is not made by the guardian of his own spontaneous movement, or is made in pursuance of a duty which the state has imposed upon him. The position of the guardian is closely analogous to the position of subordinate political superiors; who hold their delegated powers of direct or judicial legislation as mere trustees for the sovereign granters.

Again: the master has legal rights, over or against his slave, which are conferred by the state upon the master for his own benefit. And, since they are conferred upon him for his own benefit, he is not legally bound to exercise or use them. Now if, in pursuance of these rights, he sets a law to his slave, the law is compounded of a positive law and a positive moral rule. Being made by sovereign authority, and clothed by the sovereign with sanctions, the law made by the master is properly a positive law. But, since it is made by the master of his own spontaneous movement, or is not made by the master in pursuance of a legal duty, it is properly a rule of positive morality, as well as a positive law. Though the law set by the master is set circuitously by the sovereign, it is set or established by the sovereign at the pleasure of the subject author. The master is not the instrument of the sovereign or state, but the sovereign or state is rather the instrument of the master.

Before I dismiss the subject of the present note, I must make two remarks.

1. Of laws made by men as private persons, some are frequently styled 'laws *autonomic*.' Or it is frequently said of some of these laws, that they are made through an αὐτονομία residing in the subject authors. Now laws *autonomic*, or *autonomical*, are laws made by subjects, as private persons, in pursuance of legal rights: that is to say, in pursuance of legal rights which they are free to exercise or not, or in pursuance of legal rights which are not saddled with trusts. A law of the kind is styled *autonomic*, because it is made by its author of his own spontaneous disposition, or not in pursuance of a duty imposed upon him by the state.

It is clear, however, that the term *autonomic* is not exclusively applicable to laws of the kind in question. The term will apply to every law which is not made by its author in pursuance of a legal duty. It will apply, for instance, to every law which is made immediately or directly by a monarch or sovereign number: independence of legal duty being of the essence of sovereignty.

2. Laws which are positive law as viewed from one aspect, but which are positive morality as viewed from another, I place simply or absolutely in the first of those capital classes. If affecting exquisite precision, I placed them in each of those classes, I could hardly indicate the boundary by which those classes are severed without resorting to expressions of repulsive complexity and length.

man *is* in a state of nature, he cannot impose the law in the character of sovereign, and cannot impose the law in pursuance of a legal right. And the law being *imperative* (and therefore proceeding from a *determinate* source) is a law properly so called: though, for want of a sovereign author proximate or remote, it is not a positive law but a rule of positive morality.

An imperative law set by a sovereign to a sovereign, or by one supreme government to another supreme government, is an example of rules of the second kind. Since no supreme government is in a state of subjection to another, an imperative law set by a sovereign to a sovereign is not set by its author in the character of political superior. Nor is it set by its author in pursuance of a legal right: for every legal right is conferred by a supreme government, and is conferred on a person or persons in a state of subjection to the granter. Consequently, an imperative law set by a sovereign to a sovereign is not a positive law or a law strictly so called. But being *imperative* (and therefore proceeding from a *determinate* source), it amounts to a law in the proper signification of the term, although it is purely or simply a rule of positive morality.

If they be set by subjects as private persons, and be not set by their authors in pursuance of legal rights, the laws following are examples of rules of the third kind: namely, imperative laws set by parents to children; imperative laws set by masters to servants; imperative laws set by lenders to borrowers; imperative laws set by patrons to parasites. Being *imperative* (and therefore proceeding from *determinate* sources), the laws foregoing are laws properly so called: though, if they be set by subjects as private persons, and be not set by their authors in pursuance of legal rights, they are not positive laws but rules of positive morality.

Again: A club or society of men, signifying its collective pleasure by a vote of its assembled members, passes or makes a law to be kept by its members severally under pain of exclusion from its meetings. Now if it be made by subjects as private persons, and be not made by its authors in pursuance of a legal right, the law voted and passed by the assembled members of the club is a further example of rules of the third kind. If it be made by subjects as private persons, and be not made by its authors in pursuance of a legal right, it is not a positive law or a law strictly so called. But being an *imperative* law (and the body by which it is set being therefore *determinate*), it may be styled a *law* or *rule* with absolute precision or propriety, although it is purely or simply a rule of positive morality.

The positive moral rules which are laws improperly so called, are *laws set or imposed by general opinion:* that is to say, by the general opinion of any class or any society of persons. For example, Some are set or imposed by the general opinion of persons who are members of a profession or calling: others, by that of persons who inhabit a town or province: others, by that of a nation or independent political society: others, by that of a larger society formed of various nations.

A few species of the laws which are set by general opinion have gotten appropriate names.—For example, There are laws or rules imposed upon gentlemen by opinions current amongst gentlemen. And these are usually styled *the rules of honour,* or *the laws* or *law of honour.*—There are laws or rules imposed upon people of fashion by opinions current in the fashionable world. And these are usually styled *the law set by fashion.*—There are laws which regard the conduct of independent political societies in their various relations to one another: Or, rather, there are laws which regard the conduct of sovereigns or supreme governments in their various relations to one another. And laws or rules of this species, which are imposed upon nations or sovereigns by opinions current amongst nations, are usually styled *the law of nations* or *international law.*

Now a law set or imposed by general opinion is a law improperly so called. It is styled a *law* or *rule* by an analogical extension of the term. When we speak of a law set by general opinion, we denote, by that expression, the following fact:—Some *indeterminate* body or *uncertain* aggregate of persons regards a kind of conduct with a sentiment of aversion or liking: Or (changing the expression) that indeterminate body opines unfavourably or favourably of a given kind of conduct. In *consequence* of that sentiment, or in *consequence* of that opinion, it is likely that they or some of them will be displeased with a party who shall pursue or not pursue conduct of that kind. And, in *consequence* of that displeasure, it is likely that *some* party (*what* party being undetermined) will visit the party provoking it with some evil or another.

The body by whose opinion the law is said to be set, does not *command,* expressly or tacitly, that conduct of the given kind shall be forborne or pursued. For, since it is not a body precisely determined or certain, it cannot, *as a body,* express or intimate a wish. *As a body,* it cannot *signify* a wish by oral or written words, or by positive or negative deportment. The so called *law* or *rule* which its opinion is said to impose, is merely the *sentiment* which it feels, or is merely the *opinion* which it holds, in regard to a kind of conduct.

A determinate member of the body, who opines or feels with the body, may doubtless be moved or impelled, by that very opinion or sentiment, to *command* that conduct of the kind shall be forborne or pursued. But the command expressed or intimated by that determinate party is not a law or rule imposed by general opinion. It is a law properly so called, set by a determinate author.— For example, The so called law of nations consists of opinions or sentiments current among nations generally. It therefore is not law properly so called. But one supreme government may doubtless *command* another to forbear from a kind of conduct which the law of nations condemns. And, though it is fashioned on law which is law improperly so called, this command is a law in the proper signification of the term. Speaking precisely, the command is a rule of positive morality set by a determinate author. For, as no supreme government is in a state of subjection to another, the government commanding does not command in its character of political superior. If the government receiving the command were in a state of subjection to the other, the command, though fashioned on the law of nations, would amount to a positive law.

The foregoing description of a law set by general opinion imports the following consequences:—that the party who will enforce it against any future transgressor is never determinate and assignable. The party who actually enforces it against an actual transgressor is, of necessity, certain. In other words, if an actual transgressor be harmed in consequence of the breach of the law, and in consequence of that displeasure which the breach of the law has provoked, he receives the harm from a party, who, of necessity, is certain. But that certain party is not the executor of a *command* proceeding from the uncertain body. He has not been authorised by that uncertain body to enforce that so called law which its opinion is said to establish. He is not in the position of a minister of justice appointed by the sovereign or state to execute commands which it issues. He harms the actual offender against the so called law or (to speak in analogical language) he applies the sanction annexed to it, of his own spontaneous movement. Consequently, though a party who actually enforces it is, of necessity, certain, the party who will enforce it against any future offender is never determinate and assignable.

It follows from the foregoing reasons, that a so called law set by general opinion is not a law in the proper signification of the term. It also follows from the same reasons, that it is not armed with a sanction, and does not impose a duty, in the proper acceptation of the expressions. For a sanction properly so called is an evil annexed to a command. And duty properly so called is an obnoxiousness to evils of the kind.

# 44

## H. L. A. Hart

H. L. A. Hart (1906–     ), Professor of Jurisprudence at **Oxford**
University and considered by many the leading philosopher in the field,
defends a revised version of positivism and challenges 'exaggerations'
of American legal realism.

# POSITIVISM AND THE SEPARATION OF
# LAW AND MORALS*

In this article I shall discuss and attempt to defend a view which Mr. Justice
Holmes, among others, held and for which he and they have been much criticized.
But I wish first to say why I think that Holmes, whatever the vicissitudes of his
American reputation may be, will always remain for Englishmen a heroic figure
in jurisprudence. This will be so because he magically combined two qualities:
one of them is imaginative power, which English legal thinking has often lacked;
the other is clarity, which English legal thinking usually possesses. The English
lawyer who turns to read Holmes is made to see that what he had taken to be
settled and stable is really always on the move. To make this discovery with
Holmes is to be with a guide whose words may leave you unconvinced, sometimes even repelled, but never mystified. Like our own Austin, with whom
Holmes shared many ideals and thoughts, Holmes was sometimes clearly wrong;
but again like Austin, when this was so he was always wrong clearly. This surely
is a sovereign virtue in jurisprudence. Clarity I know is said not to be enough;
this may be true, but there are still questions in jurisprudence where the issues
are confused because they are discussed in a style which Holmes would have
spurned for its obscurity. Perhaps this is inevitable: jurisprudence trembles so
uncertainly on the margin of many subjects that there will always be need for
someone, in Bentham's phrase, "to pluck the mask of Mystery" from its face.
This is true, to a pre-eminent degree, of the subject of this article. Contemporary
voices tell us we must recognize something obscurred by the legal "positivists"
whose day is now over: that there is a "point of intersection between law and
morals",[1] or that what *is* and what *ought* to be are somehow indissolubly fused
or inseparable,[2] though the positivists denied it. What do these phrases mean?

*H. L. A. Hart, "Legal Positivism and the Separation of Law and Morals," *Harvard Law Review,*
LXXXI (1958), p. 598ff. Reprinted by permission of the author and the Harvard Law Review
Association. Copyright © 1958 by The Harvard Law Review Association. The footnotes have
been numbered.
[1] D'Entreves, *Natural Law* 116 (2d ed. 1952).
[2] Fuller, *The Law in Quest of Itself* 12 (1940); Brecht, "The Myth of Is and Ought", 54 Harv.
L. Rev. 811 (1941); Fuller, "Human Purpose and Natural Law", 53 J. Philos. 697 (1956).

Or rather which of the many things that they *could* mean, *do* they mean? Which of them do "positivists" deny and why is it wrong to do so—

I

I shall present the subject as part of the history of an idea. At the close of the eighteenth century and the beginning of the nineteenth the most earnest thinkers in England about legal and social problems and the architects of great reforms were the great Utilitarians. Two of them, Bentham and Austin, constantly insisted on the need to distinguish, firmly and with the maximum of clarity, law as it is from law as it ought to be. This theme haunts their work, and they condemned the natural-law thinkers precisely because they had blurred this apparently simple but vital distinction. By contrast, at the present time in this country and to a lesser extent in England, this separation between law and morals is held to be superficial and wrong. Some critics have thought that it blinds men to the true nature of law and its roots in social life.[3] Others have thought it not only intellectually misleading but corrupting in practice, at its worst apt to weaken resistance to state tyranny or absolutism,[4] and at its best apt to bring law into disrespect. The nonpejorative name "Legal Positivism," like most terms which are used as missiles in intellectual battles, has come to stand for a baffling multitude of different sins. One of them is the sin, real or alleged, of insisting, as Austin and Bentham did, on the separation of law as it is and law as it ought to be.

How then has this reversal of the wheel come about? What are the theoretical errors in this distinction? Have the practical consequences of stressing the distinction as Bentham and Austin did been bad? Should we now reject it or keep it? In considering these questions we should recall the social philosophy which went along with the Utilitarians' insistence on this distinction. They stood firmly but on their own utilitarian ground for all the principles of liberalism in law and government. No one has ever combined, with such even-minded sanity as the Utilitarians, the passion for reform with respect for law together with a due recognition of the need to control the abuse of power even

---

[3] See Friedmann, *Legal Theory* 154, 294–95 (3d ed. 1953). Friedmann also says of Austin that "by his sharp distinction between the science of legislation and the science of law," he "inaugurated an era of legal positivism and self-sufficiency which enabled the rising national State to assert its authority undisturbed by juristic doubts." *Id*, at 416. Yet, "the existence of a highly organised State which claimed sovereignty and unconditional obedience of the citizen" is said to be "the political condition which makes analytical positivism possible." *Id*. at 163. There is therefore some difficulty in determining which, in this account, is to be hen and which egg (analytical positivism or political condition). Apart from this, there seems to be little evidence that any national State rising in or after 1832 (when the *Province of Jurisprudence Determined* was first published) was enabled to assert its authority by Austin's work or "the era of legal positivism" which he "inaugurated."

[4] See Radbruch, "Die Erneuerung des Rechts," 2 *Die Wandlung* 8 (Germany 1947); Radbruch, "Gesetzliches Unrecht und Übergesetzliches Recht," 1 *Suddeutsche Juristen- Zeitung* 105 (Germany 1946) (reprinted in Radbruch, *Rechtsphilosophie* 347 (4th ed. 1950). Radbruch's views are discussed at pp. 458–462 *infra*.

when power is in the hands of reformers. One by one in Bentham's works you can identify the elements of the *Rechtsstaat* and all the principles for the defense of which the terminology of natural law has in our day been revived. Here are liberty of speech, and of press, the right of association, the need that laws should be published and made widely known before they are enforced, the need to control administrative agencies, the insistence that there should be no criminal liability without fault, and the importance of the principle of legality, *nulla poena sine lege*. Some, I know, find the political and moral insight of the Utilitarians a very simple one, but we should not mistake this simplicity for superficiality nor forget how favorably their simplicities compare with the profundities of other thinkers. Take only one example: Bentham on salvery. He says the question at issue is not whether those who are held as slaves can reason, but simply whether they suffer. Does this not compare well with the discussion of the question in terms of whether or not there are some men whom Nature has fitted only to be the living instruments of others? We owe it to Bentham more than anyone else that we have stopped discussing this and similar questions of social policy in that form.

So Bentham and Austin were not dry analysts fiddling with verbal distinctions while cities burned, but were the vanguard of a movement which laboured with passionate intensity and much success to bring about a better society and better laws. Why then did they insist on the separation of law as it is and law as it ought to be? What did they mean? Let us first see what they said. Austin formulated the doctrine:

The existence of law is one thing; its merit or demerit is another. Whether it be or be not is one enquiry; whether it be or be not conformable to an assumed standard, is a different enquiry. A law, which actually exists, is a law, though we happen to dislike it, or though it vary from the text, by which we regulate our approbation and disapprobation. This truth, when formally announced as an abstract proposition, is so simple and glaring that it seems idle to insist upon it. But simple and glaring as it is, when enunciated in abstract expressions the enumeration of the instances in which it has been forgotten would fill a volume.

Sir William Blackstone, for example, says in his "Commentaries," that the laws of God are superior in obligation to all other laws; that no human laws should be suffered to contradict them; that human laws are of no validity if contrary to them; and that all valid laws derive their force from that Divine original.

Now, he *may* mean that all human laws ought to conform to the Divine laws. If this be his meaning, I assent to it without hesitation. . . . Perhaps, again, he means that human lawgivers are themselves obliged by the Divine laws to fashion the laws which they impose by that ultimate standard, because if they do not, God will punish them. To this also I entirely assent. . . .

But the meaning of this passage of Blackstone, if it has a meaning, seems rather to be this: that no human law which coniflcts with the Divine law is obligatory or binding; in other words, that no human law which conflicts with the Divine law *is a law* . . . .[5]

---

[5] Austin, *The Province of Jurisprudence Determined*, 184–85 (Library of Ideas ed. 1954).

Austin's protest against blurring the distinction between what law is and what it ought to be is quite general: it is a mistake, whatever our standard of what ought to be, whatever "the text by which we regulate our approbation or disapprobation." His examples, however, are always a confusion between law as it is and law as morality would require it to be. For him, it must be remembered, the fundamental principles of morality were God's commands, to which utility was an "index": besides this there was the actual accepted morality of a social group or "positive" morality.

Bentham insisted on this distinction without characterizing morality by reference to God but only, of course, by reference to the principles of utility. Both thinkers' prime reason for this insistence was to enable men to see steadily the precise issues posed by the existence of morally bad laws, and to understand the specific character of the authority of a legal order. Benthams' general recipe for life under the government of laws was simple: it was "to obey punctually; to censure freely".[6] But Bentham was especially aware, as an anxious spectator of the French revolution, that this was not enough: the time might come in any society when the law's commands were so evil that the question of resistance had to be faced, and it was then essential that the issues at stake at this point should neither be oversimplified nor obscured.[7] Yet, this was precisely what the confusion between law and morals had done and Bentham found that the confusion had spread symmetrically in two different directions. On the one hand Bentham had in mind the anarchist who argues thus: "This ought not to be the law, therefore it is not and I am free not merely to censure but to disregard it." On the other hand he thought of the reactionary who argues: "This is the law, therefore it is what it ought to be," and thus stifles criticism at its birth. Both errors, Bentham thought, were to be found in Blackstone: there was his incautious statement that human laws were invalid if contrary to the law of God,[8] and "that spirit of obsequious *quietism* that seems constitutional in our Author" which "will scarce ever let him recognise a difference" between what is and what ought to be.[9] This indeed was for Bentham the occupational disease of lawyers: "[I]n the eyes of lawyers—not to speak of their dupes—that is to say,

---

[6] Bentham, *A Fragment on Government,* in I *Works* 221, 230 (Bowring ed. 1859) (preface, 16th para.)
[7] See Bentham, *Principles of Legislation,* in *The Theory of Legislation* 1, 65 n.* (Ogden ed. 1931) (c. XII, 2d para, n.*).
Here we touch upon the most difficult of questions. If the law is not what is ought to be; if it openly combats the principle of utility; ought we to obey it? Ought we to violate it? Ought we to remain neuter between the law which commands an evil, and morality which forbids it? See also Bentham, *A Fragment on Government,* in I *Works* 221, 287–88 (Bowring ed. 1859) (c. IV, 20th-25th paras.).
[8] 1 Blackstone, *Commentaries* *41. Bentham criticized "this dangerous maxim," saying "the natural tendency of such a doctrine is to impel a man, by the force of conscience, to rise up in arms against any law whatever that he happens not to like." Bentham, *A Fragment on Government,* in I *Works* 221, 287 (Bowring ed. 1859) (c. IV, 19th para.). See also Bentham, *A Comment on the Commentaries* 49 (1928) (c. III). For an expression of a fear lest anarchy result from such a doctrine, combined with a recognition that resistance may be justified on grounds of utility, see Austin, *op. cit. supra* note 12, at 186.
[9] Bentham, *A Fragment on Government,* in I *Works* 221, 294 (Bowring ed. 1859) (c. V, 10th para.).

as yet, the generality of non-lawyers—the *is* and *ought to be* . . . were one and indivisible".[10] There are therefore two dangers between which insistence on this distinction will help us to steer: the danger that law and its authority may be dissolved in man's conceptions of what law ought to be and the danger that the existing law may supplant morality as a final test of conduct and so escape criticism.

In view of later criticisms it is also important to distinguish several things that the Utilitarians did not mean by insisting on their separation of law and morals. They certainly accepted many of the things that might be called "the intersection of law and morals." First, they never denied that, as a matter of historical fact, the development of legal systems had been powerfully influenced by moral opinion, and, conversely, that moral standards had been profoundly influenced by law, so that the content of many legal rules mirrored moral rules or principles. It is not in fact always easy to trace this historical causal connection, but Bentham was certainly ready to admit its existence; so too Austin spoke of the "frequent coincidence"[11] of positive law and morality and attributed the confusion of what law is with what law ought to be to this very fact.

Secondly, neither Bentham nor his followers denied that by explicit legal provisions moral principles might at different points be brought into a legal system and form part of its rules, or that courts might be legally bound to decide in accordance with what they thought just or best. Bentham indeed recognized, as Austin did not, that even the supreme legislative power might be subjected to legal restraints by a constitution and would not have denied that moral principles, like those of the fifth amendment, might form the content of such legal constitutional restraints. Austin differed in thinking that restraints on the supreme legislative power could not have the force of law, but would remain merely political or moral checks; but of course he would have recognized that a statute, for example, might confer a delegated legislative power and restrict the area of its exercise by reference to moral principles.

What both Bentham and Austin were anxious to assert were the following two simple things: first, in the absence of an expressed constitutional or legal provision, it could not follow from the mere fact that a rule violated standards of morality that it was not a rule of law; and, conversely, it could not follow from the mere fact that a rule was morally desirable that it was a rule of law.

The history of this simple doctrine in the nineteenth century is too long and too intricate to trace here. Let me summarize it by saying that after it was propounded to the world by Austin it dominated English jurisprudence and constitutes part of the framework of most of those curiously English and perhaps unsatisfactory productions—the omnibus surveys of the whole field of jurisprudence. A succession of these were published after a full text of Austin's lectures finally appeared in 1863. In each of them the utilitarian separation of law and morals is treated as something that enables lawyers to attain a new

---

[10] Bentham, *A Commentary on Humphreys' Real Property Code,* in 5 *Works* 389 (Bowring ed. 1843).
[11] Austin, *op. cit. supra* note 12, at 162.

clarity. Austin was said by one of his English successors, Amos, "to have delivered the law from the dead body of morality that still clung to it";[12] and even Maine, who was critical of Austin at many points, did not question this part of his doctrine. In the United States men like N. St. John Green,[13] Gray, and Holmes considered that insistence on this distinction had enabled the understanding of law as a means of social control to get off to a fruitful new start; they welcomed it both as self-evident and as illuminating—as a revealing tautology. This distinction is, of course, one of the main themes of Holmes' most famous essay "The Path of the Law",[14] but the place it had in the estimation of these American writers is best seen in what Gray wrote at the turn of the century in *The Nature and Sources of the Law*. He said:

> The great gain in its fundamental conceptions which Jurisprudence made during the last century was the recognition of the truth that the Law of a State . . . is not an ideal, but something which actually exists. . . . [I]t is not that which ought to be, but that which is. To fix this definitely in the Jurisprudence of the Common Law, is the feat that Austin accomplished.[15]

## II

So much for the doctrine in the heyday of its success. Let us turn now to some of the criticisms. Undoubtedly, when Bentham and Austin insisted on the distinction between law as it is and as it ought to be, they had in mind *particular* laws the meanings of which were clear and so not in dispute, and they were concerned to argue that such laws, even if morally outrageous, were still laws. It is, however, necessary, in considering the criticisms which later developed, to consider more than those criticisms which were directed to this particular point if we are to get at the root of the dissatisfaction felt; we must also take account of the objection that, even if what the Utilitarians said on this particular point were true, their insistence on it, in a terminology suggesting a general cleavage between what is and ought to be law, obscured the fact that at other points there is an essential point of contact between the two. So in what follows I shall consider not only criticism of the particular point which the Utilitarians had in mind, but also the claim that an essential connection between law and morals emerges if we examine how laws, the meanings of which are in dispute, are interpreted and applied in concrete cases; and that this connection emerges again

---

[12] Amos, *The Science of Law* 4 (5th ed. 1881). See also Markby, *Elements of Law* 4–5 (5th ed. 1896):

Austin, by establishing the distinction between positive law and morals, not only laid the foundation for a science of law, but cleared the conception of law . . . of a number of pernicious consequences to which . . . it had been supposed to lead. Positive laws, as Austin has shown, must be legally binding, and yet a law may be unjust . . . He has admitted that law itself may be immoral, in which case it may be our moral duty to disobey it . . . .

*Cf.* Holland, *Jurisprudence* 1–20 (1880).

[13] See Green Book Review, 6 Am. L. Rev. 57, 61 (1871). Reprinted in Green, *Essays and Notes on the Law of Tort and Crime* 31, 35 (1933).

[14] 10 Harv. L. Rev. 457 (1897).

[15] Gray, *The Nature and Sources of the Law* 94 (1st ed. 1909) (§213).

if we widen our point of view and ask, not whether every particular rule of law must satisfy a moral minimum in order to be a law, but whether a system of rules which altogether failed to do this could be a legal system.

There is, however, one major initial complexity by which criticism has been much confused. We must remember that the Utilitarians combined with their insistence on the separation of law and morals two other equally famous but distinct doctrines. One was the important truth that a purely analytical study of legal concepts, a study of the meaning of the distinctive vocabulary of the law, was as vital to our understanding of the nature of law as historical or sociological studies, though of course it could not supplant them. The other doctrine was the famous imperative theory of law—that law is essentially a command.

These three doctrines constitute the utilitarian tradition in jurisprudence; yet they are distinct doctrines. It is possible to endorse the separation between law and morals and to value analytical inquiries into the meaning of legal concepts and yet think it wrong to conceive of law as essentially a command. One source of great confusion in the criticism of the separation of law and morals was the belief that the falsity of any one of these three doctrines in the utilitarian tradition showed the other two to be false; what was worse was the failure to see that there were three quite separate doctrines in this tradition. The indiscriminate use of the label "positivism" to designate ambiguously each one of these three separate doctrines (together with some others which the Utilitarians never professed) has perhaps confused the issue more than any other single factor.[16] Some of the early American critics of the Austinian doctrine were, however, admirably clear on just this matter. Gray, for example, added at the end of the tribute to Austin, which I have already quoted, the words, "He may have been wrong in treating the Law of the State as being the command of the sovereign"[17] and he touched shrewdly on many points where the command theory is defective. But other critics have been less clearheaded and

---

[16] It may help to identify five (there may be more) meanings of "positivism" bandied about in contemporary jurisprudence:

(1) the contention that laws are commands of human beings, see pp. 446–450 *infra,*

(2) the contention that there is no necessary connection between law and morals or law as it is and ought to be, see pp. 442–445 *supra,*

(3) the contention that the analysis (or study of the meaning) of legal concepts is (a) worth pursuing and (b) to be distinguished from historical inquiries into the causes or origins of laws, from sociological inquiries into the relation of law and other social phenomena, and from the criticism or appraisal of law whether in terms of morals, social aims, "functions," or otherwise, see pp. 452–453 *infra,*

(4) the contention that a legal system is a "closed logical system" in which correct legal decisions can be deduced by logical means from predetermined legal rules without reference to social aims, policies, moral standards, see pp. 452–453 *infra,* and

(5) the contention that moral judgments cannot be established or defended, as statements of facts can, by rational argument, evidence, or proof ("noncognitivism" in ethics), see pp. 465–467 *infra.*

Bentham and Austin held the views described in (1), (2), and (3) but not those in (4) and (5). Opinion (4) is often ascribed to analytical jurists, see pp. 452–453 *infra,* but I know of no "analyst" who held this view.

[17] Gray, *The Nature and Sources of the Law* 94–95 (2d ed. 1921).

have thought that the inadequacies of the command theory which gradually came to light were sufficient to demonstrate the falsity of the separation of law and morals.

This was a mistake, but a natural one. To see how natural it was we must look a little more closely at the command idea. The famous theory that law is a command was a part of a wider and more ambitious claim. Austin said that the notion of a command was "the *key* to the sciences of jurisprudence and morals",[18] and contemporary attempts to elucidate moral judgments in terms of "imperative" or "prescriptive" utterances echo this ambitious claim. But the command theory, viewed as an effort to identify even the quintessence of law, let alone the quintessence of morals, seems breathtaking in its simplicity and quite inadequate. There is much, even in the simplest legal system, that is distorted if presented as a command. Yet the Utilitarians thought that the essence of a legal system could be conveyed if the notion of a command were supplemented by that of a habit of obedience. The simple scheme was this: What is a command? It is simply an expression by one person of the desire that another person should do or abstain from some action, accompanied by a threat of punishment which is likely to follow disobedience. Commands are laws if two conditions are satisfied: first, they must be general; second, they must be commanded by what (as both Bentham and Austin claimed) exists in every political society whatever its constitutional form, namely, a person or a group of persons who are in receipt of habitual obedience from most of the society but pay no such obedience to others. These persons are its sovereign. Thus law is the command of the uncommanded commanders of society—the creation of the legally untrammelled will of the sovereign who is by definition outside the law.

It is easy to see that this account of a legal system is threadbare. One can also see why it might seem that its inadequacy is due to the omission of some essential connection with morality. The situation which the simple trilogy of command, sanction, and sovereign avails to describe, if you take these notions at all precisely, is like that of a gunman saying to his victim, "Give me your money or your life." The only difference is that in the case of a legal system the gunman says it to a large number of people who are accustomed to the racket and habitually surrender to it. Law surely is not the gunman situation writ large, and legal order is surely not to be thus simply identified with compulsion.

This scheme, despite the points of obvious analogy between a statute and a command, omits some of the most characteristic elements of law. Let me cite a few. It is wrong to think of a legislature (and a fortiori an electorate) with a changing membership, as a group of persons habitually obeyed: this simple idea is suited only to a monarch sufficiently long-lived for a "habit" to grow up. Even if we waive this point, nothing which legislators do makes law unless they comply with fundamental accepted rules specifying the essential lawmaking procedures. This is true even in a system having a simple unitary constitution

[18] Austin, *op cit. supra* note 12, at 13.

like the British. These fundamental accepted rules specifying what the legislature must do to legislate are not commands habitually obeyed, nor can they be expressed as habits of obedience to persons. They lie at the root of a legal system, and what is most missing in the utilitarian scheme is an analysis of what it is for a social group and its officials to accept such rules. This notion, not that of a command as Austin claimed, is the "key to the science of jurisprudence," or at least one of the keys.

Again, Austin, in the case of a democracy, looked past the legislators to the electorate as "the sovereign" (or in England as part of it). He thought that in the United States the mass of the electors to the state and federal legislatures were the sovereign whose commands, given by their "agents" in the legislatures, were law. But on this footing the whole notion of the sovereign outside the law being "habitually obeyed" by the "bulk" of the population must go: for in this case the "bulk" obeys the bulk, that is, it obeys itself. Plainly the general acceptance of the authority of a lawmaking procedure, irrespective of the changing individuals who operate it from time to time, can be only distorted by an analysis in terms of mass habitual obedience to certain persons who are by definition outside the law, just as the cognate but much simpler phenomenon of the general social acceptance of a rule, say of taking off the hat when entering a church, would be distorted if represented as habitual obedience by the mass to specific persons.

Other critics dimly sensed a further and more important defect in the command theory, yet blurred the edge of an important criticism by assuming that the defect was due to the failure to insist upon some important connection between law and morals. This more radical defect is as follows. The picture that the command theory draws of life under law is essentially a simple relationship of the commander to the commanded, of superior to inferior, of top to bottom; the relationship is vertical between the commanders or authors of the law conceived of as essentially outside the law and those who are commanded and subject to the law. In this picture no place, or only an accidental or subordinate place, is afforded for a distinction between types of legal rules which are in fact radically different. Some laws require men to act in certain ways or to abstain from acting whether they wish to or not. The criminal law consists largely of rules of this sort: like commands they are simply "obeyed" or "disobeyed." But other legal rules are presented to society in quite different ways and have quite different functions. They provide facilities more or less elaborate for individuals to create structures of rights and duties for the conduct of life within the coercive framework of the law. Such are the rules enabling individuals to make contracts, wills, and trusts, and generally to mould their legal relations with others. Such rules, unlike the criminal law, are not factors designed to obstruct wishes and choices of an antisocial sort. On the contrary, these rules provide facilities for the realization of wishes and choices. They do not say (like commands) "do this whether you wish it or not," but rather "if you wish to do this, here is the way to do it." Under these rules we exercise powers, make claims, and assert rights. These phrases mark off characteristic features of laws that confer rights and powers; they are laws which are, so to speak, put at the disposition of individuals in a way in which the criminal law is not. Much ingenuity has gone into the task of "reducing" laws of this second sort to some complex variant of laws of the first sort. The effort to show that laws conferring rights are "really" only conditional stipulations of sanctions to be exacted from the person ultimately under a legal duty characterizes much of Keslen's work.[19] Yet to urge this is really just to exhibit dogmatic determination to suppress one aspect of the legal system in order to maintain the theory that the stipulation of a sanction, like Austin's command, represents the quintessence of law. One might as well urge that the rules of baseball were "really" only complex conditional directions to the scorer and that this showed their real or "essential" nature.

One of the first jurists in England to break with the Austinian tradition, Salmond, complained that the analysis in terms of commands left the notion of a right unprovided with a place.[20] But he confused the point. He argued first, and correctly, that if laws are merely commands it is inexplicable that we should have come to speak of legal rights and powers as conferred or arising under them, but then wrongly concluded that the rules of a legal system must necessarily be connected with moral rules or principles of justice and that only on this footing could the phenomenon of legal rights be explained. Otherwise, Salmond thought, we would have to say that a mere "verbal coincidence" connects the concepts of legal and moral right. Similarly, continental critics of the Utilitarians, always alive to the complexity of the notion of a subjective right, insisted that the command theory gave it no place. Hägerström insisted that if laws were merely commands the notion of an individual's right was really inexplicable, for commands are, as he said, something which we either obey or we do not obey; they do not confer rights.[21] But, he too, concluded that moral, or, as he put it, common-sense, notions of justice must therefore be necessarily involved in the analysis of any legal structure elaborate enough to confer rights.

Yet, surely these arguments are confused. Rules that confer rights, though distinct from commands, need not be moral rules or coincide with them. Rights, after all, exist under the rules of ceremonies, games, and in many other spheres regulated by rules which are irrelevant to the question of justice or what the law ought to be. Nor need rules which confer rights be just or morally good rules. The rights of a master over his slaves show us that. "Their merit or

---

[19] See, *e.g.*, Kelsen, *General Theory of Law and State* 58–61, 143–44 (1945). According to Kelsen, all laws, not only those conferring rights and powers, are reducible to such "primary norms" conditionally stipulating sanctions.

[20] Salmond, *The First Principles of Jurisprudence* 97–98 (1893). He protested against "the creed of what is termed the English school of jurisprudence," because it "attempted to deprive the idea of law of that ethical significance which is one of its most essential elements." *Id.* at 9, 10.

[21] Hagerstrom, *Inquiries into the Nature of Law and Morals* 217 (Olivecrona ed. 1953): "[T]he whole theory of the subjective rights of private individuals . . . is incompatible with the imperative theory." See also *id.* at 221:
The description of them [claims to legal protection] as rights is wholly derived from the idea that the law which is concerned with them is a true expression of rights and duties in the sense in which the popular notion of justice understands these terms.

demerit," as Austin termed it, depends on how rights are distributed in society and over whom or what they are exercised. These critics indeed revealed the inadequacy of the simple notions of command and habit for the analysis of law; at many points it is apparent that the social acceptance of a rule or standard of authority (even if it is motivated only by fear or superstition or rests on inertia) must be brought into the analysis and cannot itself be reduced to the two simple terms. Yet nothing in this showed the utilitarian insistence on the distinction between the existence of law and its "merits" to be wrong.

III

I now turn to a distinctively American criticism of the separation of the law that is from the law that ought to be. It emerged from the critical study of the judicial process with which American jurisprudence has been on the whole so beneficially occupied. The most skeptical of these critics—the loosely named "Realists" of the 1930's—perhaps too naively accepted the conceptual framework of the natural sciences as adequate for the characterization of law and for the analysis of rule-guided action of which a living system of law at least partly consists. But they opened men's eyes to what actually goes on when courts decide cases, and the contrast they drew between the actual facts of judicial decision and the traditional terminology for describing it as if it were a wholly logical operation was usually illuminating; for in spite of some exaggeration the "Realists" made us acutely conscious of one cardinal feature of human language and human thought, emphasis on which is vital not only for the understanding of law but in areas of philosophy far beyond the confines of jurisprudence. The insight of this school may be presented in the following example. A legal rule forbids you to take a vehicle into the public park. Plainly this forbids an automobile, but what about bicycles, roller skates, toy automobiles? What about airplanes? Are these, as we say, to be called "vehicles" for the purpose of the rule or not? If we are to communicate with each other at all, and if, as in the most elementary form of law, we are to express our intentions that a certain type of behavior be regulated by rules, then the general words we use—like "vehicle" in the case I consider—must have some standard instance in which no doubts are felt about its application. There must be a core of settled meaning, but there will be, as well, a penumbra of debatable cases in which words are neither obviously applicable nor obviously ruled out. These cases will each have some features in common with the standard case; they will lack others or be accompanied by features not present in the standard case. Human invention and natural processes continually throw up such variants on the familiar, and if we are to say that these ranges of facts do or do not fall under existing rules, then the classifier must make a decision which is not dictated to him, for the facts and phenomena to which we fit our words and apply our rules are as it were *dumb*. The toy automobile cannot speak up and say, "I am a vehicle for the purpose of this legal rule," nor can the roller skates chorus, "We are not a vehicle." Fact situations do not await us neatly labeled, creased, and folded, nor is their legal classification written on them to be simply read off by the judge. Instead, in applying legal rules, someone must take the responsibility of deciding that words do or do not cover some case in hand with all the practical consequences involved in this decision.

We may call the problems which arise outside the hard core of standard instances or settled meaning "problems of the penumbra"; they are always with us whether in relation to such trivial things as the regulation of the use of the public park or in relation to the multidimensional generalities of a constitution. If a penumbra of uncertainty must surround all legal rules, then their application to specific cases in the penumbral area cannot be a matter of logical deduction, and so deductive reasoning, which for generations has been cherished as the very perfection of human reasoning, cannot serve as a model for what judges, or indeed anyone, should do in bringing particular cases under general rules. In this area men cannot live by deduction alone. And it follows that if legal arguments and legal decisions of penumbral questions are to be rational, their rationality must lie in something other than a logical relation to premises. So if it is rational or "sound" to argue and to decide that for the purposes of this rule an airplane is not a vehicle, this argument must be sound or rational without being logically conclusive. What is it then that makes such decisions correct or at least better than alternative decisions? Again, it seems true to say that the criterion which makes a decision sound on such cases is some concept of what the law ought to be; it is easy to slide from that into saying that it must be a moral judgment about what law ought to be. So here we touch upon a point of necessary "intersection between law and morals" which demonstrates the falsity or, at any rate, the misleading character of the Utilitarians' emphatic insistence on the separation of law as it is and ought to be. Surely, Bentham and Austin could only have written as they did because they misunderstood or neglected this aspect of the judicial process, because they ignored the problems of the penumbra.

The misconception of the judicial process which ignores the problems of the penumbra and which views the process as consisting pre-eminently in deductive reasoning is often stigmatized as the error of "formalism" or "literalism." My question now is, how and to what extent does the demonstration of this error show the utilitarian distinction to be wrong or misleading? Here there are many issues which have been confused, but I can only disentangle some. The charge of formalism has been leveled both at the "positivist" legal theorist and at the courts, but of course it must be a very different charge in each case. Leveled at the legal theorist, the charge means that he has made a theoretical mistake about the character of legal decision; he has thought of the reasoning involved as consisting in deduction from premises in which the judges' practical choices or decisions play no part. It would be easy to show that Austin was guiltless of this error; only an entire misconception of what analytical jurisprudence is and why he thought it important has led to the view that he, or any other analyst, believed that the law was a closed logical system in which judges deduced their decisions from premises.[22] On the contrary, he was very much alive to the character of language, to its vagueness or open character;[23] he thought that in the penumbral situation judges must necessarily legislate, and, in accents that sometimes recall those of the late Judge Jerome Frank, he berated the common-law judges for legislating feebly and timidly and for blindly relying on real or fancied analogies with past cases instead of adapting their decisions to the growing needs of society as revealed by the moral standard of utility. The villains of this piece, responsible for the conception of the judge as an automaton, are not the Utilitarian thinkers. The responsibility, if it is to be laid at the door of any theorist, is with thinkers like Blackstone and, at an earlier stage, Montesquieu. The root of this evil is preoccupation with the separation of powers and Blackstone's "childish fiction" (as Austin termed it) that judges only "find," never "make", law.

But we are concerned with "formalism" as a vice not of jurists but of judges. What precisely is it for a judge to commit this error, to be a "formalist," "automatic," a "slot machine?" Curiously enough the literature which is full of the denunciation of these vices never makes this clear in concrete terms; instead we have only descriptions which cannot mean what they appear to say: it is said that in the formalist error courts make an excessive use of logic, take a thing to "a dryly logical extreme",[24] or make an excessive use of analytical methods. But just how in being a formalist does a judge make an excessive use of logic? It is clear that the essence of his error is to give some general term an interpretation which is blind to social values and consequences (or which is in some other way stupid or perhaps merely disliked by critics). But logic does not prescribe interpretation of terms; it dictates neither the stupid nor intelligent interpretation of any expression. Logic only tells you hypothetically that *if* you give a certain term a certain interpretation then a certain conclusion follows. Logic is silent on how to classify particulars—and this is the heart of a judicial decision. So this reference to logic and to logical extremes is a misnomer for something else. which must be this. A judge has to apply a rule to a concrete

---

[22] This misunderstanding of analytical jurisprudence is to be found in, among others, Stone, *The Province and Function of Law* 141 (1950):

In short, rejecting the implied assumption that all propositions of all parts of the law must be logically consistent with each other and proceed on a single set of definitions . . . he [Cardozo, J.,] denied that the law is actually what the analytical jurist, *for his limited purposes,* assumes it to be.

See also *id.* at 49, 52, 138, 140; Friedman, *Legal Theory* 209 (3d ed. 1953). This misunderstanding seems to depend on the unexamined and false belief that analytical studies of the meaning of legal terms would be impossible or absurd if, to reach sound decisions in particular cases, more than a capacity for formal logical reasoning from unambiguous and clear predetermined premises is required.

[23] See the discussion of vagueness and uncertainty in law, in Austin, *op. cit. supra* note 12, at 202–05, 207, in which Austin recognized that, in consequence of this vagueness, often only "fallible tests" can be provided for determining whether particular cases fall under general expressions.

[24] Hynes v. New York Cent. R.R., 231 N.Y. 229, 235, 131 N.E. 898, 900 (1921); see Pound, *Interpretations of Legal History* 123 (2d ed. 1930); Stone, *op. cit. supra* note 32, at 140–41.

case—perhaps the rule that one may not take a stolen "vehicle" across state lines, and in this case an airplane has been taken.[25] He either does not see or pretends not to see that the general terms of this rule are susceptible of different interpretations and that he has a choice left open uncontrolled by linguistic conventions. He ignores, or is blind to, the fact that he is in the area of the penumbra and is not dealing with a standard case. Instead of choosing in the light of social aims, the judge fixes the meaning in a different way. He either takes the meaning that the word most obviously suggests in its ordinary nonlegal context to ordinary men, or one which the word has been given in some other legal context, or, still worse, he thinks of a standard case and then arbitrarily identifies certain features in it—for example, in the case of a vehicle, (1) normally used on land, (2) capable of carrying a human person, (3) capable of being self-propelled—and treats these three as always necessary and always sufficient conditions for the use in all contexts of the word "vehicle," irrespective of the social consequences of giving it this interpretation. This choice, not "logic," would force the judge to include a toy motor car (if electrically propelled) and to exclude bicycles and the airplane. In all this there is possibly great stupidity but no more "logic," and no less, than in cases in which the interpretation given to a general term and the consequent application of some general rule to a particular case is consciously controlled by some identified social aim.

Decisions made in a fashion as blind as this would scarcely deserve the name of decisions; we might as well toss a penny in applying a rule of law. But it is at least doubtful whether any judicial decisions (even in England) have been quite as automatic as this. Rather, either the interpretations stigmatized as automatic have resulted from the conviction that it is fairer in a criminal statute to take a meaning which would jump to the mind of the ordinary man at the cost even of defeating other values, and this itself is a social policy (though possibly a bad one); or much more frequently, what is stigmatized as "mechanical" and "automatic" is a determined choice made indeed in the light of a social aim but of a conservative social aim. Certainly many of the Supreme Court decisions at the turn of the century which have been so stigmatized[26] represent clear choices in penumbral area to give effect to a policy of a conservative type. This is peculiarly true of Mr. Justice Peckham's opinions defining the spheres of police power and due process.[27]

But how does the wrongness of deciding cases in an automatic and mechanical way and the rightness of deciding cases by reference to social purposes show that the utilitarian insistence on the distinction between what the law is and what it ought to be is wrong? I take it that no one who wished to use these vices of formalism as proof that the distinction between what is and what ought

[25] See McBoyle v. United States, 283 U.S. 25 (1931).
[26] See, *e.g.*, Pound, "Mechanical Jurisprudence," 8 Colum. L. Rev. 605, 615–16 (1908).
[27] See, *e.g.*, Lochner v. New York, 198 U.S. 45 (1905). Justice Peckham's opinion that there were no reasonable grounds for interfering with the right of free contract by determining the hours of labor in the occupation of a baker may indeed be a wrongheaded piece of conservatism but there is nothing automatic or mechanical about it.

to be is mistaken would deny that the decisions stigmatized as automatic are law; nor would he deny that the system in which such automatic decisions are made is a legal system. Surely he would say that they are law, but they are bad law, they ought not to be law. But this would be to use the distinction, not to refute it; and of course both Bentham and Austin used it to attack judges for failing to decide penumbral cases in accordance with the growing needs of society.

Clearly, if the demonstration of the errors of formalism is to show the utilitarian distinction to be wrong, the point must be drastically restated. The point must be not merely that a judicial decision to be rational must be made in the light of some conception of what ought to be, but that the aims, the social policies and purposes to which judges should appeal if their decisions are to be rational, are themselves to be considered as part of the law in some suitably wide sense of "law" which is held to be more illuminating than that used by the Utilitarians. This restatement of the point would have the following consequence: instead of saying that the recurrence of penumbral questions shows us that legal rules are essentially incomplete, and that, when they fail to determine decisions, judges must legislate and so exercise a creative choice between alternatives, we shall say that the social policies which guide the judge's choice are in a sense there for them to discover; the judges are only "drawing out" of the rule what, if it is properly understood, is "latent" within it. To call this judicial legislation is to obscure some essential continuity between the clear cases of the rule's application and the penumbral decisions. I shall question later whether this way of talking is salutory, but I wish at this time to point out something obvious, but likely, if not stated, to tangle the issues. It does not follow that, because the opposite of a decision reached blindly in the formalist or literalist manner is a decision intelligently reached by reference to some conception of what ought to be, we have a junction of law and morals. We must, I think. beware of thinking in a too simple-minded fashion about the word "ought." This is not because there is no distinction to be made between law as it is and ought to be. Far from it. It is because the distinction should be between what is and what from many different points of view ought to be. The word "ought" merely reflects the presence of some standard of criticism; one of these standards is a moral standard but not all standards are moral. We say to our neighbour, "You ought not to lie," and that may certainly be a moral judgment, but we should remember that the baffled poisoner may say, "I ought to have given her a second dose." The point here is that intelligent decisions which we oppose to mechanical or formal decisions are not necessarily identical with decisions defensible on moral grounds. We may say of many a decision: "Yes, that is right; that is as it ought to be," and we may mean only that some accepted purpose or policy has been thereby advanced; we may not mean to endorse the moral propriety of the policy or the decision. So the contrast between the mechanical decision and the intelligent one can be reproduced inside a system dedicated to the pursuit of the most evil aims. It does not exist as a contrast to be found only in legal systems which, like our own, widely recognize principles of justice and moral claims of individuals.

An example may make this point plainer. With us the task of sentencing in criminal cases is the one that seems most obviously to demand from the judge the exercise of moral judgment. Here the factors to be weighed seem clearly to be moral factors: society must not be exposed to wanton attack; to much misery must not be inflicted on either the victim or his dependents; efforts must be made to enable him to lead a better life and regain a position in the society whose laws he has violated. To a judge striking the balance among these claims, with all the discretion and perplexities involved, his task seems as plain an example of the exercise of moral judgment as could be; and it seems to be the polar opposite of some mechanical application of a tariff of penalities fixing a sentence careless of the moral claims which in our system have to be weighed. So here intelligent and rational decision is guided however uncertainly by moral aims. But we have only to vary the example to see that this need not necessarily be so and surely, if it need not necessarily be so, the Utilitarian point remains unshaken. Under the Nazi regime men were sentenced by courts for criticism of the regime. Here the choice of sentence might be guided exclusively by consideration of what was needed to maintain the state's tyranny effectively. What sentence would both terrorize the public at large and keep the friends and family of the prisoner in suspense so that both hope and fear would cooperate as factors making for subservience? The prisoner of such a system would be regarded simply as an object to be used in pursuit of these aims. Yet, in contrast with a mechanical decision, decision on these grounds would be intelligent and purposive, and from one point of view the decision would be as it ought to be. Of course, I am not unaware that a whole philosophical tradition has sought to demonstrate the fact that we cannot correctly call decisions or behavior truly rational unless they are in conformity with moral aims and principles. But the example I have used seems to me to serve at least as a warning that we cannot use the errors of formalism as something which per se demonstrates the falsity of the utilitarian insistence on the distinction between law as it is and law as *morally* it ought to be.

We can now return to the main point. If it is true that the intelligent decision of penumbral questions is one made not mechanically but in the light of aims, purposes, and policies, though not necessarily in the light of anything we would call moral principles, is it wise to express this important fact by saying that the firm utilitarian distinction between what the law is and what it ought to be should be dropped? Perhaps the claim that it is wise cannot be theoretically refuted for it is, in effect, an *invitation* to revise our conception of what a legal rule is. We are invited to include in the "rule" the various aims and policies in the light of which its penumbral cases are decided on the ground that these aims have, because of their importance, as much right to be called law as the core of legal rules whose meaning is settled. But though an invitation cannot be refuted, it may be refused and I would proffer two reasons for refusing this invitation. First, everything we have learned about the judicial process can be expressed in other less mysterious ways. We can say laws are incurably incomplete and we must decide the penumbral cases rationally by reference to social aims. I think Holmes, who had such a vivid appreciation of the fact that "general propositions do not decide concrete cases," would have put it that way. Second, to insist on the utilitarian distinction is to emphasize that the hard core of settled meaning is law in some centrally important sense and that even if there are borderlines, there must first be lines. If this were not so the notion of rules controlling courts' decisions would be senseless as some of the "Realists"—in their most extreme moods, and, I think, on bad grounds—claimed.[28]

By contrast, to soften the distinction, to assert mysteriously that there is some fused identity between law as it is and as it ought to be, is to suggest that all legal questions are fundamentally like those of the penumbra. It is to assert that there is no central element of actual law to be seen in the core of central meaning which rules have, that there is nothing in the nature of a legal rule inconsistent with *all* questions being open to reconsideration in the light of social policy. Of course, it is good to be occupied with the penumbra. Its problems are rightly the daily diet of the law schools. But to be occupied with the penumbra is one thing, to be preoccupied with it another. And preoccupation with the penumbra is, if I may say so, as rich a source of confusion in the American legal tradition as formalism in the English. Of course we might abandon the notion that rules have authority; we might cease to attach force or even meaning to an argument that a case falls clearly within a rule and the scope of a precedent. We might call all such reasoning "automatic" or "mechanical," which is already the routine invective of the courts. But until we decide that this *is* what we want, we should not encourage it by obliterating the Utilitarian distinction.

IV

The third criticism of the separation of law and morals is of a very different character; it certainly is less an intellectual argument against the Utilitarian distinction than a passionate appeal supported not by detailed reasoning but by reminders of a terrible experience. For it consists of the testimony of those who have descended into Hell, and, like Ulysses or Dante, brought back a message for human beings. Only in this case the Hell was not beneath or beyond earth, but on it; it was a Hell created on earth by men for other men.

This appeal comes from those German thinkers who lived through the Nazi regime and reflected upon its evil manifestations in the legal system. One of these thinkers, Gustav Radbruch, had himself shared the "positivist" doctrine until the Nazi tyranny, but he was converted by this experience and so his appeal to other

---

[28] One recantation of this extreme position is worth mention in the present context. In the first edition of *The Bramble Bush,* Professor Llewellyn committed himself wholeheartedly to the view that "what these officials do about disputes is, to my mind, the law itself" and that "*rules* . . . are important so far as they help you . . . predict what judges will do . . . That is all their importance, except as pretty playthings." Llewellyn, *The Bramble Bush* 3, 5 (1st ed. 1930). In the second edition he said that these were "unhappy words when not more fully developed, and they are plainly at best a very partial statement of the whole truth . . . [O]ne office of law is to control officials in some part, and to guide them even . . . where no thoroughgoing control is possible, or is desired. . . . [T]he words fail to take proper account . . . of the office of the institution of law as an instrument of conscious shaping . . . " Llewellyn, *The Bramble Bush* 9 (2d ed. 1951).

men to discard the doctrine of the separation of law and morals has the special poignancy of a recantation. What is important about this criticism is that it really does confront the particular point which Bentham and Austin had in mind in urging the separation of law as it is and as it ought to be. These German thinkers put their insistence on the need to join together what the Utilitarians separated just where this separation was of most importance in the eyes of the Utilitarians; for they were concerned with the problem posed by the existence of morally evil laws.

Before his conversion Radbruch held that resistance to law was a matter for the personal conscience, to be thought out by the individual as a moral problem, and the validity of a law could not be disproved by showing that its requirements were morally evil or even by showing that the effect of compliance with the law would be more evil than the effect of disobedience. Austin, it may be recalled, was emphatic in condemning those who said that if human laws conflicted with the fundamental principles of morality then they cease to be laws, as talking "stark nonsense."

> The most pernicious laws, and therefore those which are most opposed to the will of God, have been and are continually enforced as laws by judicial tribunals. Suppose an act innocuous, or positively beneficial, be prohibited by the sovereign under the penalty of death; if I commit this act, I shall be tried and condemned, and if I object to the sentence, that it is contrary to the law of God . . . the court of justice will demonstrate the inconclusiveness of my reasoning by hanging me up, in pursuance of the law of which I have impugned the validity. An exception, demurrer, or plea, founded on the law of God was never heard in a Court of Justice, from the creation of the world down to the present moment.[29]

These are strong, indeed brutal words, but we must remember that they went along—in the case of Austin and, of course, Bentham—with the conviction that if laws reached a certain degree of iniquity then there would be a plain moral obligation to resist them and to withhold obedience. We shall see, when we consider the alternatives, that this simple presentation of the human dilemma which may arise has much to be said for it.

Radbruch, however, had concluded from the ease with which the Nazi regime had exploited subservience to mere law—or expressed, as he thought, in the "positivist" slogan "law as law" *(Gesetz als Gesetz)*—and from the failure of the German legal profession to protest against the enormities which they were required to perpetrate in the name of law, that "positivism" (meaning here the insistence on the separation of law as it is from law as it ought to be) had powerfully contributed to the horrors. His considered reflections led him to the doctrine that the fundamental principles of humanitarian morality were part of the very concept of *Recht* or Legality and that no positive enactment or statute, however clearly it was expressed and however clearly it conformed

[29] Austin, *The Province of Jurisprudence Determined* 185 (Library of Ideas ed. 1954).

with the formal criteria of validity of a given legal system could be valid if it contravened basic principles of morality. This doctrine can be appreciated fully only if the nuances imported by the German word *Recht* are grasped. But it is clear that the doctrine meant that every lawyer and judge should denounce statutes that transgressed the fundamental principles not as merely immoral or wrong but as having no legal character, and enactments which on this ground lack the quality of law should not be taken into account in working out the legal position of any given individual in particular circumstances. The striking recantation of his previous doctrine is unfortunately omitted from the translation of his works, but it should be read by all who wish to think afresh on the question of the interconnection of law and morals.[30]

It is impossible to read without sympathy Radbruch's passionate demand that the German legal conscience should be open to the demands of morality and his complaint that this has been too little the case in the German tradition. On the other hand there is an extraordinary naïveté in the view that insensitiveness to the demands of morality and subservience to state power in a people like the Germans should have arisen from the belief that law might be law though it failed to conform with the minimum requirements of morality. Rather this terrible history prompts inquiry into why emphasis on the slogan "law is law," and the distinction between law and morals, acquired a sinister character in Germany, but elsewhere, as with the Utilitarians themselves, went along with the most enlightened liberal attitudes. But something more disturbing than naïveté is latent in Radbruch's whole presentation of the issues to which the existence of morally iniquitous laws give rise. It is not, I think, uncharitable to say that we can see in his argument that he has only half digested the spiritual message of liberalism which he is seeking to convey to the legal profession. For everything that he says is really dependent upon an enormous overvaluation of the importance of the bare fact that a rule may be said to be a valid rule of law, as if this, once declared, was conclusive of the final moral question: "Ought this rule of law to be obeyed?" Surely the truly liberal answer to any sinister use of the slogan "law is law" or of the distinction between law and morals is, "Very well, but that does not conclude the question. Law is not morality; do not let it supplant morality."

However, we are not left to a mere academic discussion in order to evaluate the plea which Radbruch made for the revision of the distinction between law and morals. After the war Radbruch's conception of law as containing in itself the essential moral principle of humanitarianism was applied in practice by German courts in certain cases in which local war criminals, spies, and informers under the Nazi regime were punished. The special importance of these cases is that the persons accused of these crimes claimed that what they had done was

---

[30] See Radbruch, "Gesetzliches Unrecht und Übergesetzliches Recht," 1 *Suddeutsche Juristen-Zeitung* 105 (Germany 1946) (reprinted in Radbruch, *Rechtsphilosophie* 347 (4th ed. 1950). I have used the translation of part of this essay and of Radbruch, "Die Erneuerung des Rechts," 2 *Die Wandlung* 8 (Germany 1947), prepared by Professor Lon Fuller of the Harvard Law School as a mimeographed supplement to the readings in jurisprudence used in his course at Harvard.

not illegal under the laws of the regime in force at the time these actions were performed. This plea was met with the reply that the laws upon which they relied were invalid as contravening the fundamental principles of morality. Let me cite briefly one of these cases.[31]

In 1944 a woman, wishing to be rid of her husband, denounced him to the authorities for insulting remarks he had made about Hitler while home on leave from the German army. The wife was under no legal duty to report his acts, though what he had said was apparently in violation of statutes making it illegal to make statements detrimental to the government of the Third Reich or to impair by any means the military defence of the German people. The husband was arrested and sentenced to death, apparently pursuant to these statutes, though he was not executed but was sent to the front. In 1949 the wife was prosecuted in a West German court for an offense which we would describe as illegally depriving a person of his freedom (rechtswiarige Freiheitsberaubung). This was punishable as a crime under the German Criminal Code of 1871 which had remained in force continuously since its enactment. The wife pleaded that her husband's imprisonment was pursuant to the Nazi statutes and hence that she had committed no crime. The court of appeal to which the case ultimately came held that the wife was guilty of procuring the deprivation of her husband's liberty by denouncing him to the German courts, even though he had been sentenced by a court for having violated a statute, since, to quote the words of the court, the statute "was contrary to the sound conscience and sense of justice of all decent human beings." This reasoning was followed in many cases which have been hailed as a triumph of the doctrines of natural law and as signaling the overthrow of positivism. The unqualified satisfaction with this result seems to me to be hysteria. Many of us might applaud the objective—that of punishing a woman for an outrageously immoral act—but this was secured only by declaring a statute established since 1934 not to have the force of law, and at least the wisdom of this course must be doubted. There were, of course, two other choices. One was to let the woman go unpunished; one can sympathize with and endorse the view that this might have been a bad thing to do. The other was to face the fact that if the woman were to be punished it must be pursuant to the introduction of a frankly retrospective law and with a full consciousness of what

[31] Judgment of July 27, 1949, Oberlandesgericht, Bamberg, 5 *Suddeutsche Juristen-Zeitung* 207 (Germany 1950), 64 Harv. L. Rev. 1005 (1951); see Friedmann, *Legal Theory* 457 (3d ed. 1953). The text has been left as originally written, but it has been shown by Dr. H. O. Pappe of the Australian National University in his article. "On the Validity of Judicial Decisions in the Nazi Era," in 23 Modern Law Review (1960), 260, that the report of the case in 64 Harvard Law Review which was followed by the author is misleading. As Dr. Pappe shows, in the actual case the German court after accepting the theoretical possibility that statutes might be invalid if in conflict with Natural Law held that the Nazi statutes in question could not be held to violate it; the accused was held guilty of unlawfully depriving her husband of liberty, since she had no duty to inform against him but did so for purely personal reasons and must have realized that to do so was in the circumstance "contrary to the sound conscience and sense of justice of all decent human beings." Accordingly, the case as discussed in the text must now be regarded as a hypothetical one. Dr. Pappe's careful analysis of a decision in a similar case in the German Supreme Court should be studied. (*op. cit.*, 268 ft.)

was sacrificed in securing her punishment in this way. Odious as retrospective criminal legislation and punishment may be, to have pursued it openly in this case would at least have had the merits of candour. It would have made plain that in punishing a woman a choice had to be made between two evils, that of leaving her unpunished and that of sacrificing a very precious principle of morality endorsed by most legal systems. Surely if we have learned anything from the history of morals it is that the thing to do with a moral quandary is not to hide it. Like nettles, the occasions when life forces us to choose between the lesser of two evils must be grasped with the consciousness that they are what they are. The vice of this use of the principle that, at certain limiting points, what is utterly immoral cannot be law or lawful is that it will serve to cloak the true nature of the problems with which we are faced and will encourage the romantic optimism that all the values we cherish ultimately will fit into a single system, that no one of them has to be sacrificed or compromised to accommodate another.

> All Discord Harmony not understood
> All Partial Evil Universal Good

This is surely untrue and there is an insincerity in any formulation of our problem which allows us to describe the treatment of the dilemma as if it were the disposition of the ordinary case.

It may seem perhaps to make too much of forms, even perhaps of words, to emphasize one way of disposing of this difficult case as compared with another which might have led, so far as the woman was concerned, to exactly the same result. Why should we dramatize the difference between them? We might punish the woman under a new retrospective law and declare overtly that we were doing something inconsistent with our principles as the lesser of two evils; or we might allow the case to pass as one in which we do not point out precisely where we sacrifice such a principle. But candour is not just one among many minor virtues of the administration of law, just as it is not merely a minor virtue of morality. For if we adopt Radbruch's view, and with him and the German courts make our protest against evil law in the form of an assertion that certain rules cannot be law because of their moral iniquity, we confuse one of the most powerful, because it is the simplest, forms of moral criticism. If with the Utilitarians we speak plainly, we say that laws may be law but too evil to be obeyed. This is a moral condemnation which everyone can understand and it makes an immediate and obvious claim to moral attention. If, on the other hand, we formulate our objection as an assertion that these evil things are not law, here is an assertion which many people do not believe, and if they are disposed to consider it at all, it would seem to raise a whole host of philosophical issues before it can be accepted. So perhaps the most important single lesson to be learned from this form of the denial of the Utilitarian distinction is the one that the Utilitarians were most concerned to teach: when we have the ample resources of plain speech we must not present the moral criticism of institutions as propositions of a disputable philosophy.

V

I have endeavored to show that, in spite of all that has been learned and experienced since the Utilitarians wrote, and in spite of the defects of other parts of their doctrine, their protest against the confusion of what is and what ought to be law has a moral as well as an intellectual value. Yet it may well be said that, though this distinction is valid and important if applied to any particular law of a system, it is at least misleading if we attempt to apply it to "law," that is, to the notion of a legal system, and that if we insist, as I have, on the narrower truth (or truism), we obscure a wider (or deeper) truth. After all, it may be urged, we have learned that there are many things which are untrue of laws taken separately, but which are true and important in a legal system considered as a whole. For example, the connection between law and sanctions and between the existence of law and its "efficacy" must be understood in this more general way. It is surely not arguable (without some desperate extension of the word "sanction" or artificial narrowing of the word "law") that every law in a municipal legal system must have a sanction, yet it is at least plausible to argue that a legal system must, to be a legal system, provide sanctions for certain of its rules. So too, a rule of law may be said to exist though enforced or obeyed in only a minority of cases, but this could not be said of a legal system as a whole. Perhaps the differences with respect to laws taken separately and a legal system as a whole are also true of the connection between moral (or some other) conceptions of what law ought to be and law in this wider sense.

This line of argument, found (at least in embryo form) in Austin, where he draws attention to the fact that every developed legal system contains certain fundamental notions which are "necessary" and "bottomed in the common nature of man,"[32] is worth pursuing—up to a point—and I shall say briefly why and how far this is so.

We must avoid, if we can, the arid wastes of inappropriate definition, for, in relation to a concept as many-sided and vague as that of a legal system, disputes about the "essential" character, or necessity to the whole, of any single element soon begin to look like disputes about whether chess could be "chess" if played without pawns. There is a wish, which may be understandable, to cut straight through the question whether a legal system, to be a legal system, must measure up to some moral or other standard with simple statements of fact: for example, that no system which utterly failed in this respect has ever existed or could endure; that the normally fulfilled assumption that a legal system aims at some form of justice colours the whole way in which we interpret specific rules in particular cases, and if this normally fulfilled assumption were not fulfilled no one would have any reason to obey except fear (and probably not that) and still less, of course, any moral obligation to obey. The connection

[32] Austin, "Uses of the Study of Jurisprudence," in *The Province of Jurisprudence Determined* 365, 373, 367–69 (Library of Ideas, ed. 1954).

between law and moral standards and principles of justice is therefore as little arbitrary and as "necessary" as the connection between law and sanctions, and the pursuit of the question whether this necessity is logical (part of the "meaning" of law) or merely factual or casual can safely be left as an innocent pastime for philosophers.

Yet in two respects I should wish to go further (even though this involves the use of a philosophical fantasy) and show what could intelligibly be meant by the claim that certain provisions in a legal system are "necessary." The world in which we live, and we who live in it, may one day change in many different ways; and if this change were radical enough not only would certain statements of fact now true be false and vice versa, but whole ways of thinking and talking which constitute our present conceptual apparatus, through which we see the world and each other, would lapse. We have only to consider how the whole of our social, moral, and legal life, as we understand it now, depends on the contingent fact that though our bodies do change in shape, size, and other physical properties they do not do this so drastically nor with such quicksilver rapidity and irregularity that we cannot identify each other as the same persistent individual over considerable spans of time. Though this is but a contingent fact which may one day be different, on it at present rest huge structures of our thought and principles of action and social life. Similarly, consider the following possibility (not because it is more than a possibility but because it reveals why we think certain things necessary in a legal system and what we mean by this): suppose that men were to become invulnerable to attack by each other, were clad perhaps like giant land crabs with an impenetrable carapace, and could extract the food they needed from the air by some internal chemical process. In such circumstances (the details of which can be left to science fiction) rules forbidding the free use of violence and rules constituting the minimum form of property—with its rights and duties sufficient to enable food to grow and be retained until eaten—would not have the necessary nonarbitrary status which they have for us, constituted as we are in a world like ours. At present, and until such radical changes supervene, such rules are so fundamental that if a legal system did not have them there would be no point in having any other rules at all. Such rules overlap with basic moral principles vetoing murder, violence, and theft; and so we can add to the factual statement that all legal systems in fact coincide with morality at such vital points, the statement that this is, in this sense, necessarily so. And why not call it a "natural" necessity?

Of course even this much depends on the fact that in asking what content a legal system must have we take this question to be worth asking only if we who consider it cherish the humble aim of survival in close proximity to our fellows. Natural-law theory, however, in all its protean guises, attempts to push the argument much further and to assert that human beings are equally devoted to and united in their conception of aims (the pursuit of knowledge, justice to their fellow men) other than that of survival, and these dictate a further necessary content to a legal system (over and above my humble minimum) without which it would be pointless. Of course we must be careful not to exaggerate the differences among human beings, but it seems to me that above this minimum the purposes men have for living in society are too conflicting and varying to make possible much extension of the argument that some fuller overlap of legal rules and moral standards is "necessary" in this sense.

Another aspect of the matter deserves attention. If we attach to a legal system the minimum meaning that it must consist of general rules—general both in the sense that they refer to courses of action, not single actions, and to multiplicities of men, not single individuals—this meaning connotes the principle of treating like cases alike, though the criteria of when cases are alike will be, so far, only the general elements specified in the rules. It is, however, true that *one* essential element of the concept of justice is the principle of treating like cases alike. This is justice in the administration of the law, not justice of the law. So there is, in the very notion of law consisting of general rules, something which prevents us from treating it as if morally it is utterly neutral, without any necessary contact with moral principles. Natural procedural justice consists therefore of those principles of objectivity and impartiality in the administration of the law which implement just this aspect of law and which are designed to ensure that rules are applied only to what are genuinely cases of the rule or at least to minimize the risks of inequalities in this sense.

These two reasons (or excuses) for talking of a certain overlap between legal and moral standards as necessary and natural, of course, should not satisfy anyone who is really disturbed by the Utilitarian or "positivist" insistence that law and morality are distinct. This is so because a legal system that satisfied these minimum requirements might apply, with the most pedantic impartiality as between the persons affected, laws which were hideously oppressive, and might deny to a vast rightless slave population the minimum benefits of protection from violence and theft. The stink of such societies is, after all, still in our nostrils and to argue that they have (or had) no legal system would only involve the repetition of the argument. Only if the rules failed to provide these essential benefits and protection for anyone—even for a salve-owning group— would the minimum be unsatisfied and the system sink to the status of a set of meaningless taboos. Of course no one denied those benefits would have any reason to obey except fear and would have every moral reason to revolt.

VI

I should be less than candid if I did not, in conclusion, consider something which, I suspect, most troubles those who react strongly against "legal positivism." Emphasis on the distinction between law as it is and law as it ought to be may be taken to depend upon and to entail what are called 'subjectivist' and "relativist" or "noncognitive" theories concerning the very nature of moral judgments, moral distinctions, or "values." Of course the Utilitarians themselves (as distinct from later positivists like Kelsen) did not countenance any such theories, however unsatisfactory their moral philosophy may appear to us now. Austin thought ultimate moral principles were the commands of God, known to us by revelation or through the "index" of utility, and Bentham thought they were verifiable propositions about utility. Nonetheless I think (though I cannot prove) that insistence upon the distinction between law as it is and ought to be has been, under the general head of "positivism" confused with a moral theory according to which statements of what is the case ("statements of fact") belong to a category or type radically different from statements of what ought to be ("value statements"). It may therefore be well to dispel this source of confusion.

There are many contemporary variants of this type of moral theory: according to some, judgments of what ought to be, or ought to be done, either are or include as essential elements expressions of "feeling," "emotion," or "attitudes" or "subjective preferences"; in others such judgements both express feelings or emotions or attitudes and enjoin others to share them. In other variants such judgements indicate that a particular case falls under a general principle or policy of action which the speaker has "chosen" or to which he is "committed" and which is itself not a recognition of what is the case but analogous to a general "imperative" or command addressed to all including the speaker himself. Common to all these variants is the insistence that judgments of what ought to be done, because they contain such "noncognitive" elements, cannot be argued for or established by rational methods as statements of fact can be, and cannot be shown to follow from any statement of fact but only from other judgments of what ought to be done in conjunction with some statement of fact. We cannot, on such a theory, demonstrate, *e.g.*, that an action was wrong, ought not to have been done, merely by showing that it consisted of the deliberate infliction of pain solely for the gratification of the agent. We only show it to be wrong if we add to those verifiable "cognitive" statements of fact a general principle not itself verifiable or "cognitive" that the infliction of pain in such circumstances is wrong, ought not to be done. Together with this general distinction between statements of what is and what ought to be go sharp parallel distinctions between statements about means and statements of moral ends. We can rationally discover and debate what are appropriate means to given ends, but ends are not rationally discoverable or debatable; they are "fiats of the will," expressions of "emotions," "preferences," or "attitudes."

Against all such views (which are of course far subtler than this crude survey can convey) others urge that all these sharp distinctions between is and ought, fact and value, means and ends, cognitive and noncognitive, are wrong. In acknowledging ultimate ends or moral values we are recognizing something as much imposed upon us by the character of the world in which we live, as little a matter of choice, attitude, feeling, emotion as the truth of factual judgments about what is the case. The characteristic moral argument is not one in which the parties are reduced to expressing or kindling feelings or emotions or issuing exhortations or commands to each other but one by which parties come to acknowledge after closer examination and reflection that an initially disputed case falls within the ambit of a vaguely apprehended principle (itself no more "subjective," no more a "fiat of our will" than any other principle of classification) and this has as much title to be called "cognitive" or "rational" as any other initially disputed classification of particulars.

Let us now suppose that we accept this rejection of "noncognitive" theories of morality and this denial of the drastic distinction in type between statements of what is and what ought to be, and that moral judgments are as rationally defensible as any other kind of judgments. What would follow from this as to the nature of the connection between law as it is and law as it ought to be? Surely, from this alone, nothing. Laws, however morally iniquitous, would still (so far as this point is concerned) be laws. The only difference which the acceptance of this view of the nature of moral judgments would make would be that the moral iniquity of such laws would be something that could be demonstrated; it would surely follow merely from a statement of what the rule required to be done that the rule was morally wrong and so ought not to be law or conversely that it was morally desirable and ought to be law. But the demonstration of this would not show the rule not to be (or to be) law. Proof that the principles by which we evaluate or condemn laws are rationally discoverable, and not mere "fiats of the will," leaves untouched the fact that there are laws which may have any degree of iniquity or stupidity and still be laws. And conversely there are rules that have every moral qualification to be laws and yet are not laws.

Surely something further or more specific must be said if disproof of "noncognitivism" or kindred theories in ethics is to be relevant to the distinction between law as it is and law as it ought to be, and to lead to the abandonment at some piont or some softening of this distinction. No one has done more than Professor Lon Fuller of the Harvard Law School in his various writings to make clear such a line of argument and I will end by criticising what I take to be its central point. It is a point which again emerges when we consider not those legal rules or parts of legal rules the meanings of which are clear and excite no debate but the interpretation of rules in concrete cases where doubts are initially felt and argument develops about their meaning. In no legal system is the scope of legal rules restricted to the range of concrete instances which were present or are believed to have been present in the minds of legislators; this indeed is one of the important differences between a legal rule and a command. Yet, when rules are recognized as applying to instances beyond any that legislators did or could have considered, their extension to such new cases often presents itself not as a deliberate choice or fiat on the part of those who so interpret the rule. It appears neither as a decision to give the rule a new or extended meaning nor as a guess as to what legislators, dead perhaps in the eighteenth century, would have said had they been alive in the twentieth century. Rather, the inclusion of the new case under the rule takes its place as a natural elaboration of the rule, as something implementing a "purpose" which it seems natural to attribute (in some sense) to the rule itself rather than to any particular person dead or alive. The Utilitarian description of such interpretative extension of old rules to new cases as judicial legislation fails to do justice to this phenomenon; it gives no hint of the differences between a deliberate fiat or decision to treat the new case in the same way as past cases and a recognition (in which there is little that is deliberate or even voluntary) that inclusion of the new case under the rule will implement or articulate a continuing and identical purpose, hitherto less specifically apprehended.

Perhaps many lawyers and judges will see in this language something that precisely fits their experience; others may think it a romantic gloss on facts better stated in the Utilitarian language of judicial "legislation" or in the modern American terminology of "creative choice."

To make the point clear Professor Fuller uses a nonlegal example from the philosopher Wittgenstein which is, I think, illuminating.

Someone says to me: "Show the children a game." I teach them gaming with dice and the other says "I did not mean that sort of game." Must the exclusion of the game with dice have come before his mind when he gave me the order?[33]

Something important does seem to me to be touched on in this example. Perhaps there are the following (distinguishable) points. First, we normally do interpret not only what people are trying to do but what they say in the light of assumed common human objectives so that unless the contrary were expressly indicated we would not interpret an instruction to show a young child a game as a mandate to introduce him to gambling even though in other contexts the word "game" would be naturally so interpreted. Second, very often, the speaker whose words are thus interpreted might say: "Yes, that's what I mean [or "that's what I meant all along"] though I never thought of it until you put this particular case to me." Third, when we thus recognize, perhaps after argument or consultation with others, a particular case not specifically envisaged beforehand as falling within the ambit of some vaguely expressed instruction, we may find this experience falsified by description of it as a mere decision on our part so to treat the particular case, and that we can only describe this faithfully as coming to realize and to articulate what we "really" want or our "true purpose"—phrases which Professor Fuller uses later in the same article.[34]

I am sure that many philosophical discussions of the character of moral argument would benefit from attention to cases of the sort instanced by Professor Fuller. Such attention would help to provide a corrective to the view that there is a sharp separation between "ends" and "means" and that in debating "ends" we can only work on each other nonrationally, and that rational argument is reserved for discussion of "means," But I think the relevance of his point to the issue whether it is correct or wise to insist on the distinction between law as it is and law as it ought to be is very small indeed. Its net effect is that in interpreting legal rules there are some cases which we find after reflection to be so natural an elaboration or articulation of the rule that to think of and refer to this as "legislation," "making law," or a "fiat" on our part would be misleading. So, the argument must be, it would be misleading to distinguish in

---

[33] Fuller, "Human Purpose and Natural Law," 53 J. Philos. 697, 700 (1956).
[34] *Id.* at 701, 702.

such cases between what the rule is and what it ought to be—at least in some sense of ought. We think it ought to include the new case and come to see after reflection that it really does. But even if this way of presenting a recognizable experience as an example of a fusion between is and ought to be is admitted, two caveats must be borne in mind. The first is that "ought" in this case need have nothing to do with morals for the reasons explained already in section III: there may be just the same sense that a new case will implement and articulate the purpose of a rule in interpreting the rules of a game or some hideously immoral code of oppression whose immorality is appreciated by those called in to interpret it. They too can see what the "spirit" of the game they are playing requires in previously unenvisaged cases. More important is this: after all is said and done we must remember how rare in the law is the phenomenon held to justify this way of talking, how exceptional is this feeling that one way of deciding a case is imposed upon us as the only natural or rational elaboration of some rule. Surely it cannot be doubted that, for most cases of interpretation, the language of choice between alternatives, "judicial legislation" or even "fiat" (though not arbitrary fiat), better conveys the realities of the situation.

Within the framework of relatively well-settled law there jostle too many alternatives too nearly equal in attraction between which judge and lawyer must uncertainly pick their way to make appropriate here language which may well describe those experiences which we have in interpreting our own or others' principles of conduct, intention, or wishes, when we are not conscious of exercising a deliberate choice, but rather of recognising something awaiting recognition. To use in the description of the interpretation of laws the suggested terminology of a fusion or inability to separate what is law and ought to be will serve (like earlier stories that judges only find, never make, law) only to conceal the facts, that here if anywhere we live among uncertainties between which we have to choose, and that the existing law imposes only limits on our choice and not the choice itself.

# 45

## Lon Fuller

Lon Fuller (1902–    ), Carter Professor of Jurisprudence at Harvard University and a leading American legal realist, proposes an inner morality of law itself.

# WAYS TO FAIL TO MAKE LAW*

## EIGHT WAYS TO FAIL TO MAKE LAW

Rex came to the throne filled with the zeal of a reformer. He considered that the greatest failure of his predecessors had been in the field of law. For generations the legal system had known nothing like a basic reform. Procedures of trial were cumbersome, the rules of law spoke in the archaic tongue of another age, justice was expensive, the judges were slovenly and sometimes corrupt. Rex was resolved to remedy all this and to make his name in history as a great lawgiver. It was his unhappy fate to fail in this ambition. Indeed, he failed spectacularly, since not only did he not succeed in introducing the needed reforms, but he never even succeeded in creating any law at all, good or bad.

His first official act was, however, dramatic and propitious. Since he needed a clean slate on which to write, he announced to his subjects the immediate repeal of all existing law, of whatever kind. He then set about drafting a new code. Unfortunately, trained as a lonely prince, his education had been very defective. In particular he found himself incapable of making even the simplest generalizations. Though not lacking in confidence when it came to deciding specific controversies, the effort to give articulate reasons for any conclusion strained his capacities to the breaking point.

Becoming aware of his limitations, Rex gave up the project of a code and announced to his subjects that henceforth he would act as a judge in any disputes that might arise among them. In this way under the stimulus of a variety of cases he hoped that his latent powers of generalization might develop and, proceeding case by case, he would gradually work out a system of rules that could be incorporated in a code. Unfortunately the defects in his education were more deep-seated than he had supposed. The venture failed completely. After he had handed down literally hundreds of decisions neither he nor his subjects could detect in those decisions any pattern whatsoever. Such tentatives toward generalization as were to be found in his opinions only compounded

*Lon Fuller, from *The Morality of Law*, New Haven, Yale University Press, 1964, pp. 33-41.

the confusion, for they gave false leads to his subjects and threw his own meager powers of judgment off balance in the decision of later cases.

After this fiasco Rex realized it was necessary to take a fresh start. His first move was to subscribe to a course of lessons in generalization. With his intellectual powers thus fortified, he resumed the project of a code and, after many hours of solitary labor, succeeded in preparing a fairly lengthy document. He was still not confident, however, that he had fully overcome his previous defects. Accordingly, he announced to his subjects that he had written out a code and would henceforth be governed by it in deciding cases, but that for an indefinite future the contents of the code would remain an official state secret, known only to him and his scrivener. To Rex's surprise this sensible plan was deeply resented by his subjects. They declared it was very unpleasant to have one's case decided by rules when there was no way of knowing what those rules were.

Stunned by this rejection Rex undertook an earnest inventory of his personal strengths and weaknesses. He decided that life had taught him one clear lesson, namely, that it is easier to decide things with the aid of hindsight than it is to attempt to foresee and control the future. Not only did hindsight make it easier to decide cases, but—and this was of supreme importance to Rex—it made it easier to give reasons. Deciding to capitalize on this insight, Rex hit on the following plan. At the beginning of each calendar year he would decide all the controversies that had arisen among his subjects during the preceding year. He would accompany his decisions with a full statement of reasons. Naturally, the reasons thus given would be understood as not controlling decisions in future years, for that would be to defeat the whole purpose of the new arrangement, which was to gain the advantages of hindsight. Rex confidently announced the new plan to his subjects, observing that he was going to publish the full text of his judgments with the rules applied by him, thus meeting the chief objection to the old plan. Rex's subjects received this announcement in silence, then quietly explained through their leaders that when they said they needed to know the rules, they meant they needed to know them *in advance* so they could act on them. Rex muttered something to the effect that they might have made that point a little clearer, but said he would see what could be done.

Rex now realized that there was no escape from a published code declaring the rules to be applied in future disputes. Continuing his lessons in generalization, Rex worked diligently on a revised code, and finally announced that it would shortly be published. This announcement was received with universal gratification. The dismay of Rex's subjects was all the more intense, therefore, when his code became available and it was discovered that it was truly a masterpiece of obscurity. Legal experts who studied it declared that there was not a single sentence in it that could be understood either by an ordinary citizen or by a trained lawyer. Indignation became general and soon a picket appeared before the royal palace carrying a sign that read, "How can anybody follow a rule that nobody can understand?"

The code was quickly withdrawn. Recognizing for the first time that he needed assistance, Rex put a staff of experts to work on a revision. He instructed them to leave the substance untouched, but to clarify the expression throughout. The resulting code was a model of clarity, but as it was studied it became apparent that its new clarity had merely brought to light that it was honeycomed with contradictions. It was reliably reported that there was not a single provision in the code that was not nullified by another provision inconsistent with it. A picket again appeared before the royal residence carrying a sign that read, "This time the king made himself clear—in both directions."

Once again the code was withdrawn for revision. By now, however, Rex had lost his patience with his subjects and the negative attitude they seemed to adopt toward everything he tried to do for them. He decided to teach them a lesson and put an end to their carping. He instructed his experts to purge the code of contradictions, but at the same time to stiffen drastically every requirement contained in it and to add a long list of new crimes. Thus, where before the citizen summoned to the throne was given ten days in which to report, in the revision the time was cut to ten seconds. It was made a crime, punishable by ten years' imprisonment, to cough, sneeze, hiccough, faint or fall down in the presence of the king. It was made treason not to understand, believe in, and correctly profess the doctrine of evolutionary, democratic redemption.

When the new code was published a near revolution resulted. Leading citizens declared their intention to flout its provisions. Someone discovered in an ancient author a passage that seemed apt: "To command what cannot be done is not to make law; it is to unmake law, for a command that cannot be obeyed serves no end but confusion, fear and chaos." Soon this passage was being quoted in a hundred petitions to the king.

The code was again withdrawn and a staff of experts charged with the task of revision. Rex's instructions to the experts were that whenever they encountered a rule requiring an impossibility, it should be revised to make compliance possible. It turned out that to accomplish this result every provision in the code had to be substantially rewritten. The final result was, however, a triumph of draftsmanship. It was clear, consistent with itself, and demanded nothing of the subject that did not lie easily within his powers. It was printed and distributed free of charge on every street corner.

However, before the effective date for the new code had arrived, it was discovered that so much time had been spent in successive revisions of Rex's original draft, that the substance of the code had been seriously overtaken by events. Ever since Rex assumed the throne there had been a suspension of ordinary legal processes and this had brought about important economic and institutional changes within the country. Accommodation to these altered conditions required many changes of substance in the law. Accordingly as soon as the new code became legally effective, it was subjected to a daily stream of amendments. Again popular discontent mounted; an anonymous pamphlet appeared on the streets carrying scurrilous cartoons of the king and a leading article with the title: "A law that changes every day is worse than no law at all."

Within a short time this source of discontent began to cure itself as the pace of amendment gradually slackened. Before this had occurred to any noticeable degree, however, Rex announced an important decision. Reflecting on the misadventures of his reign, he concluded that much of the trouble lay in bad advice he had received from experts. He accordingly declared he was reassuming the judicial power in his own person. In this way he could directly control the application of the new code and insure his country against another crisis. He began to spend practically all of his time hearing and deciding cases arising under the new code.

As the king proceeded with this task, it seemed to bring to a belated blossoming his long dormant powers of generalization. His opinions began, indeed, to reveal a confident and almost exuberant virtuosity as he deftly distinguished his own previous decisions, exposed the principles on which he acted, and laid down guide lines for the disposition of future controversies. For Rex's subjects a new day seemed about to dawn when they could finally conform their conduct to a coherent body of rules.

This hope was, however, soon shattered. As the bound volumes of Rex's judgments became available and were subjected to closer study, his subjects were appalled to discover that there existed no discernible relation between those judgments and the code they purported to apply. Insofar as it found expression in the actual disposition of controversies, the new code might just as well not have existed at all. Yet in virtually every one of his decisions Rex declared and redeclared the code to be the basic law of his kingdom.

Leading citizens began to hold private meetings to discuss what measures, short of open revolt, could be taken to get the king away from the bench and back on the throne. While these discussions were going on Rex suddenly died, old before his time and deeply disillusioned with his subjects.

The first act of his successor, Rex II, was to announce that he was taking the powers of government away from the lawyers and placing them in the hands of psychiatrists and experts in public relations. This way, he explained, people could be made happy without rules.

### THE CONSEQUENCES OF FAILURE

Rex's bungling career as legislator and judge illustrates that the attempt to create and maintain a system of legal rules may miscarry in at least eight ways; there are in this enterprise, if you will, eight distinct routes to disaster. The first and most obvious lies in a failure to achieve rules at all, so that every issue must be decided on an ad hoc basis. The other routes are: (2) a failure to publicize, or at least to make available to the affected party, the rules he is expected to observe; (3) the abuse of retroactive legislation, which not only cannot itself guide action, but undercuts the integrity of rules prospective in effect, since it puts them under the threat of retrospective change; (4) a failure to make rules understandable; (5) the enactment of contradictory rules or (6) rules that require conduct beyond the powers of the affected party; (7)

introducing such frequent changes in the rules that the subject cannot orient his action by them; and, finally, (8) a failure of congruence between the rules as announced and their actual administration.

A total failure in any one of these eight directions does not simply result in a bad system of law; it results in something that is not properly called a legal system at all, except perhaps in the Pickwickian sense in which a void contract can still be said to be one kind of contract. Certainly there can be no rational ground for asserting that a man can have a moral obligation to obey a legal rule that does not exist, or is kept secret from him, or that came into existence only after he had acted, or was unintelligible, or was contradicted by another rule of the same system, or commanded the impossible, or changed every minute. It may not be impossible for a man to obey a rule that is disregarded by those charged with its administration, but at some point obedience becomes futile—as futile, in fact, as casting a vote that will never be counted. As the sociologist Simmel has observed, there is a kind of reciprocity between government and the citizen with respect to the observance of rules.[1] Government says to the citizen in effect, "These are the rules we expect you to follow. If you follow them, you have our assurance that they are the rules that will be applied to your conduct." When this bond of reciprocity is finally and completely ruptured by government, nothing is left on which to ground the citizen's duty to observe the rules.

The citizen's predicament becomes more difficult when, though there is no total failure in any direction, there is a general and drastic deterioration in legality, such as occurred in Germany under Hitler.[2] A situation begins to develop, for example, in which though some laws are published, others, including the most important, are not. Though most laws are prospective in effect, so free a use is made of retrospective legislation that no law is immune to change ex post facto if it suits the convenience of those in power. For the trial of criminal cases concerned with loyalty to the regime, special military tribunals are established and these tribunals disregard, whenever it suits their convenience, the rules that are supposed to control their decisions. Increasingly the

[1] *The Sociology of Georg Simmel* (1950), trans. Wolff, §4, "Interaction in the Idea of 'Law,'" pp. 186–89; see also Chapter 4, "Subordination under a Principle," pp. 250–67. Simmel's discussion is worthy of study by those concerned with defining the conditions under which the ideal of "the rule of law" can be realized.
[2] I have discussed some of the features of this deterioration in my article, "Positivism and Fidelity to Law," 71 *Harvard Law Review* 630, 648–57 (1958). This article makes no attempt at a comprehensive survey of all the postwar judicial decisions in Germany concerned with events occurring during the Hitler regime. Some of the later decisions rested the nullity of judgments rendered by the courts under Hitler not on the ground that the statutes applied were void, but on the ground that the Nazi judges misinterpreted the statutes of their own government. See Pappe, "On the Validity of Judicial Decisions in the Nazi Era," 23 *Modern Law Review* 260–74 (1960). Dr. Pappe makes more of this distinction than seems to me appropriate. After all, the meaning of a statute depends in part on accepted modes of interpretation. Can it be said that the postwar German courts gave full effect to Nazi laws when they interpreted them by their own standards instead of the quite different standards current during the Nazi regime? Moreover, with statutes of the kind involved, filled as they were with vague phrases and unrestricted delegations of power, it seems a little out of place to strain over questions of their proper interpretation.

principal object of government seems to be, not that of giving the citizen rules by which to shape his conduct, but to frighten him into impotence. As such a situation develops, the problem faced by the citizen is not so simple as that of a voter who knows with certainty that his ballot will not be counted. It is more like that of the voter who knows that the odds are against his ballot being counted at all, and that if it is counted, there is a good chance that it will be counted for the side against which he actually voted. A citizen in this predicament has to decide for himself whether to stay with the system and cast his ballot as a kind of symbolic act expressing the hope of a better day. So it was with the German citizen under Hitler faced with deciding whether he had an obligation to obey such portions of the laws as the Nazi terror had left intact.

In situations like these there can be no simple principle by which to test the citizen's obligation of fidelity to law, any more than there can be such a principle for testing his right to engage in a general revolution. One thing is, however, clear. A mere respect for constituted authority must not be confused with fidelity to law. Rex's subjects, for example, remained faithful to him as king throughout his long and inept reign. They were not faithful to his law, for he never made any.

# Bibliography

For general legal reference the following annual publications are recommended: *Harvard Law School Library Annual Bibliography* (Cambridge, Harvard University Printing Office), *Index to Legal Periodicals* (American Association of Law Libraries), and *Law books in Print* (Dobbs Ferry, N.Y., Glanville Publishers, Inc.). *Black's Law Dictionary* (St. Paul, Minn., West Publishing Co.) is a convenient one volume dictionary of legal terms. R.W.M. Dias, *Bibliography of Jurisprudence* (London, Butterworth 1964) offers an extensive survey of jurisprudential materials. Karl Llewellyn appends a bibliography of the literature of American legal realism prior to 1931 to "Some Realism on Realism" which is reprinted with the article above in Chapter 1. A basic negligence bibliography appears in notes to Walter Blum and Harry Kalvern, "The Empty Cabinet of Dr. Calabresi" reprinted in Chapter III above. The listings below follow topical chapter headings which in many instances overlap in subject-matter. Related topical listings should, therefore, be consulted.

## I. *General Legal Theory*

Allen, C. K., *Law in the Making*. Oxford, Clarendon Press, 1927.

Ames, J. B., *Lectures on Legal History and Miscellaneous Legal Essays*. Cambridge, Harvard University Press, 1930.

Anderson, J. N. D., "Reflections on Law, Natural, Divine and Positive," *Journal of the Transactions of the Victoria Institute of the Philosophical Society of Great Britain*, Vol.89 (1957).

*Aquinas: Selected Political Writings*, A. P. D'Entrèves, ed., J. G. Dawson, trans., Oxford, Basil Blackwell, 1948.

Austin, J., *Lectures on Jurisprudence*, London, John Murray, 1873.

———, *Province of Jurisprudence Determined*, New York, Humanities Press, 1967.

Barry, B. M., *Political Argument*, New York, Humanities Press, 1965.

Bégin, R. F., *Natural Law and Positive Law*, Washington, Catholic University of America Press, 1959.

Bentham, J., *A Defence of Usuary*, 2nd ed., London, T. Payne, 1790.

———, *A Fragment on Government*, Oxford, Clarendon Press, 1891.

———, *An Introduction to the Principles of Morals and Legislation*, Oxford, Basil Blackwell, 1948.

———, *The Limits of Jurisprudence Defined*, New York, Columbia University Press, 1945.

———, *The Principles of Morals and Legislation*, New York, Hafner, New York, 1948.

———, *Theory of Legislation*, New York, Harcourt, Brace and Co., 1931.

Blackstone, W., *Commentaries on the Law of England*, B. C. Gavit, ed., St. Paul, Minn., West, 1941.

Bodenheimer, E., *Jurisprudence: The Philosophy and Method of Law*, Cambridge, Harvard University Press, 1962.

———, "Modern Analytical Jurisprudence and the Limits of Its Usefulness," *U. of Pa. L. Rev.*, Vol. 104 (1956).

———, *Treatise on Justice*, New York, Philosophical Library, 1967.

Brandt, R., *Ethical Theories*, Englewood Cliffs, N.J., Prentice-Hall, Inc., 1957.

Brusiin, O., "Legal Theory: Some Considerations," *Arch. Rechts-Sozial-Philos.*, Vol. 43 (1957).

Buckland, W. W., *Some Reflections on Jurisprudence*, Cambridge, Cambridge University Press, 1945.

Cairns, H., *Law and the Social Sciences*, New York, Harcourt, Brace and Co., 1935.

————, *Legal Philosophy from Plato to Hegel*, Baltimore, Johns Hopkins University Press, 1949.

————, *Theory of Legal Science*, Hackensack, N.J., Rothman, 1969.

Cardozo, B., *The Growth of the Law*, New Haven, Yale University Press, 1963.

————, *The Nature of the Judicial Process*, New Haven, Yale UniversityPress, 1921.

————, *The Paradoxes of Legal Science*, New York, Columbia University Press, 1928.

Carnes, J. R., "Whether There Is A Natural Law," *Ethics*, Vol. 78 (1967).

Castberg, F., *Problems of Legal Philosophy*, 2nd. ed., London, G. Allen, 1958.

Cogley, J. (and others), *Natural Law and Modern Society*, Cleveland, The World Publishing Co., 1963.

Cohen, F. S., *Ethical System and Legal Ideals: An Essay on the Foundation of Legal Criticism*, Ithica, Cornell University Press, 1959.

————, "Transcendental Nonsense and the Functional Approach," *Col. L. Rev.*, Vol. 35, 1935.

Cohen, J. A., *The Criminal Process in the People's Republic of China 1949–1963*, Cambridge, Harvard University Press, 1968.

Cohen, M. R., "Jurisprudence as a Philosophical Discipline," *J. of Philos.*, Vol. 9 (1913).

————, *Law and the Social Order*, New York, Harcourt Brace & Co., 1933.

————, *Reason and the Law*, New York, Collier Books, 1961.

————, and F. Cohen, *Readings in Jurisprudence and Legal Philosophy*, New York, Prentice-Hall, 1951.

Cook, W. W., "Hohfeld's Contribution to the Science of Law," *Yale L. J.*, Vol. 28 (1919).

Cowan, T. A., "Experimental Jurisprudence and the 'Pure Theory of Law'," *Phil. and Phen. Research*, Vol. 11 (1950).

————, "A Postulate Set for Experimental Jurisprudence," *Philos. Sci.*, Vol. 18 (1951).

Dabin, J., *General Theory of Law* (in *The Legal Philosophies of Lask, Radbruch and Dabin*, Cambridge, Harvard University Press, 1950).

Deane, H. A., *The Political and Social Ideas of St. Augustine*, New York, Columbia University Press, 1963.

Del. Vecchio, G., *General Principles of Law*, F. Forte, trans., Boston, Boston University Press, 1958.

————, *Justice: An Historical and Philosophical Essay*, Chicago, Aldine, 1958.

————, *Philosophy of Law*, T.O. Martin, trans,. Washington, Catholic University Press, 1953.

D'Entrèves, A. P., *Natural Law*, London, Hutchinson, 1951.

————, *Notion of the State: An Introduction to Political Theory*, London, Oxford University Press, 1967.

Dewey, J., "Logical Method and Law," *Cornell L. Quarterly*, Vol. 17 (1924).

Dias, R. W. M., *Jurisprudence*, 2nd ed., London, Butterworth, 1964.

Dicey, A. V., *Conflict of Laws*, 7th ed. by J. H. C. Morris (and others), London, Stevens, 1958.

Dillard, I., ed., *The Spirit of Liberty, Papers and Addresses of Learned Hand*, 3rd. ed., New York, Knopf, 1960.

Duguit, L., *Law and the Modern State,* F. and H. T. Laski, trans., New York, B. W. Huebsch, 1919 (repub. Fertig, 1968).

Dworkin, R., "The Model of Rules," *U. of Chic. L. Rev.,* Vol. 35 (1967).

Ehrlich, E., *Fundamental Principles of the Sociology of Law,* W. L. Moll, trans., New York, Russell & Russell, Inc. (repub. 1962).

Frank, J., *Courts on Trial: Myth and Reality in American Justice, Princeton,* Princeton University Press, 1949.

———, *Law and the Modern Mind,* London, Stevens, 1949.

———, "What Courts Do In Fact," *Ill. L. Rev.,* Vol. 26 (1932).

Friedmann, W. G., *Law in a Changing Society,* Berkeley, University of California Press, 1959.

———, *Legal Theory,* 5th ed., New York, Columbia University Press, 1967.

Friedrich, C. J., *The Philosophy of Law in Historical Perspective,* 2nd ed., Chicago, University of Chicago Press, 1963.

———, "Karl Llewellyn's Legal Realism in Retrospect," *Ethics,* Vol. 74 (1964).

Freund, P. A., *On Law and Justice,* Cambridge, Harvard University Press, 1968.

Fuller, L. L., *Anatomy of Law,* New York, Praeger, 1968.

———, "Human Purpose and Natural Law," *J. Philos.,* Vol. 53 (1955).

———, *Law in Quest of Itself,* Boston, Beacon Press, 1960.

———, *Legal Fictions,* Stanford, Stanford University Press, 1967.

———, *The Morality of Law,* New Haven, Yale University Press, 1964.

———, *Problems of Jurisprudence,* New York, Foundation Press, 1949.

Garlan, E. N., *Legal Realism and Justice,* New York, Columbia University Press, 1941.

Geny, F., *Method d'Interpretation et Sources en Droit Prive Positif: Critical Essay,* 2nd ed., English trans. by Louisiana State Law Institute, St. Paul, Minn., West, 1963.

Golding, M. P., "Kelsen and the Concept of 'Legal System'," *Arch-Rechts-Sozialphilos.,* Vol. 47 (1961).

———, ed., *The Nature of Law: Readings in Legal Philosophy,* New York, Random House, 1966.

Goldsmith, M., *Hobbes' Science of Politics,* New York, Columbia University Press, 1965.

Goodhart, A. L., *English Contributions to the Philosophy of Law,* New York, Oxford University Press, 1949.

Gray, J. C., *Nature and Sources of Law,* New York, Columbia University Press, 1909.

Grotius, H., *Law of War and Peace,* F. W. Kelsey, trans., New York, Liberal Arts, 1963.

Guest, A. G., ed., *Oxford Essays in Jurisprudence,* Oxford, Oxford University Press, 1961.

Hagerstrom, A., *Inquiries into the Nature of Law and Morals,* Broad, trans., Stockholm, Almquist and Wiksell, 1953.

Hall, R. L., *Freedom Through Law,* New York, Columbia University Press, New York, 1952.

Hall, J., "Analytic Philosophy and Jurisprudence," *Ethics,* Vol. 77 (1966).

———, *Comparative Law and Social Theory,* Baton Rouge, Louisiana State University Press, 1963.

———, *Readings in Jurisprudence,* New York, Bobbs-Merrill, 1938.

———, *Studios in Jurisprudence and Criminal Theory,* New York, Oceana, 1958.

Hand, L., *The Bill of Rights,* Cambridge, Harvard University Press, 1958.

———, *The Spirit of Liberty,* Papers and Addresses of Learned Hand, 3rd ed., I. Dillard, ed., New York, Knopf, 1960.

Harding, A. L., *Natural Law and Natural Rights,* Dallas, S.M.U. Press, 1955.

Hart, H. L. A., "Analytical Jurisprudence in Mid-Twentieth Century: A Reply to Professor Bodenheimer," *U. of Pa. L. Rev.,* Vol. 105 (1957).

————, *The Concept of Law*, Oxford, Clarendon, Press 1961.

————, "Definition and Theory in Jurisprudence," *Law Quart. Rev.*, Vol. 70 (1954).

Hazard, J. N. and I. Shapiro, *The Soviet Legal System*, Dobbs Ferry, N.Y., Oceana Publications, 1962.

Hegel, G. F., *Philosophy of Right*, Knox, trans., Oxford, Clarendon Press, 1942.

Henson, R. O., ed., *Landmarks of Law*, Boston, Beacon Press, 1960.

Hobbes, T., *Leviathan*, New York, Liberal Arts, 1958.

*Hobbes Studies by Leo Strauss and Others*, Oxford, Blackwell, 1965.

Holmes, O. W., Jr., *Collected Legal Papers*, New York, Harcourt, Brace, 1902.

————, *The Common Law*, Boston, Little, Brown and Co., 1923.

————, "Natural Law," *Harvard L. Rev.*, Vol. 32 (1918).

Hook, S., ed., *Law and Philosophy*, New York, New York University Press, 1964.

————, *The Paradoxes of Freedom*, Berkeley, University of California Press, 1962.

————, *Reason, Social Myths and Democracy*, New York, Harper and Row, 1966.

Hughes, G., ed., *Law, Reason and Justice*: Essays in Legal Philosophy, New York, New York University Press, 1969.

Ihering, R., *Law as a Means to an End*, I. Husik, trans., Hackensack, N. J., Rothman, 1968.

————, *Struggle for Law*, J. S. Labor, trans., Chicago, Callaghan & Co., 1879.

Jenkins, I., "The Genesis of Positive Law," *Arch. Rechts-Social Philos.*, Vol. 50 (1964).

Kant, I., *The Metaphysical Elements of Justice*, J. Ladd, trans., New York, Liberal Arts, 1965.

————, *The Philosophy of Law*, W. Hastie, trans., Edinburgh, T. T. Clark, 1887.

Kantorowicz, H., *The Definition of Law*, Cambridge, Cambridge University Press, 1958.

Kelsen, H., *The Communist Theory of Law*, New York, Praeger, 1955.

————, "Le Droit Naturel," *Rev. Inter. Philos.*, Vol. 17 (1963).

————, "Foundations of Democracy," *Ethics*, Supp. Vol. 66 (1955).

————, *General Theory of Law and State*, A Wedberg, trans., New York, Russell and Russell, 1961.

————, *Pure Theory of Law*, M. Knight, trans. (from 2nd German ed.), Berkeley, University of California Press, 1967.

————, *What is Justice*, Berkeley, University of California Press, 1957.

Kleinz, J. P., "Mandate of Heaven: The Natural Law in the World Today," *Duns Scotus Philosophical Association*, Vol. 27 (1963).

Kocourek, A., *Jural Relations*, 2nd ed., New York, Bobbs-Merrill, 1927.

Laslett, P., ed., *Philosophy, Politics and Society* (First Series), Oxford, Blackwell, 1956.

————, and W. G. Runciman, eds., *Philosophy, Politics and Society* (Second Series), Oxford, Blackwell, 1962.

————, eds., *Philosophy, Politics and Society* (Third Series), New York, Barnes & Noble, 1967.

Lee, K. R., "Hart's Primary and Secondary Rules," *Mind*, Vol. 77 (1968).

*The Legal Philosophies of Lask, Radbruch and Dabin*, K. Wilk, trans., Cambridge, Harvard University Press, 1950.

Levy, B., *Cardozo at the Frontiers of Legal Thinking*, rev. ed. Cleveland, Case-Western Reserve University Press, 1969.

Llewellyn, K. N., *Bramble Bush*, New York, Oceana, 1960.

————, *Common Law Tradition*, Boston, Little, Brown & Co., 1960.

————, *Jurisprudence*, Chicago, University of Chicago Press, 1962.

————, "A Realistic Jurisprudence—The Next Stop," *Col. L. Rev.*, Vol. 30 (1930).

————, "Some Realism About Realism," *Harvard L. Rev.*, Vol. 44 (1931).

Lloyd, D., *Idea of Law*, Harmondsworth, Middlesex, Penguin, 1964.

————, *Introduction to Jurisprudence*, London, Stevens, 1959.

Luijpen, W. A., *Phenomenology of Natural Law*, Pittsburg, Duquesne University Press, 1967.

McIlwain, C. H., *Constitutionalism: Ancient and Modern*, Ithaca, Great Seal Books, 1958.

MacIver, R. M., *The Web of Government*, New York, Macmillan, 1947.

Maine, H. J. S., *Ancient Law*, Boston, Beacon Press, 1963.

Maitland, F. W. and F. Pollock, *History of English Law*, 2nd ed. reissued, London, Cambridge University Press, 1968.

Maritain, J., *Man and State*, Chicago, University of Chicago Press, 1951.

*Melanges en l'honneur de Jean Dabin*, Vol. I. *Theories générale du droit*, Vol. II. *Droit positif*, Bruxelles, Etablissements Emile Bruylant, 1963.

Mendelsohn, S., *Criminal Jurisprudence of the Ancient Hebrews*, 2nd ed., New York, Hermon Press, reissued 1968 (1891).

Miller, P. G. E., *Legal Minds in America from Independence to the Civil War*, New York, Doubleday, 1962.

Morris, C., *Great Legal Philosophers: Selected Readings in Jurisprudence*, Philadelphia, University of Pennsylvania Press, 1962.

Morris, H., ed., *Freedom and Responsibility*, Stanford, Stanford University Press, 1961.

Murray, J. C., S. J., *We Hold These Truths*, New York, Sheed & Ward, 1960.

*Natural Law and Natural Rights*, Dallas, S.M.U. Press, 1955.

Newman, R. A., ed., *Essays in Jurisprudence in Honor of Roscoe Pound*, New York, Bobbs-Merrill, 1962.

Olafson, F. A., ed., *Society, Law and Morality*, Englewood Cliffs, N. J., Prentice-Hall, Inc., 1961.

Olivecrona, K., *Law as Fact*, London, Oxford University Press, 1939.

Paton, G. W., *Jurisprudence*, 2nd ed., D. P. Derham, ed., Oxford, Clarendon Press, 1964.

Patterson, E. N., *Jurisprudence: Men and Ideas of the Law*, Brooklyn, Foundation Press, 1953.

Peczenik, A., "Juristic Definition of Law", *Ethics*, Vol. 78 (1968).

Peters, R. S. and S. I. Benn, *Social Principles and the Democratic State*, London, George Allen & Unwin, Ltd., 1959.

Perelman, Ch., "What the Philosopher May Learn from the Law," *Nat. L. Forum* Vol. II (1966).

Petrazycki, L., *Law and Morality*, H. W. Babb, trans., Cambridge, Harvard University Press, 1955.

Pollock, F., *The History of English Law Before the Time of Edward I*, 2nd ed., London,, Cambridge University Press, 1968.

————, *Jurisprudence and Legal Essays*, A. L. Goodhart, ed., New York, St. Martins Press, 1961.

Pound, R., *Criminal Justice in America*, New York, Holt, 1945.

————, *Development of Constitutional Guarantees of Liberty*, New Haven, Yale University Press, 1963.

————, "Fifty Years of Jurisprudence," *Harvard L. Rev.*, Vol. 50 (1937).

————, *Introduction to the Philosophy of Law*, rev. ed., New Haven, Yale University Press, 1954.

————, *Jurisprudence*, 5 vols., St. Paul, Minn., West, 1959.

————, *Justice According to Law,* New Haven, Yale, 1951.

————, *New Paths of Law,* Lincoln, Neb., University of Nebraska Press, 1950.

————, *Social Control Through Law,* New Haven, Yale University Press, 1942.

————, *The Spirit of the Common Law,* Boston, Beacon Press, 1963.

Quinton, A., ed., *Political Philosophy,* Oxford, Oxford University Press, 1967.

Renner, K., *Institutions of Private Law and Their Social Functions,* O. Kahn-Freund, ed., London, Routledge & Kegan paul, Ltd., 1949.

Rommen, H. A., *The Natural Law,* T. Hanley, trans., St. Louis, B. Herder Book Co., 1949.

Ross, A., *Directives and Norms,* London, Routledge & Kegan Paul, 1968.

————, *On Law and Justice,* Berkeley, University of California Press, 1959.

————, *Towards a Realistic Jurisprudence,* A. I. Fausboll, trans., Copenhagen, E. Munksgaard, 1946.

Rumble, W. E., Jr., *American Legal Realism: Skepticism, Reform, and the Judicial Process,* Ithaca, Cornell University Press, 1968.

————, "The Paradox of American Legal Realism," *Ethics,* Vol. 75 (1965).

Sartorius, R. E., "The Concept of Law," *Arch. Rechts-Sozialphilos.,* Vol. 52 (1966).

Sayre, P., "An Introduction to the Philosophy of Law," *Iowa L. Rev.,* Vol. 36, (1951).

Sèiichi, A., "An Aspect of the Epistemological Problem of Natural Law," *Rev. Inter. Philos.,* Vol. 17 (1963).

Shklar, J. N., *Legalism,* Cambridge, Harvard University Press, 1964.

————, *Political Theory and Ideology,* New York, Macmillan, 1966.

Sidorsky, D., "A 'Paradox' in Some Interpretations of Natural Law" (Abstract), *J. of Philos.,* Vol. 62 (1965).

Simon, R. J., ed., *Sociology of Law: Interdisciplinary Readings,* San Francisco, Chandler, 1968.

*Soviet Legal Philosophy,* H. W. Babb, ed., Cambridge, Harvard University Press, 1951.

Stammler, R., *Theory of Justice,* New York, Macmillan, 1925 (reissued by Rothman, 1968).

Stone, J., " 'The Nature of Things' on the Way to Positivism? Reflections on a Concrete Natural Law," *Arch. Rechts-Sozial Philos.,* Vol. 50 (1964).

————, "Roscoe Pound and Sociological Jurisprudence," *Harvard L. Rev.,* Vol. 78 (1965).

Strauss, L., *Natural Right and History,* Chicago, University of Chicago Press, 1953.

Summers, R. S., *Essays in Legal Philosophy,* Berkeley, University of California Press, 1968.

————, "The New Analytical Jurists," *N.Y.U. L. Rev.,* Vol. 41 (1966).

Tammelo, I., "Contemporary Developments of the Imperative Theory of Law: A Survey and Appraisal," *Arch. Rechts-Sozialphilos.,* Vol. 49 (1963).

Tarde, G. de, *Penal Philosophy,* Boston, Little, Brown and Co., 1912.

Vinogradoff, P., *Common Sense in Law,* 3rd ed., rev. by H. G. Hanbury, Oxford, Oxford University Press, 1959.

————, *Collected Papers,* New York, Oceana, 1966.

Wasserstrom, R., *The Judicial Decision,* Stanford, Stanford University Press, 1961.

Weber, M., *Max Weber on Law in Economy and Society,* M. Rheinstein and E. Shils, eds., Cambridge, Harvard University Press, 1954.

Weiss, P., "The Nature and Locus of Natural Law," *J. Philos,.* Vol. 53 (1956).

Wild, J., *Plato's Modern Enemies and the Theory of Natural Law,* Chicago, Chicago University Press, 1953.

Woelf, P., *Politics and Jurisprudence,* Chicago, Loyola University Press, 1966.

Wolheim, R., "The Nature of Law," *Political Studies,* Vol. 2 (1954).

Zerby, L. K., "Some Remarks on the Philosophy of Law," *J. Philos.,* Vol. 46 (1949).


II. *Legal Rights*


Aiken, H. D., "Rights, Human and Otherwise," *Monist,* Vol. 52 (1968).

Ayer, A. J. (and others), *Les Fondement des Droits de l'homme,* Firenze, La Nuova Italia, 1966.

Bedau, H., "The Right to Life," *Monist,* Vol. 52 (1968).

Berman, H. J., "Human Rights in the Soviet Union," *How. L. J.,* Vol. 11 (1965).

Blackstone, W. T., "Equality and Human Rights," *Monist,* Vol. 52 (1967).

Blaustein, A., ed., *Civil Rights and the American Negro: A Documentary History,* New York, Trident, 1968.

Brown, S. M., "Inalienable Rights," *Phil. Rev.,* Vol. 64 (1955).

Cahn, E. N., *Great Rights,* New York, Macmillan, 1963.

Commager, H. S., *Freedom, Loyalty, Dissent,* Oxford, Oxford University Press, 1954.

Corbin, A. L., "Jural Relations and Their Classification," *Yale L. J.,* Vol. 30 (1921).

———, "Legal Analysis and Terminology," *Yale L. J.,* Vol. 29 (1919).

Cox, A., M. D. Howe and J. R. Wiggins, *Civil Rights, The Constitution and The Courts,* Cambridge, Harvard University Press, 1967.

Ellin, J., "Wasserstrom and Feinberg on Human Rights," *J. Philos.,* Vol. 62, (1965).

Elsen, S. H., and A. Rosett, "Protections for the Suspect Under Miranda v. Arizona," *Col. L. R.,* Vol. 67 (1967).

Feuer, L. S., "Natural Rights," in Atti. XII, *Congr. Intern. Filos.,* VIII, Firenze, Sansoni, 1961.

Fitch, F. B., "A Revision of Hohfeld's Theory of Legal Concepts," *Log. et Anal.,* Vol. 10 (1967).

Feinberg, J., "Duties, Rights and Claims," *Amer. Phil. Quar.,* Vol. 3 (1966).

———, "Wasserstrom on Human Rights," *J. Philos.,* Vol. 61 (1964).

Frankena, W. K., "Natural and Inalienable Rights," *Phil. Rev.,* Vol. 64 (1955).

Friedrich, C. J., ed., *Liberty,* (Nomos IV), New York, Atherton Press, 1962.

Gale, R. M., "Natural Law and Human Rights," *Philos, and Phen. Research.* Vol. 20 (1960).

Goble, G. W., "A Redefinition of Basic Legal Terms," *Col. L. Rev.,* Vol. 35 (1935).

Golding, M. P., "Towards a Theory of Human Rights," *Monist,* Vol. 52 (1968).

Greenberg, J., "The Supreme Court, Civil Rights and Civil Dissonance," *Yale L. J.,* Vol. 77 (1968).

Gross, H., *Privacy – Its Legal Protection,* New York, Oceana, 1964.

Hart, H. L. A., "Are There Any Natural Rights," *Phil. Rev.,* Vol. 64 (1955).

———, "The Ascription of Responsibility and Rights," *Proc. Arist. Soc.,* Vol. 49 (1948–9).

———, "Definition and Theory in Jurisprudence," *Law Quart. Rev.* ,Vol. 70 (1954).

Hazard, J. N., *Settling Disputes in Soviet Society,* New York, Columbia University Press, 1960.

Helm, P., "Defeasibility and Open Texture," *Analysis,* Vol. 28 (1968).

Hohfeld, W. N., *Fundamental Legal Conceptions,* W. W. Cook, ed., New Haven, Yale University Press, 1919.

Hook, S., "Intelligence and Human Rights," Mem. XIII, *Congr. Intern. Filos.,* VIII (1961).

———, *Political Power and Personal Freedom,* New York Collier Books, 1962.

Kaufman, A. S., "A Sketch of a Liberal Theory of Fundamental Human Rights," *Monist,* Vol. 52 (1968).

King, M. L., Jr., *Why We Can't Wait,* New York, Harper & Row, 1964

Kocourek, A., "The Hohfeld System of Fundamental Legal Concepts, "*Ill L. Quar.,* Vol. 15 (1920).

———, *Jural Relations,* New York, Bobbs-Merrill, 1927.

———, "Plurality of Advantage and Disadvantage in Jural Relation," *Mich. L. Rev.,* Vol. 19 (1920).

———, "Polarized and Unpolarized Legal Relations," *Ky. L. J.,* Vol. 9 (1921).

———, "Rights in Rem," *Pa. L. Rev.,* Vol. 68 (1920).

———, "Terminology and Classification in Fundamental Jural Relations," *Amer. L. School Rev.,* Vol. 4 (1921).

———, "Various Definitions of Jural Relations," *Col. L. Rev.,* Vol. 20 (1920).

Konvitz, M. R., *Bill of Rights Reader: Reading Constitutional Cases,* 4th ed., Ithaca, Cornell University Press, 1968.

———, *Expanding Liberties,* New York, Viking, 1967.

Locke, J., *Two Treatises of Government,* P. Laslett, ed., Cambridge, Cambridge University Press, 1964.

Macdonald, M., "Natural Rights," in *Philosophy, Politics and Society* (First Series), P. Laslett, ed., Oxford, Blackwell, 1956.

Maher, F. K. H., "The Kinds of Legal Rights," *Melbourne Univ. L. Rev.,* Vol. 5 (1965).

Melden, A. I., and W. K. Frankena, "Human Rights," *Proc. Amer. Phil. Assn.,* Vol. 1 (1952).

———, *Rights and Right Conduct,* Oxford, Oxford University Press, 1959.

*Miranda v. Arizona,* 384 U.S. 436 (in *Criminological Controversies,* R. D. Knudten, ed., New York, Appleton-Century-Crofts, 1968).

Nielson, K., "Scepticism and Human Rights," *Monist,* Vol. 52 (1968).

Pound, R., "Legal Rights," *Inter. Jour. Eth.,* Vol. 26 (1915).

Radin, M., "A Restatement of Hohfeld," *Harvard L. Rev.* Vol. 51 (1938).

Reich, C., "Individual Rights and Social Welfare: The Emerging Legal Issue," *Yale L. J.,* Vol. 74 (1965).

———, "The New Property," *Yale L. J.,* Vol. 73 (1964).

Roshwald, M., "The Concept of Human Rights," *Phil. and Phen. Research.,* Vol. 19 (1958–9).

Sovern, M. I., *Legal Restraints on Racial Discrimination in Employment,* New York, 20th Century Fund, 1966.

Strauss, L., *Natural Right and History,* Chicago, University of Chicago Press, 1953.

Sundby, N. R., "Legal Right in Scandanavian Analyses," *Nat. L. Forum,* Vol.13(1968).

Towe, T. E., "Fundamental Rights in the Soviet Union: A Comparative Approach," *U. of Pa. L.R.,* Vol. 115 (1967).

Van Alstyne, W. W., "The Demise of the Right-Privilege Distinction in Constitutional Law," *Harv. L. Rev.,* Vol. 81 (1968).

Vinogradoff, P., "The Foundations of a Theory of Rights," *Yale L. J.,* Vol. 34, (1924).

Wainwright, W. J., "Natural Rights," *Amer. Phil. Quar.,* Vol. 4 (1967).

Wasserstrom, R., "Rights, Human Rights and Racial Discrimination," *J. Philos.,* Vol. 61 (1964).

Williams, G. L., *Sanctity of Life and the Criminal Law*, New York, Knopf, 1957.
Woozley, A. D., "Legal Duties, Offences, and Sanctions," *Mind*, Vol. 77 (1968).


III. *Legal Liability*

Blum, W. J., and H. Kalvern, Jr., *Public Law Perspectives on a Private Law Problem; Auto Compensation Plans*, Boston, Little Brown and Co., 1965.
Ehrenzweig, A. A., *Negligence Without Fault: Trends Toward an Enterprise Liability for Insurable Loss*, Berkeley, University of California Press, 1951.
———, "A Psychoanalysis of Negligence," *Northwestern L. Rev.*, Vol. 47 (1953).
Fleming, J. G., *The Law of Torts*, Sydney, Law Book Co., of Australia, 1957
Friedmann, W. G., "Social Insurance and the Principles of Tort Liability," Harv. L. Rev., Vol. 63 (1949).
Gregory, C. O., and H. Kalven, *Cases and Materials on Torts*, Boston, Little, Brown and Co., 1959.
Harper, F. V., and F. James, Jr., *The Law of Torts*, Boston Little Brown and Co., 1956.
Green, N., *Essays on Tort and Crime*, Menasha, Wis., George Banta Publishing Co., 1933.
Hart, H. L. A. and A. M. Honoré, *Causation in the Law*, Oxford, Clarendon Press, 1959.
Hart, H. L. A., "Negligence, *Mens Rea* and Criminal Responsibility," in A. G. Guest, ed., *Oxford Essays in Jurisprudence*, London, Oxford University Press, 1961.
Holmes, O. W., Jr., *The Common Law*, Boston, Little, Brown and Co., 1881.
Keeton, R. E., and J. O'Connell, *Basic Protection for the Traffic Victim*, 1965.
Kircheimer, O., "Criminal Omissions," *Harv. L. Rev,*, Vol. 55 (1942).
Michael, J., and H. Wechsler, *Criminal Law and Its Administration*, Brooklyn, Foundation Press, 1940.
Montrose, J. L., "Is Negligence and Ethical or a Sociological Concept?" *Mod. L. Rev.*, Vol. 21 (1958).
Morris, C., "Duty, Negligence and Causation." *U. of Pa. L. Rev.*, Vol. 61 (1952).
———, "Proof of Negligence," *Northwestern L. Rev.*, Vol. 47 (1953)
———, *Studies in Torts*, Brooklyn, Foundation Press, 1952.
Paton, G. W., "Negligence," *Australian L. Jour.*, Vol. 23 (1949).
Pollock, F., *Law of Torts*, 15th ed., P.A. Landon, ed., London, Stevens, 1951.
Prosser, W. L., *Handbook of the Law of Torts*, 2nd ed., St. Paul, Minn., West Publishing Co., 1955.
Radin, M., "A Speculative Inquiry into the Nature of Torts," *Texas L. Rev.* Vol. 21 (1943).
Radzinowicz, L., and J. W. C. Turner, eds., *The Modern Approach to Criminal Law*, London, Macmillan, 1948.
Salmond, J., *Torts*, 12th ed., R. F. V. Heuston, ed., London, Sweet and Maxwell, 1957.
Wasserstrom, R., "Strict Liability in the Criminal Law," *Stan. L. Rev.*, Vol. 12 (1960).
Williams, G., *Joint Torts and Contributory Negligence*, London, Stevens, 1951.


IV. *Legal Responsibility*

Allen, R. C., E. Z. Ferster, and H. Weihofen, *Mental Impairment and Legal Incompetency*, Englewood Cliffs, N.J., Prentice Hall, 1968.
Allen, R. C., E. Z. Ferster, and J. G. Rubin, eds., *Readings in Law and Psychiatry*, Baltimore, Johns Hopkins University Press, 1968.
Anscombe, G. E. M., *Intention*, Oxford, Basil Blackwell, 1957.

Alexander, P., and A. Macintyre, "Cause and Cure in Psychotheraphy" (Symposium), *Proc. Arist. Soc.,* Supp. Vol. 29 (1955)

Barnes, W. H. F. W. D., Falk, and A. D. Jones, "Intention, Motive and Responsibility" (Symposium), *Proc. Arist. Soc.,* Supp. Vol. 19 (1945).

Beccaria, C. B., *On Crimes and Punishments,* New York, Liberal Arts, 1963.

Berman, H. J., and J. B. Quigley, Jr., "Comment on the Presupposition of Innocence Under Soviet Law," *U.C.L.A. L. Rev.,* Vol. 15 (1968).

Biggs, J., *The Guilty Mind: Psychiatry and the Law of Homicide,* New York, Harcourt, Brace, 1955.

——, *The Guilty Mind,* Baltimore, John Hopkins Press, 1967.

Board, R. G., "Operational Criteria for Determining Legal Insanity," *Col. L. Rev.,* Vol. 61 (1961).

F. H. Bradley, *Ethical Studies,* London, Oxford University Press, 1927.

——, "Responsibility," *Jour, Crim. L. and C:iminol.,* Vol. 2 (1911).

Brandt, R. B., "Blameworthiness and Obligation," in A. I. Melden, ed., *Essays in Moral Philosophy,* Seattle, University of Washington Press, 1958.

Cook, W. W., "Act, Intention and Motive," *Yale L. J.,* Vol. 26 (1917).

Cooper, P. G., "Collective Responsibility," *Phil.,* Vol. 43 (1968).

Cross, R., *An Introduction to Criminal Law,* 5th ed., London, Butterworth, 1964.

Davis, P. E., ed., *Moral Duty and Legal Responsibility: A Philosophical Legal Casebook,* New York, Appleton-Century, Crofts, 1966.

Edwards, J. L. J., "Automatism and Criminal Responsibility," *Mod. L. Rev.,* Vol. 21 (1958).

——, "Criminal Degrees of Knowledge," *Mod. L. Rev.,* Vol. 17 (1954).

——, *"Mens Rea" in Statutory Offenses,* London, Macmillan, 1955.

Ehrenzweig, A. A., "A Psychoanalysis of the Insanity Pleas — Clues to the Problems of Criminal Responsibility and Insanity in the Death Cell," *Yale L. J.,* Vol. 73 (1964).

Falk, W. D., " 'Ought' and Motivation," *Proc. Arist. Soc.,* Vol. 48 (1947-48).

Feinberg, J., "Collective Responsibility," *J. Philos.,* Vol. 65 (1968).

——, "Problematic Responsibility in Law and Morals," *Phil. Rev.,* Vol. 71 (1962).

Fingarette, H., "The Concept of Mental Disease in Criminal Law Insanity Tests," *U. of Chic. L. R.,* Vol. 33 (1966).

Fitzgerald, P. J., *Crime and Punishment,* Oxford, Oxford University Press, 1962.

——, "Voluntary and Involuntary Act" in A. G. Guest, ed., *Oxford Essays in Jurisprudence,* Oxford, Oxford University Press, 1961.

Fox, S. J., "Physical Disorder, Consciousness, and Criminal Liability," *Col. L. Rev.,* Vol. 63 (1963).

Freedman, R., W. Overholser and M. S. Guttmacher, "Mental Disease or Defect Excluding Responsibility—A Psychiatric View of the American Law Institute Model Penal Code Proposal," *Amer. J. Psychiatry,* Vol. 18 (1961).

Friedrich, C. J., ed., *Responsibility* (Nomos III), New York, Liberal Arts, 1960.

Frym, M., "Criminal Intent," *Texas L. Rev.,* Vol. 31 (1953).

Geach, P. T., "Ascriptivism," *Phil. Rev.,* Vol. 69 (1960).

Ginsberg, M., *The Nature of Responsibility,* London, Clark Hall Fellowship, 1953.

Glueck, S., *Law and Psychiatry,* Baltimore, Johns Hopkins Press, 1962.

——, and E. Glueck, *Ventures in Criminology,* Cambridge, Harvard University Press, 1964.

Goldstein, A. S., *The Insanity Defense,* New Haven Yale University Press, 1967.

Goldstein, J., "Psychoanalysis and Jurisprudence," *Yale L. J.,* Vol. 77 (1968).

Guttmacher, M. S., and A. Weihofen, *Psychiatry and the Law,* New York, Norton, 1953.

Hall, J., *General Principles of Criminal Law,* 2nd ed., Indianapolis, Bobbs-Merrill, 1960.

———, "Negligent Behavior Should be Excluded from Penal Liability, "*Col. L. Rev.,* Vol. 63 (1963).

———, "Psychiatry and Criminal Responsibility," *Yale L. J.,* Vol. 65 (1956).

———, *Studies in Jurisprudence and Criminal Theory,* New York, Oceana Publications, 1958.

Hampshire, S., *Thought and Action,* London, Chatto and Windus, 1959.

Hart, H. L. A., *Punishment and Responsibility,* New York, Oxford University Press, 1968.

———, and A. M. Honore, *Causation in the Law,* Oxford, Clarendon Press, 1959.

Hart, H. M., "The Aims of the Criminal Law," *Law and Contemp. Prob.,* Vol. 23 (1958).

Houlgate, L. D., "Ignorantia Juris, A Plea for Justice," *Ethics,* Vol. 78 (1967).

Hughes, G., "Criminal Omissions," *Yale L. J.,* Vol. 67 (1958).

Jaspers, K., *The Question of German Guilt,* E. B. Ashton, trans., New York, Putnam, 1961.

Jeffrey, C. R., *Criminal Responsibility and Mental Disease,* Springfield Ill., Charles C. Thomas, 1967.

Jones, H., *Crime and the Penal System,* 2nd ed., London, University Tutorial Press, Ltd., 1962.

Katz, J., J., Goldstein and A. M. Dershowitz, *Psychoanalysis, Psychiatry and the Law,* New York, The Free Press, 1967.

Krasnowiecki, J. Z., "A Logical Problem in the Law of Mistake as to Person," *Phil. Quar.,* Vol. 10 (1960).

Kuh, R. H., "The Insanity Defense—An Effort to Combine Law and Reason." *U. Pa. L. Rev.,* Vol. 110 (1962).

Lewis, H. D., "Collective Responsibility," *Phil.,* Vol. 23 (1948).

Lindner, R., *Rebel Without a Cause,* New York, Grune & Stratton, 1944.

Lombroso, C., *Crime, Its Causes and Remedies,* Horton, trans., Boston, Little, Brown & Co., 1911.

Michael, J., and H. Wechsler, *Criminal Law and Its Administration: Cases: Statutes and Commentaries,* New York, Foundation Press, 1940.

Miller, J., "The Criminal Act," in M. Radin and A. M. Kidd, eds., *Legal Essays in Honor of Orin Kip McMurray,* Berkeley, University of California Press, 1935.

Morris, H., ed., *Freedom and Responsibility: Readings in Philosophy and Law,* Stanford, Stanford University Press, 1961.

Mueller, G. O. W., "Mens Rea and the Law Without It," *West Virginia L. Rev.,* Vol. 53 (1955).

———, "On Common Law Mens Rea," *Minn. L. Rev.,* Vol. 18 (1958).

O'Brien, V. P., *The Measure of Responsibility in Persons Influenced by Emotions,* Washington, Catholic University of America Press, 1948.

Overholser, W., *The Psychiatrist and the Law,* New York, Harcourt-Brace-World, 1953.

Pitcher, G., "Hart on Action and Responsibility," *Phil. Rev.,* Vol. 69 (1960).

Prevezer, S., "Automatism and Involuntary Conduct," *Crim. L. Rev.,* (1958).

Raab, F. R., "Moralist Looks at the Durham and M'Naghten Rules," *Minn. L. Rev.,* Vol. 46 (1961).

Reid, J. P., "Criminal Insanity and Psychiatric Evidence: The Challenge of Blocker," *How. L. J.,* Vol. 8 (1962).

Roche, P. Q., *The Criminal Mind,* New York, Farrar, Strauss & Cudahy, 1958.

Rome, H. P., "McNaughton, Durham and Psychiatry," *F.R.D.,* Vol. 34 (1964).

Rubin, S., *Psychiatry and the Criminal Law,* Dobbs Ferry, N.Y., Oceana, 1965.

Ryle, G., *The Concept of Mind,* London, Hutchinson's University Library, 1949.

Schafer, S., *Victim and His Criminal*, New York, Random House, 1968.

Schwartz, L. H., " 'Mental Disease'; The Groundwork for Legal Analysis and Legislative Actions," *U. Pa. L. Rev.*, Vol. III (1963).

Silber, J. R., "Being and Doing: A Study of Status Responsibility and Voluntary Responsibility," *U. of Chic. L. Rev.*, Vol. 35 (1967).

Smith, J. C., "Guilty Mind in the Criminal Law," *Law Quar. Rev.*, Vol. 76 (1960).

Stoljar, S., "Ascriptive and Prescriptive Responsibility," *Mind*, Vol. 68 (1959).

Szasz, T. S., *Law, Liberty and Psychiatry*, New York, Macmillan, 1963.

———, *The Myth of Mental Illness*, New York, Hoeber-Harper, 1961.

Tarde, G. de, *Penal Philosophy*, Boston, Little, Brown and Co., 1912.

Wasserstrom, R. A., "H. L. A. Hart and the Doctrines of Mens Rea and Criminal Responsibility," *U. of Chic. L.R.*, Vol. 34 (1967).

———, "Strict Liability in the Criminal Law," *Stan. L. Rev.*, Vol. 12 (1960).

Wechsler, H., "The Criteria of Criminal Responsibility," *U. of Chic. L. Rev.*, Vol. 22 (1955).

Weinreb, L. L., *Criminal Law: Cases, Comment, Questions*, New York, Foundation Press, 1969.

Weiss, P., "Social, Legal and Ethical Responsibility," *Ethics*, Vol. 57 (1946).

Williams, G., *Criminal Law*, 2nd ed., London, Stevens, 1961.

Wootton, B., *Crime and Criminal Law*, London, Stevens, 1963.

———, "Diminished Responsibility: A Layman's View," *L. Q. Rev.*, Vol. 76 (1960).

———, *Social Science and Social Pathology*, London, G. Allen & Unwin, 1967.

## V. *Punishment*

Armstrong, K. G., "The Retributivist Strikes Back," *Mind*, Vol. 70 (1961).

Baier, K., "Is Punishment Retributive," *Analysis*, Vol. 16 (1955-6).

Bedau, H., ed., *The Death Penalty in America*, 2nd ed., Garden City, Doubeday Anchor Books, 1967.

Benn, S. I., "An Approach to the Problems of Punishment," *Philos.*, Vol. 33 (1958).

Doyle, J. F., "Justice and Legal Punishment," *Philos.*, Vol. 42 (1967).

Flew, A., "The Justification of Punishment," *Philos.*, Vol. 29, 1954.

Gahringer, R. E., "Punishment as Language," *Ethics*, Vol. 71 (1960).

———, "Punishment and Responsibility," *J. Philos.*, Vol. 66 (1969).

Hart, H. L. A., *Punishment and Responsibility*, New York. Oxford University Press, 1968.

Hazelrigg, L., ed., *Prison Within Society: A Reader in Penology*, Doubleday, 1968.

Hodges, D. C., "Punishment," *Philos. and Phenomenol. Res.*, Vol. 18 (1957-8).

Holton, T., "Prevention of Delinquency Through Legal Counselling: A Proposal for Improved Juvenile Representation," *Col. L. Rev.*, Vol. 68 (1968).

Kaufman, A. S., "The Reform Theory of Punishment," *Ethics*, Vol. 71 (1960).

Mabbot, J. D., "Professor Flew on Punishment," *Philos.*, Vol. 30 (1955).

———, "Freewill and Punishment," in *Contemporary British Philosophy* (Third Series), H. D. Lewis, ed., New York, Macmillan, 1961.

McCloskey, H. J., "The complexity of the Concepts of Punishment," *Philos.*, Vol. 37 (1962).

———, "Utilitarian and Retributive Punishment," *J. Philos.*, Vol. 64 (1967).

McPherson, T., "Punishment, Definition and Justification," *Analysis*, Vol. 28 (1967).

Madden, E. H., ed., *Philosophical Perspectives on Punishment*, Springfield, Ill., C. C. Thomas 1968.

Menninger, K., *The Crime of Punishment*, New York, Viking, 1969.

*Model Penal Code*, Philadelphia, American Law Institute, 1962.

Morris, H., "Persons and Punishment," *Monist*, Vol. 52 (1968).

Packer, H. L., *Limits of Criminal Sanction*, Stanford, Stanford University Press, 1968.

Pakenham, F., *The Idea of Punishment*, London, Geoffrey Chapman, 1961.

Pincoffs, E. L., *Rationale of Legal Punishment*, Humanities Press, New York, 1966.

Rawls, J. B., "Two Concepts of Rules," *Phil, Rev.*, Vol. 64 (1955).

*Royal Commission on Capital Punishment* 1949-53 *Report*, London, Her Majesty's Stationery Office, 1953.

Sellin, T., "The Death Penalty" (Attached to *Model Penal Code*, Tent, Draft No. 9), Philadelphia, American Law Institute, 1959.

Smith, J. M., "Punishment: A Conceptual Map and a Normative Claim," *Ethics*, Vol. 75 (1965).

Stromberg, T., "Some Reflections on the Concept of Punishment," *Theoria*, Vol. 23 (1957).

Strong, E. W., "Justification of Juridical Punishment," *Ethics*, Vol. 79 (1969).

Van Der Haag, E., "On Deterrence and the Death Penalty," *Ethics*, Vol. 78 (1968).

Walker, O. S., "Why Should Irresponsible Offenders Be Excused," *J. Philos.*, Vol. 66 (1969).

Wechsler, H., "Codification of Criminal Law in the United States: The Model Penal Code," *Col. L. Rev.*, Vol. 68 (1968).

Wootton, B., *Crime and Criminal Law*, London, Stevens, 1963.

## VI. Legal Obligation and the Rule of Law

Abraham, H. J., *Freedom and the Court: Civil Rights and Civil Liberties in the United States*, New York, Oxford University Press, 1967.

Adams, T. F., *Law Enforcement: An Introduction to the Police Role in the Country*, Englewood Cliffs, N.J., Prentice-Hall, Inc., 1968.

Baynes, D. C., *Conscience, Obligation and the Law: The Moral Binding Power of the Civil Law*, Chicago Loyola University Press 1966.

Bedau H. A., ed., *Civil Disobedience: Theory and Practice*, New York, Pegasus, 1969.

————, "On Civil Disobedience," *J. Philos.*, Vol. 58 (1961).

Bienen, H., *Violence and Social Change*, Chicago, University of Chicago Press, 1968.

Black, C. L., Jr., "The Problem of the Compatibility of Civil Disobedience with American Institutions of Government," *Texas L. Rev.*, Vol. 43 (1965).

Blackstone, W. T., "Civil Disobedience: Is It Justified," *Georgia L. Rev.*, Vol. 3 1969.

Brandt, R., "The Concept of Obligation and Duty," *Mind*, Vol. 73 (1964).

Brown, B. F., Review: Bayne: *Conscience, Obligation and the Law: Moral Binding Power of the Civil Law*, U. of Pa. L.R., Vol. 115 (1967).

Brown S. M., Jr., "Civil Disobedience," *J. Philoso.*, Vol. 58 (1961).

Carnes, J. R., "Why Should I Obey the Law?" *Ethics*, Vol. 71 (1960).

Cohen, C., "Civil Disobedience and the Law," *Rutgers, L. Rev.*, Vol. 21 (1966).

————, "Conscientious Objection," *Ethics*, Vol. 78 (1968).

Dahl, R. A., *Modern Political Analysis*, Englewood Cliffs, N.J., Prentice-Hall, 1963.

Friedrich, C. J., ed., *Authority* (Nomos I), Cambridge, Harvard University Press, 1958.

————, *Constitutional Reason of State*, Providence, R.I., Brown University Press, 1957.

————, ed., *Revolution* (Nomos VIII), New York, Atherton, 1966.

Gert, B., "On Justifying Violence," *J. Philos.*, Vol. 66 (1969).

D'Entrèves, A. P., "Legality and Legitimacy," *Rev. Meta.*, Vol. 16 (1962-3).

Douglas, W. O., *Points of Rebellion*, New York, Vintage, 1970.

Dworkin, R., "On Not Prosecuting Civil Disobedience," *The New York Review of Books*, Vol. 10 (June 6, 1968).

Ellin, J., "Fidelity to Law," *Soundings*, Vol. 51 (1968).

Fortas, A., *Concerning Dissent and Civil Disobedience*, New York, New American Library, 1968.

Freund, P. A., *The Supreme Court of the United States, Its Business and Purposes*, New York, Meridian Press, 1961.

Gewirth, A., "Civil Disobedience, Law and Morality; An Examination of Justice Fortas' Doctrine," *Monist*, Vol. 54 (1970).

Ghandi, M. K., *Law and Lawyers*, S. B. Kher, ed., Navajivan, 1962.

――――, *Non-Violent Resistance (Satyagrapha)*, K. Bharatan, ed., New York, Schocken, 1961.

Hale, R. L., "Law Making by Unofficial Minorities," *Col. L. Rev.*, Vol. 20 (1920).

Harding, W., ed., *Variorum Civil Disobedience*, New York, Twayne, 1968.

Hart, H., and H. Wechsler, *Federal Courts and the Federal System*, New York, Foundation Press, 1953.

Hart, H., "The Relation Between State and Federal Law," *Col. L. Rev.*, Vol. 54 (1954).

Hazard, J., The Soviet System of Government, 3rd ed., Chicago, *University of Chicago Press*, 1964.

Hook, S., "Social Protest and Civil Disobedience," *Humanist*, Vol. 27 (1967).

Jennings, W. I., *The Law and the Constitution*, 5th ed., London, University of London Press, 1959.

Keeton, M., "The Morality of Civil Disobedience," *Texas L. Rev.*, Vol. 43 (1965).

Laski, H. J., *Authority in the Modern State*, Hamden, Conn., Archon, reissued 1968.

Liebman, M., "Civil Disobedience – A Threat to Our Society," *Amer. Bar. Assn. J.*, Vol. 51 (1965).

Lynd, S., "Civil Disobedience and Non-violent Destruction," *Humanist*, Vol. 28 (1968).

――――, *Intellectual Origins of American Radicalism*, New York, Pantheon Books, 1968.

――――, ed., *Non violence in America: A Documentary History*, New York, Bobbs-Merrill, 1966.

MacFarlane, L. J., "Justifying Political Disobedience," *Ethics*, Vol. 79 (1968).

McIver, R., *The Modern State*, London, Oxford University Press, 1926.

Marsh, M., "The Rule of Law as a Supra-National Concept," in *Oxford Essays in Jurisprudence*, A. G. Guest, ed., London, Oxford University Press, 1961.

Marshall, B., "The Protest Movement and the Law," *Virginia L. Rev.*, Vol. 71 (1965).

Mayer, P., ed., *The Pacifist Conscience*, London, Rupert Hart-Davis, 1966.

Murphy, J. G., "Allegiance and Lawful Government," *Ethics*, Vol. 79 (1968).

Pappe, H. O., "On the Validity of Judicial Decisions in the Nazi Era," *Modern L. Rev.*, Vol. 23 (1960).

Plamenatz, J. P., *Consent, Freedom and Political Obligation*, 2nd ed., Oxford, Oxford University Press, 1968.

Prichard, H. A., *Moral Obligation*, Oxford, Clarendon Press, 1949.

Prosch, H., "Limits to the Moral Claim in Civil Disobedience," *Ethics*, Vol. 75 (1965).

――――, "Towards an Ethic of Civil Disobedience," *Ethics*, Vol. 77 (1967).

Quinton, A., ed., *Political Philosophy*, New York, Oxford University Press, 1967.

Roche, J. P., *Courts and Rights: The American Judiciary in Action*, 2nd ed., New York, Random House, 1966.

Rucker, D., "The Moral Grounds of Civil Disobedience," *Ethics,* Vol. 76 (1966).

Russell, B. *Authority and the Individual,* London, George Allen & Unwin, 1965.

Sartorius, R., "Utilitarianism and Obligation," *J. Philos,.* Vol. 66 (1969).

Schlissel, L., ed., *Conscience in America: A Documentary History of Conscientious Objection in America,* 1757-1967, New York, Dutton, 1968.

Schwarz, W., "The Right of Resistance," *Ethics,* Vol. 74 (1964)

"Sentencing in Cases of Civil Disobedience" (Notes), *Col. L. Rev.,* Vol. 68 (1968).

Sibley, M. Q., "Nonviolence and Revolution, *Humanist,* Vol. 28 (1968)

———, ed., *The Quiet Battle: Writings on the Theory and Practice of Nonviolent Resistance,* Garden City, Doubleday, 1963.

Spitz, D., "Democracy and the Problem of Civil Disobedience," *Amer. Pol. Sci. Rev.,* Vol. 48 (1954).

———, ed., *Political Theory and Social Change,* New York, Atherton, 1967.

Spock, B., "Vietnam and Civil Disobedience," *Humanist,* Vol. 28, 1968.

Thompson, S. M., "The Authority of Law, *Ethics,* Vol. 75 (1964).

Thoreau, H., *Variorum Civil Disobedience,* annotation and introduction by W. Harding, New York, Twayne, 1967.

*U.S. President's Commission on Law Enforcement and the Administration of Justice,* New York, Avon, 1968.

Vile, M. J. C., *Constitutionalism and the Separation of Powers,* Oxford, Oxford University Press, 1967.

Walzer, M., "The Obligation to Disobey," *Ethics,* Vol. 77 (1967).

Wasserstrom, R., "Disobeying the Law," *J. Philos.,* Vol. 58 (1961).

———, "The Obligation to Obey the Law," *U.C.L.A. L. Rev.,* Vol. 10 (1963).

Wolff, R. P., "On Violence," *J. Philos.,* Vol. 66 (1969).

———, *The Rule of Law,* New York, Simon and Schuster, Inc., (announced).

Woodward, B., "Vietnam and the Law," *Commentary,* Vol. 46 No. 5 (1968).

Wyzanski, C. E., Jr., "Constitutionalism: Limitation and Affirmation" in *Government Under Law.,* A. Sutherland, ed., Cambridge, Cambridge University Press, 1956.

Zinn, H., *Disobedience and Democracy: Nine Fallacies on Law and Order,* New York Random House, 1968.

VII. *Judicial Reasoning*

Abraham, H. J., *Judicial Process,* 2nd. ed., Oxford, Oxford University Press, 1968.

"Abuse of Discretion: Administrative Expertize v. Judicial Surveillance" (Comment), *U. of Pa. L. R.,* Vol. 115 (1966).

Berman, H. J., *Soviet Criminal Law Procedure: The RSFSR Codes,* 1966.

Boasson, C., *The Use of Logic in Legal Reasoning,* Amsterdam, North-Holland Pub. Co., 1966.

Bodenheimer, E., "Neglected Theory of Legal Reasoning," *J. Legal Ed.,* Vol. 21 (1969).

Boonin, L. G., "Concerning the Authoritative Status of Legal Rules, "*Ethics,* Vol. 74 (1964).

———, "The Logic of Legal Decisions," *Ethics,* Vol. 75 (1965).

———, "The Meaning and Existence of Rules," *Ethics,* Vol. 76 (1965).

Cardozo, B. N., *The Nature of the Judicial Process,* New Haven, Yale University Press, 1921.

———, *Paradoxes of Legal Science,* New York, Columbia University Press, 1928.

Chroust, A. H., "Law: Reason, Legalism, and the Judicial Process," *Ethics,* Vol. 74 (1963)

Cohen, F. S., "Field Theory and Judicial Logic," *Yale L.J.,* Vol. 59 (1950).

———, "Transcendental Nonsense and the Functional Approach," *Col. L. Rev.*, Vol. 35 (1935).

Cohen, M. R., *Law and the Social Order*, New York, Harcourt, Brace and Co., 1933.

———, "The Process of Judicial Legislation," *Amer. L. Rev.*, Vol. 48 (1914).

———, *Reason and the Law*, New York, The Free Press, 1950.

Cross, R., *Evidence*, 2nd ed., London, Butterworths, 1963.

———, *Precedent in English Law*, Oxford, Clarendon Press, 1961.

Dewey, J., "Logical Method and Law", *Cornell L.Q.*, Vol. 17 (1924).

Dickinson, J., "Legal Rules: Their Application and Elaboration," *U. of Pa. L. Rev.*, Vol. 79 (1931).

———, "Legal Rules: Their Function in the Process of Decision, "*U. of Pa. L.* Rev., Vol. 79 (1931).

Dworkin, R., "Judicial Discretion," *J. Philos.*, Vol. 60 (1963).

———, "The Model of Rules," *U. of Chic. L. Rev.*, Vol. 35 (1967).

———, "Wasserstrom: The Judicial Decision," *Ethics*, Vol. 75 (1964).

Emmet, D., *Rules, Roles and Relations,*" London, Macmillan, 1966.

Frank, J., *Courts on Trial*, Princeton, N.J., Princeton University Press, 1950.

Frankfurter, F., " Some Reflections on the Reading of Statutes," *Col, L. Rev.*, Vol. 47 (1947).

Friedrich, C. J., ed., *Rational Decision* (Nomos VII), New York, Atherton, 1964.

Fuller, L., *Legal Fictions*, Stanford, Stanford University Press, 1967.

Golding, M. P., "Principled Decision-Making and the Supreme Court," *Col. L. Rev.*, Vol. 63 (1963).

Gottlieb, G., *Logic of Choice: An Investigation of the Concepts of Rule and Rationality*, New York, Macmillan, 1968.

Gray, J. C., "Judicial Precedents," *Harvard L. Rev.*, Vol. 9 (1895).

Guest, A. G., "Logic in the Law," in *Oxford Essays in Jurisprudence*, A. G. Guest, ed., Oxford, Oxford University Press, 1961.

Halper, T., "Logic in Judicial Reasoning," *Indiana L. J.*, Vol. 44 (1968).

Hart, H. M., Jr. and J. T. McNaughton, "Some Aspects of Evidence and Inference in the Law," *Daedalus*, Vol. 87 (1958).

Hart, H., and H. Wechsler, *Judicial Code and Rules of Procedure in the Federal Courts*, New York, Fogundation Press, 1962.

Hill, A., "The Law-Making Power of the Federal Courts: Constitutional Pre-emption, *Col. L. Rev.*, Vol. 67 (1967).

Hughes, G., "Rules, Policy and Decision Making," *Yale L. J.*, Vol. 77 (1968).

Hunter, J. F. M., "The Logic of Social Contracts," *Dialogue*, Vol. 5 (1966-7).

Jensen, O. C., *The Nature of Legal Argument*, Oxford, Basil Blackwell, 1957.

Kalven, H., Jr., and H. Zeisel, *The American Jury*, Boston. Little, Brown, & Co., 1966.

Kelly, D. S., "Legal Concepts, Logical Functions, and Statements of Fact," *Tasmania U. L. R.*, Vol. 3 (1968).

"Legalism: Jurisprudence Round Table 1965," (J. Shklar and Others), *Legal Ed.*, Vol. 19 (1966).

Levi, E. A., *An Introduction to Legal Reasoning*, Chicago, University of Chicago Press, 1949.

Llewellyn, K., *The Common Law Tradition: Deciding Appeals*, Boston, Little, Brown & Co., 1960.

Lunstedt, A. V., *Legal Thinking Revised*, The Hague, Netherlands, Nijhoff, 1956.

McBride, W. L., "Essential Role of Models and Analogies in the Philosophy of Law," *N.Y.U. L. Rev.*, Vol. 43 (1968).

Mullock, P., "The 'Logic' of Legal Reasoning," *Mind*, Vol. 75 (1966).

Murphy, J. G., "Law Logic," *Ethics*, Vol. 77 (1967).

Perry, T. D., "Judicial Method and the Concept of Reasoning," *Ethics*, Vol. 80 (1969).

Pound, R., "The End of Law as Developed in Legal Rules and Doctrines," *Harvard L. Rev.*, Vol. 27 (1914).

———, "Mechanical Jurisprudence," *Col. L. Rev.*, Vol. 8 (1908).

Powell, T. R., *Vagaries and Varieties in Constitutional Interpretation*, Columbia University Press, New York, 1956.

Radin, M., *Law as Logic and Experience*, New Haven, Yale University Press, 1940.

———, "Theory of Judicial Decision," *Amer. B. A. J.*, Vol. II (1925).

Rinaldi, F., "Logic and the Law of the Future," *Aust. Law*, Vol. 7 (1967).

Rostow, E. V., *Sovereign Prerogative: The Supreme Court and the Quest for Law*, New Haven, Yale University Press, 1962.

Rumble, W. E., Jr., "Rule-Skepticism and the Role of the Judge," *Jour. Pub. L.*, Vol. 15 (1966).

Sartorius, R. E., "The Justification of Judicial Decision," *Ethics*, Vol. 78 (1968).

Schaefer, W. V., "Precedent and Policy," *U. of Chic. L. Rev.*, Vol. 34 (1966).

Schubert, G., *The Judicial Mind: The Attitudes and Ideologies of Supreme Court Justices 1946-1963*, Evanston, III., Northwestern University Press, 1965.

Singer, M. G., "Moral Rules and Principles," in A. I. Melden, ed., *Essays in Moral Philosophy*, Seatle, University of Washington Press, 1958.

Smith, J. C., "Law, Language and Philosophy," *U. of Brit. Columb. L.R,.* Vol. 3 (1968).

Stevens, R., "Hedley Byrne v. Heller: Judicial Creativity and Doctrinal Possibility," *Mod. L. R.*, Vol. 27 (1964).

Stone, J., *Legal System and Lawyers' Reasonings*, Stanford, Stanford University Press, 1964.

Summers, R. S., "Logic in the Law," *Mind*, Vol. 72 (1963).

Wasserstrom, R. A., *The Judicial Decison: Toward a Theory of Legal Justification*, Stanford, Stanford University Press, 1961.

Wechsler, H., "Challenge of a Model Penal Code, " *Harvard L. Rev.*, Vol. 65 (1952).

———, " Towards Neutral Principles of Constitutional Law," *Harvard L. Rev.*,Vol. 73 (1959).

Woozley, A. D., "The Existence of Rules," *Nous*, Vol. 1 (1967).

———, "What is Wrong with Retrospective Law," *Phil. Quart.*, Vol. 18 (1968).

Yntema, H. E., "The Rational Basis of Legal Science," *Col. L. Rev.*, Vol. 31 (1931).

## VIII. *Justice*

Barry, B. M., "Justice and the Common Good," *Analysis*, Vol. 21 (1960-1).

Baxster, I. F. G., "Justice and Mysticism, "*Rev. Inter. Philos.*, Vol. 17 (1963)

Bedau, H., ed., *Justice and Equality*, Englewood Cliffs, N.J. Prentice Hall, 1970.

Blackshield, A., "Empirical and Rationalist Theories of Justice," *Arch. Rechts-Sozial-philos.*, Vol. 48 (1962).

Blackstone, W. T., "On the Meaning and Justification of the Equality Principle," *Ethics*, Vol. 77 (1967).

Bodenheimer, E., *Treatise on Justice*, New York, Philosophical Library, 1967.

Breitel, C. D., "Criminal Law and Criminal Justice," *Utah Law Rev.*, (1966).

Bourke, V. J., "Foundations of Justice," *Proc. Amer. Cathol. Philos, Assoc.*, Vol. 36 (1962).

Brandt, R. B., *Ethical Theory*, Englewood Cliffs, N.J., Prentice-Hall, 1959.

————, ed., *Social Justice*, Englewood Cliffs, N. J., Prentice-Hall, 1962.

Brown, B. F., "Justice in the Natural and Civil Law," *Proc. Amer. Cathol. Philos. Assoc.*, Vol. 36 (1962).

Cahn, E. N., *Sense of Injustice*, Bloomington, Ind., Indiana University Press, 1964.

Conquest, R., ed., *Justice and the Legal System in the U.S.S.R.*, New York. Frederick A. Praeger, 1968.

Cook. W. W., "The Powers of the Courts of Equity," *Col. L. Rev.*, Vol. 15 (1915).

Del Vecchio, G., "Equality and Inequality in Relation to Justice," *Natural L. Forum*, Vol. 11 (1966).

————, *Justice: An Historical and Philosophical Essay*, Lady Guttrie, trans., A. H. Campbell ed., Edinburgh, The University Press, 1952.

Eckhoff, T., *Justice and the Rule of Law*, Oslo, Johan Grundt Tanum Forlag, 1966.

Emmons, D. C., "Justice Reassessed," *Amer. Phil. Quar.*, Vol. 4 (1967).

Franklin, M., "A New Conception of the Relation Between Law and Equity," *Philos. and Phenom. Res.*, Vol. 11 (1951).

Fried, C., "Natural Law and the Concept of Justice," *Ethics*, Vol. 1 74 (1963-4).

Friedrich, C. J., and J. Chapman, eds., *Justice* (Nomos VI). New York, Atherton, 1963.

————, ed., *Public Interest* (Nomos V), New York, Atherton, 1962.

Garlan, E. N., *Legal Realism and Justice*, New York. Columbia University Press, 1941.

Gerats, C. H., and D. Roach, "The Object of Social Justice," *Proc. Amer. Cathol. Philos. Assoc.*, Vol. 36 (1962).

Ginsberg, M., "The Concept of Justice," *Philos.*, Vol. 38 (1963).

Gleisser, M., *Juries and Justice*, New York, Barnes & Noble, 1968.

Grincel, C. W., "Justice and the Philosophers," *Proc. Amer, Cathol. Philos. Assoc.*, Vol. 36 (1962).

Hanbury, H. G., *Modern Equity*, 8th ed., London, Stevens, 1962.

Hannaford, R., "Equal Freedom vs Equal Treatment," *Ethics*, Vol. 79 (1968).

Jaffe, R., *The Pragmatic Conception of Justice*, (U. of Calif. Pub. in Philos., 34), Berkeley, University of California Press, 1960.

Kecton, R. E., *Venturing to Do Justice, Reforming Private Law*, Cambridge, Harvard University Press, 1969.

Kelsen, H., *What Is Justice*, Berkeley, University of California Press, 1957.

Kent, E. A., "Justice as Respect for Person," *Southern J. of Philos.*, Vol., 6 (1968).

Ladd, J., Review of *Treatise on Justice*, by E. Bodenheimer, *Col. L. Rev.*, Vol. 68 (1968).

Lakoff, S. A., *Equality in Political Philosopy*, Cambridge, Harvard University Press, 1964.

Lloyd, A. C., "Natural Justice," *Philos. Quar.*, Vol. 12 (1962).

Lundstedt, V., *Law and Justice*, Stockholm, Almquist & Wiksell, 1952.

Macadam, J. I., "The Precepts of Justice," *Mind*, Vol. 77 (1968).

Maitland, F. W., *Equity*, Cambridge, *Cambridge University Press*, 1913.

Malik, C., "Justice in the International Order," *Proc. Amer. Cathol. Philos. Assoc.*, Vol 36 (1962).

Martin, W. O., "The Intentionality of Distributive Justice," *Proc. Amer. Cathol. Philos, Assoc.*, Vol 36 (1962).

Morris, C., "A Dissent to Dr. Waelder's Theory of Justice," *U. of Pa. L. Rev.*, Vol. 115 (1966).

Newman, R. A., *Equity and Laws: A Comparative Study*, New York, Oceana Publications, 1961.

Oesterle, J. A., "Justice in Society – The State and the Individual," *Proc. Amer. Cathol. Philos. Assoc.*, Vol. 36 (1962).

Olfson, R. A., ed., *Justice and Social Policy*, Englewood Cliffs, N. J., Prentice-Hall, 1961.

Pennock, J. R., and J. W. Chapman, eds., *Equality* (Nomos IX), New York, Atherton, 1967.

Perelman, Ch., *The Idea of Justice and the Problem of Argument*, New York, Humanities Press, 1963.

———, *Justice*, New York, Random House, 1967.

Pound, R., *Justice According to Law*, New Haven, Yale University Press, 1951.

Rawls, J., "Distributive Justice: Some Addenda," *Nat. L. Forum.*, Vol. 13 (1968).

———, "Justice and Constitutional Liberty," in *Justice* (Nomos VI), C. J. Friedrich and J. Chapman, eds., New York, Atherton, 1963.

———, "Justice as Fairness," *J. Philos.*, Vol. 55 (1957).

———, "Justice as Fairness," *Philos. Rev.*, Vol. 68 (1958).

———, "The Sense of Justice," *Philos. Rev.*, Vol. 72 (1963).

Rescher, N., *Distributive Justice*, Indianapolis, Bobbs-Merrill, 1966.

Ross, A., *On Law and Justice*, M. Dutton, trans., Berkeley, University of California Press, 1959.

Runciman, W. G., *Relative Deprivation and Social Justice*, London, Routledge & K. Paul. 1966.

Stone, J., *Human Law and Human Justice*, Stanford, Stanford University Press, 1965.

———, *Social Dimensions of Law and Justice*, Stanford, Stanford University Press, 1966.

Summers, R. S., "H. L. A. Hart on Justice," *J. Philos.*, Vol. 59 (1962).

Tillich, P. J., *Love Power and Justice*, New York, Oxford University Press, 1954.

Vlastos, G., "Justice and Psychic Harmony in the Republic," *J. Philos.*, Vol. 66 (1969).

———, "The Argument in the *Republic* that 'Justice Pays', "*J. Philos.*, Vol. 65 (1968).

Waelder, R., "The Concept of Justice and the Quest for a Perfectly Just Society," *U. of Pa. L. Rev.*, Vol. 115 (1966).

———, "A Reply to Professor Morris' Statement of Dissent," *U. of Pa. L. Rev.*, Vol. 115 (1966).

Wolff, R. P., "A Refutation of Rawls' Theorem on Justice," *J. Philos.*, Vol. 63 (1966).

## IX. Property

Abrams, C., *Forbidden Neighbors*, New York, Harpers, 1955.

———, *The City Is the New Frontier*, New York, Harper & Row, 1965.

———, *The Future of Housing*, New York, Harper Bros., 1946.

———, *Revolution in Land*, New York, Harper Bros., 1939.

Alluntis, F., "Private Property and Natural Law," *Stud in Philos. and the Hist. of Philos.*, Vol. 2 (1963).

Arnold, T. W., *The Folklore of Capitalism*, New Haven, Yale University Press, 1937.

Babcock, R. F., *The Zoning Game*, Madison, Wis., University of Wisconsin Press, 1966.

Bentham, J., "A Commentary on Humphreys' Real Property Code," in *Works*, Vol. 5, Bowring, ed., Edinburgh, W. Tait, 1843.

Berger, C. J., *Land Ownership and Uses: Cases, Statutes and Other Materials*, Boston, Little, Brown, 1968.

Berle, A.A., Jr., *The American Economic Republic.* New York, Harcourt, Brace & World, 1963.

———, and G. C. Means, *The Modern Corporation and Private Property*, New York Macmillan, 1933.

———, *Power Without Property*, New York, Harcourt, Brace, 1959.

————, "Property, Production and Revolution," *Col. L. Rev.*, Vol. 65 (1965).

————, *The Three Faces of Power*, New York, Harcourt, Brace & World, 1967.

Carey, H., "Real Property," *Jour. Leg. Pol. Soc.*, Vol. 1 (1943).

*The Case for Regional Planning*, New Haven, Yale University Press, 1947.

Casner, A. J. and W. B. Leach, *Cases and Text on Property*, Boston, Little, Brown and Co., 1950.

Cohen, F., "Dialogue on Private Property," *Rutgers L. Rev.*, Vol. 9 (1954).

Cohen, M. R., "Property and Sovereignty," in *Law and the Social Order*, New York, Harcourt Brace & Co., 1933.

Coker, F. W., ed., *Democracy, Liberty and Property*, New York, Macmillan, 1942.

Commons, J. R., *Legal Foundations; of Capitalism*, New York, Macmillan, 1924.

————, and J. B. Andrews, *Principles of Labor Legislation*, 4th ed., New York, Harper Bros., 1936.

Cotton, R., "Tenant Unions: Collective Bargaining and the Low-Income Tenant," *Yale L. J.*, Vol. 77 (1968),

Cook, W. W., "Privileges of Labor Unions in the Struggle for Life," *Yale L. J.*, Vol. 27 (1918).

Darling, F. F., and J. P. Milton, eds,. *Future Environments of North America*,        Garden City, N.Y., The Natural History Press, 1966.

Delafows, J., *Land Use Controls in the United States*, Cambridge, Harvard University Press, 1962.

De Vos, A., *Pollution Reader*, Montreal, Harvest House, 1968.

Dewhurst, J. F., *America's Needs and Resources*, New York, Twentieth Century Fund, 1955.

Eldredge, H. W., ed., *Taming Megapolis*, 2 Vols, Garden City, N.Y., Doubleday Anchor Books, 1967.

Ely, R. T., and Wehrwein, G. S., *Land Economics*, New York, Macmillan, 1940.

————, *Property and Contract in Their Relations to the Distribution of Wealth*, 2 Vols., New York, Macmillan, 1914.

Ewald, W. R., Jr., ed., *Environment for Man—The Next Fifty Years*, Bloomington, Ind., Indiana University Press, 1966.

Ferman, L. A., ed., *Poverty in America: Book of Readings*, Rev., ed., Ann Arbor, University of Michigan, 1968.

Friedman, L. M., "The Dynastic Trust," *Yale. L. J.*, Vol. 73 (1964).

————, and J. Ladinsky, "Social Change and the Law of Industrial Accidents, *Col. L. Rev.*, Vol. 67 (1967).

Galbraith, J. K., Jr., *American Capitalism*, Boston, Houghton Mifflin Co., 1952.

Gans, H., "Social and Physical Planning for the Elimination of Urban Poverty, *Wash. L. Quar.*, Vol. 2 (1963).

Gellhorn, W., "Poverty and Legality: The Law's Slow Awakening," *Wash. & Mary, L. Rev.*, Vol. 9 (1967).

Gide, C., and C. Rist, *History of Economic Doctrine*, 2nd ed., R. Richards, trans., Boston, D. C. Heath & Co., 1913.

Gough, J. W., *John Locke's Political Philosophy*, Oxford, Clarendon Press, 1950.

Haar, C. M., *Land Planning Law in a Free Society*, Cambridge, Harvard University Press, 1951.

————, *Land-Use Planning: A Case Book on the Use, Misuse, and Reuse of Urban Land*, Boston, Little, Brown and Co., 1959.

————, ed., *Law and Land: Anglo-American Planning Practice*, Cambridge, Harvard University Press, 1964.

Hale, Robert, L., "Rate Making and the Revision of the Property Concept," *Col. L. Rev.*, Vol. 22 (1922).

Hallowell, A. I., "The Nature and Function of Property as a Social Institution," *Jour. Leg. Pol. Soc.*, Vol. 1 (1943).

Hamilton, W. H., *The Pattern of Competition*, New York, Columbia University Press, 1940.

———, " 'Property' According to John Locke." *Yale L. J.*, Vol. 41 (1932).

———, "Property Rights in the Market," *Jour. Leg. Pol. Soc.*, Vol. 1 (1943).

Harris, D. R., "The Concept of Possession in English Law." in *Oxford Essays in Jurisprudence*, A. G. Guest, ed., Oxford, Oxford University Press, 1961.

Hazard, J. N., "Soviet Property Law: A Case Study Approach," in *Soviet Society*, Boston, Houghton Mifflin Co., 1961.

Hecht, N., "From Seisin to Sit-in: Evolving Property Concepts," *Bost. Univ. L. Rev.*, Vol. 44 (1964).

Heller, D., "Public Landlords and Private Tenants: The Eviction of 'Undesirables' From Public Housing Projects," *Yale L. J.*, Vol. 77 (1968).

Hobhouse, L. T., "Historical Evolution of Property in Fact and in Idea," in *Property: Its Rights and Duties*, 3rd. ed., London, Macmillan & Co., 1915.

Honoré, A. M., "Ownership," in *Oxford Essays in Jurisprudence*, A. G. Guest, ed., Oxford, Oxford University Press, 1961.

Hoselitz, B. F., and W. E. Moore, *Industrialization and Society*, New York, Humanities Press, 1963.

Hufschmidt, M. M., ed., *Regional Planning*, New York, Praeger, 1969.

James, H., "The Rule of Law and the Welfare State," *Col. L. Rev.*, Vol. 58 (1958).

Jones, J. W., "Forms of Ownership," *Tulane, L. R.*, Vol. 22 (1947).

Kapp, W., *The Social Costs of Private Enterprise*, Cambridge, Harvard University Press, 1950.

Kruse, L. F. V., *The Right of Property*, 2 vol., London, Oxford University Press, 1939.

Landsberg, H. H., I. L. Fischman and J. L. Fisher, *Resources in America's Future: Patterns of Requirements and Availabilities*, 1960-2000, Baltimore Johns Hopkins Press, 1963.

Larkin, W. P., *Property in the Eighteenth Century*, Cork, Cork University Press, 1930.

Lefcoe, G., *Land Development Law, Cases and Materials*, New York, Bobbs-Merrill, 1966.

Llewellyn, K., "What Price Contract—An Essay in Perspective," *Yale L. J.*, Vol. 40 (1931).

Lowie, R. H., "Property Rights and Coercive Powers of Plains Indian Military Societies" *Jour, Leg. Pol. Soc.*, Vol. 1 (1943).

McDougal, M. S., and D. Haber, *Property, Wealth, Land: Allocation, Planning, and Development.* Charlottesville, Va., Michie Casebook Corporation, 1948.

McLaughlin, J. A., *Cases on the Federal Anti-Trust Laws of the United States*, New York, The Ad Press, 1930.

McPherson, C. B., *The Political Theory of Possessive Individualism*, Oxford, Clarendon Press, 1962.

———, *The Real World of Democracy*, Oxford, Clarendon Press, 1966.

Mandelker, D. R., *Case Studies in Land Planning and Development*, Indianapolis, Boss-Merrill, 1968.

———, *Green Belts and Urban Growth*, Madison, Wis., University of Wisconsin Press, 1962.

———, *Managing Our Urban Environment: Cases, Text and Problems*, Indianapolis, Bobbs-Merrill, 1966.

———, "The Role of Law in the Planning Process," *Law and Contem. Prob.* Vol. 30 (1964).

Marx, K., *Capital*, New York, The Modern Library, 1959.

————, *Economic and Philosophic Manuscripts of* 1844, Moscow, Foreign Language Publishing House, 1961.

————, and F. Engels, *The German Ideology*, New York, International Publishers, 1947.

Maxwell, R. C., and S. A. Riesenfeld, *California Security Transactions*, St. Paul, Minn., West, 1957.

Megarry, R. E., and H. W. R. Wade, *The Law of Real Property*, 2nd ed., London, Stevens, 1957.

Michelman, F. I., "Property, Utility and Fairness: Comments on the Ethical Foundations of 'Just Compensation' Law", *Harvard L. Rev.*, Vol. 80 (1967).

Mill, J. S., *Principles of Political Economy*, W. J. Ashley, ed., New York, Kelly, 1909.

Moore, W. E., "The Emergence of New Property Conceptions in America," *Jour. Leg. Pol. Soc.*, Vol. 1 (1943).

Moulds, H., "Private Property in Locke's State of Nature," *The Amer. Jour. of Econ. and Soc.*, Vol 23 (1964).

Myrdal, G., *The Political Element in the Development of Economic Theory*, P. Streeter, trans., Cambridge, Harvard University Press, 1954.

Neumann, F., *The Democratic and Authoritarian State*, Glencoe, Ill., Free Press of Glencoe, 1968).

Newman, R. A., *Newman on Trusts*, 2nd ed., Brooklyn, Foundation Press, 1955.

Noyes, C. R., *Economic Man in Relation to His Natural Environment*, New York, Columbia University Press, 1948.

————, *The Institution of Property*, New York, Longmans, Green and Co., 1936.

————, "Property and Sovereignty," *Jour. Leg. Pol. Soc.*, Vol 1 (1943).

Okun, B., and R. W. Richardson, eds., *Studies in Economic Development*, New York, Holt, Rinehart and Winston, 1961.

Philbrick, F. S., "Changing Conceptions of Property in Law," *U. of Pa. L. R.*, Vol. 45 (1938).

Polanyi, K., *The Great Transformation*, New York, Farrar and Rinehart, 1944.

Pooley, B. J., *The Evolution of British Planning Legislation*, Ann Arbor, Mich., Michigan Legal Publications, 1960.

————, *Planning and Zoning in the United States*, Ann Arbor, University of Michigan Law School, 1961.

Pound, R., "The Law of Property and Recent Juristic Thought," *Amer. Bar. Assoc. Jour.*, Vol. 25 (1939).

————, "Liberty of Contract," *Yale L. J.*, Vol. 18 (1909).

Powell, R. B., "The Relotionship Between Property Rights and Civil Rights," *Hastings L. J.*, Vol. 15 (1963).

Powell, R. R., *Law of Real Property*, New York. Bender, 1953-61.

Powell, T. R., "Collective Bargaining Before the Supreme Court," *Pol. Sci. Quar.*, Vol. 33 (1918).

*Property, Its Rights and Duties*, 3rd ed., London, Macmillan and Co., 1915.

Proudhon, P. J., *What Is Property*, New York, Dover, 1970.

Reich, C. A., "The Law of the Planned Society," *Yale L. J.*, Vol. 75 (1966).

————, "The New Property," *Yale, L. J.*, Vol. 73 (1964).

Renner, K., *The Institutions of Private Law*, O. Kahn, ed., London  Routledge and Kegan Paul, 1949.

*Restatement of Property*, Philadelphia, American Law Institute, 1938.

Riesenfeld, S. A., and R. C. Maxwell. *Modern Social Legislation*, Brolokyn, Foundation Press, 1951.

Rozos, G. T., *Five Types of Philosophical Theory of Property*, New York, Columbia University Ph.D. Dissertation, 1958.

Rudden, B., "Soviet Housing Law," *Int'l. and Comp. L.Q.*, Vol. 12 (1963).

Sax, J. L., "Takings and the Police Power," *Yale L. J.*, Vol. 74 (1964).

Schlatter, R., *Private Property: The History of an Idea*, New Brunswick, N.J., Rutgers University Press, 1951.

Schneider, H. W., "Pragmatism and Property," *Jour, Leg. Pol. Soc.*, Vol. 1, (1943).

Schwartz, B., *The Rights of Property*, New York, Macmillan, 1965.

Smith, A., *Wealth of Nations*, London, Methuen & Co., 1920.

Speth, J. S., Jr., "Judicial Review of Displace Relocation in Urban Renewal," Yale, L. J., Vol. 77 (1968).

Stelzer, I. M., *Selected Antitrust Cases*, Rev. ed., Homewood, Ill., Richard D. Irwink, Inc., 1961.

Summers, W. L., "Property in Oil and Gas," *Yale L. J.*, Vol. 29 (1919).

Tawney, R. H., *The Acquisitive Society*, New York, Harcourt, Brace & Howe, 1920.

Vignaux, P., "Some Ideas on Property in the French Labor Movement," *Jour. Leg. Pol. Soc.*, Vol. I (1943).

Whyte, W. H., *Last Landscape*, New York, Doubleday, 1968.

Williams, H. R., ed., *Cases and Materials on the Law of Property*, Brooklyn, Foundation Press, 1954.

Wingo, L. Jr., *Cities and Space: The Future Use of Urban Land*, Baltimore, Johns Hopkins Press, 1966.

## X. *Law and Morality*

Ames, J. B., "Law and Morals," *Harvard, L. Rev.*, Vol. 22 (1908).

Bentham, J., *An Introduction to the Principles of Morals and Legislation*, Oxford, Basil Blackwell, 1948.

Bedau, H., ed., *Conflict of Loyalties: Selective Conscientious Objection*, New York, Pegasus, 1968.

Blackshield, A. R., "Hart-Devlin Controversy in 1965," *Sidney. L. Rev.*, Vol. 5 (1967).

Blackstone, W. T., "On the Meaning and Justification of the Equality Principle," *Ethics*, Vol. 77 (1967).

Blanshard, P., *Religion and the Schools: The Great Controversy*, New York, Beacon Press, 1963.

Bockle, F., *Law and Conscience*, M. J. Donnelly, trans., London, Sheed & Ward, 1966.

Brecht, A., "The Myth of Is and Ought," *Harvard L. Rev.*, Vol. 54 (1941).

Carney, F. S., "Religion and the Legislation of Morals," *Soundings*, Vol. 51 (1968).

Cahn, E. N., *Moral Decision: Right and Wrong in the Light of American Law*, Bloomingdon, Ind., Indiana University Press, 1955.

*Challenge and Progress of Homosexual Law Reform*, Council on Religion and the Homosexual, 1968.

Cohen, F. S., "The Ethical Basis of Legal Criticism," *Yale L. J.*, Vol. 41 (1931).

————, *Ethical Systems and Legal Ideas*, New York, Furman, 1933.

————, "Modern Ethics and the Law," *Brooklyn L. Rev.*, Vol. 4 (1934).

Cohen, M. R., "Moral Aspects of the Criminal Law," *Yale L. J.*, Vol. 49 (1940).

Dallmayr, F. R., "Functionalism, Justice and Equality, "*Ethics*, Vol. 78 (1967).

Devlin, P.. *The Enforcement of Morals*, Oxford, Oxford University Press, 1959.

Drinin, R. F., *Religion, The Courts and Public Policy*, New York, McGraw-Hill, 1963.

Dworkin, R., "Lord Devlin and the Enforcement of Morals," *Yale L. J.,* Vol. 75 (1966).
——, "Philosophy, Morality and the Law—Observations Prompted by Professor Fuller's Novel Claim," *U. of Pa. L. Rev.,* Vol. 113 (1965).
Ernst, M. L., and A. U. Schwartz, *Censorship: The Search for the Obscene,* New York, Macmillan, 1964.
Fried, C., "Natural Law and the Concept of Justice," *Ethics,* Vol. 74 (1964).
Fuller, L., "Human Purpose and Natural Law." *J. Philos.,* Vol. 53 (1956).
——, *The Morality of Law,* New Haven, Yale University Press, 1964.
——, "Positivism and Fidelity to Law, *"Harvard L. Rev.,* Vol. 81 (1958).
Goodhart, A. L., *English Law and the Moral Law,* London, Stevens & Sons, 1953.
Grisez, G. D., "The Moral Basis of Law," *Thomist,* Vol. 32 (1968).
Hägerström, A., *Inquiries into the Nature of Law and Morals,* Broad, trans., Stockholm, Almquist and Wiksell, 1953.
Hanworth, L., "The Language of Justice," *Southern J. Philos.,* Vol. 4 (1966).
Hart, H. L. A., *Law, Liberty and Morality,* New York, Vintage Books, 1963.
——, "Legal Positivism and the Separation of Law and Morals," *Harvard L. Rev.,* Vol. 81 (1958).
——, "Social Solidarity and the Enforcement of Morality," *U. of Chic. L. Rev.,* Vol. 35 (1967).
Hedenius, I., "On Law and Morals," *J. Philos.,* Vol. 56 (1959).
Jones, H., "The Practice of Justice," *Washington U. L. Quar.,* (1966).
Ison, T. G., "Enforcement of Morals,.' *Univ, Brit. Col. L. Rev.,* Vol 3 (1967).
Kemp, J., *Reason, Action and Morality,* New York, Humanities Press, 1964.
Konvitz, M. R., *Religious Liberty and Conscience:* A Constitutional Inquiry, New York, Viking, 1968.
Knudten, R. D., ed., *Criminological Controversies,* New York, Appleton-Century-Crofts, 1968.
Lewis, J. U., "Moral Obligation and the Concept of Law," *Rurgers L. Rev.,* Vol. 23 (1968)
Louch, A. R. "Sins and Crimes," *Philos.,* Vol. 43 (1968).
McClosky, H. J., "A Critique of the Ideals of Liberty," *Mind,* Vol. 74 (1965).
McNeilly, F. S., "The Enforcibility of Law," *Nous,* Vol. 2 (1968).
Meiklejohn, D., *Freedom and the Public: Public and Private Morality,* Syracuse, Syracuse University Press, 1965.
Nagel, E., "The Enforcement of Morals," *Humanist,* Vol. 28 (1968).
Northrop, F. S. C., "Law, Language and Morals," *Yale L. J.,* Vol. 71 (1962).
Nozick, R., "Moral Complication and Moral Structure," *Nat. L. Forum,* Vol. 13 (1968).
Petrazycki, L., *Law and Morality,* Babb, trans., Cambridge, Harvard University Press, 1955.
Pfeffer, L., *Church and State Freedom,* Rev. ed., Boston, Beacon Press, 1967.
Schwarz, A., "No Imposition of Religion: The Establishment Clause Value," *Yale L. J.,* Vol. 77 (1968).
Schlissel, L., ed., *Conscience in America,* New York, Dutton, 1968.
Shklar, J., *Legalism,* Cambridge, Harvard University Press, 1964.
Strauss, E. B., "Moral Responsibility and the Law," *The Dublin Rev.,* Vol. 118 (1954).
Stumpf, S. E., *Morality and Law,* Nashville, Vanderbilt University Press, 1966.
Summers, R. S., " 'Is' and 'Ought' in Legal Philosophy," *Philos. Quar.,* Vol. 13 (1963).
——, "Professor Fuller on Morality and Law," *J. Leg. Ed.,* Vol. 18 (1965).
Swomley, J. M., *Religion, the State and the Schools,* New York, Pegasns, 1968.
Taylor, R., "Law and Morality," *N.Y.U. L. Rev.,* Vol. 43 (1968).
Weiss, P., "Social, Legal and Ethical Responsibility," *Ethics,* Vol. 58 (1946).

# Index